Social Problems and Social Movements

James DeFronzo
University of Connecticut

Jungyun Gill
Stonehill College

ROWMAN & LITTLEFIELD
Lanham • Boulder • New York • London

Executive Editor: Nancy Roberts
Assistant Editor: Megan Manzano
Senior Marketing Manager: Amy Whitaker
Interior Designer: Kathy Mrozek

Credits and acknowledgments for material borrowed from other sources, and reproduced with permission, appear on the appropriate page within the text.

Published by Rowman & Littlefield
An imprint of The Rowman & Littlefield Publishing Group, Inc.
4501 Forbes Boulevard, Suite 200, Lanham, Maryland 20706
www.rowman.com

6 Tinworth Street, London SE11 5AL, United Kingdom

British Library Cataloguing in Publication Information Available

Library of Congress Cataloging-in-Publication Data

Names: DeFronzo, James, author. | Gill, Jungyun, author.
Title: Social problems and social movements / James DeFronzo, University of Connecticut, Jungyun Gill, Stonehill College.
Description: Lanham : Rowman & Littlefield, [2020] | Includes bibliographical references and index.
Identifiers: LCCN 2018053699 (print) | LCCN 2018060894 (ebook) | ISBN 9781442221550 (electronic) | ISBN 9781442221543 (pbk. : alk. paper)
Subjects: LCSH: Social problems—United States. | Social movements—United States.
Classification: LCC HN57 (ebook) | LCC HN57 .D43 2020 (print) | DDC 361.10973—dc23
LC record available at https://lccn.loc.gov/2018053699

♾™ The paper used in this publication meets the minimum requirements of American National Standard for Information Sciences—Permanence of Paper for Printed Library Materials, ANSI/NISO Z39.48-1992.

Printed in the United States of America

BRIEF CONTENTS

CONTENTS

LIST OF BOXES

Our central aim is to make your social problems course a journey of discovery and empowerment that enhances your ability to make our society, and, when and where possible, our world, better. We begin by encouraging readers to always use the sociological perspective, the sociological imagination. This perspective links the most personal elements of an individual's life to social forces. It helps us comprehend how our experiences, feelings, thoughts, and actions, as well as those of other people, are affected by culture, social structure, and technological and social change. Understanding the nature and importance of social and cultural factors that shape our lives helps people develop the collective means to change aspects of society that cause social problems.

There are numerous issues that draw public concern including poverty, inequality, discrimination based on characteristics such as race, ethnicity, gender or sexual orientation, the status of immigrants and refugees, health care insurance, crime and corruption, and the functioning of the criminal justice system. Many people are also worried about drug abuse, particularly the surge in opioid addiction and overdose deaths, sexual harassment and exploitation, threats to the environment, terrorism, the continuing danger of nuclear war, and the epidemic of gun massacres at schools and other places that the U.S., more than any other technologically advanced nation experiences.

In addition, many believe there are threats to democracy in the United States. The huge role of money in the U.S. political system means that the concentration of wealth in a tiny percentage of the population gives that group more power and influence than other citizens. Beyond that trend, accusations of political leaders' attempts to suppress the free press and restrict voting rights, coupled with government officials repeatedly lying and tolerating or even fostering corruption at the highest levels, leads many to conclude that our country is threatened by growing authoritarianism. Further, intelligence agencies have agreed that a foreign power has made serious attempts to interfere in U.S. elections to defeat candidates it opposes and promote those it approves.

We believe that we should not rely just on politicians to tackle social problems. Rather everyone should search out the facts on important issues, consider the validity of others' points of view, and evaluate situations in terms of your personal moral principles and the ideals of the United States. Then you should take action not only through political means like supporting candidates' campaigns and voting, but also by participating in social movements aimed at addressing social problems. Through bringing attention to social problems, educating people about them, and mobilizing public opinion, social movements can force politicians to act despite the influence of special interests that try to prevent them from responding.

Social movements, from reform efforts to revolutions, have played a role in addressing social problems in the past. And today social movement activism is needed more than ever given the failures of politicians and government officials.

Perhaps nothing more clearly emphasizes the potential effectiveness of social movement activism in the U.S. than the Never Again movement begun by students at Marjory Stoneman Douglas High School in Parkland, Florida, after a former student used an assault rifle to murder 14 of their classmates, a teacher, a coach and the school's athletic director on February 14, 2018. Rather than leave the matter to politicians in a state which had been one of the easiest for persons as young as 18 to obtain an assault rifle, many of the school's students responded ferociously by traveling to the state capital Tallahassee, and demanding action to ban the sale of assault rifles, raise the legal age for purchasing a firearm, and more effectively restrict seriously mentally ill persons' access to guns. An international 17 minute (one minute for each victim) student walkout was scheduled for March 14, one month after the tragedy. The March for Our Lives in Washington, D.C., and many other U.S. cities was scheduled for March 24. Students vowed to work to remove from office any government official who did not support reasonable, common sense gun control measures. Apparently shocked by the Parkland massacre and the student survivors' movement, several businesses decided to raise the age limit for buying guns to 21, and others stopped selling assault rifles. And more companies ended special benefits they had provided to members of the National Rifle Association (NRA) because they perceived the NRA as typically blocking gun reforms through its influence and financial backing of government officials. The Florida state legislature responded with some reforms including raising the age for purchasing guns to 21 and providing more money for student mental health services and school safety measures.

Our approach emphasizes the role of social movements in dealing with social problems and improving society. To better prepare students for activism, the second chapter of our book explains how social movements can address social problems and change society, and describes sociological explanations for the development of social movements. The third chapter describes the powerful forces that participants in social movements addressing social problems must contend with in order to achieve success. Each following chapter presents overviews of social problems and then provides examples of how working together can bring about positive change.

ORGANIZATION OF THE TEXT

Social Problems and Social Movements is organized into 15 chapters with examples of major social movements provided throughout the book. To illustrate how the depth of social problems and the approaches for solving them can differ from place to place, many chapters present inter-state and international comparisons. Chapters 4 through 15 also include analyses of social problems from the points of view of major sociological theoretical frameworks such as the structural-functional, conflict, racial/ethnic-conflict, feminist-conflict, and symbolic-interactionist approaches.

Chapter 1, The Sociology of Social Problems, defines the concept "social problem" and explains how a particular condition or pattern of behavior becomes recognized as a social problem. This chapter next explains the sociological perspective, the sociological imagination, and illustrates its application to a serious social problem, the rise of criminal youth gangs. Chapter 1 also compares the major sociological theoretical frameworks that are applied to social problems. Finally, this chapter describes the various types of research sociologists use to develop a better understanding of a problem, its cause, and its possible solution. Aspects of the Tea-Party, Occupy, and Free Higher Education movements are covered.

Chapter 2, The Sociology of Social Movements, explains what a social movement is, the important role of social movements in addressing social problems, and the different types of social movements. The chapter also presents sociological explanations for the development of social movements and the stages social movements often go through. The important role of students in social movements is described as well as how social movements bring about social change. The role of music in social movements is discussed and aspects of actual social movements are covered including the Civil Rights, Anti-Vietnam War, U.S. Women's, Anti-Sweatshop, Pro-Life, Pro-Choice, Arab Uprising, and other movements.

Chapter 3, The Sociology of Power: Economics, Wealth, and Politics, describes the power frameworks that participants in social movements addressing social problems must deal with in order to achieve success. The first major power framework is economic. This chapter describes the tremendous level of wealth inequality in the U.S. and how money influences politics and government. It also explains how wealth and power influence conceptions of social problems and the success or failure of social movements. A second framework of power is key structural characteristics of the U.S. political system that have the potential for undermining the will of the majority of voters, such as the electoral college system at the federal level and the gerrymandering of political districts at the state level. Social movements covered in this chapter include the Anti-Electoral College movement and the Post 2016 Election Women's March.

Chapter 4, Poverty, describes how poverty is measured, the dimensions of poverty in the U.S., child poverty in the U.S. compared to other technologically advanced nations, the working poor, explanations for poverty, and the consequences of poverty. Government assistance programs, welfare reform, and proposed solutions to poverty are explained. Social movements covered in this chapter include Martin Luther King Junior and the movement to improve the lives of the working poor, and the American Labor Union movement.

Chapter 5, Race, Ethnicity, and Immigration, describes the concepts of race, ethnicity, and racism, and the level of diversity in the U.S. It also explains the role of immigration, controversies about immigration, different types of racial/ethnic relations, and what is meant by stereotypes, prejudice, and discrimination. This chapter in addition explains white privilege, color-blind racism, institutional discrimination, race and the criminal justice system, and the major causes of prejudice, and describes movements for equality of opportunity and the various approaches to reducing prejudice and discrimination. Movements covered include the anti-racist Charlottesville, Virginia, protests; the Dreamers' movement; the U.S. Nativist movement; the anti-slavery Abolitionist movement; the German anti-Nazi White Rose Movement; the South African anti-Apartheid movement; Racial Profiling and the Trayvon Martin movement; and the U.S. African American Freedom movement from ratification of the Constitution to the present.

Chapter 6, Gender and Sexual Orientation, explains gender identity, gender binary, sexism, gender stereotypes, gender discrimination, gender inequality, different types of sexual orientation, and homophobia. This chapter also covers cultural sexism, institutional sexism, cultural and institutional bias against LGBT persons, different types of feminism, and sexual assault on college and university campuses. Movements covered include the U.S. Women's movement, the Gay and Lesbian Rights movement, and the Me Too movement.

Chapter 7, The Family, describes the different concepts and types of marriage and family worldwide, how marriage and family have changed over time in the U.S., and family related social problems such as intimate partner violence, child abuse and elder abuse, and the causes and prevention of violence in the family. This chapter also covers divorce and the impacts of divorce, trends in unwed parenthood and efforts to reduce teen pregnancy, mass incarceration and the African American family, and how technologically advanced nations provide assistance to families and children. Movements covered include the Movement for the Legalization of Same Sex Marriage and the Child Protection movement.

Chapter 8, Education and Media, describes the differences in literacy rates and academic achievement among social groups in the U.S. as well as among nations and the factors that may be responsible for these differences, the impacts of class, race, ethnicity, and gender on academic performance, contrasting approaches to improving academic performance, and the college student debt issue. School racial and economic segregation and school crime, the school to prison pipeline, bullying, and discipline problems are also covered. The second half of the chapter explains factors that affect media authorities' decisions to broadcast a particular potential news story or ignore it, media issues concerning objectivity, the "fake news" issue, media access inequality, media and crime, and the role of mass media and social media in social activism. The learning of history through movies is also discussed. Movement topics covered include Education and Student movements, and media and social movements.

Chapter 9, Health Care and Well-Being, describes inequalities in health and health care among nations as well as among social groups in the U.S., the effects of globalization on health, the HIV/AIDS problem and the world's reaction to it, major preventable threats to health, efforts to improve access to health care in the U.S., and government programs to provide healthcare. This chapter also explains factors characterizing high life expectancy states compared to low life expectancy states and the Patient Protection and Affordable Care Act (Obamacare). Problems of dealing with mental health and the impact of deinstitutionalization of persons with mental health issues are covered. The effects of the U.S. Labor Union movement, the Civil Rights movement, the Feminist movement, and the Gay Rights movement on improving health care access are also described.

Chapter 10, Crime and Criminal Justice, describes the major forms of crime (such as street crime, white collar crime, cyber crime, organized crime, political crime, serial murder and mass murder), the major types of crime data, changes in patterns of crime over time, the characteristics of criminals, and mass incarceration in the U.S. The chapter also presents biological, psychiatric and sociological approaches to explaining crime, the types of criminal behavior best explained by each approach, and sociological theories of criminal behavior. Movements covered include the Movement to Legalize Marijuana; the Black Lives Matter movement; and the Parkland, Florida, Marjory Stoneman Douglas High School students' Never Again movement.

Chapter 11, Globalization, Technology, and Global Inequalities, explains globalization, the role of technology in globalization, the positive and negative aspects of globalization, and the effects of globalization on poverty and inequality. Chapter 11 also explains the Modernization, World Systems, and Dependency theories of globalization and approaches for reducing the harmful consequences of globalization, including Thomas Piketty's proposal to stop the trend towards ever increasing wealth inequality through worldwide progressive taxation of capital. Global Revolutionary movements are described as well as global techniques to conceal criminal financial activities.

Chapter 12, Population, Urbanization and Aging, describes the major population problems confronting nations around the world and attempts to solve these problems, such as providing education to women and girls in developing countries. The chapter further explains the role of immigration in the U.S. population and the effects of aging on the populations of technologically advanced nations. This chapter also identifies social problems related to urbanization and urban areas in the U.S. and around the world and describes responses to these problems. Malala Yousafzai's Global Girls' Right to Education movement is presented.

Chapter 13, The Environment, describes the major environmental problems facing the U.S. and the world, including global warming, climate change, air pollution, water pollution, land pollution, electronic waste and radioactive waste disposal, and the problems of environmental injustice and environmental racism. This chapter also explains the causes of environmental problems and attempts to reduce them such as green energy. It also describes changes in federal environmental policy by the new administration following the 2016 election. Examples of environmental disasters described in the chapter include the British Petroleum Deep Water Horizon Oil Spill and the Flint, Michigan, Environmental Disaster. Movement activist efforts covered include Lois Gibbs Environmental Activist in response to the Love Canal hazardous waste contamination of residential areas and the Global Water Justice movement.

Chapter 14, Drug Abuse and Human Trafficking, describes what drugs and drug abuse are, the types and levels of drug use around the world and in the U.S., and the consequences of drug abuse. The chapter also explains why many people use drugs and various efforts and proposals to reduce drug abuse. The second part of the chapter describes the forms and characteristics of human trafficking, its causes, and efforts to combat human trafficking. Examples of the inter-relation of drugs and politics in the chapter include Mexican Organized Crime, Corruption and the Murder of 43 College Students, and Drugs, Monarchs and the Contra War. The chapter also has a feature on Sex Trafficking and Sex Slavery and describes the Movement against Human Trafficking.

Chapter 15, War, Rebellion, and Terrorism, explains the concepts of war, rebellion, and terrorism, the causes of war and rebellion, and how war and rebellion can be interrelated. The chapter also describes the consequences of war and rebellion, war crimes, and strategies to establish and maintain peace. The U.S. shift to an all volunteer army, the issue of a cultural gap between many civilians and the military, and the growth of private military firms are discussed. This chapter in addition describes major forms of terrorism and explains the causes of terrorism and different approaches to combating terrorism. The chapter also presents the issue of whether the U.S. should join the International Criminal Court. Movements covered include War, Sexual Violence, and the Movement to End Sexual Assault in the Military and Islamic Fundamentalist Terrorist Movements: Al Qaeda and ISIS.

PEDAGOGICAL FEATURES

Chapter Objectives

Each chapter begins with a set of chapter objectives. Chapter objectives serve as a guide to student readers and assist them in anticipating the most important elements of the chapter.

Chapter Opening Vignettes

Following the chapter objectives, each chapter opens with a brief account of an event, situation or personal experience that illustrates an important aspect of the chapter's content.

Theoretical Analyses of Social Problems

Chapters include analyses of social problems from the points of view of major sociological theoretical frameworks such as the structural-functional, conflict, racial/ethnic-conflict, feminist and symbolic-interactionist approaches.

Inter-State and International Comparisons

To illustrate how the depth of social problems and the approaches for solving them can differ from place to place, inter-state and international comparisons are presented in many chapters.

Social Movements

Social Movements boxes provide important examples of how people organize and work together to solve the social problems described in the text. Some of the movements covered include the Free Higher Education Movement, the Student Movement against Sweatshops, the African American Freedom Movement, and the Child Protection Movement.

Special Topics

Special Topics boxes provide key information about or illustrate a particular aspect of the social problem under discussion. Boxes include *Why Did European Nations Develop More Extensive Social Welfare Systems?, Technologically Advanced Countries' Assistance to Working Families and Their Children, Suppressing Health Research for Political Reasons, The British Petroleum Deep Water Horizon Oil Spill* and the *Flint, Michigan, Environmental Disaster.*

Key Terms

Key terms are defined on the page of the chapter where they first appear, and they are referenced at the end of the chapter. A complete glossary is included at the end of the text.

End of Chapter Materials

The end of each chapter contains a chapter review, key terms list, and discussion questions.

ANCILLARIES

This book is accompanied by an ancillary package that is designed to enhance the experience of both instructors and students.

For Instructors

Instructor's Manual and Test Bank. For each chapter in the text, the Instructor's Manual provides student learning objectives, key terms with definitions, discussion questions, and Web resources. The Test Bank includes a variety of multiple choice, true/false, and short answer questions and is available in either Word or Respondus format. The Instructor's Manual and Test Bank is available to adopters for download on the text's catalog page at https://rowman.com/ISBN/9781442221543.

PowerPoint® Slides. The PowerPoint slides provide lecture slides for every chapter and charts and figures from the text. The presentation is available to adopters for download on the text's catalog page at https://rowman.com/ISBN/9781442221543.

For Students

Companion Website. Accompanying the text is an open-access Companion Website designed to reinforce key topics and help students to master key vocabulary and concepts through flashcards and self-graded quizzes. Students can access the companion website from their computers or mobile devices at https://textbooks.rowman.com/defronzo.

ACKNOWLEDGMENTS

Many people played important roles in the creation of this book. Foremost is Nancy Roberts, executive acquisition editor, of Rowman & Littlefield who encouraged, guided and assisted us through the writing and revisions of the manuscript. Megan Manzano, R&L assistant editor, also played a crucial role in editing and preparing the manuscript for production. We are also very grateful to Sarah Stanton, former R&L senior acquisitions editor, who originally accepted our proposal for this book and assisted us in the early stages of the book's development. Thanks also to Karen Trost, Karen Trost Editorial Services, who provided valuable editing of early versions of several chapters. For the production phase of the book, we are greatly appreciative of the work of Alden Perkins, R&L senior production editor; Integra's Ramanan Sundararajan, team lead-project management; and Integra's Surej Unnikrishnan, project lead, rights and permission. We also express gratitude for the essential efforts of other members of the R&L and Integra communities in the development of this book. In addition, we wish to express thanks to the manuscript reviewers whose comments and suggestions benefitted us greatly and to all those who contributed in other ways, including obtaining the photographs used throughout the book.

Jungyun is very grateful to her colleagues at Stonehill College, especially professors Erica Tucker and Ann Marie Rocheleau, for their friendship and encouragement. She is also deeply indebted to the members of her family and her friends, in particular her mother, Bok-Dan Kim, and her father, Sang-Deuk Gil, her wonderful husband, Jim, and his parents Mary Pavano DeFronzo and Armand DeFronzo, her sister Jungha and brothers Chunghoon and Woongchan, her brother-in-law, Namho Kang, and her sisters-in-law, Bo-na Gong and Kyungim Choi, her fantastic nephews Jimin, Jihyun, and Doeun and niece Yunsil, her husband's brother, Donald DeFronzo, his wife Diane Bracha DeFronzo, her husband's sister Margaret Pastore and partner David Timm, David, Monica, Grace, and Matthew Hermanowski DeFronzo, Victoria and Karen DeFronzo, Michael Pastore, cousin Connie Manafort, and many other cousins.

James would like to thank his fantastic wife Jungyun for all her support and encouragement. He is very grateful to fellow faculty members, and thousands of students at the University of Connecticut and Indiana University, including Professor Lance Hannon of Villanova University and Monica Cuddy, who encouraged his work on social problems and social movements. He is also grateful for the support and encouragement provided by all the relatives Jungyun mentioned above and many friends he met at Fairfield University, Indiana University and Stonehill College, including Professor Walter Ellis now of Hillsborough College, Professor Roger Gocking of Mercy College, John McVarish of Massachusetts, Tom and Brenda Lewandowski of Indiana and wpi@workersproject.org, Sue Cook of Indiana, Professors Jane Prochnow and Bill Tunmer of the University of Canterbury and Massey University, New Zealand, Ted Rhodes and Joni Pascal and Wendy Kimsey and Dave Fowler of California, and Deanna Levanti and Bill Braun of Ivory Silo Farm, Massachusetts. James would like to especially express thanks for the inspiration provided by his brother, Donald DeFronzo, progressive mayor of their home city, New Britain, Connecticut, elected to five terms as state senator and primary senate sponsor of Connecticut's public campaign financing law, state Commissioner of the Department of Administrative Services, and Professor of Public Policy and Practical Politics at Central Connecticut State University who has worked tirelessly in and out of government for universal social justice and equality of opportunity.

Thanks also go to the reviewers who read all or part of the initial manuscript: Cari Beecham-Bautista, College of DuPage; Teresa DeCrescenzo, California State University-Northridge; Keri Diggins, Scottsdale Community College; Laura Workman Eells, McPherson College; Albert Fu, Kutztown University; Scott Hamilton, Dallas County Community College Districts; Angela Lewellyn Jones, Elon University; David G. LoConto, New Mexico State University; Deanna McGaughey-Summers, University of Louisville; Sadie Pendaz-Foster, Normandale Community College; Amy Stich, Northern Illinois University; Peter J. Venturelli, Valparaiso University.

ABOUT THE AUTHORS

James DeFronzo is emeritus faculty of Sociology at the University of Connecticut. He has published research and theoretical articles in the areas of criminology, political sociology, social movements, military sociology, gender, substance abuse, demography, and social psychology. His books include *The Iraq War: Origins and Consequences*, the three volume *Revolutionary Movements in World History* (used in more than sixty countries), and five editions of *Revolutions and Revolutionary Movements* (described in *Choice* (2015) as "likely the best college-level survey of revolutionary movements.")

Jungyun Gill is an associate professor of Sociology in the Sociology and Criminology Department at Stonehill College. She has published and presented research and theoretical works in the areas of gender, families, transnational adoptions, child welfare, mental health, social movements, political sociology, military sociology and Asian racial identity. Her book *Unequal Motherhoods and the Adoption of Asian Children: Birth, Foster and Adoptive Mothers* (2017) explores the personal, organizational and political aspects of the adoption of Asian children by U.S. residents and the experiences of the three types of mothers, birth, foster and adoptive, intimately involved in international interracial adoption.

CHAPTER 1

The Sociology of Social Problems

CHAPTER OBJECTIVES

- Define "social problem."
- Apply the concept of the sociological imagination.
- Compare the major sociological perspectives on social problems.
- Explain how the major types of sociological research are used to understand social problems.

WOULD YOU LIKE TO LIVE IN AN AMERICA *where women are forbidden to vote or hold public office, most Americans face poverty in old age, and parents have to pay thousands of dollars for their child's education from first grade through high school? Things that many Americans take for granted are the results of great popular struggles against inequality and injustice. Progressive social change throughout history has involved some people recognizing that terrible conditions and unfair practices are not necessarily inevitable or preordained and then convincing others to join them in doing something about it.*

In 2008 the United States was hit by an economic downturn so severe that many people lost their jobs and many homeowners found themselves "under water": their homes had dropped in value so drastically that they actually owed more than they were worth. In response, two popular protests arose, each gaining the support of millions of Americans: the conservative Tea Party movement and the liberal Occupy Wall Street movement. Most participants in the Tea Party movement, named after the American rebels who protested against a British tax on tea by tossing British tea into Boston harbor in 1773, believe harmful intervention by the federal government, including "bailout" programs for banks and corporations, is the main cause of serious social problems. In contrast, the Occupy Wall Street movement believes that the actions of the country's economic elite (the wealthiest one percent) are the real cause of major problems, which is why this is also referred to as the 99 Percent Movement. Ninety-nine Percenters believe that harmful policies, including – but not limited to – drastic reduction in taxes on the rich and allowing banks and big business to act in reckless ways without fear of punishment, result from control of government by wealthy people and powerful corporations. They claim that a strong government that really acts in the interests of most people is needed to create fairer laws and policies.

Both the Tea Party and Occupy movements had significant impacts. The Tea Party movement pulled the Republican Party further to the right and helped get many more conservative candidates Republican nominations to run for office. It also turned out large numbers of voters in key elections, such as the crucial 2010 midterm election discussed in Chapter 3, which resulted in far more Republican-controlled state legislatures and governorships and increased Republican members in the House of Representatives. The Occupy Movement propelled the issue of increasing economic inequality into the political spotlight and set the stage for the nearly successful effort of Vermont Senator and self-described democratic socialist Bernie Sanders to win the Democratic presidential nomination in 2016.

What the Tea Party and Occupy Wall Street movements have in common is the view that the cause of many serious social problems is not so much personal failings or choices but powerful social forces. In this sense, both groups are employing a perspective that sociologists call the "sociological imagination." This first chapter defines "social problems" and the sociological imagination, describes the different sociological perspectives, and explains the different methods used to conduct research into social problems in an attempt to find solutions.

WHAT IS A SOCIAL PROBLEM?

A **social problem** is a condition or a type of behavior that many people believe is harmful. Some conditions clearly hurt people, such as lacking enough money to buy basic food, shelter, and clothing; being unable to find a job; or suffering from the effects of a polluted environment. However, the extent to which any of these or other conditions or behaviors becomes social problems is based not only on the reality of their existence but on the level of public concern. For example, extreme poverty existed in parts of the United States in the 1950s, but many Americans were totally unaware of the level of suffering it inflicted. In 1962, writer and social activist Michael Harrington published a compelling book about impoverished Americans, *The Other America*, which caught the attention of the entire nation, including President John F. Kennedy. The book became assigned reading in thousands of college courses from coast to coast. Soon poverty became widely viewed as a social problem, leading to the federal government's "war on poverty" and programs that many Americans rely on today, such as Medicaid (federal government health care for the poor), Medicare (government health care for those 65 or older), food stamps, and more comprehensive Social Security benefits. This illustrates that any social problem has two important components: its **objective element** and its **subjective element**. In this case the objective element is the reality of the conditions of poverty: the reality of insufficient access to food, health services, and education; and high rates of infant mortality, preventable diseases, and illiteracy. The subjective element of poverty is the level of public concern about these objective conditions, the desire to alleviate them, and the belief that this is possible.

The objective elements of a social problem may either be personally experienced or measured in some way. For example, you can determine how many people are unemployed, or go bankrupt because of inability to pay medical expenses. Interpreting how troubling these situations are in terms of deeply held conceptions of right and wrong is a subjective element that can be measured through public opinion surveys.

The process in the development of a social problem begins when someone (a claims maker) makes an argument (a **claim**) that a condition or behavior is harmful and tries to convince others why something must be done about it and what specific actions are needed (Best 2013). The **claims maker** may be an expert in a related field, someone with personal experience, or a social activist who tries to assemble evidence supporting a claim that a condition or behavior is a social problem. As a writer and social activist, Michael Harrington, the author of *The Other America*, is an example of the latter. The next step is gaining favorable coverage from the media. If this effort is successful, the public will react by coming to view the objective condition or behavior as a problem. Claims makers may also try to mobilize large numbers of people in a movement to work together to deal with the problem and force lawmakers to do something about it. The effectiveness of the actions taken by lawmakers can then be evaluated.

social problem A condition or a type of behavior that many people believe is harmful.

objective element Reality of the existence of a condition or behavior recognized as a social problem.

subjective element Level of public concern about a condition or behavior recognized as a social problem.

claim An argument that a condition or behavior is harmful.

claims maker An expert in a related field, someone with personal experience, or a social activist who tries to assemble evidence supporting a claim that a condition or behavior is a social problem.

Social Movements: The Movement for Free Higher Education

Protest against student debt

Since 1970, college tuition in the United States has increased faster than the rate of inflation. During the same period, inflation-adjusted household income has risen very little except for the upper ten percent of the population. The average tuition and fees in 2016 dollars for public four-year colleges and for private nonprofit four-year colleges more than tripled between the 1971–1972 and 2016–2017 academic years. (College Board 2017). Student loan debt for those graduating in 2016 averaged $37,172 and by 2017 an estimated forty-four million Americans had student loan debt (Picchi 2016; Student Loan Hero 2017).

In comparison, after the German state of Lower Saxony ended tuition fees in October of 2014, all public higher education in Germany became tuition free. This was achieved through a sustained student movement advocating that education is a basic human right necessary to ensure equality of opportunity. Every German state will now fund at least one undergraduate degree and a consecutive master's degree (Hermanns 2014). The German free higher education movement began in 1999 in response to several German states introducing college tuition fees. Some two hundred student unions, political parties, labor unions, and other groups created the Alliance Against Tuition Fees. Student protests all over Germany forced an end to the fees.

Many Americans believe that tuition-free universities and colleges can also be achieved in the United States. Like the German activists, they claim this would vastly increase equality of opportunity. Heather Gautney, a sociologist at Fordham University, and Adolph Reed, a political scientist at the University of Pennsylvania, have been national supporters of the U.S. free higher education campaign. The movement calls for an end to tuition for persons who meet admission requirements at all four-year or two-year public institutions of higher learning (Gautney and Reed 2015; Reed 2005; Reed and Gautney 2015). This would ensure that students from working-class and middle-class families have access to college educations. Government funding of free tuition and fees is estimated to cost about one percent or less of the federal budget.

As a step toward universal free higher education, in his January 20, 2015, State of the Union Address, President Barack Obama proposed two years of free community college education throughout the nation for persons having at least a 2.5 grade point average (LoBianco 2015). Supporters asserted that this program would provide students with skills necessary for high-technology and advanced manufacturing jobs. Other students aiming for four-year degrees would be helped by earning two years of college credits free at a community college, which they could then transfer to a four-year institution. In lower-income and working-class neighborhoods two years of free community college has the potential of making going to college the new norm (Bryant 2015). But could such a revolutionary measure actually succeed in the face of conservative opposition? Is a massive youth movement for free higher education possible in the United States, where the dominant culture has fostered a psychological acceptance of the unearned privilege of children from affluent families? During the 2016 presidential campaign, one of the major candidates, Bernie Sanders, who enjoyed overwhelming support among Democratic voters under the age of thirty, called for free public college education for all Americans.

What are your thoughts?
Do you think that college education should be free to qualified persons? How could this be achieved in the United States?

The Social Context of Social Problems

To learn about social problems, how they develop, and how people work together to deal with them, it is important to understand their context: the essential features of the societies in which they arise. These include the basic components of social structure and culture.

Social structure is the expression for relatively stable patterns of social behavior and relationships among people. It means how a society is organized. A **social institution** is a continuing pattern of social relationships intended to fulfill people's basic needs and aspirations and carry out functions essential to the operation of society. The most important institutions include the family, education, the economy, politics and government, health care, organized religion, and the communications media. Within these broad institutions, others exist to carry out specialized functions, such as the criminal justice system within government. Conditions generated by institutions may become social problems. For example, the creation of laws by the government that unfairly favor some people over others, such as tax laws that benefit the wealthy over the middle class, may come to be viewed as a social problem. A major aspect of social structure is **social stratification**, which refers to inequality among people with regard to important social factors including access to education, income, property, power, and prestige. For example, a child born into a family in the wealthiest one percent of the population is likely to be educated in private high schools where tuition and fees often equal or exceed the cost of attending America's top universities. Social stratification can be a major source of social problems if inequality of access becomes too great. Whereas social structure refers to how society is organized, **culture** refers to the knowledge, ways of thinking, shared understandings of behavior, and physical objects that characterize a people's way of life. The elements of culture particularly important for understanding social problems are values, norms, beliefs, and symbols. *Values*, which define what is good, desirable, beautiful, and worth working for, are the goals that culture gives people to strive to achieve in life and, in so doing, feel fulfilled and good about themselves. People's values can influence whether they view specific conditions or behaviors as social problems. For example, since most Americans share the value of equality of opportunity they tend to view poverty, which limits access to educational opportunity, as a social problem.

Just as culture provides values for people to strive for, it also provides guidelines for how to behave in society to achieve and maintain them. *Norms* are shared rules for behavior. The mildest norms, called *folkways*, are general expectations for behavior in particular social situations, like shaking hands when being introduced to someone new. *Mores* are stronger, more widely observed norms with greater moral significance, such as respectful behavior at a religious service. *Laws* are rules for behavior enforced by government. While laws are often also mores, this is not always the case. The National Prohibition Act of 1919 (Volstead Act), which violated the alcohol consumption folkways of many people in the United States by prohibiting the sale of alcoholic beverages, was enacted to help solve social problems such as domestic violence, child abuse, and homicide; these crimes were believed to be committed more often by drunken men. Making the sale of alcohol a crime appeared

social structure Relatively stable patterns of social behavior and relationships among people.

social institution A continuing pattern of social relationships intended to fulfill people's basic needs and aspirations and carry out functions essential to the operation of society.

social stratification Inequality among people with regard to important social factors including access to education, income, property, power, and prestige.

culture The knowledge, ways of thinking, shared understandings of behavior, and physical objects that characterize a people's way of life.

to worsen other social problems, however. Organized crime surged as groups illegally produced or imported and sold alcoholic beverages to the enormous American market. Corruption increased tremendously, as gangsters used their huge profits to bribe police officers, judges, and government officials, who often had no personal moral opposition to alcohol. As this example illustrates, laws intended to reduce social problems can in fact contribute to or escalate harmful social conditions. Another example can be seen in the effects of laws enacted between 1980 and 2007 to grow the economy more rapidly, which greatly reduced financial regulations; these measures vastly increased economic inequality and contributed to the 2008 economic recession that caused the rise of the Tea Party and Occupy Wall Street movements.

Beliefs are another important element of culture. They are the ideas people have about what is true and how things should be. This includes why certain events occur or conditions exist. Beliefs may be based on experience or values and norms, or on what is learned from family, friends, school, recognized experts, or communication media like TV or the Internet. Consider global climate change. Beliefs affect whether someone thinks it actually exists, whether it is a problem, and whether people or government can do anything about it. A *symbol* is anything, including words, objects, or images, which represents something beyond itself. A symbol conveys a meaning to people. The logo of a profitable oil corporation may bring feelings of well-being to its executives and shareholders but provoke hostility from those who blame it for environmental pollution. The emotions elicited by a particular symbol can play a significant role in the mobilization of people to respond to a social problem.

Values, norms, beliefs, and symbols are not necessarily the same for every member of a particular culture. A **subculture** refers to a specific set of values, norms, beliefs, symbols, and behaviors shared by a group of people unique enough to significantly distinguish them from the other members of a culture. Subcultures can be based on factors such as occupation, wealth, religion, age, region, ethnicity, or patterns of recreation. For example, Wall Street financial executives tend to share a set of values and norms somewhat different from members of labor unions such as the International Brotherhood of Teamsters, which includes truck drivers, warehouse workers, locomotive engineers, and airline pilots. Among religious groups in the United States, the evangelical Protestant subculture is more socially conservative and reliant on literal interpretations of the Bible than other Protestant churches such as the Methodists, Congregationalists, Presbyterians, and Episcopalians.

Opposing Explanations for Social Problems

The elements of social structure and culture just described can have a powerful influence on which conditions or patterns of behavior are recognized as social problems and what people decide to do about them. For example, growing wealth inequality may worry middle- and working-class people, who believe that economic and political power is being concentrated in the hands of a few. In contrast, those in the upper class may view inequality as a necessary byproduct of the economic growth that is beneficial to all members of society.

subculture A specific set of values, norms, beliefs, symbols, and behaviors shared by a group of people unique enough to significantly distinguish them from the other members of a culture.

Another example of opposing beliefs is the relationship between guns and crime. Many believe that easy access to handguns causes violent crimes such as homicide, but many others view gun ownership as a solution to crime. The latter point of view gained support after a mass murder in Killeen, Texas, in 1991; a man drove his pickup truck through the front window of a restaurant and proceeded to shoot and kill twenty-three people, resulting in the most lethal shooting rampage in the United States at that time. Dr. Suzanna Hupp, a chiropractor who was having lunch with her parents, had left her handgun in her car in obedience to Texas law; she survived, but both of her parents were killed. Believing she could have stopped the killings if she had taken her gun into the restaurant, Hupp campaigned in Texas and throughout the country for the passage of laws that would permit citizens with no criminal records to carry guns. Texas passed such a law in 1995, and a number of other states followed suit. Hundreds of thousands more people now carry guns legally, and many believe this change in law has helped deter crime. Others feel that more gun carrying increases the risk that arguments or incidents such as road rage will lead to shootings that otherwise would not happen (Donohue, Aneja, and Weber 2017; Ewing 2017).

Special Topics: What Are Today's Greatest Social Problems?

What are the most serious problems facing society? Two polls of thirty-six thousand individuals in twenty-three countries on six continents conducted by the British Broadcasting Company identified the following as major social problems (BBC 2010, 2011):

- extreme poverty
- unemployment
- corruption
- crime
- pollution
- the costs of food and energy
- human rights abuses
- war
- terrorism
- climate change

Views on which problems were the most serious, however, varied widely around the globe. Residents of India, Nigeria, and Turkey were especially worried about corruption. In China and Russia, the greatest concern was the cost of food and energy. In Mexico, Brazil, and Ecuador, crime and violence were seen as the greatest problems.

In 2017, the United Nations identified these same problems along with additional concerns (United Nations 2017a): ensuring access to clean water, enhancing the rights and opportunities of women and children, protecting refugees fleeing war and other threats, and safeguarding and promoting democracy around the world.

What are your thoughts?

Let's start by looking a little closer to home. What do you think are the seven most important social problems in the United States today? Rank them beginning with the most serious. Record your answers in the blanks and then compare your choices to those in the table below.

1. _____
2. _____
3. _____
4. _____
5. _____
6. _____
7. _____

(continued)

Special Topics (*continued*)

TABLE 1.1	Results of Gallup National Survey: Most Important Problems (March 2017)
1) Dissatisfaction with government/Poor leadership	
2) Immigration/Illegal aliens	
3) Unemployment/jobs	
4) The economy in general	
5) Healthcare	
6) Unifying the country	
7) Race relations/Racism	
8) Education	
9) National security	
10) Federal budget deficit/Federal debt	

Source: Gallup 2017.

USING THE SOCIOLOGICAL IMAGINATION TO ADDRESS SOCIAL PROBLEMS

One of sociology's greatest tools for understanding and analyzing social problems is the sociological imagination. As described by legendary American sociologist C. Wright Mills, the **sociological imagination** is the ability to relate the most personal elements and problems (what Mills called "personal troubles") of an individual's life to social forces and the flow of history. It helps us understand how our experiences, feelings, thoughts, and actions, as well as those of other people, are affected by the structure of society, culture, and social change (Mills 1959:6–7). A personal problem becomes a social problem (what Mills called a "public issue") when society comes to view its cause as a result of social forces rather than personal characteristics.

A sociological analysis of the development of the gang problem in Los Angeles provides an excellent application of the sociological

sociological imagination The ability to relate the most personal elements and problems of an individual's life to social forces and the flow of history.

Demonstration in favor of more effective gun laws and gun law enforcement

imagination to a social problem. During and following World War II, Los Angeles experienced a huge industrial boom as major corporations established or expanded factories there, including automobile manufacturers. Firms recruited thousands of African Americans for well-paying manufacturing jobs, who then purchased homes and entered the middle class. The large majority of African-American children were born into two-parent families. However, in the 1960s the manufacturing plants began to move out of Los Angeles.

As advancing technology eliminated some industrial jobs, companies pulled up stakes to locate their plants in countries where they could increase their profits by paying much lower wages. The workers who lost their jobs generally did not receive training or assistance to help them develop new skills. In a short time, the Los Angeles African American middle class was decimated; the income enabling family support disappeared with the factories. More and more children began growing up in single-parent households lacking a stable male role model. As economic opportunity declined and family structure weakened, membership in new criminal youth gangs surged. Two of the most powerful gangs, the Bloods and the Crips, were founded in 1970 (Peralta 2009). The gangs provided status, a family-type environment complete with older male role models, and economic opportunities through drug trafficking. In the 1980s and 1990s, homicide rates in Los Angeles reached record levels as young members of rival gangs killed each other.

Someone watching the news coverage of gang violence in Los Angeles might conclude that an inherent immorality of African American young people caused the gang violence and drug dealing. Applying the sociological imagination allows you to see a more accurate picture: the social origins of the violent behavior of gang members. The gang youth were often the children or grandchildren of perfectly

Shut-down factory

law-abiding citizens. It was the change in economic and social conditions that created a generation with different attitudes and patterns of behavior. In identifying the underlying social causes of criminal youth gangs, sociological analysis also points to potential social solutions to this social problem. Perhaps government policy should prevent companies from moving manufacturing to other countries or provide incentives to move plants back to areas in the United States where unemployment levels are high. The sociological imagination allows identification of such measures as policies that could help solve the youth gang problem.

SOCIOLOGICAL PERSPECTIVES ON SOCIAL PROBLEMS

When you apply the sociological imagination, you look for links between personal characteristics and experiences, and social forces. However, a complete understanding of the nature of those social forces requires an understanding of the nature of society itself. Sociologists have developed three major conceptual frameworks to describe how society works: the structural-functional, conflict, and symbolic-interactionist perspectives. These three perspectives serve as general frameworks on which to build distinct **theories** or explanations for the existence of particular social conditions or patterns of behavior. These approaches can be presented as mutually exclusive conceptions of society, but the most accurate and productive approach is to view them as complementary: Each one identifies important social processes that may be more or less relevant to a particular situation. In addition, each theoretical perspective suggests how social problems may develop and what can be done to address them.

theory An explanation for the existence of particular social conditions or patterns of behavior.

Structural-Functional Perspective

The **structural-functional perspective**, also referred to as structural functionalism, is a conceptual framework that views society as a system of interdependent parts carrying out functions crucial to the well-being of the other parts and the system as a whole. For example, the structural-functional point of view considers the institution of the family to have the primary responsibility for maintaining the physical and emotional well-being of children, socializing them, and teaching them basic morality and how to treat other people with respect. The educational system has the function of providing the knowledge and skills for people to become productive participants in the economy. The economy combines people's knowledge and talents with technology and resources to produce goods and services, and the political system maintains order and defends society against threats. Functionalists note that institutions can have both intended and publicly recognized functions called **manifest functions**, as well as other equally real but unintended and often not well-understood functions referred to as **latent functions**. For example, the manifest function of elementary school is to educate children and provide them with a basic foundation for more advanced learning. It also has the real latent functions of supervising and protecting young children while their parents and/or guardians are at work. The structural-functional perspective provides three major approaches to explaining the development of social problems: social pathology, social disorganization, and social dysfunction.

Social Pathology The early pioneers of structural functionalism, Frenchmen August Comte (Coser 1977) and Emile Durkheim (1892) and the Englishman Herbert Spencer (Turner, Beeghley, and Powers 2006), viewed society as analogous to a living organism that can be healthy, evolve to a higher state, or become ill (suffer from a disease). This approach is referred to as **social pathology**. From this point of view society becomes sick and plagued with harmful conditions for several possible reasons. One is the failure to adequately teach children the cultural values and norms necessary to fit in with and abide by the rules of society. This could result from the breakdown of the family or the educational system, or the weakening of religion leading to other institutions being unable to adequately carry out their functions. Other events that might have such effects could be war or epidemics that drastically reduce the size of a society's healthy population and workforce and drain its resources.

Inspired by ideas of biological evolutionists such as Charles Darwin and Jean-Baptiste Lamarck, Spencer argued that the presence of too many morally or physically defective people could prevent a society from evolving to a higher state. Spencer created the expression "survival of the fittest" to represent his belief that people and societies were more likely to evolve if each individual enjoyed or suffered the consequences of his or her abilities and actions. The most "fit" would survive and prosper. Consistent with this view, he was generally against government intervention in society to aid the weak or poor or to redistribute income or resources. Spencer's view of society, which became known as "social Darwinism," provided supposedly scientific rationalizations for the

structural-functional perspective A conceptual framework that views society as a system of interdependent parts carrying out functions crucial to the well-being of the other parts and the system as a whole.

manifest functions Intended and publicly recognized functions.

latent functions Unintended and often hidden or not well-understood functions.

social pathology A structural-functional perspective that likens society to a living organism that can be healthy, evolve to a higher state, or become ill.

views of some European leaders who believed that their societies were inherently superior and had the right to dominate over nonwhite peoples. It also supported local politicians in their efforts to oppose social welfare systems, which would help "unfit" people survive and interfere with the process of evolution.

Social Disorganization A second functionalist explanation for social problems emerged from the work of sociologists at the University of Chicago, including Ernest Burgess and Robert Park. Observing the massive influx of immigrants from rural areas and other countries who arrived to work in the surging industrial economy, these social scientists concluded that social change that occurs too quickly causes social disorganization, the disruption of the functioning of social institutions. Schools were unprepared for the huge flood of children, good housing was scarce, and the cultural composition of neighborhoods changed rapidly and often kept changing. Many people became disillusioned when their norms did not fit with urban life or help them achieve their goals. This situation, being without meaningful or useful norms, is called **anomie**. Family life suffered and crime soared. Functionalist Robert Merton (1957) developed a theory about crime as a social problem based on the concepts of social disorganization and anomie. He claimed that because the United States had a highly materialist culture but very unequal access to legitimate opportunities such as education and jobs, those without opportunities become highly frustrated. Many of them respond by "innovating," creating illegal patterns of behavior to obtain the materialistic values of their culture unachievable by legitimate means.

Social Dysfunction Robert Merton described another cause of social problems: **social dysfunction**. According to this approach, the positive functions of social institutions may simultaneously create harmful (dysfunctional) conditions. For example, improvements in technology make an economic system more productive (a positive function) but may eliminate jobs and increase unemployment and poverty; these dysfunctions can disrupt or degrade the functioning of the overall society. Similarly, the use of certain energy resources, such as coal, to provide electrical power may cause environmental damage. Society must continuously be on the lookout for dysfunctions caused by its social institutions.

Conflict Perspective

The **conflict perspective** is a conceptual approach that views society as characterized by inequalities that advantage some groups and disadvantage others, leading to conflict and the potential for social change. In contrast to the structural-functional perspective, which implies that change is generally gradual except for the occasional impact of a breakthrough scientific discovery or technological innovation, advocates of the conflict approach argue that, throughout history, social change has often been rapid and sweeping. They view social change as the product of social conflict such as that experienced in the American, French, Russian, Chinese, and Arab Spring revolutions, in which large mobilized masses of the population broke the chains of power and coercion that held the

social disorganization A structural-functional perspective that sees problems being caused by social change that occurs too quickly, or anything else that disrupts the functioning of social institutions.

anomie State of lacking meaningful or useful norms (also referred to as normlessness).

social dysfunction A structural-functional perspective asserting that harmful conditions may be created by the positive functions of social institutions.

conflict perspective A conceptual approach that views society as characterized by inequalities that advantage some groups and disadvantage others, leading to conflict and the potential for social change.

old society together. The basis of conflict ranges from inequalities based on economic class, race, gender, sexual orientation, or other factors to differences of opinion on issues such as abortion or gun ownership.

The conflict perspective emerged from the work of the German social theorist Karl Marx (Marx 1867; Marx and Engels 1848). Marx's nineteenth-century analysis of societies throughout history led him to promote the idea that society is the product of the use of technology to obtain or produce the necessities of life and improve living conditions. As technology and the economy change over time, so does the structure and culture of society. Marx focused on the shift from agricultural economies to the industrial economies shaped by advancing technology and capitalist investments. He argued that in all societies those who dominate the economy also dominate the political system as well as other major institutions, and try to shape the institutions and culture to protect their interests.

According to Marx, as those at the top of a capitalist society (the *bourgeoisie*) expand their wealth and power, inequality grows to a level unbearable for the working-class majority of the population (the *proletariat*) because of deteriorating living standards. Eventually the proletariat launch a rebellion to overthrow the bourgeoisie. The goal of a proletarian revolution is the establishment of a new economic and social system called *socialism*, in which major resources, big businesses, and large industries are collectively owned, and income and opportunities are distributed more equally. Obviously, no sweeping transformation from capitalism to socialism has occurred in the technologically advanced societies, but Marx's ideas have inspired several modern forms of the conflict approach.

Economic-Conflict Perspective The **economic-conflict perspective** focuses on factors such as poverty, the concentration of power in the hands of the wealthy, and the profit motive of capitalist culture as major causes of social problems. The capitalist system's pursuit of profits at the expense of human welfare is the ultimate cause of harmful economic conditions and the social problems that arise from them. These social problems include street and white-collar crime, environmental pollution, political corruption, war, and many others. According to this view, the solution to social problems lies in efforts by the majority to develop a more humane economic system; replacing an intensely profit driven system should greatly reduce inequality and eliminate poverty.

Racial/Ethnic-Conflict Perspective The **racial/ethnic-conflict perspective** emphasizes that inequality and conflict are not only rooted in economic factors; they can also result from discrimination against people on the basis of skin color or ethnic heritage. The settlers of the colonies that became the United States, primarily white Protestants from Britain and other northern European countries, established a culture that ranked themselves on top, with all other racial and religious groups below. This had a dramatic influence on political rights and economic opportunities. Slavery was the worst example, but following the end of slavery after the Civil War, racism and cultural prejudice continued to flourish, limiting access to jobs and education, along with the right

economic-conflict perspective A conflict perspective that focuses on factors such as poverty, the concentration of power in the hands of the wealthy, and the profit motive of capitalist culture as major causes of social problems.

racial/ethnic-conflict perspective A conflict perspective that focuses on discrimination based on skin color or ethnic heritage as the cause of social problems.

to vote and a positive social identity. Despite massive struggles against racism and ethnic prejudice, including the civil rights movement of the 1950s and 60s, many Americans still discriminate on the basis of race and/or ethnicity. This disadvantages certain groups, increasing their risk of being poor and their probability of engagement in and victimization by crime.

Feminist-Conflict Perspective The **feminist-conflict perspective** focuses on gender inequality. Gender was neglected by early sociologists, whose studies were dominated by the male point of view. Feminist scholars note that functionalists like Talcott Parsons adopted the position that women's biology (the ability to bear children) determined their role in society, limiting them to child-rearing and caring for the household. However, they viewed the original conflict perspective as inadequate because it paid too little attention to the oppression of women inherent in *patriarchy*, the male dominated social system characteristic of almost all societies. Feminists view patriarchy as the cause of many social problems, including physical and sexual violence against women, gender discrimination, and the high female poverty rate. Feminist sociologists make women the central focus of sociological analysis. Gender inequality is not due to women's "nature." It is instead the product of self-serving patriarchal beliefs that men created about women's "appropriate" social roles, capabilities, and limitations. Feminist theorists believe research on social problems should focus on improvements to society, especially efforts to eliminate inequality between men and women in all areas of life.

False and True Consciousness in the Conflict Perspective All conflict theories are concerned with the importance of moving people away from a state of **false consciousness**, a lack of understanding about the existence or cause of a harmful condition or behavior. The aim is to replace false consciousness with **true consciousness** of the existence and cause of a harmful condition or behavior. (Marx in his theory called true consciousness *class consciousness*, the awareness of real economic interests and how they are affected by existing social arrangements.) According to the conflict perspective, those who benefit from existing social arrangements promote false consciousness in those they dominate and exploit. For example, in the past governing elites in many societies fostered cultural beliefs and religious doctrines that made workers, slaves, and/or women believe that their limited opportunities were due to their own inferiority or to the will of their Creator. Social activists attempt to create true consciousness by making people aware of harmful conditions and by promoting the idea that these conditions can be eliminated if people work together.

Symbolic-Interactionist Perspective

Both the structural-functional and conflict approaches are macrosociological in that they analyze society on a large scale, focusing on social institutions and the relationships of population groups to those institutions. The **symbolic-interactionist perspective** (also called symbolic

feminist-conflict perspective A conflict perspective that focuses on gender inequality as the cause of social problems.

false consciousness A lack of understanding about the existence or cause of a harmful condition or behavior.

true consciousness Awareness of the existence and real cause of a harmful condition or behavior and that this harmful condition or behavior can be eliminated if people work together.

symbolic-interactionist perspective A sociological perspective that focuses on the analysis of person-to-person interaction and the actual meanings people give to their experiences and environments.

interactionism), in comparison, is a microsociological approach that focuses on the analysis of person-to-person interaction and the actual meanings people give to their experiences and environments. This perspective attempts to explain the origin of certain harmful conditions or behaviors at a more personal level. Adopting the learning theory of crime developed by the famous criminologist Edwin Sutherland, symbolic interactionists believe that many lawbreakers, from professional burglars to corporate white-collar criminals, become criminals by learning certain attitudes and skills from others.

According to symbolic interactionism, society is continually constructed through social interaction. American pioneers of this perspective Charles Horton Cooley and George Herbert Mead (Turner, Beeghley, and Powers 2006) believed that a person's sense of self and personality are not simply the outgrowth of genetic makeup. Rather, the self is continuously constructed through ongoing human interaction. Cooley called this concept the *looking glass self*. People's understanding of their own identity, as well as traits such as values, beliefs, attitudes, and behavior toward others, all originate from how they think others perceive them and what they expect of them.

Two other sociologists, W. I. Thomas and Dorothy Swaine Thomas (1928:572), developed an important contribution to symbolic interactionism and the study of social problems called the Thomas theorem. According to the Thomas theorem, if situations are defined as real, their consequences are real. In other words, people's subjective interpretations of reality, rather than objective reality, determine how they behave. Consider the aforementioned belief held that women's biology naturally limits their capabilities and confines them to childrearing and taking care of household chores. This belief prevented many men and women from recognizing women's true capabilities and that an oppressive social system, not nature, was limiting women's potential for achievement. Symbolic interactionism identifies why people learn to ignore certain conditions or behaviors and define them as "normal," or come to see them as social problems.

The Benefit of a Combined Perspective

Each of the three major perspectives has both important insights and limitations that suggest they might be best used in combination. The structural-functional perspective fits with what appear to be the normal patterns of interdependency that people experience every day, and the concepts of social disorganization and social dysfunction are appealing explanations for harmful conditions. It views inequality as created by the superior abilities and efforts of individuals functioning within the social system. The structural-functional perspective, however, tends to ignore excessive inequalities and divisions based on factors such as class, race, and gender, as well as the roles of coercion, exploitation, oppression, and discrimination, assuming that the organization of society is inherently functional. In addition, it neglects the importance of privileged status in protecting and increasing advantages and power.

The conflict perspective, in contrast, is criticized for overlooking evidence that large sectors of society seem to function relatively smoothly for extended periods of time, providing valuable goods and services through a process of exchange and interdependency. It is also criticized for exaggerating the degree of division and conflict in society to levels that are unrealistic, except during periods of exceptional conflict. However, the conflict approach does direct attention to how the wealthy can dominate government and shape laws to benefit them and allow them to exert great influence over the mass media and other institutions that influence the masses. The conflict perspective appears better suited than the structural-functional perspective to explaining the development of certain objective conditions, such as economic inequality and environmental pollution, that come to be viewed as social problems. Although the structural-functional approach provides a broad overview of how society functions, the conflict perspective is better at uncovering how particular social arrangements benefit certain groups more than others.

Symbolic-interactionism focuses on how people construct their understandings of society through communication. Thus, it is especially useful in understanding how a particular condition or behavior comes to be viewed as a social problem. The symbolic-interactionist perspective emphasizes the microsociological processes of learning and interaction, in comparison to the structural-functional and conflict macrosociological approaches that focus mainly on social structure. But symbolic-interactionism has been criticized for not paying enough attention to the influence of social structures on people's lives and learning experiences. For example, many young people become involved in certain criminal behaviors like drug dealing or burglary because they learn them from others, but having these learning experiences is much more likely to happen to young people who live in high-poverty areas where decent-paying jobs are scarce. Like the conflict perspective, symbolic-interactionism stresses the importance of exploring who wants people to believe a particular social condition or behavior is not a problem, who wants them to believe it is, and what they are attempting to accomplish.

SOCIOLOGICAL RESEARCH ON SOCIAL PROBLEMS

In modern societies when a condition or a behavior becomes widely viewed as a social problem, it is likely to become the subject of scientific research in order to develop a better understanding of the problem, its cause, and potential solutions. Social activists may cite research findings to bolster their points of view. Politicians and organizations often rely on research to guide them in formulating policies and allocating resources to deal with social problems. Ideally, everyone should understand the essential features and basic types of social research and how to evaluate the significance and validity of research findings.

The research process begins with a **research question**, the topic that the researcher wants to investigate (Babbie 2016; Neuman 2011). For example, a researcher concerned with the problem of millions of Americans lacking health insurance might decide to investigate how

research question The topic that the researcher wants to investigate.

other wealthy, technologically advanced nations provide universal health care coverage for their citizens. Or a researcher concerned with the unemployment problem might examine how effective community colleges are in providing new skills for laid-off workers that actually result in getting jobs. A second step is to learn what is known about the topic from previous research. This is called the **literature review**. This can help the researcher decide what type of research to conduct and what further aspects her or his research will involve.

Depending on the research question and what previous research has revealed about the topic, a study may be exploratory, descriptive, explanatory, or applied. An *exploratory study* is useful as a starting point when there is little or no prior research on the issue. It can provide guidance for the design of later studies. For example, if a new pattern of behavior develops, such as prostitution among teenagers from middle-class families, a researcher might initially explore the topic by interviewing some of the young people and law enforcement officers involved. This effort could lead to the identification of key groups involved in the activity and an improved understanding that guides the researcher in developing descriptive studies. *Descriptive studies* gather detailed observations on the characteristics of the condition or behavior that exploratory or past research indicates are important to examine. If sufficient descriptive material is available, a sociologist might conduct an *explanatory study* that attempts to explain why a particular social condition or pattern of behavior exists. For example, if a series of descriptive studies finds that most of the members of juvenile gangs are high-school dropouts, a sociologist might develop a theory that poor academic performance causes young people to join gangs.

In the gang example, academic performance and gang membership are referred to as variables. A **variable** is anything that can have two or more values and can be measured in some way. When you decide how to measure a variable, you are operationalizing it. For example, let's consider the theory that poor academic performance causes young people to join gangs. The variable for academic performance could be operationalized as a student's grade point average. This variable is called the **independent variable**. An independent variable is the one that the theory says determines the value of another variable called the **dependent variable**. In our example, gang membership is the dependent variable. Here it could be operationalized simply as "joined" or "did not join." An explanatory study involves testing a **hypothesis**. A hypothesis is a prediction derived from a theory about how one variable is related to another variable. If the hypothesis is found to be true, then the theory receives support. Say that a sociologist tests the hypothesis that young people join gangs after receiving poor grades. The researcher is gathering information not only to see if there is a link between a low grade point average and joining a gang but to determine which comes first. If the study finds that a person joins a gang *after* getting a low grade point average, the hypothesis is confirmed. But if the study finds that young people with high grade point averages join gangs and *then* their grade point averages go down, the hypothesis is not confirmed.

If repeated studies continue to confirm a theory, then some type of intervention might be developed. For example, if subsequent studies

literature review A researcher's review of previous research on her or his topic of interest.

variable Anything that can have two or more values and can be measured in some way.

independent variable The variable that a theory says determines the value of another variable.

dependent variable The variable whose value is determined by the independent variable.

hypothesis A prediction derived from a theory about how one variable is related to another variable.

Responding to a multiple-choice question on a questionnaire survey

applied research (also called evaluation research) Testing the effectiveness of any program, strategy, or policy intended to affect society.

survey research A type of research that involves asking people questions about a topic.

sample The persons chosen for a study to represent a larger population you want to learn about.

experiment The type of research in which the independent variable is manipulated to see if this is followed by the predicted change in the dependent variable while controlling for other factors thought to affect the dependent variable.

confirm that young people's poor school performance is followed by joining gangs, a special tutoring program might be created to assist children whose grades begin to deteriorate. Testing the effectiveness of such a program or any strategy or policy intended to affect society is called **applied research**.

Survey Research

Once you have decided on your research question and whether your study is exploratory, descriptive, explanatory, or applied, you need to select your research method. **Survey research**, one of the most widely used sociological research methods, involves asking people questions about a topic. The survey approach includes personal interviews and questionnaire surveys. The *personal interview* is a relatively intimate form of survey research in which the interviewer meets face-to-face or over the telephone or similar electronic devices with research participants to ask questions about a topic. The interactive nature of the interview allows the researcher to ask follow-up questions to obtain an in-depth understanding of the respondent's thoughts and feelings about a subject, but interviews are relatively time consuming, expensive to conduct, and lack anonymity. Respondents may be unwilling to give honest verbal answers to certain questions. Relatively brief personal interviews, typically conducted by phone leading up to a major election to gauge support for candidates or issues on the ballot, may be conducted by news agencies, universities, or other institutions to inform the public, or by partisan political groups or consulting firms to help them advise their candidates or groups.

Questionnaire surveys are a relatively quick and inexpensive way to gather a lot of information from a lot of people. Questionnaires may be mailed, passed out in person, or sent electronically. Since they are anonymous and can be filled out in private, participants are more likely to give honest responses than in face-to-face interviews. On the other hand, questionnaires often provide more superficial information than well-constructed interviews, and the response rate is low. When conducting personal interviews or questionnaire surveys, you must make sure that the people in the **sample** (the persons chosen for a study to represent a larger population about which you want to learn) have been selected in such a way that they are representative of the population that interests you. For example, say that you would like to know the opinions of nurses throughout the United States about access to affordable health care. Since it's impractical to question hundreds of thousands of nurses, you would randomly select a sample of nurses to interview.

Experiments

The **experiment** is a form of research especially useful for testing for a cause-and-effect relationship between variables. The independent variable is manipulated while other factors thought to affect the dependent variable are controlled. If manipulation of the independent variable is followed by the predicted change in the dependent variable, there is evidence of a causal relationship. In 2010 George Mason University professor David Weisburd was awarded the Stockholm Prize in Criminology for his experiments showing that concentrating police patrols in high-crime areas did not just shift criminal behavior to other locations but actually reduced it (Greif 2010). In one crucial experiment in a large Midwestern city, 110 high-crime city blocks or crime "hot spots" were identified. The hot spots were randomly assigned either to the *experimental (treatment) condition* (concentrating police patrols) or to the *control* or *untreated condition* (not concentrating police patrols) (Weisburd 2005). Preventive police patrols were two to three times more frequent in the blocks in the experimental condition than in the blocks in the control condition. The results showed a decrease in crime in the blocks with heightened police patrols compared to those with the standard number of police patrols.

One potential limitation of experiments is that the more tightly the researcher controls the elements of the experiment, the more unrealistic the experimental condition may become, which decreases the relevance of the findings to life outside the experimental setting.

Field Research

Field research, often called *ethnography*, involves gathering data on assumed natural behavior in the field, the real-world setting. This involves careful observation and accurate recording of people's behavior and the meanings and explanations they give to their own actions. This may be accomplished by taking plentiful notes while making the observations or from memory following a period of observations or by recording observations electronically. The researcher may simply observe people's behavior. Or she or he may actually participate in their activities and possibly form a long-term relationship with the people whose behavior she or he is observing. This second option is called **participant observation**. Mitchell Duneier's (2000) *Sidewalk* is an important participant observer study. In this five-year effort the author observed, interviewed, and worked as an assistant for poor sidewalk book and other merchandise vendors, many of them homeless persons, and sold magazines himself on three New York City blocks. Duneier's research revealed the struggles and strategies of these individuals trying to earn a living in their typically illegal businesses. Another notable example of participant observer research is Jeffrey Kidder's (2005) "Style and Action: A Decoding of Bike Messenger Symbols" in which he worked for a year as a New York City bicycle messenger learning about the experiences, thoughts, interactions, and way of life of people involved in this unique, exciting, and potentially dangerous job.

Field research is intended to provide a much deeper and comprehensive understanding of social behavior than is possible through the use of surveys or experiments. It is especially well suited for studying groups of special interest to society (such as juvenile gangs), unique occupations or subcultures, and unusual activities such as episodes of social conflict or protest.

field research A type of research that involves gathering data on what is assumed to be natural behavior in a real-world setting.

participant observation A type of research that involves the researcher actually participating in the activities of the people she or he is observing.

Focus Groups

A **focus group** is a group discussion, usually one to two hours in length, in which group members are asked to focus on a selected topic under the guidance of a researcher who acts as a moderator and facilitator. According to Morgan (1996:2), "The hallmark of focus groups is their explicit use of group interaction to produce data and insights that would be less accessible without the interaction found in a group." Focus groups can be used, for example, to evaluate alternate approaches to winning support for a particular cause, political candidate, or product. Morgan (1996:34–35) indicates that, except for special circumstances, the groups should be composed of strangers who are similar in terms of race, class, gender, and age. Similarity is thought to facilitate free communication, and strangers are more likely to express their ideas openly. Morgan also recommends that a focus group be limited to six to ten members and have a well-structured plan with a predetermined set of essential questions.

Secondary Data Analysis

Secondary data analysis involves analyzing data that have been collected by others. Secondary data can be obtained from the U.S. Census; the FBI Uniform Crime Reports; large surveys such as the National Election Survey, the General Social Survey, and the National Crime Victimization Survey; or any government, business, institutional, or historical records or documents. Social scientists can use such data to gain insights into the size, characteristics, and causes of social problems. For example, in 2012 the Center for Public Integrity (Ginley 2012) published the results of a study of state laws and policies about the provision of information to the public regarding government finances and private lobbyists, political campaigns financing, and ethics enforcement. States received scores on their level of vulnerability to corruption. None of the states achieved an "A" rating. The five states receiving B-level grades were California, Connecticut, Nebraska, New Jersey, and Washington State. More than 50 percent of the states scored below a C–, and eight (Georgia, Maine, Michigan, North Dakota, South Carolina, South Dakota, Virginia, and Wyoming), got an "F." Later research showed generally similar state rankings (Kusnetz 2015). While Virginia reduced its vulnerability to corruption, there was little evidence of any improvement for the large majority of states.

Historical and Comparative Research

Historical and comparative research, sociological analyses and comparisons of societies, was the preferred research method of early social theorists, including Comte, Spencer, and Durkheim. Marx's historical and comparative analyses led to the development of conflict theory. After studying a number of societies, another German sociologist, Max Weber (1904–1905; 1915), concluded that the development of unique ideas could bring about massive social change. He claimed that major religions, such as Catholicism, Buddhism, and Hinduism, lacked the qualities of the Protestant work ethic that gave rise to the spirit of capitalism and the rapid capitalist acceleration of technological advances, productivity, and commerce in northern Europe following the Protestant Reformation.

focus group A group discussion, usually one to two hours in length, in which group members are asked to focus on a selected topic under the guidance of a researcher who acts as a moderator and facilitator.

secondary data analysis A type of research that involves analyzing data that have been collected by others.

historical and comparative research Sociological analyses and comparisons of societies.

A contemporary example of historical and comparative research is an attempt by multiple researchers to identify the factors that brought about revolutions during the twentieth and twenty-first centuries (DeFronzo 2015; Foran 2005; Goldfrank 1979; Goldstone 1980, 1982; Goodwin 2001). This work involved examining the pre-revolution population, economic, and political characteristics of each nation; reviewing the writings, ideologies, and biographies of revolutionary leaders; evaluating the actions of governments; and analyzing newspaper and eye witness accounts. Elements strongly related to revolution included high levels of discontent in wide sectors of a society's population; divisions among the elite; unifying motivations that cut across economic class lines and unite the majority of a society's population behind the goal of revolution; severe political crises that paralyzed the administrative and coercive capabilities of the state; and a permissive world context in which other nations do not intervene effectively to prevent revolution.

Examine the data in the table below:

1. What research questions would you like to develop?
2. Is your study going to be exploratory, descriptive, explanatory, or applied?
3. What research method would you like to employ for your study?

Why do you think your method is most suitable for your study?

TABLE 1.2		Differences in Health Care Insurance and Health				
		2013–2016 Average Percentage of People without Health Insurance	2016 Infant Mortality Rate (Deaths per 1,000 Live Births)	2016 Stroke Mortality Rate (Deaths per 100,000 Population)	2016 Cancer Mortality Rate (Deaths per 100,000 Population)	2016 Heart Disease Mortality Rate (Deaths per 100,000 Population)
The ten most uninsured states	Texas	18.7%	5.7	42.0	148.5	167.7
	Alaska	16.2%	5.4	39.0	158.7	141.0
	Florida	15.6%	6.1	37.3	146.9	146.2
	Georgia	15.4%	7.5	44.3	160.2	179.0
	Oklahoma	15.2%	7.4	41.8	177.8	228.2
	Nevada	14.9%	5.7	35.9	157.3	205.9

(continued)

| TABLE 1.2 | Differences in Health Care Insurance and Health (*continued*) |

		2013–2016 Average Percentage of People without Health Insurance	2016 Infant Mortality Rate (Deaths per 1,000 Live Births)	2016 Stroke Mortality Rate (Deaths per 100,000 Population)	2016 Cancer Mortality Rate (Deaths per 100,000 Population)	2016 Heart Disease Mortality Rate (Deaths per 100,000 Population)
	Mississippi	14.0%	8.6	50.6	187.7	233.1
	Louisiana	13.4%	8.0	46.0	171.9	213.1
	New Mexico	13.3%	6.2	35.5	138.8	150.6
	Arizona	12.9%	5.4	29.8	136.8	138.9
Average		**15.0%**	**6.6**	**40.2**	**158.5**	**180.4**
The ten states with the smallest percent uninsured	Pennsylvania	7.6%	6.1	37.0	164.7	176.2
	Rhode Island	7.3%	5.7	26.8	158.0	152.4
	Delaware	7.1%	7.9	41.6	170.8	163.2
	Wisconsin	6.9%	6.3	33.3	158.0	154.9
	Connecticut	6.8%	4.8	26.3	144.9	144.3
	Iowa	5.9%	6.1	32.3	159.8	162.8
	Minnesota	5.7%	5.1	32.5	148.6	114.9
	Vermont	4.9%	0.0	29.2	158.4	158.8
	Hawaii	4.9%	6.1	34.3	128.7	127.0
	Massachusetts	3.1%	3.9	27.9	150.2	134.8
Average		**6.0%**	**5.2**	**32.1**	**154.2**	**148.9**

Sources: Percentage Uninsured from U.S. Census, 2013 to 2016 1-Year American Community Surveys.

Health Data – Centers for Disease Control, 2017 https://www.cdc.gov/nchs/pressroom/sosmap/nhis_insured/nhisunin-sured.htm

CHAPTER REVIEW

What Is a Social Problem?

A social problem is a condition or a type of behavior that many people believe is harmful. The extent to which conditions or behaviors become social problems is based not only on the reality of their existence (objective element) but on the level of public concern (subjective element). Social institutions and social stratification provide a structural context for social problems. The cultural context of social problems includes values, norms, beliefs, and symbols.

Using the Sociological Imagination to Address Social Problems

The sociological imagination is the ability to relate the most personal elements and problems of an individual's life to social forces and historical events. It helps you to understand how your experiences, feelings, thoughts, and actions, and those of other people, are affected by the structure of society, culture, and social change. Personal problems become social problems when they come to be viewed as caused by social forces rather than by personal characteristics.

Sociological Perspectives on Social Problems

There are three primary sociological perspectives. The structural-functional perspective, which views society as a system of interdependent parts carrying out functions crucial to the well-being of the other parts and the system as a whole, includes three major approaches: social pathology, social disorganization, and social dysfunction. The conflict perspective views society as characterized by inequalities that advantage some groups and disadvantage others, and that lead to conflict and the potential for social change. Modern forms of the conflict approach include the economic-conflict, racial/ethnic-conflict, and feminist-conflict perspectives. The symbolic-interactionist perspective is a microsociological approach that views behavior and consciousness as the products of the meanings people develop through the process of person-to-person interaction.

Sociological Research on Social Problems

Sociological research methods include survey research (asking people questions), experiments, field research (observing natural behavior in a real-world setting), focus groups, secondary data analysis (using data collected by others), and historical and comparative research.

KEY TERMS

anomie, p. 12
applied research (also called evaluation research), p. 18
claim, p. 3
claims maker, p. 3
conflict perspective, p. 12
culture, p. 5
dependent variable, p. 17
economic-conflict perspective, p. 13
experiment, p. 18
false consciousness, p. 14
feminist-conflict perspective, p. 14
field research, p. 19
focus group, p. 20
historical and comparative research, p. 20

hypothesis, p. 17
independent variable, p. 17
latent functions, p. 11
literature review, p. 17
manifest functions, p. 11
objective element, p. 3
participant observation, p. 19
racial/ethnic-conflict perspective, p. 13
research question, p. 16
sample, p. 18
secondary data analysis, p. 20
social disorganization, p. 12
social dysfunction, p. 12
social institution, p. 5
social pathology, p. 11

social problem, p. 3
social stratification, p. 5
social structure, p. 5
sociological imagination, p. 8
structural-functional perspective, p. 11
subculture, p. 6

subjective element, p. 3
survey research, p. 18
symbolic-interactionist perspective, p. 14
theory, p. 10
true consciousness, p. 14
variable, p. 17

DISCUSSION QUESTIONS

1. Why do people differ regarding what conditions or behaviors they consider to be social problems?

2. Select a major social problem and describe opposing points of view about its causes.

3. Using your sociological imagination, explain how a personal issue that you or someone you know experiences is affected by social forces.

4. Who do you think is best suited for solving social problems: the federal government, local government, private individuals working together, business people, or some other group? Does the type of social problem affect your choice? Explain your answer.

5. What are the major social problems on your campus? What do you think can be done about them?

6. Select one of today's social institutions, such as the economy, politics and government, religion, or the media. Which sociological perspective (structural-functional, conflict or symbolic-interactionist) is best suited for explaining the way this institution operates?

7. Pick a major social problem. Which method or methods of sociological research would you select to study this social problem?

CHAPTER 2

The Sociology of Social Movements

CHAPTER OBJECTIVES

- Explain the important role of social movements in addressing social problems.
- Describe the different types of social movements.
- Identify the contrasting sociological explanations for the development and success of social movements.
- Outline the stages of development and decline of social movements.
- Explain how social movements can change society.

AFTER EARNING A BS IN COMPUTER ENGINEERING *from Cairo University and an MBA in marketing and finance from the American University of Egypt, Wael Ghonim became head of marketing for Google Middle East and North Africa. Although he had a career with Google, Ghonim's aspiration was to liberate his country from Hosni Mubarak's dictatorship and bring democracy to Egypt. Wael became a cyber activist and worked on prodemocracy websites. He created a Facebook page in 2010 called "We are all Khaled Said," named after a young businessman who police dragged from an Internet café and beat to death after Said exposed police corruption online. Through the posting of videos, photos, and news stories, the Facebook page rapidly became one of Egypt's most popular activist social media outlets, with hundreds of thousands of followers (BBC 2011, 2014; CBS News 2011).*

An uprising in nearby Tunisia began in December 2010 and forced out its corrupt leader on January 14, 2011. This inspired the thirty-year-old Ghonim to launch Egypt's own revolution. He requested through the Facebook page that all of his followers tell as many people as possible to stage protests for democracy and against tyranny, corruption, torture, and unemployment on January 25, 2011. Hundreds of thousands turned out for the protests in Cairo, Alexandria, and other cities, prompting the regime's security forces to seize Ghonim. On January 27, the government tried to stop the growing revolution by shutting down the Internet. Google and many other organizations and individuals demanded Ghonim's release. He was set free after twelve days and emerged as a heroic symbol of the revolutionary struggle. For weeks the country was in turmoil as police tried to evict protestors from key areas of major cities, but popular momentum for change proved unstoppable. On February 9, hundreds of thousands of workers went on strike around the country, and on the 11th Mubarak was forced to resign, ending his thirty-year reign. Time magazine recognized Ghonim as one of the one hundred most influential persons of 2011 (Time 2013).

Later developments showed that although the events of January and February 2011 ended one dictatorship, they did not achieve democracy in Egypt. The revolution for democracy and social justice in that nation and others around the world continues, but Wael Ghonim's actions demonstrate how one courageous individual can play a key role in sparking a massive social movement to address social problems.

As described in Chapter 1, the *sociological imagination* explains the role of social forces in our lives. When people believe that social forces cause a social problem, they often organize a collective effort called a social movement to do something about it. This chapter explores what social movements are, why and how they occur, and their stages of development, as well as their effectiveness in bringing about social change.

WHAT IS A SOCIAL MOVEMENT?

As you learned in the last chapter, a *social problem* exists when there is widespread belief that a condition or pattern of behavior is harmful. A **social movement** is a persistent and organized effort involving the mobilization of large numbers of people to work together to either bring about what they believe to be beneficial social change or resist or reverse what they believe to be harmful social change. Social movements are among the most dramatic events the world has ever known. The United States has experienced great movements such as the abolitionist movement to end slavery in the nineteenth century, the women's suffrage movement to win the vote for women in the nineteenth and early twentieth centuries, and the civil rights movement in the 1950s and 1960s to end racial discrimination. Along with certain national election campaigns, social movements have become the most important collective force for bringing about change in the country's history.

Social movements can be classified in a number of ways. One can first consider whether the movement intends to bring about or resist change. An **innovative (liberal) movement** intends to introduce something new with regard to culture, patterns of behavior, policies, or institutions. For example, a liberal movement exists to legalize marijuana. A **conservative movement** has the goal of maintaining things the way they are (resisting change), such as the movement to prevent legalization of marijuana where it remains illegal. A **reactionary movement** seeks to resurrect cultural elements, patterns of behavior, or institutions of the past ("bring back the good old days"). An example would be a movement that wants to return to banning same-sex marriage.

Movements can also be classified in terms of which aspects of society are targeted for change. Is change sought in patterns of behavior, culture, policies, or institutions? Are the changes meant to affect everyone, or only a particular group of people? A **reform movement** calls for change in patterns of behavior, culture, and/or policy, but does not try to replace entire social institutions. Supporters of reform movements appeal to policymakers, attempt to elect candidates, and sometimes bring cases before courts to achieve their goals. Movements involving civil rights, women's rights, sexual orientation, and the rights of people with disabilities all call for acceptance by the larger culture to ensure equal access to all social institutions but do not aim to replace them. Antiwar and environmental movements are also considered reform movements because they call for changes in government policy rather than sweeping institutional change.

A **revolutionary movement** in contrast, aims to bring about great structural change by replacing one or more major social institutions. In the eighteenth century, the American Revolution succeeded in changing the political system of the original thirteen colonies by freeing colonists from British monarchical control and creating a democratic form of government. In the late eighteenth century and early nineteenth century, the French Revolution ended a monarchy and established a republic. More contemporary examples of successful revolutions include the 1979 Iranian Revolution that replaced a monarchy with a fundamentalist Islamic republic, the revolutions that swept away one-party political

social movement A persistent and organized effort involving the mobilization of large numbers of people to work together to either bring about what they believe to be beneficial social change or resist or reverse what they believe to be harmful social change.

innovative (liberal) movement A social movement that intends to introduce something new with regard to culture, patterns of behavior, policies, or institutions.

conservative movement A social movement with the goal of maintaining things the way they are.

reactionary movement A social movement that seeks to resurrect cultural elements, patterns of behavior, or institutions of the past.

reform movement A social movement that calls for changes in patterns of behavior, culture, and/or policy, but does not try to replace entire social institutions.

revolutionary movement A social movement that aims to bring about great structural change by replacing one or more major social institutions.

systems in Eastern Europe and the former Soviet Union from 1989 to 1991, and the anti-apartheid movement in South Africa that ended the system of white political domination there in 1994. Even more recently, the 1996–2008 Nepalese Revolution replaced a monarchy with democracy, and the Arab uprisings (collectively called the Arab Awakening or Arab Spring), which began in Tunisia on December 17, 2010, changed the forms of government in Tunisia, Egypt, and Libya, and may affect even more Arab societies in the coming years.

Social movements can also be classified in other ways. The major goal of an **identity movement** is to spread understanding of mechanisms of domination, including cultural elements such as oppressive language, to destroy debilitating stereotypes, ways of thinking, and talking that are "the means and products of group subordination" (Gill and DeFronzo 2009:212). These movements attempt to create a new identity for the oppressed group "that provides a sense of empowerment, pride, self-confidence and equality" and also actively confront "the larger public's norms, beliefs, behaviors, and ways of thinking" (Gill and DeFronzo 2009:212). Identity movements develop among persons who perceive themselves to be the target of discrimination based on an ascribed characteristic such as race, nationality, physical characteristics, gender, sexual orientation, or other fixed traits. For example, the feminist movement attacks the traditional view of women as lacking the intelligence, will, emotional stability, or toughness to successfully participate in all areas of life by focusing attention on women who have made great achievements in politics, science, and business. This movement also promotes traits traditionally associated with women, such as compassion and cooperativeness, as crucial to the well-being of society. The purpose of the feminist movement is to provide all women with psychological empowerment and positive identities, and to replace stereotypes that limit their roles or define them as inferior with a global conception of women as equal to men.

Numerous factors can give rise to identity movements, including "exposure to concepts of freedom and liberation that were intended for the benefit of other groups, but have direct liberation implications to the members of another subordinated group" (Gill and DeFronzo 2009:212). Although reform movements can be clearly differentiated from revolutionary movements, other ways of classifying social movements are not mutually exclusive and can overlap. Reform movements to expand the opportunities of certain categories of people and revolutionary movements to free whole populations from foreign control are also to some extent identity movements because of their efforts to beneficially change the cultural identities of disadvantaged groups.

Some sociologists believe that, in the first half of the twentieth century, social movements in the most technologically advanced societies centered on economic goals. These dealt mainly with the redistribution of wealth and income and were based primarily on the industrial and urban work forces. In the second half, there was a perceived shift to identity movements and movements focusing on government policies. These **new social movements** were concerned with moral and quality-of-life issues and the establishment of new collective identities. Examples of new social movements include peace movements (like the anti–Vietnam War Movement of the 1960s and early 1970s) and

identity movement
A social movement aimed at creating a new identity for an oppressed group that provides a sense of empowerment, pride, self-confidence, and equality.

new social movements Social movements that arose during the second half of the twentieth century and are concerned with moral and quality-of-life issues and the establishment of new collective identities.

movements focusing on the environment, women's rights, gay rights, and animal rights. Critics claim that this division is artificial, because movements concerned with moral and quality-of-life issues coexisted with workers' labor movements during the period of industrialization (Pichardo 1997), and new social movements often have economic as well as moral and identity goals.

Certain movements, sometimes called **alternative movements**, aim to change a single type of behavior. For example, the temperance movement of the nineteenth and early twentieth centuries, similar in focus to today's antidrug movement, tried to convince people not to drink alcohol because of suspected links to child and spousal abuse, other violent crimes, and social ills. Another example is an abstinence movement. Abstinence movements such as True Love Waits advocate sexual relations only after marriage. **Redemptive movements** intend to bring about a more total transformation of the individual by encouraging people to adopt a new moral-religious outlook that will affect a wide range of personal behaviors. Examples include religious revivalist or fundamentalist movements that demand a deeper demonstration of commitment to the faith. **Transnational movements** are active in more than one country. Examples include the women's, environmental, and human rights movements, and movements promoting democracy. See table 2.1 for a summary of the different types of social movements, along with examples of each. It is important to note that some movements are more than one type. For example, the feminist movement has aspects that permit it to be classified as an innovative (liberal) movement, a reform movement, an identity movement, a new social movement, and a transnational movement.

Student Participation in Movements for Social Change

Student activism ranges from protests against university administrations to mobilizations that have contributed to the downfall of governments. Many students, brimming with idealism, have initiated social movements or joined existing ones. The Social Movements box describes an important social movement action that began with a sit-in at a lunch counter by four college students in 1960. In the years that followed, hundreds of thousands of students became active in the civil rights movement, as well as the antiwar, women's, environmental, and gay rights movements. Today, students are involved in movements fighting for social justice and human rights and participating in activist groups, such as the new Students for a Democratic Society, successor to the massive Vietnam War-era student organization of the same name.

As noted in the first chapter, one issue spurring youth to initiate protests is the increasing cost of higher education. In 2011, student loan debt reached about one trillion dollars and was estimated to be greater than all combined credit card debt in the United States (Cauchon 2011). This trend continued into 2018 when student debt reached $1.5 trillion owed by 44.2 million persons (Friedman 2018). In reaction to enormous tuition hikes, thousands of students enrolled in schools in the California State University system have participated in massive

alternative movements Social movements that aim to change a single type of behavior.

redemptive movements Social movements that encourage people to adopt a new moral-religious outlook that will affect a wide range of personal behaviors.

transnational movements Social movements active in more than one country.

TABLE 2.1	Types of Social Movements	
Type of Movement	**Goals**	**Examples**
Innovative (Liberal)	Introduce new cultural elements, patterns of interaction, policy, or institutions	Legalize marijuana movement
Conservative	Maintain things the way they are	Keep marijuana illegal movement
Reactionary	Bring back old cultural elements, patterns of behavior, policy, or institutions	Movement opposing same-sex marriage
Reform	Change cultural elements, patterns of behavior, and/or policy, but do not replace institutions	U.S. civil rights movement
Revolutionary	Bring about great structural change by replacing one or more major social institutions	American Revolution, French Revolution
Identity	Create positive cultural and personal identities for members of groups that have been the target of prejudice and discrimination	Gay rights movement
New social	Achieve moral, quality-of-life, self-actualization, and other noneconomic goals	Anti–Vietnam War movement, environmental movement
Alternative	Change one specific type of behavior	Temperance movement, abstinence movement
Redemptive	Total moral change of individuals affecting multiple behaviors	Religious fundamentalist movement
Transnational	Achieve aims in more than one country	Human rights movement

protest demonstrations beginning in the fall of 2009. Angus Johnston, a history professor at the City University of New York who studies student activism, estimated that at least 160 student protests occurred in the United States during the 2014 fall semester alone, mostly involving issues related to sexual assault and sexism on campus, university governance and student rights, and tuition and funding (Johnston 2014; Wong 2015). UCLA's Higher Education Research Institute (2016) reported that in its Fall 2015 survey of 141,189 first-year full-time students entering four-year colleges and universities across the United States, about 9 percent said that there was a "very good chance" they would participate in student demonstrations and protests while in college. This was the highest percentage in the annual survey's fifty-year history. Those expecting to participate varied from about 6 percent of Native American and Asian students to 7 percent of white, 10 percent

Social movement activists engaged in a protest demonstration

of Latino and 16 percent of black students. The trend toward increasing U.S. student activism appeared to continue (Smith 2017).

Internationally, students are active in social movements in many countries. The Internet, cell phones, and social media have provided new means for reform and revolutionary ideas to spread and inspire millions, and for people to organize and coordinate their actions. This was clearly demonstrated in the protests that broke out in Arab nations beginning in December 2010, described in part in this chapter's introduction. Since then students have used social media to organize other major protests, including Hong Kong students' huge prodemocracy demonstrations in 2014 (Epatko and Daly 2014; McKirdy 2017), and many protests in the United States (Curwen, Song, and Gordon 2015). Young people will continue to play a central role in prodemocracy and human rights movements around the world.

Here are several online resources for learning more about current student movements in the United States:

United States Student Association

http://www.usstudents.org/work/debt/

The American Association of University Women

http://www.aauw.org/

Youth Activism Project

http://youthactivismproject.org/publications/

Nation Topics – Student Movements

http://www.thenation.com/node/153/student-movements#axzz2c-qinUdKO

Students for a Democratic Society

http://www.newsds.org/

Social Movements: A Social Movement Action Originating at a Lunch Counter

Lunch counter sit-in at Woolworth's store, Greensboro, North Carolina

On February 1, 1960, four African American freshmen attending the Agricultural and Technical University of North Carolina – Joseph McNeil, Franklin McCain, Ezell Blair Jr. (who later changed his name to Jibreel Khazan), and David Richmond – were inspired by earlier protests against racist segregationist policies to sit down at the whites-only lunch counter at a Woolworth's store in Greensboro,

North Carolina. Although the staff refused to serve them, they refused to leave. Hundreds of students participated in lunch counter sit-ins over the next few days, not just in Greensboro, but in other cities and states as well. This launched a boycott of stores with service segregation policies. Responding to economic losses, Woolworth's desegregated its entire national chain of stores the following July, an important victory for the growing civil rights movement.

Ask yourself:

1. What social movements are students/ student groups on your campus currently involved in?
2. What movement-related actions or activities have students engaged in recently?
3. To what extent are the students involved in a movement on your campus linked to a national or transnational social movement?

WHY DO SOCIAL MOVEMENTS BEGIN?

Because social movements have played such important roles in shaping human history, social scientists have studied them and come up with a number of explanations for why they develop. One approach is to explain why people are or become discontented with a particular condition or pattern of behavior. It is easy to understand why some events provoke widespread anger. For example, if for some reason all of the public school teachers in California were suddenly subjected to a 25 percent cut in pay, you would expect that most California teachers would be outraged and engage in some form of public protest. It's harder to predict whether other, comparable social situations will produce widespread outrage. For example, the average salary for public school teachers in Indiana is about 30 percent less than the California average, but there have not been any major protests by Indiana teachers about their inferior salaries (Herron 2018; Will 2018). Why not? A number of factors help determine why people react (or don't react). One major type of explanation is deprivation theory, of which there are two forms.

Absolute Deprivation and Relative Deprivation Theories

According to **absolute deprivation theory**, social movements develop when people are unable to obtain adequate food, shelter, or other basic needs. However, history shows that people living in poverty over a period of generations develop the cultural outlook that their situation is fated and unchangeable. Similarly, the existence of wide gaps in wealth levels of groups in a society does not seem sufficient to bring about social movements. Social movements, including revolutionary movements, appear to develop not just as a result of deprivation or inequality but because of expectations and moral beliefs concerning fairness and social justice (DeFronzo 2015; Fullerton 2006). In other words, living conditions or political limitations only become intolerable when people come to view them as unacceptable relative to how they think things should be. Gurr (1970:46–56) describes three ways this view, called **relative deprivation theory**, can develop:

1. *Decremental deprivation.* Decremental deprivation involves a rapid drop in living standards caused by an event such as a sudden severe economic downturn. People feel deprived relative to their former living standards. For example, after the Great Depression began in 1929, the United States experienced a great surge in participation in the labor movement; more workers joined labor unions in the 1930s than ever before in the nation's history. The new economic and political power of the great labor unions, such as the United Auto Workers and the International Brotherhood of Teamsters, won higher wages, health insurance, pensions, and other benefits from employers, which helped raise millions of workers into the middle class.

2. *Progressive deprivation.* According to a study of economic trends preceding several major revolutions (Davies 1962), progressive deprivation occurs when a society experiences a prolonged period of economic progress and improved living standards followed by a period of sharp decline. Since people expect things to keep getting better as they had in previous years, a wide gap develops between expectations and worsening conditions. Both the American Revolution and the Russian Revolution of 1917 fit this pattern.

3. *Aspirational deprivation.* Aspirational deprivation occurs when people gain new information convincing them that their living conditions are unacceptable and can be changed, causing discontent to rise and support for social movements to increase. For example, in the 1960s and 70s many younger Catholic priests and nuns in Latin American countries adopted liberation theology (Berryman 1987), a social justice orientation holding that clergy should confront and criticize unjust social conditions, including poverty and inequality of opportunity, in addition to dealing with spiritual needs. Clergy informed their impoverished parishioners that poverty was not the result of God's will but caused by the selfishness and greed of certain people, and that these unjust

absolute deprivation theory The idea that social movements develop when people are unable to obtain adequate food, shelter, or other basic needs.

relative deprivation theory The idea that living conditions or political limitations only become intolerable when people come to view them as unacceptable relative to their conception of the way they think things should be.

conditions could and should be changed through group action. In response, many parishioners organized protests and even created social movements to demand change. When these efforts were repressed, some turned to armed revolutionary struggle, as in the successful revolution in Nicaragua in 1979 portrayed in a somewhat fictionalized fashion in the movie *Under Fire*.

People may also experience relative deprivation when they witness a condition or a pattern of behavior that they find unacceptable in terms of deeply held personal moral standards. This helps explain why many people participate in movements even though they do not personally suffer from the conditions they want to change. *Moral relative deprivation* explains why many college students participate in social movements dealing with issues that may be remote from their personal experiences (Gill and DeFronzo 2009:205), as in campus mobilizations against South African apartheid in the 1980s and early 1990s. In that movement the immediate aim was to get colleges to stop investing in South Africa until Nelson Mandela, the leader of the African National Congress, was freed from prison and democratic elections were held. A more recent example is the student movement against sweatshops (see the Social Movements feature).

Social Movements: The Student Movement against Sweatshops

Students protest against sweatshops

The US anti-sweatshop movement is one of the largest American student movements since campuses mobilized in the 1980s and early 1990s to force an end to apartheid in South Africa. The elimination of sweatshops is far more difficult because sending jobs to other nations where workers' wages are much lower has become an integral part of the global economic system. Sweatshops are also a way for business interests to weaken labor unions and limit or lower American workers' wages.

A *sweatshop* is essentially any business or manufacturing setting in which workers are very poorly paid or forced to work under harsh or unsafe conditions. Corporations in the United States and other countries obtain products from factories in developing countries in order to increase profits. Sweatshops have also operated much closer to home. Some U.S. businesses hire illegal immigrants desperate for any kind of job and afraid to complain to legal authorities about abusive conditions.

Social Movements (*continued*)

The vast majority of the price of products relying on sweatshop labor goes to the store, advertising, materials, shipping, and the contractor employing the workers. For example, according to the *Asia Times* (Guerin 2006), labor costs in Indonesia are only about 6 percent of production costs, so if the cost of making a dress is $50, the worker who made it receives $3. If the dress is sold at stores in the United States for $100, doubling the worker's wage would only increase the American consumer's cost to $103! This seemingly paltry sum would make a huge difference for the Indonesian worker, but the unregulated market is continually under pressure to minimize labor costs rather than show concern for worker welfare.

Since it is impractical to organize workers at the tens of thousands of sweatshops in dozens of developing countries around the world, or even at the hundreds of sweatshops in American cities, student activists, including those in the United Students Against Sweatshops (2017; Dreier 2001; Featherstone, 2002) movement, have instead focused on educating consumers in the United States about sweatshops and what they can do about them. This includes refusal to buy products from corporations that utilize sweatshops and campus demonstrations to convince college officials to stop selling the rights for college logos to clothing manufacturers that rely on sweatshops. The anti-sweatshop movement is also working with labor unions in the United States, as hundreds of thousands of American workers in the garment industry have lost their jobs due to this type of corporate outsourcing, and millions have been forced to settle for lower wages or benefits under the threat that their jobs could be shipped to another part of the world.

Anti-sweatshop movement activists want U.S. companies, colleges, and government agencies to agree to and enforce a policy mandating that workers are paid livable wages and are permitted to form labor unions if they wish, and that companies provide safe work places visited regularly by independent inspectors.

For more information, visit United Students Against Sweatshops: http://usas.org/.

What are your thoughts?

1. Do you think that companies that use sweatshops should be prevented from selling sweatshop products in the United States? Why or why not?
2. Do you think that stores should be prevented from selling sweatshop products? Why or why not?

Resource Mobilization Theory

According to **resource mobilization theory**, people motivated to create a social movement must have access to necessary resources to succeed (Jenkins 1983). Useful resources include funding, effective leaders, and access to social networks through which new participants can be recruited. Other beneficial resources can be the support of powerful persons, aid from previously established social movement organizations, and assistance from important moral figures who can bestow legitimacy on the movement and its goals. For example, the civil rights movement benefitted from the support of many African American churches (Morris 1986) and their leaders, including Martin Luther King Jr. Their congregations provided meeting places, participants, and financial

resource mobilization theory The idea that people motivated to create a social movement must have access to necessary resources to succeed.

contributions, and their preexisting intercity and interstate connections served as avenues for geographic expansion and long-distance coordination of efforts.

Political Opportunities Theory

Another view posits that the level of people's grievances and the available resources are not sufficient explanations of social movements (Goodwin and Jasper 1999). According to **political opportunities theory** (also called *political process theory*) (Meyer 2004), political context is key to explaining social movements and their effects on society (McAdam 1982; McAdam, McCarthy, and Zald 1996; Tarrow 1992). Social movements arise at times when political circumstances for their success are favorable. In other words, people only initiate a social movement when they perceive that the political climate will allow them to organize successfully and achieve their goals. In addition, a social movement that is already underway will often attempt to use its influence to make the political environment more favorable.

This perspective focuses on how the external political environment facilitates or interferes with initiating a social movement, recruiting and mobilizing participants, and getting access to resources. On the flip side, it also explores how a social movement influences political campaigns and government policies and how a movement can alter the political context in which it operates (McAdam, McCarthy, and Zald 1996). For example, the movement to prohibit alcoholic beverages was affected by the enemy in World War I being Germany, a major exporter of beer, and that many German Americans owned breweries in the United States. Supporters of Prohibition portrayed the liquor industry as foreign controlled and subversive, leading to prohibition, the federal ban on alcoholic beverages from 1920 to 1933.

In another example, the civil rights movement benefitted from increased support and favorable actions by the Democratic Party and Democratic government officials, including the passage of the Civil Rights Act of 1964 (Bump 2015). This, in turn, caused many African American voters to switch to the Democratic Party. McAdam (1982) and Tilly (1978) argue that for a social movement to develop, the availability of political opportunities must be coupled with a concept similar to the *true consciousness* described in the discussion of the conflict perspective in Chapter 1. *Cognitive liberation* is a three-phase change in people's thinking about a situation (Nepstad 1997):

1. People decide that an existing condition or social arrangement is unjust.

2. They come to believe it can be changed and demand change.

3. They gain confidence that through working together they will possess the power to achieve that goal.

political opportunities theory The idea that political context is key in explaining social movements and their effects on society.

The Social Movements feature illustrates political opportunities theory in the context of two opposing social movements. It also describes how both movements attempt to influence the political environment.

Social Movements: The Influence of the Pro-Life and Pro-Choice Movements on State and National Politics and Policies

Pro-choice and pro-life demonstrators

The pro-life and pro-choice movements are two major opposing social movements that clearly aim to influence the political environment. Both have worked for decades to elect government leaders who favor creating and enforcing laws in line with their contrasting positions on abortion and have had tremendous impacts on U.S. politics. The pro-life movement attempts to ban abortion completely. In contrast, the pro-choice movement aims to continue the legal status of and accessibility to abortion in a wide range of circumstances. It also focuses on educating women about contraception to make abortion a last resort. Both movements have significant resources and political opportunities, especially in certain states. The pro-life movement enjoys the support of many evangelical Protestant leaders, bishops and priests of the Catholic Church, and many Republican governors and legislators (especially in southern states). The pro-choice movement benefits from the support of feminist groups and many Democratic office holders (particularly in northern and West Coast states).

In 2011 the pro-life movement persuaded legislatures in nineteen states to pass a record-breaking number of laws restricting abortion (Guttmacher Institute 2011). These included requirements for special counseling and longer waiting periods for those seeking abortions, and banning abortion at or after twenty weeks of pregnancy unless the woman's life is endangered or there is a substantial danger of major irreversible physical harm. Between 2011 and 2015 thirty-one states enacted a total of 288 additional restrictions on abortion (Ertelt 2016). In the 2016 election, those involved in the pro-life movement mostly supported Donald Trump, who promised to nominate conservatives to the Supreme Court likely to rule in favor of curtailing or ending access to abortion. Fulfilling his promise, President Trump nominated Neil Gorsuch, whom the Senate confirmed to the Supreme Court on April 7, 2017, and Brett Kavanaugh, whom the Senate confirmed to the Supreme Court on October 6, 2018.

What are your thoughts?

1. Do you think that government, either state or federal, should have the power regulate abortion? Why or why not?

Leadership Theory

Leadership theory asserts that the emergence and success of social movements requires exceptional leaders. Leaders can be classified into three types (DeFronzo 2008). **Charismatic leaders**, usually the type most widely recognized by the public, emotionally inspire others through their words and their actions and by presenting the movement as an essential moral struggle. Famous charismatic leaders include Mahatma Gandhi of India's revolutionary movement for independence and democracy, Martin Luther King Jr. of the American civil rights

leadership theory The idea that the emergence and success of social movements requires exceptional leaders.

charismatic leader A type of leader who emotionally inspires others through words and actions and by presenting the movement as an essential moral struggle.

movement, and Nelson Mandela of South Africa's anti-apartheid struggle. An important charismatic leader of the suffrage movement was Susan B. Anthony, who served as spokeswoman of the movement and traveled the country extensively giving speeches calling for women's right to vote (*Encyclopedia Britannica* 2017). An **intellectual leader** provides a social movement with ideology explaining the problem, its cause, and the need for action. A movement's ideology should be consistent with widely held values. For example, in the United States this could involve linking the movement with fulfilling the ideals of freedom, individual human rights, and equality of opportunity. An intellectual leader of the women's suffrage movement was Elizabeth Cady Stanton. She authored the "Declaration of Sentiments" (modeled after the Declaration of Independence), asserting that women and men are entitled to equal rights, which was signed by participants at the first women's rights convention at Seneca Falls, New York, in 1848. Stanton provided her fellow suffragists with radical ideas for the time such as women's rights to own property, serve on juries, receive equitable wages, and withhold sex from their husbands. She also wrote a number of Susan B. Anthony's speeches (Andrews 2015). A **managerial leader** transforms the ideals and goals of the movement into organization and coordinated action. Carrie Chapman Catt was an exceptional managerial leader of the suffrage movement who organized and led the movement's "Winning Strategy" plan. This was a disciplined and often successful effort to win the right for women to vote in a succession of individual states by getting states to hold referenda on the issue (U.S. House of Representatives 2017b). As more and more states allowed their women residents the right to vote, pressure mounted on the federal government to do the same. In some social movements, a single person may perform more than one of the three leadership roles.

Leaders must decide on strategy and tactics. In the context of social movements, **strategy** is a general approach for achieving movement goals. The strategy of nonviolence was employed by the movements led by Mahatma Gandhi and Martin Luther King Jr. Strategies can include sub-strategies, such as legal demonstrations, collecting signatures on petitions, or illegal but peaceful occupations of buildings. A movement's strategy can be affected by public response and government actions. The anti-apartheid movement led by Nelson Mandela relied on a nonviolent strategy at first. In response to violent repression by the South African white minority government, it eventually shifted to violent resistance involving bombings of economic and military targets and mobile, small-unit (guerilla) warfare. When white leaders finally agreed to democratic elections, the anti-apartheid movement reverted to its nonviolent strategy, which led to Mandela's election as president in 1994.

While strategy represents a general approach to advancing a movement, **tactics** are the immediate actions used to implement it. McAdam (1997:343–351) describes several tactics operating within the civil rights movement's strategy of nonviolence: bus boycotts, in which people refused to ride buses until the policy of racially segregated seating was eliminated; the aforementioned sit-ins by African Americans at whites-only eating facilities; and freedom rides, in which African Americans and white Americans traveled together on buses across state

intellectual leader A type of leader who provides a social movement with ideology explaining the problem, its cause, and the need for action.

managerial leader A type of leader who transforms the ideals and goals of the movement into organization and coordinated action.

strategy A general approach for achieving movement goals.

tactics The immediate actions used to implement a strategy.

Martin Luther King Jr. giving a speech

lines to bring public attention to the states refusing to comply with Supreme Court rulings that forbade racial segregation on buses and in bus terminals.

Framing Theory

Framing theory describes the processes through which an individual comes to embrace the ideology of, and supports and participates in, a social movement (Best 2013; Snow and Benford 1988; Snow, Rochford, Worden, and Benford 1986). Advocates of framing theory believe that other theories are all incomplete explanations of social movements. They argue that one of the important tasks of a social movement's leaders is to present or "frame" a social movement in terms of the core values held by people the movement seeks to recruit. Whatever social structural conditions are present, a social movement is unlikely to develop unless leaders accomplish this. *Framing* is the process of describing the movement in such a way that it makes sense, appeals to as many people as possible, and fulfills one or more deeply held values. Framing is similar to the process of claims making described in Chapter 1. Snow and Benford (1988) explain that social movements interpret and provide meanings for conditions, actions, and events in a manner that is intended to mobilize potential participants, obtain acceptance and support from the larger public, and undermine the efforts of movement opponents. Framing accomplishes three tasks:

1. *Diagnosis.* Diagnostic framing explains why a condition or pattern of behavior is a problem and what – or who – causes it.

2. *Prognosis.* Prognostic framing proposes a solution and a plan of action, including strategy and tactics, for social movement participants.

framing theory The idea that a social movement emerges because of framing: the process of describing a social movement in such a way that it makes sense, appeals to as many people as possible, and fulfills one or more deeply held values.

3. *Motivation.* Motivational framing explains why people need to act to deal with the problem.

The leaders of a social movement try to shape its public image to show that its goal and underlying ideology align with deeply held cultural values. For example, in the United States the leaders of the movements to end slavery and to obtain equal opportunity for women both sought to rally mass support by referring to values expressed in key documents of the American Revolution. Among the most cited is a phrase from the Declaration of Independence stating that all people are entitled to equal opportunities for "life, liberty and the pursuit of happiness."

Multi-Factor Theory

Despite the attention given in recent years to the theories of social movements described above (such as the resource mobilization, political opportunity, and framing theories), many sociologists are drawn to Smelser's (1962) multifactor ("value added") theory for a more comprehensive explanation of social movements. This theory was developed to explain not just social movements but a wide range of collective behavior including riots, vigilantism, collective panics, and crazes or fads. Although Smelser formulated his theory from the structural-functional perspective, the nature of the subject matter and the inherent logic of his analysis results in a theory that has elements in common with the conflict and symbolic-interactionist approaches. Here are Smelser's six factors that explain the development of a social movement:

1. *Structural conduciveness.* It is the underlying characteristics of a society that make the development of a social movement possible and influence what type of movement emerges. For example, if a government blocks all means of communication, it may be difficult for a movement to emerge. As you have already learned, the development of the Internet and social media, along with the increased use of cell phones, played a major role in the Arab Awakening protests in the winter and spring of 2011 that toppled governments in Tunisia, Egypt, and Libya.

2. *Structural strain.* Factors such as absolute or relative deprivation in terms of expectations, aspirations, or moral ideals cause large-scale discontent. In Tunisia and other Arab nations that experienced massive explosions of protest in late 2010 and 2011, people became intensely frustrated by repressive dictatorships, brutal and corrupt security forces, and limited economic opportunities.

3. *Growth and spread of a generalized belief (ideology).* This is the development of a shared common explanation for the cause of the condition generating discontent and a belief that something can and should be done about it. In the Arab uprisings, most people believed the dictatorships to be the central cause of problems and that large-scale protests were necessary to remove them.

4. *Precipitating factors.* These are dramatic events that confirm or justify the generalized belief and provoke people to action. The self-immolation of a poverty-stricken, twenty-six-year-old

multifactor theory The idea that a social movement emerges and is shaped by multiple factors including communication, discontent, shared beliefs, dramatic events, movement leadership's ability to mobilize people, and the response of those in power.

Tunisian street vendor, Mohamed Bouazizi, on December 17, 2010, sparked the Tunisian rebellion. He had been harassed repeatedly and then beaten by police after trying to sell produce to support his mother and siblings. This tragic and desperate act against a corrupt dictatorship ignited massive protests against the government, which then spread to other Arab nations.

5. *Mobilization.* Leaders encourage and organize movement supporters in mass protests and related activities such as boycotts, petitions, campaigns for (or against) certain political candidates, court battles, and other measures to achieve movement goals.

6. *Operation of social control.* Depending on the movement, those with power in society may support it, attempt to manipulate it by influencing one of the first five factors, oppose it, or even attempt to violently repress it. In Tunisia and Egypt, government repression was overwhelmed by popular protest.

STAGES OF SOCIAL MOVEMENTS

Social movements tend to go through a number of stages of development. A well-known model of these stages was developed by Armand L. Mauss (1975). Mauss stressed the importance of focusing on the continual interactions between movements, government, and the larger social environment. His research led him to conclude that movements typically, though not always, go through five phases: incipiency, coalescence, institutionalization, fragmentation, and demise. For some social movements there is also a sixth phase, revival.

Incipiency

The first stage of a social movement, its **incipiency**, begins when a large number of people become distressed by a particular situation. For example, during the 1960s the government claimed that a war of aggression was being waged against a small nation in Southeast Asia called South Vietnam. Soon many college professors contradicted the government's story, asserting that the war was a continuation of decades of Vietnamese resistance to colonialism. They claimed that, according to the Geneva Accords, which ended the 1946–1954 "French-Indochina War," South Vietnam should not even exist as a separate nation. In their view, the fighting was essentially a civil war between the Vietnamese. This conflicting assessment provoked outrage among many college students, who believed that their government had deceived them and launched an immoral and unjustified war, and discontent soon spread around the country. The development of this antiwar movement caused the United States to experience one of its greatest periods of internal strife since the Civil War.

Coalescence

In the second stage, **coalescence**, a social movement becomes more organized and develops resource-gathering capabilities. Coalescence of the antiwar movement was facilitated by the involvement of veterans of

incipiency The first stage of a social movement, which begins when a large number of people become distressed by a particular situation.

coalescence The second stage of a social movement, in which it becomes more organized and develops resource-gathering capabilities.

institutionalization The third stage of a social movement, in which the government takes official notice of the movement and tries to cope with it and the movement establishes one or more geographically extensive or even national social movement organizations.

fragmentation The fourth stage of a social movement, in which it breaks apart, typically after a period of some success, because movement participants disagree about whether essential goals have really been achieved.

the civil rights movement, including Martin Luther King Jr. He joined the antiwar movement and participated in the 1967 march from Central Park to the United Nations headquarters, one of the largest antiwar protest marches in U.S. history.

Institutionalization

As the mass media pays increased attention, **institutionalization** occurs when the government takes official notice of a movement and tries to cope with it and the movement establishes one or more geographically extensive or even national social movement organizations (SMOs). In this stage the government typically addresses the movement in some way, ranging from promising to investigate the problem that the movement is publicizing to enacting policies or passing legislation to deal with it. In the case of the civil rights movement, the U.S. government acted to bring about desegregation of public facilities and schools and to combat racial discrimination in employment. In responding to the antiwar movement, the government pledged to work for peace, entered into peace negotiations, and began to reduce the number of U.S. soldiers in Vietnam. Major SMOs of the antiwar movement included the National Coordinating Committee to End the War in Vietnam and Vietnam Veterans Against the War. Examples of SMOs for the civil rights movement include Martin Luther King Jr.'s Southern Christian Leadership Conference and the National Association for the Advancement of Colored People.

Fragmentation

Fragmentation is the breaking apart of a movement, typically after a period of some success, because movement participants disagree about whether essential goals have really been achieved. Those who

U.S. military veterans protest against the Vietnam War

feel the movement's mission has not actually been accomplished may propose new strategies, tactics, or actions. For example, after the federal government passed the Civil Rights Act of 1964 and the Voting Rights Act of 1965, some movement participants became less active. But Martin Luther King Jr. believed that not enough had really been done to help low-income Americans. He and several others then organized the Poor People Campaign in early 1968 in pursuit of more job opportunities and better health care and housing for the nation's poor (Lohr 2008). In the case of the antiwar movement, despite government claims it was trying to end the war by engaging in peace negotiations and reducing U.S. troop strength in Vietnam, the war continued for years. After the 1968 assassinations of two major charismatic opponents of the war – Martin Luther King Jr. and Senator Robert Kennedy of New York – some deserted the nonviolent antiwar movement (in particular, a group called the Weather Underground) to engage in violent actions, such as bombings of government facilities and corporate headquarters.

Demise

Eventually a movement may meet its **demise**, or come to an end because it has achieved its goal, lost popular support, or been repressed. For example, the abolitionist movement lost its reason for existence upon slavery's elimination following the Civil War. The conclusion of the Vietnam conflict in 1975 brought an end to the antiwar movement. In some societies extreme repression can destroy a movement, and this can occur even before a movement passes through the early stages. The Nazi regime crushed Germany's gay movement in the 1930s–1940s (Broich 2017), and the Argentine dictatorship violently suppressed socialist movements in the "dirty war" of the late 1970s and early 1980s (Finchelstein 2014).

Revival

Although this phase is not a part of Mauss's normal movement-stages model, he noted that some movements that appeared to meet their demise did not totally end but instead experienced **revival**, re-emerging in the same or a modified form. For example, once the women's suffrage movement succeeded in obtaining the right for women to vote in 1920, it appeared to decline for decades. But in the 1960s it began a strong revival as the feminist movement, aimed at addressing a range of issues related to economic, educational, sports, and military equality of opportunity for women. More recently, some view the Black Lives Matter movement as a revival of the 1950s–1960s civil rights movement (Harris 2015).

SOCIAL MOVEMENTS AND SOCIAL CHANGE

Social movements can change society in both intended and unintended ways, some widely recognized and others not as clearly understood. For example, the women's movement of the 1960s opened the

demise The fifth stage of a social movement, in which it comes to an end because it has achieved its goal, lost popular support, or been repressed.

revival An additional stage of some social movements that occurs if they re-emerge in the same or a modified form.

Social Movements: Music, Entertainers, and Social Movements

Pete Seeger and Bruce Springsteen perform protest music

Music has played a major role in energizing supporters of social movements. The famous civil rights anthem "We Shall Overcome" has become a worldwide protest song. It was derived from a tune that had its origins in an early twentieth-century gospel hymn and was sung by striking African American workers in the 1940s. The moving French revolutionary march, "La Marseillaise," has played a similarly inspiring role for revolutionary movements around the globe. Throughout American history, music has inspired and energized participants in great social struggles including the labor, civil rights, and peace movements (Alterman 2012; Eyerman and Jamison 1998; Lynskey 2011; Rosenthal and Flacks 2012; Weissman 2010).

Today a number of prominent musical artists are involved in social activism. Ani DeFranco, a well-known and admired American singer, songwriter, guitarist, and poet, is active in the women's movement and has become a feminist icon. Joan Baez is another legendary American singer and songwriter who has participated in human rights and many other social movements. Jay-Z is a rap artist involved in urban antiviolence campaigns.

Bruce Springsteen, who has sold more than 120 million albums world-wide, supported the Obama election campaign in 2008. Before an estimated four hundred thousand people at the Lincoln Memorial the night before Obama's inauguration, Springsteen performed his own song "The Rising" and sang Woody Guthrie's "This Land Is Your Land" with activist musician Pete Seeger. "This Land Is Your Land," widely interpreted as critical of economic inequality, became one of America's most famous folk songs. Seeger, an admirer and friend of Guthrie's, was also a legendary folk song writer, singer, and activist and was a supporter of the civil rights, antiwar and environmental movements.

Springsteen used his 2012 album "Wrecking Ball" to express his outrage at the suffering people experienced because of the 2008 financial crisis in the United States. In the April 30, 2012, issue of the *Nation*, Springsteen is quoted as saying, "I had friends losing their homes, and nobody went to jail… . Previous to Occupy Wall Street, there was no pushback: there was no movement, there was no voice that was saying just how outrageous – that a basic theft had occurred that struck at the heart of what the entire American idea is about" (p. 15).

What are your thoughts?
Visit the websites below to learn more about protest and social movement songs.

http://www.rollingstone.com/music/lists/
readers-poll-the-10-best-protest-songs-of-
all-time-20141203/crosby-stills-nash-and-
young-ohio-20141203

https://newsone.com/1460645/top-10-civil-
rights-protest-songs-of-all-time/

http://www.grinningplanet.com/6001/
environmental-songs.htm

1. Listen to or read the lyrics of several of the songs on these websites. What do you think are the essential elements of a great social movement song?

way for an enormous increase in female labor-force participation. At the same time, the United States experienced skyrocketing burglary rates. Before long a link between the two trends became apparent. Since burglars prefer to enter unguarded buildings, the increasing number of homes with two working adults provided millions of new vulnerable targets. This, in turn, stimulated rapid growth of the private security industry and sales of home alarms and other security devices.

Because of its democratic political system, social movements in the United States have primarily been reform movements aimed at changing aspects of social behavior and culture and encouraging full and equal participation by all population groups in American institutions. The women's suffrage movement and the civil rights movement both brought about major cultural, psychological, behavioral, and legal changes. In the first two decades of the twentieth century women were not allowed to vote, and for the first six public and private facilities in many parts of the country were racially segregated. Pressure from these and other social movements has played a significant role in overcoming deeply embedded racism, sexism, and ignorance. In the 1950s and 1960s a series of laws and court rulings banned racial discrimination in jury selection, real estate practices and home mortgages, and access to schools and colleges. Interracial marriages and adoptions have increased. The numbers of women and racial minorities in high positions in politics and government, economic institutions, and the military continue to grow.

For the first time in U.S. history, the top two candidates for the 2008 Democratic nomination for president were a woman, Hillary Clinton, and an African American, Barack Obama; on the Republican side, another woman, Sarah Palin, became the party's vice presidential candidate. The influence of the gay liberation movement was reflected in the dramatic change in majority public opinion in favor of permitting same-sex marriage. The cultural shift toward greater equality has been greatest among young adults. Despite all of these changes in culture and institutional access, significant levels of prejudice, discrimination, and inequality of opportunity remain. Continuing gender discrimination in income led to the passage of the Lilly Ledbetter Fair Pay Act, which President Obama signed into law on January 29, 2009. Legal measures and cultural changes appear to have reduced certain forms of racial and gender discrimination significantly, but it is clear that much more needs to be accomplished in these areas. Since the 1970s economic inequality has increased, upward social mobility has decreased, the middle class is shrinking, and money has become an increasingly dominant influence in the U.S. political system; some even argue that it has become less democratic. These trends have sparked a resurgence of social movements with an economic focus, possibly leading to significant social change in the future.

Social Movements: The U.S. Women's Movement and the 2012, 2016, and 2018 Elections

In the nineteenth and early twentieth centuries, American women engaged in a long and difficult struggle to win the right to vote and hold political office. After decades of protests, the Nineteenth Amendment finally allowed women to participate in elections. Today women serve as governors, state legislators, U.S. representatives, and U.S. senators. Democrat Geraldine Ferraro and Republican Sarah Palin ran as their party's candidates for vice president in the 1984 and 2008 elections, respectively. And Hillary Clinton, after almost winning her party's nomination for president in 2008, was nominated as the Democratic presidential candidate in 2016. She was the choice of 2.86 million more voters than Republican candidate Donald Trump, who won the Electoral College.

Women's rights was a major issue in the 2012, 2016 and 2018 elections. Many Democrats accused Republican candidates and the Republican Party leadership of attempting to roll back generations of women's rights advances. At stake, according to women's groups, were women's right to equal pay for equal work, affordable access to contraception, and the right to choose whether to continue a pregnancy. In the 2012 election, exit polls indicated that 55 percent of women voters cast their ballot for the Democratic presidential candidate, Barack Obama, while 44 percent chose Republican candidate Mitt Romney (CNN 2012). In the 2016 election the gender gap was similar. Exit polls showed women voted 54 percent for Democrat Hillary Clinton and 41 percent for Republican Donald Trump; 5 percent voted for another candidate or declined to answer (CNN 2016).

The results of the 2018 midterm elections meant that there would be twenty-four

TABLE 2.2 | Women Senators in 2019

Democrats		Republicans	
Tammy Baldwin	Wisconsin	Marsha Blackburn	Tennessee
Maria Cantwell	Washington	Shelly Capito	West Virginia
Catherine Cortez Masto	Nevada	Susan Collins	Maine
Tammy Duckworth	Illinois	Joni Ernst	Iowa
Diane Feinstein	California	Deb Fischer	Nebraska
Kirsten Gillibrand	New York	Cindy Hyde-Smith	Mississippi
Kamala Harris	California	Lisa Murkowski	Alaska
Margaret Hassan	New Hampshire		
Mazie Hirono	Hawaii		
Amy Klobuchar	Minnesota		
Patty Murray	Washington		
Jacky Rosen	Nevada		
Jeanne Shaheen	New Hampshire		
Kyrsten Sinema	Arizona		
Tina Smith	Minnesota		
Debbie Stabenow	Michigan		
Elizabeth Warren	Massachusetts		

Social Movements (*continued*)

women senators in 2019, the most in U.S. history (Center for Women and Politics – Rutgers Eagleton Institute of Politics 2018; U.S. Senate 2018). As shown in the table above, seventeen are Democrats and seven are Republicans.

Ask yourself:

1. Do you think there should be a higher percentage of women in government in the United States? Why or why not?
2. Do you think that the two major parties are equally supportive of women in government? Why or why not?

CHAPTER REVIEW

What Is a Social Movement?

A social movement is the mobilization of large numbers of people to work together to deal with a social problem. It is a persistent and organized effort to either bring about what participants believe to be beneficial social change or in some cases resist or reverse change viewed as harmful. An innovative (liberal) movement intends to introduce something new with regard to culture, patterns of behavior, policies, or institutions. A conservative movement aims to maintain things the way they are. Reactionary movements seek to resurrect cultural elements, patterns of behavior, or institutions of the past.

Reform movements call for change in patterns of behavior, culture and/or policy, but do not try to replace whole social institutions. Revolutionary movements, in contrast, aim at bringing about great structural change by replacing one or more major social institutions. Social movements can also be classified as identity, new social, alternative, redemptive, and transnational movements.

Why Do Social Movements Begin?

Theories about why social movements occur include absolute deprivation theory, relative deprivation theory, resource mobilization theory, political opportunities theory, leadership theory, framing theory, and multifactor theory. The most sensible way to understand social movements may be to use a comprehensive multifactor approach that shows how a combination of different elements affects the emergence and outcomes of social movements.

Stages of Social Movements

Social movements addressing social problems can go through a series of stages, including incipience, coalescence, institutionalization, fragmentation, demise, and possibly revival.

Social Movements and Social Change

Social movements have played an enormous role in combating discrimination against and in expanding rights for various groups in American society. They have and continue to affect American elections at the local and national level as well as those in other nations.

KEY TERMS

absolute deprivation theory, p. 33
alternative movements, p. 29
charismatic leader, p. 37
coalescence, p. 41
conservative movement, p. 27

demise, p. 43
fragmentation, p. 42
framing theory, p. 39
identity movement, p. 28
incipiency, p. 41

innovative (liberal) movement, p. 27
institutionalization, p. 42
intellectual leader, p. 38
leadership theory, p. 37
managerial leader, p. 38
multifactor theory, p. 40
new social movements, p. 28
political opportunities theory, p. 36
reactionary movement, p. 27
redemptive movements, p. 29

reform movement, p. 27
relative deprivation theory, p. 33
resource mobilization theory, p. 35
revival, p. 43
revolutionary movement, p. 27
social movement, p. 27
strategy, p. 38
tactics, p. 38
transnational movements, p. 29

DISCUSSION QUESTIONS

1. Based on what you have learned in this chapter, why do you think some people become involved in social movements and others do not?

2. Select a major social movement and describe what type you think it is and why.

3. Are there any current social movements you would view as revolutionary rather than reform? Explain your answer.

4. Pick a major current social movement, the theory you think best explains its development, and describe why.

5. Pick a major current social movement and describe what stage it is in and why.

6. Pick a major social movement. Which method or methods of sociological research described in Chapter 1 would you use to study it?

7. Describe a recent social movement that succeeded and brought about significant social change.

CHAPTER 3

The Sociology of Power: Economics, Wealth, and Politics

CHAPTER OBJECTIVES

- Describe major types of political and economic systems around the world.
- Describe the growth of the size and power of corporations.
- Describe class, income inequality, wealth inequality, and social mobility in the United States.

- Explain major economic and political factors that affect access to power in the United States.
- Explain major as well as controversial aspects of the U.S. political system and the impact of money on politics.
- Explain how wealth and power influence conceptions of social problems and the development and success or failure of social movements that address them.

IN IOWA ON THE NIGHT *before the 2012 presidential election President Barack Obama spoke to a crowd of supporters.*

> *What the protectors of the status quo in Washington are counting on now is that you'll get worn down by all the squabbling. You'll get fed up with the dysfunction. You'll walk away and leave them to make decisions that affect every American. ... The folks at the top in this country, it turns out they don't need another champion in Washington. They'll always have a seat at the table. They'll always have access and influence. The people who need a champion are the Americans whose letters I read late at night ... The laid-off furniture worker who's retraining at the age of 55 for a new career at a community college ... The cooks and the waiters and cleaning staff, working overtime in a hotel in Des Moines or Vegas, trying to save enough to buy a first home or send their kid to college ... The teacher in an overcrowded classroom with outdated schoolbooks, digging into her own pocket to buy school supplies, not always feeling like she's got the support she needs, but showing up every day because she knows that this might be the day that she's got a breakthrough and she makes a difference in one child's life. All those kids in inner cities, small farm towns – kids dreaming of becoming scientists or doctors, engineers or entrepreneurs, diplomats or even a President – they need a champion in Washington, because the future will never have as many lobbyists as the status quo – children don't have lobbyists the way oil companies or banks do. But it's the dreams of those children that will be our saving grace (White House 2012).*

Four years later Donald Trump won the electoral college and the presidency in part by expressing the view that government and economic elites had continued to ignore the interests of millions of Americans. In his inaugural address he stated,

> *For too long, a small group in our nation's capital has reaped the rewards of government while the people have borne the cost. Washington flourished – but the people did not share in its wealth. Politicians prospered – but the jobs left, and the factories closed. The establishment protected itself, but not the citizens of our country... . Mothers and children trapped in poverty in our inner cities; rusted-out factories scattered like tombstones across the landscape of our nation; an education system, flush with cash, but which leaves our young and beautiful students deprived of knowledge; and the crime and gangs and drugs that have stolen too many lives and robbed our country of so much unrealized potential" (USA Today 2017).*

While many Americans questioned the accuracy or sincerity of President Trump's words, his criticisms of U.S. trade policies and neglect of workers interests were similar to the views expressed by the unsuccessful leftist candidate for the Democratic nomination, Vermont Senator Bernie Sanders.

One of the few ways most Americans can counter entrenched privilege is to ensure that government works on their behalf. This chapter looks at how economic resources have become concentrated in the hands of a relatively small percentage of Americans, how this powerful fraction of the population exerts enormous influence over domestic and foreign policy, and how this structural characteristic of society can both generate harmful social conditions and interfere with social movements that address them. Through the vigorous efforts of millions of Americans, however, social movements and elections sometimes still succeed in changing society for the better.

Governments and economic systems are major structures of power that affect the development of social problems and the fate of social movements that emerge to combat them. The United States is a capitalist democracy. To understand what that means, it is helpful to describe the characteristics of different types of political and economic systems.

GOVERNMENT TYPES

A *democracy* is a form of government where the people exercise political power and participate directly or indirectly in creating laws and policies and in selecting the top government leaders (Goldstone 1998a). Essential elements include legal equality of all citizens under the law, the ability to obtain truthful information on any condition or issue, and the ability to participate in free elections. Modern democracies like the United States, Canada, Mexico, India, France, and South Korea are *democratic republics* in which the people elect representatives, such as senators or members of parliament, who vote on legislation on behalf of the citizens who elected them. The excerpt from former president Obama's speech at the opening of this chapter is an appeal to Americans to make use of their democracy to influence government, policymaking and who gets elected to power.

Oligarchic republics portray themselves as democracies but in reality are dominated by a small number of individuals or families whose power is generally based on wealth. In the nineteenth and early twentieth centuries, many countries in South and Central America fit this pattern. In more recent times, oligarchy appeared to be developing in Russia after the 1991 fall of the Soviet Union. Enormously valuable resources and industries, formerly owned by the Russian people through their government, rapidly fell into the hands of private individuals. Some of them became billionaires in what many Russians now regard as the greatest theft in history.

Authoritarian governments severely limit participation in politics. These include civilian and military dictatorships and authoritarian one-party states. In a *dictatorship* a single person or a small group, like a council of military officers, rules with little or no legal restrictions on their actions. Chile, for example, was ruled by a military dictatorship from 1973 to 1989. An *absolute monarchy* is a dictatorship where the ruler is the member of a royal family that holds power typically on the basis of heredity from generation to generation. The Kingdom of Saudi Arabia is an example.

Dozens of nations at one time had governments controlled by only one political party. These included some of the most brutal authoritarian regimes in history, such as Fascist Italy (1922–1943), Nazi Germany (1933–1945), and the Soviet Union under Stalin (1927–1953). In 2017, Communist Parties had exclusive control of governments in China, Cuba, North Korea, Laos, and Vietnam.

Another type of government, the *Islamic republic*, emerged with the 1979 Iranian Revolution. In an Islamic republic Islamic religious law is prominent in the constitution and legal system. Women's rights and clothing styles tend to be severely limited.

ECONOMIC AND CLASS SYSTEMS

Capitalism

The United States has **capitalism** as its economic system, wherein resources, industry and businesses, and other means of producing goods or services are privately owned. The primary motive for economic activity is profit. Most goods and services are sold and bought in competitive markets (Collins 1998). The culture of capitalist societies teaches that people are primarily motivated by self-interest and that society works best when it recognizes this. The Scottish economist Adam Smith stated in his book *The Wealth of Nations* (1776 [2012]) that the best possible capitalist system is one where there is no government regulation and no barriers to trade either within or between nations. Competition motivates people to continually improve products and services so everyone's overall well-being continuously improves. According to Smith, people enjoy a great deal of personal freedom in this system since social order is based on the need to cooperate in voluntary economic interactions for mutual benefit rather than on government coercion.

capitalism The economic system in which resources, industry and businesses, and other means of producing goods or services are privately owned, the primary motive for economic activity is profit, and most goods and services are sold and bought in competitive markets.

But capitalism is not always associated with political freedom. For example, during 1970s and 1980s the capitalist economies of Chile and South Korea grew under conservative military dictatorships. Smith also failed to anticipate the development of giant corporations that would make business relations far more impersonal and often less competitive than during his time. And capitalism can generate harmful conditions. The search for higher profits has often devastated entire towns and cities as corporations reduced labor costs by replacing workers with machines or moving factories to countries where wages were lower.

Karl Marx (1818–1883), a German social theorist, provided another influential analysis of capitalism. He believed that from ancient times people invented tools (technology) to become more secure and enjoy better lives. Improvements in technology continuously changed the economy and other aspects of society, including culture. Marx viewed capitalism as a revolutionary force, dramatically improving productivity through the industrial revolution and smashing past traditions and ways of life. But whereas Adam Smith believed capitalism was permanent, Marx saw it as a temporary stage in the ongoing development of society (Marx and Engels 1848 [1998]; Marx 1875 [1994]). He believed that the majority of people, once familiar with science and rational thinking, would want a more developed stage of society: **socialism**.

Socialism

The vision of a future society that possessed full equality and social justice has developed in many cultures throughout history. Some believed this would be a gift from God. Others thought it could evolve as a product of human moral and intellectual development. But Marx believed it would be achieved through class conflict. The working class or **proletariat**, composed of all workers from unskilled laborers to engineers and scientists who sell their labor for wage, would defeat the wealthy business owners, the **bourgeoisie**, and establish the first society in history controlled by and run for the welfare of the vast majority of people. Major resources and industries were to be socially (collectively) owned, and people would enjoy equality of opportunity. Health care, education, and basic nutrition would be provided to all either freely or at low cost. The culture of socialist societies would motivate people to work not only for personal gain but also out of a sense of responsibility for their fellow citizens.

Although Marx argued that social institutions and culture were shaped largely by the nature of a society's technology and economy (his concept of historical materialism), he also believed in the power of ideas. Marx thought that his ideas and those of other revolutionary intellectuals would inspire frustrated workers by explaining the root cause of their problems and providing them with a plan for a better society.

According to Marx, after the world shifted to socialism, governments would be less repressive. The greater efficiency and productivity of socialism would lead to enormous growth in technology and wealth. Since antagonistic classes would eventually cease to exist, social change would no longer be the product of class conflict but instead flow more directly from technological advances. This would mark the achievement of the highest state of society, communism.

It's obvious that several of Marx's major predictions failed. The class system did not split into only two classes, a minority of the very rich and a majority that was very poor. A large middle class emerged instead. Advances in technology improved living conditions for most people. In addition, capitalist leaders had the advantage of being able to read Marx's works and take steps to avert a proletarian revolution

socialism Ideally, an economic and social system characterized by equality of opportunity and social justice in which major resources and industries are socially (collectively) owned and health care, education, and basic nutrition are provided to all either freely or at low cost.

proletariat In Marx's theory, the working class, composed of all workers from unskilled to highly trained who sell their labor for a wage.

bourgeoisie In Marx's theory, the wealthy business owners.

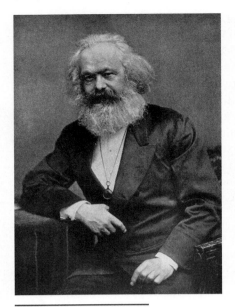

Karl Marx

by initiating reforms. They allowed workers to form labor unions to seek higher wages and better working and living conditions. In addition, Marx underestimated how access to resources of less developed societies would provide capitalist leaders in the developed countries the capacity to improve their workers' lives while simultaneously continuing to enrich themselves. As living conditions for the proletariat improved, the motivation for a workers' revolution subsided. Socialist revolutions instead occurred in less developed societies like Russia, China, and Vietnam. These societies often failed to live up to Marx's ideals by imposing limits on political freedom and by lagging behind the economic development of advanced capitalist nations.

The Reality of Blended Systems

While we tend to believe countries are either capitalist or socialist, in reality almost all countries have a blend of capitalist and socialist features.

capitalist-socialist societies Nations with predominantly capitalist economies where resources, businesses, and industries are mainly privately owned but which adopted measures advocated by socialist movements such as universal public education for children, publicly funded health care systems, and social security retirement systems.

Capitalist-Socialist Societies Many nations have predominantly capitalist economies where resources, businesses, and industries are mainly privately owned. Governments in these countries publicly embrace capitalist ideology. In some, like the United States, the government plays a limited role in the economy. In others like South Korea and Japan, government is active in coordinating between companies that secure resources and those involved in manufacturing and the export of products. Nations that began with nearly totally capitalist economies have eventually adopted measures advocated by socialist movements such as universal public education for children, socialized health care systems in which people pay little or nothing for essential medical services, and social security retirement systems. Leaders in capitalist nations viewed such reforms as beneficial to the economic system because they created a more highly educated population needed for advancing technology, and a healthier, happier work force that could look forward to retiring without having to live in poverty. These socialist aspects of mainly capitalist systems also reduced disruptive class conflict. Scandinavian countries are prime examples of predominantly capitalist economies that provide extensive social welfare programs.

socialist-capitalist societies Nations where resources and major industries are owned primarily by the state but where a significant expansion of capitalist business activity from selling crops in open markets to owning industries and businesses for profit has taken place.

Socialist-Capitalist Societies Revolutions in countries like China, Cuba, and Vietnam led to the adoption of socialist economic systems where resources and major industries are owned primarily by the state. The governments identify with socialist ideology and have a strong role in the economy. But economic progress was often unsatisfactory. Eventually, while retaining Communist Party governments, a significant expansion of capitalist business activity from selling crops in open markets to starting, owning, and running industries and businesses for profit was allowed. Even foreign investments were permitted.

Are There Links between Types of Economies and Types of Political Systems?

Living in a society that has a capitalist economy and where there is freedom of speech and religion and elections to choose leaders, many Americans feel that capitalism and democracy go hand in hand. Is this true?

It seems largely true for advanced capitalist societies. But there are examples of authoritarian societies with capitalist economies. In the oil-rich monarchies of the Middle East, resources and property are mostly privately owned, yet they are dictatorships that severely limit freedom of expression and women's rights. Nazi Germany and Fascist Italy both had capitalist economies with property mainly privately owned. Other nations such as South Korea, Malaysia, Singapore, Chile, Brazil, and Argentina spent long periods under military dictatorships while they simultaneously had capitalist economies. And China has allowed a vast increase in capitalist business activity while maintaining its one-party government.

THE GROWTH OF THE SIZE AND POWER OF CORPORATIONS

A **corporation** is a business organization that is given a charter by a government recognizing it as a separate legal entity having rights, assets, responsibilities, and liabilities separate from those of its owners or employees. This arrangement protects the property of executives from being seized to cover debts or lawsuits concerning damages caused by the corporation. Only the assets owned specifically by the corporation are at risk. Karl Marx believed that continuing technological development, ongoing division of labor, increasing rationality, and the pursuit of profit would shift the economy from relatively small competitive capitalist enterprises to very large corporations characterized by much less real competition.

Marx believed that companies that were good at the division of labor process and rationally coordinating the specific tasks of workers would surpass those that weren't. When Ford Motor Company, for example, introduced assembly-line production, a few vehicle manufacturers with sufficient resources followed suit. Some of those that could not went out of business.

In such a system, production of goods would eventually become concentrated in a small number of companies. There would, in effect, be only a few real sources (*oligopoly*) or one source (*monopoly*) for each major commodity or service such as oil, cars, computers, or banking. Social theorists following Marx's lead later referred to this situation as monopoly capitalism and predicted giant corporations would be able to set similar prices for products, control supply, maintain high profit levels, and prevent government oversight or interference. Executives would enjoy high salaries but in reality take virtually no personal risks.

corporation A business organization that is given a charter by a government recognizing it as a separate legal entity having rights, assets, responsibilities, and liabilities separate from those of its owners or employees.

Émile Durkheim and Max Weber, the other major classical sociological theorists who wrote mainly after Marx, did not share Marx's expectation that capitalism would lead to proletarian socialist revolution. Rather, they felt the problems caused by capitalism could be dealt with through reforms. Durkheim (1893) believed, in fact, that increasing division of labor, which he viewed as the essential trend in the process of economic and social development, was forming a new basis of social cohesion by making people more interdependent on one another. Weber saw the division of labor as part of the trend toward rationalizing business and government organizations (1924). Like Marx, he believed that those businesses that were the most rational in investment, research, and division and coordination of labor would eclipse those run less rationally.

While complete monopolies generally do not exist in most parts of the world, economic concentration has occurred to a significant degree. Though many thousands of small businesses still play significant roles, large corporations dominate the U.S. economy.

Modern Concentrated Economic Power

The Internal Revenue Service (2016a) indicated that in 2012 close to six million U.S. corporations submitted tax returns. While four out of five corporations were relatively small businesses with assets under $500,000, less than one twentieth of one percent (3,051 corporations) had assets above $2.5 billion. This very tiny fraction actually held 81 percent of all corporate assets. The value of this wealth was approximately twenty times the 2012 U.S. national budget and about six times the entire U.S. national debt (White House 2014). The power of the large corporations is not only due to their vast assets and revenues. Many have moved beyond their initial areas of industry or business through mergers or purchases of other companies, or simply by branching into new fields for added profits or security. These types of corporations, **conglomerates**, operate in multiple economic sectors. General Electric, for example, manufactures electrical equipment, appliances, and jet engines, and is also involved in oil and gas exploration, mining, finance, health care, and software services. Further, corporations often display more cooperation and unity than competition. The very top leadership tends to come from similar upper-class backgrounds and elite universities and schools of business. Individuals on one corporation board of directors often serve on the board(s) of other corporations. This connective framework, referred to as *interlocking directorates*, constitutes a means for information and points of view to be shared, and planning, actions, and policies coordinated through face-to-face interaction.

The gigantic size and transnational character of the biggest corporations has important consequences. Rationally utilizing world resources can advance technology and lifestyles in the rich capitalist societies, which can later benefit people in other societies. For example, the development of cell phones allows people in both developed and lesser-developed countries to have personal phones. Telephone communication using cell phones and satellites spares developing nations much of the time and enormous cost of building land line telephone systems.

conglomerate A corporation that operates in multiple economic sectors.

But the size and international character of major corporations gives them much more leverage against workers and labor unions. They can move their operations from unionized states to states with little tradition of unions or to other countries with low labor costs and weak enforcement of safety or environmental regulations. Often the only way, if given a chance at all, for American workers to keep their jobs is to accept lower wages and reduced benefits. At the same time, corporations reward executives with huge salaries and bonuses for increasing profits. Big corporations received huge infusions of taxpayer dollars to keep them operating after the economic crisis of 2008. The claim was they were too big to fail;allowing them to do so would wreck the overall economy.

CLASS AND ECONOMIC INEQUALITY IN THE UNITED STATES

Around the world people are ranked or "stratified" in terms of social and economic characteristics such as how much education, prestige, income, or power they have. Some agriculture-based societies, such as preindustrial India, had caste systems. In a caste system you stay in the rank you are born into throughout your life. Most modern societies, in contrast, have **social class systems** based on both birth and achievement. This means social mobility is possible by moving either up or down. People who have similar ranks on economic characteristics are viewed as members of the same social class.

THE U.S. SOCIAL CLASS SYSTEM

Sociologists (Gilbert 2018) who have studied stratification describe the United States as having six major classes.

Upper Class

The upper class, also sometimes referred to as the capitalist class, about one percent of the population, is mostly composed of high-ranking corporate executives and big-business owners, successful investors, top government officials, highly paid media, entertainment and sports celebrities, and heirs of large fortunes. Apart from sports and entertainment stars, it is common for members of this category to have attended Ivy League or other highly selective colleges and often have postgraduate degrees. In 2015 the typical household income for this category was about $1.5 million (Gilbert 2018). Some sociologists (Baltzell 1987) distinguish between an upper-upper class and a lower-upper class. Upper-upper class people are members of families that have been in the United States since colonial times and have been wealthy for generations. The Bush family of presidents George H. W. Bush and George W. Bush is a prominent example. People in the lower-upper class are the "new rich." They are from families that have only recently acquired wealth. Bill Gates, the founder of Microsoft, is a good example.

social class system
A social and economic stratification system typically based on both birth and achievement within which it is possible to move either up or down.

Upper-Middle Class

The upper-middle class is about 14 percent of the population. Members are typically professional workers like medical doctors, engineers, scientists, judges, lawyers, mid-level business executives, or the owners of medium-sized businesses or very successful small businesses. Most are college graduates and many have postgraduate degrees. Household incomes for this category were typically around $200,000 in 2015, with some as high as $500,000 (Gilbert 2018).

Middle Class

This class includes about 30 percent of the U.S. population. Incomes on average are around $85,000 for households in this class. Members are white-collar workers such as teachers and lower-level business managers or small-business owners. Many have some college education or other education beyond high school. Many high-skill, high-income blue-collar workers such as electricians are also in this class.

Working Class

The working class, also sometimes referred to as the lower-middle class, includes many semiskilled blue-collar persons, such as workers in auto and truck factories, as well as those in lower paid white-collar positions such as clerical workers. Most are high school graduates. The working class is another approximately 25 percent of the population. The typical household income in this class was about $40,000 in 2015.

Lower Classes

The lower classes are about 30 percent of the U.S. population.

The working poor, about 15 percent of the population, sometimes called the upper lower class, is composed of persons in low-paid unskilled blue-collar jobs and low-paid service jobs. Household incomes for this category were typically around $25,000 in 2015.

The underclass, approximately 15 percent of the population, sometimes referred to as the lower-lower class, is composed of persons who rarely or only occasionally participate in the labor force and rely heavily on government assistance. Household incomes were around $15,000.

ECONOMIC INEQUALITY

Income Inequality

income The money a person receives from working, investments, or other sources.

wealth The total worth of all assets a person owns minus any debts he or she has.

Economic inequality refers to differences among people in terms of income and wealth. **Income** is money a person receives from working, investments, or other sources. **Wealth** is the total worth of all assets a person owns minus any debts he or she has. Assets include interest-earning assets such as bank accounts, capital assets such as stocks or bonds, and property assets such as home ownership. In 1970, the top income fifth in the U.S. population received around 43.3 percent of all income. But by 2016, this had risen to 51.5 percent. The shares of the other income fifths in 2016, 22.9 percent, 14.2 percent, 8.3 percent, and 3.1 percent, respectively, had all fallen during this period (U.S. Census 2017a; Statista 2018b). Growth in the top fifth's income share was disproportionate due to the huge income increase for the top one percent. According to the U.S. Congressional Budget Office (2018), the household income after government assistance transfers and taxes of the top one percent grew by 228 percent from 1979 to 2014, while that of the rest of the top fifth grew by a much lower 73 per-

Social disparity in wealth

cent. For the middle three-fifths of the population, income growth was 42 percent. Income growth for the lowest fifth of the population was 69 percent. The income growth for the lowest fifth of the population (and to a lesser extent for the next highest fifth) was significantly more than it would have been because households in this category benefited greatly beginning mainly in 2014 from the effects the Affordable Care Act, the expansion of Medicaid, and the Obama administration's reduced taxes on low-income persons (Congressional Budget Office 2018).

Why did income rise so dramatically for the top one percent? One reason is that a large part of income for many very rich persons is their gains from investments in stock. Income from selling stocks owned for more than a year, capital gains, was taxed at around 15 percent, much lower than the tax rate on income earned in a high-salary paycheck, which was as high as 35 percent (Consumerism Commentary 2013). Because the top one percent keeps larger proportions of their income, they are more able to buy stocks and other investments with low or no taxes, like tax-free bonds, increasing both their wealth and the proportion of their minimally taxed income.

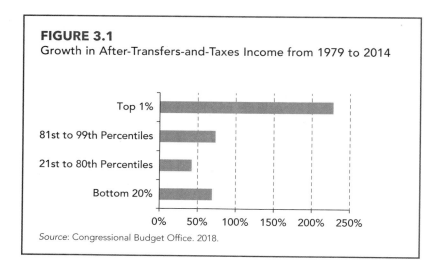

FIGURE 3.1
Growth in After-Transfers-and-Taxes Income from 1979 to 2014

Source: Congressional Budget Office. 2018.

Thomas Volscho and Nathan Kelly published a comprehensive study on income going to the top one percent, "The Rise of the Super-Rich," in the *American Sociological Review* (2012). Examining data for 1949–2008, they found that Republican control of Congress raised the proportion of national income going to the wealthy. Decline in labor union membership played a separate role in greater income going to the rich. In terms of specific policies, lowering taxes on high-income persons and on capital gains from stock helped increase income for the top one percent.

Another factor affecting income inequality is changing job structure. Technological innovation has replaced tens of thousands of workers with robotic machines. Corporations moved much manufacturing to developing nations, where labor costs are much lower. At the same time, the income of corporate executive officers soared while the average worker's pay stagnated. In 1965 the CEOs of America's top 350 firms earned about 20 times the average pay of a worker in the firm's main industry, but CEOs earned more than 271 times their average worker's pay in 2016 (Mishel and Schieder 2017). The average CEO compensation increased 973 percent from 1978 to 2016, but there was only an 11.2 percent growth in average worker compensation. CEO pay has grown far faster than corporate profits, stock prices, or the wages of college graduates. In 2016, according to an AFL-CIO analysis of available data, the CEOs of S&P 500 Index companies received an average total compensation of about $13.1 million, about 347 times more than that earned by production and nonsupervisory workers (AFL-CIO 2018).

Income Inequality Internationally

The Organization of Economic Co-operation and Development (OECD 2016) collects data on income for its more than thirty member nations. Table 3.1 shows two widely used measures of income inequality for each nation, the **Gini coefficient** and the ratio representing how much greater the income of the top ten percent of the country's population is compared to the bottom ten percent. The Gini coefficient can range from zero (meaning everyone has the same income) to one (meaning a single person has all the income). The top 10 percent vs. the bottom 10 percent income ratio is the average income of the top 10 percent as a multiple of the average income of the bottom 10 percent of the income scale. As in calculating the Gini coefficient, income data used to calculate the ratio is after taxes and transfers and is adjusted for differences in household size. Among the OECD nations, Turkey, the United States, Chile, and Mexico had the greatest gaps in income between the top ten percent and the bottom ten percent.

Wealth Inequality

Gini coefficient A measure of income inequality that ranges from zero (meaning everyone has the same income) to one (meaning a single person has all the income).

Ownership of wealth is much more unequal than income. According to economist Edward N. Wolff, the top 20 percent of wealth holders owned 89.9 percent of all wealth in 2016. The top one percent owned 39.6 percent of all wealth, the next 4 percent owned 27.1 percent, and the next 5 percent owned 12.1 percent (Wolff 2017).

TABLE 3.1	Income Distribution-OECD 2016

Country	Gini Coefficient	Top 10% vs. Bottom 10%	Country	Gini Coefficient	Top 10% vs. Bottom 10%
Demark	0.25	5.2	Ireland	0.30	7.4
Slovenia	0.25	5.4	France	0.31	7.4
Slovak Republic	0.25	5.7	Canada	0.32	8.6
Norway	0.25	6.2	Australia	0.33	8.8
Czech Republic	0.26	5.4	Italy	0.33	11.4
Iceland	0.26	5.6	New Zealand	0.33	8.2
Finland	0.26	5.5	Spain	0.34	11.7
Belgium	0.27	5.9	Japan	0.34	10.7
Sweden	0.27	6.3	Portugal	0.34	10.1
Austria	0.28	7.0	Estonia	0.34	9.7
Netherlands	0.28	6.6	Greece	0.34	12.3
Switzerland	0.28	6.7	United Kingdom	0.35	10.5
Hungary	0.29	7.2	Israel	0.38	12.5
Germany	0.29	6.6	United States	0.40	18.8
Poland	0.30	7.4	Turkey	0.41	15.2
South Korea	0.30	10.1	Mexico	0.48	30.5
Luxembourg	0.30	7.1	Chile	0.50	26.5

Source: OECD 2016.

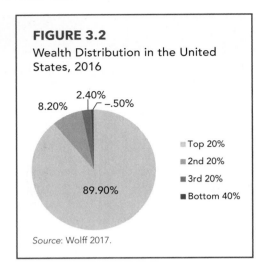

FIGURE 3.2
Wealth Distribution in the United States, 2016

2.40%
8.20% —.50%
89.90%

- Top 20%
- 2nd 20%
- 3rd 20%
- Bottom 40%

Source: Wolff 2017.

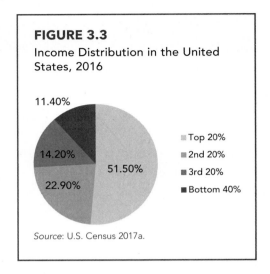

FIGURE 3.3
Income Distribution in the United States, 2016

11.40%
14.20%
22.90%
51.50%

- Top 20%
- 2nd 20%
- 3rd 20%
- Bottom 40%

Source: U.S. Census 2017a.

In the United States stock ownership has generated wealth faster than real estate in the form of home ownership since 1890 (Olick 2014). Home ownership is often the major component of wealth for middle-class persons, rather than stock.

The superrich and other powerful individuals have access to a global network that helps hide the money, property, and financial dealings of wealthy people, corrupt business persons and politicians, and criminal organizations. In April 2016 international news media revealed that someone had leaked 11.5 million electronic files, the so-called Panama Papers, from the Panamanian law firm Mossack Fonseca (Peralta 2016). This company is one of many around the world in places like Panama, the British Virgin Islands, the Cayman Islands, and other countries that assist people in hiding income and wealth. One of the likely purposes is to avoid paying taxes. As much as 8 percent of the world's total wealth ($7.6 trillion) is concealed from governments in secretive financial accounts and instruments, causing a loss to the United States alone of an estimated $37 billion in unpaid taxes annually (Harding 2016; Semple, Ahmed, and Lipton 2016).

Research indicates that most Americans want greater equality of wealth. A study carried out by professors at Harvard and Duke Universities in December of 2005 (Norton and Ariely 2011) asked 5,522 U.S. residents in a nationally representative sample to estimate the level of wealth inequality in the United States (what percentage of wealth was owned by the wealthiest one-fifth of the population, the next one-fifth, etc.) and what they thought would be the ideal levels. The authors note that at the time of their study the top one-fifth of the U.S. population owned about 84 percent of the country's wealth. But on average respondents thought the top one-fifth owned much less, 59 percent. The estimates were very similar regardless of gender, income, or political party. Amazingly, when asked what an ideal wealth distribution should be, the average response was that the top one-fifth of Americans should own just 32 percent of all wealth! The respondents also thought the next two-fifths of the population should own about 22 percent of

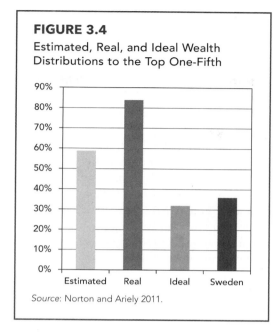

FIGURE 3.4

Estimated, Real, and Ideal Wealth Distributions to the Top One-Fifth

Source: Norton and Ariely 2011.

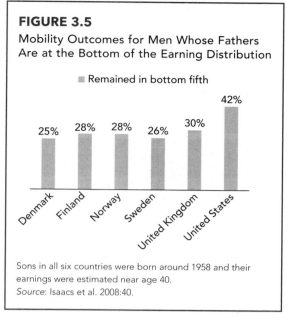

FIGURE 3.5

Mobility Outcomes for Men Whose Fathers Are at the Bottom of the Earning Distribution

Sons in all six countries were born around 1958 and their earnings were estimated near age 40.
Source: Isaacs et al. 2008:40.

the wealth each, the next fifth about 14 percent and the bottom fifth about 10 percent (in reality the actual percentages for the two lowest fifths at the time of the study were 0.2 percent and 0.1 percent, respectively). What the respondents considered ideal was similar to the real wealth distribution in Sweden (36 percent of wealth owned by the top one-fifth). There were only minor gender, class, or political-orientation differences in wealth distribution ideals among respondents, although women, lower-income individuals and Democrat-leaning persons were slightly more equalitarian.

The results of this study raise an interesting question. If the large majority of Americans favor a much more equalitarian distribution of wealth, why is wealth ownership so highly concentrated in the United States?

SOCIAL MOBILITY

Another issue regarding inequality is **social mobility**, the upward or downward movement on the economic ladder within a lifetime or between generations. For example, when a person born in poverty works her or his way into the middle class, this is called upward social mobility. The possibility of upward social mobility, at least for men, has been declining in recent decades (Kopczuk, Saez, and Song 2010). Research also suggests that upward social mobility decreases when economic inequality increases (Krueger 2012). Among advanced industrial nations, the United States appears to have not only high economic inequality but also relatively low social mobility (Krugman 2012).

In the United States and the United Kingdom, about half of parental earnings advantages are passed on to sons. If trends hold consistent, it would take an average of six generations for this advantage to disappear. Paternal earnings had the least effect on sons' earnings in Canada,

social mobility The upward or downward movement on the economic ladder within a lifetime or between generations.

Norway, Finland, and Denmark, where less than 20 percent of income advantages are passed on to children. The implication of these statistics is that in these countries it would take three, not six, generations, to essentially cancel out the effects of being born into a wealthy family (Isaacs et al. 2008). A more recent study by Miles Corak (2016) found that among twenty-four middle-income and high-income countries, the United States ranks 16th in the level of intergenerational earnings mobility.

States with high union membership like New York, New Jersey, Michigan, Connecticut, Pennsylvania, Massachusetts, and Maryland have higher social mobility than states like North Carolina, South Carolina, Texas, Oklahoma, Louisiana, and Mississippi, which have relatively low union membership (Madland and Bunker 2012; Pew Research Center 2012a). Unions push for higher wages, worker training programs, better public education, and adequate social assistance programs, all of which help lower-income people become upwardly mobile.

POWER IN THE UNITED STATES

Americans are proud that their country was born from a revolution against tyranny. While slavery and the exclusion of women from politics were glaringly inconsistent with its founding ideals of freedom and democracy, the United States has progressed toward fulfilling them. Political sociologists, however, disagree on just how democratic the United States really is. Do all Americans actually enjoy equal ability to influence government policies, or is it more accurate to say that a relatively small percentage of Americans exercise power? The view that political power is exercised by ordinary Americans through elections and through the organizations they support is called **pluralism** (Dahl and Rae 2005; Lipset 1981). The contrasting view is that a relatively small percentage dominates the political system. This is referred to as the power elite/ruling class perspective (Mills 1967; Domhoff 2012, 2013). The authors of this book believe that the exercise of political power in the United States shifts over time and due to circumstances along a continuum with the pluralism model at one end and the power elite/ruling class model at the other.

The Power Elite

C. Wright Mills, in *The Power Elite* (1967), and G. William Domhoff, in *Who Rules America* (2013), studied power in American society. Mills, analyzing U.S. society shortly after World War II, believed people occupying the top positions in major business corporations, the federal government, and the armed forces constituted the **power elite** that made the most important decisions. Mills believed they tended to be united in their interests and views. Members of the business elite served in top government positions and government office holders often took corporate jobs after leaving the public sector.

Domhoff, in contrast, concluded that the economic elite, composed of members of the upper class active in business or politics, along with other major corporate leaders, is in reality the dominant power elite.

pluralism The view that political power is exercised by ordinary Americans through elections and through the organizations they support.

power elite According to Mills, the power elite are people occupying the top positions in major business corporations, the federal government, and the armed forces who made the most important decisions. According to Domhoff, the dominant power elite is the economic elite.

A Ruling Class?

According to Domhoff (2012, 2013), the economic power elite is the **ruling class** in the United States. The members of this class control the major corporations and also heavily influence nonprofit foundations and research organizations that the public looks to for supposedly impartial research on important issues. Domhoff claims the upper class tries to determine what issues come to the public's attention and what views the public should adopt. It maintains a high degree of unity through interlocking corporate directorates, a network of exclusive social clubs and schools where its children are taught a distinctive self-serving upper-class perspective on the nation and the world, and intermarriage. The members of the economic power elite cooperate and support one another and the same polices because of their overwhelmingly similar economic interests and attitudes.

THE POLITICAL SYSTEM AND POLITICAL POWER

Money and Elections

One reason the upper class has so much influence over government is that running for political office in the United States is very expensive. Because politicians are so dependent on money, wealthy individuals and corporations can influence the candidate selection process and determine which candidates succeed by either providing or withholding contributions. Once elected, many office holders have to spend enormous amounts of time fundraising for the next election. This means they have less time to devote to seriously studying important issues or social problems. This is especially true of members of the House of Representatives, who have to stand for election every two years. The Campaign Finance Institute (2018) reported that in the 2016 election the average campaign spending for each of the two major-party candidates for House of Representatives races was $1,128,559. The average expenditure for a winning House candidate was $1,516,021, more than double what the losing candidate spent. This suggests that to hold the seat a representative has to raise about $2,077 every day. If the candidate is not independently wealthy, she or he must raise funds from people or groups who often expect favors in return for their money. The average 2016 spending of a person running for a Senate seat was $8,277,186, with the winning candidate spending $10,464,068. So to be re-elected a senator has to raise about $4,776 each day of her or his six year term! The graph shows that, controlling for inflation, the total money spent on House and Senate campaigns more than doubled between 1974 and 2016.

The 5 to 4 Supreme Court decision on January 21, 2010, in *Citizen's United v. the Federal Election Commission* eased restrictions on election spending and political activity by special interest groups and corporations (Legal Information Institute 2010; CBSNEWS 2012). This allowed political action committees (PACs), organizations that raised contributions within specified limits to support or defeat a political candidate, to become Super PACs that could now raise unlimited contributions

ruling class According to Domhoff, the economic power elite.

FIGURE 3.6

Congressional Campaign Expenditures: 1974–2016 (Adjusted for Inflation, 2016 Dollars)

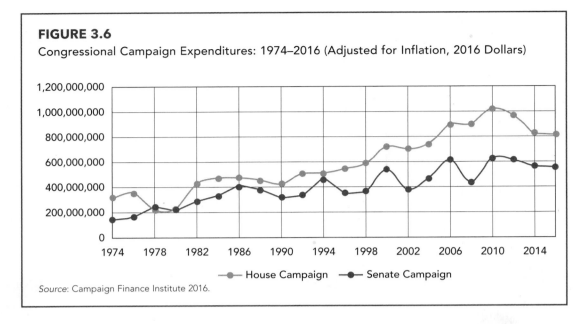

Source: Campaign Finance Institute 2016.

from individuals, corporations, or other groups (Goyette 2012). The enormous role of money in politics disillusions many to the point where they do not even bother to vote. Some legislators at the state level have attempted to provide public financing for political campaigns as a way of reducing the power of money from private interests in politics. In 2005, for example, Connecticut passed one of the nation's first public financing of political campaign laws (Craven 2009).

In the 2016 presidential campaign the *New York Times* (2016) reported that by February 9, dozens of wealthy individuals had contributed a million dollars or more to candidates' campaigns or political organizations supporting candidates' campaigns. Among the Republicans, Donald Trump had contributed over $12 million to his own campaign. Ted Cruz's effort had received several multimillion-dollar contributions including one for about $11 million and another for about $10 million. On the Democratic side, Hillary Clinton also benefitted from multi-million-dollar contributors, including one who provided $7 million. Of the major candidates, only self-proclaimed democratic socialist Bernie Sanders lacked any million-dollar contributors. His campaign was financed mainly by a large number of relatively small contributions (Campaign Finance Institute 2016).

Who Votes?

International Comparisons The American Revolution created the first democratic republic in the modern world and spurred the international democratic movement. Yet voter turnout in the United States is relatively low. Among 196 nations which held their most recent national legislative elections during 2001–2015, voter turnout in the United States for 2014, 42.5 percent, ranked 185th (Solijonov 2016). U.S. voter turnout in the presidential election year of 2016, 61.4 percent

(U.S. Census 2017b), would have ranked 126th on the list. On average, less than two-thirds of the U.S. voting age population vote, whereas Australia, Belgium, Demark, Ecuador, Italy, New Zealand, Sweden, and Uruguay are among forty nations with an average turnout over 75 percent (Solijonov 2016). A number of things affect voter turnout. For example, Latin American countries typically hold elections on Sundays, when it is easier for people to vote, while the United States holds elections on a workday (Planas 2012). Also, some nations have compulsory voting, including eighteen among the 125 countries with higher voter turnout than the United States had in its 2016 election.

Factors Affecting the Decision to Vote Voting is related to education, income, age, gender, and race/ethnicity. Decades of research show that older people and persons with higher levels of income and education are more likely to vote (U.S. Census 2017b; McDonald 2018). For example, in the 2016 election nearly 73 percent of persons aged 65 to 74 voted, compared to only 43 percent of those aged 18 to 24. About 80 percent of those with household incomes of $150,000 or above voted, compared to about 62 percent in the $40,000 to $49,999 range, and only about 41 percent of those with incomes under $10,000 (U.S. Census 2017b). Among racial/ethnic groups, 65.3 percent of non-Hispanic white citizens voted in the 2016 election compared to 59.4 percent of black, 49 percent of Asian, and 47.6 percent of Hispanic citizens.

Since the 1980 presidential election, women have been more likely than men to vote in national elections (Center for Women and Politics 2017). In the 2016 presidential election, women voters outnumbered male voters by about 9.9 million (U.S. Census 2017b), with 63.3 percent of women voting compared to 59.3 percent of men (Center for American Women and Politics 2018). In 2016 women voted at higher rates among blacks, Hispanics, and non-Hispanic whites. And since 2004, Asian/Pacific Islander women voted at rates higher than or nearly equal to the rates for Asian/Pacific Islander men.

Mass-membership organizations like the National Women's Organization, the American Association of Retired People, and the National Rifle Association often mobilize their members to vote. Members of labor unions are more likely to vote, and states with greater union membership have higher voter turnout than other states. Leighley and Nagler (2006) found evidence that the decline in union membership, from 29.3 percent of the workforce in 1964 to 12.6 percent in 2004, contributed to the drop in voter turnout during this period. In 2016, union membership dropped further to 10.7 percent (Bureau of Labor Statistics 2017).

STRUCTURAL FLAWS IN THE POLITICAL SYSTEM

One of the controversial aspects of the U.S. political system is the electoral college method of electing the president. This has sometimes led to the defeat of the presidential candidate for which most people voted. In the 2000 presidential election, for example, Al Gore won over 500,000 more votes than George W. Bush. But Bush became president instead

Social Movements: The Anti-Electoral College Movement

Anti-electoral college demonstrator

The 2016 election outcome spurred a new social movement to abolish the electoral college. Many Americans were shocked into awareness that the electoral college can hand victory to a presidential candidate who loses the popular vote by millions.

Why does the United States have the electoral college system rather than direct popular election of the president? The answer is that when the Constitution was being written in the 1780s, certain compromises were made to get the political leaders of all thirteen states to join into a single nation. First, some of the Founders opposed direct popular election out of fear that some charismatic but dangerous demagogue could appeal to the prejudices of the uneducated mass of eighteenth-century Americans and become the country's leader. Instead, they wanted the final decision to be made by well-educated "electors" in each state who could chose to ignore their voters' choice. Second, the electoral college system appealed to slave states. The slave states wanted to be able to protect the institution of slavery on which they were economically dependent. Since the number of members of the House of Representatives from each state was to be based on state population, the slave states demanded that the Constitution allow them to count every five unfree persons (slaves) as three additional free persons. This allowed the slave states to have more representatives in the House than if population counting was based solely on free residents. This also gave the slave states more power in

selecting the president through the electoral college because the number of electors in each state is based on the total of its two senators plus the number of its representatives. The electoral college also gave disproportionally greater influence to small states since each state gets two electors based on its two senators regardless of population. This means, for example, that in 2016 each voter in Wyoming had about three times the influence in selecting the president as a voter in California. Two original motives for the electoral college no longer exist. Slavery has been abolished. And the electoral college can actually give more influence to less-educated rather than better-educated Americans, opposite to what the Founders intended. For the 2016 election, analysis of 125,000 Gallup respondents surveyed during 2015 and the 2016 presidential campaign indicated that, controlling for other factors, Trump supporters were less likely to have four-year college degrees (Rothwell and Diego-Rosell 2016).

In 2017 multiple efforts were underway to replace the electoral college with a direct popular vote for president. This, however, is difficult. It would require a constitutional amendment approved by two-thirds of both the U.S. House of Representatives and Senate and then ratified by three-quarters of the state legislatures. Since the electoral college system has allowed two Republican candidates to serve as president in the twenty-first century despite losing the popular vote, no electoral college replacement legislation is likely as long as Republicans control the Senate. One effort to replace the electoral college was the Moveon.org petition signed by about six hundred thousand Americans within three months of the 2016 election (Moveon.org 2017).

Ask yourself:
Why or why not is the electoral college a democratic method of electing the president? What advantages or drawbacks would there be if the electoral college was replaced by direct popular vote of the president?

because he officially won the state of Florida by 537 votes (although the conservative-dominated Supreme Court stopped the recount of Florida's votes). And in 2016 the difference between the popular vote result and the electoral college result was even more shocking. Although Hillary Clinton won nationally by over 2.86 million votes, Donald Trump became president because he won the electoral college by taking the states of Pennsylvania, Michigan, and Wisconsin by a combined total of about 78,000 votes.

The U.S. Senate can also counter the will of the majority of Americans because it gives disproportionate influence to states with small populations. For example, the two senators from the state with the smallest population, Wyoming, representing about 576,000 people, have the same power in the Senate as the two senators from California, representing over 38 million people.

Certain practices in the U.S. Senate and the House of Representatives can also impede the spirit of democracy. In the House of Representatives, the Speaker, who leads the representatives of the majority party in the House, can refuse to bring a bill before the full House for a vote even though there are plenty of votes to pass it. In the Senate a big problem is the filibuster rule. This allows a small group of senators or even just one senator to talk continuously on a proposed bill unless at least sixty senators vote to call for a vote on the proposed legislation.

The Impact of the 2010 Midterm Elections

Voter turnout for midterm elections tends to be much lower than for presidential elections. For example, while about 62 percent of potential voters voted in the 2008 presidential election, the turnout for the 2010 midterm election was around 42 percent, meaning about forty-two million fewer voters (McDonald 2018). Especially significant was that the decline in voter turnout was much greater for groups that tended to vote Democratic. The drop in the percentages of young persons, people of color, and women, all of whom had voted disproportionately for the Democratic candidate, Obama, in 2008, was significantly greater than the drop in non-Hispanic white males and older voters who had disproportionately voted for the Republican candidate John McCain. This meant that Republican-leaning voters played a much bigger role in determining the outcome of the 2010 election. Fear of Obama's Affordable Health Care Act and that he would try to drastically reduce gun ownership motivated many to vote Republican in 2010. The Tea Party movement, launched in early 2009, proved effective in getting Republican nominations for candidates it favored and in turning out millions of voters to elect them.

The outcome of the 2010 elections had major impacts. The results switched the House of Representatives from Democratic to Republican control. The outcomes at the state level gave Republicans control of both state legislative bodies in twenty-five states, compared to sixteen for the Democrats. Republicans also dominated one of the legislative bodies in another eight states. Overall, this was the greatest Republican state legislative advantage since 1952 (Storey 2010). In addition, thirty states had Republican governors (Republican Governors Association 2013). This is important because, following the 2010 census, states had to redraw boundaries for congressional districts and state legislative districts (Daley 2016). In many states, when one party is in control of both legislative bodies and the governorship it can create voting districts to give itself an advantage in coming elections. This practice, called "gerrymandering," involves rearranging boundaries so that the party in control of the state government adds to or subtracts territory from voting districts, making it likely that its candidates can win by a safe margin, say 55 to 60 percent of the vote. Voters leaning toward the opposing party are then heavily concentrated in a relatively small number of voting districts.

Gerrymandering had enormous consequences for the 2012 elections. The great Republican advantage in redistricting appeared to be a major reason why the Republican Party retained control of the House of Representatives by thirty-two seats despite Democratic candidates for the House winning about 1.1 million more votes nationwide than Republican candidates (Office of the Clerk, House of Representatives 2013; Palmer and Cooper 2012). The trend of Republicans winning a significantly higher percent of seats in the House than the proportion of the popular vote their candidates received continued in later elections. In 2016, for example, Republican candidates won 49.1 percent of the House popular vote but took 55.4 percent (241) of the seats (Cook 2016; House of Representatives 2017). The Democrats won 48 percent of the House popular vote but took only 44.6 percent of the seats (194).

Several states also illustrate the impact of redistricting. In 2012, more voters in Wisconsin voted for Democratic than Republican candidates for the state's seats in Congress and the state legislature. But the way the Republican-controlled state government conducted redistricting contributed to Republicans taking five of Wisconsin's eight seats in the House of Representatives and Republican majorities in both the Wisconsin State Senate and the Wisconsin State Assembly (Palmer and Cooper 2012). Redistricting also helped ensure that thirteen of Pennsylvania's eighteen members of the House of Representatives elected in 2012 were Republicans despite Democratic candidates receiving 83,000 more votes than Republicans statewide. A similar pattern occurred in Ohio and Virginia.

The 2010 midterm elections had other important consequences. In several states with historically strong labor union movements, such as Ohio, Wisconsin, and Michigan, Republican governments passed laws to weaken unions. Ohio's state constitution, however, permits citizens to approve or reject certain government actions. Public sentiment was so opposed to Senate Bill 5, which restricted public employee collective bargaining rights, that voters in a special referendum on November 8, 2011, overturned it by a wide margin (Thrush 2011). Republican-controlled state governments also passed laws requiring new forms of voter identification to prevent noncitizens from voting or people voting more than once. Critics claimed,

FIGURE 3.7

Pennsylvania's Strangely Shaped 7th Congressional District in December 2011.

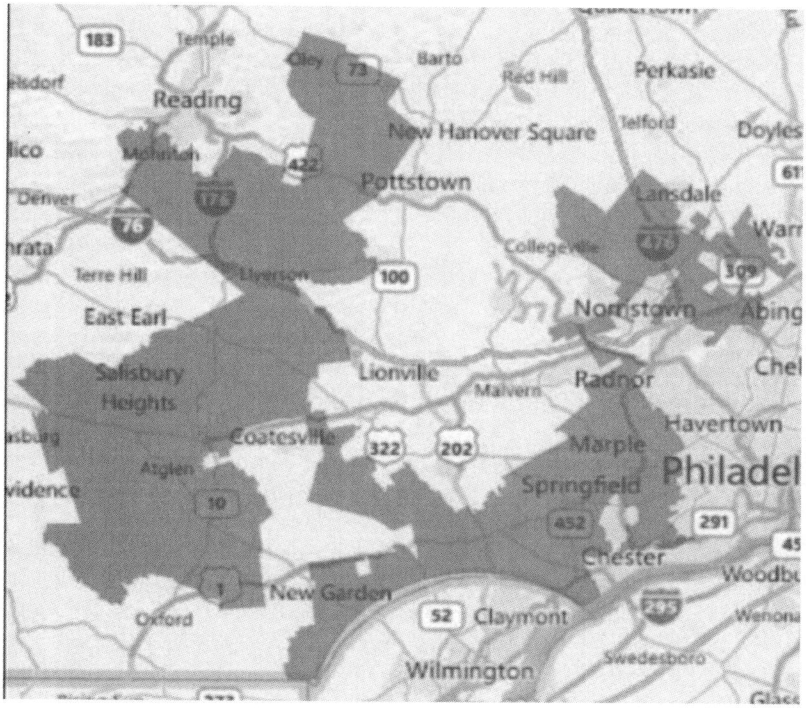

however, that there was no evidence of any significant voter fraud and that the real reason for the new voter IDs was to make it harder for Democratic-leaning groups, such as poor people, minorities, and college students, to vote. Several state governments also reduced the number of early voting days, making it more difficult for lower-income working people and minorities to vote. On election day 2012, many voters in Ohio and Florida had to wait in line for three hours or more to exercise their democratic right to vote. Similar problems were reported on election day in 2016 in key states, including Florida, Michigan, North Carolina, Ohio, and Pennsylvania (Wolf and McCoy 2016).

THE ARMED FORCES

Military leaders appear clearly subordinate in power to both economic and federal governmental elites in the United States. Yet the armed forces have direct physical control of the most powerful technologies of violence in the world. Although since the end of the draft in 1973 only a

Special Topics: Whatever Happened to Lincoln's Republican Party?

Millions of Americans saw the hit movie *Lincoln* in 2012, which told the story of the struggle to pass the 13th Amendment to abolish slavery. Abraham Lincoln was the first Republican president. He campaigned in 1860 to prevent the expansion of slavery to U.S. territories that were not yet states. In the election, Lincoln won only the northern states of the east and the Midwest, plus California and Oregon. Missouri, Kentucky, Virginia, Maryland, Delaware, and all the states farther south went to other candidates.

A century and a half later, the pattern for the Republican Party's presidential candidate Mitt Romney in 2012 was nearly the reverse of Lincoln's in 1860. Romney took only a single state that Lincoln won, Indiana. Instead, Romney won all of the states of the Civil War Confederacy that seceded because of the election of a Republican president in 1860 except for Virginia and Florida. What has changed about the Republican Party and the United States to bring about this remarkable geographic shift?

Several factors played a role. One was the changing tactics of Republican big business interests. Wealthy capitalists have consistently been among the main supporters of the Republican Party, but their means of obtaining high profits through low labor costs changed over time. In the 1850s and 1860s many industrialists' desire for cheap labor coincided with the goal of the abolitionist movement to end slavery. Transforming millions of slaves into free laborers would increase competition among workers for jobs, allowing employers to keep wages low. But after the rise of labor unions in the North (which successfully increased wages for workers), many manufacturers decided to move factories to nonunion southern states where labor costs were lower. Thus, over time Republican big business interests shifted southward.

Racial attitudes also played a role in moving the base of the Republican Party to the south. The events motivating racially biased white voters to shift from the Democratic Party to the Republican Party were the strong pro-civil rights stand taken by the Democratic Kennedy administration and, in particular, the Civil Rights Act of 1964 and the Voting Rights Act of 1965 passed under the Democratic Johnson administration. These anti-racist federal laws made economic and political discrimination on the basis of race, including interfering with the right to vote, illegal. This caused many white voters in the south to look for an alternative to the Democratic Party. The Republican Party began to attract them not by being openly racist but by adopting the limited government, extreme states' rights position. This had once been used by proslavery politicians, most notoriously John C. Calhoun of South Carolina, to defend the institution of slavery before the Civil War (Tanenhaus 2013). After this shift, he Republican Party steadily gained electoral strength in the South. Except for the successful presidential campaigns of white southern Democrats, Jimmy Carter of Georgia in 1976 and Bill Clinton of Arkansas in 1992 and 1996, the white vote in the South has gone overwhelmingly Republican. While in the 2008 presidential election Democrat Barack Obama won 53 percent of the white vote in California, 54 percent in Wisconsin, 52 percent in New York, and 65 percent in Vermont, only 28 percent of whites voted for him in Texas, 11 percent in Mississippi, and 10 percent in Alabama (Tilove 2008). The percent of whites voting for Obama in staunchly Republican northern states like Idaho, Utah, and Wyoming was over 32 percent, much higher than in Deep South states.

In the 2016 election, however, Donald Trump altered the pattern of recent presidential elections by taking the northern states of Pennsylvania, Michigan, and Wisconsin by a combined total of about 78,000 votes. This allowed him to win the electoral college despite losing the popular vote by slightly over 2.86 million votes.

What do you think?

What are the pros or cons of having only two major political parties in the United States? What are the benefits or drawbacks of being a member of a political party?

small proportion of the population serves in the military (less than one percent at any time), advanced technology has increased the lethality of modern weapons far beyond what was available in the past. In other words, fewer people have the ability to destroy more property and kill more people much more efficiently and with considerably reduced personal risk than ever before in history.

Studies show that there has been a trend for an increasing cultural and political gap between military personnel and most American civilians. Research indicates that since the end of the draft the military tended to become more conservative and more pro-Republican (Holsti 1999, 2001). Furthermore, without the draft military personnel tend to come disproportionately from southern states and western states (except for California) and from households in which a parent was a member of the armed forces. Some sociologists have raised the question of whether civilian control of the military could be jeopardized if the social and political distance between the armed forces and civilian leadership continues to grow.

ECONOMIC AND POLITICAL POWER AND MOVEMENTS FOR CHANGE

Despite economic and political forces that impede progressive movements, committed people working together can change and have changed society for the better. Two great engines of beneficial social change, idealism and science, play major roles in social movements overcoming social injustice.

American society was founded on the core ideals of "equality" and "unalienable rights" of "life, liberty and the pursuit of happiness." But financial interests and deeply held traditional prejudices originally excluded people of color and women. One of the world's first sociologists, Harriet Martineau (1802–1876), noted the stark moral inconsistencies between the ideals and realities of early American society. She made the clearest prediction of how the contradictions would bring social change (Lengermann and Niebrugge 2007). Martineau was born in England and, though barred from receiving a university education because of her gender, achieved great fame as a social analyst and writer. In 1834 she travelled to the United States, visiting twenty of the then twenty-four states and meeting hundreds of ordinary citizens as well as many political, business, and religious leaders. Martineau believed the most essential values of American society were expressed in the Declaration of Independence, "that all men are created equal," and that governments have that right to exist and exercise authority only when they derive "their just powers from the consent of the governed." She concluded that economic interests and harmful traditions like racism and sexism were responsible for deviations from America's central moral principles: slavery, the political and economic powerlessness of women, and great inequality of property ownership. These contradicted the concepts that all people are created equal and that people should only be governed through their own consent (Martineau believed that great inequality of property results in government by the rich rather than by the people). Martineau predicted that the inconsistency between America's core ideals and slavery, the subordination of women, and wealth inequality would generate a process of social change that would bring social reality ever closer to its essential ideals.

Reflecting Martineau's prediction, at his second inauguration on January 23, 2013, President Obama emphasized the importance of people working together to bring America closer to its central ideals.

Social Movements: The Women's March and the Post-Election Movements

Participants in the Women's March

The surprise election of Donald Trump by the electoral college immediately provoked post-election anti-Trump movements. To many Americans, Trump appeared to be an extremely dishonest (possibly psychopathic) con man who had bragged that as a celebrity he could kiss women and even grab them between their legs. Disappointment quickly gave way to anger and horror that such a person could and would become president. This outrage soon found an outlet in an idea by Teresa Shook, a retired attorney and grandmother of four girls living in Hawaii. Teresa, after seeing the result on election night, posted a call on a Facebook event page that women should march in Washington to protest. When she woke the next morning, some 10,000 women responded that they wanted to march. Then the number climbed dramatically. On January 21, a crowd estimated at 500,000 marched in the nation's capital, around three times the number estimated to have shown up for the inauguration the day

before (Sheth 2017). Scientists at the University of Connecticut and the University of Denver estimated the total marching in dozens of cities around the United States to protest Trump to be at least 3.2 million.

President Trump's January 27 executive order on immigration prompted a new series of protests in many other cities and airports. That order indefinitely barred Syrian refugees from entering the United States and imposed a ninety-day ban on travel to the United States from seven Muslim majority countries: Iran, Iraq, Libya, Somalia, Sudan, Syria, and Yemen (Caldwell 2017). Critics of the executive order claimed it was intended as a ban on Muslim immigrants from these countries.

By late January, scientists announced a March for Science to assert a role for science in policymaking in the face of prominent Republicans' denials of climate change and other seemingly non-science-based statements. On Earth Day April 22, 2017, hundreds of thousands marched for science in more than six hundred cities around the world, including Washington, D.C., Boston, Chicago, Los Angeles, San Francisco, and New York (Lapook 2017). Given the publicly stated agenda of President Trump and Republican leaders in Congress, activists anticipated that these demonstrations would be followed by new protests.

What do you think?

What types of social movements do you think will occur most frequently in the next few years? Are there any you might join?

"'We hold these truths to be self-evident, that all men are created equal; that they are endowed by their Creator with certain unalienable rights; that among these are life, liberty, and the pursuit of happiness.' Today we continue a never-ending journey to bridge the meaning of those words with the realities of our time. For history tells us that while these truths may be self-evident, they've never been self-executing... . The patriots of 1776 did not fight to replace the tyranny of a king with the privileges of a few or the rule of a mob. They gave to us a republic, a government of, and by, and for the people" (White House 2013).

CHAPTER REVIEW

Government Types

Contemporary government types around the world include democratic republics, oligarchic republics, authoritarian governments, dictatorships, absolute monarchies, one-party states, and Islamic republics.

Economic and Class Systems

Capitalism is an economic system wherein resources, industry and businesses, and other means of producing goods or services are privately owned. The primary motive for economic activity is profit, and most goods and services are sold and bought in competitive markets. Socialism ideally is an economic and social system characterized by equality of opportunity and social justice in which major resources and industries are socially (collectively) owned and health care, education, and basic nutrition are provided to all either freely or at low cost. In reality almost all countries have a blend of capitalist and socialist features. Capitalist-socialist societies are nations with predominantly capitalist economies where resources, businesses, and industries are mainly privately owned but which have adopted measures advocated by socialist movements such as universal public education for children, publicly funded health care systems, and social security retirement systems. Socialist-capitalist societies are nations where resources and major industries are owned primarily by the state but where a significant expansion of capitalist business activity from selling crops in open markets to owning industries and businesses for profit has taken place. History shows that there is no necessary link

between a country's economic system and its type of political system.

Growth of the Size and Power of Corporations

Contemporary capitalist economies are dominated by huge corporations. In the United States, one twentieth of one percent of all corporations owns over 80 percent of all corporate assets. This concentrated economic power exerts enormous influence over politicians and government. While large corporations have played a major role in the development of new technologies, the fact that they are privately owned and controlled means their policies do not necessarily benefit the majority of people and may even cause harm in order to maximize profits. Many are responsible for sending millions of U.S. jobs to other countries. Some helped convince government leaders to lower taxes on wealthy individuals and ease regulations on financial activities involving stocks and mortgages. These actions contributed to increasing income and wealth inequality, and to causing the great economic recession that began in 2008.

Class and Economic Inequality in the United States

Around the world people are ranked or "stratified" in terms of social and economic characteristics such as how much education, prestige, income, or power they have. Whereas some pre-industrial agriculture-based societies had caste systems where you stay in the rank you are born into throughout your life, most modern societies have social class systems based on both birth and achievement. This means social mobility is possible by moving either up or down. People who have similar ranks on economic characteristics are viewed as members of the same social class.

U.S. Social Class System

The United States has six major social classes: the upper class, about 1 percent of the population, is composed of high-ranking corporate executives and business owners, certain top government officials, highly paid media, entertainment and sports celebrities, and heirs of large fortunes; the upper-middle class, about 14 percent of Americans, are professional workers like medical doctors, engineers, scientists, judges, lawyers, mid-level business executives, or the owners of medium-sized businesses or very successful small businesses; the middle class includes about 30 percent of the U.S. population who are white collar workers such as teachers and lower-level business mangers or small-business owners and highly skilled blue-collar workers such as electricians; the working class (also called the lower-middle class), about 25 percent of the population, includes many semiskilled blue-collar workers, such as workers in car and truck factories, as well as those in lower-paid white-collar positions such as clerical workers; the working poor about 15 percent of population, sometimes called the upper-lower class, is composed of persons in low-paid unskilled blue-collar jobs and low-paid service jobs; and the *underclass*, approximately 15 percent of the population, sometimes referred to as the lower-lower class, is composed of persons who rarely or only occasionally participate in the labor force and rely heavily on government assistance.

Economic Inequality

Economic inequality refers to differences among people in terms of income and wealth. Income is money a person receives from working, investments, or other sources. Wealth is the total worth of all assets a person owns minus any debts he or she has. Wealth inequality is much greater than income inequality, and both increased significantly in the United States since the early 1980s.

Social Mobility

Social mobility is the upward or downward movement on the economic ladder within a lifetime or between generations. Among advanced industrial nations, the United States appears to have not only high economic inequality but also relatively low social mobility.

Power in the United States

The view that political power is exercised by ordinary Americans through elections and through the organizations they support is called pluralism. The contrasting view that a relatively small percentage dominates the political system is called the power-elite/ruling-class perspective. In reality, the exercise of power in the United States seems to be a continuum between the power-elite and ruling-class models at one end and the pluralist, democratic model at the other. Some acts of government appear mainly influenced by the preferences of elite groups, while at other times policies result from a more democratic process.

The Political System and Political Power

In the United States, money plays an enormous role in politics. Politicians spend much of their time raising money for political campaigns and then are expected to repay donors with political favors. An important way for most Americans to exercise political power is through voting. But voter participation is relatively low in the United States compared to other democracies. Research shows that highly educated people, higher-income persons, older Americans, and women are more likely to vote.

Structural Flaws in the Political System

The U.S. political system has several structural characteristics that have sometimes defeated the will of the majority of voters. One is the electoral college, an aspect of the original Constitution created in great part to advantage slave-owning states and protect slavery, which has repeatedly allowed candidates receiving a minority of the popular vote to become president.

Another is the U.S. Senate, which gives as much power to senators representing a few hundred thousand voters as those representing many millions.

The results of the 2010 interim election led to the redistricting of many voting districts in ways that give a conservative minority an advantage in voting for members of the House of Representatives and also state legislatures in a number of states. State legislatures controlled by conservatives attacked labor unions and were accused of attempting a level of voter suppression not seen in America since the days of the segregationist South.

The Armed Forces
Military leaders appear clearly subordinate in power to both economic and federal governmental elites in the United States. Yet the armed forces have direct physical control of the most powerful technologies of violence in the world. Research indicates that since the end of the draft the military has tended to become more conservative.

Economic and Political Power and Movements for Change
Economic and political inequalities affect the development and success of social movements. Modern technology allows movement activists to communicate more rapidly with each other and with vast audiences. Showing how harmful conditions and policies contradict the basic core values of American society can continue to win victories for movements advocating progressive change and social justice.

KEY TERMS

bourgeoisie, p. 53
capitalism, p. 52
capitalist-socialist societies, p. 54
conglomerate, p. 56
corporation, p. 55
Gini coefficient, p. 60
income, p. 58
pluralism, p. 64

power elite, p. 64
proletariat, p. 53
ruling class, p. 65
social class system, p. 57
social mobility, p. 63
socialism, p. 53
socialist-capitalist societies, p. 54
wealth, p. 58

DISCUSSION QUESTIONS

1. What type of economic system is best suited to support and preserve a democratic political system? Explain your point of view.

2. Why do you think that in the twenty-first century some countries are still governed by authoritarian regimes, or even monarchies?

3. What do you view as the greatest threat to American democracy? Explain your position.

4. Do you think that reducing the level of economic inequality in the United States would be beneficial or harmful? Explain your point of view.

5. Should limits be set on the role of money in the U.S. political system? Explain your point of view.

6. What can be done to increase the percentage of people who vote in elections in the United States?

7. Should changes be made to the U.S. political system to make it more democratic? If yes, what changes? In any case, explain your position.

CHAPTER 4

Poverty

CHAPTER OBJECTIVES

- Explain the difference between absolute and relative poverty.
- Describe how poverty is measured in the United States.
- Describe the major consequences of poverty.
- Describe the difficulties of the working poor.
- Explain major points of view on the causes of poverty.

- Describe the structural-functional, conflict, and symbolic-interactionist perspectives on poverty.
- Describe the proposed solutions to poverty and the programs developed to reduce poverty and its effects.

MANY AMERICANS ARE THE DESCENDANTS *of people who came to the United States to escape poverty. The vast majority were poor not because they were lazy, or had no ambition, or lacked moral standards. Millions of immigrants from Germany, Ireland, Mexico, Italy, Poland, and other nations had virtually no hope of escaping poverty if they remained in their homelands no matter how hard they worked or how morally upright they were. It was the economic and political structures of those societies that kept them poor. Their welcome to the United States is enshrined in the words on the base of the Statue of Liberty: "Give me your tired, your poor, your huddled masses yearning to breathe free, the wretched refuse of your teeming shore. Send these, the homeless, tempest-tost to me, I lift my lamp beside the golden door."*

Does contemporary America welcome the poor? Or do government officials today really want only the highly educated and those with outstanding talents to become part of our nation? As discussed in Chapter 3, the United States has higher income inequality and wealth gaps and lower social mobility than other advanced countries. One in every seven Americans, including one in every five American children, lives in poverty. Even more troubling, for many Americans hard work does not seem to result in an escape from poverty. Millions work at minimum- or near-minimum wage jobs forty hours a week but remain poor. What do most Americans today think are the primary causes of poverty? Is it mainly individual limitations and personal moral failings? Or do economic and political factors play major roles?

WHAT IS POVERTY?

Poverty can be viewed in either absolute or relative terms. **Absolute poverty** means a person or family does not have access to basic things, including food, clean water, clothing, housing, sanitation, health care, and education, needed to survive and maintain health and well-being. **Relative poverty**, in contrast, refers to people having so much less in material goods and style of life than others that they are seen as "poor" in terms of social standards even if they do not suffer absolute poverty. For example, if you live in a $300,000 condominium in Greenwich, Connecticut, where the average price of homes for sale in June 2017 was about $4 million (Trulia 2017), you might well be seen as or feel poor in a relative sense compared to your neighbors.

absolute poverty Not having access to basic things, including food, clean water, clothing, housing, sanitation, health care, and education, needed to survive and maintain health and well-being.

relative poverty Having so much less in material goods and style of life than others that people are seen as "poor" in terms of social standards even if they do not suffer absolute poverty.

Definition and Measurement of Poverty in the United States

The federal government defines and measures poverty using the concept of absolute poverty. During 1963–1964 Mollie Orshansky of the Social Security Administration developed what became the basis for the "poverty threshold," which has been used by the government to count the number of poor people in the country (Fisher 1997). This threshold delineates the income level needed to purchase the minimum resources necessary for survival. Anyone whose income falls below it is considered to be in poverty. Orshanky based the threshold on data from the Department of Agriculture, which indicated that families typically spent about one third of their income on food at that time. She calculated the poverty threshold by simply multiplying by three the amount of money required to purchase the cheapest food plan developed by the Department, the "emergency" program for minimal-required nutrition. Dozens of separate poverty thresholds are calculated for households of different sizes and composition. For example, the federal poverty income threshold for a household with two adults and two children in 2016 was $24,339 and $24,858 in 2017 (U.S. Census 2018c). The thresholds are adjusted annually according to changes in the consumer price index (CPI). This absolute measurement of poverty, though, has several problems. Since the early 1960s, when Orshansky developed the formula for the poverty line, the portion of family income spent on food has steadily decreased while costs for housing, child care, health care, and transportation became much more expensive. In other words, families spend less than one third of their income on food these days but have to spend more on other necessary items. This likely results in an underestimate of absolute poverty. Another limitation is that the official federal measurement of poverty does not consider different costs of living in different geographic areas. This means that poverty is underestimated in areas where the cost of living is high and overestimated in places where the cost of living is low. Table 4.1 displays federal poverty thresholds for 2017 by size of family and number of related children.

A Profile of the Poor

The percent living in poverty has changed over time. In 1960 about 22 percent of Americans were estimated to be poor (DeNavas-Walt, Proctor, and Smith 2011). Then the poverty rate significantly decreased to about 12 percent in 1969 due to President Lyndon Johnson's "War on Poverty." The poverty rate has since increased in part due to the recession that began in 2008 reaching 15.9 percent of the population in 2011 (48.5 million people) and 2012 (48.8 million people) (U.S. Census 2013). One in three Americans had at least one spell of poverty lasting two or more months during the period of 2009–2011 (Mangahas 2013). In 2016, about 12.7 percent of Americans (40.6 million people) had incomes below the poverty thresholds (U.S. Census 2017a). The risk of being poor varies by region, race and ethnicity, gender, family type,

TABLE 4.1	Poverty Thresholds for 2017 by Size of Family and Number of Related Children under 18 Years (in Dollars)

| Size of Family Unit | Related Children under 18 Years | | | | | | | | |
	None	One	Two	Three	Four	Five	Six	Seven	Eight or More
One Person (Unrelated Individual)									
Under Age 65	12,752								
Age 65 and Older	11,756								
Two People									
Householder Under Age 65	16,414	16,895							
Householder Age 65 and Older	14,816	16,831							
Three People	19,173	19,730	19,749						
Four People	25,283	25,696	24,858	24,944					
Five People	30,490	30,933	29,986	29,253	28,805				
Six People	35,069	35,208	34,482	33,787	32,753	32,140			
Seven People	40,351	40,603	39,734	39,129	38,001	36,685	35,242		
Eight People	45,129	45,528	44,708	43,990	42,971	41,678	40,332	39,990	
Nine People or More	54,287	54,550	53,825	53,216	52,216	50,840	49,595	49,287	47,389

Source: U.S. Census 2018c.

and age. Northeastern states have the lowest poverty rates, followed by the Midwest and the West. Generally, Southern states have higher poverty levels. During 2015–2016 New Hampshire had the lowest state poverty rate, about 6.8 percent (U.S. Census 2017a). Kentucky, Louisiana, Mississippi, and New Mexico all had over 17 percent in poverty. White non-Hispanic persons, and Asians had below-average poverty rates in 2016 of 8.8 percent and 10.1 percent, respectively.

Blacks and Hispanics had above-average poverty rates, 22.0 percent and 19.4 percent, respectively. Only 5.1 percent of families with two married parents present were poor. In comparison, for single parent male-headed families the poverty rate was 13.1 percent and for single parent female-headed families it was 26.6 percent.

The most disturbing aspect of this social problem is the enormous number of children (persons under eighteen) growing up in poverty. In 2016, 13.3 million children, 18 percent of all children, were living in poverty (U.S. Census 2017a). The U.S. Census American Community Survey (2016b) indicated that in ten states, Alabama, Arizona, Arkansas, Georgia, Kentucky, Louisiana, Mississippi, New Mexico, South Carolina, and Tennessee, as well as the District of Colombia, more than one in four children was poor.

The United Nations Children's Fund (UNICEF) collects data to measure child poverty internationally. UNICEF defines "child relative income poverty" as the percentage of children (0–17) in households with income less than 60 percent of the median household income in a nation, a method different from that used to define poverty in the United States (UNICEF 2017b). Table 4.2 shows, that among technologically developed nations, the United States has had one of the highest levels of children living in "child relative income poverty."

Many people have stereotypes of poor Americans as people who are lazy and unwilling to work and therefore deserve to live in poverty. But this view is inaccurate for most of the poor. Over one-third of the poor are children. Further, more than one-third of the poor adults are working, but despite their labor they earn incomes that are below the poverty level. These persons and other workers whose incomes are above but close to the poverty threshold are referred to as the **working poor** described earlier in Chapter 3.

working poor People who work and earn a wage, but whose earnings are near or below the poverty level.

TABLE 4.2	Child Relative Income Poverty in Technologically Advanced Nations		
Country 2014	**Child Relative Income Poverty**	**Country 2014**	**Child Relative Income Poverty**
Denmark	9.2	Austria	18.2
Norway	10.2	Belgium	18.8
Finland	10.9	United Kingdom	19.7
South Korea	11.5	New Zealand	19.8
Netherlands	13.7	Canada	22.2
Czech Republic	14.7	Poland	22.3
Switzerland	14.8	Hungary	25.0
Sweden	15.1	Italy	25.1
Germany	15.1	Greece	25.5
Australia	17.5	Portugal	25.6
France	17.7	United States	29.4
Japan	18.2	Spain	30.5

Source: UNICEF 2017.

CONSEQUENCES OF POVERTY

People in poverty are less likely to be able to provide themselves and their children with a safe environment and a hopeful future. Poverty increases the likelihood of poor health, exposure to environmental toxins, limited educational opportunities, family troubles, poor housing, homelessness, political apathy, and crime victimization.

Health

Living in poverty increases the risks of health problems and engaging in health-damaging behaviors. One problem is poor nutrition. Millions of low-income people experience "food insecurity," the lack of reliable access to enough nutritious food to lead healthy and productive lives.

Research shows that food-insecure adults and children are more likely to be overweight or obese because those who eat less or skip meals to meet food budgets may overeat when food becomes available (Food Research and Action Center 2011). Children who come to school hungry often have difficulty concentrating on their work. Even if the school provides free lunches for all students, learning ability can be impaired during the morning hours. Nutrition-based learning problems early in life can rob young people of the intellectual foundation they need for success in later schooling.

Poverty and economic insecurity generate anxiety. Partly as a result, poor people are more likely to use tobacco and to seek relief through drug and alcohol abuse. Because many lack health insurance, they often delay seeking medical assistance until an illness that could have been successfully treated at an early stage (or even prevented) is far advanced. Eventually they may go to a hospital emergency room where treatment must be provided whether or not a patient can pay for it. All these factors contribute to a relatively high infant mortality rate (the number of children who die in the first year of life per 1,000 births) among the poor. The Centers for Disease Control and Prevention (2018) reported that infant mortality has been about 60 percent higher for infants in poverty households than those in non-poverty households. The U.S. infant mortality rate was 5.8 in 2017, significantly higher than those of the large majority of Organization of Economic Co-operation and Development (OECD) advanced industrialized nations (Central Intelligence Agency 2018a).

Poverty also makes people more vulnerable to natural disasters, where having a car and emergency equipment and supplies can affect survival. The over 1,800 who perished when Hurricane Katrina struck in 2005 were disproportionately low-income persons.

Family Troubles

Lack of income can cause stress that leads to conflict between partners, divorce, and child or elderly neglect or mistreatment. Low-income parents are more likely to use physical punishment on their children, increasing the likelihood that discipline turns into physical abuse. Poor parents are often unable to afford child care when they are working or searching for employment. This can make children more vulnerable to accidents, predators, or the influences of gangs.

Growing up in poverty also increases the likelihood of teenage pregnancy (Harding 2003). Having a child early in life is related to dropping out of high school before graduation. This in turn can seriously limit future income opportunities.

Limited Education

Children growing up in poverty tend to be at greater risk of lacking family resources and support to do well in school, have high academic and job aspirations, or develop confidence in their academic abilities (American Psychological Association 2018). Many children from low-income households go to schools with serious limitations, such as overcrowded classrooms, shortages of educational equipment, supplies and up-to-date textbooks, and less-experienced or less-qualified faculty (Kozol 1991, 2005, 2013). According to the National Center for Educational Statistics (2016e), students from households with incomes in the lower 25 percent were more than four times more likely to drop out of high school in 2015 than students from households with incomes in the top 25 percent. High schools with low graduation rates tend to be located in areas with high levels of poverty, unemployment, and crime.

Poor Housing Conditions

The poor typically live in dilapidated houses or apartments in older buildings. These often have faulty plumbing and heating systems, pest infestation, and lead paint that causes lead poisoning, especially of young children. Public housing projects have helped, but the supply is limited. Poor families typically spend a high proportion of their incomes on rent. In urban areas, the housing affordable to the poor often has higher levels of air pollution because of nearby industries or heavy motor vehicle traffic. In many areas near low-rent housing there are old shut down factories and the contaminated land they sit on, another source of toxic pollution. Rather than pay for the costly clean-up of the sites, some corporations chose to continue paying taxes on them and leave them as is.

Homelessness

Hundreds of thousands of Americans spend nights in homeless shelters, on the streets, or in makeshift shelters made of various discarded materials. On a surveyed night in January in 2014 about 578,424 people were homeless throughout the United States, including about 50,000 military veterans. Most homeless persons (401,051, or about 70 percent) were in emergency shelters or transitional housing, with 177,373 unsheltered (U.S. Department of Housing and Urban Development 2014). This represents a 10 percent reduction in the overall number of homeless people since 2010. The National Alliance to End Homelessness (2016) reported a further decline of people homeless on a January night in 2015 to 564,708. It's estimated that each year about 3.5 million people, including over 2 million children, experience at least temporary **homelessness** (National Student Campaign against Hunger and Homelessness 2016). Besides military veterans and poor families, the homeless population includes victims of domestic violence, substance abusers, released prison or jail inmates, and physically ill or severely mentally ill persons.

Without free universal health care, many homeless people are unable to get help for mental illness or substance abuse, making it impossible for them to hold jobs even when employment is available. Still, research suggests that between 40 and 45 percent of homeless adults work at least part time (U.S. Department of Housing and Urban Development 2013a). But their income is still too low for them to afford rent.

homelessness Not having a home to call your own and instead having to spend nights in homeless shelters, on the streets, or in makeshift shelters made of various discarded materials.

Homelessness

Crime

If you watch TV shows on real crimes such as homicide, you may observe that the perpetrators and victims are overwhelmingly low-income persons. In fact, many crimes involving person-to-person violence or theft, so-called street crimes like assault and robbery, disproportionately involve lower-income persons. Limited economic opportunity increases the likelihood that a poor person will commit violent crime.

But people of all social classes engage in serious exploitive or criminal behavior. Often upper-class perpetrators of such acts go unpunished because people in their social class have disproportionately had the power to write laws that define their damaging behavior as lawful. If they do break laws, their access to extensive legal resources often helps them avoid conviction or prison. In Chapter 10, "Crime and Criminal Justice," we will discuss street crime as well as harmful behaviors perpetrated by middle- or upper-income persons.

The police and criminal justice system, following public opinion and the dictates of existing legal codes, focus primarily on street crimes. It is therefore much more likely that low-income persons will go to prison than higher-income individuals. Another factor affecting the class focus of criminal punishment is that thousands of people living in urban areas that have been stripped of their industries have turned to drug trafficking. America's federal and state prisons are bulging with poor and minority inmates convicted of drug-related offenses. But it's much less likely that affluent persons using drugs will spend any time in prison.

The higher criminal punishment rates for the poor are not just due to greater involvement in certain forms of crime. It also reflects quality of legal representation. Most lower-income persons accused of crimes are represented by overburdened attorneys paid by the state. These public defenders often lack access to resources like private detectives or funds to hire expert witnesses or pay for DNA testing that might aid their clients. The vast majority of accused low-income persons are under great pressure from both the prosecution, intent on avoiding spending taxpayers' money on trials, and their own defense attorneys to plead guilty to charges and accept a prison sentence rather than go to trial and risk a much harsher punishment if convicted. Around 90 percent or more of both federal and state court cases are resolved through plea bargains rather than criminal trials (Bureau of Justice Assistance 2011; Jackson 2017; Mangino 2014). Once low-income persons have a criminal record, opportunities for getting a job with a decent wage decline, and they are more likely to remain poor. In almost all states they also lose the right to vote while in prison and in most states for some period after release (*New York Times* 2009, 2012).

Barriers to Political Participation

You might think, more than any other group in society, the poor would be motivated to make use of their one way to influence politics and government, the ballot box. But as noted in Chapter 3, the lower one's income, the less likely a person is to vote. Part of the problem is the link between poverty and conviction for street crimes.

In the 2016 election, between five and six million mostly low-income people were barred from voting because of their criminal records (Chalabi 2017; Uggen, Larson, and Shannon 2016). In Alabama, Florida, Kentucky, Mississippi, Tennessee, and Virginia, the states with the strongest restrictions on former inmates participating in elections, more than 7 percent of adults were banned from voting (Uggen et al. 2016).

Another problem is that many poor people believe that elected officials are not really interested or able to help them get access to jobs with livable wages. Why get your hopes up when the government gives corporate CEOs exclusive power to decide whether jobs will exist or not in your community?

POWERLESSNESS OF THE WORKING POOR

Wages paid for different jobs are supposedly set by the marketplace. In reality, power or lack of it also affects what people get paid. The wealthy have so much influence over lawmaking and tax policies that they ensure very high incomes for the positions they hold. This occurs even when their performance is disastrous, as in the behavior of corporate executives leading up to the economic recession of 2008. As analyst Nate Silver (2012) points out, top securities rating companies, whom investors look to for unbiased evaluations of the soundness of investments, gave dangerously insecure investment funds some of their top ratings. Executives were making lots of money. To disclose the real level of risk would have lowered their incomes. When the crash came, the government provided hundreds of millions of tax payer dollars to "bail out" large corporations. Then once the economic recovery began, many of the same executives resumed making enormous incomes.

In comparison, many working people have little or no power to compel employers to pay livable wages. The federal minimum wage in 2017 was $7.25 per hour (Minimum-Wage.org 2018). A worker with a full-time forty-hour work week receiving this wage makes $15,080. This

Special Topics: Martin Luther King Jr., the Working Poor, and the Memphis Sanitation Workers' Strike

Memphis sanitation workers strike

We all know that Martin Luther King Jr. was a towering leader of the civil rights movement. But many of us are not aware that he was also a major leader of the multiethnic, multiracial Poor People's movement and the anti-Vietnam war movement (Carson 2001; Wright 2007). King was willing to confront any type of social injustice, regardless of the political consequences. He opposed all racial discrimination and economic injustice worldwide. King believed that African Americans should not take part in what he

(*continued*)

Special Topics (*continued*)

viewed as an unjust war in Vietnam or participate in the economic exploitation of poor people in other countries just to win benefits for themselves at home from powerful politicians. King was also distinctive among major civil rights leaders in his calling for change to the U.S. economic system and criticizing its excessive emphasis on profit making.

King and other progressive social activists made plans to launch a new social movement, the multiracial Poor People's Campaign. King told members of the Southern Christian Leadership Conference's May 1967 meeting in Frogmore, South Carolina, that the American civil rights movement was turning into a much broader human rights movement (Wright 2007), including economic human rights. He also asserted that the era of reform was transforming into one of revolution. A huge Poor People's march was set for May 1968 in Washington, D.C.

In the meantime, King lent support to working poor people in Memphis, Tennessee. He believed that their struggle exemplified the need for social justice that the Poor People's Campaign would draw attention to nationally (Educator Resources 2013; Global Freedom Struggle 2013; Honey 2007). Sanitation workers in Memphis received pay so low that many had to rely on welfare and food stamps to survive. They were often denied overtime pay for late-night shifts and had to use old trucks that were frequently in poor condition. When it rained, African American sanitation workers could not take shelter anywhere except in the back of the garbage trucks with the trash. Seeking to improve their situation, sanitation workers formed a labor union and were granted a charter by the American Federation of State, County, and Municipal Workers (AFSCME) as Local 1733 in 1964.

During a February 1, 1968 rainstorm, two workers, Echol Cole and Robert Walker, climbed into the trash compartment of their truck to stay dry and were crushed to death by the accidentally triggered compactor mechanism. In response to this tragedy, and to win safer working conditions and higher wages, over 1,100 Memphis Department of Public Works employees, led by Local 1733 president T. O. Jones, went on strike. The national AFSCME leadership gave support once the strike was underway.

Martin Luther King Jr. came to Memphis to help call national attention to the strikers' cause and participate in their protests. On the night of April 3, King gave his famous "Promised Land" speech to a crowd of enthusiastic sanitation workers. The next evening, as King was on the balcony of his Lorraine Motel room preparing to go to dinner, he was shot and killed.

Four days later, on April 8, his wife Coretta Scott King, union leaders, and other activists led 42,000 people in a silent march through the streets of Memphis to honor him and convince the city government to agree to the strikers' goals. The national AFSCME leadership pledged continued support for the striking workers. On April 16, the Memphis city council agreed to recognize the local union as the representative of the sanitation workers and to raise workers' wages.

Coretta Scott King and other movement leaders worked hard to launch the Poor People's Campaign on May 12. They demanded an Economic Bill of Rights that would ensure jobs with adequate pay to all those able to work, sufficient support for those unable to work, and access to land and capital for poor people to use in starting farms or other businesses. They also wanted poor people to be able to effectively participate in government (Wright 2007). Black, white, Hispanic, and Native American activists engaged in weeks of protests in the nation's capital. But absent the leadership of the assassinated Martin Luther King Jr., the Poor People's Campaign ultimately achieved little. The economic human rights revolution King envisioned remains for a new generation to achieve.

is about $9,778 below the poverty threshold, $24,858, for a family of two adults and two children under eighteen years of age in 2017 (U.S. Census 2018c). Some states such as Texas had the same minimum wage as the federal government. But other states had higher minimum wages. In Delaware, Florida, and Illinois, for instance, the minimum wage in 2017 was $8.25 per hour (National Conference of State Legislatures 2018). That's an income of $17,160 per year, still about $7,698 below the federal poverty threshold for the same type of family. The state of Washington had the highest state minimum wage in 2017, $11.50 per hour. This would yield an annual income of $23,920, still $938 short of the federal poverty threshold. This means that many of the working poor throughout the country often do not make enough to pay for all their basic necessities, let alone save money for an emergency. A large proportion continually falls into debt on a regular basis. They work as farm laborers, fast food servers, unskilled industrial employees, or at other low-skill, nonunionized jobs. These types of jobs usually lack health insurance, parental leave, vacation days, or sick days (Seccombe 2007; U.S. Bureau of Labor Statistics 2012). Many of the working poor are single mothers who attempt to join the labor force but find that the jobs available to them often lack the pay levels or benefits they need to support their families and pay for child care while working. Faced with expenses and debts they cannot pay, many of these women leave the work force and apply for welfare assistance to help feed and shelter their children and obtain necessary medical care.

CAUSES OF POVERTY

Shipler (2005) argues that there are multiple, often interlocking causes for why particular persons or families are poor. Poverty can be due to social background, like being born into a family without the resources to provide a good education. Growing up in a neglectful or abusive household can impact children in ways that interfere with their ability to trust others or accept the authority of teachers. Even where a single parent sets a great example, and works multiple jobs to provide for her or his children, lack of proper supervision may leave children vulnerable to victimization or expose them to negative role models. This in turn can lead to bad behavior and decision making that damage a child's future. There are also cultural, economic, and political components to poverty. Understanding them and their interrelationships can point the way to comprehensive approaches to dealing with this social problem. Social scientists, as well as the public in general, speak of three broad causes: people's individual characteristics, social structure, and cultural factors.

Individual Characteristics

American culture is filled with stories of people like Abraham Lincoln who used their wits, talents, and hard work to pull themselves out of poverty and become enormously successful. This is the cultural theme of rugged individualism. Many believe that personal characteristics like high aspirations, a strong work ethic, a positive moral code, and persistent effort are sufficient to overcome any family or class disadvantages. The corresponding view of the poor is that they are responsible for their own situation by being lazy, lacking ambition and good moral values, and always looking for the government to take care of them.

Interestingly, these ideas are widespread. For example, the "Poverty in America" study conducted by NPR, Harvard University's Kennedy School of Government, and the Kaiser Foundation (NPR 2001), based on a 2001 national survey of almost two thousand persons eighteen years or older, asked respondents: "In your opinion, which is the bigger cause of poverty today – that people are not doing enough to help themselves out of poverty, or that circumstances beyond their control cause them to be poor?" Forty-five percent chose "circumstances beyond their control cause them to be poor," but 48 percent chose "people are not doing enough to help themselves out of poverty."

Additional research, however, indicates that low-income persons tend to assert that their own situation results from things beyond their control (Seccombe 2007) like physical disability, injury, illness, or child-rearing responsibilities that prevent holding a job, or a scarcity of jobs with sufficient income to escape poverty. The individualistic view of the poor in the United States contrasts with how European Union citizens perceive the cause of poverty. According to a 2010 survey of twenty seven European Union member countries, only 15 percent of respondents view "laziness and lack of willpower" as the cause of poverty, whereas 48 percent attribute the cause to "injustice in society," 14 percent to being "unlucky," and 16 percent to "an inevitable part of progress" (7 percent responded "don't know" or gave no response) (European Commission 2010).

Social Structure

Many people believe that characteristics of social structure cause poverty. In the "Poverty in America" survey referenced above (NPR 2001), 27 percent of respondents with incomes more than twice the federal poverty level blamed poverty on "a shortage of jobs," compared to 47 percent with incomes between the poverty level and twice the level, and 62 percent below the poverty line. Corresponding percentages for "too many jobs being part time or low wage" are 50 percent, 61 percent, and 70 percent, and for "medical bills" 54 percent, 68 percent, and 71 percent. In addition, about 46 percent of respondents in each of the three income categories blamed "poor quality public schools" and "the welfare system."

There are three distinctive approaches to explaining how social structure generates poverty. One centers on the nature of the capitalist economic system, another on economic change, and a third on the welfare system (Seccombe 2007).

Capitalism Although capitalism has been a very productive economic system, many believe it inherently causes poverty for a large segment of the population. As noted in Chapter 3, Marx argued that the capitalist class uses its influence over government to enact laws that serve its profit-making and wealth-accumulation interests rather than those of lower-income people. He believed that many workers do not receive what they really deserve for their labor. The capitalist class is able to maintain this situation in part because they make sure there is a "reserve labor force" of unemployed people. Thus, those that have jobs can be forced to accept low wages because of the threat of being replaced by the unemployed. To ensure high profits, capitalism needs a sizeable proportion of people in poverty.

Economic Change This explanation holds that poverty is due to shifts in economic activity. Technological advances have led to the elimination of millions of good-paying U.S. manufacturing jobs either through the increased use of automated machinery or the improved ability to set up new industrial plants in developing countries where labor costs are extremely low. As a result, millions of Americans lost the opportunity to climb out of poverty into the middle class (Wilson 2009).

The Welfare System Political conservatives believe that certain social programs intended to help poor people instead foster dependency on government handouts. Rather than encouraging people to gain job skills, seek employment, and support themselves, they argue that welfare assistance motivates behavior that ensures continued government aid. According to this view, women growing up in low-income households get pregnant, and have babies outside of marriage in order to qualify for welfare benefits. This increases the number of poor children and the percentage of children growing up in one-parent households, where they are less likely to develop the moral traits and cognitive skills to become productive members of society.

But some researchers view the current welfare system as a cause of poverty not because it provides too much aid to poor people, but in certain ways too little. Seccombe (2007) reported that most of the women in her study of families receiving welfare believed that the existing welfare system actually discouraged them from working. They felt that the types of jobs they could get, often minimum or near minimum wage jobs, typically lacked the pay and types of benefits, like health care coverage, that could make them economically self-sufficient. Instead, working at such jobs deprives them of health care coverage and other assistance provided by welfare programs and endangers the well-being of their children. Seccombe's data indicated that rather than reacting to a mother's employment by cutting crucial benefits and potentially harming her children, the welfare system could facilitate mothers joining the work force by assisting with health care, child care, housing, and transportation needs.

Cultural Factors

Oscar Lewis (1966) introduced the **culture of poverty** concept in 1966. It states that in response to long-term structural conditions like unemployment, minimum wage jobs, and poor-quality schools, poor people develop a subculture of values, norms, beliefs, attitudes, and behaviors that help them adapt to their situation. Seccombe (2007) argues that the

culture of poverty The concept that in response to long-term structural conditions like unemployment, minimum wage jobs, and poor-quality schools, poor people develop a subculture of values, norms, beliefs, attitudes, and behaviors that help them adapt to their situation.

culture of poverty concept combines aspects of the individual characteristics and the social structure explanations. The poverty subculture leads to individual traits seen as deviant and self-defeating by society. People influenced by the culture of poverty are said to view relying on government aid, involvement in gangs, and activities such as selling drugs, substance abuse, early sexual intercourse, and unmarried parenting as normal in their social world. The subculture of poverty is transmitted from one generation to the next, blinding people to opportunities to escape poverty. Thus, the subculture of poverty becomes another cause of poverty independent of structural conditions.

Wilson (1987, 1996, 2009) thinks poverty subculture can be eliminated by changing structural conditions. He blames economic factors and social and geographic isolation, rather than race, as the causes of poverty among urban African Americans. Wilson argues the removal of good-paying manufacturing jobs had catastrophic impacts on people in inner cities. Increases in male unemployment drastically decreased the number of men whose incomes could support a family. What followed was growth in the percentage of children born outside marriage and then raised in single-parent households. Many of these children grew up with little direct interaction with successful male role models and with severely limited economic opportunities. Wilson's work implies that the culture of poverty can be overcome by job opportunities. Seccombe (2007) claims her research shows that the culture of poverty can be penetrated because people raised in it often respond positively to educational opportunities.

SOCIOLOGICAL PERSPECTIVES ON POVERTY

Structural-Functional Perspective

The structural-functional perspective holds that since economic inequality and poverty have existed in most societies, they must fulfill a necessary positive function (Davis and Moore 1945). This function is that they help in the recruitment of people for important jobs, like computer engineer, medical doctor, and nuclear physicist, that can only be performed by highly intelligent, talented people who undergo extensive education. Only very high pay levels for these jobs can motivate the small number of gifted people to spend the time and effort for the required training. Other jobs that are far less important can be done by almost anyone, and require much less training. So differences in pay for different jobs (income inequality) makes sure society functions properly and produces benefits for everyone. Just as a good income is an incentive to study and work hard, poverty is the unpleasant fate that awaits those who don't.

Criticisms have been leveled at the structural-functional explanation for inequality and poverty. Pay levels for certain jobs do not reflect their importance to society, or the intelligence, or the length of training necessary to do them. For example, the pay of many athletes is far above that of child care workers. But which is more important to society? Scientists, often brilliant people with PhDs in chemistry, physics, or biology, who spent many years in training and whose work steadily advances knowledge and technology, typically make far less than corporate CEOs. And speaking of CEOs, how many of them failed miserably in the years leading up to the great recession of 2008 but continued to enjoy enormous paychecks? This indicates that differences in rewards for different occupations are based as much or more on who controls power rather than on the importance of jobs.

Another problem with the structural-functional justification of economic inequality is that it permits individuals to build up huge fortunes. This eventually interferes with the basic mechanism the theory claims is necessary for recruiting talented people to perform the economic roles requiring the highest levels of intelligence and training. The problem is that as the cost of advanced education climbs higher and higher and the income and wealth gaps widen, many talented children born into low-income families are simply unable to access the educations that could prepare them for occupations they could perform better than others fortunate enough to grow up in affluent families. Thus, over time, increasing economic inequality becomes dysfunctional for the operation of society.

Symbolic-Interactionist Perspective

The symbolic-interactionist approach focuses on how the problem of poverty is socially constructed and portrayed through communication. This process helps determine people's views on what causes poverty and what they think about poor people. One description of the poor is that they are responsible for their own poverty. Therefore the only way to deal with poverty is to "reform" those poor people capable of being changed into hardworking citizens. In contrast, other people promote the idea that poverty is caused mainly by how a society is organized. Thus, changing society could reduce poverty. The symbolic-interactionist perspective attempts to analyze the methods each side uses to win support for its views.

The symbolic-interactionist perspective has been criticized for promoting the view that poverty is a problem only when some people define an economic environment as harmful. It tends to neglect consideration of the factors – individual, structural, or cultural – that may cause desperate economic conditions.

Conflict Perspective

The social conflict approach asserts that poverty is only inevitable in certain types of societies. Most people are poor not because of personal characteristics but rather because the society in which they live makes them poor.

Marxist Perspective As described earlier, Marxists believe that capitalism thrives on maintaining a "reserve labor force" of poor people. This pressures many workers to accept low wages. At the international level, corporate executives increase profits by eliminating millions of

U.S. jobs and shipping them to countries where extreme poverty causes people to work for very low pay. This leaves many Americans either jobless or with access to only low-paying jobs and in poverty.

Racial/Ethnic-Conflict Perspective This perspective argues that poverty is linked to discrimination on the basis of skin color and ethnic heritage. Many people still harbor negative attitudes toward members of other racial and ethnic groups. This prejudice helps explain why it is about three times more likely that African American children and Hispanic children grow up in poverty than non-Hispanic white children.

Feminist-Conflict Perspective The feminist-conflict perspective focuses on how gender inequality affects poverty. In 2016, the percentage of families in poverty with two married parents present was only 5.1 (U.S. Census 2017a). But the poverty rate for single-parent female-headed families was 26.6 percent, about twice the rate for single-parent male-headed families, 13.1 percent. What accounts for the very high rate of poverty for female-headed families? The feminist perspective identifies two factors. The first is that in our patriarchal society the responsibility for child care falls mainly to women. Fulfilling that role prevents many women from earning a wage high enough to avoid poverty. The second is that the occupations most open to women typically pay considerably less than those dominated by men and that when in the same occupations women often earn less than men anyway.

Intersectional View The intersectional view emphasizes that economic factors, race/ethnicity, and gender each independently affect the probability that a person will live in poverty. Thus those at the intersection of the disadvantaged positions in regard to class, race/ethnicity, and gender, like unskilled, African American or Hispanic women (along with their children), have the highest poverty rates.

The conflict perspective on poverty is criticized in part for tending to neglect the important role that material incentives can play in economic development. Critics note, for example, that the economies of China and Vietnam began to increase in productivity more rapidly once they abandoned strict socialist policies and allowed for expanded profit-making opportunities and enterprises.

PROPOSED SOLUTIONS TO POVERTY

Encourage Personal Reliance

Conservatives assert that there are very few people on the verge of starving to death in the United States. They believe that almost all Americans labeled as poor are poor only in a relative sense. Most low-income Americans would not be considered poor in many other countries because they have things like televisions, refrigerators, and air conditioning (U.S. Energy Information Administration 2018).

Social Movements: The U.S. Labor Union Movement

Achievements of the U.S. labor union movement

Wealthy individuals typically oppose economically oriented social movements among lower-income people. They have viewed these movements as threatening their freedom of action, profit levels, and sometimes the capitalist system itself. A major example is the U.S. labor union movement.

During the colonial period, workers were often required to labor twelve-hour days, six days a week. Some workers came up with the idea of cooperating with one another and agreeing that everyone at their place of employment would refuse to work unless their demands for fair wages, shorter hours, and better and safer working conditions were met. In the early United States, courts consistently ruled that such efforts by workers were illegal criminal conspiracies. But this trend was broken in 1836 when a Connecticut court ruled in favor of striking union leaders and in 1842 when a Massachusetts court ruled that labor unions were basically legal.

Major labor conflicts at times brought some cities and regions to near-civil war conditions, such as the American Railway Union strike of 1894 that began in Pullman, Illinois, and spread to many other states; the Ludlow, Colorado, coal strike of 1913–1914; the 1921 Battle of Blair Mountain in the coal country of southern West Virginia; the Minneapolis Teamsters strike of 1934; and the 1936–1937 United Auto Workers strike in Flint, Michigan.

As workers organized into labor unions in the nineteenth and early twentieth centuries, several distinct union movement strategies and ideologies emerged. The first American unions were typically *craft unions* such as the United Cigar Wrappers Union led by Samuel Gompers. These were unions of highly skilled workers whose labor could not be easily replaced because it required long periods of training. Craft unions tended to limit membership so as to control the training and supply of highly skilled workers. This helped ensure both the power of the union and relatively high wages for members. A number of craft unions banded together in 1886 to form a federation, the American Federation of Labor (AFL), also led by Gompers (AFL-CIO 2017). Another type of union was formed on the basis of a whole industry rather than a particular skill. Major examples of these *industrial unions* are the United Steel Workers, the United Auto Workers, and the United Mine Workers. When industrial unions were formed, they typically included some skilled, but mostly semiskilled and unskilled workers who were relatively easy to replace. It was in the interest of industrial unions to allow all ethnic and racial groups into the union so that none of these groups was hostile to the union. Otherwise it would be easier for employers to recruit members of an excluded group as strikebreakers. Industrial unions grew dramatically in membership in the 1930s under the pro-union president Franklin Delano Roosevelt. These unions formed their own federation, the Congress of Industrial Organizations (CIO), in 1938. In 1956, the two great union federations united to form the AFL-CIO.

Unions also differed in terms of ideology. "Business unionism" became the dominant union ideology and was best represented in the craft unions of the AFL, such as the United Carpenters and Joiners Union. Business unionism is the view that the main purpose of unions is to serve as the business organization of their members, functioning to improve their well-being within the

(continued)

Social Movements (*continued*)

capitalist system. "Revolutionary unionism," in contrast, asserts that the long-range aim of workers should be to replace the capitalist economy with a socialist economy. One major revolutionary union movement was the Industrial Workers of the World (IWW), founded in 1905 (Zinn 2003). Many IWW members were imprisoned for opposing U.S. participation in World War I, and membership declined after 1918.

Collectively, workers' strikes and threats of strikes helped increase the wages and benefits of labor union members, improve their working conditions, and those of millions of other Americans. This contributed to the huge expansion of the nation's middle class. The union movement's achievements included, for example, reducing the work day from twelve to ten hours and then to eight hours. Although the steady loss of manufacturing jobs to other countries and other factors described in Chapter 3 and this chapter led to a decline in union membership, unions are still a significant economic and political force.

Many conservatives also believe that character flaws like laziness and lack of morals are mostly to blame for poverty. They argue that aid to low-income people will simply encourage dependency on government, so severely limiting welfare assistance is the best way to fight poverty. This would force poor people to develop skills to support themselves through their own labor. Welfare aid should be provided only to those who lack income through no fault of their own, like very young children and severely disabled persons. If government assistance is given to any able-bodied Americans, like returning military veterans, it should be extremely short term.

More Effective Government Programs

Many political leaders view poverty as a significant problem. Being poor may not always mean being on the verge of starvation, but it does typically mean a lack of ability to pay for important services like health care, education, and transportation. Being locked out of what America has to offer to those born into more affluent circumstances can be stressful and depressing.

While personal characteristics can contribute to poverty, liberals see the major cause as the economy. Outsourcing jobs increases poverty by forcing workers to accept lower wages and by weakening or destroying labor unions that helped protect workers in the past.

Liberals advocate a wider range of aid. More comprehensive assistance would include free technical training to make individuals more attractive as prospective employees. Free preschool and day care would make it more feasible for a single parent to hold a job while ensuring the welfare of her or his children.

Supporters of the living wage movement argue that there should be a minimum living wage set for each local area. This would take into account geographic differences in the costs of essential goods and services (Nadeau and Glasmeier 2016). Researchers at the Massachusetts Institute of Technology have developed a living wage calculator for counties and cities to serve as a guide for citizens and lawmakers (Living Wage Calculator 2016).

Change Social Structure

Some politicians advocate reducing economic inequality so that people have a better chance of escaping poverty. Another structural approach is to provide tax breaks and other advantages for those who create jobs in the United States. Any benefits the government gives corporations for moving jobs to other countries, like low-cost loans, must be ended. Corporations would have to prove that any proposed overseas investment would not result in a net loss of U.S. jobs.

EXISTING ASSISTANCE PROGRAMS

The Great Depression and Social Welfare

The Great Depression of the 1930s provided the impetus for the first major federal welfare programs during the administration of President Franklin D. Roosevelt. The *Social Security Act* of 1935 is possibly the single biggest anti-poverty legislation in the country's history. Before that act, millions of elderly Americans lived in poverty; because of Social Security, relatively few retired Americans fell below the poverty line during the great recession that began in 2008. Social Security, like federal unemployment assistance and Medicare (health care for persons aged sixty-five and over), is a *social insurance program* into which payments are made while a person is working. Then at some specified time the person is eligible to receive benefits from the program.

Another type of federal assistance is an *entitlement program*, also called a *categorical program*. Eligibility is based not on paying into the program but on simply being in a certain "category" of persons. One of the most important and ultimately controversial categorical entitlement program began in 1935 under the title *Aid to Dependent Children*, later renamed in 1962 *Aid to Families with Dependent Children* (AFDC). AFDC provided single parents and their children with monthly income. It was criticized, however, for several reasons. One was that it encouraged dependency on welfare rather than working for a living. Another was that women were more likely to qualify for AFDC if they were not married. And the amount they received was higher the more children they had. Critics argued that AFDC encouraged single-parent, female-headed families (Whittington and Alm 2003) and having more children outside of marriage to increase AFDC benefits. The number of people on AFDC increased over the years, as did the length of time recipients stayed in the program.

Welfare Reform of 1996

Criticisms of AFDC led to the welfare reform legislation of 1996, backed both by many Republicans and Democratic members of Congress, the *Personal Responsibility and Work Opportunity Reconciliation Act* (PRWORA). PRWORA was intended to make it clear that federal assistance to adults was only temporary and that its purpose was to help people become self-sufficient by getting and keeping a job. AFDC was replaced with the *Temporary Assistance for Needy Families* (TANF) program. Unlike AFDC, the federal government limits TANF assistance for adults with children to only sixty months of a person's entire life and for adults without children to twenty-four months. The federal government made individual states responsible for determining eligibility for TANF and for ensuring that recipients seek and obtain a job. To receive TANF a person must enroll in job training, search for a job, or actually work at a job.

The number of families receiving AFDC had begun to decline after 1994 (U.S. Department of Health and Human Services 2012), two years before PRWORA was enacted. The number of families receiving the new federal assistance (TANF) fell at a more rapid rate between 1996 (when PRWORA became law) and 2000, and more slowly after that until the devastating economic recession of 2008. Then the numbers began to increase. The employment rate for adult AFDC/TANF recipients rose from 6.6 percent in 1992 to 38.3 percent in 1999, and then declined to 29 percent in 2010 before rising to 51.9 percent in 2016 (U.S. Department of Health and Human Services 2017).

The proportion of children born to unmarried women rose steadily from 5 percent in 1960 to 32 percent in 1995 (Child Trends Data Bank 2018). One aim of PRWORA was to reverse this trend. The percentage of children born outside of marriage briefly stabilized in the mid-1990s but then rose from 32 percent in 1997 to 41 percent in 2008. This was followed by a decline to 39.8 percent in 2016 (Centers for Disease Control and Prevention 2017f).

Several other major federal government programs that help low-income persons are described below. It is important to keep in mind that individual states have their own programs to assist poor persons. There are also aid projects run by religious and other private organizations.

Other Assistance Programs

Medicaid *Medicaid* ensures medical care for disabled and poor persons by sending government payments to health care providers. Since the 1996 welfare reform, individual states are allowed to determine their own eligibility rules and qualifying income levels for this program. Partly as a result, many poor people have failed to receive Medicaid. However, the Patient Protection and Affordable Health Care Act attempted to remedy this situation by stating that beginning in 2014, most individual adults under the age of sixty-five with incomes under about $15,000 should be allowed by the states to qualify for Medicaid (Healthcare.gov 2016).

Supplemental Nutritional Assistance Program The *Supplemental Nutritional Assistance Program (SNAP)*, formerly called the Food Stamp Program, provides federal assistance to low-income people to purchase prepackaged food. While administered by the U.S. Department of Agriculture, SNAP benefits are distributed by the individual states. In the past, recipients were given paper coupons (stamps) to use in stores to pay for food. The stores would then receive money payments from the government when they turned in the stamps. Now a number of states provide SNAP recipients with electronic debit cards instead of paper coupons. The debit cards allow for assigned benefits to be transmitted almost instantaneously to the recipients' cards. The cards also facilitate stores' reimbursements from the government. Since the SNAP debit card functions similarly to a bank card, other people purchasing groceries may be totally unaware when a SNAP card is used, protecting users from feeling stigmatized for receiving assistance (U.S. Department of Agriculture 2017).

Housing Assistance The federal government has established several programs to help people obtain or maintain housing. These range from promoting the building or revitalization of low-cost housing, to helping homeowners avoid foreclosure, to assisting low-income people in paying rent.

Education Aid Federal and state governments assist low-income people in getting an education. Some programs aid a child's intellectual and emotional development and physical well-being. Others provide financial assistance for academically qualified low-income persons to pay for their educations. The *Head Start Program*, begun in 1965, is aimed at providing preschool education for children born into low-income families. Initially children three to five years old could enter the program. Later in the 1990s, after research indicated the importance of a child's experiences in the first few years of life, a new program, called *Early Head Start* and covering children from birth to age three, was established. To be eligible for Head Start/Early Head Start a child's family income must generally be below the poverty level set by federal government guidelines (U.S. Department of Health and Human Services 2018a; 2018b;, 2018c). Children from homeless families, foster families, and families receiving public assistance such as TANF are also eligible. Enrolled children get health and dental care and meals.

Research shows that children who participate in Head Start perform better in school and are more likely to graduate high school and attend

Children in a Head Start program

college than children from similar low-income families who did not (Deming 2009; Garces, Thomas Duncan, and Currie 2002). But some studies suggest that for many children the benefits tend to fade away after a few years (Lee and Loeb 1995). What determines whether the positive effects of Head Start are lasting appears to be the types of schools children attend after Head Start. When Head Start children attend schools in areas of concentrated poverty where schools are deficient and most other students are from poor families, the benefits of Head Start tend to disappear.

At the other end of the educational process, the federal government provides Pell grants to low-income students to attend college (Federal Student Aid 2017). Other forms of federal college assistance include teach grants (where the recipient agrees to become a teacher) and low-interest loans.

***Earned Income Tax Credit* (EITC)** EITC is a federal income tax credit for working heads of families based on the number of children and the earned income of the family (IRS 2017). It is a refundable tax credit for low- to moderate-income working families enacted in 1975 in part to offset required Social Security contributions and to act as an incentive for people to work. Llobrera and Zahradnik (2004) estimate that the EITC lifted 2.7 million children out of poverty in 2002, as well as 2.2 million adults. In 2016, twenty-five states and the District of Columbia also provided their own versions of EITC (IRS 2016b).

Childbirth-Related Leave Policies and Publicly Supported Child Care

Some 183 countries of the 185 for which information is available provide paid leave for at least some working women (Addati, Cassirer, and Gilchrist 2014). And at least 79 countries out of 167 for which data are available provide paid leave for at least some working fathers. In comparison, the U.S federal government does not guarantee any paid maternity leave, although several states do, including California, Hawaii, New Jersey, New York, and Rhode Island. In addition, some women in the United States may receive paid maternity leave through their employer. The other country with no paid maternity leave is Papua New Guinea (Addati et al. 2014; Bernard 2013; Gibson 2016). It's important to note, however, that the percentage of women workers covered by national paid maternity leave laws varies greatly around the world. In less-developed countries, under 20 percent of working women may be covered; in some European countries more than 90 percent are covered. Worldwide it is estimated that less than 41 percent of women workers are legally entitled to maternity leave (Addati et al. 2014; Bernard 2013; Gibson 2016). Categories excluded from coverage are typically workers at small businesses, agricultural workers, or domestic workers. Another significant issue is that many women who are legally entitled to paid maternity leave do not actually get it for reasons such as lack of effective enforcement of the maternity leave law, lack of awareness of it, discriminatory practices, or reluctance to rely on a government assistance program. In Japan, for example, although 66 to 89 percent of working women are estimated to be covered by the maternity leave law, only somewhere between 33 and 65 percent actually use it. Table 4.3 shows the characteristics of maternity leave laws for the United States and nine other technologically advanced nations according to a global study conducted by the International Labor Organization (Addati et al. 2014).

The U.S. Family and Medical Leave Act (FMLA), passed in 1993, provided the possibility of twelve weeks of job-protected unpaid

TABLE 4.3	Maternity Leave in the United States and Other Selected Technologically Advanced Countries			
Country	Length of Maternity Leave	Amount of Maternity Leave Cash Benefits (% of previous earnings)	Estimate of Maternity Leave Law Coverage (% of working women legally covered)	Source of Funding of Maternity Leave Cash Benefits
United States	12 weeks (federal)	Unpaid	33%–65%	No federal program for payments
Canada	17 weeks (federal)	55% for 15 weeks up to a ceiling	66%–89%	Social insurance
France	16 weeks	100% up to a ceiling	90%–100%	Social insurance
Germany	14 weeks	100%	66%–89%	Social insurance and employers
Italy	22 weeks	80%	66%–89%	Social insurance
Japan	14 weeks	66.7%	66%–89%	Social insurance and public funds
Russian Federation	20 weeks	100% up to a ceiling	90%–100%	Social insurance
Sweden	14 weeks	80%	90%–100%	Social insurance
Spain	16 weeks	100%	66%–89%	Social insurance
United Kingdom	52 weeks	6 weeks paid at 90%; lower of 90%/flat rate for weeks 7–39; weeks 40–52 unpaid	66%–89%	Public funds and employers

Source: Addati et al. 2014.

maternity or paternity leave for some working parents. To qualify a person must be employed by a business with at least fifty employees and have worked there at least 1,250 hours during the previous year (Waldfogel 2001). About 40 percent of U.S. working parents did not qualify for unpaid leave (Bernard 2013). And many parents cannot afford weeks without pay and do not take the leave, or take less than twelve weeks.

Special Topics: Why Did European Nations Develop More Extensive Social Welfare Systems?

Europeans have access to more extensive social welfare than people in the United States (Moller et al. 2003). This includes health care that is essentially free, government provided day care and preschool services, lengthy parental leave, longer annual vacations, and low-cost public university educations. Visitors from countries like Sweden often wonder why the United States lacks a social welfare system like theirs.

One reason is that throughout much of U.S. history, when severe economic recessions occurred in eastern cities millions of poor people headed west to settle land in lightly populated territories that would later become states. Alleviating economic hardship through acquiring free frontier land and developing it into privately owned productive farms and ranches helped foster a tradition of "rugged individualism," especially in much of the Midwest and West.

The social safety valve of emigration from crowded eastern cities to the frontier meant that many Americans were much less receptive to collective solutions to poverty like socialist political movements. In contrast, Europeans often supported socialist ideas and participated in massive political movements that threatened upper-class wealth. In response, European leaders like Germany's Otto von Bismarck enacted social welfare reforms to calm socialist-oriented workers.

After the 1917 Russian Revolution, increased fear of workers' revolutions motivated European governments to create more comprehensive education, health care, and pension programs. But the distant Russian Revolution did not have a similar effect on American political leaders until the Great Depression of the 1930s.

An additional factor limiting the development of the social welfare system was the country's heterogeneous population. Because the United States is a nation formed from waves of foreign immigrants and was linguistically, religiously, culturally, and racially divided, it was more difficult for Americans to communicate and cooperate with one another in political movements. It also delayed Americans identifying with one another as equal members of the same national family. To provide some collective security against unexpected hardships, the tendency in the United States was for each group to form its own mutual aid or insurance arrangements rather than working all together for one universal system. In comparison, most European societies were much more ethnically and religiously homogeneous. This facilitated workers' movements; it also made it more likely that wealthier people would view all fellow citizens as members of their own national family and consent to social welfare programs.

But now there is no frontier for economically distressed Americans to settle. In addition, social surveys indicate that racial, ethnic, and other group-centered prejudices have declined significantly. Americans today are much more likely to see their fellow citizens as members of a common national family whose well-being should be a universal goal. Also, admiration of other nations' social welfare systems has become more widespread. These factors contributed to the U.S. movement for federal health care insurance.

CHAPTER REVIEW

What Is Poverty?
Poverty can be viewed in either absolute or relative terms. Absolute poverty means a person or family does not have access to basic things, including food, clean water, clothing, housing, sanitation, health care, and education, needed to survive and maintain health and well-being. Relative poverty, in contrast, refers to people having so much less in material goods and style of life than others that they are seen as "poor" in terms of social standards even if they do not suffer absolute poverty.

Consequences of Poverty
People in poverty are less likely to be able to provide themselves and their children with a safe environment and a hopeful future. Poverty increases the likelihood of poor health, exposure to environmental toxins, limited educational opportunities, family troubles, poor housing, homelessness, political apathy, and crime victimization.

Powerlessness of the Working Poor
Many working Americans do not earn enough to pay for basic necessities, save for an emergency, or lift themselves out of poverty. They work as farm laborers, fast food servers, unskilled industrial employees, or at other low-skill, nonunionized jobs. These types of jobs usually lack health insurance, parental leave, vacation days, and sick days.

The federal minimum wage in 2017 was $7.25 per hour. A worker with a full-time forty-hour workweek receiving this wage makes $15,080. This is about $9,778 below the poverty threshold, $24,858, for a family of two adults and two children under eighteen years of age in 2017.

Causes of Poverty
There are three broad explanations for what causes poverty. The individual characteristics view holds that most people are poor because of personal limitations such as low intelligence or faulty personality traits. The structural view blames aspects of social structure. The Marxist version claims that capitalism concentrates wealth in a small minority, resulting in high inequality. Keeping a significant proportion of the population poor helps capitalists keep wages low and profits high. The cultural view asserts that structural conditions like unemployment, low income, and poor living conditions cause the development of an adaptive subculture of poverty. The deviant values and norms of the poverty subculture become a separate cause for poverty independent of structural factors.

Sociological Perspectives on Poverty
The structural-functional perspective holds that economic inequality and poverty can have positive functions for society. High rewards motivate people to study and work hard to become qualified to fulfill society's most important roles. And the unpleasantness of poverty is a deterrent for those who would otherwise be lazy. The symbolic-interactionist approach focuses on understanding how people's views of poverty and poor people are socially constructed by various interest groups through communication. This process helps determine what, if anything, people think should be done about poverty. The conflict approach asserts that poverty is only inevitable in certain types of societies. Most people are poor not because of personal characteristics but because their being poor serves someone else's interests or is the result of corporations' excessive pursuit of profits.

Proposed Solutions to Poverty
Many believe that poverty can be reduced if more people are taught to develop a strong work ethic and pride in taking personal responsibility for themselves. Another view is that more intelligently designed and effective government programs, like providing free child and day care services, can help people get and keep jobs that will allow them and their families to escape poverty. Some believe that extensive structural changes to the economic system and government, like forcing corporations to create millions of jobs in the United States, would alleviate poverty.

Existing Assistance Programs

In 1935, in the midst of the Great Depression, the federal government created huge social welfare programs like Social Security to provide income after retirement and Aid to Families with Dependent Children (AFDC) to ensure the basic needs of low-income children. The 1996 welfare reform replaced AFDC with Temporary Assistance for Needy Families, which emphasizes that assistance for adults has a time limit and requires efforts to obtain employment. Other important programs to help low-income persons include Medicaid, the Supplemental Nutritional Assistance Program, and Head Start, as well as the Earned Income Tax Credit that has helped lift several million working families above the poverty line.

Other advanced industrial countries developed more extensive social welfare systems than the United States. Debate continues regarding possible approaches to dealing with poverty and whether it can be eliminated.

KEY TERMS

absolute poverty, p. 79
culture of poverty, p. 91
homelessness, p. 85

relative poverty, p. 79
working poor, p. 82

DISCUSSION QUESTIONS

1. Why do you think the United States has a higher percentage of children in poverty than many other highly developed nations?

2. In your opinion, which sociological perspective best explains why a lot of poverty exists in the United States? What are the reasons for your choice?

3. What do you think should be done to improve the situation for working poor people in the United States?

4. Which existing government program do you think has been most effective in reducing poverty in the United States? What are the reasons for your choice?

5. Why have existing government programs been unable to eliminate poverty in the United States?

6. What do you think would be the best way or ways to reduce poverty in the United States?

CHAPTER 5

Race, Ethnicity, and Immigration

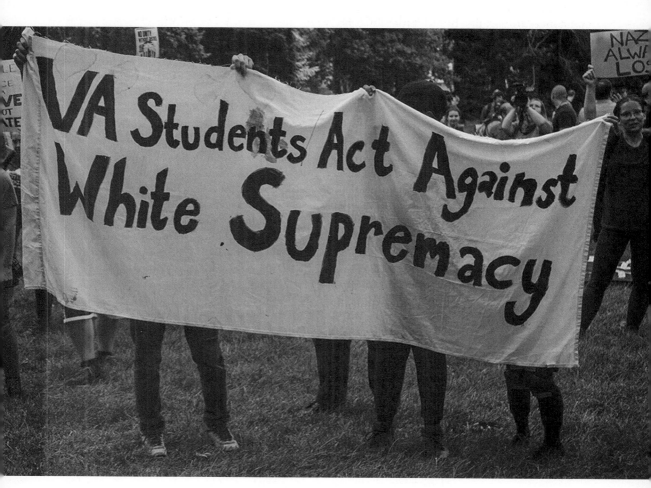

CHAPTER OBJECTIVES

- Describe the concepts of race, ethnicity, racism, and diversity in the United States.
- Explain the role of immigration in the United States and controversies about immigration.
- Explain the different types of racial/ethnic relations.

- Explain stereotypes, prejudice, and discrimination.
- Explain what is meant by white privilege and institutional discrimination.
- Describe the major causes of prejudice.
- Compare major sociological approaches to prejudice and discrimination.
- Describe movements for equality of opportunity and the various approaches to reducing prejudice and discrimination.

IN FEBRUARY 2017, *the municipal government of Charlottesville, Virginia, home of the University of Virginia, decided to remove a statue of Confederate General Robert E. Lee from the city's Emancipation Park. Many in the community wanted the statue gone because Lee led an army fighting to preserve slavery and was responsible for the deaths of tens of thousands who fought to end it. They also viewed this and other Confederate monuments as symbols of white domination and racism. Like most Confederate monuments (Drum 2017), the Lee statue in Charlottesville was commissioned in the early twentieth century when the Ku Klux Klan (KKK) grew to its largest size and targeted not only blacks but Jewish and Catholic immigrants as well. The purpose of the surge in Confederate statue construction is now widely seen as a means of reasserting white Protestant traditions and political control against perceived threats from nonwhites and culturally foreign invaders. While some people objected to removing the statue because they saw it as part of Virginia's history, protests against the decision were spearheaded by assorted white extremist groups, including the Ku Klux Klan and neo-Nazis. They planned a "Unite the Right Rally" for August 11–12, 2017, to protest the statue's removal and what they viewed as a growing attack on their version of American traditions. One right-wing militia showed up armed with semiautomatic rifles wearing military-style camouflage clothing and were at first mistaken for Virginia National Guard troops by local officials.*

On the night of August 11, hundreds of torch-bearing whites marched in Charlottesville chanting Nazi-reminiscent slogans such as "blood and soil" and "Jews will not replace us." The next day, near the Lee statue, counterprotesters from the community, the University of Virginia, and various left-wing groups confronted the Unite the Right marchers, chanting "No Nazis, No KKK, No fascist USA!" Several fights broke out between members of the opposing demonstrations. Then, as the confrontations appeared to be coming to an end, a car driven by a white man alleged to be a Nazi sympathizer crashed into a crowd of people opposing the Nazis, the KKK, and their associates. Heather Heyer, a thirty-two-year-old paralegal from Charlottesville, was killed and nineteen others were injured. On the same day a Virginia State Police helicopter covering the events in Charlottesville crashed, killing troopers Berke Bates and H. Jay Cullen (Weiner 2017). Local authorities and the governor of Virginia placed blame for the tragedy primarily on the white extremists. But President Trump, who had been supported in his election campaign by leaders of KKK and Nazis groups, shocked the nation, including leading figures in his own Republican Party, by blaming "many sides" and seeming to charge the anti-Nazis and anti-KKK demonstrators with equal responsibility (CNN 2017a). David Duke, a former leader of the KKK, and Richard B. Spencer, former editor of Alternative Right *magazine, praised Trump's statement (Thrush and Haberman 2017). On September 6, the Charlottesville city council voted unanimously to also remove the statue of Confederate General Thomas "Stonewall" Jackson (Hedgpeth 2017).*

The election and reelection of Barack Obama as president of the United States were remarkable achievements for a nation in which enslavement of Africans was once legal and an immense source of wealth for many white Americans. Obama's opportunity was the product of a series of social movements and conflicts over race relations including the abolitionist campaign against slavery, the Civil War, the struggle against white supremacist terrorists, and the modern civil rights movement. In the process, court battles and legislation eliminated legal barriers to equal participation in society, government, and the economy. The attitudes toward race and ethnicity of millions of Americans changed dramatically, which is reflected not only in the election of nonwhite and Hispanic political candidates to high office but also in the increase in interracial marriages and the portrayal of interracial and multiethnic relationships in TV and film dramas and comedies.

Even after all this change, however, there is a significant potential for racial conflict and violence, as illustrated by the events at Charlottesville. People are still often treated differently and have different opportunities in life on the basis of race and ethnicity. Sometimes this is because of open hostility toward a particular race or ethnic group. But often the processes resulting in racial or ethnic disadvantage are more covert and less widely recognized. One example of indirect but devastating inequality of opportunity is mass incarceration. African Americans are about six times more likely to be imprisoned than whites. As a result of the loss of industry and decent-paying jobs from dozens of American cities, the structure of drug laws and enforcement, and persisting bias in the criminal justice system, millions of African American men have spent time in prison, jail, and/or under correctional supervision, with enormous sociological impact. With so many men away from home, family life has suffered. After release from prison, a criminal record makes it hard to compete for even low-wage jobs. It is difficult to enact social change to address this problem because so many affected people have lost the right to vote or are unable to participate in social movements because they are incarcerated (Alexander 2012; Oliver 2008). If they think about them at all, many white Americans view these effects as well-deserved consequences of engaging in crime, ignoring racism altogether.

RACE, ETHNICITY, AND RACISM

What are Race, Ethnicity, and Racism?

In the past race was often defined biologically as a set of genetic characteristics linked to particular physical traits, including skin color, eye color, and hair color and texture, as well as vulnerability to particular diseases. These differences were thought to have arisen over many thousands of years as the result of adaptations to local ecological and climatic conditions, as well as geographic isolation. However, it has been argued that there is no such thing as clearly distinctive biological races because migration and intermarriage have intermixed genetic characteristics among virtually all peoples. In addition, despite differences in physical appearance, the genetic makeup of all human beings appears to be more than 98 percent identical, so the physical traits associated with race are limited to a very small fraction of human genes.

Social scientists, in comparison, view **race** as a socially constructed category of persons who share one or more biologically based traits that people consider especially important. Historically, skin color has been the most central determinant of race. Of secondary importance are traits like hair color and texture, and the shape of facial characteristics such as eyes, nose, and lips. People can differ from one another in many ways, but it is these few physical traits that various societies have used to designate racial membership, affecting access to political rights and economic opportunity. At certain times throughout history, people with particular physical traits have been socially defined as members of a superior race, an inferior race, or a dangerous race, and this has had enormous social consequences. For hundreds of years, people in one particular racial group have claimed superiority over another on religious or supposedly scientific grounds. In the "religious" type, a mark placed by God on a sinner has been interpreted as the different skin color of the sinner and his or her descendants. On the "scientific" side, physical characteristics have been associated with differences in personality traits, abilities, and behavior. For example, German Nazi "scientists" claimed that Aryans (in Nazi ideology, Western European whites not of Jewish descent) were biologically and intellectually superior to other people. As Nazi forces captured one country after another, their "scientists" physically examined local people to see if any qualified as Aryans rather than members of "inferior" groups.

Unlike race, which is socially constructed in terms of one or more physical characteristics, ethnicity has no biological aspect at all. **Ethnicity** refers to a social category of people who share the same cultural heritage, often – but not always – involving a common language and a common religion. For example, the two largest ethnicities (ethnic groups) in the United States are Hispanic/Latino and German, both representing around 16 percent of the population each (U.S. Census 2017g).

Racism is the belief that people of one race are superior to people of another race or of all other races. Throughout history people have made this claim in order to obtain material or psychological benefits. In the

race A socially constructed category of persons who share one or more physical traits such as skin color that affect access to political rights, economic opportunities, and other forms of resources and power.

ethnicity A social category of people who share the same cultural heritage, often involving a common language and a common religion.

racism The belief that people of one race are superior to people of another race or of all other races.

United States, claims of white racial superiority were used to rationalize the slavery of Africans whose exploited labor enriched many whites and played a major role in the country's economic development. Europeans often used racist beliefs to justify their domination of Africa, the Americas, and much of Asia, including China, India, and Vietnam. During the Spanish–American War, British author Rudyard Kipling articulated the idea that Europeans and white Americans had the duty to dominate and educate inferior people around the world in his famous poem "The White Man's Burden" to civilize "your new-caught sullen peoples, half devil and half child" (Kipling 1899). Such thinking supported white control and economic exploitation of hundreds of millions of people and vast areas around the globe.

Minorities (also referred to as minority groups) are categories of people who are subjected to disadvantages such as barriers to educational, employment, or political opportunities because of their physical or cultural characteristics, or other reasons such as sexual orientation. In many societies, certain racial and ethnic groups have been treated as minorities. For example, in the United States African Americans have historically been a minority group.

Racial and Ethnic Diversity in the United States

The federal government asks U.S. residents on census questionnaires whether they are of Hispanic/Latino cultural background and also to identify their race. Table 5.1 summarizes the results for the 2000 and 2010 censuses and the 2016 American Community Survey. One of the most significant findings is the decreasing percentage of the population that is non-Hispanic/Latino white. In 2000, this group comprised 69.1 percent of the total population but declined to 62.0 percent in 2016. The increase in the number of Hispanics/Latinos was seven times greater than the increase in the number of non-Hispanic/Latino whites between 2000 and 2016, and the increase in the numbers of African Americans and Asian Americans were both about twice as great. If these trends continue, it is projected that non-Hispanic/Latino whites will constitute less than half the U.S. population by the year 2045, making the United States even more of a multiracial and multicultural society than it is today (Frey 2018; U.S. Census 2018a).

The U.S. census also asks people to describe themselves in terms of the nationality of their ancestors. Responses indicate that virtually every nationality in the world is represented in the United States. Table 5.2 shows the ten largest nationality groups in the United States in each of five broad categories.

The census provides a useful approximation of the ethnic composition of the United States, but the questionnaire survey the government uses as a research method (see Chapter 1) has several shortcomings. First, your nationality may not be the same as your ethnicity; this is especially true of certain countries. For example, a South African could be Zulu, Afrikaner, or from one of about a dozen other ethnic groups. Another problem is that some people choose to report their nationality using a much broader category, such as "European" or "African." Finally,

minorities Categories of people who are subjected to disadvantages such as barriers to educational, employment, or political opportunities because of their physical or cultural characteristics, or other reasons such as sexual orientation.

TABLE 5.1	Population by Hispanic or Latino Origin and by Race for the United States: 2000, 2010, and 2016							
	2000		**2010**		**2016**		**Change from 2000 to 2016**	
	Number	**%**	**Number**	**%**	**Number**	**%**	**Number**	**%**
Hispanic or Latino Origin								
Total Population	281,421,906	100	308,745,538	100	318,558,162	100	37,136,256	13.2
Hispanic or Latino	35,305,818	12.5	50,477,594	16.3	55,199,107	17.3	19,893,289	56.3
Not Hispanic or Latino	246,116,088	87.5	258,267,944	83.7	263,359,055	82.7	17,242,967	7.01
Not Hispanic or Latino Whites	194,552,774	69.1	196,817,552	63.7	197,362,672	62	2,809,898	1.44
Race								
Total Population	281,421,906	100	308,745,538	100	318,558,162	100	37,136,256	13.2
One Race	274,595,678	97.6	299.736,465	97.1	308,805,215	96.9	34,209,537	12.5
White	211,460,626	75.1	223,553,265	72.4	233,657,078	73.3	22,196,452	10.5
Black or African American	34,658,190	12.3	38,929,319	12.6	40,241,818	12.6	5,583,628	16.1
American Indian or Alaska Native	2,475,956	0.9	2,932,248	0.9	2,597,817	0.8	121,861	4.92
Asian	10,242,998	3.6	14,674,252	4.8	16,614,625	5.2	6,371,627	62.2
Native Hawaiian or Other Pacific Islander	398,835	0.1	540,013	0.2	560,021	0.2	161,186	40.4
Other	15,359,073	5.5	19,107,368	6.2	15,133,856	4.8	−225,217	−1.5
Two or More Races	6,826,228	2.4	9,009,073	2.9	9,752,947	3.1	2,926,719	42.9

Sources: The source for the 2000 and 2010 data is the U.S. Census (2011c), and the source for the 2016 data is the U.S. Census 2016 American Community Survey (2018b).

TABLE 5.2	Top Ten European, Hispanic/Latino, Sub-Saharan African, Asian, and Middle Eastern-North African Nationalities in the United States				
Top Ten European Nationalities in the U.S	**Top Ten Hispanic/Latino Nationalities in the U.S**	**Top Ten Sub-Saharan African Nationalities in the U.S**	**Top Ten Asian Nationalities in the U.S**	**Top Ten Middle Eastern-North African Nationalities in the United States**
German 47,911,129	Mexican 31,798,258	Nigerian 264,550	Chinese 3,361,879	Lebanese 501,988
Irish 34,670,009	Puerto Rican 4,623,716	Ethiopian 202,715	Asian Indian 2,908,204	Iranian 463,552
English 25,927,345	Cuban 1,785,547	Somali 120,102	Filipino 2,538,325	Turkish 195,283
Italian 17,250,211	Salvadoran 1,648,968	Cape Verdean 95,003	Vietnamese 1,669,447	Egyptian 190,078
Polish 9,569,207	Dominican 1,414,703	Ghanaian 91,322	Korean 1,449,876	Syrian 148,214
French 8,761,677	Guatemalan 1,044,209	South African 57,491	Japanese 756,898	Israeli 129,359
Scottish 5,460,679	Colombian 908,734	Kenyan 51,749	Pakistani 351,049	Iraqi 105,981
Dutch 4,645,906	Honduran 633,401	Liberian 51,296	Cambodian 253,830	Palestinian 93,438
Norwegian 4,470,081	Ecuadorian 564,631	Sudanese 42,249	Hmong 241,308	Moroccan 82,073
Swedish 4,088,555	Peruvian 531,358	Sierra Leonean 16,929	Thai 189,889	Jordanian 61,664

Sources: U.S. Census (2011d) and U.S. Census American Community Surveys 2010 and 2011 (2017g).

many people have parents from more than one ethnic or national background, so they may be unsure of how to answer this question.

IMMIGRATION

Immigration is the movement of people into a country from another to take up residency. The vast majority of Americans either immigrated to the United States themselves or are the descendants of someone who

immigration The movement of people into a country from another to take up residence.

did, which accounts for our incredible racial and ethnic diversity. Immigration has been a continuous process since the country was founded. Hundreds of German Hessian mercenary soldiers paid by the British to fight in the American Revolution chose to become American citizens rather than return to Germany. Irish Catholic immigrants poured into the United States between the Revolutionary and Civil Wars, especially during the tragic 1845–1851 Irish Potato Famine, so many that the Union and Confederate armies both had Irish units. The great wave of immigration following the Civil War included southern and eastern Europeans.

The American Nativist Movement Against Immigration in the Nineteenth and Early Twentieth Centuries

Earlier immigrant groups often resented later ones, as the former they perceived the latter threatened their racial domination, culture, moral standards, safety, access to political power, jobs, or other interests. They sometimes launched an effort to bar certain groups from entering the United States. A **nativist movement** is one that aims to prevent people viewed as racially, culturally, or morally different, or otherwise threatening to the interests of residents, from entering a country. In reaction to the huge surge in arrivals from Catholic countries, many American Protestants began a major political effort to limit or end non-Protestant immigration to the United States. They argued that the new immigrants were prone to crime and immoral behavior and were more loyal to a foreign monarch, the Catholic pope in Rome, than to the American government. A large nativist political party, the "Know Nothings," began winning state level victories in the 1850s. However, it was the Northern victory in the Civil War that gave birth to the organization that would play the largest role in the anti-immigrant campaign, the Ku Klux Klan (KKK). The Klan, founded in 1865 in Pulaski, Tennessee, by Confederate military veterans, used intimidation, violence, and political strength to make sure that the Confederacy's defeat would not result in racial equality. By the early twentieth century the Klan had broadened its goals to include the protection of white Protestant America from Catholic and Jewish immigrants and had become a truly national organization of about four million members. The KKK emerged as a strong political force in a number of states outside the South, especially Indiana and Colorado (Goldberg 1991), but its popularity and influence plummeted after 1925. During that year, members of the Colorado Klan were charged with profiting from criminal activity including prostitution, gambling, bootlegging, and corruption, and the head of the Indiana Klan was arrested for rape and murder.

nativist movement A movement that aims to prevent people viewed as racially, culturally, or morally different, or otherwise threatening to the interests of residents, from entering a country.

The nativist movement prompted Congress to pass the Immigration Act of 1924, which greatly limited immigration by setting quotas for different countries. It also required for the first time that immigrants obtain visas to enter the United States. Before it was enacted, if immigrants made it to the immigration center at Ellis Island with some money to initially support themselves, were in apparent good physical and mental health and able to pass a simple IQ test in their own language, they were admitted (Matza 2017; Ngai 2004). The intent of this law was to drastically reduce the flow of non-Protestant, non-English-speaking, often darker-skinned people into the United States from countries in southern Europe. A section of this act also prevented entry into the United States of persons ineligible for citizenship. This effectively excluded Asians from immigrating to the United States because of earlier legislation (the Naturalization Acts of 1790 and 1795). Passage of this law and the huge unemployment rates in the United States following the onset of the Great Depression in 1929 kept the number of legal U.S. immigrants low for decades.

The Elimination of Immigration Quotas in the 1960s

By the 1960s, the immigration quota system was seen as a product of past racist policy. Southern Europeans had come to be viewed as white, and most Protestants no longer feared Catholicism, so the 1965 Immigration and Nationality (Harter-Celler) Act abolished immigration quotas, anticipating that immigration into the United States from countries like Italy and Greece would increase. Instead of quotas, preferences were to be given to people with important skills or who already had families in the United States. Within a few years a new surge of immigrants came from Latin America, Asia, and Africa, which led to a new immigration law in 1986, the Immigration Reform and Control Act (IRCA). This was the first law to impose penalties on those who hired illegal immigrants. IRCA also granted legal status to illegal immigrants who had entered the United States before January 1, 1982, lived in the country continuously, and agreed to pay a fine and any back taxes. An estimated three million persons were granted legal residency as a result of IRCA.

The Continuing Debate over Immigration

Most Americans accept legal immigration of persons with high levels of education and valuable skills, such as doctors, nurses, engineers, and scientists. The primary concern is about the hundreds of thousands of persons, often desperately poor, who cross the border illegally to find new economic opportunities. These illegal immigrants are accused of using social services and schools funded by taxpayer dollars, taking jobs away from citizens, lowering wages by working for low pay, and engaging in criminal activity.

One view is that the best approach is to provide a pathway to legal residency for all illegal immigrants without serious criminal records, especially for those whose parents brought them into the country as children. Of the estimated 11 million undocumented persons, 2.7 percent (300,000) are estimated to have felony (any crime punishable by death or imprisonment for more than one year) convictions (Chishti and Mittelstadt 2016; Yee, Davis, and Patel 2017). Estimates of the percentage of the general population which has been convicted of felony crimes range from 2.7 percent to around 6 percent (Bureau of Justice Statistics 2017; Shannon et al. 2011). Typically this proposal is accompanied by a call for more effective control of borders. Another point of view contends that the only fair approach is to strictly enforce the law and deport all illegal aliens to their countries of origin. Proposals for stopping illegal immigration include extending fortified border fences, greatly increasing personnel patrolling the borders, giving government officials and police more power to enforce immigration law, and even the use of military force. In 2010, Arizona enacted a controversial state law that made failure to carry immigration documents a crime and gave police broad authority to detain anyone they suspected of being in the United States illegally (Archibold 2010). However, the country as a whole seemed to be moving toward acceptance of the proposed "DREAM Act" (see boxed feature), which aimed to provide many undocumented immigrants without criminal records the opportunity to gain legal status while strengthening barriers to illegal immigration. In the 2016 presidential campaign, Republican candidate Donald Trump asserted that illegal immigration and unsatisfactorily vetted immigrants were major threats to national security and promised that if elected president he would build a wall along the border between the United States and Mexico. The Center for Immigration Studies (Warren and Kerwin 2017) reported, however, that in 2014 about 42 percent of all undocumented U.S. residents had overstayed their legal visas rather than crossed the border illegally and that in 2014 approximately two-thirds of those who joined the undocumented population were overstays.

While millions of Americans supported Trump's views on immigration, the white nationalist movement and the alt-right movement, which participated in the Unite the Right Rally in Charlottesville described at the beginning of this chapter, have been among the most active in calling for restrictions on immigration. The white nationalist movement, which includes the KKK and neo-Nazi groups, claims it's trying to ensure the survival of the white race. American white nationalists believe that U.S. national identity should be based on the white race and white ethnic groups' cultures. Their views range from white supremacy and advocating an all-white nation to tolerating some nonwhites as long as whites remain the large majority of the population and in control of the government, the economy, and other major institutions (Taub 2016). Alt-righters, who have been disproportionately young white males active on the Internet, also have a range of views and some overlap with white nationalists. They tend to oppose multiculturalism, political correctness, and feminism (NPR 2016) and focus on defending Western civilization and American traditional culture from contamination by Islam or other non-American influences. For these reasons many white nationalists and alt-righters go beyond just opposing illegal immigration to also call for severely limiting legal immigration to whites from English-speaking or European nations.

Americans more sympathetic to undocumented immigrants claim that the vast majority are law-abiding, tax-paying persons who have come to the United States to escape poverty and sometimes dangerous conditions in their home countries, and that building a wall and mass deportations would emotionally devastate many families and possibly harm the U.S. economy. They also argue that punishment should be directed at the people and companies who hire undocumented immigrants rather than at poor persons drawn across the border by the hope of a better life.

Social Movements: The Dreamers' Movement

Pro-DREAM Act demonstrators

According to the United We Dream website (United We Dream 2017), the Dreamers' Movement had its origins in the mid-2000s when a number of groups, most prominently the National Immigration Law Center, created a coalition of immigration reform activists to work for equal educational opportunities for undocumented youth. Student mobilization for access to colleges and universities and a path to citizenship for undocumented young people led to the formation of activist groups around the country, including the California Dream Network, the New York State Youth Leadership Council, the Student Immigrant Movement in Massachusetts, and the University Leadership Initiative in Austin, Texas, collectively known as the Dreamers' Movement. The movement supported passage of the Development, Relief, and Education for Alien Minors (DREAM) Act, proposed federal legislation which would provide a route to U.S. citizenship for immigrant youth brought into the country as children. Supporters of the DREAM Act noted that of the approximately 3,300,000 students who graduate high school every year in the United States, 65,000 (or about 2 percent) are undocumented persons who crossed the border with their parents when they were

very young children and have grown up in the United States. The DREAM Act would provide undocumented high-school graduates who had entered the country when they were younger than sixteen and have "good moral character" eligibility "for a 6 year long conditional path to citizenship that requires completion of a college degree or two years of military service" (DREAM Act Portal 2017). In 2010, the DREAM Act received only fifty-five of the sixty votes necessary in the Senate to advance the legislation, killing the bill for the foreseeable future. In response, President Obama in 2012 issued an executive order creating the Deferred Action for Child Arrivals (DACA) program. DACA allowed hundreds of thousands of young people brought to the United States illegally as children to remain in the country. Applicants could not have serious criminal records and must have entered the United States before 2007, when they were under the age of sixteen. DACA recipients were allowed to work legally in the United States for two-year renewable periods (Heinrich and Arkin 2017). In September 2017 President Trump announced DACA would end in six months but invited Congress to take action on the program (Koppan 2017). The Dreamers' Movement and the larger question of whether to provide a route to citizenship for millions of otherwise law-abiding undocumented immigrants continues as a major issue in U.S. politics.

What are your thoughts?

What do you think should be done with illegal immigrants who were brought to the United States as children and have not committed any serious crimes? What about their parents?

Trump also called for extreme vetting of anyone who wanted to immigrate to the United States. In 2017, President Trump issued an executive order intended to temporarily ban persons from seven predominately Muslim nations (Iran, Iraq, Libya, Somalia, Sudan, Syria, and Yemen; later, Iraq was dropped from the list). In his first speech to Congress, President Trump stated that immigration should be based on merit (*Los Angeles Times* 2017).

There are three other major issues related to undocumented immigrants: "anchor babies," "maternity tourism," and sanctuary cities. The term *anchor babies* refers to babies born to illegal immigrants in the United States, who by virtue of the 14th Amendment are automatically granted U.S. citizenship. Many people believe that these babies "anchor" their undocumented parents to the United States; in other words, it is difficult to deport them since doing so would separate them from their children. The 14th Amendment also appears to have led to a practice called *maternity tourism* (also called *birth tourism*) (Martinez and Meeks 2015), in which pregnant women from other nations travel to the United States just before giving birth so that their newborns qualify as American citizens. Critics argue that the 14th Amendment was intended to ensure the citizenship of former slaves and should not have been interpreted in a way that allows any baby born in the United States to become an American citizen.

Sanctuary cities are certain cities in the United States with municipal governments that have policies designed to avoid detecting undocumented immigrants and/or assisting federal authorities in their apprehension or prosecution. This often includes prohibiting city police or other municipal employees from asking about a person's immigration status. There are an estimated 340 sanctuary cities that in some way limit cooperation with Immigration and Customs Enforcement (ICE) (Foley 2015; Kaplan 2017). Some leaders in sanctuary cities support their position by arguing that identifying undocumented immigrants in the process of police work or other city services would discourage them from reporting crimes or seeking needed assistance. ICE disagrees, asserting that state and local officials should support the country's immigration laws and that removing criminals from the country would reduce crime (ICE 2017).

TYPES OF RACIAL/ETHNIC RELATIONS

When different racial or ethnic groups encounter and interact with each other, one of several patterns can develop. These include mutually beneficial trade and cultural exchanges, genocide, slavery, removal and segregation, colonialism, assimilation, and racial and ethnic pluralism.

Mutually Beneficial Trade and Cultural Exchanges

Throughout history, peoples of different races and ethnicities often began their relationships by interacting with each other for mutual benefit. For example, for many generations Europeans and the people of China and

India engaged in trade along the approximately four-thousand-mile Silk Road. Recall that Christopher's Columbus's original intention in setting out on his voyage, which led to the discovery of the "New World" in 1492, was to find a much faster water route to China and India.

However, when one group believed it was militarily superior and was not getting what it wanted from others through trade, it resorted to violence in order to take what it wanted. For example, in the seventeenth century Dutch people began settling in the southernmost part of Africa. They traded with the local indigenous people, who had herds of cattle and sheep and engaged in farming. When the locals resisted demands to give up more and more of what they had, the white settlers used their guns to take the land and cattle, and within a short time transformed the local people into impoverished servants and slaves. Religious leaders among the Dutch settlers justified this practice by claiming that God intended them to take over the land and wealth of southern Africa and create a Christian South Africa.

Genocide

Genocide refers to the deliberate attempt to annihilate, in whole or in part, a racial, ethnic, national, or religious group. It has sometimes occurred when a society with superior weapons comes in contact with another society living in an area with valuable resources. White settlement led to a rapid decline of the Native American populations of North and South America. Many thousands perished from the loss of land and resources to the settlers, from harsh forced labor, and from famine. Others died in wars attempting to resist the tide of foreigners. Millions more were killed by diseases brought by the European immigrants for which the native population had little immunity, although in most cases this does not appear to have been an intentional method of extermination. In the 2010 census, only about two percent of the U.S. population reported Native American ancestry (U.S. Census 2014).

Another major reason for genocide is hatred of a group blamed for victimizing a category of people that now has the opportunity to retaliate. For example, the German Nazis blamed Jews for all sorts of things: Germany's loss in World War I, the poverty of millions of Germans, the creation of Marxism and Germany's great enemy the Soviet Union, and attempting to destroy the "racial purity" of the German people. The Nazis claimed their policy of repressing Jews was necessary to protect Germany. Many ethnic Hutus in Rwanda blamed the Tutsis minority for past collaboration with European colonialists and for exploitation of the Hutu majority. In 1994, Hutu extremists in the government, military, and mass media led a genocidal massacre of hundreds of thousands of Tutsis. This tragedy, which might have been prevented or greatly limited by fast intervention by other nations, greatly increased international commitment to preventing future genocide.

Slavery

At some point in human history, conquerors concluded that rather than killing people they defeated in war, it would be useful to make some into

genocide The deliberate attempt to annihilate, in whole or in part, a racial, ethnic, national, or religious group.

slaves. **Slavery**, a situation in which one person is owned by another and must do whatever the latter demands, has existed since ancient times. Racial difference was not necessarily a basis for enslavement. For example, the Romans enslaved many people they conquered in other parts of Europe, such as Germans, Britons, and Greeks, as well as Jews and Arabs from the Middle East. The Roman economy benefitted greatly from the skills and labor of hundreds of thousands of slaves. Roman justification for enslavement was typically it being punishment for fighting against Rome, not a claim of racial superiority.

Slavery in the American South was justified using of a number of arguments:

- It was essential to the economies of both the Southern states and the Northern states, since cotton produced by slaves was the biggest U.S. export before the Civil War.

- Many prominent figures in the Bible's Old Testament were slaveholders.

- Europeans were racially superior to Africans and Africans lived better under American slavery than they did as free persons in Africa.

- God supported slavery, and a slave was sinning against God if he or she disobeyed slaveowners or tried to escape.

Removal and Segregation

There are many examples of a dominant category of people expelling or removing another category of people from one geographic area to another or barring them from certain locations. The Indian Removal Act of 1830 pushed the Cherokees and other tribes out of southeastern states to territories west of the Mississippi (Library of Congress 2017). An estimated four thousand Cherokees died on the forced march west known as "the Trail of Tears." From the end of the Civil War until the 1960s much of the United States was characterized by legally enforced racial segregation. **Segregation** is the separation of a race, ethnic group, class, religious group, or other group from the rest of society. South Africa had a system of institutionalized segregation, called **apartheid** (apartness or separateness). After 1948 the South African government re-enforced apartheid by removing many thousands of blacks from urban areas where they had lived and worked close to whites. Most indigenous Africans under apartheid were allowed to live in only the 13 percent of the country designated as black "homelands." If they had work contracts in white-owned mines or factories or as servants for white households, the contracted workers lived in barracks-style buildings or houses in black "townships" separated from the white population. Apartheid finally ended in 1994 after a revolutionary struggle led by Nelson Mandela.

Colonialism

Colonialism is a process in which a typically more technologically advanced nation subdues and dominates the people of a lesser-developed area in order to benefit from their resources. Around the early sixteenth

slavery A situation in which one person is owned by another and must do whatever the latter demands.

segregation The separation of a race, ethnic group, class, religious group, or other group from the rest of society.

apartheid A system of segregation in South Africa.

colonialism A process in which a typically more technologically advanced nation subdues and dominates the people of a lesser-developed area in order to benefit from their resources.

century, European countries began a process of colonizing North and South America, Africa, and much of Asia and the Middle East. The process has three main facets: political, economic, and cultural-psychological.

- **Political**. The colonizing country takes control of the area, usually through force or the threat of force. For example, during 1847–1883 French forces in a series of wars defeated the Vietnamese and gained control of Vietnam, Cambodia, and Laos, which they then collectively called "French Indochina"

- **Economic**. The colonizing country develops, reshapes, and exploits the economy and resources of the colonized area in ways that most benefit the colonizing nation. For example, when the Spanish conquered areas in the Americas, they often forced the local native population to switch from farming to mining gold, as gold was far more valuable to Spain than agricultural produce.

- **Cultural-Psychological**. The colonizing power spreads its cultural values, norms, and way of thinking to the colonized peoples in order to get the people of the colonized area (or at least their ruling class) to willingly cooperate with the colonizing country. For example, once in control of Vietnam, the French began mining the country's mineral resources and vastly expanded rice cultivation in the Mekong Delta to produce a huge amount for sale on the world market, benefitting France's economy. The French also built schools in Vietnam to teach the Vietnamese the French language and give them a knowledge and love of French culture, but many Vietnamese objected to being controlled and exploited. Eventually a successful Vietnamese revolutionary anti-colonial movement pushed the French out in 1954, but hundreds of thousands perished in the process. The Vietnamese revolution was one of many national liberation movements in Asia, Africa, and South America against foreign imperialism. The box below describes aspects of the Bolivian indigenous people's struggle against imperialism.

Special Topics: The Decolonization Constitution of the Plurinational State of Bolivia

Evo Morales, a labor union leader of Amerindian ancestry, first won the presidency of Bolivia in December 2005. Morales believes his party's success represents a historic victory of indigenous people against colonialism and racial and cultural repression (Postero 2010:18). After his inauguration on January 22, 2006, Morales fulfilled his pledge to hold an election for a Constituent Assembly to write a new constitution. The assembly was to provide the people with the opportunity to bring about revolutionary structural change in their political and economic systems without violence. After much debate and discussion, the new constitution was approved by approximately two-thirds of voters in a national referendum in January 2009 (Regalsky 2010:36).

The constitution renamed the "Republic of Bolivia" as the "Plurinational State of Bolivia." This new name signifies that Bolivia is peopled by diverse ethnic and racial groups, all entitled to equal rights. It "decolonizes" the formerly racially and culturally oppressed indigenous peoples by condemning "all forms of dictatorship, colonialism, neocolonialism,

(*continued*)

Special Topics (*continued*)

and imperialism" (Constitution of the Plurinational State of Bolivia 2009). The document also includes the following provisions:

- **Natural resources**. Natural resources are owned by the Bolivian people. "On behalf of the Bolivian people," the government controls hydrocarbon production and marketing.
- **Water and sanitation**. Access to water and sanitation are identified as human rights and are not subject to privatization.
- **Education and health care**. Education and health care are to be provided for free.
- **Elimination of poverty**. The state must work to eliminate poverty and bring about equal access to ".productive resources" such as land, tools, materials, knowledge, and financing
- **Employment**. While protecting private or collectively owned property, the constitution requires safe working conditions and decent wages.
- **Taxation**. Bolivians are to be taxed "in proportion to their economic capacity."
- **Elimination of violence**. "All forms of violence against children and adolescents, both in the family and in society," are banned and punished.
- **Voting**. Citizens are given the right to initiate legislation, vote on proposals through referenda, and vote to recall any elected officials except judges.

In the first election under the new constitution, Morales was re-elected president with 64 percent of the vote, and his party won large majorities in both houses of the Bolivian legislature.

Before 2006, foreign corporations controlled the extraction of natural gas in Bolivia, when, where, and how much to sell, and the price. Despite being one of the most mineral-rich countries in the world, foreign interests had exploited the country's resources in the past so that most Bolivians were among the very poorest people in South America. Morales's government gave Bolivians control of their extracted hydrocarbons all the way to the point of sale, with the ability to decide how much to sell, to whom, and at what price. Bolivia's share of revenue generated by the sale of hydrocarbons increased from 18 percent to 50 percent (Kaup 2010:129), and its income from hydrocarbons climbed from about $287 million in 2004, to $1.57 billion in 2007 (Kaup 2010:129), to around $6.57 billion in 2014 (U.S. Department of Energy 2016). Much of the new revenue went to improving social conditions and wages for the country's poor, causing income inequality to decline significantly (CIA 2017c).

What are your thoughts?

1. What do you think about Bolivia's Constitution of the Plurinational State of Bolivia?
2. Should the constitution of a country specify what share of revenue it should receive from foreign corporations for its resources? Why or why not?

Assimilation

Assimilation refers to the process through which a culturally distinct group gradually adopts the dominant culture in a society. For example, millions of people immigrated to the United States from Italy and Poland between the second half of the nineteenth and early twentieth centuries. Within two generations, the overwhelming majority of both groups had largely adopted U.S. culture, although most remained Catholic. These highly assimilated groups, having adopted the majority

assimilation The process through which a culturally distinct group gradually adopts the dominant culture in a society.

American culture, began to intermarry with each other and other earlier-arrived ethnic groups like the Irish and the Germans. This high degree of assimilation of immigrants led to America being described as a "melting pot," in which many different groups became culturally integrated within a very short time (Crossman 2017).

Racial and Ethnic Pluralism/Multicultural Pluralism

Racial and ethnic pluralism refers to a social environment in which all racial and ethnic categories have the same level of civil rights, economic opportunity, and respect, regardless of their level of assimilation to the dominant culture. For example, the Global Center for Pluralism (2016) regards Canada as one of the world's most successful racially and ethnically pluralistic nations. It notes that Canada is home to indigenous peoples, a large French-speaking minority, and many immigrants. In 2011 over 20 percent of its population was foreign born, coming mainly from Africa, Asia, the Middle East, and Latin America. **Multicultural pluralism** refers to a social environment in which no group is socially disadvantaged; in addition, racial and ethnic groups maintain a high level of cultural distinctiveness. Many Americans claim to support social equality for all racial and ethnic groups. However, support for multicultural pluralism, such as allowing certain ethnic groups to use another language in preference to English, is more limited.

The box below describes three social movements that confronted legally supported white supremacy: The American abolitionist movement against slavery, the German White Rose student movement against Nazism and the South African multiracial movement against apartheid.

racial and ethnic pluralism A social environment in which all racial and ethnic categories have the same level of civil rights, economic opportunity, and respect, regardless of their level of assimilation to the dominant culture.

multicultural pluralism A social environment in which no group is socially disadvantaged and racial and ethnic groups maintain a high level of cultural distinctiveness.

Social Movements: Evil Can Be Legal: Government-Supported Ideologies of Racial Domination and the Movements that Challenged Them

Slavery in the United States: The American Abolitionist Social Movement

The United States Constitution of 1789 protected slavery. The Fugitive Slave Act of 1850 required police throughout the United States, including in the non-slave states, to return runaway slaves to their owners. Anyone who helped a slave escape or hid or assisted him or her was considered a criminal subject to imprisonment and fines. But some Americans were so morally outraged over slavery that they committed themselves to destroying it.

Activists formed the abolitionist movement, which demanded the immediate end of slavery. Abolitionists, such as journalist William Lloyd Garrison, escaped slaves Frederick Douglas and Harriet Tubman, and author Harriet Beecher Stowe, were initially seen by many as radicals. In her widely read anti-slavery novel *Uncle Tom's Cabin*, Stowe, who had lost a young son to cholera, poured her own feelings of loss into her depiction of a slave woman whose owner decided to sell off her son. The book's effective depiction of the humanity of slaves and of the effects of slavery on families and children

(continued)

Social Movements (*continued*)

informed hundreds of thousands of readers of its cruelty. The courage of abolitionist activists and escaped slaves in the face of often vicious federal and state government repression helped convince millions that slavery was morally wrong and that they needed to take a stand against it.

The White Rose Movement

During World War II, a group of students at the University of Munich secretly organized the White Rose movement in a brave attempt to oppose the Nazi government. Some of these activists were medical students who, after being forced into military service, witnessed Nazi atrocities against civilians and captured Russian soldiers and learned of massacres of Jews on the Eastern Front. The White Rose movement secretly produced leaflets to promote passive resistance against the war and Hitler's regime, including one that read: "A victory of fascist Germany in this war would have immeasurable frightful consequences... . The day of reckoning has come – the reckoning of German youth with the most abominable tyrant our people have ever been forced to endure... . The name of Germany is dishonored for all time if German youth does not finally rise, take revenge, smash its tormentors. Students! The German people look to us" (Trueman 2011).

Inspired by their Catholic beliefs, White Rose leaders Sophie Scholl and her brother Hans distributed leaflets at the university. After being observed doing so, they and four other leaders were arrested and executed by the Nazi regime. Today in Germany and around the world they are considered heroes.

The Anti-Apartheid Movement

As you have already learned, apartheid existed in South Africa for decades. Under apartheid, anyone working for racial equality was condemned as a traitor and a communist. Despite the risks, anti-apartheid movements emerged, and millions of South Africans of all races struggled against the racist state. At the heart of the anti-apartheid movement were the African National Congress (ANC) and its two main allies, the Congress of South African Trade Unions (COSATU) and the South African Communist Party (SACP). Out of a fear of communism and that a post-apartheid government in mineral-rich South Africa could become an ally of the Soviet Union, Western European nations and the United States continued to trade with the white racist government of South Africa and at times aided it militarily. South Africa's allies only began to apply significant pressure to change when the Soviet Union disintegrated and the Cold War came to an end in the early 1990s. With few options remaining, the white government released Nelson Mandela, an ANC leader who had been imprisoned as a convicted traitor and terrorist for twenty-seven years. After several years of massive anti-apartheid labor union strikes and popular demonstrations, the white regime ultimately permitted democratic elections, which the ANC won, allowing Mandela to become South Africa's first post-apartheid president.

What are your thoughts?

Is anything legal that you consider evil in the United States? Why do you think it is evil and why do think it is legal?

PREJUDICE AND DISCRIMINATION

Many people experience disadvantages, such as limitations of opportunities in life or psychological or even physical harm, because they are members of a particular social group. This section presents the topics of prejudice and stereotypes, discrimination, white privilege, and institutional discrimination, and attempts to explain both the obvious and more subtle ways people encounter barriers or mistreatment simply because of who they are.

Prejudice and Stereotypes

Prejudice refers to prejudging people before getting to know them personally, and often involves negative feelings, attitudes, and stereotypes directed toward every individual in an entire race, ethnic group, religion, social class, or other social group. For example, at one time many Americans felt hostile toward Catholics because they believed that all members of the Catholic faith were more loyal to the head of their church, the Pope in Rome, than to the U.S. Constitution and democracy. This made it difficult for a Catholic to be nominated for and win the presidency until well into the twentieth century. Such a belief about all Catholics is called a stereotype. A **stereotype** is a set of expectations for the behavior, moral character, capabilities, or limitations of a person. Stereotypes can be positive or negative. For example, some people stereotype Asians as being great at math. In a more negative example, after it became known that Islamic extremists carried out the 9/11 attacks, some Americans began to stereotype all Islamic Americans as hostile to the United States and supporters of terrorism. Stereotypes are more likely to exist when the people holding them have little or no experience interacting as equals with the category of people they stereotype. Personal contact among people in different groups often breaks down stereotypes. One of the authors of this book witnessed how person-to-person interaction can destroy stereotypes when interviewing a young white couple from Kentucky who had moved to Indianapolis. One part of the interview included a list of questions about attitudes toward African Americans. The couple consistently gave the most positive answers possible, indicating that African Americans were kind, hard-working and good people, and they loved having them as neighbors in their apartment building. At one point the husband indicated that their attitudes about African Americans had changed dramatically since coming to Indianapolis, explaining that shortly after they arrived in the city with their infant son his wife became seriously ill. Over the next couple of months, their African American neighbors regularly brought meals, took care of their child, and assisted the recovering mother until she was well. This experience broke down their old stereotypes and changed their lives and views toward people of another race.

Discrimination

In contrast to prejudice, which refers to feelings, attitudes, and expectations, discrimination refers to behavior. **Discrimination** is treating people a certain way because they are members of a particular social category. Prejudice and discrimination often occur together, but not always. There can be situations in which an unprejudiced person might be forced to discriminate. For example, if laws forbid the hiring of gay teachers, a school principal with no personal anti-gay prejudice might be forced to discriminate against a gay job applicant. On the other hand, a personally prejudiced principal may be prohibited by law from discriminating against a gay teacher.

prejudice Prejudgment of people before getting to know them personally, often involving negative feelings, attitudes, and stereotypes directed toward every individual in an entire race, ethnic group, religion, social class, or other social group.

stereotype A set of expectations for the behavior, moral character, capabilities, or limitations of a person based on their membership in a social category.

discrimination Treating people a certain way because they are members of a particular social category.

White Privilege

Throughout U.S. history, white people, especially white men, have enjoyed privileges. Millions of white Americans benefitted from the labor of African slaves. After slavery was abolished, other white advantages continued. According to W. E. B. Du Bois (1935), benefits for white workers were both material and psychological. Certain types of jobs, like positions in law enforcement, were reserved primarily for whites. However, even low-paid white workers enjoyed a high "public and psychological wage" because of their whiteness (Du Bois 1935:700). Unlike African Americans and other minority groups, even poor whites were generally treated politely by fellow citizens and were unrestricted in their movements, access to public buildings and private businesses, and ability to vote. Psychologically, poor whites could pride themselves on being better treated than nonwhites and on having higher status in society. Maintaining this racial division benefitted big-business owners, who could keep wages low by pitting white workers against nonwhite workers.

Even today there is still a need for awareness that being white provides advantages (Rothenberg 2015). In her widely cited paper "White Privilege: Unpacking the Invisible Knapsack," Peggy McIntosh (1988) described **white privilege** as advantages that white persons enjoy, often without awareness, over nonwhite persons. She explained that white Americans carry with them at all times "an invisible weightless knapsack" of unearned assets that they benefit from without appreciating that they received them because of their race. She argues that many white people were taught to "see racism only in individual acts of meanness, not in invisible systems conferring dominance" on their racial group.

The dozens of everyday advantages McIntosh finds in the knapsack of white privilege include things like: not having to warn your children that other children might be unpleasant to them because of the way they look; easy access to picture books, holiday cards, dolls, toys, and magazines featuring people of your own race; being able to move to a new location without worrying about hostility from prejudiced neighbors; not wondering whether a police officer pulling you over is profiling you; being able to go shopping without fear of being followed around the store on suspicion of shoplifting; and having relatively easy access to legal or medical services.

Making people aware of white privilege can be an important step in the process of extending the same privileges to everyone regardless of the color of their skin.

Institutional Discrimination

Institutional discrimination refers to the operation of institutions in a way that discriminates against a category of people. For example, prior to the Educational Amendments Act of 1972 and its Title IX component, federally funded educational institutions were allowed to discriminate against women by not providing them with equal educational opportunities, including in college sports. **Institutional racism** refers to discrimination by institutions on the basis of race. Institutional

white privilege Advantages that white persons enjoy, often without awareness, over nonwhite persons.

institutional discrimination The operation of institutions in a way that discriminates against a category of people.

institutional racism The operation of institutions in a way that discriminates against people on the basis of race.

racism has plagued the American economic, criminal justice, military, health care, and educational systems. For example, before President Truman's 1948 Executive Order No. 9981 the U.S. armed forces had racially segregated military units, and before the 1954 Supreme Court ruling in *Brown v. Board of Education* many states had racially segregated schools. A contemporary example is that schools with high percentages of African American students are often less well-funded and well-staffed than other schools. In addition, standardized academic aptitudes tests tend to put African American youth and certain other minorities at a disadvantage when they use language unfamiliar to these groups or assume educational experiences they have not had.

Discrimination in the Criminal Justice System The criminal justice system discriminates against African Americans in multiple ways; this includes everything from **racial profiling**, the practice of targeting people for suspicion of crime based on their race, ethnicity, religion, or national origin rather than on observing or detecting them engaged in a specific behavior (National Institute of Justice 2018), to the level of criminal charges to the harshness of punishment (Alexander 2012). For example, the penalty for possession of crack cocaine, the form often used among low-income groups that are disproportionately African American in many urban areas, is much higher than the penalty for powder cocaine, which is used more often by high-income, disproportionately white groups. From 1986 through 2009, the federal penalty for possession of one thousand grams of powder cocaine was ten years, but a person with only ten grams of crack cocaine could get the same ten-year sentence (*Washington Post* 2010), partly because crack cocaine was more often associated with violent crime. Thus, a much higher percentage of African Americans served long prison sentences for cocaine trafficking or possession than white Americans. In an attempt to somewhat level the playing field, in 2010 Congress reduced the disparity in harshness of punishment from one hundred to one to eighteen to one (Shapiro 2010).

At the state level, research has commonly found that killers of white Americans are much more likely to receive the death penalty than killers of African Americans. The highest percentage sentenced to death – and most likely to be executed – are African Americans convicted of killing white victims (Jacobs et al. 2007). Another example of institutional discrimination is racial profiling by law enforcement personnel. In many communities, African Americans are much more likely than whites to be stopped and questioned by police solely on the basis of race. The killing of Trayvon Martin, described in the following boxed feature, is viewed as an example of the potentially tragic consequences of racial profiling. Legal scholar Michelle Alexander (2012) provides a convincing data analysis to show that the functioning of the criminal justice system, particularly in its war on drugs, has resulted in mass incarceration of black males in the United States. More African Americans were in prison or otherwise under correctional supervision when Barack Obama was president than were slaves in 1850. According to Wagner and Sawyer (2018), about one in five persons incarcerated in

racial profiling The practice of targeting people for suspicion of crime based on their race, ethnicity, religion, or national origin rather than on observing or detecting them engaged in a specific behavior.

the United States in state and federal prisons, local jails, and youth correctional facilities are there for nonviolent drug offenses such as possession or trafficking. Drug laws are widely seen as one of the reasons why blacks are about six times more likely to be incarcerated than whites

Social Movements: Racial Profiling and the Trayvon Martin Movement

Demonstrators protesting the killing of Trayvon Martin and racial profiling

On February 26, 2012, Trayvon Martin, an unarmed seventeen-year-old African American high-school student, was returning from a store to a residence in a gated community in Sanford, Florida. He was spotted by twenty-eight year-old George Zimmerman, reportedly the neighborhood watch coordinator. Zimmerman, who was carrying a licensed hand gun, viewed Martin as a suspicious person. Zimmerman called the Sanford Police Department to report his observation. Soon after the conversation with the police dispatcher – who suggested that Zimmerman should not personally approach Martin – some type of interaction occurred between the two, resulting in Zimmerman shooting and killing Martin (Blow 2012). Zimmerman was not arrested at first, but after widespread protest he was charged with second-degree murder. Although Zimmerman was working as an insurance underwriter, he was completing an associate's degree in criminal justice at a Florida college and had frequent communication with friends in local law enforcement. His profiling of a black male teenager walking in a gated complex as a probable danger

to the community appeared to reflect racial profiling among many police (Melber 2013).

Zimmerman's defense lawyers relied in part on Florida's "stand your ground" law. This law allows a person, even if he or she began an aggressive confrontation, to use lethal violence against the person he or she attacked if that person responds with violence that is viewed as life threatening. Critics claim that, in effect, this law permits the killer who survived the confrontation to be legally treated as the victim and considered innocent, as long as there are no witnesses or video recordings proving otherwise. A *Tampa Bay Times* study of some two hundred cases found that the stand your ground defense allowed the defendant to go free about 70 percent of the time (Hundley, Martin, and Humburg 2012). As in other studies, the race of the victim mattered. When the person killed was white, the defendant invoking stand your ground escaped punishment 59 percent of the time. But when the person killed was black, 73 percent of the killers went free. On July 13, 2013, a Florida jury found Zimmerman not guilty.

This killing spurred the creation of the Black Lives Matter movement against unjustified law enforcement use of lethal violence, racial profiling, and other perceived biases of the criminal justice system. Tens of thousands of people have become actively involved. The movement targets states and police departments with the worst reputations for racially based abuse of human rights.

What are your thoughts?

Do you think that racial profiling is ever justified in police work? Why or why not? What is your opinion of the stand your ground law?

(Sentencing Project 2017). In contemporary U.S. society, where overt racial discrimination is illegal and most people claim to be *color-blind* (against racism), the disproportionate arrest and imprisonment of African Americans is often viewed as evidence of color-blind racial discrimination. **Color-blind racial discrimination** (also referred to as color-blind racism) is behavior or institutional practices that have the effect of discriminating against people of a certain race even though the publicly stated basis for differential treatment is not race (Bonilla-Silva 2018). For example, the antidrug law that has harsher punishment for the type of cocaine use more common among blacks than for the type of cocaine use more common among whites has been viewed as a form of color-blind racial discrimination. Alexander argues that, because people with a criminal record can be permanently and legally discriminated against, many African Americans have lifelong difficulties getting a job, improving their education, and depending on the state, even voting.

Housing Discrimination Racially based housing discrimination has had devastating effects on many African Americans. Historically, lack of access to mortgage loans, limiting their residences to areas with low property values, and overcharging for real estate services and purchases put African Americans at a long-term economic disadvantage. Millions of white Americans received government assistance through programs like the GI Bill to buy homes anywhere in the United States, but African Americans either could not buy homes at all or were limited to specific areas. Mortgage companies and banks engaged in *redlining*. This originally meant literally drawing a red line around certain neighborhoods or areas on a map (usually populated mainly by minorities) and then refusing to provide home loans within these areas on the grounds that it was too risky. In addition, real estate companies would steer minority home buyers away from white residential areas. Since building up equity through owning a home is the main way most working- and middle-class people accumulate wealth, denial of home ownership increased the wealth gap between African Americans and white Americans.

Although the 1968 Federal Fair Housing Act and the 1974 Equal Credit Opportunity Act banned housing and lending discrimination, some of this behavior persisted. Research published by the U.S. Department of Housing and Urban Development (HUD) in 2013 revealed continuing housing discrimination. The study, which was conducted by the Obama administration in 2012, employed pairs of testers (one white and one from a minority group) in more than eight thousand separate tests in twenty-eight metropolitan areas around the United States. The pairs of testers were the same age and gender and presented the same financial qualifications to buy or rent a home. Unlike the earlier 1977 HUD housing discrimination study, in which some realtors refused to work with minority buyers at all, the minority testers in the 2012 study were usually shown at least one property. The results indicated that Hispanics were treated about the same as whites when it came to buying but were given fewer opportunities for renting. African American and Asian testers were provided with fewer opportunities for both renting

color-blind racial discrimination (also referred to as color-blind racism) Behavior or institutional practices that have the effect of discriminating against people of a certain race even though the publicly stated basis for differential treatment is not race.

FIGURE 5.1

Racial and Ethnic Differences in Household Income and Wealth

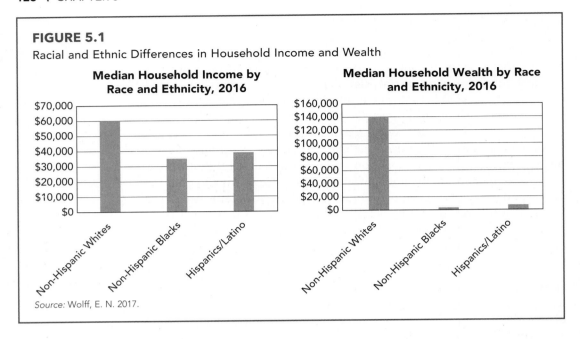

Source: Wolff, E. N. 2017.

and buying. In other words, many real estate agents still appeared to be steering minorities away from certain properties by not disclosing that they were available. Real estate agents informed African American buyers about 17 percent fewer homes for sale and showed them about 18 percent fewer homes than whites. Asian buyers were told about 15 percent fewer available units and were shown nearly 19 percent fewer homes (Gamboa 2013; Sokou 2013).

As noted above, home ownership has been a major way many working- and middle-class people have accumulated assets in the past. But housing discrimination interfered with the ability of the targets of discrimination to build up wealth. In 2016 the median household income for non-Hispanic whites was about $60,000, whereas for non-Hispanic blacks it was $35,000 and for Hispanics/Latinos $39,000 (Wolff 2017). But the wealth gap among these groups was much larger. The median net worth for non-Hispanic whites in 2016 was $140,500, while for non-Hispanic blacks it was $3,400 and for Hispanics/Latinos $6,300. These numbers in part reflect the fact that while 15.5 percent of non-Hispanic whites had zero or negative net worth in 2016 (they owed more than the worth of their assets), 37 percent of non-Hispanic blacks and 32.8 percent of Hispanics/Latinos had zero or negative net worth. The differences in income and wealth are displayed in the figures above.

CAUSES OF PREJUDICE

What causes people to be prejudiced? This is important to explore since prejudice is a primary, though, as noted earlier, not the only motivation for discrimination. Social scientists point to personality type, situational factors, culture, and social structure.

Personality Type

Following the terrible destruction of World War II launched by authoritarian governments in Nazi Germany, imperial Japan, and Fascist Italy, sociologists and psychologists searched for an explanation as to why supposedly highly cultured people in the twentieth century would engage in such savagery and mass murder. A group of researchers led by Theodor Adorno (1993) found that some people have an *authoritarian personality type* that predisposes them to prejudice against other groups. Such people tend to feel insecure because of typically emotionally cold, strict, demanding parents who viewed life and society in sharply contrasting terms of right and wrong and passed on this rigid way of thinking to their children. Their feelings of insecurity and simplistic way of viewing the world makes people with an authoritarian personality prone to using stereotypes when thinking about other racial or ethnic groups. Believing they are the members of a superior race or ethnic group make them feel better about themselves.

Situation

Research by psychologists (Dollard 1980; Whitley and Kite 2009) and others suggest that people who experience a lot of frustration become prone to aggressive behavior, including hostility toward minority groups. When unable to strike out at the real cause of frustration, a person chooses a vulnerable substitute, a scapegoat, on which to displace his or her aggression. The term *scapegoat* comes from the Jewish Day of Atonement, Yom Kippur. In ancient times, a goat would be sent out into the countryside after a high priest had symbolically placed all his people's sins upon it. You might expect, from this point of view, that people who experience serious frustrations such as job loss or marital difficulties would be more prone to prejudice. Another form of frustration linked to prejudice is *status anxiety*, the idea that people who have low status in income, education, or job prestige feel compelled to blame some inferior group for their troubles. For example, during apartheid in South Africa, more lower-middle-class and working-class white Afrikaners were opposed to racial equality than whites with higher levels of income and education (DeFronzo 2015). Similarly, white Americans with lower levels of education and income have been more prone to overt expressions of racial or ethnic prejudice.

Culture

Socialization in a culture that values one race or ethnic group over others is a major cause of prejudice. Children raised in families where parents express hostility toward other racial or ethnic groups tend to adopt these attitudes themselves within the first few years of life (Van Ausdale and Feagin 2001). These ideas may either be reinforced or countered by what is learned from friends, nonfamily social groups (like sports teams), schools, and the mass media. People tend to avoid social contact with members of the groups against which they have learned to be biased, limiting the person-to-person interactions that could undermine and disprove it. Diversity in educational settings can be very important for reducing prejudice because it brings together people of different backgrounds.

Social Structure

The structure of a society's economy can be a powerful cause of prejudice. According to this view, the development of racist ideology in the United States was caused mainly by the huge expansion of cotton growing in the South, especially after 1800. This expansion resulted from the invention of the cotton gin, which allowed seeds to be separated from fiber about fifty times faster than doing it by hand. In addition, increased demand for cotton in Europe prompted the forced removal of Native Americans from tens of millions of acres of fertile land in the southern states, and encouraged utilization of the cheap labor of millions of slaves. So the economic benefit of slavery to whites motivated the development of an ideology of white supremacy that became a major element of American culture.

SOCIOLOGICAL PERSPECTIVES ON PREJUDICE AND DISCRIMINATION

Each of the major sociological conceptual frameworks provides insights on how to reduce prejudice and discrimination. The structural-functional approach highlights the importance of understanding how prejudice and discrimination against any social group can be dysfunctional for society. The economic-conflict approach suggests that a fairer economic system would reduce racial and ethnic prejudice and discrimination. The **critical race theory** conflict view states that victims of racism will play a central role in eliminating it. And the symbolic-interactionist perspective describes the importance of emphasizing the inconsistency between prejudice and discrimination and core American values.

Structural-Functional Perspective

A simple functionalist analysis suggests that for a social system to work smoothly all members of society must accept and adjust to existing social relations. For example, in a society based on slavery, everyone, including the slaves, should be taught to accept slavery.

A deeper functional analysis attempts to determine potential dysfunctions of an existing system and whether they are serious enough to require social change. One of the most obvious dysfunctions of a society structured to deny a large category of people access to equal opportunity is the loss of talent that might otherwise have benefitted society as a whole. Consider the accomplishments of today's brilliant African American scientists, politicians, businesspersons, artists, entertainers, and others who would have been unable to contribute their achievements to humanity if they had been slaves like their ancestors. A comprehensive functional analysis views any significant denial of access to opportunity as potentially harmful to the entire society.

critical race theory A conflict approach stating that because racism is profoundly integrated into American institutions, culture, and everyday social life and activities, the only way to spread awareness of and remove it is through the insights and narratives of people of color.

Conflict Perspective

As you have already learned, the conflict approach focuses on inequalities that advantage certain groups and disadvantage others. From the Marxist conflict perspective, these inequalities benefit the capitalist employers. Although in the United States the large majority of the people are in the middle and working classes, it is difficult for them to unite against the upper class because of their racial and ethnic differences. The inherent economic insecurity of the capitalist economic system promotes intergroup hostility and prejudice as each race or ethnicity competes against the others. According to this view, overthrowing the rule of the rich and creating a fairer economic system would greatly reduce racial and ethnic prejudice.

Another conflict orientation, critical race theory, states that racism became and remains profoundly integrated into American institutions, culture, and everyday social life and activities (Han 2008). It operates in ways that are often not even noticed or understood from the subjective perspective of white Americans, who benefit from its existence. The only way to expose this embedded and sometimes subtle racism is through the standpoint of people of color, whose narratives can uniquely reveal the influence of race and racism on their daily lives and challenge the color-blind claims of the privileged majority group. Only though such exposure will all people become aware of the depth and pervasiveness of racism and then be able to consider the level of social change necessary to address the problem.

Symbolic-Interactionist Perspective

According to the symbolic-interactionist perspective, the dominant group in a society characterized by great inequality tries to maintain social stability by socializing all its members, including those most disadvantaged, to believe in and accept the existing way of life. The dominant group attempts to influence the cultural values and beliefs of the exploited groups, control their learning experiences, and shape their identities, including what people think of themselves and their capabilities. For example, most slaves were forbidden from practicing their original religion or using their African names, and were prevented from learning how to read and write to keep them from becoming knowledgeable about and proficient in the culture of the dominant whites.

Despite the focus on acceptance, this perspective also provides insights into how oppressed people can free themselves from the identity and cultural restraints imposed on them by the dominant group and mobilize social movements to fight for change. The **African American freedom movement** (of which the civil rights movement from the mid-1950s to the late 1960s was a major component), for example, attempted to communicate to members of the dominant group that their own moral well-being required equal treatment and opportunity for all. Political campaigns, demonstrations, and educational efforts forced the larger public to recognize inconsistencies between core American values and past ways of thinking and acting toward minorities. Social movements like this create new group identities that provide feelings of

African American freedom movement The struggle for equal rights for African Americans throughout American history.

Social Movements: The African American Freedom Movement

The African American struggle against prejudice and discrimination has a long history. Following the American Revolution, African Americans were bitterly disappointed that the new U.S. Constitution protected slavery. Many slaves and free blacks resisted, and some even participated in slave rebellions that were quickly and brutally repressed. The U.S. Supreme Court repeatedly ruled in favor of slave owners. Congress even passed legislation that made it a crime to aid escaped slaves. In 1860, the election of Abraham Lincoln, who opposed the expansion of slavery to the western territories, dramatically ended the proslavery orientation of the federal government and provoked the Southern states to secede and begin the Civil War.

As the Civil War was coming to an end in 1865, Congress passed the 13th Amendment to the Constitution that, once ratified by the states, abolished slavery. During the Union forces' occupation of former Confederate states during Reconstruction, African Americans participated in politics and elections in large numbers. However, after federal forces withdrew in 1875, white-controlled Southern state governments began preventing former slaves from voting and enacted "Jim Crow" laws that ensured racial segregation and white social, political, and economic domination. In the 1896 *Plessy v. Ferguson* case, the U.S. Supreme Court ruled that the concept of "separate but equal" schools and other publicly funded facilities was constitutional, reinforcing this trend.

Activists W. E. B. Du Bois, William Monroe Trotter, and others founded the Niagara Movement in July 1905, which demanded immediate equal political and economic rights for African Americans and helped inspire the 1910 creation of the National Association for the Advancement of Colored People (NAACP).

Protests and court cases brought by African American activists led to President Franklin Roosevelt banning racial employment discrimination in defense industries in 1941, the Supreme Court ruling against segregation in interstate transportation in 1947, President Harry Truman banning racial segregation in the military in 1948, and the 1954 Supreme Court declaration that racially segregated schools were unconstitutional (Carson 2006).

In 1955, after Rosa Parks was arrested for refusing to give up her bus seat to a white person, the African American residents of Montgomery, Alabama, launched a new mass participation protest phase of the freedom movement by boycotting segregated buses. This prompted a Supreme Court ruling that segregation on public buses was unconstitutional. The bus boycott is viewed by many as the beginning of what is called the *civil rights movement* phase of the African American freedom movement.

The civil rights period of the 1950s and 60s witnessed a number of organizations with distinct orientations: reformist, cultural nationalist, and revolutionary. The NAACP, Congress of Racial Equality (CORE), and Southern Christian Leadership Conference (SCLC) were generally reformist and attempted to open up America's existing institutions to full and equal participation through court battles, proposals and support of legislation, efforts to elect anti-racist candidates to government office, and nonviolent civil disobedience such as sit-ins.

The most prominent cultural nationalist organization was the Nation of Islam. Its leaders advocated the adoption of a more authentic African based cultural heritage in reaction to what was viewed as slave culture and a psychology of submission to whites. Because the last names of many African Americans were derived from those of former slave owners, the Nation of Islam wanted its members to take new names and embrace Islam, the religion that many Africans had practiced before being brought to America, to achieve real social and psychological freedom. For example, world heavyweight boxing champion Cassius Clay took the name Muhammad Ali upon joining the Nation of Islam.

Social Movements (*continued*)

In contrast to both the reformers and the cultural nationalists, the revolutionaries believed that African American freedom required major institutional change, including replacement of the capitalist economic system with a socialist economy. They felt that distributing income and wealth more equally, eliminating poverty, and ensuring the availability of decent-paying jobs would eliminate much of the underlying motivation for racism. The main revolutionary organization was the Black Panther Party, founded in Oakland California in 1966 by Bobby Seale, Huey Newton, and their associates. Newton asserted that "racism cannot be eliminated until capitalism is eliminated" (1971:202). The Panthers strongly opposed U.S. military involvement in Vietnam and publicly advocated that African Americans own firearms and have the right to self-defense. Local police departments often appeared hostile to the Panthers, and the group even caught the attention of the FBI. Hundreds of Black Panther Party members were arrested, and some were killed in confrontations with police. By the end of the mid-1970s, the influence of the Panthers and other militant political groups faded.

While activism declined in the 1970s, the protests of the 1950s and 1960s had led Congress to pass several major human rights laws:

- The Civil Rights Act of 1964 outlawed segregation in public accommodations and banned racial discrimination in hiring and in programs receiving federal funds.
- The Voting Rights Act of 1965 prohibited any state or local government from interfering with the right to vote "on account of race or color" (Ourdocuments.gov 2013).
- In 1972, the Equal Employment Opportunity Act reinforced the ban on employment discrimination based on race; in addition, it banned discrimination based on sex or religion.

Public opinion surveys have indicated that support for overt racism has declined significantly, but institutional discrimination and color-blind discrimination continues. These forms of discrimination occur through policies such as drug laws and self-defense ("stand your ground") laws that significantly disadvantage minorities. For example, a number of state legislatures have passed or are attempting to pass laws requiring identification cards to fight voter fraud, which critics claim is virtually nonexistent (Farley 2017). Such laws are seen as making it much harder for minority and low-income persons to vote because getting the new identification cards costs time and money. Another example is gerrymandering in congressional and state voting districts, described in Chapter 3, which can reduce the effect of minority votes and provides conservative white voters with excessive influence over who gets elected (Axios 2017; Daley 2017).

On June 25, 2013, the U.S. Supreme Court ruled five to four to strike a central provision of the Voting Rights Act of 1965. The court majority stated that voter registration information and other data on which the law was based is now out of date (Gunier et al. 2013; U.S. Supreme Court 2013). The decision appears to remove the authority of the federal government to oversee the voting process in nine mostly southern states, along with certain districts in other states suspected of interfering with U.S. citizens' right to vote in the past. This could make it much easier for state and local governments to prevent many low-income racial- or ethnic-minority citizens from voting through methods such as requiring voter IDs, which are difficult or inconvenient to obtain, or not providing enough voting locations in heavily minority areas.

What are your thoughts?

(1) Do you think that movement organizations with the cultural nationalist or revolutionary orientations provide any positive contributions to efforts to increase equality of opportunity in society? Why or why not?

(2) Which do you think would do the best job of ensuring that every qualified person has the ability to vote, the federal government or state governments? Why?

empowerment, pride, and self-confidence that further encourages mass participation in the struggle for social justice.

PROPOSED SOLUTIONS TO PREJUDICE AND DISCRIMINATION

Social movement activism contributed to multiple efforts aimed at reducing prejudice and discrimination. These included innovative programs and new policies in the areas of education, the economy, and government.

The Role of Education

National social surveys conducted from 1972 through 2008 have shown that among whites a higher level of education is linked to less racial prejudice and decreased support of discrimination (Bobo et al. 2012). Many institutions of higher education now offer courses on multiculturalism that attempt to combat harmful negative stereotypes of racial and ethnic minorities. A central aim is to heighten appreciation for diversity by spreading knowledge about how each group's culture and achievements have contributed to American society. Research has also shown that mutual prejudices between groups have often been significantly reduced when members of the groups become involved in interacting and cooperating with one another to accomplish tasks as students do in the schoolroom (Dovidio and Gaertner 1999). Providing the points of view of minority-group persons can help identify the presence of prejudice and decrease its influence on all members of society.

Economic Reform

Sociological and psychological theories and research suggest that certain economic factors can influence the degree of race and ethnic prejudice. High levels of employment and employment security appear to reduce intergroup hostility. A strong economy that ensures that good-paying jobs are plentiful and layoffs of workers are rare should reduce prejudice. Corporations can be encouraged through economic incentives and appeals to patriotism to develop new manufacturing facilities and jobs in the United States. Modern industrial technology often requires much higher skill levels than in the past, so another strategy to keep unemployment low would be the extensive provision of free or low-cost technical educational and training opportunities. Reducing economic frustration and anxiety is a promising approach to eliminating racial and ethnic tensions.

affirmative action programs Policies aimed at recruiting minority persons to make up for past discrimination and create a workforce or student body more representative of the entire population.

Political Reform

Political policies can play a major role in fostering an equalitarian society free of discrimination. A number of government agencies and private businesses and institutions have established **affirmative action programs**, policies aimed at recruiting minority persons to make up for past discrimination and create a workforce or student body more representative of the entire population. The U.S Supreme Court has generally supported the constitutionality of such efforts, but has imposed some limitations.

The government is ultimately responsible for preventing racial and ethnic discrimination, and can intervene in the economy to promote full employment and investment in the United States and to ensure that hard work will be rewarded with fair pay and economic security. If local or state authorities attempt to interfere, directly or indirectly, with the ability of people to vote, the federal government must act to protect this essential democratic right.

The role of government in combating racism and ethnic prejudice is also manifested in **hate crime** legislation and enforcement. According to the Federal Bureau of Investigation (2016a), a hate crime is a traditional offense like murder, arson, or vandalism with an added element of bias. For the purposes of collecting statistics, the FBI has defined a hate crime as a "criminal offense against a person or property motivated in whole or in part by an offender's bias against a race, religion, disability, sexual orientation, ethnicity, gender, or gender identity."

Most states have some kind of hate crime law, but the laws vary widely in the types of bias that are covered and in the level of commitment by the criminal justice system. For example, according to the Anti-Defamation League (2016), a number of states, such as Arizona, California, Connecticut, Hawaii, Illinois, Iowa, Maine, Minnesota, New Hampshire, New Jersey, New York, Pennsylvania, Texas, Washington, and Vermont, have fairly comprehensive hate crime laws covering race, religion, ethnicity, sexual orientation, gender, and disability. Some have added hate crimes motivated by bias against transgender persons. A hate crime is considered an offense not only against a specific victim, but against entire communities, which can be put into a state of fear (terrorized) by the crime. In effect, hate crime laws can be viewed as a criminal justice defense against certain forms of domestic terrorism.

hate crime A criminal offense against a person or property motivated in whole or in part by an offender's bias against a race, religion, disability, sexual orientation, ethnicity, gender, or gender identity.

Nelson Mandela and his view on hateful prejudice and how to end it

No one is born hating another person because of the color of his skin, or his background, or his religion. People must learn to hate, and if they can learn to hate, they can be taught to love, for love comes more naturally to the human heart than its opposite.

Nelson Mandela
July 18, 1918 – December 5, 2013

CHAPTER REVIEW

Race, Ethnicity, and Racism

Race is a socially constructed category of persons who share one or more biologically based traits that people consider especially important. Historically, skin color has been the central determinant of race. Unlike race, ethnicity has no biological aspect. Ethnicity refers to a group of people who share the same cultural heritage, which usually involves a common language and a common religion. A minority group is any category of people who are subjected to disadvantages because of their physical or cultural characteristics, sexual orientation, or gender identity, such as barriers to educational and job opportunities or the ability to vote. Racism is the belief that people of one race are superior to persons of another race. People make claims of superiority in order to obtain material and psychological benefits. Claims of white racial superiority helped justify the slavery of Africans whose exploited labor played a major role in U.S. economic development. Europeans often used racist beliefs to justify their domination of Africa, the Americas, and much of Asia.

Types of Racial/Ethnic Relations

When different racial or ethnic groups encounter and interact with each other, one of several patterns can develop: mutually beneficial trade and cultural exchanges, genocide, slavery, removal and segregation, colonialism, assimilation, racial and ethnic pluralism, or multicultural pluralism.

Immigration

Many Americans accept legal immigration of persons with valuable skills, such as doctors, nurses, engineers, and scientists. The main concern is over the hundreds of thousands of persons who enter the United States illegally. According to one view, the best approach is to provide a pathway to legal residency for illegal immigrants with no serious criminal records, especially children whose parents brought them into the country. Another point of view contends that the right approach is strict enforcement of the law and deportation of undocumented aliens of all ages to their countries of origin.

Prejudice and Discrimination

Prejudice refers to prejudging people before getting to know them personally, often involving negative feelings, attitudes, and stereotypes directed toward every individual in an entire race, ethnic group, or religion. A stereotype is a set of expectations for a person's behavior, moral character, capabilities, or limitations based on her or his membership in a social category. In contrast to prejudice, which refers to feelings, attitudes, and expectations, discrimination refers to behavior. Discrimination means treating people a certain way because they are members of a particular category. Discrimination can be carried out by individuals or institutions, such as the criminal justice system or the housing industry.

Causes of Prejudice

Explanations for the causes of prejudice include personality type, situational factors, culture, and social structure. Research indicates that people with the authoritarian personality type are more prone to prejudice. So are people who experience economic insecurity or status anxiety. Many people are prejudiced because they learn prejudice from family and friends. In addition, a racist ideology, like that of white supremacy, can develop to justify economic exploitation of another group and its resources.

Sociological Perspectives about Prejudice and Discrimination

Applying sociological perspectives, structural-functional analysis suggests that one of the most obvious dysfunctions of a society structured to deny a large category of people access to equal opportunity is the loss of talent that might otherwise benefit society as a whole.

The conflict approach focuses on inequalities that advantage certain racial or ethnic groups and disadvantage others. Critical race theory, one version of the conflict approach, argues that racism is so embedded in American institutions and everyday life that much of it is not comprehended by whites and can only be adequately exposed by the narratives and analyses of people of color.

The symbolic-interactionist perspective describes how people learn to accept or reject the social structure and social roles that society imposes on them. The dominant group attempts to influence the cultural values and beliefs of the exploited groups, control their learning experiences, and shape their identities. Social movements attempt to create new group identities that provide feelings of empowerment, pride, and self-confidence and encourage mass participation in the struggle for social justice.

Proposed Solutions to Prejudice and Discrimination

Attempts to reduce prejudice, discrimination, and conflict among racial and ethnic groups include education (such as courses on multiculturalism that combat harmful negative stereotypes of racial and ethnic minorities), efforts to decrease economic frustration and anxiety, and government actions to prevent racial and ethnic discrimination.

KEY TERMS

affirmative action programs, p. 134
African American freedom movement, p. 131
apartheid, p. 118
assimilation, p. 120
colonialism, p. 118
color-blind racial discrimination, p. 127
critical race theory, p. 130
discrimination, p. 123
ethnicity, p. 108
genocide, p. 117
hate crime, p. 135
immigration, p. 111
institutional discrimination, p. 124

institutional racism, p. 124
minorities, p. 109
multicultural pluralism, p. 121
nativist movement, p. 112
prejudice, p. 123
race, p. 108
racial and ethnic pluralism, p. 121
racial profiling, p. 125
racism, p. 108
segregation, p. 118
slavery, p. 118
stereotype, p. 123
white privilege, p. 124

DISCUSSION QUESTIONS

1. Is race or ethnic prejudice a significant problem in the town or city where you grew up? What about at your high school or college?

2. Is racial/ethnic diversity good for the United States? Explain your point of view.

3. Are legal immigrants from non-European countries a threat to U.S. society, or are they beneficial? Explain your point of view.

4. What is the best way to reduce racial/ethnic prejudice and discrimination?

5. Do you favor affirmative action policies at institutions of higher learning? Why or why not?

6. Are criminal justice policies biased against racial or ethnic minorities in the United States? Why or why not?

7. Are state laws that require increased voter identification at polling places justified to prevent voter fraud or intended to reduce the number of persons in certain categories who are allowed to vote? Explain your point of view.

CHAPTER 6

Gender and Sexual Orientation

CHAPTER OBJECTIVES

- Explain the concepts of gender identity, gender binary, and sexism.
- Explain gender stereotypes, gender discrimination, and gender inequality.
- Describe the factors involved in cultural sexism and institutional sexism.
- Describe the movement for gender equality.

- Explain the different types of feminism.
- Explain different types of sexual orientation and homophobia.
- Describe the movement to end discrimination on the basis of sexual orientation.

WOMEN AND PEOPLE OF SAME-SEX orientation have both suffered historically from prejudice, stereotyping, and discrimination. But, beginning with women obtaining the vote in 1920, rights once reserved only to heterosexual males have been steadily won by both groups. Although bias and barriers remain, one of the best examples of progress is the election on November 7, 2012, of seven-term Democratic congresswoman Tammy Baldwin as the junior U.S. senator from Wisconsin. She is the first openly gay or lesbian person to be elected to the Senate, as well as Wisconsin's first woman senator. Tammy Baldwin, unlike many lesbians, had the advantage of being born in a progressive city, Madison, and in a state, Wisconsin, with a relatively liberal political history. Raised by supportive family members, she graduated first in her class from Madison West High School and went on to attend Smith College in Massachusetts, majoring in mathematics and government. After graduation she earned a degree from the University of Wisconsin Law School in 1989. Beginning in local government on the Dane County Board of Supervisors representing downtown Madison, she steadily rose in political prominence and won Wisconsin's 2nd Congressional District in 1999, becoming the second openly gay member of Congress after Barney Frank of Massachusetts (Biography 2016). She held that House seat until elected to the Senate to which she was re-elected in 2018. During her political career she has been a strong supporter of universal health care and equal rights for lesbian, gay, bisexual, and transgender persons.

SEX, GENDER, AND SEXUAL ORIENTATION

Sex refers to being biologically (physically) male or female. This includes a person's chromosomal, chemical, reproductive, and anatomical characteristics such as external genitalia. The vast majority of people, probably over 99 percent, have either the XX sex chromosome structure (statistically normal female) or the XY sex chromosome structure (statistically normal male). Rare sex-determining chromosome types include, but are not limited to, the XXX female, the XXY male, and the XYY male. People who have combinations of the physical characteristics that normally signify male or female are referred to as "intersex" (American Psychological Association 2011).

The concept of **gender**, in comparison, refers to the understanding that people have of what it means to be a male or female in their particular culture or social group. Gender is a social construct, meaning that it is the product of learning and social interaction. People learn from being socialized into their culture what behaviors and psychological traits are expected of men or women. Their conceptions are continually reinforced and/or modified through communication. The cultural belief that men and women have distinct personality traits, capabilities, and strengths and weaknesses has been referred to as the "**gender binary**" (Wade and Ferree

sex Being biologically (physically) male or female in terms of a person's chromosomal, chemical, reproductive, and anatomical characteristics such as external genitalia.

gender A social construct that is the product of people learning from their culture and interactions with others what behaviors and psychological traits are expected of men or women.

gender binary The cultural belief that men and women have distinct personality traits, capabilities, and strengths and weaknesses.

gender identity How one's sense of gender corresponds to biological sex characteristics.

cisgender identity Having a gender identity that is the same as the person's sex identity assigned at birth (the same as her or his physical sex characteristics) .

transgender identity Having a gender identity that is the opposite of the person's physical sex characteristics.

cisnormativity The individual or institutional assumption that everyone is cisgender and cisgender identities are superior to transgender identities.

doing gender How people try to display masculinity or femininity through attitudes, traits, clothing, symbols, and behaviors that represent the gender they want to present to others.

sexism Prejudice or discrimination against a person on the basis of sex or gender identity.

sexual orientation A person's sexual attraction and/or emotional-romantic attraction to persons of the opposite sex, same sex, or both sexes.

heteronormativity The individual or institutional assumption that everyone is heterosexual and heterosexual orientation is superior to other sexual orientations.

coming out The process of identifying and accepting one's own sexual orientation or gender identity (coming out to oneself) and of publicly acknowledging it to others (coming out to others).

2015:10). It assumes there are only two types of people, men and women. This culturally embedded concept also implies that all men consistently share the stereotypical male traits and all women the stereotypical female traits. So the gender binary undermines not only similarities between men and women but also variations within men and women. Our social interactions, culture, and institutions are built upon the gender binary. This system especially disadvantages those whose gender identity is ambiguous and does not conform to the binary concept of gender.

Gender identity refers to how one's sense of gender corresponds to biological sex characteristics. When a person feels masculine and has male physical characteristics, his gender identity is male. Similarly, when a person feels feminine and has female physical characteristics her gender identity is female. When a person's gender identity is the same as the sex identity assigned at birth (the same as her or his physical sex characteristics), the person has a **cisgender identity**. But a person whose sense of gender is the opposite of her or his physical sex characteristics has a **transgender identity**. **Cisnormativity** refers to the individual or institutional assumption that everyone is cisgender and cisgender identities are superior to transgender identities. In their social interactions, people try to display masculinity or femininity through attitudes, traits, clothing, symbols, and behaviors that represent the gender they want to present to others. This is often referred to as "gender expression" by psychologists or **doing gender** by sociologists. Sex and gender identity, like race and class, have been the target of prejudice and discrimination. **Sexism** refers to prejudice or discrimination against a person on the basis of sex or gender identity. It is usually based on the belief that one sex or gender identity is naturally superior.

Sexual orientation refers to a person's sexual attraction and/or emotional-romantic attraction to persons of the opposite sex (*heterosexual* orientation), same sex (*homosexual* orientation), or both sexes (*bisexual* orientation). A person can also feel sexual and romantic attraction to people of any sex or gender identity and think that sex and gender identities are irrelevant in determining whom they will be sexually and emotionally attracted to (*pansexual* orientation). Also, a person can have a lack of or low level of sexual attraction to others or desire for sex (*asexual* orientation). **Heteronormativity** is the individual or institutional assumption that everyone is heterosexual and heterosexual orientation is superior to other sexual orientations. **Coming out** refers to the process of identifying and accepting one's own sexual orientation or gender identity (coming out to oneself) and of publicly acknowledging it to others (coming out to others).

SOCIOLOGICAL PERSPECTIVES ON GENDER AND SEXUAL ORIENTATION INEQUALITY

Structural-Functional Perspective

The structural-functional approach suggests that both gender inequality and sex orientation inequality originate in the primitive economic and health conditions of early humanity. In ancient times, when people survived through hunting and gathering and primitive agriculture, a necessary functional division of labor took place between men and women. Because women's mobility was limited due to frequent pregnancy, child birth, and nursing, they specialized in domestic activities like nurturing and rearing children and tending to farms. The men specialized in activities that took them away from home, often for long periods of time, like hunting large game or warfare. This functional division of labor was coupled with differences in personality. Men developed and had to display *instrumental ("masculine") traits* such as aggressiveness, toughness, independence, and resourcefulness, which helped them survive in a dangerous and difficult environment. Women developed *expressive ("feminine") traits* like warmth and emotional supportiveness important for nurturing young children and maintaining intimate relationships. Since death rates were high and life spans were on average relatively short, and also because children's labor was useful in pre-industrial farming, high birth rates were viewed as a functional necessity. This attitude privileged heterosexual sex, which could produce children, over homosexual sex. Culture, including religion in many societies, confirmed these gender roles and heterosexuality as normative.

As nations industrialized, the gender role specialization that emerged over thousands of years was maintained. The structural-functional perspective viewed the instrumental role of men and the expressive role of women as complimentary and important for the health and stability of families (Parsons and Bales 1956). In other words, women carried out the expressive functions of raising children, catering to the emotional needs of family members and ensuring the smooth running of the household while men engaged in the instrumental functions of making money and financially supporting the family. And children were to be brought up with heterosexual sexual orientations so that they could later form heterosexual relationships and produce children.

Conflict Perspective

Economic-Conflict Perspective The economic-conflict perspective makes an assumption about how gender role differences first developed similar to that of the structural-functional perspective. That is, because of women's frequent pregnancy, a sexual division of labor took place.

As technological advances steadily increased the ability to modify and manipulate the outer environment, men, due to their instrumental specialization, had nearly complete control over the tools, machines, weapons, and wealth that were the main bases of power. As the power gap between men and women grew, men came to define women as inferiors and ultimately as a valued form of property. Women became increasingly economically dependent on men. This was reinforced through men's control of law and culture, including religion, which generally supported male domination. Karl Marx's long-time friend Friederich Engels (1884) argued that as advancing technology allowed men to accumulate property, they developed the institution of the family as a way to ensure that they could pass their property on to their biological sons. Engels also noted that poor men who were exploited by employers would often take out their frustrations on women, making females the most exploited people under the capitalist system. According to Engels, a socialist economic system would end poverty, relieve the economically generated frustration of working men, and thus end the oppression of women.

But advancing technology also created the means (scientific research, machinery, computers, and robotics, etc.) for women and men to play more equal economic roles. Differences in size and physical strength between men and women became less relevant to carrying out important and productive economic roles. Women's participation in the economy, however, was impeded by discrimination and by the "false consciousness" of inferiority implanted in many women by socialization to the male-dominated culture. The economic- conflict perspective views barriers to female labor force participation at all levels as interfering with the achievement of the economic system's full productivity since so much talent is wasted when capable women are left out. Over time this contradiction between the needs of the economy and wasting female talent contributes to fostering a social movement recognizing the right of women to have opportunities equal to those of men.

The economic-conflict approach also has implications for eliminating sexual orientation inequality. As progress in science and technology made it possible for women to perform on an equal level with men, it also caused other changes that helped lead to greater public acceptance of homosexuality. First, medical technology reduced infant mortality and increased life spans. Second, more and more of the population came to live in relatively crowded urban areas. Both of these trends meant that families with large numbers of children were no longer necessary for the economy and the welfare of society. These developments undermined the argument that the function of sex was only to generate births. Sex came to be seen as legitimate simply as a source of pleasure and as a way to express love. Since reproduction was no longer a necessary goal of sexual encounters, homosexual relations for love, enjoyment, and fulfillment came to be more acceptable since most heterosexual activity involved the same motivations.

Feminist-Conflict Perspective The feminist conflict perspective considers various explanations for the formation of male-dominated societies, the subordination of women, and the development of gender personality differences. Susan Brownmiller (1975), for example, argued that female subordination had its origin in the willingness of men to use violence and rape against women. Because men's physical advantages allowed them to use force to intimidate and terrorize women, women had little choice but to become dependent on and submissive to some men in order to obtain protection from the aggression of men in general.

Others who advocate the feminist-conflict approach accept ideas of the economic-conflict perspective, such as early technological advances increasing the power gap between males and females due to men's instrumental specialization. As the power gap between men and women expanded, women became more economically dependent on men. Men rewarded women who submitted and punished or even killed women who rebelled, and enshrined rationales for the subordination of women in the cultures and religions of virtually all major civilizations. Many feminist-conflict theorists argue, however, that this may have little to do with capitalism, as Engels thought, since male domination of government, law, and social life persisted in societies that experienced socialist revolutions.

Male domination may be based on causes deeper than the nature of the economic system. Some feminist conflict theorists believe that lesbian sexual relationships free women from dependency on and control by men.

Racial/Ethnic-Conflict Perspective The racial/ethnic-conflict perspective, while sharing many of the ideas of the economic-conflict and feminist-conflict perspectives, has emphasized the concept of intersectionality developed by black feminists (Collins 2008; Combahee River Collective 1978; Crenshaw 2016; Crenshaw and Adewunmi 2014) Intersectionality emphasizes the importance of the impact of the intersection of different forms of oppression. Among the most victimized members of society are women who not only suffer sexist discrimination but also class prejudice because of low income, racial/ethnic prejudice because of color or ethnicity, and sexual orientation hostility because of same-sex relationships.

Symbolic-Interactionist Perspective

The symbolic-interactionist perspective emphasizes interpersonal interaction, learning experiences, and labeling in analyzing the causes and effects of gender inequality and sexual orientation inequality. People develop an understanding of what's expected of males and females from learning the values and norms of their culture, from seeing which gender holds positions of power in social institutions, and from interpreting the expectations of others with whom they interact. Until relatively recently, many girls grew up believing that they lacked the capability to do well in subjects like math and science and were often concerned about being high achievers because they feared social rejection and being unpopular. This turned into a self-fulfilling prophesy in which many females would not even make an effort to excel in these areas.

In the past individuals also learned that society expected males and females to be heterosexual and condemned those who were not. This situation caused anxiety and even depression among those who worried that they were not "normal" and feared the reactions of parents, friends, and employers if their sexual orientation became known.

Bessie Coleman and Amelia Earhart, pilots who overcame sexist stereotypes to lead the way for women aviators

The symbolic-interactionist perspective indicates that the social liberation of women and persons with same-sex orientation or transgender identity requires both a positive self-concept and an effort to transform culture and the attitudes of other people. One factor that contributed to the development of movements to achieve these goals was earlier involvement in the social movements for African American civil rights and peace in Vietnam. Activists in these movements were exposed to ideas of freedom and justice that had direct implications for the members of other subordinated groups. Many women and gays and lesbians who participated in these efforts became convinced that movements were needed to win social justice and equality of opportunity for themselves and people like them. The modern women's movement and LGBT (lesbian, gay, bisexual, and transgender) rights movement were intended to achieve these aims. These collective efforts are identity movements. As noted in Chapter 2, the major aim of an identity movement is to spread understanding of mechanisms of domination and repression, including cultural elements such as negative stereotypes and oppressive language, to bring about change. The goal is to destroy debilitating identities and ways of thinking and talking that are "the means and products of group subordination" (Gill and DeFronzo 2009:212). The women's movement and the LGBT movement attempt to create new identities that provide "a sense of empowerment, pride, self-confidence and equality" and also actively confront and change "the larger public's norms, beliefs, behaviors, and ways of thinking" (Gill and DeFronzo 2009:212) about women and people of non-heterosexual orientation.

GENDER INEQUALITY AND DISCRIMINATION

Gender is a central organizing principle of societies. People construct their conceptions of gender from witnessing and experiencing the roles men and women play in institutions, from learning gender-related values and norms from culture, and from direct interactions with other persons. All three major sociological perspectives provide explanations for why men have historically dominated societies. These perspectives point to cultural and structural forms of sexism. *Cultural sexism* refers to how elements of culture, including traditions, stereotypes, values, norms, and symbols, promote the idea that one sex or gender identity is inherently superior. *Institutional (structural) sexism* (similar to institutional racism) refers to how society and its institutions are organized to privilege or discriminate against persons on the basis of their sex or gender identity.

CULTURAL SEXISM: SEXIST TRADITIONS, STEREOTYPES, VALUES, NORMS, AND SYMBOLS

Family

The family has functioned as the initial learning environment through which children are first exposed to what it meant to be a girl or a boy. Clothing and blankets for little girls are often pink but blue for little boys. Parents, relatives, and friends typically buy very distinctive types of toys that serve as meaningful symbols of what children are expected to play with in preparation for adult roles: dolls, doll houses, tea sets, and toy ovens for little girls; and miniature trucks, steam shovels, trains, airplanes, toy soldiers, and toy guns for little boys. All of this is reinforced by the sex-typed behavior of parents, with the moms preparing dinners, washing laundry or vacuuming the rugs while the dads mowed the lawn or watched football or baseball on TV or played these sports with their sons.

Only recently have men begun to do an increased share of child care and household chores, but women still on average do much more. For example, the U.S. Bureau of Labor Statistics "American Time Use Survey" (2015) found that while in 2003 only 35 percent of men reported doing food preparation and food cleanup on an average day, this rose to 43 percent in 2014. But still in 2014 the daily women's share of food preparation and cleanup was 69 percent. Also in 2014, on an average day only 20 percent of men did housework such as cleaning the house or doing the laundry, compared to 49 percent of women. The survey further revealed that on an average day in households with children under the age of six, women spent one hour providing primary childcare such as feeding or bathing a child, compared to only twenty-three minutes for men. Another study published in the *Journal of Marriage and the Family* (Yavorsky, Dush, and Schoppe-Sullivan 2015) analyzed time-use diaries kept by duel-earner couples in the three months before the birth of their first child and for the nine months after the birth. The results indicated that once the baby had arrived, mothers on average spent about two more hours in unpaid work per day, much of it child care, than before; the increase in unpaid work for the fathers was only about forty minutes.

Schools

Children's conceptions of gender and the capabilities of females and males can be influenced by school factors such as the gender-relevant content of books, the way teachers treat and respond to girls and boys, and the advice given by counselors. Studies of children's picture books have shown repeatedly that they tend to display traditional stereotypes of males and females. Hamilton et al. (2006), for example, analyzed two hundred top children's picture books published between 1995 and 2001. They pointed out that while earlier research had found considerable underrepresentation of girls and women and gender stereotyping of those that did appear, there were hopes that bias would decrease over time. They found, however, that the level of gender bias in children's picture books was about the same as in the 1980s. There were almost twice as many male compared to female main characters, with the males much more likely to appear in pictures. Male main characters were less than one-third as likely as female main characters to be involved in nurturing or caring for others. Both male and female characters were overwhelmingly portrayed in gender-stereotyped occupations and while males had a wider range of jobs, more females than males appeared to have no paid jobs at all.

Another important factor in females' academic achievement and career choices is the attitudes and expectations that girls perceive from their teachers. Lavy and Sand (2015) found, for example, that primary school teachers' biases regarding boys' and girls' capabilities affect their academic achievements in both middle school and high school, including their decisions on taking advanced-level math or science courses in high school. Primary school teachers' biases in favor of boys had a positive effect on boys' achievements and enrollment in advanced math courses in high school and a negative effect on girls' achievements and enrollments in advanced math courses. The overall findings indicate that since enrollment in advanced math and science courses in high school is typically a prerequisite for higher education in fields such as engineering, computer science, and other sciences, teachers' gender-biased interactions with students early in their schooling have long-term impacts on future career paths and earning levels in adulthood. The researchers also found that the effect was larger for children whose mothers had lower educational attainment than their fathers, and for girls from low socio-economic backgrounds.

Language

Language can teach gender stereotypes to children and reinforce them in adults. In the past, for instance, it was typical to use expressions referring to someone in a position of power or in certain occupations as male. Business executives were collectively referred to as "businessmen" (rather than "businesspersons") even though some were women, and heads of boards of directors "chairmen" (rather than "chairpersons"). This use of words conveys the message that men are expected to exercise power and that for women to do so is abnormal. Another biased practice is to use male pronouns such as he or him when the sex of the person is not known, as in referring to a police officer driving "his" police vehicle rather than "his or her" police vehicle.

The way people use language and words can also teach sexism, even unintentionally, in other ways. This includes always placing the male before the female, as in saying "boys and girls" rather than "girls and boys." Using female pronouns in referring to cars or ships or planes ("she's a beauty") can also convey sexist meanings by signaling a female label implies male ownership. Finally, one of the most insidious sexist uses of language is attempts to insult, criticize, or motivate boys or men by referring to them as "girls" or "bitches." This unavoidably conveys the meaning that there is something inferior about being female. Furthermore, our language is also based on the gender binary and reinforces cisnormativity. This is prominent in our use of pronouns. Over time there have been attempts to make our language more gender neutral, including new gender-neutral pronouns such as "ze" (instead of he or she) and "hir" (instead of his or her).

Media

The mass media provide endless opportunities for communication and entertainment. But media also conveys powerful gender stereotypes. One type is extreme body images for both females and males, often in part the result of Photoshop editing or plastic surgery of one type or another. Female models are typically extremely thin, presenting an ideal body image that is virtually impossible for the large majority of women to achieve, much less maintain. The image that male models and actors present is similarly nearly impossible for most men. Movies frequently present men and women in gender-stereotyped ways: Males are often adept at using violence, whereas women are typically in need of protection and saving.

Gender stereotypes also play a role with regard to the people who bring us TV news. Male TV news anchors appear to have significantly longer job longevity than females (Gutgold 2010). Women have brought numerous law suits against TV stations and networks on the grounds of age discrimination (Acuna 2012). Music videos also project gender stereotypes. In her review of research on sexualization and racism in music videos, Maddy Coy (2014) argues that sexism has served as a profitable marketing tool for music companies through explicitly sexual displays of women's bodies, especially those of black women. Research indicates that music videos show traditional gender stereotyping, portraying men as dominant and aggressive while women are shown largely as sex objects. A study of forty-one rap music videos (Hunter 2011), for example, described women dancing like strippers for men's entertainment.

Religion

The founders of Christianity, Islam, Judaism, Buddhism, and Confucianism were male, as are the contemporary leaders of these religions. Their ancient texts typically contain statements suggesting male superiority. For example, the old testament of the Judeo-Christian tradition refers to God creating man and then creating woman from man to be his companion. Islam, in some countries forces, women to wear clothing (burqa) that conceals virtually all parts of their bodies except hands and eyes. In general, religions historically fostered stereotypical gender roles, with the father as the head of the household and the mother assigned primary responsibility for child care. Women who tried to be independent of men or violate religiously supported gender stereotypes were often punished or shunned by religious authorities. Joan of Arc, although later canonized as a Catholic saint, was executed in part for violating religious law by wearing men's clothing.

Although women tend to be more religious than men in terms of believing in God, believing in an afterlife, reporting that religion is important in their lives, attending religious services, and saying prayers (Pew Religious Landscape Study 2014a), they have in the past been barred from becoming Catholic priests, orthodox Jewish rabbis, or Islamic clergy. However, several Protestant denominations have allowed women to become clergy, including the Episcopalians, the Southern Baptist Convention, the Evangelical Lutheran Church of America, and the United Methodist Church (Religionstolerance.org 2015). By 2011, for example, about one in four clergy in the United Methodist Church were women (Keaton 2013).

INSTITUTIONAL SEXISM

Education

Educational opportunities for women were limited in the early history of the United States. Eventually the country's need for more teachers led to some colleges opening their doors to women. But for decades most women pursued higher education for careers that were extensions of women's traditional gender role orientation as caregivers such as nurses and educators.

Females are now more likely to graduate high school than males (Child Trends 2017) and have significantly higher high school senior grade point averages (Russell Sage Foundation 2013). Women are also now more likely to obtain college bachelor's and master's degrees than men. And the number of advanced degrees earned by women in engineering, physical sciences, life sciences, business, and in medical, dental, and law schools has generally increased since the early 1970s. But on many college campuses women are at significant risk of experiencing sexual harassment or even sexual assault, as described in the special feature below.

Research indicates that both male and female university science professors tend to have a bias against women graduate students in scientific fields (Pollack 2013). A study conducted by researchers at Yale University (Moss-Racusin et al. 2012) surveying professors in physics, chemistry, and biology at six major research universities around the United States found that, on average, they viewed an application for the position of laboratory manager from a young male scientist more favorably than an application from a young female scientist with identical qualifications and accomplishments. And in cases where the female applicant was selected for the position, the salary she was offered was on average about $26,000, compared to about $30,000 for the male. Interestingly, the female professors seemed to display the same gender bias against women applicants as the male professors. Bias against women aspiring to careers in science and certain other professions may be another reason for sizeable differences between men and women in postgraduate fields of study, as indicated in the figure below.

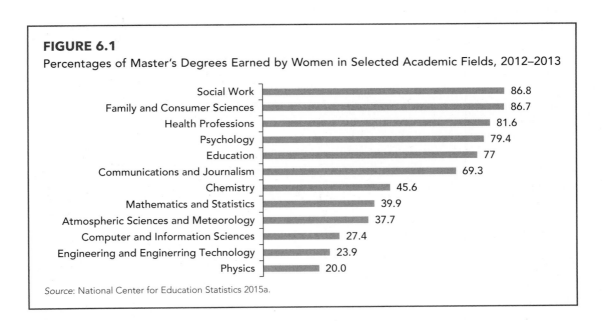

FIGURE 6.1

Percentages of Master's Degrees Earned by Women in Selected Academic Fields, 2012–2013

Field	Percentage
Social Work	86.8
Family and Consumer Sciences	86.7
Health Professions	81.6
Psychology	79.4
Education	77
Communications and Journalism	69.3
Chemistry	45.6
Mathematics and Statistics	39.9
Atmospheric Sciences and Meteorology	37.7
Computer and Information Sciences	27.4
Engineering and Enginerring Technology	23.9
Physics	20.0

Source: National Center for Education Statistics 2015a.

Special Topics: Sexual Assault on Campus

People like to think of universities and colleges as safe places where young adults acquire the knowledge and skills to ensure productive and happy futures. But in reality many college campuses pose a high risk of sexual assault. The findings of a Association of American Universities (AAU) study (Cantor et al. 2015) indicate that about 23 percent of undergraduate university women experience nonconsensual sexual contact before they graduate (as do about 5 percent of undergraduate men). The research involved 150,072 respondents (89,115 females and 60,957 males) at twenty-seven universities. Nonconsensual sexual contact included sexual penetration or sexual touching. Penetration meant inserting a penis, finger or object inside another person's vagina or anus, or mouth or tongue contact with another person's genitals. Sexual touching referred to kissing or touching another person's breast, chest, crotch, groin, or buttocks, or grabbing, groping, or rubbing another person in a sexual way, even over the person's clothes.

The AAU study indicated that 10.8 percent of undergraduate women experienced nonconsensual sexual penetration (completed or attempted) before graduation and that the risk was greatest for freshmen. The most dangerous period for freshmen women may be between student orientation and Thanksgiving break because they are often independent of family for the first time and unfamiliar with the new environment and potential threats (Booth 2015). The AAU survey found that use of alcohol or drugs increased risk of nonconsensual sexual contact. For undergraduate females, about half of nonconsensual sexual penetration occurred because of physical force and the other half because of being incapacitated by things like alcohol or drugs. Undergraduate victims reported that the offender was a friend or acquaintance about 40 percent of the time, someone they had dated or been intimate with before 24 percent, and a stranger 29 percent of the time, respectively. Only about 26 percent of

females experiencing nonconsensual sexual penetration by force reported it to authorities and only 14 percent did so for penetration by incapacitation. Reasons given for not reporting included thinking the offense was not serious enough, feeling too embarrassed or ashamed or that it would be too emotionally distressing, or because a victim did not think that anything could be done about it.

The study also asked respondents about experiences of sexual harassment (sexually oriented behaviors that interfere with academic work, limit ability to engage in an academic program, or create a hostile, offensive, or intimidating academic, work, or social environment). The research indicated that about 62 percent of female undergraduates said they had been sexually harassed by behaviors such as inappropriate remarks about their appearance, body or sexual behavior, or offensive or insulting sexual jokes or stories.

The percentage of female undergraduates saying they were the victims of nonconsensual sexual contact ranged from 13 percent at one university to 30 percent at another and sexual harassment ranged from 49 percent to 74 percent. When asked whether it was very or extremely likely that the university would conduct a fair investigation of a report of sexual assault or sexual misconduct, the percentages ranged from a high of 67 percent at one university to a low of only 26 percent at another. For students who experienced the most serious victimization, nonconsensual penetration by physical force, reporting the assault to a university agency ranged from a high of 46 percent and to a low of only 17 percent.

The research also discovered that most students who witnessed an intoxicated person at risk of having a nonconsensual sexual encounter or a person behaving in a sexually violent or harassing way did nothing about it. This problem has led to student activism encouraging both females and males to intervene when they see a person

(continued)

Special Topics (*continued*)

in danger of being sexually victimized. For example, female students at Syracuse University organized "The Girl Code Movement" to mobilize college women. Instead of being bystanders, they actively intervene to prevent at-risk students from being sexually assaulted (Booth 2015). Many people believe that education about sexual assault on campus should begin long before college. Males students at Dover-Sherborn Regional High School in Dover, Massachusetts, for example, began a movement called Stand with Everyone Against Rape (SWEAR) to educate teenage boys about sexual assault and its consequences. The effort spread to other Boston-area schools.

Ask yourself:

How serious a problem is sexual assault on your campus? What can you do about it?

Work and Income

Although the difference between female and male wage levels, the *gender wage gap*, is large, it has declined significantly over the last four decades. While for full-time, year-round workers female median annual earnings was only 60.2 percent of males' in 1980, it was 78.6 percent of males' in 2015 (Hegewisch and DuMonthier 2016). And while the median usual weekly earnings of women was 64.2 percent of males' in 1980, it was 81.1 percent of males' in 2015. For both men and women, earnings increase as years of education increase. However, women's earnings are less than men's earnings at all the levels of academic achievement, and the gender wage gap is wider at higher levels of education, as shown in the figure below.

FIGURE 6.2

Median Usual Weekly Earnings of Full-time Workers, Ages 25 and Older, by Level of Education and Gender, 2015

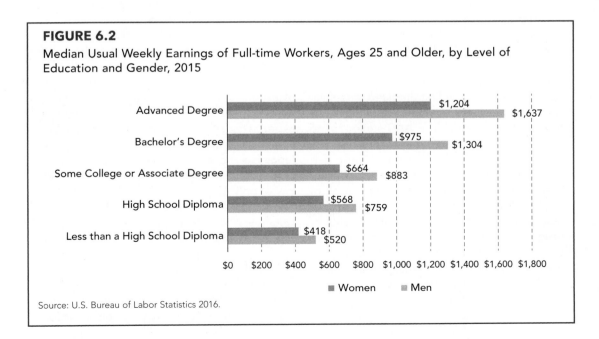

Source: U.S. Bureau of Labor Statistics 2016.

The occupations with the highest percentages of women workers reflect the traditional stereotype of women as nurturers and helpers. Women comprise over 80 percent of workers in occupations such as secretaries and administrative assistants, receptionists and information clerks, teacher assistants, registered nurses, nursing, psychiatric, and home health aides, personal care aides, bookkeeping, accounting and auditing clerks, maids and housekeeping cleaners, general office clerks, and elementary and middle school teachers (Institute for Women's Policy Research 2016). In most of these female-dominated job categories the minority of workers who were men had a median weekly income higher than that of women. The average median weekly earnings for full-time working women in these overwhelmingly female occupations in 2015 was about $647 and for men about $717. This implies that male workers may enjoy the *"glass escalator"* effect, the invisible advantages that male workers in female-dominated occupations have regarding performance evaluation and promotion (Williams 1992; Wingfield 2009).

Occupations with the smallest proportions of women workers tend to reflect the traditional stereotype of men as being tough, strong, leaders, producers in the economy outside the home, and mobile. Women are under 30 percent of workers in job categories such as carpenters, construction laborers, auto mechanics, electricians, drivers in sales operations and truck drivers, grounds maintenance workers, freight movers, first-line supervisors of production and operating workers, software developers, wholesale and manufacturing sales representatives, production workers, and general and operations managers (Institute for Women's Policy Research 2016). The average median weekly earnings for full-time working women in the top twelve overwhelmingly male occupations in 2015 for which data were available (seven of the twelve occupations) was about $792, while that for men was about $1,007. Although women tended to earn more in these male-dominated jobs than in the predominantly female occupations, the gender wage gap was greater, as shown in the table below.

TABLE 6.1 | The Gender Wage Gap for Full-Time Workers, 2015

	Percent in an Occupation Who Are Women	Women's Median Weekly Earnings	Men's Median Weekly Earnings	Women's Earnings as a Percent of Men's
All Full-Time Workers	44.3%	$726	$895	81.1%
Twelve Occupations with the Highest Percentages of Female Workers				
Secretaries and Administrative Assistants	94.4%	$683	$786	86.9%
Teacher Assistants	92.2%	$530	N/A	N/A
Receptionists and Information Clerks	91.6%	$569	$619	91.9%

TABLE 6.1 | The Gender Wage Gap for Full-Time Workers, 2015 (*continued*)

	Percent in an Occupation Who Are Women	Women's Median Weekly Earnings	Men's Median Weekly Earnings	Women's Earnings as a Percent of Men's
Book Keeping, Accounting and Auditing Clerks	88.7%	$692	$690	100.3%
Nursing, Psychiatric and Home Health Aides	88.4%	$457	$526	86.9%
Registered Nurses	88.3%	$1,098	$1,222	89.9%
Maids and Housekeeping Cleaners	84.7%	$407	$475	85.7%
Office Clerks	83.2%	$622	$609	102.1%
Personal Care Aides	81.2%	$441	$537	82.1%
Elementary and Middle School Teachers	80.6%	$957	$1,077	88.9%
Cashiers	69.4%	$405	$471	86.0%
First-Line Supervisors of Office and Administrative Support Workers	66.5%	$781	$878	89%
Twelve Occupations with the Lowest Percentages of Female Workers				
Carpenters	1.2%	N/A	$687	N/A
Construction Laborers	2.1%	N/A	$642	N/A
Automotive Service Technicians and Mechanics	2.3%	N/A	$724	N/A
Electricians	2.9%	N/A	$891	N/A
Driver/Sales Workers and Truck Drivers	3.9%	$632	$751	84.2%
Grounds Maintenance Workers	4.5%	N/A	$473	N/A
Laborers and Freight, Stock and Material Movers, Hand	15.3%	$455	$547	83.2%
First-Line Supervisors of Production and Operating Workers	17.0%	$623	$924	67.4%
Software Developers, Applications and Systems Software	18.0%	$1,415	$1,751	80.8%
Production Workers	24.0%	$501	$666	75.2%
General and Operations Managers	24.5%	$1002	$1,347	74.4%
Sales Representatives, Wholesale and Manufacturing	25.9%	$917	$1066	86.0%

Source: Institute for Women's Policy Research 2016.

The income gaps between women and men are caused by several factors. One is that women work disproportionately in occupations with lower income levels. This seems largely the result of socialization to traditional gender stereotypes and gender bias in the educational system. Second, even when men and women are in the same occupations, women often have lower earnings levels because their careers have been interrupted more often than men's careers. This may result in less overall experience and seniority for women, both of which can affect pay levels. One reason for interrupted women's careers is that pregnancy and childbirth, especially in the absence of comprehensive child care programs, often compel women to temporarily withdraw from the labor force, putting them at a disadvantage when they go back to work. Another reason is that some married women give priority to their husband's careers, leaving their own jobs when, for example, their spouses' companies transferred them to a new geographic location. Still another factor has been sexual harassment that can cause a woman to leave a job for another that provides a safer, less offensive work environment. It appears, though, that these factors cannot completely explain the gender wage gap, indicating that gender discrimination also plays a significant role (American Association of University Women 2016). Even in high-paying occupations women's advancement can be blocked by the so-called "**glass ceiling**," an invisible and often subtle yet powerful barrier of male prejudice and "old boy" networks that prevent female promotion beyond a certain level. And women, even in high-level positions, have experienced sexual harassment and even sexual assault from bosses or co-workers. In response, many women have mobilized to fight back as described in the special feature on the Me Too movement below.

glass ceiling An invisible and often subtle yet powerful barrier of male prejudice and "old boy" networks that prevent female promotion beyond a certain level.

Social Movements: The Me Too Movement

Me Too movement demonstrators

Tamara Burke began the Me Too movement in 2006 to help people who survived sexual violence, especially women of color in low-income communities. A basic goal of the movement is to provide emotional strength and a feeling of not being alone to a survivor of sexual assault through statements of support from other survivors. According to the Me Too movement website (https://metoomvmnt .org), the "movement has built a community of survivors from all walks of life" who have helped "to de-stigmatize survivors by highlighting the breadth and impact sexual violence has on thousands of women." The

(continued)

Social Movements (*continued*)

movement is committed to helping survivors not only heal but lead the effort to disrupt "all systems that allow sexual violence to flourish."

The size and influence of the Me Too movement grew as women came forward to accuse powerful, wealthy, and famous persons of sexual harassment and assault. One major event in this momentum-building process occurred when prominent Fox News anchor Gretchen Carlson launched a sexual harassment lawsuit against Roger Ailes, chairman of Fox News, in early July 2016 (Grynbaum and Koblin 2016). Ailes was accused of forcing Carlson out of Fox because she rejected his sexual advances and because she objected to repetitive sexual harassment in the Fox newsroom. On July 21, Ailes resigned as Fox News chairman and CEO (McShane 2016). Fox News then lost its most popular broadcast personality, Bill O'Reilly, in April of 2017 (Steele and Schmidt 2017) after allegations that he engaged in sexual harassment. Fox News was strongly criticized after an April 1, 2017, *New York Times* article revealed that it and its parent company, 21st Century Fox, had repeatedly supported O'Reilly through settlements with five women who had accused him of inappropriate behavior; the settlements totaled $13 million. More than fifty advertisers withdrew from O'Reilly's show, women's rights organizations demanded he be removed, and employees at Fox expressed concern that the company was insincere about the pledge it had made after the Ailes scandal that it would ensure a safe working environment for women. The Fox News scandals were soon followed by a deluge of rape and sexual harassment charges by numerous prominent actresses against famed Hollywood producer Harvey Weinstein. Weinstein was fired from his company in early October 2017 (Al Mukhtar, Gold, and Buchanan 2018). The successful toppling of these three powerful men spurred other women to come forward with stories of unpunished sexual aggression. Following the accusations against Harvey Weinstein, actress Alyssa Milano popularized the expression "Me Too" when she tweeted it and encouraged victims of sexual assault and harassment to come forward to "give people a sense of the magnitude of the problem" (Chuck 2017). With 24 hours of Milano's October 15, 2017, tweet, "Me Too" had been posted millions of times online through Facebook or Twitter, often with a personal story of sexual assault or harassment (Radu 2017). Messages came from eighty-five countries. The tremendous mobilization of women, men, institutions, and many private businesses in support of Me Too and the punishment of powerful men accused of repetitive sexual assault or harassment raised hope that a significant moral and cultural change was in progress. The goals are that more victims will be believed when they accuse perpetrators, that law enforcement and other institutions will be more effective in punishing offenders, that work environments will be safer, and that sexually aggressive behavior will decline.

Within a few months of the Weinstein firing and Milano's call for women to come forward, dozens of prominent men in the entertainment or news industries had been fired or forced to resign in the face of a wave of accusations of sexually inappropriate behavior (Al Mukhtar et al. 2018). In the U.S. Congress and in a number of state governments, demands were raised and legislation proposed to make it easier for women or men to bring forward charges of sexual assault and harassment (Davis 2017; O'Brien 2018).

What are your thoughts?
Do you feel that the Me Too movement will have a lasting effect in the United States or in other countries? Why or why not?

Politics and Government

American women have fought for political rights and social justice for themselves and other disadvantaged groups since the time of the American Revolution. They participated in the abolitionist movement to free the slaves and the labor union movement to win better conditions and wages for workers. And they demanded the right to vote and run for political office. Their determined efforts finally succeeded with the ratification of the 19th Amendment to the Constitution in 1920. But for decades women's roles in politics and government were limited. Several factors contributed to this situation. One was sexist prejudice against women holding political power. Another is the power of money in politics. The men who had high-income positions and wealth supported male candidates for political office. When women did try to run for political office, it was usually only after having and raising children. Entering politics at a later age meant that women could often run only for local- or state-level office. The modern women's movement helped open more opportunities for women in politics. In March 2017, 19 percent of the House of Representatives and 21 percent of the Senate were women (Center for American Women and Politics 2017; U.S. House of Representatives 2017a). Of the 83 women House members, 62 were Democrats and 21 were Republicans; of the 21 woman Senators, 16 were Democrats and 5 were Republicans. This meant that the United States ranked 104th among all nations in the proportion of national legislators who were women (Inter-Parliamentary Union 2017). The world average was about 23 percent for single-house parliaments or lower-house parliaments. While the five nations with the highest percentages of women in single-house parliaments or lower-house parliaments were Rwanda (61 percent), Bolivia (53 percent), Cuba (49 percent), Iceland (48 percent), and Nicaragua (46 percent), the Nordic countries had the highest regional average, about 42 percent. However, it is important to note that in 2017, dozens of countries (including Rwanda and Bolivia) had quota laws requiring that a set minimum percentage of candidates or, in some cases actual officeholders, be women. And in some countries' political parties set their own voluntary quotas for women candidates (Quota Project 2017). The results of the 2018 midterm elections meant that the 2019 House of Representatives would have an all time high of 102 women representatives (89 Democratic women representatives and 13 Republican women representatives), including 43 women of color (42 Democratic and 1 Republican). (Center for American Women and Politics 2018). And the 2019 Senate would have a new high of 24 women senators (17 Democratic women senators and 7 Republican women senators). This means the percent of women in Congress would climb from 20.6 percent in 2018 to 23.6 percent in 2019.

The highest-ranking women ever in the U.S. government include Speaker of the House Nancy Pelosi (2007–2011; 2019-) and Secretaries of State Madeleine Albright (1997–2001), Condoleezza Rice (2001–2005), and Hillary Clinton (2009–2013). Two women have been nominated for vice president, Democrat Geraldine Ferraro in 1984 and Republican Sarah Palin in 2008. Democrat Hillary Clinton was nominated for president in 2016. She won the national popular vote by 2.86 million but lost to the Republican candidate in the electoral college.

The Military

Men have long dominated armed forces around the world. Archeological research indicates, though, that in some nomadic cultures of central Asia (ancient Scythia), many women became effective warriors because proficiency at two key skills gave them equality with men in combat: horse riding and rapid, accurate use of bows and arrows from galloping steeds (Mayor 2014). Advanced weapons technology, such as jet fighters and missile-firing ships, submarines, and drones, has provided women with an even greater capability in modern combat.

Beginning with the American Revolution, increasing numbers of women participated in military campaigns as cooks, laundresses, and nurses. Some women became spies, and others disguised themselves as men to serve as combat soldiers (Abbott 2014; History.org 2016; Wood 2016). During World War I more than twelve thousand women enlisted as nurses and support staff in the military and four hundred died. Back in the United States, many women took over the work of men away in the armed forces becoming, for example, 24 percent of aircraft factory workers. In World War II, more than 350,000 women served in the U.S. military in noncombat roles such as nurses, ambulance drivers, pilots, mechanics, and administrative workers. Thousands more served in the Korean War and the Vietnam War. In 1976 women were finally admitted to the military service academies of the army, navy, and air force.

In 1991 Congress authorized women pilots to fly combat missions and during the 1991–1992 Persian Gulf War; around forty-one thousand women served in the combat zones. Later, women participated in the Afghan, Iraq, and anti-terrorism wars.

In 2015 there were approximately 165,000 enlisted women and 35,000 officers making up about 15 percent of U.S. military personnel. About 7 percent of all generals and admirals were women (CNN 2013a; Wood 2016). On December 3, 2015, Defense Secretary Ashton Carter announced that all combat roles would in the future be open to women (Lamothe 2015).

Despite the enormous progress women have made in the armed forces, they have been, as in other areas of work, often victimized by sexual harassment and sexual assault (Cox 2016a; U.S. Department of Defense 2016; Dick and Ziering 2012; Philipps 2014; Schemo 2003). Even at the country's elite military academies, sexual assault has been a problem. A survey by the inspector general of the Defense Department given to women who graduated from the U.S. Air Force Academy in May 2003 indicated that 12 percent of the female cadets had been the victims of rape or attempted rape at some time during their four years at the academy. The majority never reported their victimization to authorities. Women who had come forward in the past to report being assaulted claimed that the attackers were seldom punished. So other women came

Woman fighter pilot

to believe the rapists would be protected by male military authorities, whereas the rape victims who complained would be punished or even have their careers ended if they sought justice. There were charges that male officers and cadets who tried to expose cases of rape were also punished by military officials. The disclosures prompted some members of Congress to demand that sexual assault charges be investigated and adjudicated by civilian rather than military officials. But the process has been left in the hands of military officials who promised to do a better and fairer job in the future. The total number of sexual assaults reported to authorities at the service academies almost tripled between 2008 and 2015 (reaching 91 during the 2014–2015 academic year, with 80 women and 11 men making reports). Some believe that the increased reporting of sexual assault at the academies is not the result of increases in assault but rather increased faith that authorities will go after the rapists rather than punish the rape victims. The U.S. women's movement for equal political, economic, and social rights is described in the social movement special feature below.

Social Movements: The U.S. Women's Movement

U.S. women's movement demonstration

While the American Revolution was fought to establish the principle that "all men are created equal," women were not included. Women were not allowed to vote or hold government positions, or even own property if they were married. Higher educational opportunities were virtually nonexistent, and women were generally confined to household and farm chores and rearing children.

The country's need for better-educated citizens led to the training of women as teachers. In 1833 Oberlin College became the first coeducational college in the United States. Some women teachers, whose incomes allowed them to be economically independent of men, such as Susan B. Anthony, became organizers of the women's movement. Women's rights leaders organized the 1848 New York Seneca Falls Women's Rights Convention. Participants at Seneca Falls, including Elizabeth Cady Stanton, Lucretia Mott, and the African American abolitionist Frederick Douglas, called for women's rights to vote and hold political office. Following Seneca Falls, the movement for women's right to vote (the suffrage movement) grew rapidly. Activists moved from town to town educating people about the movement.

African American women's suffrage organizations, like Mary Shadd Cary's Colored Women's Progressive Franchise Association, founded in 1895, called for a universal suffrage amendment to allow all women to vote in all elections (Beeman 2006). In 1912 two white women activists, Alice Paul and Lucy Burns, introduced demonstration tactics and marches, including protests outside the White House, to gain the right to vote.

By the end of 1913, nine states, beginning with Colorado in 1893 and including Utah, Idaho, Washington, California, Kansas,

(continued)

Social Movements (*continued*)

Oregon, Arizona, and Illinois, gave women the right to vote. Finally, on June 4, 1919, Congress passed the 19th Amendment to the Constitution, giving all women the right to vote. It became law when ratified by the 36th state to do so, Tennessee, on August 18, 1920. Following ratification, white women's activism appeared to subside somewhat. But African American women activists played important roles in the ongoing women's movement and fighting for racial justice, such as integration of the armed forces in the late 1940s and the emergence of the modern civil rights movement in the early 1950s. The overall women's movement was re-energized by the publication in 1963 of Betty Friedan's *The Feminine Mystique*, in which she described the frustration of college-educated women confined to homemaking roles. Many women, awakened by Friedan's book, sought fulfillment through involvement in the civil rights and anti—Vietnam War movements. But they discovered that male activists in these movements were typically not very concerned with discrimination against women. In response, female activists formed new independent women's movement organizations. The most prominent was the National Organization for Women (NOW), created by college-educated and professional white women in 1966. NOW worked for pro-choice abortion rights legislation and for passage of the Equal Rights Amendment (ERA). Originally written by Alice Paul in 1923, the ERA states: "Equality of rights under the law shall not be denied or abridged by the United States or by any state on account of sex" (equalrightsamendment.org 2016). Though approved by Congress in 1972, the ERA was ratified by only thiry-five states and did not become law. In 1972 Congress also passed Title IX, which bans sex discrimination in any school educational program or activity receiving federal financial aid. As a result, women's enrollment in male-dominated academic areas and participation in sports dramatically increased. Another important achievement was the 1978 Pregnancy Discrimination Act, which banned employment discrimination against pregnant women.

The contemporary women's movement has several major branches. The liberal feminist branch aims for total equality of opportunity for women by removing barriers to full participation in all areas of society. The socialist feminist branch holds that capitalism is responsible for the oppression of women by oppressing large numbers of men and exploiting women's paid and unpaid labor. Exploited men take out their frustrations on women, making females the most oppressed people under capitalism. Replacing a harsh capitalistic system with a more socialist one would end deprivation, relieve economically generated frustration, and thus end oppression of women. The radical feminist branch sees male oppression of women as predating any particular political or economic system, so it is unlikely to be ended by simply removing institutional barriers to equal opportunity or by changing the economic system. Radical feminists disagree about what can actually be done to end patriarchy. Some believe that avoiding heterosexual relationships and creating exclusively female partnerships and living environments is the only way to escape male domination. Others suggest that modern technology may provide the means to reproduce children without pregnancy. This would eliminate the main characteristic of women that prevented them from more effectively competing with men and has been at the root of the traditional social construct of gender that underpins patriarchy. The women's movement in the United States and worldwide continues to struggle against injustice and for greater equality of opportunity and social and political rights.

What are your thoughts?

Do you believe there is still a need for a women's movement? What issues should the women's movement focus most of its attention on?

POPULATION ESTIMATES: LESBIAN, GAY, BISEXUAL, AND TRANSGENDER PERSONS

The actual number of gay, lesbian, bisexual, and transgender (LGBT) persons has been difficult to measure in social surveys. Many people answer a question about sexual orientation by giving the response they believe the interviewer expects to hear or considers acceptable

TABLE 6.2	Percentage of Population Lesbian, Gay, Bisexual, or Transgender: States and DC 2012				
States and DC	**LGBT %**	**States**	**LGBT%**	**States**	**LGBT%**
DC	10.0%	New Jersey	3.7%	West Virginia	3.1%
Hawaii	5.1%	Indiana	3.7%	Minnesota	2.9%
Vermont	4.9%	Kansas	3.7%	Virginia	2.9%
Oregon	4.9%	Ohio	3.6%	South Carolina	2.9%
Maine	4.8%	Georgia	3.5%	Wyoming	2.9%
Rhode Island	4.5%	Florida	3.5%	New Mexico	2.9%
Massachusetts	4.4%	Arkansas	3.5%	Wisconsin	2.8%
South Dakota	4.4%	Connecticut	3.4%	Iowa	2.8%
Nevada	4.2%	Delaware	3.4%	Alabama	2.8%
California	4.0%	Oklahoma	3.4%	Pennsylvania	2.7%
Washington	4.0%	Alaska	3.4%	Nebraska	2.7%
Kentucky	3.9%	Maryland	3.3%	Idaho	2.7%
Arizona	3.9%	Missouri	3.3%	Utah	2.7%
New York	3.8%	North Carolina	3.3%	Tennessee	2.6%
Michigan	3.8%	Texas	3.3%	Mississippi	2.6%
Illinois	3.8%	Louisiana	3.2%	Montana	2.6%
New Hampshire	3.7%	Colorado	3.2%	North Dakota	1.7%

Source: Gates and Newport 2013b.

(heterosexual) rather than their true sexual orientation. This is called "social desirability bias." Existing studies provide estimates that from 2.3 percent to about 8 percent of the U.S. population is LGBT. The CDC's National Health Interview Survey of 2013, which surveyed 33,557 adults between the ages of eighteen and sixty-four, found that 1.6 percent of respondents identified themselves as gay or lesbian and 0.7 percent as bisexual, while 96.6 percent labeled themselves as heterosexual, and 1.1 percent declined to answer, said "I don't know the answer," or said they were "something else" (Somashekhar 2014). However, a Gallup survey administered nationally in the summer of 2012 to 121,290 individuals found that 3.4 percent identified themselves as LGBT, with another 4.4 percent saying they "don't know" or just refusing to answer the question (Gates and Newport 2013a). This is similar to results of a number of earlier surveys with smaller samples. In an attempt to avoid social desirability bias, Coffman, Coffman, and Ericson (2013) showed that asking questions about sexuality in a way that more strongly assures respondents of total anonymity than more typical survey methods increased the percent of persons identifying themselves as nonheterosexual by about two-thirds. This suggests that the results obtained from most social surveys significantly underestimate the actual percentage of LGBT individuals. Despite the potential shortcomings of survey research on the size of the LGBT population, the large Gallup study permits estimates by states and metropolitan areas. The table below indicates that the highest percentage of persons self-identifying as LGBT was in the District of Columbia and lowest in the state of North Dakota.

Sexual orientation minorities may resettle in certain urban areas to escape prejudice. The table below shows the twenty-six of the largest fifty U.S. metropolitan areas with 4 percent or more of their populations identifying as LGBT in the Gallup Daily Tracking Survey of 374,000 respondents administered during June 2012–December 2014.

Of the fifty largest metropolitan areas, the three with the lowest LBGT percentages in 2012–2014 were Memphis, TN-MS-AR (3.1%), Pittsburgh, PA (3.0%), and Birmingham-Hoover, AL (2.6%).

WHAT CAUSES SEXUAL ORIENTATION?

A number of explanations have been offered for differences in sexual orientation (American Psychological Association 2008; Cornuelle and Pillard 2010; Långström et al. 2010; Reiss 2016; van Anders 2015; Wilson and Widom 2010). Some are biological, ranging from brain characteristics, to hormonal differences at specific stages of development, to various aspects of genes, or even birth order. Others focus on family factors like the relationship between child and mother or between child and father. Another type of explanation is that sexual abuse during childhood might affect sexual orientation in some people. And a further theory is that culture and learning experiences through interaction with other people can have an

TABLE 6.3	Metropolitan Areas with 4 Percent or More of Their Populations Lesbian, Gay, Bisexual, or Transgender: 2012–2014 Gallup Tracking Survey	
San Francisco-Oakland-Hayward, CA		6.2%
Portland-Vancouver-Hillsboro, OR-WA		5.4%
Austin-Round, TX		5.3%
New Orleans-Metairie, LA		5.1%
Seattle-Tacoma-Bellevue, WA		4.8%
Boston-Cambridge-Newton, MA-NH		4.8%
Salt Lake City, UT		4.7%
Los Angeles-Long Beach-Anaheim, CA		4.6%
Denver-Aurora-Lakewood, CO		4.6%
Hartford-West Hartford-East Hartford, CT		4.6%
Louisville/Jefferson County, KY-IN		4.5%
Virginia Beach-Norfolk-Newport News, VA-NC		4.4%
Providence-Warwick, RI-MA		4.4%
Las Vegas-Henderson-Paradise, NV		4.3%
Columbus, OH		4.3%
Jacksonville, FL		4.3%
Miami-Fort Lauderdale-West Palm Beach, FL		4.2%
Indianapolis-Carmel-Anderson, IN		4.2%
Atlanta-Sandy Springs-Roswell, GA		4.2%
Orlando-Kissimmee-Sanford, FL		4.1%
Tampa-St. Petersburg-Clearwater, FL		4.1%
Phoenix-Mesa-Scottsdale, AZ		4.1%
New York-Newark-Jersey City, NY-NJ-PA		4.0%
San Antonio-New Braunfels, TX		4.0%
Washington-Arlington-Alexandria, DC-VA-MD-WV		4.0%
Riverside-San Bernardino-Ontario, CA		4.0%

Source: Newport and Gates 2015.

impact on sexual orientation. Some even argue that sexual orientation is a matter of choice. While there is disagreement over these ideas, it seems clear that those who believe that sexual orientation is due to biology tend to be more supportive of equal civil, economic, legal, and political rights for nonheterosexuals, whereas those who feel that sexual orientation is more due to learning experiences or to free choice tend to be less supportive (Haider-Markel and Mark 2008). A national Gallup poll in 2014 found that 42 percent of the adults surveyed said they believed that people are gay because they were born gay, while 37 percent believed being gay is the result of factors such as upbringing and environment (McCarthy 2014a). In comparison, when Gallup first asked about beliefs on the origin of same-sex orientation in 1977, only 13 percent of those surveyed said being gay was a characteristic people were born with; 56 percent said being gay was the result of upbringing and environment. People with college educations, high-income persons, Democrats, liberals, those who seldom attend church, and women were more likely to express the belief that being lesbian or gay is something with which people are born.

CULTURAL BIAS AGAINST LGBT

Many Americans have been influenced by culture and other learning experiences to be *heterosexist* and *homophobic*. *Heterosexism* refers to the belief that heterosexuality is the inherently normative and superior sexual orientation and to any act or omission that discriminates against nonheterosexuals. *Homophobia* is an umbrella term to refer to negative feelings and attitudes toward persons who are perceived to be LGBT, as well as the belief that homosexuality and *transgender identity* are inherently deviant. *Transphobia* refers to negative feelings, attitudes, and discrimination specifically toward transgender people or persons with gender ambiguity.

Religion

Many religions, though not all, support heterosexism, and some foster homophobia. In the United States, people who attend religious services frequently tend in general to be less favorable toward homosexuality (Pew Research Center 2014a). Conservative Protestant churches, the Catholic Church, Orthodox Judaism, and Islam all ban engaging in homosexual activity. However, there are great differences among the members of American religious groups in attitudes toward homosexuality. The figure below shows the percent of Americans of different religions surveyed in 2011 who opposed allowing gays and lesbians to marry legally.

The United Church of Christ, the U.S. Presbyterian Church and the Evangelical Lutheran Church in America have adopted the most accepting attitudes toward homosexuality (Religious Tolerance.org 2016). Many congregations within the Society of Friends (Quakers) also have an accepting view of same-sex relations.

Family and Peers

People's attitudes toward homosexuality and transgender identity tend to be influenced by those of their parents (Cossman 2004; Raiz 2006). The more parents' express heterosexism and homophobia, the more likely their children are to do the same. Children also tend to reflect their friends' attitudes toward LGBT persons. Males are more homophobic than females, especially toward male homosexuality (Kite and Whitley 1996; LaMar and Kite 1998). In a survey based on a national sample of 1,065 elementary students in 3rd to 6th grades and 1,099 elementary school teachers of kindergarten to 6th grade, 45 percent of students reported that they hear other kids saying "that's so gay" or "you're so gay" often or all the time, and 49 percent of teachers said they hear students use the word "gay" in a negative way sometimes, often, or very often. In addition, 26 percent of students and teachers in the survey also reported hearing students use homophobic words like "fag" or "lesbo" at least sometimes (GLSEN 2012). Boys and men often insult each other not only by calling each other "girls," "ladies," "pussies," or "bitches," but also by hurling labels like "homo," "gay," "fag," "faggot," "queer," "punk," or "sissy" (Kimmel 2008). This is part of what Michael S. Kimmel calls the "guy code," in which males assert masculinity by crudely accusing others of femininity or homosexuality (2008:44–69). The emotional stress felt by boys who are the repeated targets of these kinds of taunts has sometimes resulted in suicidal thoughts or acts of violence in revenge. Family and peers are the immediate elements of social environment that implant and reinforce the cultural tradition of heterosexism and culturally embedded homophobia or impart more accepting attitudes in children. Considering institutional discrimination toward LGBT people, family acceptance of LGBT family members can

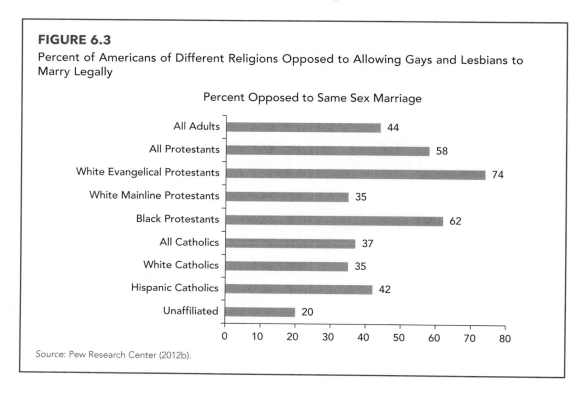

FIGURE 6.3

Percent of Americans of Different Religions Opposed to Allowing Gays and Lesbians to Marry Legally

Percent Opposed to Same Sex Marriage

All Adults	44
All Protestants	58
White Evangelical Protestants	74
White Mainline Protestants	35
Black Protestants	62
All Catholics	37
White Catholics	35
Hispanic Catholics	42
Unaffiliated	20

Source: Pew Research Center (2012b).

have a very significant effect for the well-being of LGBT people. According to a survey of 6,450 transgender and gender nonconforming persons (Grant et al. 2011), 57% experienced significant family rejection, while 43% maintained their family ties. Those who were rejected by their family were far more likely to attempt suicide (51%), experience homelessness (26%), and use drugs or alcohol (32%) compared to those who were accepted by their family (32%, 9%, and 19%, respectively).

Schools and Media

Schools and the mass media long avoided coverage of homosexuality or the contributions to society throughout history of people with same-sex orientation. This has left many heterosexual persons ignorant of homosexuality for much of their lives and vulnerable to accepting negative stereotypes of gays and lesbians when they did learn about people with same-sex orientation. The gay and lesbian rights movement, more inclusive coverage of gays and lesbian figures in schools in some parts of the country (CNN 2011), and the explosion of TV shows in the 1990s onward century featuring gay or lesbian hosts and stars helped reshape culture and public opinion toward a more positive view. Transgender issues became more visible partially due to the success of shows like *Orange is the New Black*, in which Laverne Cox, a transgender activist, portrayed a male-to-female transgender character. Change in attitudes toward the rights of gays and lesbians has been dramatic. While in 1996 only 27 percent of U.S. adults supported legalization of same-sex marriage, the percentage rose to 58 percent in 2015 (Gallup 2016). Many LGBT persons also feel that things have improved. Ninety-two percent of over eleven hundred LGBT adults in a national survey stated they believed that over the last ten years society has become more accepting of LGBT persons (Pew Research Center 2013).

INSTITUTIONAL (STRUCTURAL) BIAS AGAINST LGBT

LGBT persons have historically been denied equal rights and suffered harassment and discrimination. In the national survey of LGBT adults cited above, 58%stated that at some point in their lives they had been victimized by slurs or jokes because of sexual orientation or gender identity, 39% said that they experienced rejection by a relative or friend, 30% said they had been physically assaulted or threatened, 29% said say they had been made to feel unwelcome at a place of religious worship, and 21% said they had experienced unfair treatment by an employer (Pew Research Center 2013). The study of the 6,450 transgender and gender nonconforming people mentioned earlier found that 41% of the participants reported attempting suicide, 61% experienced being physically assaulted, and 64% experienced being sexually assaulted. Nine out of ten respondents also reported experiencing harassment or mistreatment on the job or took actions like hiding who they are to avoid mistreatment in the workplace. This study found that discrimination was even more devastating for transgender people of color (Grant et al. 2011). Major strides have been made to breakdown heterosexist institutional barriers, but more is needed to achieve full equality for LGBT people.

Family

In many states same-sex orientation persons were not allowed to legally marry. This changed when the Supreme Court ruled in the summer of 2015 that the Constitution guarantees same-sex couples the right to marry anywhere in the United States. However, only nine states give LGBT persons the same adoption rights as heterosexuals (Human Rights Campaign 2016a).

Education

Students are more likely to do well academically if they feel the school environment is safe and free from threats, intimidation and harassment. But many students who identify as LGBT have often been victimized at their schools from the early grades by other students' use of homophobic language, shoving, or even physical attacks (National Education Administration 2015). Children subjected to this type of harassment and bullying are much more prone to becoming depressed or suicidal, involved in alcohol or other drug use, carrying a weapon to school, being truant, or totally dropping out of school. Though harassment of LGBT students appears to have declined in many schools (Hammond 2013), it remains a serious problem, meriting efforts from teachers and school administrators to make schools more secure and comfortable for all students.

Work

Disclosure of sexual orientation can endanger friendships or respect of coworkers, prevent promotion, or even result in being fired. But public opinion polls show that about three-quarters of Americans oppose job discrimination against LGBT persons (Krehely 2011; Toumayan 2015). In 2014 President Obama signed an executive order forbidding discrimination against LGBT persons working for the federal government or for businesses contracting work from the federal government (Bendery 2014). The measure makes it illegal to harass or fire employees of federal contractors because of their sexual orientation or gender identity. The federal contractors' aspect of the executive order affected about twenty-four thousand businesses with approximately twenty-eight million workers, nearly 20 percent of the U.S. workforce in 2014.

Twenty states and the District of Columbia have laws banning job discrimination against LGBT persons, but eighteen states have no law against harassment, discrimination, or the firing of LGBT persons (Human Rights Campaign 2016b). Other states are in between, with some barring discrimination only for same-sex orientation but not transgender persons or outlawing LGBT discrimination only for state government jobs but not for the private sector.

Politics, Government, and the Military

Besides the United States, a number of northern and western European countries, and several in South America, such as Brazil, Argentina, and Uruguay, have legal same-sex marriage. But more than seventy countries have laws against homosexuality. Most are in Africa, the Middle East, or southern Asia (Erasing76crimes.com 2015). Many use imprisonment and some capital punishment. According to Terri Rupar (2014), the death penalty for homosexuality can be imposed in at least five countries: Iran, Mauritania, Saudi Arabia, Sudan, and Yemen.

Worldwide, LGBT persons have been elected to political office in more than forty-five countries. In the United States, Kathy Kozachenko became the first openly same-sex orientation person to be elected to public office by winning a seat on the Ann Arbor, Michigan, city council in 1974. Since then openly gay politicians have been elected to city, state, and federal government positions. As noted earlier, on November 7, 2012, seven-term Wisconsin Democratic congresswoman Tammy Baldwin became the first openly gay person to be elected to the U.S. Senate.

People with a same-sex orientation were historically barred from the U.S. armed forces. But by 2009, gays were allowed to serve in the militaries of more than twenty countries, including Austria, Belgium, Canada, the Czech Republic, Estonia, Finland, France, Ireland, Israel, Italy, Lithuania, Netherlands, New Zealand, Norway, Slovenia, South Africa, Spain, Sweden, Switzerland, and the United Kingdom (Palm Center 2009). Finally, in 2010 the U.S. Senate voted to allow lesbians and gays to openly serve in the armed forces and President Obama signed the bill into law (Associated Press 2010).

Social Movements: The Gay and Lesbian Rights Movement

Gay and lesbian rights movement demonstrators

The gay and lesbian rights movement's cultural goals include eliminating homophobia, expanding acceptance of family types beyond the traditional heterosexual nuclear family, and transforming traditional social constructions of masculinity and femininity (Bernstein 2002). The movement's political and economic goals include gaining equal legal rights and protection from discrimination.

Henry Gerber organized the first American gay rights organization, the Society for Human Rights, in Chicago in 1924, publishing the *Friendship and Freedom* newsletter, the first U.S. publication for homosexuals. But the society was soon shut down because most government and religious leaders, as well as the majority of the public, strongly opposed homosexuality, and many viewed it as a moral failing that could spread if not suppressed.

Alfred Kinsey's research in his 1948 *Sexual Behavior in the Human Male* revealed, however, that millions of men, far more than most Americans thought, engaged in homosexual relations. This finding conflicted with the traditional stereotype that homosexuality was confined to a small deviant minority. One of those influenced by Kinsey's work, Harry Hays, left the American Communist Party and in 1950 founded the Mattachine Society in Los Angeles, the first national gay rights organization. The group's goals included improving the public's attitudes toward

Social Movements (*continued*)

homosexuals and gaining complete access for homosexuals to mainstream American society. Yet the American Psychiatric Association, in its 1952 *Diagnostic and Statistical Manual of Mental Disorders*, described homosexuality as a sociopathic personality disturbance and in the early 1950s hundreds of homosexuals were dismissed from government jobs as security risks (Burton 2015; Goldfarb 2018; PBS 2011, 2013b).

In 1955 the first U.S. lesbian rights organization, the Daughters of Bilitis, was founded in San Francisco. The following year Evelyn Hooker's research paper "The Adjustment of the Male Overt Homosexual" indicated that homosexual and heterosexual males were clinically similar. In 1958 the U.S. Supreme Court issued its first decision in favor of homosexuals, ruling that publication of the LGBT magazine *One: The Homosexual Magazine* was protected by the First Amendment. But throughout the United States, actually engaging in homosexual activity was a crime. This changed when Illinois decriminalized homosexuality by repealing its sodomy laws in 1962.

Inspired by African American sit-ins at all-white lunch counters in 1960, Mattachine Society members protested against the New York Liquor Commission's ban on serving homosexuals by holding a "sip-in" at the Greenwich Village's Julius Bar in 1966. The New York City Commission on Human Rights then declared that homosexuals should be served. That same year, after a confrontation between transgender customers and police at an all-night San Francisco diner, activists founded the National Transsexual Counseling Unit, the first peer-run advocacy and support organization of its kind in the world. Then, on June 28, 1969, customers at the Stonewall Inn in Greenwich Village rioted when police raided it around one o'clock in the morning. The popular gay tavern had been repeatedly raided by police since its opening in 1967 in an effort to remove supposed sexual deviants from the area. The three-day Stonewall rebellion re-energized the gay rights movement

and is seen as the beginning of the modern LGBT movement. The Gay Liberation Front was formed immediately after Stonewall and fought for greater LGBT visibility and political power through diverse tactics such as the "coming out" campaign. On June 28, 1970, Stonewall was commemorated by a march, considered the first gay pride parade, in New York City. Annual gay pride parades soon spread to other cities.

The American Psychiatric Association removed homosexuality from its list of mental disorders on December 15, 1973. The following January, Kathy Kozachenko won a seat on the Ann Arbor City Council, becoming the first openly gay person elected to public office in the United States. On November 8, 1977, openly gay activist Harvey Milk was elected to the San Francisco Board of Supervisors. He introduced an ordinance to protect gays and lesbians from being fired from their jobs and led the successful effort to defeat a proposed ban on homosexual teachers in California, Proposition 6.

But on November 27, 1978, Dan White, a former city supervisor, assassinated Milk and Mayor George Mascone. Convicted of voluntary manslaughter, White received only a seven-year sentence, provoking outrage and a series of protests called the "White Night Riots." (In 2008 the critically acclaimed movie about Milk's life and accomplishments, *Milk*, won more support for the movement.) Milk's assassination spurred seventy-five thousand people to participate in the National March on Washington for Lesbian and Gay Rights on October 14, 1979. The Democrats in August 1980 put forth the first major party platform supporting homosexual rights, and in 1982 Wisconsin became the first state to ban discrimination based on sexual orientation.

The AIDS epidemic brought many LGBT people into the political process because of the feeling that the Reagan administration was ignoring it. On March 10, 1987, New Yorkers concerned about the spreading AIDS epidemic created ACT UP (AIDS Coalition to Unleash Power) that staged demonstrations

(*continued*)

Social Movements (*continued*)

against pharmaceutical companies they believed profiteered from selling high-priced AIDS drugs to desperate patients. Then on October 11 hundreds of thousands demanded effective action to deal with AIDS. During this second National March on Washington for Lesbian and Gay Rights, the Names Project AIDS Memorial Quilt was displayed for the first time on the D.C. National Mall. The quilt, composed of hundreds of panels commemorating individual AIDS victims, covered a space larger than a football field (Names Project Foundation 2016). In 1988, the CDC mailed a brochure, *Understanding AIDS*, to every U.S. household, and in 1990 President George H. W. Bush signed a law providing federal assistance to AIDS victims. The next year, the New York-based Visual AIDS organization adopted the red ribbon as a sign of support for HIV/AIDS victims. The red ribbon became a prominent symbol of the movement. The CDC (2015b) claims that approximately 658,507 Americans have died from AIDS and that 1,218,400 persons aged thirteen years and older are living with HIV.

The Department of Defense in 1993 prohibited the military from rejecting applicants based simply on their sexual orientation. But it forbad engaging in homosexual acts or an applicant making a statement that he or she is a homosexual. This was known as the "Don't Ask, Don't Tell" policy. Three years later President Bill Clinton signed the Defense of Marriage Act (DOMA) that proclaimed no state was required to recognize a same-sex marriage performed in another state. In 1998 Coretta Scott King, widow of Martin Luther King Jr., called on activists in the civil rights movement to join the fight against homophobia. The Ellen DeGeneres Show began in 2003, and its success indicated that Americans were becoming more accepting of gay and lesbian celebrities.

Vermont became the first state to legalize civil unions between same-sex couples in 2000, and in 2003 the Supreme Court ruled

that sodomy laws are unconstitutional. Then on March 18, 2004, Massachusetts became the first state to legalize gay marriage. New Hampshire, Vermont, Connecticut, Iowa, and Washington D.C. soon followed. But in 2008 anti-gay activists succeeded in convincing the majority of California voters to approve Proposition 8, making same-sex marriage illegal in that state.

Responding to outrage at anti-gay crimes such as the torture and murder of Matthew Shepard in Laramie, Wyoming, in 1998, Congress expanded the 1969 Federal Hate Crime Law in 2009 to include crimes motivated by a victim's actual or perceived gender, sexual orientation, gender identity, or disability. The next year a federal judge in San Francisco ruled Proposition 8 unconstitutional and that gays and lesbians have the right to marry. And in 2010 the U.S. Senate voted 65–31 to repeal the "Don't Ask, Don't Tell" policy, allowing gays and lesbians to serve openly in the U.S. armed forces (Associated Press. 2010). By the end of 2011 the gay rights movement succeeded in shifting public opinion in favor legalizing same-sex marriage (Pew Research Center 2017). Two dozen more states had legalized same-sex marriage. Then on June 26, 2015, same-sex marriage became legal throughout the United States when the Supreme Court ruled that state laws against it were unconstitutional.

Many states still did not provide a full range of rights or protections for LGBT people in areas such as employment discrimination, housing discrimination, or prevention of harassment in schools based on sexual orientation or gender identity (*Guardian* 2016). The LGBT rights movement continued to fight for equal rights.

Ask yourself:

Have you ever witnessed harassment or bullying of an LGBT person? What do you think was the most crucial factor in the growth of the LGBT rights movement?

Sex, Gender, and Sexual Orientation

Sex refers to the concept of being biologically (physically) male or female. The concept of gender, in comparison, refers to the understanding that people have for what it means to be a male or female in their particular culture or social group. It is a social construct, meaning that it is the product of learning and social interaction. Gender binary is the cultural belief that men and women have distinct personality traits, capabilities, and strengths and weaknesses. Gender identity refers to how one's sense of gender corresponds to biological sex characteristics.

When a person's gender identity is the same as the sex identity assigned at birth, the person has a cisgender identity. But a person whose sense of gender is the opposite of her or his physical sex characteristics has a transgender identity. Cisnormativity refers to the individual or institutional assumption that everyone is cisgender and cisgender identities are superior to transgender identities. Sexism refers to prejudice or discrimination against a person on the basis of sex or gender identity. It is usually based on the belief that one sex or gender identity is naturally superior. Doing gender is displaying masculinity or femininity through attitudes, traits, clothing, symbols, and behaviors that represent the gender a person wants to present to others.

Sexual orientation refers to a person's sexual attraction and/or emotional-romantic attraction to persons of the opposite sex (heterosexual orientation), same sex (homosexual orientation), or both sexes (bisexual orientation). A person can also feel sexual and romantic attraction to people of any sex or gender identity (*pansexual orientation*), or a person can have a lack of sexual attraction to others or desire for sex (*asexual orientation*). Heteronormativity is the individual or institutional assumption that everyone is heterosexual and heterosexual orientation is superior to other sexual orientations. Coming out refers to the process of identifying and accepting one's own sexual orientation or gender identity (coming out to oneself) and of publicly acknowledging it to others (coming out to others).

Sociological Perspectives on Gender and Sexual Orientation Inequality

The structural-functional perspective views both traditional gender roles and heterosexuality as functional for society. The conflict approach holds that heterosexual male power, including control over the economy and government, and traditional culture fostered prejudice and discrimination against both women and nonheterosexuals. The symbolic-interactionist perspective emphasizes interpersonal interaction, learning experiences, and labeling in analyzing the causes and effects of gender inequality and sexual orientation inequality.

Gender Inequality and Discrimination

Cultural sexism refers to how elements of culture, including traditions, stereotypes, values, norms, and symbols, promote the idea that one sex or gender identity is inherently superior. Institutional (structural) sexism refers to how society and its institutions are organized to privilege or discriminate against persons on the basis of their sex or gender identity.

Cultural Sexism: Sexist Traditions, Stereotypes, Values, Norms, and Symbols

Children generally first learn their culture's concepts of gender roles in the family from things like the types of toys they are given. Later, in elementary school, they are often exposed to traditional gender stereotypes in picture books and are influenced by teachers' different expectations for girls and boys. Certain aspects of language, such as specific words and the ways in which they are used, convey the message that men are, in certain ways, superior to women and reinforce traditional gender stereotypes. Mass media has tended to portray women as sex objects.

Institutional Sexism

Although significant progress has been made, institutional sexism is reflected by continuing biases against women in certain areas of postgraduate education and male domination of scientific occupations, managerial and executive jobs, and positions of influence in organized religion. Women have made great strides in government but still comprise less than one quarter of the U.S. Congress. In the armed forces sexual assault is a major problem, but military officials appear to be taking more effective steps to prevent it, and modern technology has facilitated a wider role for women in combat.

Population Estimates: Lesbian, Gay, Bisexual, and Transgender Persons

Existing studies provide estimates that from 2.3 percent to about 8 percent of the U.S. population is LGBT. The percentage of people self-identifying as LGBT varies significantly around the country. Sexual orientation minorities may resettle in certain urban areas to escape prejudice.

What Causes Sexual Orientation?

A number of explanations have been offered for differences in sexual orientation. Some are biological, ranging from brain characteristics to hormonal differences at specific stages of development, to various aspects of genes, or even birth order. Others focus on family factors like the relationship between child and mother or between child and father. Another type of explanation is that sexual abuse during childhood might affect sexual orientation in some people. And a further theory is that culture and learning experiences through interaction with other people can have an impact on sexual orientation. Some even argue that sexual orientation is a matter of choice. People with college educations, high-income persons, Democrats, liberals, those who seldom attend church, and women are more likely to express the belief that being lesbian or gay is something with which people are born.

Cultural Bias against LGBT

Heterosexism refers to the belief that heterosexuality is the inherently normative and superior sexual orientation and to discrimination against nonheterosexuals. *Homophobia* is an umbrella term to refer to negative feelings and attitudes toward persons who are perceived to be lesbian, gay, bisexual, or transgender as well as the belief that homosexuality and transgender identity are inherently deviant. *Transphobia* refers to negative feelings, attitudes, and discrimination specifically toward transgender people or persons with gender ambiguity.

While some religious groups have become more accepting of gays and lesbians, major religions continue to oppose homosexuality. Family and peers are key elements of the social environment influencing attitudes toward LGBT persons, as are schools and the mass media. Overall public opinion surveys indicate that most people have become more supportive of equal rights for LGBT persons.

Institutional (Structural) Bias against LGBT

LGBT persons have historically been denied equal rights and suffered harassment and discrimination. In many states, same-sex persons were not allowed to legally marry. This changed when the Supreme Court ruled in the summer of 2015 that the Constitution guarantees same-sex couples the right to marry anywhere in the United States. Many students who identify as LGBT have often been victimized at their schools from early grades onward by other students' use of homophobic language, shoving, or even physical attacks Though harassment of LGBT students appears to have declined in many schools, it remains a serious problem.

Disclosure of sexual orientation may endanger one's job or prevent promotion. But public opinion polls show that about three-quarters of Americans oppose job discrimination against LGBT persons. Many teachers and school administrators have sought to make the school environment more secure and comfortable for LGBT students. The Obama administration acted in 2014 to protect LGBT persons who work for the federal government or its contractors from discrimination based on sexual orientation or gender identity. But many states do not provide similar protection. Congress has allowed people of same-sex orientation to serve openly in the armed forces, and increasing numbers of LGBT persons are being elected to political office. But legislatures and governors in several states oppose further measures on behalf of LGBT persons.

KEY TERMS

cisgender identity, p. 140
cisnormativity, p. 140
coming out, p. 140
doing gender, p. 140
gender, p. 139
gender binary, p. 139
gender identity, p. 140

glass ceiling, p. 153
heteronormativity, p. 140
sex, p. 139
sexism, p. 140
sexual orientation, p. 140
transgender identity, p. 140

DISCUSSION QUESTIONS

1. Do you think sexism is a significant problem in the United States today? What about at your college?

2. Which sociological perceptive do you think best explains gender inequality in the United States? Why?

3. Do you think that gender equality in jobs, income, and politics will ever be achieved in the United States? Why or why not?

4. Do you think prejudice based on sexual orientation is a significant problem at your college? If yes, in what way?

5. Why do you think attitudes toward LGBT persons became much more accepting and positive in the twenty-first century?

6. Do you think that that discrimination against people on the basis of sexual orientation will ever be eliminated in the United States? Why or why not?

CHAPTER 7

The Family

CHAPTER OBJECTIVES

- Explain the different types and concepts of marriage and family worldwide.
- Describe how marriage and the family have changed overtime in the United States.
- Describe family-related social problems such as intimate partner violence, child abuse, and elder abuse, and the causes and prevention of violence in the family.

- Describe family-related social movements such as the movement for the legalization of same-sex marriage and the child protection movement.
- Describe trends in unwed parenthood and efforts to reduce teen pregnancy.
- Explain how technologically advanced nations provide assistance to families.

IN 2011 A BRUTAL CIVIL WAR broke out in Syria between the government and opposition groups ranging from prodemocracy activists to Islamic fundamentalist extremists. The conflict continued year after year, causing the deaths of an estimated 250,000 people and the flight of millions from their homes, jobs, schools, and communities. Parents lost the ability to protect, support, and plan for the future of their children. Seeking a new life, more than two million fled to refugee camps in Lebanon, Jordan, Turkey, Macedonia, and Iraqi Kurdistan. Many applied to enter European nations, the United States, or Canada. Hundreds of thousands struck out illegally in the desperate hope of reaching nations like Germany or Sweden that offered asylum. The world was shocked by images of fathers and mothers carrying their children and meager supplies as they marched hundreds of miles, and their tearful confrontations with border guards and soldiers who repeatedly attempted to block their way in the greatest European refugee crisis since World War II.

Many Syrian families have been torn apart (UNHCR 2013). Thousands of refugee children fled with only one parent, usually their mother, and some with neither. In some cases, one or both parents had been killed or imprisoned. In others, parents were unable to leave for reasons such as the care of older relatives and sent their children away to avoid being drafted into the Syrian military or forced to join anti-government fighters. Sometimes a son was sent ahead of the rest of family to find a job and a place to live.

By the end of 2015, the United States had accepted about two thousand Syrian war refugees. The process of resettlement, which begins after the United States receives a United Nations High Commission for Refugees' family referral, can take up to 18–24 months. Once arrived, the State Department's Reception and Placement Program provides a family with financial support for rent, clothing, food and other necessities for a period of 30 to 90 days (Novacic 2015). But resistance in the United States grew to allowing in more refugees because a portion of the population feared some might be terrorists. This was illustrated by a case in 2015 in which refugee-settlement workers in Indianapolis received a letter from the governor Mike Pence blocking a Syrian refugee family of three, a father, mother and five-year-old son, the day before they were supposed to arrive. In response, the governor of Connecticut, Dannell Malloy, stepped forward and arranged for the family to be settled in his state instead (Tan 2015). The plight of Syrian refugee families provides a modern example of parents fleeing the horrors and devastation of war striving desperately to protect the welfare and future of their children.

WHAT IS A FAMILY?

Definitions and conceptions of what constitutes a **family** vary among cultures and have changed over time. The U.S. census, for example, defines a family as "two or more people related by birth, marriage, or adoption residing in the same housing unit" (U.S. Census 2011a). This is a rather narrow definition useful for compiling census statistics. However, in one sense it is nontraditional because it does not specify anything about gender and thus would include same-sex couples as families. Another important census term, **household**, is defined differently; a household consists of "all people who occupy a housing unit regardless of relationship. A household may consist of a person living alone or multiple unrelated individuals or families living together" (U.S. Census 2011a). But what is a useful definition of family for Census statistical purposes may not satisfy other institutions or large sectors of the population.

Most religious institutions have historically supported the concept that a family is formed through the marriage of a woman and a man and expands with the children they give birth to or adopt. And this is the way family was legally defined by all U.S. states and the federal government. But in 2004 Massachusetts legalized same-sex marriage when its supreme court ruled that banning such marriages violated the Constitution. Connecticut's supreme court made a similar ruling in 2008. Vermont was the first state to legalize same-sex marriage by legislative action in 2009. Same-sex marriage was eventually legalized in a total of thirty-six states and the District of Columbia by court rulings, legislative action, or popular vote. Then on June 26, 2015, the U.S. Supreme Court ruled five to four in *Obergefell v. Hodges* that same-sex couples have the constitutional right to marry throughout the United States (Stohr 2015).

Leading up to this ruling, public opinion had shifted dramatically. While in 2005 58 percent of Americans opposed legalizing same-sex marriage versus 39 percent in favor, by 2015 this reversed with 61 percent in favor of allowing gay marriage and 35 percent opposed (Clement and Barnes 2015). Similarly, public opinion about what constitutes a family has shifted to a more inclusive view. By 2010 a national survey showed that 92 percent said that a husband and wife living together without kids was a family, 40 percent said that an unmarried man and woman living together without kids was a family, and 33 percent said that a gay male couple living together without kids was a family (Berman and Francis 2010). But add kids to each of these situations and the percentages rise to 99.8 percent, 83 percent, and 64 percent, respectively. In addition, 60 percent stated that if you considered yourself a family, then you were a family.

The idea of family for most people implies that the members care for one another and cooperate for mutual benefit. The traditional conception of family was based on **kinship**. Kinship refers to being related to another person through common ancestry (sharing common DNA) or marriage or adoption. But most Americans have expanded their conception of family to include unmarried opposite-sex or same-sex

family A group of two or more people who are recognized by others as a family and identify themselves as a family.

household All people who occupy a housing unit together regardless of relationship.

kinship Being related to another person through common ancestry (sharing common DNA) or marriage or adoption.

couples who are living together and raising children. And a smaller majority includes groups of people who simply think of themselves as a family. Considering all these views, an acceptably broad modern sociological definition of family would be a group of two or more people who are recognized by others as a family and identify themselves as a family.

FAMILIES AND MARRIAGE AROUND THE WORLD

The expression *nuclear family* (also called elementary family) in its original sense refers to two parents and their children. More recently some sociologists have preferred to expand the concept to also include single parents and their children. In comparison, the expression *extended family* includes the nuclear family plus other relatives such as grandparents, aunts, uncles, and first cousins.

In many countries, especially those with weak governments, even further extended kinship networks, *clans* and *tribes*, play important social and even economic and political roles (DeFronzo 2010). A clan (or sub-tribe) includes both close relatives and more distant relatives such as second, third, and fourth cousins. "Tribe" typically refers to a set of clans characterized by a belief that they are related by blood kinship and descended from a common ancestor. In kinship-based organizations, certain members are recognized as having authority over other members. For example, the leader of an Arab tribe (called a sheik, Arabic for a man of old age) is often asked to mediate disputes. In places or at times when the government is unable to provide important functions and services such as policing, courts, security, or social assistance, people have often relied on their clans or tribes for help.

An American nuclear family

Family Authority Types

patriarchal family
Families in which the father has the greatest influence in making decisions for the family and its members.

The vast majority of the world's nations are dominated by the **patriarchal family** type. In such families the father has the greatest influence in making decisions for the family and its members. But the degree of paternal dominance varies significantly. It tends to be lower where laws support mothers' rights and where mothers have their own careers outside the household and contribute significantly to family finances. The **egalitarian family** type is a family in which the partners have equal influence in decision making and share equally in family-centered activity such as child-rearing and housework. While this appears the major family type in the United States, many studies show that in reality women still do most child care and housework in addition to their jobs. International assessments of gender equality indicate that the patriarchal family type is least prominent in Scandinavian countries, but more dominant in certain Muslim nations (World Economic Forum 2015).

egalitarian family families in which the partners have equal influence in decision making and share equally in family-centered activity such as child-rearing and housework.

matriarchal family
Families that are mother centered and in which the mother has the greatest influence.

The **matriarchal family** type, in contrast, is mother centered, with the mother having the greatest influence. But this type is rare. Small groups, including the Bribri in Costa Rica (about 13,000 people), Mosuo in China (about 40,000), the Garo in India and Bangladesh (about two million), and the Minangkabau of West Sumatra, Indonesia (about five million), have some of the qualities of matriarchy such as land or other property belonging to the mother and passed down along the mother's line to daughters (Maps of the World 2015). But usually men still dominate these societies outside the family.

forced marriage
Marriages in which one or both persons do not giving free consent to marry but are instead forced into the marriage by third parties, such as parents or religious leaders.

Types of Marriage

polygamous marriage
Marriage to two or more spouses.

There are various types of marriage around the world. Some categories are not mutually exclusive. For example, a **forced marriage** can also be a **polygamous marriage**.

Arranged marriage

Selection of Marital Partner A forced marriage involves one or both persons not giving free consent. Instead, third parties, such as parents or religious leaders, use violence, abuse, or some type of pressure to bring about the marriage (Forced Marriage Unit 2015). In many countries it would be viewed as forcible rape and a violation of human rights. An **arranged marriage** is one in which a third party, typically the families of the persons to be married, take the leading role in selecting a marriage partner. But the proposed parties to the marriage are free to decide whether to go through with it.

Both forced marriages and arranged marriages may be affected by the third parties' financial, political, religious, or racial/ethnic characteristics, or other considerations. For example, a marriage might be planned between a family with a prestigious family name that has financial problems and a wealthy family without a prestigious family name. Forced and arranged marriages occur in a number of countries but appear more common in South Asia and Africa and in Muslim, Hindu, and Sikh cultures. A study in Ontario, Canada, covering a three-year period identified 219 forced marriages, with a religious breakdown of 103 Muslim, 44 Hindu, 30 Sikh, and 10 Christian (Black 2013). An **autonomous marriage** is one in which persons freely chose who to marry.

Number of Marital Partners Monogamy or **monogamous marriage** is marriage between only two persons. With regard to number of marital partners, this is the only type of marriage legal in the United States and many other countries. Polygamy or **polygamous marriage** (also called plural marriage) is marriage involving a person being married to two or more spouses. *Polygyny*, the form of polygamy in which one man has more than one wife, is practiced in a number of Muslim countries. However, *polyandry*, the marriage of a woman to more than one husband, is not allowed. In the United States, marriage in which a man has multiple wives was outlawed by the federal government in 1862, but the practice continued to be legal in Mormon-dominated Utah (PBS 2012a). Many Americans viewed polygyny as a barbaric exploitation of women. The federal government took more actions to force Utah and the Mormon Church (The Church of Jesus Christ of Latter-Day Saints) to ban polygyny, including preventing Utah from becoming a state. In 1887 Congress passed the Edmunds-Tucker Act, which disincorporated the church and allowed the federal government to seize its assets. Finally, in 1890 the Mormon president Wilford Woodruff declared an end to church support for polygyny. The federal government then responded by returning church property and admitting Utah to the union in 1896.

CHANGES IN THE U.S. FAMILY

Age at First Marriage and Cohabitation

The U.S. family changed significantly after the mid-1950s. People began getting married later in life, and the percent of Americans remaining single or cohabiting instead of marrying increased (Pew Research Center

arranged marriage
Marriages where a third party, typically the families of the persons to be married, take the leading role in selecting a marriage partner but in which the proposed parties to the marriage are free to decide whether to go through with it.

autonomous marriage
A marriage in which persons freely chose who to marry.

monogamous marriage
Marriage between only two persons.

2014b). For example in 1960 the median age at first marriage for women was twenty, but in 2012 it had climbed to twenty-seven. And in 1960, 72 percent of adult Americans were married and only 15 percent had never married (*Economist* 2013b). But in 2011 only 51 percent were married and 28 percent had never married. As marriage rates have declined, the number of people cohabiting increased from less than half-a-million opposite-sex couples in 1960 to 8.3 million in 2015 (Child Trends Data Bank 2015a; *Huffington Post* 2013). This included 3.3 million cohabiting couples with children. More than half of all Americans aged thirty to forty-nine say they have cohabited at some point in their lives.

Opinion surveys show public acceptance of cohabitation, unmarried couples raising children, and new types of family arrangements, including same-sex marriages and parents, has been increasing and that much of this change is due to the more open attitudes of young adults (Pew Research Center 2010). For example, 72 percent of Americans aged eighteen to twenty-nine are accepting of cohabiting couples compared to only 32 percent of those sixty-five or older. Similarly, 70 percent of those in the younger age group were okay with same-sex couples raising children compared to only 36 percent of those sixty-five or older. However, large majorities of all age categories (ranging from 63 percent for persons aged eighteen to twenty-nine to 80 percent for those aged sixty-five or older) believed that it was a bad thing for society for single women to have children on their own (Pew Research Center 2010). The growth in acceptance of nontraditional families was reflected by the finding in 2015 that even among U.S. residents self-identifying as Catholics in a national representative sample, 55 percent responded that "a man and women cohabiting was acceptable and as good as any

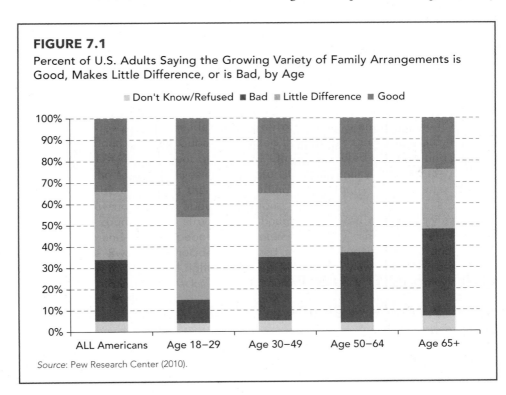

FIGURE 7.1

Percent of U.S. Adults Saying the Growing Variety of Family Arrangements is Good, Makes Little Difference, or is Bad, by Age

Don't Know/Refused ■ Bad ■ Little Difference ■ Good

Source: Pew Research Center (2010).

other way of life" and another 31 percent believed it to be "acceptable but not as good as some others" (Pew Research Center 2015a). Forty-eight percent also responded that "unmarried parents living together" was "acceptable and as good as any other arrangement for raising children," while another 35 percent responded that it was "acceptable but not as good as some others."

Divorce

The divorce rate, the number of divorces per 1,000 married women aged fifteen or older, rose from the latter half of the 1950s and reached 22.8 in 1979 (Anderson 2016; Divorcepapers.com 2015). Several factors appeared to contribute to the rise in divorce rates. One was women's increasing labor force participation and financial ability to leave unsatisfactory marital situations. Social stigma attached to divorce also decreased, and all states instituted some form of "no fault" divorce laws that made divorce easier. Until the late 1960s, a person wanting a divorce had to provide evidence of a serious fault, such as adultery or desertion, committed by her or his spouse. But under "no fault" divorce laws a person was allowed to request and be granted a divorce without showing fault by the spouse. Increased geographic mobility, which often weakens social ties to extended families, is seen as another factor that makes divorce more likely. In addition, the lengthening of people's life span has provided more opportunity for divorce.

Kennedy and Ruggles (2014) showed that the rate of ever-married people experiencing divorce leveled off between 1980 and 1990. Then it increased through 2008 and declined a little after that. About 44 percent of ever married people aged sixty to sixty-four had experienced divorce by 2010. Kennedy and Ruggles also found that for people born after 1980 there was evidence that the probability of divorce was either not increasing or was slightly declining. In 2015 the divorce rate reached a 40 year low of 16.9 (Anderson 2016). This might be due to young people marrying at a lower rate and being more selective about marriage.

As noted earlier, about 40 percent of marriages are estimated to end in divorce. Lewis and Kreider (2015) analyzed data from the 2008 through 2012 U.S. Department of Commerce American Community Surveys (ACS). The results indicated that of all persons aged fifteen and over, 49.9 percent of U.S. men and 54.5 percent of U.S. women had married, but only once. Americans with higher income and higher educational levels were more likely to have married only once. The findings also revealed that for the same population, 13.5 percent had married twice, and 3.6 percent three times or more. The large percentage who have remarried means that many children are being raised in families with a stepparent. According to a major Pew Research Center Survey (2011), about one-fifth of all adults fifty or older reported having at least one stepchild. In total, an estimated 16 percent of children live in what the U.S. Census Bureau refers to as a "**blended family**," a family with a stepparent, stepsibling, or half-sibling (Pew Research Center 2015b). About 17 percent of Hispanic children and 17 percent of black children live in a blended family, while it's 15 percent for white children and 7 percent for Asian children.

blended family A family with a stepparent, stepsibling, or half-sibling.

Impacts of Divorce on Spouses Research indicates the immediate economic impact of divorce is negative for both spouses. In heterosexual marriages, however, divorce generally reduces income and lifestyle much more for women than men (Gadalla 2009). One reason is that women usually earn less than men even when they are employed full-time. But in many cases married women have left the workforce, at least temporarily, to devote most of their time to child-rearing. So, after divorce they often find themselves with less education, work experience, or fewer or up-to-date skills to get well-paying jobs.

In terms of health and emotional well-being, divorce can have either positive or negative consequences. The person who initiates the divorce often experiences a sense of relief because she or he may feel freed from an unpleasant, stressful, conflict-ridden situation or from a domineering or abusive spouse. But some studies indicate that many divorced persons suffer from more psychological, emotional, and even health problems than married persons, especially in the period right after the divorce (Amato 2000; Lorenz et al. 2006). An increase in depression and anxiety is likely for those spouses who did not want the divorce or suffer financial problems because of the divorce.

Impacts of Divorce on Children Divorce can also have positive or negative effects on children. In some situations, divorce can rescue a child from a conflict-ridden household (Kalmijn 2015) or an emotionally and physically abusive parent, with the custodial parent providing a safer, happier home. But in many cases divorce is an emotionally difficult event for children. They may fear the loss of a loved parent and suffer continued conflict between their parents over issues such as visitation rights and schedules or child support. Other potentially stressful events can include deterioration of lifestyle if the custodial parent (usually the mother) experiences a significant loss of income. The custodial parent may move to a new home, causing the children to switch schools and separate from friends. Amato (1993) describes five possible causes for why divorce can have harmful consequences for children: (1) parental loss perspective (children's development suffers when they lose a parent); (2) parental adjustment perspective (a parent's child rearing skills are impaired by the anxieties, depression, and other problems they experience when going through a divorce); (3) interparental conflict perspective (conflict between parents leading up to and after divorce interferes with child-rearing); (4) the economic hardship perspective (a parent's significant loss of income after divorce undermines children's welfare); and (5) life stress perspective (divorce for children is accompanied by stressful events like moving, losing friends, switching schools, and losing contact with loved relatives).

Research shows that while most children whose parents divorce seem to grow into fairly normal adults, greater proportions of them, compared to other children, experience lower educational attainment, lower psychological well-being, weaker ties to both fathers and mothers, behavioral issues, and higher conflict in their own marriages (Amato and Cheadle 2005; Cavanagh and Huston 2008; Fraley and Heffernan 2013; Sigle-Rushton et al. 2014; Sun and Li 2002, 2009). In addition, it may increase the risk for being overweight/obese, at least among females (Hernandez et al. 2014). The harmful effects of divorce appear greater if it occurs early in the child's life (birth through mid- to late elementary school). For many children, the negative effects of divorce last years into the future. Evidence also indicates that marital conflict before or after the actual divorce has similar or greater harmful effects as divorce itself. Further, the establishment of a stable family situation soon after divorce reduces harmful consequences. Some research suggests that divorce impacts boys more than girls, but other findings indicate little or no gender differences.

Minimizing the Consequences of Divorce Grych's (2005) review of research shows that a high level of parental conflict has been linked to emotional and behavioral issues in children during their childhoods and later in their lives. This can include feelings of anxiety and depression, a tendency toward abusive relationships with romantic partners, and a greater probability of divorce. Research indicates that minimizing hostility and conflict between divorcing parents reduces negative effects of divorce on children and helps them adapt more easily. This is sometimes accomplished in part through divorce information programs that educate parents on the importance of not exposing their children to parental conflict, how to anticipate and respond to children's reactions to divorce, and how to share in the parenting of their children following marital separation (Center for Divorce Education 2017). A divorce mediator can also help limit conflict by assisting parents with child custody arrangements, child support, alimony, and concerns including who gets to keep the family residence or how other property is divided (James 2016). Counseling programs that help children avoid feeling respon-

A single-parent family

sible for their parents' difficulties also appear to increase the likelihood that they will come through the divorce in good shape.

People who have divorced may be eager to remarry and combine their children with those of their new spouse in a blended family. The additional rapid changes in living environment can compound difficulties caused children by their parents' divorce (Helpguide.org 2016). One suggestion is that people wait at least two years after divorce to remarry. This gives children more time to adjust to the divorce and to get to know a prospective stepparent and her or his children before moving in together. The gradual approach also allows more time for the couple to come to some understanding about factors such as parenting style.

Children Born Outside of Marriage and Single-Parent-Headed Households

In 1950 only 4 percent of U.S. children were born to unwed mothers (Familyfacts.org 2016). But this dramatically increased to 41 percent in

2009 before decreasing to 40 percent in 2015 (Child Trends Data Bank 2015a). However, in some cases unwed parents cohabit or the mother marries the biological father or another person so that the child is raised in a two-parent household.

In 1960, 8 percent of U.S. children lived with their mother alone. This rose to 24.4 percent in 2012 and then declined to 23.1 percent in 2015 (Child Trends Data Bank 2015b). In comparison, about 65 percent of U.S. children in 2015 were living with two parents, down from about 88 percent in 1960. About 4 percent lived with the father alone and 4 percent lived with some other persons, such as grandparents.

Race/Ethnic and Class Differences

Rates of divorce and children living with only one parent are lower among more-educated and higher-income Americans. There are also significant differences by race and ethnicity. In 2015, 29 percent of non-Hispanic white births were to unwed mothers, compared to 53 percent for Hispanics and 71 percent for non-Hispanic blacks (Child Trends Data Bank 2015a). Also in 2015, 83 percent of Asian American children were living with two married parents, compared to 75 percent of non-Hispanic white children, 60 percent of Hispanic children, and 34 percent of black children (Child Trends Data Bank 2015b).

SINGLE-PARENT FAMILIES

While many children from one-parent families, such as former president Barack Obama, have no serious developmental problems and go on to lead happy and productive lives, research shows that growing up with only one parent is linked to problems for some children. One disadvantage is

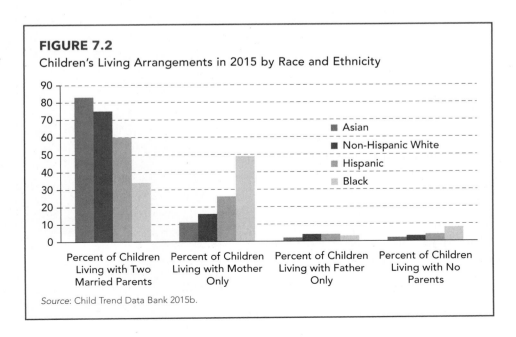

FIGURE 7.2

Children's Living Arrangements in 2015 by Race and Ethnicity

■ Asian
■ Non-Hispanic White
■ Hispanic
■ Black

Percent of Children Living with Two Married Parents

Percent of Children Living with Mother Only

Percent of Children Living with Father Only

Percent of Children Living with No Parents

Source: Child Trend Data Bank 2015b.

that when children have only one parent in the home, there is likely to be less parental interaction with and time for each child than when there are two parents. Another factor is that children in one-parent families are much more likely to grow up in poverty, attend inferior schools, have access to less health care, and have less access to important after-school educational and sports programs. In addition, children in one-parent female-headed families may suffer from the absence of a stable positive male role model. In any case, children growing up in one-parent families are at higher risk of doing poorly in school and becoming involved in youth gangs and criminal behavior.

The increase in one-parent families was particularly prominent among African Americans. In 1950, about 84 percent of black children were born to married women, but only 29 percent were in 2015. This trend for African American children was most likely due to a combination of economic changes and the impact of racism. Racial discrimination resulted in limited educational and job opportunities for African Americans and, in the northern states, residential concentration in cities. The main type of well-paying employment available for hard working African Americans was urban industrial jobs. But when these jobs disappeared due to technological change or corporations relocating factories to countries where wages were much lower, hundreds of thousands of black men were no longer able to earn enough to support families. And because of racial residential segregation and limited education, they were less able, compared to their white counterparts, to transition to well-paying white-collar employment.

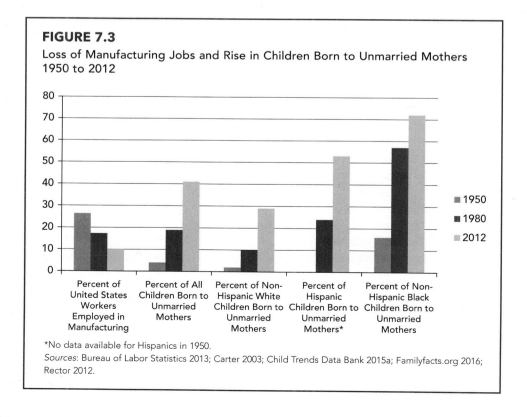

FIGURE 7.3

Loss of Manufacturing Jobs and Rise in Children Born to Unmarried Mothers 1950 to 2012

*No data available for Hispanics in 1950.

Sources: Bureau of Labor Statistics 2013; Carter 2003; Child Trends Data Bank 2015a; Familyfacts.org 2016; Rector 2012.

Mass Incarceration and the American Black Family

Another factor that many social scientists believe contributes to the large proportion of black children growing up in female-headed families is the *mass incarceration* of black men. The crackdown on drugs beginning in the 1970s led to increasing imprisonment and longer prison sentences for young black men. Western and Wildeman (2009) found that while in 1980 5.7 percent of black men aged twenty-two to thirty were in prison or jail, in 2004 it had climbed to about 13.5 percent (for those young black men with less than a college education, the proportion in prison on average each day rose to over one in five). Over the same period the percentage for similarly aged incarcerated white men went from 0.6 percent to 1.9 percent (for young white men with less than a college education, the proportion in prison increased to about one in twenty-five).

As a result of high black male incarceration and homicide victimization (see Chapter 10), there are typically only 83 black men for every 100 black women not in prison (compared to 99 white men per 100 white women not in prison) (Wolfers, Leonhardt, and Quealy 2015). This physical shortage of black men contributes to the large proportion of black female-headed families. And since persons with a criminal record have difficulty getting a job once released from prison, this further limits the number of black men who can support a family through legitimate employment.

GAY AND LESBIAN FAMILIES

The 2010 census showed there were approximately 594,000 same-sex couple households and that 115,000 reported having children (U.S. Census 2011b). Reviews of studies of same-sex families, such as that presented by the American Sociological Association in an amicus brief to the U.S. Supreme Court in 2013, indicate that children raised by same-sex parents fare as well as children raised by opposite-sex parents on measures of child development and well-being (American Sociological Association 2013). Most studies also indicate that the sexual orientation of same-sex parents does not have a significant effect on the sexual orientation of their children.

There was strong government opposition, however, to same-sex marriage. In 1996 Congress passed and President Bill Clinton signed the Defense of Marriage Act (DOMA) that stated marriage is between one man and one woman and that no state was required to recognize a same-sex marriage performed in another state. And by 2012 thirty states had banned it as well. But a number of other states permitted same-sex marriage. Massachusetts in 2004 became the first state to legalize it. New Hampshire, Vermont, Connecticut, and Iowa soon followed. In 2011, President Obama announced that the federal government would no longer enforce DOMA and the following year became the first president to support legalization of same-sex marriage. By the end of 2011, surveys consistently showed that nationally public support for same-sex marriage surpassed 50 percent (Jones 2013) and by 2015 had climbed to about 60 percent (Hook 2015). Then on June 26, 2015, the Supreme Court ruled five to four in *Obergefell v. Hodges* (Ohio) that state laws against same-sex marriage were unconstitutional. This made it legal in all states.

VIOLENCE AND ABUSE IN INTIMATE PARTNER RELATIONSHIPS

Intimate partners and family relations are sources of love, happiness, and personal fulfillment for people around the world. But in many cases, these relationships are scarred by violence, abuse, or harmful neglect of basic needs.

Intimate Partner Abuse and Violence

Intimate partner abuse can include psychological abuse, economic abuse, physical violence, and sexual abuse occurring between spouses or former spouses, cohabiting couples, or boyfriends and girlfriends. Globally, 30 percent of all women who have been in an intimate relationship have experienced physical violence and/or sexual assault by their partner (World Health Organization (WHO) 2013). In high-income nations, including the United States, Canada, western and central European nations, South Korea, Australia, and Japan, it was about 23 percent. In Europe as a whole, including Russia, it was 25 percent, about the same as in China. But WHO regions covering the Middle East, Africa, and southeast Asia all had rates of about 37 percent of women experiencing intimate partner violence. The WHO's research also indicated that women who had been the victims of partner physical or sexual abuse were more than twice as likely to have an abortion than other women, almost twice as likely to experience depression, and about 50 percent more likely to contract HIV.

According to the Breiding et al. (2014), data collected for the Centers for Disease Control and Prevention (CDC) indicated that 31.5 percent of U.S. women and 27.5 percent of men experienced some type of physical violence by an intimate partner during their lifetime. Jewkes (2002) found that heavy alcohol use is linked to the problem. And about 9 percent of women experienced intimate partner rape during their lifetime. Often intimate partner violence involves a cycle in which the assault is followed by the perpetrator apologizing and asking to be taken back, only to engage in future violence. According to the FBI's Uniform Crime Reports (FBI 2017o), 36 percent of U.S. female homicide victims in 2015 were killed by a husband or a boyfriend. During the same year, 2.5 percent of male homicide victims were killed by a wife or a girlfriend.

Income and Racial/Ethnic Differences

While Americans of all social classes experience intimate partner violence, those with low incomes are at greater risk (Jewkes 2002). CDC research indicated that 51.7% of American Indian/Alaska Native women, 51.3% of multiracial women, 41.2% of non-Hispanic black women, 30.5% of non-Hispanic white women, 29.7% of Hispanic women, and 15.3% of Asian or Pacific Islander women were victimized by intimate partner physical violence during their lifetimes (Breiding

intimate partner abuse Psychological abuse, economic abuse, physical violence, and sexual abuse occurring between spouses or former spouses, cohabiting couples, or boyfriends and girlfriends.

et al. 2014). The percentages for men were American Indian/Alaska Native, 43.0%, multiracial, 39.3%, non-Hispanic black, 36.3%, Hispanic, 27.1%, non-Hispanic white, 26.6%, and Asian or Pacific Islander, 11.5%. Because of size and strength differences, violence by men against women often inflicts more physical harm than attacks by women on men. The CDC research indicated that nationally 11.4% of multiracial women, 9.6% of non-Hispanic white women, 8.8% of non-Hispanic black women, and 6.2% of Hispanic women experienced intimate partner rape during their lifetimes.

Effects of Intimate Partner Violence

Intimate partner violence has serious psychological, social, health, and economic consequences (CDC 2015c). Many victims suffer from anxiety, low self-esteem, diminished ability to trust others, sleep disturbance, depression, and suicidal tendencies. Social impacts include increased likelihood of social isolation, homelessness, and involvement in criminal behavior, and restricted access to employment and social and health services. Intimate partner violence is associated with a wide range of health issues, including increased likelihood of smoking, drinking alcohol, illicit drug use, having unprotected sex, sexually transmitted diseases, unintended pregnancies, pregnancy difficulties, asthma, cardiovascular disease, central nervous system disorders, gastrointestinal disorders, and migraine headaches. Economic consequences taken as a whole include billions of dollars for meeting the physical and mental health care needs of victims as well as additional hundreds of millions lost to victims and the economy because of missed work days.

Decline in Intimate Partner Violence since 1994

Research data presented by the Bureau of Justice Statistics (Bureau of Justice Statistics 2013; Catalano 2013) indicates that the rate of serious intimate partner violence against females (rape or sexual assault, robbery, and aggravated assault) dropped by 73%, from 5.9 victimizations per 1,000 females age twelve or older in 1994 to 1.6 per 1,000 in 2011. The decline for male victims of intimate partner violence over the same period was 64%, from 1.1 victimizations per 1,000 in 1994 to 0.4 per 1,000 in 2011. For both males and females most of the decline came between 1994 and 2001, during a period when violent crime rates in general were falling throughout the nation.

CHILD ABUSE

child abuse Physical, sexual, psychological, or emotional maltreatment or neglect of a child (a person under age eighteen), especially by a person or persons responsible for the child's well-being.

Child abuse refers to the physical, sexual, psychological, or emotional maltreatment or neglect of a child (a person under age eighteen), especially by a person or persons responsible for the child's wellbeing.

Child neglect is the form of child abuse involving neglecting to provide for the child's basic needs such as food, health care, hygiene, shelter, clothing appropriate for the environment and weather, and proper supervision. The U.S. Department of Health and Human Services (DHHS) (2018d:19) reported that there were an estimated 676,000 victims of child abuse in 2016 (The DHHS (2018) uses the term "child maltreatment".). This represents an increase of about 3 percent from 2012. However, the state agencies that deal with child abuse may not be equally consistent in how they learn about, identify, or investigate possible cases of child abuse. This is likely because child abuse data for certain states show improbably large increases or decreases over short periods.

For example, while most states reported relatively small changes between 2012 and 2016, Maryland reported a 47 percent decrease in victims; Massachusetts, Minnesota, and Montana, on the other hand, reported very large increases of 67 percent, 87 percent, and 135 percent, respectively. Figure 7.4 shows percentages in the different categories of child abuse. "Other abuse" refers to forms of child maltreatment in addition to the major types listed by the DHHS, such as categories used only by particular states like "parent drug/alcohol abuse" or "threatened abuse" (DHHS 2018:43).

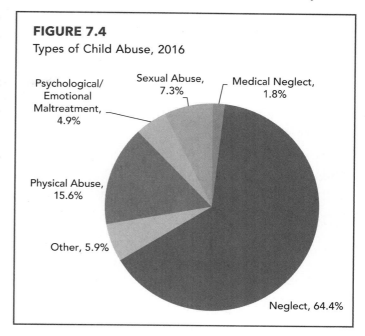

FIGURE 7.4
Types of Child Abuse, 2016

- Psychological/Emotional Maltreatment, 4.9%
- Sexual Abuse, 7.3%
- Medical Neglect, 1.8%
- Physical Abuse, 15.6%
- Other, 5.9%
- Neglect, 64.4%

Demographic Characteristics of Victims

Younger children are more likely to be abuse victims. In 2016, 29 percent of victims were under three years old. Children younger than one year had the highest victimization rate, 24.8 per 1,000 children. Children who were 1, 2, or 3 years old had victimization rates of 11.9, 11.2, and 10.6, respectively. In general, the risk of victimization decreased with age. Female children had a higher risk of victimization (9.5 per 1,000) than male children (8.7 per 1,000).

As Figure 7.5 on child abuse victims by race/ethnicity shows, the largest proportion of child abuse victims were white (44.9 percent), followed by Hispanic (22.0 percent), and African American (20.7 percent). Figure 7.6 displays rates of victimization within each racial/ethnic group.

Perpetrators and Risk Factors

The DHHS (2018) data indicates that one or both parents of an abused child committed the abuse almost nine out of ten times. But in about 13 percent of instances, a nonparent, such as a male relative, a male partner of a parent, a care provider or a neighbor, was involved.

Children living in low-income households where caregivers are under economic stress appear at greater risk. Part of the reason for more reported cases of child abuse among poverty-stricken households might be that they often receive some type of welfare assistance. This means

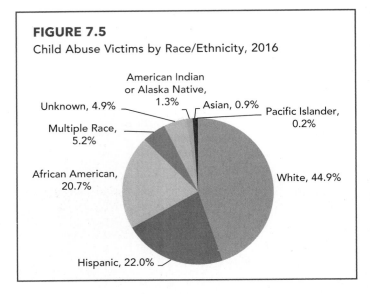

FIGURE 7.5

Child Abuse Victims by Race/Ethnicity, 2016

American Indian or Alaska Native, 1.3%

Asian, 0.9%

Pacific Islander, 0.2%

Unknown, 4.9%

Multiple Race, 5.2%

African American, 20.7%

White, 44.9%

Hispanic, 22.0%

they are generally in contact with social workers, who are required to report abuse. However, violent crime victimization in general, including homicide, is significantly more frequent among low-income Americans, and there is no reason to think that child abuse would be an exception. Factors such as mental illness, alcohol or drug abuse, being raised in a subculture of violence, being taught to respond to child misbehavior with physical punishment or having been the victim of physical, sexual, or emotional abuse as a child are associated with being more likely commit abuse. Circumstances that increase the probability of abuse are divorce or separation, loss of job, social isolation, or caretaker illness that may increase the stress of trying to care for a child.

Some evidence suggests that children with behavior or emotional problems, medical illnesses, or disabilities are at somewhat higher risk of abuse. Children in families with a large number of children or who were born from an unintended pregnancy also appear to be at greater risk.

Effects of Child Abuse

While many people who experience abuse as children appear to have no long-term effects, a significant number suffer harmful consequences. These include a tendency toward low self-esteem, lack of trust toward other people, social isolation, and being more likely to engage in law-breaking behavior, including illegal drug use and engaging in child abuse themselves.

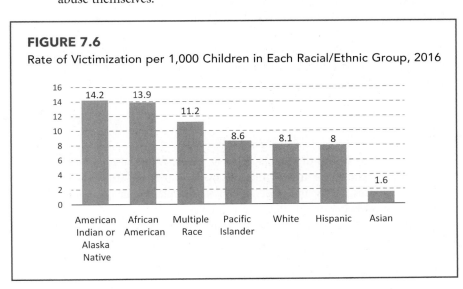

FIGURE 7.6

Rate of Victimization per 1,000 Children in Each Racial/Ethnic Group, 2016

American Indian or Alaska Native	African American	Multiple Race	Pacific Islander	White	Hispanic	Asian
14.2	13.9	11.2	8.6	8.1	8	1.6

Increase and Decrease of Child Abuse Reports

National concern about child abuse increased beginning in the 1960s. In many states, new laws were written requiring teachers and social workers to report suspected cases of abuse, and special telephone numbers were set up and publicized to facilitate reporting. In addition, "good faith" laws were passed to shield those making reports from lawsuits by suspected offenders. These changes may have contributed to an increase in the reporting of child abuse.

Between 1990 and 1994 the number of identified child abuse cases rose from 861,000 (13.4 cases per 1,000 U.S. children) to 1,032,000 (15.2

Social Movements: The Child Protection Movement

Child protection movement demonstration, Lahore, Pakistan

Major threats to children around the world include poverty; discrimination based on race, ethnicity, or other social characteristics; loss of parents to diseases (such as AIDS) or violent conflicts; forced labor; sexual abuse; trafficking; homelessness; recruitment as child soldiers; and excessively harsh or unfair treatment by criminal justice systems. In response, the United Nations' Declaration of the Rights of the Child (UNICEF 2003; UNICEF 2016) states that all children (persons under age eighteen) have the right to nutrition, health care, education, a supportive and safe environment, and protection from violence and exploitation.

The U.S. child protection movement in the nineteenth century focused on issues such as of child labor, violence against children, and children's access to education. Many children worked in the agriculture, mining, canning, and the textile industries. Massachusetts was the first state to try to reduce child labor when in 1836 it required that all children under fifteen employed in factories had to go to school at least 3 months per year. Then in 1842 it limited children's work hours to no more than 10 hours per day (Child Labor Public Education Project 2016).

In 1874, a history-changing case of child abuse came to light in New York City involving a ten-year-old girl Mary Ellen Wilson, who was repeatedly severely beaten and generally mistreated by foster parents (American Humane Association 2013). The situation was uncovered and investigated by a Methodist mission worker Etta Angell Wheeler, who, with the help of the head of the American Society for the Prevention of Cruelty to Animals, Henry Bergh, and others, persuaded

(continued)

Social Movements (*continued*)

the courts to remove Mary Ellen from the abusive household in 1874. Eventually the authorities allowed Etta's mother and then her sister to raise Mary Ellen. That same year, the New York Society for the Prevention of Cruelty to Children was created, the first organization of its kind. Similar organizations for the prevention of child abuse were soon established in many other states. Mary Ellen's case helped ignite a worldwide movement to protect children.

Child labor persisted as a serious problem in the early twentieth century, with children working for low wages at long hours under often dangerous conditions. Machinery in textile mills repeatedly caused serious injuries (Philly.com 2013). In June 1903, ninety thousand workers, 25 percent of them under the age of fifteen, began a strike at the six hundred textile mills in Kensington, Pennsylvania, about four miles northeast of Philadelphia. The Textile Workers Union called for the workweek to be reduced from sixty to fifty-five hours and that women and children not work night hours. Mary Harris Jones ("Mother Jones"), a well-known labor activist who at the time had been helping to organize West Virginia coal miners, persuaded the Kensington strike leaders to emphasize the evils of child labor. She then led a march of three hundred children, some who had been permanently maimed by machines, and other workers from Philadelphia to New York. Although the Kensington strike failed, the child workers' march drew public attention, leading Pennsylvania, New Jersey, and New York to pass child labor laws within a few years. Concern about child labor was also heightened by photographs of children working in coal mines, meatpacking houses, textile mills, canneries, and factories taken by Lewis Hine, a New York city school teacher and sociologist (National Archives 2016). But it wasn't until 1938 that federal limits were put on child labor when President Franklin Roosevelt signed the Fair Labor Standards Act.

Another significant step toward protecting children was the 1944 *Prince v. Massachusetts* Supreme Court decision. The court stated that the government has the right to overrule parents to ensure a child's well-being (Cornell University Law School 2016).

Protecting children from physical abuse re-emerged as a major public issue again in the second half of the twentieth century, when advances in medical technology began to indicate that far more child abuse was occurring than officials and the public realized. New applications of X-ray technology, for example, revealed that adults were inflicting much more serious physical injury on children than had previously been recognized. In response to public concern, all fifty states enacted new laws against caretakers' abuse of children between 1962 and 1967. Government and citizen reaction to abuse had an enormous beneficial impact. After 1992, confirmed cases of child physical abuse and sexual abuse declined by over 50 percent (Finkelhor et al. 2013).

In the area of children's criminal justice rights, two Supreme Court decisions in 1967 (*In re Gault*) and 1970 (*In re Winship*) stated, respectively, that juveniles accused of delinquency must be given similar due process as adults, such as the right to have a lawyer, the right to confront witnesses, and the right against self-incrimination, and that in cases where a juvenile is charged with an offense that would be a crime if committed by an adult, every aspect of the offense must be proven beyond a reasonable doubt (FindLaw 2016).

In 1973, the Children's Defense Fund (CDF), a national nonprofit organization that fights for children's welfare, was established (CDF 2016). That same year Hilary Clinton, newly graduated from Yale Law School, joined the CDF legal staff.

In 2014, research and media coverage again stimulated public concern about the exploitation of child labor with accounts of health problems afflicting child tobacco workers in the United States (Young 2014).

cases per 1,000 children) (Child Trends Data Bank 2015c). But after 1994 the number of cases and the rate per 1,000 children began a fairly steady decline until 1999, when 829,000 cases (rate of 11.8 per 1,000 children) were recorded. After fluctuating for several years the numbers fell again to 754,000 (rate of 10 cases per 1,000 children) in 2010. The numbers and rates above sometimes referred to two or more reports for the same child. But since the mid-2000s numbers and rates refer to individual children reported. As noted earlier, DHHS (2018) data showed that in 2016 there were approximately 676,000 child abuse victims in the United States (a rate of 9.1 abused children per 1,000 children).

ELDER ABUSE AND NEGLECT

Elder abuse refers to any behavior that harms or causes serious risk of harm to a vulnerable "senior" adult (Administration on Aging 2015). Elder abuse includes physical abuse – causing physical injury or physical pain to a senior or restraining a senior by physical or chemical means; sexual abuse – any nonconsensual sexual contact; neglect – failure to provide basic necessities such as food, health care, or shelter; exploitation – the illegal theft, misuse, or concealment of the money, property, or other assets of a senior for another person's benefit; emotional abuse – causing unnecessary emotional pain or distress to a senior through spoken words or nonverbal acts, including intimidations, humiliations, or threats; or abandonment. All fifty states have enacted elder abuse prevention laws.

Incidence and Correlates of Elder Abuse

Research on elder abuse is limited. The National Institute of Justice (NIJ 2009, 2010a) conducted a major study in 2003 involving an extensive telephone survey of more than 5,000 Americans aged sixty or older. The study found 1.6 percent (574,400 persons if projected onto the entire population aged sixty or over) stated they had been physically abused during the previous year. The perpetrators were spouses or partners in 57 percent of the cases, children or grandchildren in 10 percent, other relatives 9 percent, acquaintances 19 percent, and 3 percent strangers, while 2 percent refused to answer this question. Only 31 percent of the victims said they reported the abuse to the police. The study, in addition, found that 0.6 percent said they had been abused sexually, 5.2 percent financially, 5.1 percent emotionally, and 5.1 percent by neglect. Relatives were generally the majority of the perpetrators in all forms of abuse. The study also indicated that low income and substance abuse increased the likelihood of elder abuse.

PREVENTING FAMILY VIOLENCE

There are multiple ways to eliminate family violence.

Economic

Economic hardship, joblessness, and limited opportunity all generate stress that can lead to family violence. Government and business polices

elder abuse Any behavior that harms or causes serious risk of harm to a vulnerable "senior" adult.

oriented toward rebuilding local economies, preventing the outsourcing of jobs to other locations, training unemployed or underemployed persons to develop needed skills, and providing assistance until those able to work find employment could all contribute to reducing family violence.

Political

Male domination of the political systems in many countries is undoubtedly one reason for violence against women. Women must achieve political power though the vote and holding powerful government positions and enact laws that protect women. In many countries laws have been passed and criminal justice procedures modified to ensure that violence against women and children is more effectively identified and punished.

Cultural

Various elements of culture have contributed to family violence and must be modified or eliminated to reduce it. Patriarchy, male domination in its various forms that leads men to believe they have the right to use force against wives or children, must be eradicated, including from all of the world's religions. Cultural norms that link honor or status of any kind or solving problems to the use of violence contribute to the problem. For example, people who are brought up to believe that corporal punishment of children is appropriate are more likely to engage in child abuse in part because their use of violent discipline can cross over into what society considers abuse. The beating of children is banned in many European countries and from schools in all of them. But in the United States, corporal punishment of children in schools is still permitted in nineteen states (Walker 2016). According to the FBI's Uniform Crime Reports (FBI 2017p) there is a significantly greater occurrence of violent crime, controlling for differences in population size, in states that allow corporal punishment in school. For example, the states permitting use of corporal punishment in schools had an average homicide rate (number of homicide victims per 100,000 residents) in 2015 of 5.73, 49 percent higher than the average homicide rate for the states that do not allow corporal punishment in schools, 3.85.

Individual Characteristics

Certain individual characteristics, such as substance abuse and untreated mental illness, can increase the likelihood of engaging in family violence. Most notably, having witnessed or been the victim of family violence increases the risk of committing family violence. Breaking the cycle of intergenerational abuse is one of the great challenges in reducing family violence. After the results of a study conducted in the city of Minneapolis in the early 1980s indicated that when police respond to domestic violence by arresting the perpetrator, future violence was deterred (Sherman and Berk 1984), many states adopted a mandatory arrest policy. But other states relied on police discretion on whether or not to make an arrest or had a "pro-arrest" policy short of being mandatory (American Bar Association Commission on Domestic Violence 2007). Latter studies, however, suggested that arrest did not deter unemployed batterers and sometimes had unintended effects like discouraging victims from reporting abuse. Barbara Fedders (2010) suggested that some women may call the police hoping that they will calm the situation down or scare the perpetrator into ending the abuse. But they may not want their children to see their father being arrested and/or they may be economically dependent on the batterer's income. If the jurisdiction they live in has a mandatory arrest law, these women could decide not to call the police at all, believing that doing so would cause more harm than good.

Some type of treatment program is often available for abusers, which they may enter voluntarily or be forced to participate in by court action (Seccombe 2012). Such programs typically try to make the abuser more aware of the damage caused by abuse to partners or other family members, understand the causes of abusive behavior, and help the abuser learn how to cope with stress or anger nonviolently. However, in cases where the violence stems from deeply rooted personality traits caused by factors such as childhood trauma or ingrained patriarchal attitudes, such programs may have very little effect.

Providing Safety for Abuse Victims

One way for abuse victims to escape violence is to flee to a safe environment. Some are lucky enough to have family or friends with the ability to take them in. But for others, a domestic violence shelter provides safe refuge until a more long-term solution can be found. A number of domestic violence shelters were established by concerned citizens in the 1970s after research shed new light on the scope of both child abuse and spouse abuse. The modern children's protection and women's movements also drew national attention to these crimes. Today shelters typically provide twenty-four-hour emergency hotlines, counseling services, a place to stay from a day to months, and help in understanding criminal and civil court processes, including restraining and protective orders. They also generally provide help on transitioning to more-permanent housing and information on obtaining services such as substance abuse treatment and education and skill development for future employment (Prudence Crandall Center 2016). Some efforts have also been made in certain locations to provide shelters for pets because some abused persons have been reluctant to flee an abusive household out of fear that harm might come to their dog or cat if left behind.

TEEN PREGNANCIES AND PARENTHOOD

Teen pregnancies and marital parenthood were common in the United States in the nineteenth century when much of the country had an agricultural economy (Lindenmeyer 2008). But the rate of teen births actually reached an all-time high of 96 births per 1,000 females in the fifteen to nineteen age range in 1957. The rate then began a general

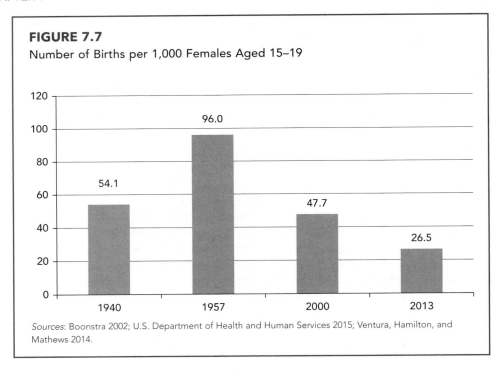

FIGURE 7.7

Number of Births per 1,000 Females Aged 15–19

Sources: Boonstra 2002; U.S. Department of Health and Human Services 2015; Ventura, Hamilton, and Mathews 2014.

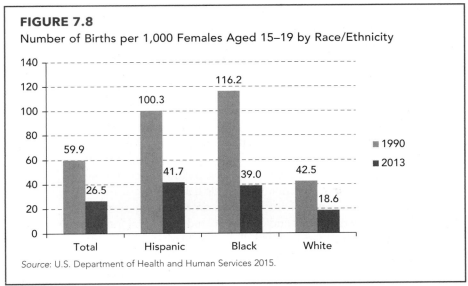

FIGURE 7.8

Number of Births per 1,000 Females Aged 15–19 by Race/Ethnicity

Source: U.S. Department of Health and Human Services 2015.

decline to 26.5 in 2013 (Boonstra 2002; U.S. Department of Health and Human Services 2015).

But the United States continues to have teen birth rates two to five times those of other highly advanced countries (Kearney and Levine 2014). In 2013 Hispanics had the highest rate (41.7), followed by blacks (39), and then whites (18.6) (U.S. Department of Health and Human Services 2015).

A further aspect of teen births is that the proportion occurring outside of marriage has steadily increased. For example, although the birth

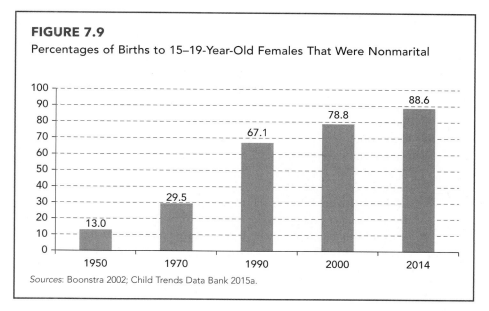

FIGURE 7.9

Percentages of Births to 15–19-Year-Old Females That Were Nonmarital

Sources: Boonstra 2002; Child Trends Data Bank 2015a.

rate for teenagers aged fifteen to nineteen was relatively high in 1950, only 13 percent of teen births were to unmarried mothers. By 2014, this was almost totally reversed, with about 89 percent of births to teenagers in the same age range occurring outside of marriage (Boonstra 2002; Child Trends Data Bank 2015a).

Causes of Teen Pregnancies

In 2010, 6 percent of teenage females became pregnant, with almost two-thirds resulting in live births, close to a third ended by abortions, and the remainder ended through miscarriages (Kost and Henshaw 2014). About 77 percent of the approximately 750,000 teen pregnancies were unplanned (U.S. Department of Health and Human Services 2015, 2016). Although teen pregnancy occurs in all social classes and racial/ethnic groups, it is more frequent in low-income neighborhoods with high levels of unemployment. Teenagers who lack positive attitudes toward school and are doing poorly academically are more likely to father or have a baby than other teenagers. In addition, research indicates that teenagers whose mothers gave birth as teens or whose mothers never attended college were more likely to have a baby. Further, teenagers who were not living with both biological parents in their early teens were more likely to have a baby.

Consequences of Teen Pregnancies

Teen pregnancies, which, as noted above, are overwhelmingly unplanned, result in a high proportion of abortions. Teens that have their babies are more likely to drop out of high school and have more limited job opportunities (U.S. Department of Health and Human Services 2016). Children born to teenagers are more likely on average to have health problems, do poorly in school, and have behavioral problems.

Preventing Teen Pregnancies

The only totally sure way to prevent unwanted pregnancies is to abstain from sexual intercourse. But for sexually active teens, the correct use of contraceptive methods (such as birth control pills, condoms, intrauterine devices, or vaginal rings) can be highly effective in reducing the risk of pregnancy. Many Americans believe that schools should only teach students that premarital sex is wrong. They argue that teaching students about contraceptive methods encourages sexual intercourse and thus causes more pregnancies, not less. But research indicates that most Americans do not support this view. For example, a study published in the *Archives of Pediatrics and Adolescent Medicine* (Bleakley, Hennessey, and Fishbein 2006) found that 82 percent of a national sample of adults favored teaching students about both the abstinence and other methods for avoiding pregnancy, with 68 percent specifically supporting teaching the proper use of condoms. Only 36 percent favored abstinence-only programs.

Research on the effectiveness of teen pregnancy prevention programs has yielded inconsistent results. Some studies indicate that trying to prevent teen pregnancy by focusing only on abstinence does not work but that programs explaining the benefits of abstinence while also showing how to use contraceptive methods have better results (Guttmacher Institute 2007). According to the Guttmacher Institute (2012), thirty-seven states required that school sex education include teaching about the benefits of abstinence. Only eighteen states and the District of Columbia mandated that school sex education include providing information about contraception.

In response to a state law passed in 2011 that required schools to teach either the abstinence-only approach to preventing teen pregnancies or "abstinence plus" programs that require teaching abstinence but allow teaching abstinence to be supplemented by teaching about contraception (Mississippi Legislature 2011), eighty of Mississippi's 151 school districts opted for abstinence only (*Huffington Post Education* 2012). But Mississippi has had one of the highest teen birth rates (Martin et al. 2013).

Another program intended to prevent teen pregnancies involves trying to give teens a realistic experience of how having a baby changes a person's life and how the baby requires constant attention. Some of these programs involve the use of high-tech computerized infant simulators (large flexible dolls). Diane de Anda (2006) conducted a study to evaluate the effectiveness of infant simulators in preventing teen pregnancy. The dolls were programmed to simulate the behavior of real babies and placed in the care of the 353 teen student subjects (94 percent ninth graders, and a few tenth and eleventh graders) for two and a half days. The simulator dolls were programmed to cry at random intervals eight to twelve times in a twenty-four-hour period, including during early morning hours. The caretaker could stop the crying by inserting a key into a slot in the doll's back until the doll stopped crying. On average the doll's crying lasted for ten to fifteen minutes. Each doll's computer recorded specific data, including how long it took for the teen to respond to the doll's crying and whether the doll was treated roughly like being dropped or hit. The results indicated that participants tended to become more aware of the impacts of having a baby on education, career plans, and social life, and the advantages of waiting longer to have a baby. However, some later research found less evidence that infant simulator programs significantly affected participants' attitudes about teen parenting (Herman, Waterhouse, and Chiquoine 2011).

Those teens who do become parents can be given assistance to help them be good caregivers and ensure their children's health and general wellbeing. This includes child care assistance, health care, financial assistance, and help continuing the parents' education. Modern infant simulator dolls can also be used to help teens who are expecting a baby be more prepared for parenting (Reality Works Experiential Learning Technology 2016).

SOCIOLOGICAL PERSPECTIVES ON FAMILY PROBLEMS

Structural-Functional Perspective

The structural-functional perspective views the family as one of the most important components of society carrying out essential social functions. These include satisfying the emotional needs of family members and providing a secure environment for childbearing and rearing. In most instances the family provides at least initial education and moral guidance for the child, encouraging concern for the welfare of other people and respect for legitimate authority. Since these functions are so crucial, the functionalist approach views strong families as the basis of society and anything that disrupts the family as a threat to the health and stability of the social system.

Structural functionalism, as originally developed in American sociology, also held that traditional gender roles are important for healthy families. That is, women are meant to carry out the expressive functions of nurturing children, catering to the emotional needs of family members, and ensuring the smooth running of the household, while men engage in the instrumental functions of working to generate an income and financially support the family.

Anything that disrupts or competes with the traditional family structure, such as divorce, having children outside of marriage, or single-parent households leads to other social problems such as poverty, child abuse, substance abuse, and juvenile delinquency and crime. Structural-functionalists also recognize that changes in other institutions, such as the economy, can disrupt the family. For example, the decline in well-paying manufacturing jobs reduced the number of men who could financially support families, leading to more children born outside of marriage and more single-parent households. In addition, rising costs of living, coupled with stagnant wages, caused more women to seek employment outside the home. This gave women more financial independence and contributed to increasing the divorce rate.

Conflict Perspective

The conflict approach recognizes the important functions carried out by the family but also claims that the family in its traditional form has perpetuated harmful inequalities.

Economic-Conflict Perspective The economic-conflict perspective argues that the family has fostered economic inequality because children tend to inherit the wealth or poverty of their parents. Frederick Engels (1884) in his *The Origin of the Family, Private Property and the State* asserted that the form of the family existing in the nineteenth century was in fact the product of humanity's capacity to produce wealth and for individuals to amass large amounts of private property. From Engel's point of view, a central purpose of the Victorian era family was to protect inheritance by ensuring that wealthy men would be able to pass their property to their sons with strong confidence that they really were their biological sons. Thus, it was important that women were virgins at the time of marriage and remained sexually faithful to their husbands. Protecting their property was also a strong motive for men to maintain total control of their wives and household finances and limit their wives to family functions. This analysis implies that shifting from a capitalist to a socialist economy should reduce male domination of society and the family. The conflict approach also points out that many U.S. businesses have influenced policies affecting families to protect their profits, like opposing extensive maternal leaves, rather than to protect the welfare of women and children. In addition, corporate policies, like the shipping of U.S. manufacturing jobs to other countries (outsourcing), has reduced the number of men who can earn enough to support a family, contributing to a decrease in the percentage of married people and an increase in the percentage of children born outside of marriage. Research indicates (Sawhill and Venator 2015) that the decline in earnings for noncollege-educated men, both white and black, probably accounts for about one-quarter of the reduction in marriages rates between 1970 and 2010.

Feminist-Conflict Perspective The feminist conflict perspective on the family focuses on gender inequalities, including men's domination over women at home and in society at large. While many feminist conflict theorists agree with elements of Engels's analysis, most also point out that patriarchy continued in many societies that experienced socialist revolutions. Feminists also point out that the patriarchal structure of families and male-dominated governmental and legal systems have contributed to men taking out their frustrations, economic or otherwise, through abuse and violence against their wives and girlfriends. Furthermore, they point out that even in homes free of spouse abuse and where women have fulfilling careers outside the home, lingering male privilege and gender stereotypes contribute to women doing most child care and housework.

Racial/Ethnic-Conflict Perspective The racial/ethnic-conflict perspective on the family describes how the frustration people of color experience from being victimized by discrimination can lead to violence against their partners. This approach also argues that the loss of well-paying manufacturing jobs from U.S. central cities severely reduced the number of African American men able to make the income necessary to support a family, leading to a scarcity of "marriageable men" and dramatic increases in children born outside of marriage, female-headed households, and female poverty (Sawhill and Venator 2015; Wilson 1987, 1996, 2010). The racial/ethnic-conflict perspective also holds that criminal justice system policies, especially the way the war on drugs has been conducted, has resulted in the mass incarceration of black men (Alexander 2012). Because employers often fear hiring people with a felony criminal record, many black men find it difficult to get any job, let alone one that pays a good wage. This in turn becomes another major factor reducing the availability of men able to support a family.

Symbolic-Interactionist Perspective

The symbolic-interactionist approach focuses on factors such as the impact of communication and the quality of family life on what children and spouses think about themselves. Children and spouses who receive love and positive messages from other family members tend to develop healthy self-esteem. But those who regularly experience psychological abuse and name-calling are often characterized by low self-esteem and may feel their family is a source of stress and pain rather than emotional support. This can result in a lack of self-confidence and damage the child's outlook on authority figures and the world. In the family the child also learns how to interact with other people, including loved ones. Children who see violence between their parents or witness or experience abuse are more likely to engage in similar behavior themselves.

Special Topics: Technologically Advanced Countries' Assistance to Working Families and Their Children

Child care for working families

Almost all technologically advanced countries have better national policies than the United States for assisting working parents and their children. The most important differences are in the areas of paid leave, child care, flexible work hours, high-quality part-time work, and universal health care.

Paid Parental Leave

Paid parental leave refers to the government providing or requiring employers to provide mothers and/or fathers with a period of time they can take off from their jobs to spend on things like taking care of newborn children or sick relatives while still receiving a significant amount of their pay and maintaining the right to return to their jobs at a later point. In many countries with paid parental leave the funding for partial salaries during the leaves is

(continued)

Special Topics (*continued*)

provided through social insurance policies to which all workers contribute. The United Nations' International Labor Organization (which has 185 member nations) states in its Convention Number 183 that all countries should provide at least 14 weeks of paid maternity leave at two-thirds of the woman's previous earnings level and that this should be funded by social insurance or government or another method where the employer is not exclusively responsible (Addati, Cassirer, and Gilchrist 2014). In 2014, 57 countries fully met or exceeded the provisions of Convention 183. Unlike the vast majority of developed nations, the United States provided no paid leave for new parents but did require 12 weeks of protected leave (meaning the employer must hold the job for the parent until he or she returns) for about 60 percent of the U.S. workforce (including full-time employees who have worked for more than one year in companies with more than fifty employees) (Schulte 2014).

Child Care

In the early 1970s, the U.S. Congress approved universal child care legislation that was intended to provide affordable, quality child care to all parents that needed it. But President Nixon, under pressure from conservatives who feared that such a government policy would undermine the family's role in child-rearing, vetoed the bill (Schulte 2014), although the government did fund some child care for the extremely poor. But in comparison, many European governments ensure that child care for working parents is either free or affordable (Gornick 2007).

Flexible Work Hours

Another factor that helps working parents take care of their children more effectively is flexible work hours. Being able to work from home when your child is sick, for example, makes a parent and child feel better. This is especially helpful for single parents and working mothers (or mothers who want to work), since women still generally play a greater role in child-rearing. The European Union requires that all member countries ensure at least 4 weeks of paid time off each year. National policy in developed countries generally provides more opportunity for flexible work hours than in the United States (Gornick 2007; Schulte 2014).

High-Quality Part-Time Work

The European Union also mandates that all of its member countries ensure that part-time workers receive pay and benefits like those of full-time workers but just prorated (proportional) to the amount of time worked below the full-time level. This makes it much more economically possible for parents to work part-time because their pay is relatively high, and they also receive some benefits.

Universal Health Care

An additional aid to working families is universal health insurance. This means that people have access to health care regardless of what job they have. It gives parents the ability to search for the type of jobs and level of work hours that best fits their families' needs without having to worry about losing access to health care for themselves and their children. This also means more economic security and less stress for both parents and children.

What Is a Family?

Public opinion surveys indicate that most Americans now consider a family to include not only a married man and woman with children but also unmarried heterosexual partners with children and same-sex partners with children. A *contemporary sociological definition of family is a group of two or more people who are recognized by others as a family and identify themselves as a family.*

Families and Marriage Around the World

A nuclear family refers to two parents and their children or a single parent and her or his children. An extended family includes a nuclear family plus other relatives such as grandparents, aunts, uncles, and first cousins.

A patriarchal family is one in which the father has the greatest influence in making decisions for the family and its members. An egalitarian family type is one in which marital partners have equal influence in decision making and share equally in family centered work such as child-rearing and housework. A matriarchal family is mother centered with the mother having the greatest influence.

A forced marriage involves one or both persons who do not give free consent. An arranged marriage is one in which a third party, typically the families of the persons to be married, take the leading role in selecting a potential marriage partner. But the proposed parties to the marriage are free to decide whether to go through with it. An autonomous marriage is one in which persons freely make the choice of who to marry without anyone forcing them or trying to select a partner for them.

Monogamous marriage is marriage between only two persons. Polygamous marriage is marriage involving a person being married to two or more spouses. Polygyny is the form of polygamy in which one man has more than one wife. Polyandry is marriage of a woman to more than one husband.

Changes in the U.S. Family

The U.S. family has changed significantly since the mid-1950s. People began getting married later in life, and the percent of Americans remaining single or cohabiting increased.

The percent of married people who divorced increased from around 1960 to 1980 due to several factors. Women's increasing labor force participation and financial independence allowed them to escape unsatisfactory marital situations. In addition, the social stigma attached to divorce declined and all states instituted "no-fault" divorce laws, making divorce easier.

Research indicates that divorce can have harmful or beneficial economic and psychological consequences for spouses. Negative impacts on children can be limited if hostility and conflict between divorcing parents is minimized.

Another significant change is that while in 1950 only 4 percent of children born in the United States were born to unwed mothers, it was 40 percent in 2015. Overall, the proportion of children raised in single-parent female-headed households increased significantly.

Single-Parent Families

Research shows that living with only one parent increases the probability of growing up in poverty and attending inadequate schools. It also increases the risk of poor academic performance and becoming involved in criminal behavior. Loss of urban industrial jobs has contributed to the dramatic rise in the proportion of African American children living in one-parent households. Another reason is the mass incarceration of black men.

Gay and Lesbian Families

Tens of thousands of children are being raised by same-sex couples. Research indicates that these children fare as well as children being raised by opposite-sex parents on various measures of child development and well-being.

Violence and Abuse in Intimate Partner and Family Relationships

Worldwide, as well as in the United States, about 30 percent of women report experiencing physical violence from a partner in an intimate relationship. Although Americans of all social classes experience intimate partner violence, those with low incomes are at greater risk. In addition, research indicates that American Indian/Alaska Native women, multiracial women, and non-Hispanic black women are at greater risk than non-Hispanic white women, Hispanic women, or Asian women. Intimate partner violence has serious harmful psychological, social, health, and economic consequences. But after 1994, intimate partner violence, like other violent crimes, has appeared to decline significantly.

Child Abuse

Child abuse refers to the physical, sexual, psychological, or emotional maltreatment or neglect of a child. Hundreds of thousands of cases are reported in the United States each year. While the largest percentage of abused children are white, the risk of being a victim has been somewhat higher for African American, American Indian/Alaskan Native, and multiracial children than for Hispanic, white, or Asian American children. Although children of all economic classes have been the victims of abuse, those living in low-income households where caregivers are under economic stress have been at greater risk. Factors such as mental illness, alcohol or drug abuse, being raised in a subculture of violence, being taught to respond to child misbehavior with physical punishment, or having been the victim of child physical, sexual, or emotional abuse are associated with being more likely commit abuse.

Elder Abuse and Neglect

Elder abuse refers to any behavior that harms or causes serious risk of harm to a vulnerable "senior" adult. Relatives are usually the perpetrators, with poverty and substance abuse increasing the likelihood of elder abuse.

Preventing Family Violence

Economic hardship, joblessness, and limited opportunity all generate stress that can lead to family violence. Male domination of the political systems in many countries is another reason for violence against women. Women must achieve political power though the vote, holding powerful government positions, and enacting laws that protect women. Various elements of culture have contributed to family violence and must be modified or eliminated to reduce it. Patriarchy, male domination in its various forms that leads men to believe they have the right to use force against wives or children, must be eradicated. Certain individual characteristics, such as substance abuse and untreated mental illness, can increase the likelihood of engaging in family violence. Most notably, having witnessed or been the victim of family violence increases the risk of committing family violence. Treatment programs are often available for abusers, but another way for abuse victims to escape violence is to flee to a safe environment such as domestic violence shelters. The problem of family violence must be addressed comprehensively on economic, political, cultural, and psychological levels.

Teen Pregnancies and Parenthood

The United States has a much higher rate of teen pregnancy than other technologically advanced nations, and the large majority of these teen births are nonmarital. Low-income teens with poor academic performance are at greater risk of pregnancy, as are those whose mothers gave birth as teens. Many teen pregnancies result in abortions. Those teens having their babies are more likely to drop out of high school and have limited educational and job opportunities. The only totally sure way to prevent unwanted pregnancies is to abstain from sexual intercourse. But for sexually active teens, the correct use of contraceptive methods can be effective in reducing the risk of pregnancy.

Sociological Perspectives on Family Problems

The structural-functional perspective views the family as the basic component of society carrying out essential social functions, including providing a secure environment for childbearing and -rearing. Anything that disrupts the family is a threat to the health of the social system.

The conflict approach claims that the family in its traditional form has perpetuated harmful inequalities. The economic-conflict perspective argues that the family has fostered economic inequality because children tend to inherit the wealth or poverty of their parents. The feminist-conflict approach points out that the patriarchal structure of families and male-dominated governmental and legal systems have contributed to men taking out their frustrations on wives and girlfriends. Even in homes where women have fulfilling careers, lingering male privilege and gender stereotypes contribute to them doing most child care and housework. The racial/ethnic-conflict perspective describes how the frustration people of color experience from being victimized by discrimination can increase the risk of family violence. This approach also describes how outsourcing American jobs and criminal justice policies leading to mass incarceration have contributed to pregnancies outside of marriage and children being raised in single parent families.

The symbolic-interactionist approach focuses on the effects of interpersonal interaction and learning experiences. Children tend to reflect in their own behavior and relationships what they experience and witness in their families.

KEY TERMS

arranged marriage, p. 177
autonomous marriage, p. 177
blended family, p. 179
child abuse, p. 186
egalitarian family, p. 176
elder abuse, p. 191
family, p. 174
forced marriage, p. 176

household, p. 174
intimate partner abuse, p. 185
kinship, p. 174
matriarchal family, p. 177
monogamous marriage, p. 177
patriarchal family, p. 176
polygamous marriage, p. 176

DISCUSSION QUESTIONS

1. What factors do you think are most responsible for the persistence of the patriarchal family type around the world?

2. Which factors and sociological perceptive do you think best explain the growth of the egalitarian family type?

3. What do you think would be the most effective way to reduce intimate partner violence in the United States? What about child abuse?

4. What do you think would be the best approach or approaches to reduce the number of teen pregnancies in the United States?

CHAPTER 8

Education and Media

CHAPTER OBJECTIVES

- Describe the differences in literacy rates and academic achievement among social groups in the United States, as well as among nations, and the factors that may be responsible for these differences.
- Describe problems in the U.S. educational system and schools.
- Explain approaches for improving academic performance.
- Explain the factors that affect media authorities' decisions to broadcast a particular potential news story or ignore it.

- Explain media issues concerning objectivity, inequality, and crime.
- Describe the roles of mass media and social media in social movements.

STUDENT EDUCATIONAL ACHIEVEMENT IN *some nations is much higher than in others. The Program for International Student Assessment (PISA) tested about 490,000 fifteen-year-old students from over sixty countries in 2015 (PISA 2017). Three main achievement categories were evaluated: mathematics, reading, and science. Excluding the several parts of the People's Republic of China that were tested in place of the whole nation, U.S. students scored 37th in math, 22nd in reading and 22nd in science. Two countries on opposite sides of the world did much better. South Korea placed 4th in math, 6th in reading and 8th in science, while Finland was 10th in math, 3rd in reading and 5th in science.*

Why did students in these two nations score so well in comparison to the United States? Actually, their paths to high student achievement appear quite different (Ripley 2013). In Korea, at the end of the normal school day millions of children head for private tutoring programs. Many do not return home until after 10 pm. It's not unusual for Korean children to sleep in some of their daytime classes to be rested for private schooling later in the day. Special classes continue in the summer. In South Korea, the key to academic achievement is devoting an enormous amount of time to study.

Finland is different. Instead of parents spending massive sums on supplementary private schooling, Finland recruits the top young intellectual talent for teaching careers, educates them at the country's finest universities, and then pays them well. Admission to a teaching program in Finland has been compared to being accepted at MIT in the United States. The Finnish strategy is to have extremely high-quality teaching throughout the public school system by having extremely high-quality teachers. More is thus achieved during the regular school day, and there is less need for private tutors. What is common to South Korea and Finland, both relatively resource-poor countries, is a national culture that puts very strong emphasis on education. High-quality human resources are viewed as essential to continued development and national welfare.

In comparison, the culture of the resource-rich United States, the nation that dominates the world economically, technologically, and militarily, has a somewhat less intense focus on educational achievement. Most U.S. parents rely on mainline schooling rather than private supplementary programs like in South Korea. And unlike Finland, many persons entering the teaching profession are students with relatively low aptitude scores who are trained in a wide range of colleges, some with minimal admission requirements. Can the United States maintain its current strength if its students continue to lag behind other nations?

SOCIOLOGICAL PERSPECTIVES ON EDUCATION

Structural-Functional Perspective

The structural-functional approach views education as a process that prepares young people to fit into and become productive members of society. Teaching children society's core values and norms ensures they will accept, rather than disrupt, the existing social system. The education process also imparts knowledge and skills to help students become intelligent and productive persons. Since ideally schools offer education to all children, society benefits because its pool of developed talent is greatly expanded. Schools can also carry out the function of identifying unique individual aptitudes, which can be developed through specialized education. Another function of education is guardianship of children. This is a latent function accompanying the directly intended teaching function. Guardianship refers to providing care and supervision for students while parents are at work or otherwise occupied.

Conflict Perspective

The conflict approach focuses on how inequality in society interferes with achieving universal educational opportunity for all and how education can in fact perpetuate inequality. This perspective notes there are tremendous differences in the quality of facilities, faculty, and instruction among schools, and that lower-income children typically attend the least-adequate schools. This limits chances for upward social mobility and perpetuates patterns of inequality. The one thing that the school system does tend to do uniformly is too indoctrinate all students to accept the existing society, with its vast inequalities, as the best possible way of life. This promotes the idea that criticizing the status quo is unpatriotic, thereby further stifling change.

Symbolic-Interactionist Perspective

This approach focuses on the interaction and communication between teachers and students. Teachers may have lower expectations for students from lower-class backgrounds. This can result in lower-income students feeling less comfortable in school and less confident in their abilities, leading to poor school performance. Thus, low expectations generate a so-called self-fulfilling prophecy, causing those of whom little is expected to in fact achieve less than they could. This preserves inequality by discouraging lower-income kids from trying to obtain the educations and careers that would allow them to enter the middle or higher classes.

However, the symbolic-interactionist perspective also helps us identify at least one aspect of education that can promote social change. It is well known that students have often played an important role in reform and revolutionary movements. If education had a totally conformist effect, this would not be possible. In reality students often learn things about their society through education that they perceive as injustices that conflict with their ideals. For example, American youth who were taught that all people are created equal and then learn about or experience discrimination have been motivated to fight for social justice for racial and ethnic minorities, women, children, people with disabilities, and sexual orientation minorities.

> **student movement** A social movement in which students are the main or leading participants.

Social Movements: Education and Student Movements

Student activists March for Our Lives, March 24, 2018

Education plus idealism can lead to the development of a **student movement**. Young people typically develop ideals about the way the world should be from the moral principles they learn early in life. Students sometimes encounter new information that conflicts with their ideals. Courses in sociology, history, or political science often make students aware of conditions (like inequality, extreme poverty, discrimination, injustice, etc.) that conflict with ideals. The result can be moral frustration that requires some type of response (Gill and DeFronzo 2009). One response is to try to change society to make it more closely reflect ideals. The circumstances of many college students, living on campus and being somewhat independent of both parental control and pressing financial concerns of family life, permit idealism to flourish and allow time for activism.

In addition to relative physical and intellectual freedom, the concentration of large numbers of students at one location facilitates rapid communication and mobilization. Research also indicates that students at colleges with a tradition of political activism are more likely to participate in student movements and protests.

One of the great student movements in U.S. history was the anti–Vietnam War movement. Students in the 1950s and early 1960s had participated in the modern civil rights movement. This was soon followed by protests against the U.S. military intervention in Vietnam. The effort was student based in part because the draft forced many young people to participate in a war they opposed, leave the country, or go to prison.

Another important factor was the information about Vietnam students learned from college courses that contradicted the administration's claim that communist aggression was responsible for the war. College students were among the first Americans to understand the tremendous gap between prowar propaganda and reality. When President Lyndon Johnson sent large U.S. forces to Vietnam, students protested. One of the first antiwar demonstrations was the May 21, 1965, Vietnam Day protest by about 10,000 persons at the University of California at Berkeley. The antiwar movement spread to other colleges in California and to other parts of the United States. By 1969, students at many colleges outside of the South opposed the war.

The student antiwar protests, coupled with the massive 1968 Vietnamese revolutionary Tet offensive, which seemed to indicate that the United States could not win the war, increased antiwar feelings in the larger population. When major political opponents of the Vietnam War, Martin Luther King Jr. and Senator Robert Kennedy, were assassinated in 1968, some student activists engaged in more extreme protest behavior. This included calling for a student boycott of classes to force

(continued)

Social Movements (*continued*)

colleges to ban Dow Chemical, the maker of the firebomb weapon napalm used by U.S. forces in Vietnam, from trying to hire students on campus. But many students felt that shutting down classes would only hurt students themselves. After this divisive tactic, a significantly weakened student antiwar movement carried on until the United States pulled out of Vietnam in 1973. The anti–Vietnam War movement served as a model for later student movements, such as those against U.S. intervention in Central America in the 1980s, South African apartheid in the 1980s and 1990s, and the invasion of Iraq in 2003.

UNEQUAL EDUCATIONAL ACHIEVEMENT WORLDWIDE

There are many nations where tens of millions of children have virtually no access to formal schooling. They rely on family members, friends, or religious or tribal leaders to teach them important skills. Lack of educational opportunity means that 758 million adults (people aged fifteen or older) worldwide are illiterate in that they lack basic reading and writing skills (UNESCO 2015). This represents 14.7 percent of the world's adults. Women are almost two-thirds of the illiterate adult population. The table below shows the twenty most literate and twenty least literate nations with populations over one million (CIA 2017d).

As reflected in the table, literacy rates vary widely around the world. In addition to the top twenty nations in the table, the United States, Australia, New Zealand, South Korea, Japan, most European, and some Latin American countries have official literacy rates in the 98 to 99 percent range. Countries with very low literacy rates generally have wide gaps between male and female literacy. For example, the male literacy rate in Niger was about 27 percent; for females it was 11 percent. Similarly, in Afghanistan the male literacy rate was about 52 percent but only 24 percent for females.

UNEQUAL EDUCATIONAL ACHIEVEMENT IN THE UNITED STATES

There are about 139,126 educational institutions in the United States (National Center for Education Statistics 2016a). This includes approximately 131,890 elementary and high schools (about 98,271 public and 33,619 private), 3,039 four-year colleges, 1,685 two-year colleges and 2,512 post-high-school nondegree schools (many providing specialized technical or career training). Total student enrollment at all levels was about 77,066,000 in October 2015, with approximately 8,605,000 children in nursery schools or kindergartens, 32,826,000 in elementary schools, 16, 535,000 in high schools, and 19,101,000 in post-high-school educational institutions (U.S. Census 2016a).

While there are many fine schools and universities in the United States, the educational system has several serious problems.

TABLE 8.1	Percent Literate for the Twenty Most Literate and Least Literate Nations with Populations over One Million
Most Literate Nations	**Least Literate Nations**
Finland 100%	Niger 19.1%
North Korea 100%	South Sudan 27%
Norway 100%	Guinea 30.4%
Latvia 99.9%	Burkina Faso 36%
Cuba 99.8%	Somalia 37.4%
Estonia 99.8%	Afghanistan 38.2 %
Azerbaijan 99.8%	Benin 38.4%
Georgia 99.8%	Mali 38.7%
Kazakhstan 99.8%	Chad 40.2 %
Lithuania 99.8%	Cote d'Ivoire 43.1%
Poland 99.8%	Sierra Leone 48.1%
Ukraine 99.8 %	Ethiopia 49.1%
Tajikistan 99.8%	Gambia 55.5%
Russia 99.7%	Senegal 57.7
Slovenia 99.7%	Pakistan 57.9%
Armenia 99.7%	Mozambique 58.8%
Belarus 99.7%	Nigeria 59.6%
Turkmenistan 99.7%	Guinea-Bissau 59.9%
Croatia 99.7%	Haiti 60.7%
Uzbekistan 99.6%	Bangladesh 61.5%

Source: CIA Country Factbook 2017 (Estimates are for the year 2015; for four countries without 2015 estimates, earlier CIA estimates are used.)

The Problem of American Students' Academic Performance

As noted in the opening section, American students on average score below students in many other technologically advanced nations on international achievement tests in math and science. While nations like Finland, South Korea, China, Estonia, and Poland have made great strides in improving their educational systems and students' educational achievement, U.S. academic performance has changed little in recent decades. In addition, there are wide gaps in academic performance among U.S. students.

Class, Race, Ethnicity, and Gender Impacts on Academic Performance

Economic Class Analyses of high school Scholastic Aptitude Test (SAT) results indicate that a students' economic class, race, and ethnicity tend to have significant impacts on scores. A *Wall Street Journal* article suggests that the SAT could be titled "Scholastic Affluence Test" because of the strong positive relationship between parental income and performance (Zumbrun 2014). A perfect score on a component of the SAT is 800, meaning that all correct answers on both the math and reading components would total 1600. The results of the 2016 SAT show that students of parents with income over $200,000 per year had an average combined math and reading score that was 60 points higher than that for students in the $140,000 to $200,000 range, 143 points higher than for students in the $60,000 to $80,000 range, and 267 points higher than for students in the less than $20,000 range (SAT 2016). The results of the 2008 SAT, the first to use family income categories similar to the more recent SAT tests, showed that the combined reading and math scores gap between those with incomes over $200,000 and those with incomes under $20,000 was 234, significantly smaller than for the 2016 SAT (SAT 2008). These big income differences appear due to several factors. One is that parents in upper income brackets generally raise their children in communities with very good teachers and school facilities or send them to high-priced private schools. So they accumulate years of superior educational experience before taking the SATs. High-income parents can also better afford to pay for tutors and special classes geared specifically to prepare children for taking the SATs. In addition, higher percentages of low-income children grow up in one-parent households. This may result is less parent–child interaction than in higher-income families and lower pre-school intellectual development.

Race and Ethnicity Race and ethnicity also have significant correlations to SAT scores. The 2016 SAT combined reading and math average for white American children was 206 points higher than the combined average for African American children and about 160 points higher than the combined average for Latino American ethnicities (SAT 2016). The combined reading and math average for Asian Americans was about 70 points higher than that for whites (due almost entirely to the higher Asian Americans' math scores). Racial and ethnic differences in SAT scores also appear due to multiple factors. Language and cultural differences in speech patterns play a role in lower reading scores and can interfere with learning math. Furthermore, teachers and facilities where many African American and Latino children go to school are often lower in quality than other schools and provide a less substantial education (Kozol 2005, 2012, 2013). Black and Hispanic children also tend to have less access to strong math and science courses (Rich 2014b). And students' educational efforts can be disrupted by threats to personal safety and gang activity, which are often more frequent at schools in low-income and minority urban areas. In addition, African American and Latino children are much more likely to be raised in one-parent households and to live in poverty (both of which can affect education, as described above).

Gender Throughout much of U.S. history, boys were taught skills to prepare them for the industrial and agricultural labor forces, whereas women were socialized to care for the home and children. As increasing numbers of individuals enrolled in college, men took courses geared for careers in science, engineering, and business; women studied for professions that reflected the traditional female nurturing role such as teaching, nursing, and social work. The women's movement and scientific research that demonstrated women's vast intellectual capabilities opened up a range of previously almost exclusively male occupations to women. A major federal law, Title IX of the Education Amendments of 1972 (U.S. Department of Education 2017), which protects people from discrimination based on sex in any educational program or activity receiving federal financial aid, played a significant role in expanding higher-educational opportunities for women. In the late 1970s, the number of women in U.S. colleges exceeded men for the first time (Borzelleca 2012). The female majority grew to about 57 percent of all college students by 2008. Graduate school enrollments generally rose faster for women than men between 1998 and 2007, and by 2008 women made up 59 percent of all first-time enrollees in graduate schools and received about 60 percent of all master's degrees and 49 percent of all doctoral degrees (Schmidt 2009). But women continued to be significantly underrepresented in the physical sciences and engineering programs. While on the 2016 SAT tests college-bound women averaged 12 points higher than college bound men on the writing test component, men's average reading test score was 2 points higher than that for women and 30 points higher on the math test (SAT 2016).

The Dropout Problem

Deficiencies in the educational system contribute to the school dropout problem. The status dropout rate is the percentage of sixteen- through twenty-four-year-olds who are not enrolled in school and have not earned a high school diploma or its equivalent, such as a General Educational Development (GED) certificate (National Center for Education Statistics 2016b; 2017b). The U.S. status dropout rate was 6.5 percent in 2014, declining significantly from 12.1 percent in 1990. The status dropout rate for males was 7.1 percent and 5.9 percent for females. The

Asian rate was 2.5 percent, for whites 5.2 percent, blacks 7.4 percent, and Hispanics 10.6 percent. Research also indicates that children from families in the income bottom 20 percent are about five times more likely to drop out of high school than children in the top 20 percent (Chapman et al. 2011). Dropouts earn about $20,241 per year, $10,386 less than persons with a high school but no college degree, and about $36,424 less than a graduate of a four-year college (Breslow 2012).

Dropouts have often been so badly educated in elementary and middle school that by the time they reach high school they are poorly prepared and become frustrated. Students who fail to pass eighth grade math or English are estimated to be seventy-five percent more likely to drop out of high school (Convissor 2014). Being held back to repeat a grade also increases the likelihood of dropping out. Some students drop out because they feel bored with school, don't see how it is relevant to their lives, or hang out with other juveniles who have dropped out. Also, various events, such as family financial difficulties, divorce or separation of parents, moving from one location to another, or pregnancy, can disrupt students' lives and increase the probability of dropping out.

Functional Illiteracy

Unfortunately, there are millions of Americans who, because of dropping out or inadequate education, are functionally illiterate. **Functional illiteracy** means lacking the level of reading or writing skills necessary to carrying out everyday tasks. Findings released by the U.S. Department of Education (Britt 2009) indicate that as many as thirty-two million adult Americans (14 percent, or one in seven) are functionally illiterate. More than half of prison inmates are estimated to be functionally illiterate, suggesting a link between illiteracy and street crimes like assault, robbery, burglary, and larceny.

The School Segregation Problem

Until the 1950s, schools in many states were racially segregated by law. In northern states, student populations also tended to be racially segregated because children typically attended neighborhood schools, and neighborhoods were racially segregated. School racial segregation laws were struck down by the 1954 Supreme Court ruling in the *Brown v. Board of Education of Topeka* (Kansas) case. The case centered on twelve-year-old Linda Brown, whose family wanted her to attend a school only four blocks from her home (Biography 2014). But a racial segregation law banned her from that all-white school and required her to attend a school for nonwhites much farther away. The U.S. Supreme Court ruled unanimously that racially segregated public facilities like schools are unconstitutional. This, in effect, opened all publicly funded educational institutions, including previously white-only colleges, to all races.

Following this Supreme Court ruling, many school districts attempted to racially integrate schools. Since whites and blacks tended to live in different neighborhoods, the solution proposed in some cities was to place students on buses and send them to schools far from their homes to achieve a proportion of students in schools similar to the racial makeup of the population. But many parents objected to their

functional illiteracy The lack of the level of reading or writing skills necessary to carry out everyday tasks.

kids having to spend unnecessary time on buses traveling to far-away schools. And many parents feared that the schools their children were bused to were inferior and less safe than those in their neighborhoods. A powerful antibusing movement developed. Many white and middle- and upper-class families escaped busing programs by moving out of the affected school districts or by placing their children in private schools. Over time, a large number of urban public school populations became so overwhelmingly poor and minority that it was impossible to bus students within a school district to achieve racially balanced schools. The busing program came to be viewed as a failure and was largely abandoned as an option for integrating schools by the twenty-first century.

Many African American and Latino students attend schools characterized by the double **school segregation** of race and poverty. According to Orfield, Kucsera, and Siegel-Hawley (2012), the typical black or Latino student attends a public school in which about 64 percent of classmates are from households with incomes below the federal poverty level. In comparison, the typical white or Asian American student going to public schools attends a school where over 60 percent of the other students are not poor.

School Crime, Bullying, and Discipline Problems

Crime School should be an absolutely safe environment. Students who feel that they are in danger can be distracted from the educational process and have difficulty learning. Crime victimization is higher for students who are poor, male, African American, or Hispanic. While crime occurs in both private and publics schools, the incidence appears to be twice as high in public schools (Robers et al. 2014). In 2014, students 12–18 years old experienced 850,100 nonfatal violent victimizations or thefts at school (National Center for Education Statistics 2016c). But while there were 181 victimizations per 1,000 students at school in 1992, the rate in 2014 was much lower, 33 victimizations per 1,000 students. School killings, while relatively rare, are terrifying to parents and students far beyond the schools where they occur. During the 1992–1993 school year, 34 young people aged 5–18 were killed at schools. The number during 2010–2011 was 11. The December 2012 Sandy Hook Elementary School massacre alone took the lives of 20 children (and 6 teachers and staff), and there were 15 other school-related homicides from July 1, 2012 to June 30, 2013 (National Center for Education Statistics 2016d).

The Youth Risk Behavior Survey (2018) reported that in 2017 about 6 percent of students in grades 9 through 12 reported that they had been threatened or injured by a weapon (such as a gun, knife, or club) on school property at least once during the 12 months before the survey. In addition, 6.7 percent said that they skipped school one or more times in the 30 days preceding the survey because they felt unsafe at school or on their way to or from school. 3.8 percent of students said they carried a weapon on school property at least one day during the 30 days preceding the survey.

Bullying The Youth Risk Behavior Survey (2018) revealed that in 2017 19 percent of students were bullied on school property during the 12

school segregation The division of students by race, ethnicity, and/or class into different schools.

months before the survey. Children who are bullied are more likely to have lower academic achievement (GPA and standardized test scores) and to skip or drop out of school (Stopbullying.gov 2014). They are also more likely to experience anxiety and depression, feel sad or lonely, and lose interest in things they used to enjoy. Although other factors play a role, bullying in rare but tragic cases has led to bullied persons committing suicide or carrying out a school shooting.

The significant amount of crime and bullying at schools, on school property, and on school buses, and terrifying mass murders at schools like Columbine High School (April 20, 1999) and Virginia Tech (April 16, 2007) have led to measures to protect students, teachers, and staff from threats to their safety. During the 2011–2012 school year, 88 percent of public schools reported that they controlled the entrance to school buildings by locking or monitoring doors, and 64 percent indicated they used security cameras (Robers et al. 2014). Other measures employed or expanded since the Sandy Hook (December 14, 2012) massacre include armed guards or armed staff members at schools, bulletproof white boards in classrooms, lockdown drills, panic button alert systems, and new lightweight, super-strong bulletproof glass to delay a shooter's access to a school until police arrive (Martin 2014).

Discipline Discipline issues such as disrespect and verbal abuse of teachers, threats to teachers or other students, fights in classrooms or hallways, and alcohol or other drug use on school property are also problems. Overall, 65 percent of public schools reported that at least one violent incident occurred at school during the 2013–14 school year (Gray and Lewis 2015). In an earlier study on school disciplinary practices for the 2009–2010 school year, 83 percent of public high schools, 67 percent of middle schools, and 18 percent of primary schools carried out at least one serious disciplinary action against students: suspensions from school lasting 5 or more days; expulsions; or transfers to specialized schools (National Center for Education Statistics 2015b). Twenty-nine percent of the 433,800 serious disciplinary actions were for physical attacks or fights, but 3 percent were for possession of a firearm or an explosive device. Other serious disciplinary actions were for the distribution, possession, or use of alcohol; the distribution, possession, or use of illegal drugs; or the use or possession of a weapon other than a firearm or explosive device. Of the serious disciplinary actions for the 2009–2010 school year, 74 percent were suspensions of 5 days or more, 20 percent were transfers to specialized schools and 6 percent were removals from school with no services for the remainder of the school year.

There is significant concern that black and Hispanic children are much more likely to be given serious school disciplinary actions or even arrested on school property than white non-Hispanic children (Associated Press 2012; Rich 2014a, 2014b). For more than two decades, many U.S. school systems have enforced "zero-tolerance" policies that require disciplinary actions for any serious rule violations such as violence, threats, theft, or possessing alcohol, illegal drugs, or weapons on school property whether or not students realized what they were doing was not permitted. The intent was to provide a safe and secure learning and work environment at schools and zero tolerance has had significant support from many teachers, school administrators, and much of the public. But critics argue there are major flaws in the policy and the way it has been enforced. One issue is whether zero tolerance is employed too strictly, with no discretion for student intentions or whether students are aware of the potential punishments for their behavior. For example, some students might carry a pocket knife to feel safe and protect themselves on their way to school and back in high-crime neighborhoods with no intent to threaten another student or a teacher. But the mere possession of the pocket knife on school property could result in suspension or expulsion. The strict enforcement of zero tolerance, critics argue, fuels the so-called school-to-prison pipeline by unnecessarily criminalizing many low-income and minority students for minor offenses or for mistakes and forcing them into lives of crime and perpetual imprisonment.

Another possible flaw in the zero-tolerance policy is that it may be used in a biased way to improve the average scores of students on standardized exams. A teachers' performance (and salary level) is often evaluated in part by her or his students' scores on standardized exams. Thus, a teacher might be more likely to recommend expulsion of a student for an offense under zero-tolerance policy who has demonstrated less academic testing ability in order to boost the overall test average for the remaining students.

There is also fear that race, ethnic, or class discrimination may influence who gets suspended or expelled from a school. For example, black students are three times as likely to be suspended and expelled compared to white students (Rich 2014b). And although black children are about 18 percent of children enrolled in preschool, nearly half of all preschool children suspended two or more times are black. It is unclear how much of the higher rates of suspension and expulsion of black and Hispanic children are due to discrimination. Some of the difference may be due to more behavioral problems among minority children, who disproportionately grow up in low-income neighborhoods characterized by relatively high levels of crime, violence, and drug use. Only research that controls for potential differences in misconduct among children can help us accurately determine how much discrimination may play a part in the suspension and expulsion of black and Hispanic children.

Nevertheless, many people are greatly concerned over the large number of children suspended, expelled, or arrested for acts on school property and possibly set on a path to adult crime and prison (American Psychological Association Zero Tolerance Task Force 2008; Rich 2014a). Social scientists and many government officials have suggested that punishments should be applied with greater flexibility. Teachers, staff, and students should have clear and shared understandings of the differences between minor and major acts of misconduct and of the associated responses and punishments. However, there is still substantial disagreement on the best approach to ensure school safety.

Soaring College Tuition and Student Debt

Since the 1970s, the cost of college tuition generally increased faster than the rate of inflation. At the same time, inflation-adjusted household income rose very little except for the richest ten percent of the population.

The average tuition and fees in 2016 dollars for private nonprofit four-year colleges for the academic year 1971–1972 was $10,832 but climbed to $33,479 for the 2016–2017 academic year (College Board 2017) . Public four-year college tuition increased from $2,531 in 1971–1972 to $9,648 in 2016–2017. The average student loan debt of a student graduating in 2016 was about $37,172, and in 2017 an estimated 44 million Americans had student loan debt (for more than 2 million, the debt exceeds $100,000) (Friedman 2018; Picchi 2016; Student Loan Hero 2017).

APPROACHES TO IMPROVING BASIC PUBLIC EDUCATION

According to a March 2017 national Gallup opinion poll, Americans included education among the ten most important problems facing the nation (Gallup 2017b). But there has been enormous disagreement over how to improve student achievement.

Criticisms of the Public School System

Critics have argued that major problems affecting the public school system include lack of accountability for student and teacher performance and lack of competition among schools, students, teachers, and administrators. In many schools, students have been promoted to the next grade regardless of how little they learned in order to avoid hurt feelings or complaints from parents. This practice of *social promotion* meant that students could graduate middle school or sometimes even high school while still functionally illiterate. To address these issues, some educational experts asserted that what was needed first was a system of standardized student achievement tests, especially for the core subjects of math and reading. This would give school and government officials accurate data on what each student had learned and how well each teacher was educating her or his students. Students who did poorly could be identified for special assistance or held back to repeat a grade. Teachers' pay could be determined, at least in part, on how well their students performed on standardized tests. Ineffective teachers would be required to obtain additional training or be removed. School principals could also be rewarded or removed in the same way. Students, teachers, and administrators would all be more accountable for their performance, increasing motivation for higher achievement.

Another proposal was to make public schools compete with one another for students as a way to force them to improve. A number of innovations may have increased school competition, although this was not necessarily the original goal in each case. A **charter school** is a publicly funded school able to operate more independently of the public school system in order to try new educational methods. Many charter schools also engage in private fundraising. And many are managed by private companies contracted by government. During the 2015–2016 academic year, there were 6,855 charter schools with about 2.85 million students, about 5.7 percent of the country's public elementary, middle, and high school students (National Center for Education Statistics

charter school A publicly funded school, often managed by a private company contracted by government, that is able to operate more independently of the school system in order to try new educational methods.

2017a). Regulations for these schools vary from state to state. Many, but not all, hire nonunion teachers.

Another innovation that began in the late 1960s is the **magnet school** (Chen 2014). One major purpose of magnet schools was to facilitate voluntary racial integration of public schools. Magnet schools are free public elementary, middle, and high schools that are run by school districts or groups of school districts. Magnet schools have an attractive central educational focus, such as science, technology, engineering, mathematics, or fine and performing arts. In order to take advantage of the special opportunities offered at a magnet school, students and their parents may choose magnet schools even though other schools are closer to where they live. Magnet schools typically appeal to a wide range of students based on their interest in the school's focus. Because of this, they often have a student body that is more diverse than neighborhood schools in terms of race, culture, and socioeconomic background. Magnet schools are often characterized by improved academic performance, fewer discipline problems, higher attendance and graduation rates, better teacher morale, lower teacher turnover rates, and higher parental engagement and satisfaction (Magnet Schools 2014). Supporters of magnet schools also claim that other public schools are forced to improve in order to compete with magnet schools for good students.

Critics of magnet schools fear that they absorb an inordinate amount of public resources, lure away many of the brightest students from other nearby public schools, and often have academic admission requirements too high to allow entrance of low-income students or those with special needs who could benefit from magnet schools (Chen 2014). By the 2015–16 school year there were an estimated 3,237 magnet schools in the United States with about 2.6 million students, about 5.2 percent of the country's public elementary, middle, and high school students (National Center for Education Statistics 2017a).

By 2017, twenty-seven states plus the District of Columbia had **school voucher programs** or a closely related type of private school option program, and several other states were considering such programs (National Conference of State Legislatures 2017c; Prothero 2017; Rios 2017). School voucher programs can provide taxpayer funds to the parents of school children to use in paying all or partial tuition at private (or in some cases public) schools of their choice. Advocates of vouchers believe they allow parents to move their children to better schools than they would otherwise be assigned by a school district. They also argue that vouchers increase competition for students and force poorly performing schools to improve. Research indicates that students using vouchers do as well or somewhat better academically than similar students in public schools. Opponents argue that voucher programs reduce desperately needed funding for public schools. They also claim that since many parents use vouchers to send their children to reli-

magnet school A free public elementary, middle, or high school run by school districts or groups of school districts that has an attractive central educational focus such as science, technology, engineering, mathematics, or fine and performing arts.

school voucher programs Programs that provide taxpayer funds to the parents of school children to use in paying all or partial tuition at private (or in some cases public) schools of their choice.

A magnet school in Los Angeles

gious schools, such as Catholic schools, voucher programs violate the First Amendment of the Constitution, which requires separation of church and state. Betsy DeVos, who became Secretary of Education in the Trump administration in 2017, is a supporter of vouchers.

There is a movement to replace many public schools with for-profit privately owned schools or publicly funded charter schools managed by for-profit private companies. Advocates of replacing public schools argue that private companies can educate children more efficiently, make changes more quickly, and get rid of poor teachers more rapidly. But critics claim existing research indicates that students at charter schools usually perform at about the same levels as public school students and that when charter schools appear to do better, the differences are very small and likely due to preventing or discouraging low-performing students from attending (Buchheit 2014; Ravitch 2014). Ravitch (2014) states that although New York Public schools are among the most highly racially segregated in the United States, New York charter schools are even more segregated. She also asserts that although New York City's privately managed charter schools teach only 6 percent of the city's school children, they have enormous political power in great part because for-profit charter schools are backed by a number of Wall Street billionaires and corporations.

Distinctive Points of View

Joel Klein (2014a), Paul Tough (2013) and Diane Ravitch (2013) have presented proposals for improving students' academic performance. Klein is a lawyer that former New York City mayor Michael Bloomberg appointed as school chancellor in 2002 to reform the school system. Klein's approach involved centralizing control of the city's more than 1,600 schools, enacting uniform standards, improving discipline and the safety of students, removing seriously underperforming teachers and principals, implementing a merit pay system to reward exceptional teachers and principals, using standardized tests to evaluate student achievement and school progress, and closing failing schools and replacing them with smaller better schools. Scores on standardized tests seemed to improve after the Klein–Bloomberg reform program. However, it appears possible that much of the improvement was due to standardized tests being made easier. When more difficult tests were used in 2010, the scores dropped far below those of the previous year (Medina 2010). The 2014 tests indicated a slight improvement from 2013, but the large majority of the city's students, more than 60 percent, still did not achieve proficiency in either math or English (Rebecca Klein 2014b).

Joel Klein believes that improving academic achievement is linked to improving the quality of teachers and principals. He advocates elevating the status and attractiveness of the teaching profession and improving teacher education. The goal is to encourage above-average college students to enter the teaching profession. Teachers and schools, according to Klein, should also be made accountable for their performance by giving parents a choice regarding what schools their children will attend. This would allow many low-income and minority children to attend good schools and also force poorly performing schools to improve or else be closed. Klein argues that improving education will help students from low-income families acquire the knowledge and skills to get good jobs and that, over time, this will reduce economic inequality.

Virtually everyone concerned with improving educational performance agrees that modern technology is needed in all schools. There is also general agreement that elevating the status of the teaching profession and motivating the most intelligent college students to become teachers could significantly improve the educational system. However, it is unclear how such a change in the status or attractiveness of the teaching profession could be brought about when American culture puts so much emphasis on achieving high levels of wealth few teachers could ever hope to obtain.

Critics of the Klein–Bloomberg approach fear that it fails to address the basic learning problems of those students most in need. Instead, it leaves them behind in public schools lacking the programs that would benefit them because resources have been diverted to charter schools. In the long run public schools would deteriorate, increasing inequality in American society.

Tough (2013), for example, reviews extensive research indicating that *cognitive education*, that is, education to impart knowledge, is only one of two crucial processes in academic achievement. The other is *character education*, meaning the development of a set of personality traits including self-control, conscientiousness, curiosity, self-confidence, and persistence in the achievement of goals (Tough 2013:xv). Tough believes that both cognitive education and strength of character are linked to economic class but that only cognitive education (such as improving the quality of teachers) has been targeted in educational reform. Research indicates that strong "character" results from a child being brought up in a warm, loving, secure, stable environment, relatively free from stress. Children with character deficiencies exist in all classes but are more common where there is intense stress, unstable, chaotic or violent family life, and extreme poverty, namely the lowest income ten percent of the population. Tough argues that educational reform that only improves teachers and school facilities will likely fail to make much of a difference for children in deep poverty. Ways must be found to build character, because character is necessary for academic achievement no matter how good schools or teachers are. This would involve ensuring economic and social support for very low-income parents to reduce stress and turmoil. Then their children would grow up with feelings of love and security and develop strong character.

Ravitch (2013) claims that a *comprehensive approach* is needed to improve the academic performance of lower income children. She argues that urban school problems are due mainly to concentrated poverty and racial segregation and that the movement for accountability has been largely taken over by people favoring privatization of public schools, which would make the situation worse for many children. Ravitch recommends providing good prenatal care for all pregnant women, high- quality preschool education for all children, small size classes, banning for-profit charter schools, having all charter schools work cooperatively with other public schools, and providing the social and medical services poor children need to do well in school. She also calls for moving away from high-stakes standardized testing of school children, ensuring that all teachers, principals, and school superintendents are professional educators, democratic control of schools through elected school boards, and reducing racial segregation and poverty.

The No Child Left Behind Program

In 2002 the federal government enacted a major reform to improve educational systems around the United States, No Child Left Behind (NCLB). The reform required all states to evaluate students through standardized tests focusing on the "core" subjects of reading and math, provide test results to parents, and make teachers and school administrators accountable for improving student performance. Schools were to provide tutoring to students who needed extra help to score satisfactorily. Schools whose students repeatedly failed to improve on standardized tests could have funding reduced or even be shut down. At first standardized test scores appeared to improve and graduation rates increased (Resmovits 2015).

However, a number of serious problems soon became apparent. Since each state could develop its own standardized tests and be penalized if too many students failed to score at proficient levels, some states created very easy tests. Thus, soon after NCLB was enacted, a number of states showed dramatic test score improvements mainly because the tests were made easy. There was also some indication that in certain cases, to boost a school's average test scores, students expected to score poorly were simply not tested. Furthermore, federal funding to states was often inadequate to provide the tutoring required under NCLB. This led some schools to divert teachers from courses like history and art to teaching the standardized test subjects, reading and math. Education shifted away from a balanced curriculum toward test taking preparation since good test performance was perceived to affect teachers' and administrators' jobs and salaries. Finally, many parents, students and teachers complained that standardized tests were culturally biased. These problems motivated the Obama administration to propose modifications to NCLB. Obama's secretary of education Arne Duncan stated that the modified NCLB would maintain required standardized testing because it was necessary to determine and inform parents and teachers how much progress students were making. But the testing process was to be streamlined by limiting the number of tests and the time allowed for schools to prepare students for tests (Payson-Denney 2015; Resmovits 2015). Further, schools were to allow time and resources for other important subjects besides reading, math, and science, like history, foreign languages, art, and physical education. In addition, the Obama administration called for increased high quality preschool education, better support for schools with low-income students, and broader evaluation of teacher and student performance rather than relying solely on standardized test scores.

Protests and Strikes by Teachers

Another approach toward improving basic public education involves teacher protests and work strikes. A number of state governments pursued policies of cutting taxes and in the process neglected the funding of public schools, especially after the recession that began in 2008. As a result of limited support, many public school students suffer from overcrowded class rooms, outdated textbooks, lack of supplies, and lack of essential teaching resources and equipment. In certain states, teachers' salaries stagnated or declined in terms of real purchasing power. Many discouraged, overworked and underpaid teachers left the teaching profession. They were often replaced by unqualified substitutes, further damaging the education of public school children. In addition, the difficulties faced by public school teachers and schools are likely at least partially responsible for the big drop in teacher education enrollments (Darling-Hammond 2018).

Desperation finally drove 20,000 West Virginia public school teachers and 13,000 school service workers to go on strike in late February 2018. Within weeks, the West Virginian teacher's strike inspired similar teacher walkouts in Oklahoma, Kentucky, Arizona, and Colorado. A national survey by the Associated Press-NORC Center for Public Affairs Research indicated that 78 percent of U.S. residents supported higher pay for teachers (Feldman and Swanson 2018). Shamed by the public revelations of the dire situations of many of their public schools and teachers, state legislators and governors scrambled to offer increased funding and teacher pay raises in order to end the strikes. The 2018 teacher strikes showed that organized workers in at least some occupations could successfully mobilize to pressure employers to improve wages and working conditions, and, in the process, combat or reverse the long-term trend toward increasing economic inequality.

MEDIA

Media refers to all forms of communication technology, including phones, radios, television, computers, the Internet, printed material, etc. Media convey information and carry out significant educational functions. Modern technology permits scientific, historical, and cultural knowledge to be shared around the world almost instantly. Media can also be used

Oklahoma Teachers' Protest, 2018

to excite, inspire, propagandize, mobilize, intimidate and terrorize. It has also provided the means for hundreds of millions of people to function as individual Internet journalists, using their smartphones to video record events and immediately transmit what they have seen and heard to the members of their social network or to the entire world.

SOCIOLOGICAL PERSPECTIVES ON MEDIA

Structural-Functional Perspective

The structural-functional perspective views media as a means to facilitate integration and interdependence among the people and institutional components of society. Improved communication can be used to reinforce a common set of values and norms (a shared culture). Media can also function internationally to facilitate global trade, financial relations, mutual understanding, cultural exchanges, and now, through the Internet and satellite communication systems, even person-to-person international interaction. The structural-functional view sees improving media and media access as playing crucial roles in the strengthening of a global social system.

Media can also have dysfunctions for society. For example, young people may spend too much time on social media and neglect schoolwork, and adults may engage in personal business or entertainment on the Internet during work time, lowering productivity.

Conflict Perspective

The conflict perspective focuses on inequality in access to media and control over media. Major news media are owned by a relatively small number of corporations. Furthermore, the news that is covered and the way it is reported often reflects financial interests and what broadcasters think their audience wants to hear rather than a truly objective coverage of events. One of the major examples of biased news was the coverage of circumstances leading up to the U.S.-led invasion of Iraq in 2003. Despite conflicting intelligence evidence, including from personnel within the CIA, major U.S. news media provided an almost totally one-sided platform for political figures who claimed, incorrectly, that Iraq possessed weapons of mass destruction. The falsely justified invasion and war cost the lives of over four thousand Americans and tens of thousands of Iraqis (DeFronzo 2010).

Because profit-oriented mass media have traditionally portrayed minorities and women by the stereotypes held by the majority of their viewers (in order to maximize the audience for their sponsors), they have played a major role in perpetuating discrimination and inequality. Research has shown, for example, that TV shows and movies watched for decades by American children presented boys as leaders and girls as followers (Barner 1999). This functioned to teach both boys and girls traditional sex roles that concealed the vast potential of women from society and even from themselves. Only recently, partly as a result of the feminist movement, have TV programs and movies begun to feature independent, self-reliant, powerful, and intelligent women and girls.

An example of media inequality in the economic sphere is high-speed, high-frequency stock trading. Many millions of trades are made by computers analyzing market activity and buying or selling stock in under a second. An estimated half of all stock trades are made this way, and some trading companies almost never have a losing day. The victims in this process are millions of individual investors and pension funds that do not have the facilities or mathematical formulas used by the high-speed trade companies. Their stock market losses help feed the profits of these companies. Even more disturbing are companies that have built or utilize electronic networks that allow them to make virtually no-risk profits by intercepting stock orders from other buyers (Batley 2014). In this process, when the company's computer detects a buy order for a large block of stock at a specific price, it quickly determines if a purchase of that stock can be made at a lower price. If it can, it buys the stock at the lower price and then sells it at the higher price that the intercepted buyer is willing to pay. All of this takes place in about a thousandth of a second or less. Even if the difference in price is small, when tens of thousands or hundreds of thousands of shares of stock are involved in each transaction, and there can be many thousands of such interceptions each day, the trading company with the advantage makes enormous profits at no risk while millions of other investors lose out.

Symbolic-Interactionist Perspective

The symbolic-interactionist perspective is concerned with the symbols, text, sounds, and imagery used in media to convey information and stories to the public and give them meaning (interpretations). It also focuses on the media's role in determining what is worth bringing to the public's attention, what the public is told about these things, what things should be considered social problems, and what the options are for solving them. The symbolic-interactionist approach further examines the motivations, goals, and capabilities of those who use media. In addition, it is concerned with how advances in technology have expanded access so that some media may be more democratic and less dominated by government and economic elites than in the past.

MEDIA ISSUES

Newsworthiness and News Objectivity

Media authorities recommend that to have **newsworthiness** and be broadcast, a particular story meet at least two of the following five criteria: significance, proximity, prominence, human interest, and timing (Mediacollege.com 2015). Significance refers in part to how many people are affected by the event or situation described in the story. The more people affected, the more important the story and the more likely it will receive media coverage. Another factor influencing significance is how much the story deviates from or disrupts normal social life or cultural norms and values. This includes, for example, huge natural disasters, major terrorist attacks, and sensational crimes like mass murders. Prominence also influences the decision to cover a story. The

newsworthiness The extent to which a story has the qualities, such as significance, proximity, prominence, human interest, and timing, to merit being presented to the public through news media.

public, in general, is more interested in things that happen to powerful or famous people, like government leaders and major entertainment and sports celebrities, than to unfamous people. Prominence may also be affected by race, ethnic, class, and other prejudices. The murder of a wealthy white person is usually expected to draw more public interest than the murder of a working-class black or Hispanic person.

Proximity – physical, social and/or cultural – is another element influencing coverage. Everything else being equal, the public tends to be more interested in stories that happen close by. A small plane crash in Minnesota, for example, will be covered in the state's newspapers and TV news broadcasts, but a similar crash in Argentina or Indonesia probably will not. But cultural proximity can often overcome great physical distance. For example, sports stories in the United Kingdom will often be covered in Australia and New Zealand but not covered at all in geographically closer countries like Iran and the Russian Federation.

Timing also influences whether a story will be covered, especially if it is only of average interest otherwise. Usually, only stories that are "new" (current, not a week or more old) are likely to be selected for coverage. In addition, stories normally of sufficient interest to the public may never be broadcast because a competing story of more importance to the public (like the 9/11 attacks or a major natural disaster such as Hurricane Katrina) dominates media attention. Human-interest stories that provoke emotions like sadness, happiness, admiration, wonder, or amusement are also attractive to many people. News programs often cover a human-interest story, like a soldier reuniting with his or her family or a young child collecting donations for a deserving cause, at the show's end to leave the audience with a good feeling.

But in reality, news directors and editors are not always free to make decisions on what stories to cover or how to cover them solely on the basis of these five factors. Another factor is avoidance of offending major program sponsors who might pull their advertising and reduce network profits. Another related consideration is to avoid offending a large sector of the public. These concerns can also interfere with **news objectivity**, the extent to which news personnel and institutions present stories truthfully and without bias to the public. For example, after the 9/11 attacks when many Americans were outraged and eager to strike back at whoever was responsible or might commit a similar terrorist attack, there was strong public support for war. News programs or talk shows that covered topics such as deaths of Afghan civilians killed by American military actions or presented opposition to the invasion of Iraq provoked a large number of complaints from both the public and advertisers who wanted their commercials to reach and be favorably received by as many people as possible. Other pressure on news programs can come from government and military leaders. These elites can punish a news organization by refusing to be interviewed by its journalists or allow it access to important information vital to producing interesting and appealing news programs.

The 2015–2016 presidential campaign and the Trump presidency provided new examples of the interrelationship of media, power, and

news objectivity The extent to which news personnel and institutions present stories truthfully and without bias to the public.

money. When Donald Trump announced his candidacy for the Republican presidential nomination on June 16, 2015, he had broad name recognition since he had been a business and television celebrity for many years. Yet many people initially did not view him as qualified to hold the presidency, and his support at first registered in single digits, behind several of the sixteen other Republican candidates. But news networks and talk shows quickly discovered that they could dramatically increase their viewership and their profits by covering Trump's speeches and rallies or inviting him as a guest. Thus, Trump benefitted from many millions of dollars of free mass media coverage compared to his Republican opponents.

Trump, however, soon accused several major media outlets of being biased and reporting "fake news," such as what he claimed were false stories about him, his family or associates, his campaign, or the policies he promoted. This included topics such as whether millions of people voted illegally for his Democratic opponent in the presidential election and whether the crowd attending his inauguration was larger or smaller than that for his predecessor Barack Obama. In February 2017 Trump was quoted in the *Los Angeles Times* (Shalby 2017) as tweeting "The FAKE NEWS media (failing @nytimes, @NBCNews, @ABC, @CBS, @CNN) is not my enemy, it is the enemy of the American People!" This hostile presidential orientation toward major news outlets raised fears that freedom of the press was endangered.

Digital Divide

Personal computers and smartphones provide access to enormous and increasing amounts of information and the ability to communicate with individuals or even millions of people almost anywhere in the world. But personal media requires financial resources for the purchase of equipment and software and payment of monthly service fees. The difference between having access to this media and not having access to this media has been referred to as the "**digital divide**." Income is significantly related to access to personal media. The PEW Research Center (Perrin and Duggin 2015) reported that in 2015 people in United States with higher education and higher income were more likely to use the Internet. Ninety-seven percent of households earning $75,000 or more used the Internet, compared to 74 percent of households earning less than $30,000.

There is also a large digital divide among nations. In 2017, about 88 percent of people in North America (Bermuda, Canada, Greenland, and the United States) used the Internet, compared to 77 percent in Europe, 68 percent in Australia and Oceana, 60 percent in Latin America and the Caribbean, 57 percent in the Middle East, 45 percent in Asia, and 28 percent in Africa (Internet World Stats 2017).

digital divide The division between those having or not having technologically advanced devices such as personal computers and smartphones that provide access to information and the ability to communicate with people almost anywhere in the world.

Media and Crime

For more than fifty years psychologists and sociologists have conducted studies to determine if exposure to violence on TV causes violent behavior. The results indicate that watching TV violence has no effect on the vast majority of viewers (Shupak 2015). But modern media has been used to

Special Topics: Learning History Through Movies

Hotel Rwanda *movie poster*

Movies can be an exciting way to tell the story of important events. For many people it may be the only way they learn about certain aspects of history. Several of the best historical movies include *Tora, Tora, Tora* (1970), about the attack on Pearl Harbor, *Midway* (1976) about the key World War II U.S. naval victory in the Pacific; *All the President's Men* (1976), about the journalists who revealed the Watergate conspiracy; *Gandhi* (1982), about India's nonviolent revolutionary leader; *Thirteen Days* (2000), about the 1962 Cuban missile crisis; *Shindler's List* (1993), about the German businessman who saved the lives of over a thousand Jews by employing them in his factories; *Hotel Rwanda* (2004), about a hotel manager who courageously struggled to provide refuge and protect people at his hotel during the Rwanda genocide; and *Selma* (2014), about the U.S. civil rights struggle to win the right to vote for blacks in the face of vicious racism.

But some very successful and Academy Award-nominated films on historical events have been criticized for not being factually accurate. One is director Oliver Stone's *JFK* (1991), about the assassination of President Kennedy. This film described efforts of New Orleans district attorney Jim Garrison to prove that the assassination was the result of a right-wing conspiracy attempting to prevent Kennedy from withdrawing from Vietnam and diminishing the power of the CIA. But critics claimed that the film, while exciting and well acted by a first-rate cast, contained factual errors and failed to adequately represent Garrison's investigative techniques.

Another controversial historical film that was financially successful and like *JFK* received multiple Academy Award nominations was director Clint Eastwood's *American Sniper* (2014), about the most lethal U.S. sniper, Navy SEAL Chris Kyle, credited with killing 160 persons in the Iraq War (Buckley 2015a). Mr. Eastwood said it had an antiwar aspect by describing the effects of war, including on soldiers and their families. Michelle Obama also felt the film described these consequences of war effectively. Critics of *American Sniper*, however, stated the film had distortions and inaccuracies. Some claimed the movie was prowar because it mislead the audience by implying Iraq had something to do with the 9/11 terrorist attacks and because it dehumanized the sniper's targets to justify killing them. Others objected to depicting Iraqis as terrorists, when many believed they were defending their country from an unjust U.S. invasion.

Although movies can make history exciting and interesting, they can also sometimes be criticized for spreading distortions and even outright falsehoods. Viewers should use multiple sources to check historical movies for accuracy.

promote or commit crime. Some people have used smartphones to bully and harass others and even video and post sexual assaults, as in the case of two former Vanderbilt football players convicted of raping a female student in a dorm room (Hastings 2015). Pedophiles have used the Internet to troll for victims, and other criminals have used it to commit fraud or steal money electronically from banks and businesses. For example, computer hackers using the Internet stole identification numbers and elevated withdrawal limits for prepaid bank cards issued by two Middle Eastern banks. On February 19, 2013, dozens of people used counterfeit prepaid bank cards with the stolen identification numbers to steal $45 million in a several-hour period from thousands of ATM bank machines in twenty-seven countries (Dye, Ax, and Finkle 2013). In New York City alone eight people in the international criminal team conducted 2,902 ATM withdraws totaling $2.4 million. The Internet has also been used by terrorists to post online magazines and videos of attacks and executions in order to attract new recruits from many countries, including the United States

According to U.S. intelligence authorities and investigators, one of the most sensational cyberattacks involved Russian citizens using the Internet in multiple ways to interfere in the 2016 presidential election to help Republican Donald Trump, the candidate viewed as more favorable to Russian interests. One aspect involved stealing emails of people working with the Democratic National Committee (Fishel 2017). Email contents reflecting discord within the party were then released periodically during the campaign to damage the chances of Democratic candidate Hillary Clinton. Another tactic was to use the Internet to spread false stories about Clinton through social media like Facebook to turn voters against her (Dougherty 2016). In addition, there were indications of Russian hacking of voter registration data bases and even attempts to hack U.S. voting systems (Perez 2017; Tribune News Service 2016).

Media can also inform the public about crime and can play a role in assisting criminal investigators and law enforcement. There are numerous true crime TV programs, such as *Dateline NBC, Forensic Files,* and *American Greed,* that describe how criminals from serial murderers to con men to corporate lawbreakers have committed their crimes. Some programs, such as *America's Most Wanted* and *The Hunt,* have sought the public's help in capturing hundreds of notorious criminals.

Law enforcement personnel have used media to detect and prevent crime, gather evidence, and locate and apprehend perpetrators (Broussard 2015; Cohen 2010; Kelly 2012). One approach is to search for indications of criminal activity and criminal networks by gathering information from social media like Facebook, YouTube, and Twitter. Many criminals use social media to brag to friends about their deeds or to organize and carry out criminal activity, like posting locations where customers can buy drugs. Just as police often establish false identities to go undercover to gather evidence on individuals and gangs, many set up social websites with false identities and profiles that make them appear to be criminals. Then they try to friend real criminals and access information and the identities of criminal associates. If there is reason to believe that an individual is particularly dangerous or a major gang figure, a law enforcement agency may obtain a court order to force a social media company to disclose all the data it has about the target. Law enforcement agencies also set up online sites people can use to submit anonymous tips about crimes and wanted persons.

MEDIA AND SOCIAL MOVEMENTS

Because technological innovations have had a revolutionary impact on communication, they have also had a great impact on how social movements emerge (Carty 2015; DeFronzo 2015). Singular subject to the Internet and social media through smartphones and personal computers has made it easier for social movements to develop by expanding the ability to bypass traditional media. It also helps overcome lack of physical closeness among potential movement participants. Personal electronic media also increase people's capacity to spread or intensify discontent with an existing condition or policy because of the individual's ability to record experiences and events on video and instantly communicate them to others via the Internet. In addition, they increase a person's ability to spread an explanation of a problem, emphasizing that the problem is due to social factors that are able to be changed through collective action. Access to the Internet also allows people to transmit images of emotionally charged episodes of repression and injustice to a much wider population in a more convincing way than ever before possible. Personalized digital media also lessens the need for clearly identifiable social movement leaders because many of the functions previously carried out top down by movement leadership, like calling for group action, can now be accomplished horizontally among movement activists with little or no fixed leadership. In addition, smartphones and other forms of digital communication allow movement participants to rapidly adjust to actions by opponents by developing new plans and tactics in response.

Digital media have played a role in important recent social movements including the Tea Party movement, the Arab Spring protests, the Occupy movement, the student loan debt movement, the Dreamers' movement, the Women's March in 2017, the Me Too movement, and the March for Our Lives in 2018.

Social movements and social media

These modern social movements combine the capabilities provided by digital media and the Internet with on-the-ground action that builds powerful ties among mobilized participants and the ability to resist repression (Carty 2015).

Digital technology, however, can also be used disrupt social movements through measures such as spreading false information or setting up counter-movement websites. Governments can use supercomputers to spy on millions of individuals through intercepting, recording, and examining their emails, text messages, telephone conversations, and book, magazine, and website preferences. Such data could be used to intimidate actual or potential activists.

CHAPTER REVIEW

Sociological Perspectives on Education

The structural-functional perspective views education as preparing young people to become productive members of society. Teaching children their culture's core values and norms ensures they will accept, rather than disrupt, the existing social system. The conflict approach focuses on how inequality interferes with achieving universal educational opportunity for all and how a flawed educational system can perpetuate inequality. The symbolic-interactionist perspective emphasizes interaction and communication between teachers and students and how this can affect student academic achievement. It also points to education's potential for bringing about social change.

Unequal Educational Achievement Worldwide

Educational achievement varies greatly around the world. U.S. students lag behind those in other developed nations in math and science.

Unequal Educational Achievement in the United States

Within the United States, educational achievement is strongly linked to economic class, race, and ethnicity. U.S. schools tend to be segregated by both economic class and race/ethnicity. Schools in white affluent areas often have better teachers and facilities. While crime on school property has declined since the early 1990s, violence, theft, and bullying are still significant problems. Zero-tolerance discipline policies have been criticized for disproportionately punishing lower-income African-American and Hispanic students. Such policies have been faulted for being too inflexible and functioning to place many minority students in the "school-to-prison pipeline" for relatively minor disciplinary issues.

College tuition has soared, making it more difficult for lower-income, working-class, and middle-class youth to afford higher education. And many of those who do go to college are left deeply in debt after graduation.

Approaches to Improving Basic Public Education

One approach for improving public education is standardized tests of reading and math to determine what students have learned and to hold teachers and school administrators accountable for student performance. Another is to introduce competition among schools to force ineffective schools to improve. Still another proposal is to improve the quality of teachers.

Charter schools were developed as laboratories for the testing of innovative teaching methods. School vouchers were introduced in some places to allow parents to use public funding to send their children to schools of their choice. Magnet schools, focusing on particular specialties like science and technology, were established to draw students of all backgrounds and achieve school racial, ethnic, and class integration voluntarily. But critics argue that in some cases these programs have drained the public school system of resources, leaving those students with the greatest needs for specialized education in schools least able to provide it. Another criticism is that major reforms have focused mainly on ways to better convey knowledge to students. But to improve the educational performance of students from very low-income households a more comprehensive approach is needed that ensures economic and social support for parents and children. Reducing family stress allows children to grow up with feelings of love and security. This results in strong character, which is necessary for a person to take advantage of educational opportunities.

In 2002 the federal government enacted No Child Left Behind. This reform required all states to evaluate students through standardized tests focusing on reading and math, provide results to parents, and make teachers and school administrators accountable for improving student performance. NCLB appeared to achieve some success but was criticized for causing schools to focus too heavily on standardized testing while neglecting important subjects like history and art.

Media

The media carries out educational functions by permitting scientific, historical, and cultural knowledge to be shared worldwide. It can also be used to excite, inspire, propagandize, mobilize, intimidate and terrorize. The media has also provided the means for hundreds of millions of people to function as individual internet journalists, using their smartphones to record events and immediately transmit what they have seen and/or heard to the members of their social network or the entire world.

Sociological Perspectives on Media

The structural-functional perspective views media as a means to facilitate understanding and interdependence among people and institutions. The conflict perspective focuses on inequality in access to media and control over media. The symbolic-interactionist perspective is concerned with the symbols, text, sounds, and imagery used in media to convey information and meanings.

Media Issues

While mainstream media ideally decide to cover particular stories on the basis of factors such as significance, proximity, prominence, human interest, and timing, and report on them objectively and without bias, in reality financial considerations play a significant role, as can powerful political interests. Access to personal media and the internet differs significantly by income level in the United States and varies greatly between developed and lesser-developed nations. Criminals use modern media to commit fraud and theft, and law enforcement use media to appeal to the public for help, investigate crimes, gather evidence, and locate suspects.

Media and Social Movements

Modern media have been employed in recent major social movements. Devices such as smartphones make it easier for movements to develop by overcoming lack of physical proximity among movement activists, supporters, and wider audiences, or lack of coverage by major media. Movement supporters use electronic means to broadcast messages, and video and audio of events through the Internet.

KEY TERMS

charter school, p. 216
digital divide, p. 225
functional illiteracy, p. 212
magnet school, p. 217
news objectivity, p. 224

newsworthiness, p. 223
school segregation, p. 213
school voucher programs, p. 217
student movement, p. 207

DISCUSSION QUESTIONS

1. What measures might be taken to reduce class and racial segregation in American public schools?

2. What approach or approaches do you think would have the best chance of improving the academic performance of low-income children in American schools?

3. What do you think would be the best approach to reducing the debt that many students accumulate when paying for a college education?

4. What factors do you think pose the greatest threat to the objective coverage and reporting of the news?

5. What measures might be taken to reduce the digital divide in the United States? What about worldwide?

CHAPTER 9

Health Care and Well-Being

CHAPTER OBJECTIVES

- Describe inequalities in health among nations as well as among groups in the United States.
- Describe the HIV/AIDS problem and the world's reaction to it.
- Explain major preventable threats to health.
- Describe the social movement for improved access to health care in the United States.

- Describe the sociological perspectives on health and heath care.
- Explain major government programs to provide healthcare in the United States.

SHOULD AMERICANS GO BANKRUPT BECAUSE *they cannot pay medical expenses? Research indicates that in 2007, three years before the passage of the Patient Protection and Affordable Care Act ("Obamacare"), about 62 percent of U.S. residents who filed for bankruptcy did so because of health care expenses (Dalen 2009; Elsevier Health Sciences 2009; Himmelstein et al. 2009). In comparison, in 1981 only about 8 percent of U.S. bankruptcies were due to medical expenses. The study also found that most health care-related bankruptcies involved middle-class persons, many of whom had health insurance that proved to be inadequate. Because in 2007 most health insurance was linked to a person's job, a health problem could cause loss of coverage if it resulted in loss of employment. About a quarter of companies cancelled insurance coverage as soon as an employee experienced a disabling illness and another quarter of firms did so within about a year (Elsevier Health Sciences 2009). Why is the United States the only industrialized nation where health care bankruptcy is such a serious problem?*

HEALTH AND HEALTH PROBLEMS WORLDWIDE

Health problems and levels of health care vary greatly around the world. There is about a thirty-four-year gap between nations with the highest average life expectancies at birth (such as Japan and Singapore, both around 85 years) and the lowest (such as Guinea-Bissau and Chad, both under 51 years). The average life span for European Union nations and the United States is 80 years. The highest in Latin America are Chile, Costa Rica, Cuba, Panama, and Puerto Rico at around 79 years, with other nations such as Argentina, Colombia, Ecuador, and Venezuela in the 76–77 year range. China is around 76 and Russia 71. Sub-Saharan Africa has the lowest life expectancy, mostly in the 50s.

Cardiovascular diseases (which include heart disease and stroke) are the major cause of death globally, accounting for about 27 percent of all deaths in 2015 (World Health Organization 2017a). Noncommunicable diseases (NCD), including cardiovascular diseases, cancers, diabetes, and chronic lung diseases, cause about 70 percent of deaths worldwide. The proportion of NCD deaths is much higher (88 percent) in high-income nations than in lower-income nations (37 percent), where infectious diseases like lower respiratory infections, **HIV/AIDS**, diarrhea, malaria, and tuberculosis cause a much larger proportion of deaths. The **under-five-child-mortality rate** (the number of children dying under five years old per 1,000 live births) is about twelve times higher in sub-Saharan African countries than in

HIV Human immunodeficiency virus.

AIDS Acquired immunodeficiency syndrome.

under-five-child-mortality rate The number of children dying under five years old per 1,000 live births.

high-income countries (UNICEF 2015). The world under-five-child-mortality rate fell from 91 in 1990 to 43 in 2015. The mortality decline is due both to the spread of modern medical technology and practices and to economic development and social change that has, for example, expanded the availability of clean water.

TABLE 9.1	Life Expectancy around the World, 2016 (CIA 2017a)				
Monaco	89.50	Austria	81.50	St. Helena, A. & T. d. C.	79.50
Singapore	85.00	Anguilla	81.40	Gibraltar	79.40
Japan	85.00	Netherlands	81.30	Denmark	79.40
Macau	84.50	Bermuda	81.30	Puerto Rico	79.40
San Marino	83.30	Isle of Man	81.20	Portugal	79.30
Iceland	83.00	New Zealand	81.20	Guam	7.10
Hong Kong	82.90	Cayman Islands	81.20	Bahrain	78.90
Andorra	82.80	Belgium	81.00	Chile	78.80
Switzerland	82.60	Finland	80.90	Cyprus	78.70
Guernsey	82.50	Ireland	80.80	Qatar	78.70
Israel	82.40	United Kingdom	80.70	Cuba	78.70
Korea, South	82.40	Germany	80.70	Czech Rep.	78.60
Luxembourg	82.30	Greece	80.50	Panama	78.60
Italy	82.20	Saint Pierre & Miquelon	80.50	Costa Rica	78.60
Australia	82.20	Malta	80.40	British Virgin Islands	78.60
Sweden	82.10	Faroe Islands	80.40	Curaçao	78.30
Liechtenstein	81.90	European Union	80.20	Albania	78.30
Jersey	81.90	Taiwan	80.10	Slovenia	78.20
Canada	81.90	Virgin Islands	80.00	St. Maarten	78.10
France	81.80	United States	79.80	Dominican Republic	78.10
Norway	81.80	Turks and Caicos Islands	79.80	No. Mariana Island	78.00
Spain	81.70	Wallis & Futuna	79.70	Kuwait	78.00

(continued)

TABLE 9.1 | Life Expectancy around the World, 2016 (CIA 2017a) *(continued)*

Saint Lucia	77.80	Mexico	75.90	Jordan	74.60
New Caledonia	77.70	Croatia	75.90	Armenia	74.60
Lebanon	77.60	Cook Islands	75.80	Bulgaria	74.50
Poland	77.60	Venezuela	75.80	Latvia	74.50
United Arab Emirates	77.50	St. Kitts & Nevis	75.70	Montserrat	74.40
French Polynesia	77.20	Colombia	75.70	Grenada	74.30
Uruguay	77.20	Maldives	75.60	Gaza Strip	73.90
Paraguay	77.20	Mauritius	75.60	Uzbekistan	73.80
Brunei	77.20	China	75.50	Brazil	73.80
Slovakia	77.10	Oman	75.50	Samoa	73.70
Argentina	77.10	Serbia	75.50	Peru	73.70
Dominica	77.00	American Samoa	75.40	Jamaica	73.60
Morocco	76.90	Saudi Arabia	75.30	Vanuatu	73.40
Aruba	76.80	Barbados	75.30	Vietnam	73.40
Algeria	76.80	St. Vincent & Grenadines	75.30	Bangladesh	73.20
Sri Lanka	76.80	Solomon Islands	75.30	Nicaragua	73.20
Ecuador	76.80	Romania	75.10	Palau	73.10
Bosnia & Herzegovina	76.70	Malaysia	75.00	Marshall Islands	73.10
Estonia	76.70	West Bank	75.00	Micronesia	72.90
Antigua & Barbuda	76.50	Iraq	74.90	Trinidad and Tobago	72.90
Libya	76.50	Lithuania	74.90	Belarus	72.70
Georgia	76.20	Syria	74.90	Fiji	72.70
Macedonia	76.20	Turkey	74.80	Indonesia	72.70
Tonga	76.20	Thailand	74.70	Egypt	72.70
Tunisia	76.10	El Salvador	74.70	Azerbaijan	72.50
Hungary	75.90	Seychelles	74.70	Greenland	72.40

(continued)

TABLE 9.1 | **Life Expectancy around the World, 2016 (CIA 2017a) (*continued*)**

Bahamas	72.40	Ghana	66.60	Burundi	60.50
Guatemala	72.30	Tuvalu	66.50	Rwanda	60.10
Suriname	72.20	Kiribati	66.20	Congo, Rep. of	59.30
Cabo Verde	72.10	Madagascar	65.90	Liberia	59.00
Ukraine	71.80	Yemen	65.50	Cote d'Ivoire	58.70
Iran	71.40	Togo	65.00	Cameroon	58.50
Honduras	71.10	Gambia	64.90	Sierra Leone	58.20
Kazakhstan	70.80	São Tomé & Principe	64.90	Zimbabwe	58.00
Russia	70.80	Eritrea	64.90	Congo, Dem. Rep.	57.30
Moldova	70.70	Cambodia	64.50	Angola	56.00
Nepal	70.70	Laos	64.30	Mali	55.80
Kyrgyzstan	70.70	Equatorial Guinea	64.20	Burkina Faso	55.50
Korea, North	70.40	Comoros	64.20	Niger	55.50
Turkmenistan	70.10	Sudan	64.10	Uganda	55.40
Bhutan	70.10	Kenya	64.00	Botswana	54.50
Mongolia	69.60	Haiti	63.80	Nigeria	53.40
Philippines	69.20	Namibia	63.60	Mozambique	53.30
Bolivia	69.20	Djibouti	63.20	Lesotho	53.00
Belize	68.70	South Africa	63.10	Zambia	52.50
India	68.50	Western Sahara	63.00	Somalia	52.40
Guyana	68.40	Mauritania	63.00	Central Afr. Rep.	52.30
Timor-Leste	68.10	Tanzania	62.20	Gabon	52.10
Pakistan	67.70	Ethiopia	62.20	Swaziland	51.60
Tajikistan	67.70	Benin	61.90	Afghanistan	51.30
Papua New G.	67.20	Senegal	61.70	Guinea-Bissau	50.60
Nauru	67.10	Malawi	61.20	Chad	50.20
Myanmar (Burma)	66.60	Guinea	60.60		

GLOBALIZATION AND HEALTH

Informational, economic, social, and political interrelationships and exchanges among the world's nations can have both beneficial and harmful effects on health. Benefits include the ability to quickly share new medical knowledge and technologies, detect serious disease outbreaks, and send resources and medical personnel to where they are needed. One potential danger of rapid travel between nations is that, without proper precautions, a disease outbreak can spread rapidly. How to prevent this was illustrated by the U.S. response to the 2014 Ebola epidemic in West Africa (White House 2014), where providing medical assistance to developing countries benefitted not only local people but also the international community by stopping a dangerous disease from spreading extensively. The 2015 Obama administration decision to ease trade and travel restrictions to and from Cuba provides another example of the positive effects of globalization. Shortly after this change in U.S. policy, New York state authorities expressed interest in obtaining a vaccine developed by Cuba for combating lung cancer (Schumaker 2015), and American doctors anticipated that a Cuban diabetes drug that seems effective and is used in more than two dozen countries would soon become available in the United States (NBC News 2015).

Effects of Global Travel and Trade

Increased international trade has spurred economic development throughout the world and has generally increased product choices for consumers. For example, high quality Japanese, Korean, and European cars have attracted millions of buyers in the United States and have also pushed American car manufacturers to improve the reliability and fuel economy of their products. But there are also drawbacks and abuses involved in global economic activity. The movement of millions of manufacturing jobs to low-wage countries has undermined American unions, decreased the income of much of the middle class, and contributed to the weakening of the family in many urban areas where it is now much harder to find a well-paying job and support a household. U.S. corporations have also been attracted to foreign locations because of lax or unenforced environmental and labor regulations. This has subjected workers to harsh or unsafe working conditions and polluted the communities where factories were located. In addition, a number of companies have promoted and marketed harmful but profitable products in other nations. For example, some American and British tobacco companies have expanded the advertising and selling of cigarettes in lesser-developed countries where anti-tobacco regulations are often lax and where many people are unaware of the health risks of smoking (Lahrichi 2015).

A Major Global Infectious Threat: HIV/AIDS

HIV refers to an infectious virus called human immunodeficiency virus, which progressively destroys the body's immune system. In its advanced stages HIV results in AIDS, or acquired immunodeficiency syndrome.

AIDS makes it impossible for a person to fight off lethal diseases. Once infected, a person has HIV for life (CDC 2017b). If HIV/AIDS goes untreated, it is usually fatal. In the United States the process of discovering HIV/AIDS began in 1979 when doctors in San Francisco, Los Angeles, and New York detected rare diseases in some gay men that typically only occurred in people with badly damaged immune systems (Weitz 2013). By 1982 the Centers for Disease Control and Prevention (CDC) officially recognized AIDS. HIV/AIDS spread rapidly in the United States, especially among the male gay population, until ways to minimize risk of infection were more widely understood and practiced. Federal and state governments were criticized for not acting rapidly to combat HIV/AIDS. The CDC (2017c) estimated that in 2015 more than 1.2 million Americans were living with HIV, with 1 in 8 unaware of the infection.

HIV can be spread through sexual intercourse (the number one cause of infection), blood, the use of unclean intravenous needles, or from an infected mother to her child during pregnancy, childbirth or through breastfeeding. There is greater risk of infection through anal than vaginal intercourse because of the higher likelihood of bleeding, facilitating HIV transmission. In both vaginal and anal intercourse, the receptor is at greater risk of infection. In 2015 Cuba became the first country to eliminate mother-to child-transmission of HIV, according to the World Health Organization (WHO) (Adams 2015). Several other countries appeared to be making similar progress.

Worldwide, heterosexual intercourse is the main way HIV spreads. HIV is thought to have originated in sub-Saharan African chimpanzees and monkeys and been transmitted to the humans who captured or killed these animals through contact with their infected blood (Carmichael 2006). It appears that HIV spread to Haiti and from Haiti to the United States (Hobbes 2014). According to the WHO (2017b), about 37 million people of all ages are infected with HIV/AIDS. Seventy percent of all those living with HIV/AIDS worldwide are in sub-Saharan Africa. Countries with the largest percentages of their adult populations infected in 2015 included Swaziland (29%), Lesotho (23%), Botswana (22%), South Africa (19%), Zimbabwçe (15%), Namibia (13%), Zambia (13%), Mozambique (11%), and Malawi (9%) (CIA 2017b).

HEALTH PROBLEMS IN THE UNITED STATES

Inequities in Health

Class and Education Economic class and education are powerfully related to health. Persons with higher incomes tend to have better health and a lower **death (mortality) rate** (number of deaths per 1,000 persons) than people with lower incomes. Research indicates that income inequality is also significantly related to the differences in other health indicators. Kaplan et al. (1996) found that the greater the share of household income going to those in the bottom 50 percent of households (in other words, the more equal the distribution of household income within a state's population), the lower the overall state death rate, the lower the percentage of people smoking tobacco, the higher the state's expenditure

death (mortality) rate Number of deaths per 1,000 persons in a population per year.

infant mortality rates The number of deaths during the first year of life per 1,000 live births per year.

on health care, and the better the condition of newborn babies. High income inequality has been found to reduce life span in analyses at the county level (Sanger-Katz 2015).

Throughout the United States, **infant mortality rates** (the number of deaths during the first year of life per 1,000 live births) vary significantly by mother's education. During 2000–2002 the infant mortality rate was 4.2 for mothers with 16 or more years of education, 6.0 for mothers with 13–15 years of education, 7.4 for mothers with 12 years of education, and 7.8 for mothers with 0–11years of education (Robert Wood Johnson Foundation 2008). In fact, in each of the fifty states and the District of Columbia, mothers with 16 or more years of education had lower infant mortality rates than mothers with less education. But the gap between the infant mortality rates of the most and least educated mothers tended to be much smaller in states with relatively low overall infant mortality rates compared to states with high overall infant mortality rates.

Race/Ethnicity African Americans have the highest mortality rate of any major racial/ethnic group in the United States (CDC 2016). They have higher death rates from heart disease, cancer, diabetes, AIDS, and homicide than non-Hispanic whites, Hispanics, American Indians/Alaskan Natives, and Asians/Pacific Islanders (CDC 2016). In 2013, the life span for Asian Americans was 86.5 years, 82.2 for Latinos, 78.9 for whites, 76.9 for Native Americans, and 74.6 for African Americans (Lewis and Burd-Sharps 2013). The fact that Latinos in the United States live longer than non-Latino whites seems somewhat surprising, since on average Latinos have less education and income. One likely reason is that U.S. Latinos, especially foreign-born Latinos, are much less likely to smoke cigarettes than whites. This factor alone may account for three-quarters of the Hispanic advantage in life span compared to whites (Scommegna 2013).

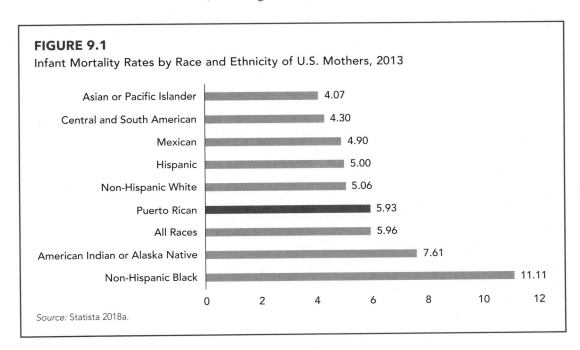

FIGURE 9.1

Infant Mortality Rates by Race and Ethnicity of U.S. Mothers, 2013

Asian or Pacific Islander	4.07
Central and South American	4.30
Mexican	4.90
Hispanic	5.00
Non-Hispanic White	5.06
Puerto Rican	5.93
All Races	5.96
American Indian or Alaska Native	7.61
Non-Hispanic Black	11.11

Source: Statista 2018a.

Infant mortality rates also differ significantly with regard to race and ethnicity (MacDorman and Matthews 2011). As shown in figure 9.1, the infant mortality rate for non-Hispanic blacks has been higher than that for major Hispanic national groups, and more than twice the rate for non-Hispanic whites and Asians/Pacific Islanders. There appear to be several reasons for relatively high African American mortality rates. These include disproportionate poverty, lower average educational attainment, a high percentage of children growing up in one-parent households, living in areas with inadequate or difficult to access health care facilities, and higher than average cigarette smoking.

Gender In the United States women live longer than men in each of the country's major racial or ethnic groupings (Infoproc 2015), on average almost five years longer. Non-Hispanic black males in 2014 had a life expectancy of 72 years, non-Hispanic white males 76.5 years, and Hispanic males 79.2 years (CDC 2017d). In comparison, non-Hispanic black women had a life expectancy of 78.1 years, non-Hispanic white women 81.1, and Hispanic women 84.0. Why do women live longer? Gender differences in behavior appear to play a significant role. Men, for example, have historically been more likely to use tobacco and illegal drugs than women. They are more often employed in dangerous occupations, including the armed forces, law enforcement, and the construction, fishing, mining, and transportation industries. Men also typically engage in more risky recreational activities and more violent behavior than women. They are more likely, for example, to participate in criminal behavior and become the victims of homicide than women. There is also some evidence of a biological advantage for women in that their immune systems and ability to repair cell damage may deteriorate more slowly than those of men (Briggs 2013; Kirkwood 2010). Women's advantage in life expectancy might be even greater if there were more women physicians especially attuned to women's health needs. But the percentage of female medical doctors has been increasing. Whereas in 1981 only 12 percent of physicians were women, 33.7 percent were women in 2016 (Kaiser Family Foundation 2017).

Research indicates, though, that more women than men suffer from chronic illnesses like multiple sclerosis and lupus and feel they are in poor health (Pearson 2013; Williams and *My Health News Daily* 2011). Women are also more likely to suffer from depression and to have been the victims of sexual assault.

Family Characteristics Research indicates that married people are likely to be healthier than persons in other statuses such as never married, divorced, or separated (Schoenborn 2004). Married people report better health and less serious psychological distress than non-married persons. Married persons are also less likely to engage in health-endangering behaviors like cigarette smoking. The exception was married men being slightly more likely to be obese. The married persons' health advantage was found in all income, race, and age subcategories examined. Existing research, however, has not been able to determine if the health differences between married people and people in other living arrangements are due to married life causing married people to be more healthy or whether all or part of the marital health advantage is due to healthier people and people with healthier behaviors being more successful in finding marriage partners and maintaining their marriages.

Other research indicates that children raised by two parents generally have fewer physical and mental health problems than children raised in single-parent, female-headed households, although some of the difference appears due to the generally lower income of female-headed households (Bramlett and Blumberg 2007).

Location The average life expectancy for the top ten states (Hawaii, Minnesota, Connecticut, California, Massachusetts, New York, Vermont, New Jersey, New Hampshire, and Utah) in 2013 was nearly 81 years while for the bottom ten states (Mississippi, West Virginia, Alabama, Louisiana, Oklahoma, Arkansas, Kentucky, Tennessee, South Carolina, and Georgia) it was 76 years (Lewis and Burd-Sharps 2013–2014). This gap is due to differences in health-related lifestyle. For example, the percent of cigarette smokers in the top ten life span states averaged 16.6, while in the ten shortest life spans states it was 25.3 percent (Mendes 2011). And the percent of population obese in the top ten life span states averaged 24.7 percent; for the ten shortest life spans states it was 33.2 percent (National Conference of State Legislatures 2015a).

Rising Costs of Health Care

The United States in 2016 spent $3.3 trillion on health care (about 17.9 percent of the country's gross domestic product), or $10,348 per U.S. resident (Centers for Medicare and Medicaid Services [CMS] 2018). The amount spent on health care grew at between 6 and 10 percent per year between 2000 and 2006 (U.S. Census 2012a). The increase in U.S. health care expenditure between 2015 and 2016 was 4.3 percent (CMS 2018), still considerably higher than the rate of inflation. The United States spends much more on health care per citizen than the other thirty-five developed OECD (Organization for Economic Cooperation and Development) nations. For example, the next three highest OECD nations in rate of health expenditure, Luxembourg, Switzerland, and Norway, spent between $1,686 and $2,884 less per capita in 2015 (OECD Key Indicators 2016). Yet 2016 life expectancy in these three nations averaged almost two and a half years longer than in the United States (CIA 2017a). Major reasons for high and rising health care costs in the United States include the general trend toward living longer, the cost of drugs, medical technology, and procedures, the cost of health care insurance, and the cost of health care administration.

Increased Life Span Americans over age 45 use a lot more prescription drugs and medical services than younger persons (CDC 2013). In 2010 about 30 percent of American men in a national sample aged

TABLE 9.2 | **Life Expectancy around the United States, 2013**

Hawaii	81.3	Rhode Island	79.9	Pennsylvania	78.5	Missouri	77.5
Minnesota	81.1	Nebraska	79.8	Texas	78.5	Georgia	77.2
Connecticut	80.8	Iowa	79.7	Montana	78.5	South Carolina	77.0
California	80.8	Arizona	79.6	Delaware	78.4	District of Columbia	76.5
Massachusetts	80.5	North Dakota	79.5	New Mexico	78.4	Tennessee	76.3
New York	80.5	Oregon	79.5	Kansas	78.7	Kentucky	76.0
Vermont	80.5	South Dakota	79.5	Alaska	78.3	Arkansas	76.0
New Jersey	80.3	Idaho	79.5	Wyoming	78.3	Oklahoma	75.9
New Hampshire	80.3	Florida	79.4	Michigan	78.2	Louisiana	75.7
Utah	80.2	Maine	79.2	Nevada	78.1	Alabama	75.4
Colorado	80.0	Virginia	79.0	Ohio	77.8	West Virginia	75.4
Wisconsin	80.0	Illinois	79.0	North Carolina	77.8	Mississippi	75.0
Washington	79.9	Maryland	78.8	Indiana	77.6		

Source: Lewis and Burd-Sharps 2013–2014.

45–64 used three or more prescription drugs within the thirty days preceding the survey, as did nearly 40 percent of 45–64 year old women. For men and women 65 years or older, the figure was about 65 percent. Improvements in medical technology have allowed many people to survive illnesses that previously would have killed them. It has also saved many children and mothers who in the past would not have survived difficult childbirths. So the mere fact that Americans are living longer is a major reason that expenditures on health care continue to rise.

Cost of Drugs, Medical Technology, and Procedures The cost of the development and manufacture of more effective drugs and medical

| TABLE 9.3 | Ten Longest and Ten Shortest Life Span States with Percentages of Smokers and Obese Persons | | | | | |

Ten Longest-Life-Span States			Ten Shortest-Life-Span States		
State	Percent Smokers	Percent Obese	State	Percent Smokers	Percent Obese
Hawaii	16%	21.8%	Georgia	21%	30.3%
Minnesota	17%	25.5%	South Carolina	24%	31.7%
Connecticut	18%	25.0%	Tennessee	25%	33.7%
California	15%	24.1%	Kentucky	29%	33.2%
Massachusetts	17%	23.6%	Arkansas	26%	34.6%
New York	19%	25.4%	Oklahoma	26%	32.5%
Vermont	18%	24.7%	Louisiana	26%	33.1%
New Jersey	18%	26.3%	Alabama	25%	32.4%
New Hampshire	17%	26.7%	West Virginia	25%	35.1%
Utah	11%	24.1%	Mississippi	26%	35.1%

Sources: Lewis and Burd-Sharps 2013–2014; Mendes 2011; National Conference of State Legislatures 2015a.

equipment, and the profits of the companies that market them, are additional factors that drive up health care costs. American drug companies state they must charge high prices for drugs to recover the expenses of research, testing, and production. But often the same drugs are sold in Canada for far less, as much as one-half to one-tenth the U.S. price (Seniors Health Insurance 2015). Modern lifesaving medical technology can be enormously expensive. The average cost of care for a low birthweight or premature infant during the first year of life in 2009 was about $49,000 (Landau 2009). The average cost of organ transplant operations in 2011 ranged from about $262,900 for kidney transplants to $561,200 for a single lung transplant to $997,700 for a heart transplant (UNOS Transplant Living 2015).

Cost of Health Care Insurance Between 1999 and 2010 the annual cost of health care insurance increased by about 8 percent per year, more than three times the rate of inflation (Healthinsurancecompanies.org

2015). For families, cost rose from $5,791 in 1999 to $13,770 in 2010. The average annual cost for employer-sponsored family health coverage grew to $16,351 in 2013, an increase of 4 percent from 2012 (though still three times the inflation rate and a little more than twice the rise in workers' wages). Workers covered by this type of family health care plan contributed an average of $4,565 toward coverage in 2013 (National Conference of State Legislatures 2015b). The average annual cost for employer-sponsored family health coverage increased to $18,764 in 2017, with workers contributing an average of $ 5,714 (National Conference of State Legislatures 2017a).

Cost of Health Care Administration Health administration costs have been defined in major research as insurance overhead (including agent and executive salaries), employers' costs to manage health benefits, hospital administration, administrative costs to practitioners, and home care administration. The United States has very high health administration costs compared to many other countries. For example, health care administration in the United States costs about two to three times per person what it costs in Canada, where every Canadian receives health care insurance coverage at birth funded by a "single payer," the Canadian government, through income, sales, and corporate taxes (Center for Healthcare Finance Information 2015; Nader 2013; Woodhandler, Campbell, and Himmelstein 2003). Many Americans believe that if the United States provided health care coverage to the population through expanding the federal government's Medicare system, which currently provides health insurance coverage to citizens aged sixty-five or over, health care administrative expenses would be reduced by hundreds of millions of dollars. However, health care experts believe this is unlikely to happen in the foreseeable future because of the economic and political influence of the more than 1,200 private health care insurance companies, and the many other medical-related health care corporations. Another way to reduce administrative costs is for the federal government to require private health care companies to standardize their computer systems so they can communicate with one another, medical practitioners, and government agencies more efficiently (Cutler, Wikler, and Basch 2012). This and related improvements like greater automation could potentially save many millions of dollars.

Consequences of the High Cost of Health Care

Because of the high cost of health care many people with no or inadequate health insurance avoid seeking medical care unless they are desperately ill or injured. They may skip taking medicine to try to make it last longer. And a serious accident or illness can force a person or family into bankruptcy. As noted earlier, the number one reason U.S. residents file for bankruptcy is medical expenses (Clear Bankruptcy 2017; Dalen 2009; Elsevier Health Sciences 2009; Himmelstein et al. 2009).

Social Movements: Health Care and Social Movements

Health care is a human right demonstration

During the twentieth and twenty-first centuries, social movements sought to achieve better living standards and greater equality of opportunity for American workers, women, people with disabilities, and racial, ethnic, and sexual orientation minorities. The civil rights movement, the gay rights movement, and movements for people with certain diseases such as AIDS typically sought changes in health care to benefit members of their group (Hoffman 2003). These included racial desegregation of hospitals and clinics, health insurance coverage of same-sex partners, and increasing the availability and affordability of AIDS drugs.

But there were few movements with the specific goal of achieving a universal health care system. Some labor organizations at times advocated this goal. But most labor unions eventually included health coverage for their members and their families as a contract demand in negotiations. The provision of health care insurance as a job benefit meant that tens of millions of U.S. workers saw little need to demand universal health care as a right of citizenship even though many fellow Americans lacked coverage. Rising costs of health care insurance, however, began consuming more and more of workers' paychecks, and by the late 1940s the two large U.S. labor union federations, the American Federation of Labor (AFL) and the Congress of Industrial Organizations (CIO), both

called for major health care reform. The Truman administration and the labor movement supported the Wagner-Murray-Dingell bill, which called for national medical insurance to be funded through social security payroll taxes. But conservative politicians branded government-mandated universal health care a socialist (or communist) program. And conservative medical physicians' associations also opposed the bill, fearing national health insurance might reduce doctors' income and independence, and the quality of medical care. By 1950, this national health insurance proposal was defeated.

The next push for health care reform occurred during the Kennedy and Johnson administrations and resulted in the 1965 establishment of Medicare, the federal program that pays for many of the medical expenses of those aged sixty-five or older regardless of income or medical history. Before Medicare, about 35 percent of people in this age bracket lacked health insurance. Many Americans believe the best way to achieve universal health care would be to simply expand Medicare to the entire population. This would be similar to the Canadian "single payer" system, where government tax funds, rather than private insurance companies, pay health care providers.

Several social trends spurred new efforts for universal health care. One was the decline in manufacturing and other jobs that had good health care insurance through labor union contracts. This left millions of Americans with no or minimal health insurance. Another factor was the dramatic rise in bankruptcies caused by illness or physical injuries to people lacking adequate health insurance. These developments increased popular demand for government intervention to ensure affordable health care.

Three modern social movements called for universal health care. Organized in 1987, the AIDS activist movement ACT UP first protested the exclusion of AIDS from insurance policy coverage and then, once coverage was available, the extremely high price for such

Social Movements (*continued*)

coverage. The proposed solution was universal health care. The civil rights movement, having achieved racial desegregation of public health facilities, turned its attention to the inability of many poor, working-class and lower-middle-class people, disproportionately African Americans, to obtain adequate health coverage. Again, the answer proposed was health care coverage for all Americans. The feminist movement also came to support this goal to diminish male domination of health care and ensure poor women's access to medical treatment.

Rising demands for universal health care played a role in the election of Democrat Bill Clinton in 1992. But rather than advocate a U.S. version of the economic and administratively simple Canadian health care system, the Clinton administration, concerned about political opposition from the insurance industry, developed a complex Health Security Bill, almost 1,400 pages long, giving private insurance companies a huge role in providing universal health care. The program was attacked by liberals as wasteful and protecting insurance companies and by conservatives as socialistic and a government takeover of health care. The effort failed.

Demand for health care reform also played a role in the election of Democrat Barack Obama in 2008. On March 23, 2010, President Obama signed the Patient Protection and Affordable Care Act (ACA) into law. This act and the related Health Care and Education Reconciliation Act of 2010 instituted comprehensive health insurance reforms. The law requires people to have health coverage or pay a penalty if they don't. Supporters viewed this legislation as a major step toward universal health care, although it relies on the private insurance industry. The ACA requires that people with preexisting conditions can no longer be denied coverage and that women cannot be charged more than men for the same insurance plan. Between 2010 and 2015 more than sixteen million people gained health care insurance coverage (White House Briefing Room 2015). A national Gallup poll found that Americans without health insurance declined from 18 percent in the fall of 2013 (when people where first able to enroll in ACA) to 11.9 percent in the first quarter of 2015 (CNN 2015a). Then the percent uninsured fell further to 10.9 percent in the last two quarters of 2015 but rose to 11.3 percent in early 2017 amid uncertainty about the ACA under the Trump administration (Thomas 2017).

PREVENTABLE ONGOING RISKS TO HEALTH
Smoking

Tobacco use was promoted widely through tobacco company advertising, the entertainment industry, and even at times the federal government. During World War II, American soldiers were sent cigarettes with their food rations. Movies and TV shows in the 1950s and 1960s featured main characters, male and female, smoking cigarettes. Research showed that by 1965 about 42 percent of Americans eighteen or older smoked (Hendrick 2008). In later years, a massive government-supported campaign, motivated by medical research, began to cause a decline in smoking. In addition, the depiction of people smoking in TV programs declined drastically in the last 50 years (Sneed 2014). But still in 2015, a little over 20 percent of Americans eighteen or older (about fifty million adults) smoked tobacco regularly (National Institute on Drug Abuse 2017e). The number of people who die from tobacco smoking annually (more than 480,000, including 42,000 from

Anti-smoking poster

secondhand smoke) is vastly greater than the deaths caused by other drugs (CDC 2015a). Most of the deaths are due to tobacco-related cancer or heart disease. In the United States tobacco use is the number one preventable cause of death.

Obesity

Obesity is the second most lethal preventable cause of death in the United States after tobacco. It is linked to an increased risk of heart disease, Type 2 diabetes, cancer, liver and gall bladder disease, and other health problems (CDC 2011, 2017a; MEDTV 2015; National Cancer Institute 2012). Obesity is defined as 30 or over on the body mass index (BMI), overweight as 25–29.9, normal as 18.5–24.9, and underweight as below 18.5. The BMI is a person's weight in kilograms divided by a person's height in meters squared. In terms of a person's height and weight, a person 5'0" tall and weighing 153 pounds or over is obese. Then, for every added inch in height an increase in weight of about 6 pounds indicates obesity. So, a 6'4" person weighing about 249 pounds or over would also generally be obese (National Heart, Lung, and Blood Institute 2017). In 2014, 27.7 percent of adult Americans were obese, 35.3 percent were overweight, 35 percent were normal weight, and 2.1 percent were underweight (McCarthy 2014b). African Americans had a higher rate of obesity (35.5 percent) than other major racial or ethnic groups. Americans in households with incomes less than $36,000 annually had a higher rate of obesity (31.9 percent) than people in higher-income households. Young adults (18–29 years old) at 17 percent obese and high-income Americans earning $90,000 or more annually at 23.1 percent obese) are among the groups least likely to be obese.

While some people tend toward obesity because of medical or genetic factors, the amount of physical activity people engage in and their patterns of food consumption play major roles. Children's lives in past generations generally involved a high level of physical activity, but today many young people become so absorbed in schoolwork, internet surfing, television, or electronic games that they don't get enough exercise. And corporate advertising campaigns often steer people toward high-calorie foods. In the United States, poor people in urban areas are at a disadvantage because healthy foods like fish, fruits, and fresh vegetables are relatively expensive and because they may lack access to big grocery stores with a wide range of healthy foods. Instead they often find themselves limited to convenience stores filled with high-calorie processed foods and to fast food restaurants featuring high-fat meals.

Fighting Obesity Health experts recommend several ways to fight obesity (Falini 2013). Parents should make sure that they have plenty of fresh fruits and vegetables available at home, as well as lean meats and fish. Avoid high-sugar beverages or junk food. They should make healthy foods a central part of their own diets so that they set a good example for their children and make physical activity a part of the daily routine for everyone in the household (such as family walks or hikes, bike rides, sports, etc.). Schools can play a role by providing healthy food options for students. They should also educate students on the health risks of obesity and how poor eating habits and lack of physical activity lead to obesity. In 2014, the Food and Drug Administration (FDA) took a major step toward helping people make informed decisions about their eating choices by requiring businesses that sell prepared foods and have more than nineteen employees to post the calories of each food item on their menus and food-related displays (Associated Press 2014a). The FDA's calorie labeling rules apply to restaurants, supermarkets selling prepared foods, coffee shops, bakeries, convenience stores, amusement parks, and vending machines. The hope is that customers will be so shocked by the calorie content of certain items that they decide to purchase lower-calorie foods and that food businesses will be motivated to provide a greater number of low-calorie healthy options.

Environmental Poisoning

Environmental poisoning is another health risk that is at least partially preventable. Major types include asbestos, carbon monoxide, and lead (Medline Plus 2015). Asbestos is a mineral once widely used in insulating houses and in shipbuilding. People in the construction and shipbuilding industries often inhaled asbestos fibers, which resulted in injuries such as scarring of the lungs and lung cancer. Carbon monoxide is a dangerous gas present in combustion fumes such as those from oil-fueled heating systems and gasoline- and diesel-powered cars and trucks that can cause headaches, dizziness, nausea, mental confusion, and even death. Carbon monoxide detectors warn people of harmful levels of the gas. Other deadly chemicals pumped into the air by coal-powered plants and oil and chemical spills poison drinking water and aquatic animals.

mental illness Any one of a number of thinking or mood disorders resulting in impaired functioning and/or debilitating feelings of distress.

Lead is another environmental threat. This metal was once widely used in cooking pots, pipes, and paint. Drinking water, breathing air, or eating food that contains lead or coming in contact with flaking lead paint in older houses can introduce lead into the body. This can result in nerve disorders, muscle or joint pain, or even infertility, and lead poisoning can interfere with memory and the ability to concentrate. Children are especially at risk for lead poisoning because it can interfere with mental and physical development and even cause brain damage.

Lower-income people in urban areas are often exposed to environmental poisons when they reside in buildings with lead paint, live close to factories or abandoned chemically contaminated industrial sites, or breathe polluted air.

MENTAL HEALTH

Mental health is the state of well-being in which a person can make good use of her or his abilities and talent, handle the typical stresses of life effectively, and be capable of contributing positively to family, friends, and community (CDC 2017e). **Mental illness** refers to any one of a number of thinking or mood disorders resulting in impaired functioning and/or debilitating feelings of distress. *The Diagnostic and Statistical Manual of Mental Disorders, 5th Edition: DSM-5* (American Psychiatric Institute 2013), the product of input from hundreds of international psychiatric professionals, describes scores of mental disorders. Research indicates that as many as 6 percent of adult Americans suffer from severe mental illness each year and a quarter or more of the population has some type of mental disorder (Rosenberg 2013; Weitz 2013). Among the major mental disorders are mood disorders, anxiety disorders, personality disorders, and psychotic disorders. Mood disorders include persisting depression and bipolar (manic depressive) disorder characterized by a strong feeling of happiness followed by intense depression. Depression appears to be the most common form of mental illness, affecting 26 percent or more of adults in the United States at some point in their lives. Anxiety disorders refer to intense anxiety displayed through phobias, panic, or obsessive-compulsive behavior. Personality disorders include the antisocial (psychopathic) personality type (characterized by lack of guilt feelings for harmful behavior) and deep-rooted negative personality traits such as paranoia or narcissism. Psychotic disorders include schizophrenia and related disorders in which a person loses touch with reality and often experiences delusions, hallucinations, and/or extreme paranoia.

Cover of the Diagnostic and Statistical Manual of Mental Disorders

Causes of Mental Illness and Links to Gender, Race, and Class

Research indicates that there are multiple causes of mental disorders. Inherited genetic characteristics make some people more vulnerable to mental illness.

Physical events such as brain injuries, a pregnant woman's exposure to poisonous chemicals, drug abuse, or being the victim of physical or emotional abuse may all contribute to mental disorders. Stress caused by poverty, war, divorce, loss of a loved one, the onset of a serious illness or disability, losing one's job, or being the victim of discrimination can also increase the risk of mental disorders. For many people, mental disorder appears to be the result of a combination of biological and environmental factors.

Mood disorders, substance abuse disorders, and schizophrenia are more common among lower-income people (Weitz 2013). While the overrepresentation of mental disorders among lower-income people may be partially due to these individuals being unable to hold jobs, research indicates that the stress of being poor plays a bigger role in explaining higher rates of mental illness among low-income persons. Once income level is controlled for, there generally does not appear to be any relationship between race and mental disorders. But some studies indicate that mood disorders are more frequent among non-Hispanic whites and substance abuse-related disorders among Hispanics and non-Hispanic whites. There appears to be no evidence of ethnic differences for schizophrenia. While mood disorders are more common among women, impulse control disorders, substance abuse-related disorders, schizophrenia, and the psychopathic personality type are more common among men. Existing research, for example, indicates that up to 3 percent of the male population may be psychopaths, compared to no more than one percent of females (Dutton 2012).

Treatments for Mental Illness

In pre-industrial societies, people with the symptoms of minor forms of mental illness could often work adequately at low-skill jobs and be helped or controlled effectively by family members (Weitz 2013). But when individuals' behavior was too bizarre or unacceptable, communities typically looked to religious leaders for guidance. Clerics might resort to prayer, exorcism, physical violence, or even killing. Religious "treatment" of disruptive behavior led to witchcraft trials and the deaths of 100,000 or more persons during the fifteenth to seventeenth centuries. Beginning around 1600, as scientific knowledge grew, societies shifted toward locking up mentally ill persons in prisons or "madhouses" where conditions where often deplorable. The process of locking up hundreds of thousands of the mentally ill, known as the Great Confinement, continued into the mid-twentieth century. Dorothea Dix (1802–1887), a social reformer and educator, succeeded in convincing authorities to bring about improved conditions and more humane treatment for confined mentally ill persons in Massachusetts and a number of other states and countries. But overall conditions in many public mental facilities remained unsatisfactory.

In the twentieth century, the developing field of psychology led to attempts to scientifically treat the mentally ill. One approach, inspired by the work of Sigmund Freud, was psychotherapy. This involved patients discussing their mental difficulties with trained therapists in the hope of eventually coming to understand and overcome the underlying cause of their problems. But psychotherapy, whatever its potential benefits, was an expensive process that only upper-class or upper-middle-class persons could afford. Other questionable medical approaches for mentally ill persons were introduced in the 1930s. These included repeated large dose injections of insulin and electroconvulsive (electroshock) therapy, which induced comas or seizures some physicians believed reduced symptoms of certain mental disorders. Another even more extreme approach was destroying part of the brain (lobotomies) to improve behavior. Each of these practices fell out of favor because of doubts about their benefits and the introduction beginning in the 1950s of psychoactive chemicals. These drugs were viewed as more humane and appeared generally more effective.

Deinstitutionalization

The number of people confined to often overcrowded and understaffed state mental hospitals reached a peak of 558,000 in 1955 (Weitz 2013). The development of Thorazine, which prevents schizophrenic hallucinations and drugs that reduce the symptoms of other harmful mental disorders played a significant role in the decline of the mental hospital population (**deinstitutionalization**) that began in the mid-1950s. By 2013, there had been an approximately 90-percent reduction in the number of state hospital beds (Smith 2013). Mentally ill persons who used prescribed psychoactive drugs were much more capable of living and working in communities. The Community Mental Health Centers Construction Act, passed by Congress in 1963, was another factor that contributed to deinstitutionalization of mentally ill persons. This legislation was intended to provide federal funding for hundreds of local mental health centers that would assist people with mental difficulties in living satisfying and productive lives. Many states took advantage of the deinstitutionalization approach to close expensive state mental hospitals. But in reality too few community mental health centers, only about half of the fifteen hundred originally intended, were built, and none of those that were built were completely funded (Smith 2013). This meant that while many people lived much better lives than they would have in state mental institutions, thousands of others failed to receive the assistance they needed. Many with serious mental illness ended up drug abusers, homeless, or in jails or prison. The three biggest mental health care providers in the United States in 2013 were correctional institutions: the Cook County (Illinois) jail, the Los Angeles County jail, and the Rikers Island (New York) jail.

SOCIOLOGICAL PERSPECTIVES ON HEALTH

Structural-Functional Perspective

The structural-functional approach views health care as an institution that contributes to the smooth functioning of society because illness interferes with people's ability to carry out their jobs and other social roles. This perspective also analyzes how changes in health technology affect society. In health care, both medical research and the medical

deinstitutionalization
The shift to treating persons designated as mentally ill to settings other than mental hospitals.

profession became highly specialized. One result was new drugs, proce-dures, and treatments that greatly reduced medical problems that once took tens of millions of lives. This included virtually wiping out infec-tious diseases such as smallpox, yellow fever, measles, polio, malaria, diphtheria, and typhoid fever, and eliminating unsafe practices associ-ated with pregnancy and childbirth in many countries. The application of these innovations worldwide, as well as improvement in sewage sys-tems and much wider availability of clean water, shifted the main causes of death to chronic diseases like heart disease and cancer. It also reduced the rate at which people died and increased average life span from about 40 to 70 or more years. This change in the causes and patterns of health and disease is referred to as the **epidemiological transition**. The epi-demiological transition, along with the movement of people from rural areas and agricultural labor to cities and urban jobs caused the related **demographic transition**. The demographic transition is the shift from high death rates and high **birth rates** characteristic of pre-industrial agricultural societies to low death rates and low birth rates character-istic of advanced urbanized industrial societies. The lower death rate, coupled with the low birth rate, had unintended consequences. In the United States the percent of retired persons grew larger while the pro-portion of active workers whose contributions fund Social Security shrank, threatening its economic viability. Saving Social Security will require changes like increasing the age for eligibility, lowering benefit payments, and/or finding alternative funding. It might also lead to poli-cies to encourage young people from other countries to legally emigrate to the United States to increase the proportion of active workers. Thus, improved health care can cause unanticipated social change.

Conflict Perspective

The conflict approach focuses on how economic, political, and social inequality affects health and health care. Throughout the world people with the most power and wealth tend to have the best health care. The gap between the health of people in the upper and lower income classes varies significantly among nations because of differences in access to health care. The United States is the only technologically advanced nation without a system to guarantee health care to all members of society. This is one reason why the United States has the highest first-day infant mor-tality (number of deaths in the first 24 hours after birth per 1,000 births) among all technologically advanced nations (Castillo 2013).

Critics claim that treating health care as a commodity to be sold for profit rather than as a basic human right affects the entire health care system by making it primarily responsive to those who can pay enough to ensure profits, rather than poor people who often have the most serious health problems. Profit-motivated drug companies have little financial incentive to produce drugs to prevent or treat diseases in underdeveloped countries where few people have the money to pay for them. The director general of the WHO, Dr. Margaret Chan, stated that the drug industry's drive for profits was a reason that no vaccine had been found for Ebola and "[a] profit-driven industry does not invest in products for markets that cannot pay" (Gladstone 2014).

epidemiological transition The shift in the cause of death in a society from being predominantly infec-tious disease to chronic disease.

demographic transition The shift from high birth rates and high death rates to low birth rates and low death rates.

birth rate The number of live births per 1,000 members of a population per year.

Health problems also put low-income people at a disadvantage in getting access to higher education, vocational training, and good jobs. And the profit motive in American health care can promote corruption among medical professionals. Some doctors and hospitals may focus on personal gain rather than patients' well-being in making diagnoses, ordering diagnostic procedures, or recommending treatment. Evidence indicates, for example, that doctors order more medical tests when they own the labs that do the testing (Tozzi 2013).

The conflict approach also emphasizes how insurance companies and pharmaceutical corporations use some of their profits to hire lobbyists and fund politicians to protect their interests.

Symbolic-Interactionist Perspective

The symbolic-interactionist approach is concerned with the definitions and meanings associated with health, illnesses, and healthcare, and how these are communicated among people and modified over time and space: in other words, how they are socially constructed. An interesting example of the social construction of behaviors as illnesses can be seen in the case of homosexuality. As Christianity developed, the Church's religious leaders proclaimed that the purpose of sex was to produce children and strongly condemned homosexuality. This religious view led to government enactment of criminal laws mandating severe punishment for homosexual behavior. Just preceding the Declaration of Independence in 1776, male homosexuals were subject to the death penalty in all thirteen British colonies in America (Crompton 1976). After the revolution, the states individually moved to drop the death penalty for homosexual behavior but replaced it with other harsh penalties.

By the early twentieth century a "progressive" movement was underway among some in medicine and psychiatry to "medicalize" homosexuality by redefining it from a sinful behavior of choice to a form of mental illness. This effort at the time was viewed as beneficial to homosexuals, because if they were defined as "sick" persons they would be less responsible for their behavior than if their homosexuality was simply a matter of choice (Herek 2012). The attempt to redefine homosexuality as an illness was embodied in the 1952 first issue of the *Diagnostic and Statistical Manual of Mental Disorders* (*DSM-1*) of the American Psychiatric Association, where homosexuality was classified as a mental disorder.

Research, however, repeatedly indicated that homosexuality was a natural state for many people, not an illness, and that on average homosexuals and heterosexuals did not differ significantly regarding symptoms of mental illness. Finally in 1986, the characterization of homosexuality as a mental disorder was removed entirely from the revised third edition of the *DSM* (*DSM-3*). Thus, the social construction of homosexuality changed over time from sinful act to mental disorder to healthy and normal act for certain people. Masturbation is another behavior that went through a similar transformation in meaning from sin to mental disorder to normal.

The symbolic-interactionist approach is also concerned with whether and how stigma becomes attached or removed from socially identified illnesses, sick people, and/or health care. The attachment of a negative stigma may be influenced by religious or political considerations, economic interests, or other factors. Although nations like Canada and Sweden that guarantee health care coverage to their citizens have among the healthiest populations in the world, opponents of universal health care stigmatized them as "socialist" in order to prevent such a system from being adopted in the United States.

The lack of a rapid response to the AIDS outbreaks in the United States and South Africa illustrate how special interests can affect the recognition, social meaning, and reaction to a health crisis. The HIV that causes AIDS appears to have originated in chimpanzees in Africa and crossed over to humans. In the United States, the disease developed disproportionately among highly stigmatized groups in the early 1980s, homosexual men and intravenous drug users. This seems to be a major reason why the response of the federal government was slow.

Special Topics: Suppressing Health Research for Political Reasons

The power of the gun lobby over the federal government

The CDC and the National Center for Injury Prevention and Control funded research on gun violence in the early 1990s. Findings, published in a series of articles in the New *England Journal of Medicine*, indicated that the presence of a gun in the home tripled the likelihood that someone living there would become the victim of a homicide (Hall 2015). Furthermore, the data showed that the risk of suicide for adolescents and young adults in homes with a gun was about ten times that for households without one. The results tended to undermine the argument that keeping a gun in the home provided security for family members.

The National Rifle Association (NRA) and progun members of Congress were concerned about the research. Congress decided to cut the CDC's budget by the specific amount that the organization had allocated to the gun research (Hall 2015). And a clause was placed in the CDC 1996 appropriations bill that effectively prevented it from funding gun research for the next 20 years: "[N]one of the funds made available for injury prevention and control at the Centers for Disease Control and Prevention may be used to advocate or promote gun control" (Omnibus Consolidated Appropriations Bill. HR 3610 1996). "Precisely what was or was not permitted under the clause was unclear. But no federal employee was willing to risk his or her career or the agency's funding to find out" (Kellermann and Rivara 2013) by granting support for new gun studies.

Thus, in the years leading up to horrific gun mass murders such as those at Virginia Tech, Sandy Hook Elementary School, Orlando, and Las Vegas, research that might have helped prevent those massacres was limited by the restrictions imposed by conservative politicians allied with the NRA.

In South Africa, the national government was also slow to respond to AIDS. But the AIDS victims there were largely heterosexuals. The main reason for the delayed response appeared to be economic and political. In the 1990s the African National Congress (ANC) won the first post-apartheid elections, promising to improve the well-being of the country's impoverished majority. But defining AIDS as a serious problem and responding rapidly would have absorbed a substantial amount of resources and interfered with economic development projects (Handley 2004).

GOVERNMENT HEALTH CARE PROGRAMS

Medicaid

Medicaid is the federal health care program for low-income people enacted in 1965. It is funded jointly by the federal government and the states and is a "means-tested" program, in that only those lacking the ability to pay for health care services are eligible. Individual states are allowed considerable freedom in determining who receives Medicaid, but all recipients are supposed to be either U.S. citizens or permanent residents. In 2010 the federal Patient Protection and Affordable Care Act (ACA) allowed expansion of Medicaid coverage to persons with income levels up to 33 percent above the poverty line. However, a number of state governments, primarily many of those with Republican-controlled governorships and legislatures, refused to expand coverage.

Children's Health Insurance Program

The Children's Health Insurance Program (CHIP), formerly known as the State Children's Health Insurance Program (SCHIP), was enacted by the federal government in 2007. CHIP provides matching funds to states so that families with children whose incomes are low but not low enough to qualify for Medicaid can purchase health insurance. Although the George W. Bush administration refused to expand the program, President Barack Obama signed the Children's Health Reauthorization Act of 2009 (Congressional Record 2009), which allowed CHIP to cover some four million more children and pregnant women.

Military Health Care

The federal government, through the Department of Defense, funds and controls the military health system (MHS). MHS provides health services to both active-duty and retired U.S. military personnel and their dependents. In 2013 it employed 60,389 civilians and 86,051 military personnel and served 9.6 million persons through 56 hospitals, 361 ambulatory care clinics, and 249 dental clinics worldwide (U.S. Department of Defense 2014).

Medicare

Medicare is the federal social insurance program set up by Congress in 1965 to pay for many of the medical expenses of those aged sixty-five or older (who have paid into the program), regardless of income or medical history. Medicare also covers certain younger people with disabilities or particular illnesses such as kidney disease (Medicare.gov 2017).

STATE AND FEDERAL HEALTH CARE REFORM

State Reforms

After repeated federal failures to create universal health care, several states, including Hawaii, Massachusetts, and Minnesota, enacted their own health care reforms to significantly increase the percent of residents with health insurance. The Massachusetts health care law of 2006, passed while Republican Mitt Romney was governor, was particularly significant since it served as a model for the Obama administration's ACA. The Massachusetts law required everyone in the state to be covered by health insurance but also provided free health insurance for residents with incomes less than 150 percent of the federal poverty line and partially subsidized insurance for those with incomes between 150 to 200 percent of the federal poverty level (Raymond 2007). The percentage of Massachusetts' non-elderly population without health insurance declined from 10.9 in 2006 to 6.3 in 2010. The percentage of non-elderly without health insurance for the entire United States in 2010 was about three times the Massachusetts figure (Kaiser Family Foundation 2012). After passage of the ACA, the percentage without health insurance declined further in Massachusetts to 4.9 by mid-2014, second to Delaware, which had only 3.3 percent without health insurance (Gallup 2014). The eleven states with the lowest percentages without health insurance also included Hawaii (6.9%), Connecticut (7.4%), Vermont (8.5%), Maryland (8.4%), Minnesota (8.8%), Rhode Island (9.3%), Pennsylvania (10.1%), and Iowa and New York tied at 10.3 percent. The ten states with the highest percentages of residents lacking health care insurance in mid-2014, according to Gallup (2014), were South Carolina (16.8%), Arizona (17.2%), Oklahoma (17.5%), Kansas (17.6%), Montana (17.9%), Louisiana (18.4%), Florida (18.9%), Georgia (20.2%), Mississippi (20.6%), and Texas (24.0%). The governments of each of the ten states with the highest proportions of population lacking health insurance refused to cooperate fully with the federal ACA.

The Affordable Health Care Act

Before the enactment of the ACA in 2010, research indicated a lack of health care insurance caused the deaths of about forty-five thousand Americans annually (Cecere 2009). The ACA mandates that people obtain health care insurance or pay a financial penalty. Businesses with more than fifty employees must provide their workers with access to health insurance. The ACA forces insurance companies to provide insurance regardless of people's pre-existing conditions and prevents charging such people higher premiums (Weitz 2013). It also stops insurance companies from limiting annual or lifetime benefits. However, since the ACA relies on hundreds of private for-profit health insurance companies, the system is complex and administrative costs are high.

By 2015 an additional sixteen million Americans had gained health care insurance coverage (White House 2015). The ten states with the biggest increases in the percentages of their populations insured between 2013 and midyear 2014, Arkansas, Kentucky, Delaware, Washington, Colorado, West Virginia, Oregon, California, New Mexico, and

Connecticut, all fully cooperated with the ACA by permitting Medicaid expansion and by setting up their own state health insurance exchanges (Gallup 2014). Exchanges are online portals where people can shop for health insurance from the competing companies. The exchanges also provide qualified consumers with premium subsidies or cost-sharing subsidies. Research indicates that the percentages of the U.S. population without health insurance declined from 18 percent in the fall of 2013 (when people where first able to enroll in the ACA) to 11.9 percent in the first quarter of 2015 (CNN 2015a). On June 25, 2015, the U.S, Supreme Court, in a 6 to 3 ruling, turned back a major threat to the ACA by declaring that it did effectively authorize federal subsidies to qualified people not only in states with their own health care insurance exchanges but also in the thirty-four states with only federal exchanges (CNN 2015b). By the end of 2016 the percent of Americans without health care insurance declined further, to 10.9 percent, although it rose to 11.3 percent in 2017 (Thomas 2017). President Donald Trump and his fellow party leaders of the Republican-controlled Senate and House of Representatives declared in 2017 that they intended to repeal and replace the ACA because of flaws like rising premiums, while many Democrats called for keeping the ACA and fixing its defects.

CHAPTER REVIEW

Health and Health Problems Worldwide

The quality of health care and types of health problems vary greatly worldwide. Noncommunicable diseases such as heart disease and cancer cause most deaths, but in lower-income countries infectious diseases still take many lives. Death rates have declined over time due to wider access to modern medical technology and to social development that has, for example, expanded the availability of clean water.

Globalization and Health

Globalization has had both beneficial and harmful effects on health. One obvious danger of rapid international travel is that a disease outbreak can spread quickly from one country to another. Benefits of globalization include the ability to share new medical knowledge and technologies, fast detection of disease outbreaks, and rapid deployment of medical resources to limit the spread of disease.

HIV/AIDS is a major infectious disease that has spread internationally. Over 1.2 million U.S. residents live with HIV/AIDS. But the HIV/AIDS problem is most severe in sub-Saharan Africa, where tens of millions are infected.

Health Problems in the United States

In the United States, health inequality is linked to class, education, race, ethnicity, gender, and family characteristics. The United States spends much more on health care per citizen than other advanced nations. Yet it lags behind many of these countries in life expectancy. Because of the high cost of health care, people with no or inadequate health insurance avoid seeking medical care unless they are desperately ill and skip taking medicine on schedule to make it last longer. Without adequate health insurance, serious accidents or illnesses force families into bankruptcy.

Social movements that sought to achieve greater equality of opportunity for workers, women, people with disabilities, and racial, ethnic, and sexual orientation minorities led to collective efforts to obtain wider availability of good health care. A recent attempt toward universal health care in the United States comparable to that in other highly developed nations was the federal Patient Protection and Affordable Health Care Act of 2010.

Preventable Ongoing Risks to Health

Preventable or at least partially preventable risks to health include tobacco smoking, obesity, and environmental poisoning. Exposure to preventable health risks vary by income, education level, race and ethnicity, and, to some extent, gender.

Mental Health

Mental illness refers to a thinking or mood disorder that causes impaired functioning and/or debilitating feelings of distress. Mental disorders can be caused by genetic characteristics, physical events such as brain injuries, exposure to poisonous chemicals, drug abuse, being the victim of physical or emotional abuse, or stress such as that caused by poverty, war, divorce, loss of a loved one, or the onset of a serious illness or disability. Beginning in the 1950s the use of psychoactive drugs helped bring about deinstitutionalization of many mentally ill persons, but outpatient treatment was often inadequate.

Sociological Perspectives on Health

The structural-functional approach emphasizes that health care maintains people's well-being and contributes to society's smooth functioning because healthy people can most effectively act out their social roles. The conflict approach focuses on how economic, political, and social inequality affects health and health care. Throughout the world, people with the most power and wealth tend to have the best health care, the healthiest lives, and the longest life spans. The symbolic-interactionist approach is concerned with the definitions and meanings associated with health, illnesses, and healthcare, and how these are communicated among people and modified over time and place.

Government Health Care Programs

Government health care programs include Medicaid, the Children's Health Insurance Program, military health care, and Medicare.

State and Federal Health Care Reform

State and federal health reform efforts in the twenty-first century led to the Massachusetts health reform of 2006, which became the primary model for the 2010 Patient Protection and Affordable Health Care Act.

KEY TERMS

AIDS, p. 232
birth rate, p. 251
death (mortality) rate, p. 237
deinstitutionalization, p. 250
demographic transition, p. 251

epidemiological transition, p. 251
HIV, p. 232
infant mortality rate, p. 238
mental illness, p. 248
under-five-child-mortality rate, p. 232

DISCUSSION QUESTIONS

1. What do you think would be the most effective ways to reduce the world's major health problems? Explain your answer.

2. What are the most serious preventable causes of health problems where you live? What do you think could be done to reduce these risks to health?

3. Which sociological perspective most effectively analyzes problems in the U.S. health care system? Explain your answer.

4. In your opinion, has the Patient Protection and Affordable Care Act had more beneficial or harmful consequences? What evidence supports your point of view?

5. What do you think would be the best way to extend health care insurance coverage to those who do not have it?

CHAPTER 10

Crime and Criminal Justice

CHAPTER OBJECTIVES

- Explain the concepts of crime and deviant behavior.
- Describe of the major types of crime data.
- Describe the major types of crime.
- Describe the characteristics of criminals.
- Explain biological, psychiatric, and sociological approaches to explaining crime.
- Explain major sociological theories of crime.

BLACKSBURG, VIRGINIA., 9:43 AM, APRIL 16, 2007: *"We've been hurt,"* nineteen-year-old Virginia Tech student Emily Haas whispered into a cell phone (Horwitz 2007). University Police Lt. Debbi Morgan could hear gunfire as she listened to Emily tell her she was lying wounded in 211 Norris Hall. *"Keep yourself safe,"* Lt. Morgan said. *"We're sending people." "Please hurry,"* Emily implored. Although she was shot twice, Emily survived. But twenty-seven other students and five professors did not.

There have been many lethal shootings at American educational institutions. Four of the worst occurred, respectively, at Columbine High School (Colorado) on April 20, 1999; Virginia Tech (Blacksburg, Virginia) on April 16, 2007; Sandy Hook Elementary School (Newtown, Connecticut) on December 14, 2012 and Marjory Stoneman Douglas High School (Parkland, Florida) on February 14, 2018. At Columbine, eighteen-year-old Eric Harris and seventeen-year-old Dylan Klebold gunned down twelve students and a teacher before killing themselves. At Virginia Tech, twenty-three-year-old senior English major Seung-Hui Cho killed thirty-two before committing suicide. At Sandy Hook, twenty-year-old Adam Lanza murdered twenty 6- and 7-year-old children and six adult staff members before taking his own life. He had earlier killed his mother. And at Marjory Stoneman Douglas High, nineteen-year-old former student Nikolas Cruz killed fourteen students, a teacher, a coach, and the school's athletic director before being apprehended by police.

Similar to most other mass murders, these school massacres were perpetrated by enraged and socially isolated males who appeared to suffer from mental illness. Nonetheless, they were able to obtain the kinds of weapons that would allow them to kill many people very rapidly. In response to school mass murders, some groups advocate widespread gun training and arming of teachers and other school staff persons. The idea is that if a shooter opens fire, armed citizens on the scene can return fire and put an end to the attack quickly to limit the damage. Another widely supported proposal is better mental health intervention so that troubled persons can be effectively identified and treated before committing acts of violence. And many people, including relatives of school shooting victims like Lori Haas, Emily Haas' mother, who became a leader of the Coalition to Stop Gun Violence (Cunningham 2013), favor stricter gun control like universal background checks to make sure that criminals and seriously mentally ill persons do not have easy access to guns. School shootings, like other forms of criminal behavior, show how crime is often the result of a combination of factors. They also illustrate how controversy and political conflict can develop over how to prevent crime.

crime Any voluntary and intentional behavior or omission that federal, state, or local government designates as a violation of criminal law and for which there is no legally accepted excuse, such as self-defense or insanity.

deviant behavior Behavior that is inconsistent with deeply and widely held norms, expectations, or standards but is not necessarily unlawful.

WHAT IS CRIME?

Crime is any voluntary and intentional behavior or omission that federal, state, or local government designates as a violation of criminal law and for which there is no legally accepted excuse, such as self-defense or insanity. Crime is different from what is meant by the expressions "deviance" or "deviant behavior." **Deviant behavior** is behavior that is inconsistent with deeply and widely held norms, expectations, or standards. But much deviant behavior is lawful. What is "deviant" can vary among different population groups and change over time. For example, homosexuality was much more widely viewed as deviance twenty years ago than today. In contrast, cigarette smoking, which was once widely accepted has become increasingly viewed as deviant behavior.

It is also true that some crimes may not be viewed as deviant by many people. For example, millions of Americans considered drinking alcohol totally normal when it was banned by the 1920 Prohibition law. And alcohol consumption was suddenly no longer a crime after the law's repeal in 1933. Something similar occurred with regard to marijuana. In January 2014, Colorado became the first state to permit recreational marijuana use, although many in the state and around the country still view marijuana use as deviant. This change of law in Colorado also illustrates a prominent feature of the U.S. justice system: its high degree of decentralization. There are fifty different state criminal justice systems, plus the District of Colombia, each with its own laws, in addition the federal legal system. Therefore, what is legal in some states may be illegal in others and, as in the case of marijuana, what is legal at the state level may be illegal at the federal level. Although this can cause inconsistency, inefficiency, and lack of coordination, it can also spur social change. If a change in law succeeds in one state, it can lead to similar changes in other states.

MEASURING THE EXTENT AND FORMS OF CRIME

Government and academic researchers have spent many millions of dollars gathering data on crime. Major sources of crime data include official statistics, victimization surveys, and self-report studies.

Official Crime Statistics

Official crime statistics come from government sources, primarily the police and the courts. For example, court records provide information on people convicted of auto theft. But courts have data only for crimes where a person has been arrested and charged. Police and sheriffs' departments provide much more comprehensive crime statistics than courts because they include crimes the police know occurred regardless of whether the perpetrator was arrested. Police data are compiled in the Federal Bureau of Investigation's (FBI) **Uniform Crime Reports (UCR)**. The FBI UCR program began publishing reports in 1930 (FBI 2017a). Law enforcement agencies around the United States were asked to voluntarily maintain accurate records on seven particular crimes in their jurisdictions and report these statistics annually. These seven crimes were to serve as indicators of all crime in the United States and so were called the "index crimes." The first four index crimes were the violent crimes of homicide, forcible rape, robbery, and aggravated assault. The UCR defined them as (U.S. Department of Justice 2017):

- **Homicide** – "Murder and nonnegligent manslaughter: the willful (nonnegligent) killing of one human being by another."

official crime statistics
Crime statistics that come from government sources, primarily the police and the courts.

Uniform Crime Reports (UCR) FBI-compiled crime statistics based on crime data supplied by thousands of law enforcement agencies around the United States.

- **Forcible rape** – "The carnal knowledge of a female forcibly and against her will. Rapes by force and attempts or assaults to rape, regardless of the age of the victim, are included. Statutory offenses (no force used – victim under age of consent) are excluded."

But note that "[i]n 2013, the FBI UCR program began collecting rape data under a revised definition within the Summary Reporting System. Previously, offense data for forcible rape were collected under the legacy UCR definition: the carnal knowledge of a female forcibly and against her will. Beginning with the 2013 data year, the term 'forcible' was removed from the offense title, and the definition was changed. The revised UCR definition of rape is: penetration, no matter how slight, of the vagina or anus with any body part or object, or oral penetration by a sex organ of another person, without the consent of the victim. Attempts or assaults to commit rape are also included in the statistics presented here; however, statutory rape and incest are excluded" (FBI 2017b). This change in definition means male victims are now included. However, in 2016 rape data were reported under both the old (legacy) definition and the new definition.

- **Robbery** – "The taking or attempting to take anything of value from the care, custody, or control of a person or persons by force or threat of force or violence and/or by putting the victim in fear."

- **Aggravated assault** – "An unlawful attack by one person upon another for the purpose of inflicting severe or aggravated bodily injury. This type of assault usually is accompanied by the use of a weapon or by means likely to produce death or great bodily harm. Simple assaults are excluded."

When the UCR was first published, the seven index crimes also included the three property crimes of burglary, motor vehicle theft, and larceny theft. In 1979, arson was added as a fourth property crime. The UCR definitions are (U.S. Department of Justice 2017):

- **Burglary** – "The unlawful entry of a structure to commit a felony or a theft. Attempted forcible entry is included."

- **Larceny theft (except motor vehicle theft)** – "The unlawful taking, carrying, leading, or riding away of property from the possession or constructive possession of another. Examples are thefts of bicycles, motor vehicle parts and accessories, shoplifting, pocketpicking, or the stealing of any property or article that is not taken by force and violence or by fraud. Attempted larcenies are included. Embezzlement, confidence games, forgery, check fraud, etc., are excluded."

- **Motor vehicle theft** – "The theft or attempted theft of a motor vehicle. A motor vehicle is self-propelled and runs on land surface and not on rails. Motorboats, construction equipment, airplanes, and farming equipment are specifically excluded from this category."

- **Arson** – "Any willful or malicious burning or attempt to burn, with or without intent to defraud, a dwelling house, public building, motor vehicle or aircraft, personal property of another, etc."

The UCR indicated that there were 1,283,058 violent crimes in the United States in 2016 using the new more comprehensive definition of rape (1,248,185 using the old definition of rape) and 7,919,035 property crimes, not including arson (arson is not included because the arson data is often incomplete) (FBI 2017b). In 2016, 118 law enforcement officers died from injuries received in the line of duty, 66 as a result of criminal acts (an increase of 61 percent from 2015) and 52 from accidents (FBI 2017c).

Currently nearly 18,000 law enforcement agencies send their statistics on crime to the FBI UCR (FBI 2017d). The annual UCR (which provides crime statistics for the entire United States, individual states, and many cities, towns, and college campuses) is available online at https://ucr.fbi.gov/ucr-publications. In order to assess the actual risk of victimization between places with greatly differing population sizes, the UCR provides both the actual number of a crime and the crime rate, the number of times that crime occurred per 100,000 residents. For example, in 2016 New York City experienced 335 homicides and New Orleans 174 (FBI 2017e). But the risk of being a victim of homicide was ten times greater in New Orleans because its homicide rate was 43.8 (43.8 homicide victims per 100,000 New Orleans residents), while the homicide rate for New York City was 3.9 (3.9 homicide victims per 100,000 New York City residents).

After many law enforcement experts expressed interest in a more comprehensive and detailed crime data system, the FBI initiated the **National Incident-Based Reporting System (NIBRS)** in 1988. In the NIBRS system, law enforcement agencies are asked to report detailed information on forty-nine specific crimes (the NIBRIS Group A Offenses) and more limited arrestee characteristics for another eleven crimes (the NIBRIS Group B Offenses) (FBI 2017f). However, in 2015, only about 36 percent of the U.S. law enforcement agencies participating in the UCR, covering a little less than a third of the U.S. population, also participated in NIBRS.

Although the UCR is a valuable source of crime data, it has several limitations. First, it tends to ignore the kinds of property crimes committed by professional and wealthy people. A second problem is that it includes only crimes known to police. Most crimes become known to police because someone chose to report them. If a crime victim chooses not to report, for example, a robbery, it will not be counted in the UCR, even though it did happen. In fact, research indicates that between 2006 and 2010, only 35 percent of rapes, 59 percent of robberies, and 55 percent of household burglaries were reported to police (Langton et al. 2012). Only homicide and motor vehicle theft become known to the police more than 80 percent of the time. So much more crime takes place than is indicated in the UCR.

A third potential flaw in police data is that it can reflect changes in the way police enforce the law or classify crimes rather than a real change in levels of criminal behavior. Police officials' desire for increased funding might motivate stricter enforcement or misclassification of crimes to make it appear that crime is getting worse and additional money is needed to more effectively deal with the problem. If, on the other hand, the police leadership favors reelection of the mayor, enforcement might be eased or some serious crimes might be classified as less serious to make it look like anti-crime policies are more successful than they really are.

National Incident-Based Reporting System (NIBRS) A more comprehensive and detailed crime data system intended to replace the UCR.

UCR Crime Trends The UCR indicates that crime rose from 1960 to 1980 and fluctuated somewhat until 1991. Then crime rates fell to early-1960s levels around 2005 and stayed at those levels or went even lower in much of the country through 2014. Between 2014 and 2016 the property crime rate fell further, by 5 percent, while the violent crime rate rose by 6.8 percent. The homicide rate, which reached its highest level in 1980, is considered the most valid UCR crime rate because homicides almost always become known to the police. The fact that changes in the rates of other violent crimes as well as burglary, larceny theft, and motor vehicle theft corresponded to the changes in the homicide rate indicates that these changes were real rather than caused by changes in the tendency to report crime. What caused crime rates to rise and then fall? Some criminologists believe that the rise in violence and property crime between 1960 and 1980 was caused by divorce increasing dramatically, which interfered with the proper upbringing of children. Since UCR violent crimes and property crimes are disproportionately committed by teenagers and young adults, some believe that the rise in the proportion of the population made up of young people in the 1960s caused crime rates to climb. Another argument is that protests against government policies like involvement in the Vietnam War contributed to a decline in respect for government in general that eroded many people's willingness to abide by laws.

One explanation for the crime decline after 1991 is that convicted criminals began receiving harsher sentences, keeping them off the streets for longer periods (Levitt 2004). Another is that the proportion of the population made up of low-income young people decreased because of the decline in birth rates. Many also believe that the increase in the number of police and implementation of more efficient and proactive police tactics played an important role. Crack cocaine use, thought to be particularly associated with violence, appeared to drop. Another explanation is that the expansion of social programs for young people and anti-child-abuse programs for parents and children also contributed to reducing crime.

Victimization Surveys

The U.S. Justice Department, recognizing that official statistics from police and courts severely undercount crimes because so many are not reported, began a new method of collecting crime data in 1973. It organized a national survey of tens of thousands of Americans asking them if they, their household members, or their businesses had been criminally victimized during the previous six months, regardless of whether they reported it to police. This **National Crime Victimization Survey (NCVS)** seeks victimization information on basically the same types of major crimes covered in the UCR with the exception of homicide. In 2015, the NCVS surveyed around 163,880 people in about 95,760 households (Bureau of Justice Statistics 2016; Truman and Morgan 2016). Based on what the NCVS found, estimates of the number of criminal victimizations of each type covered in the questionnaire were projected for the entire U.S. population. Results since the beginning of the NCVS show that about twice as much serious crime actually occurs

National Crime Victimization Survey (NCVS) A national survey of tens of thousands of Americans asking them if they, their household members, or their businesses had been criminally victimized, regardless of whether they reported it to police.

self-report crime studies
Anonymous surveys in which people are asked whether they have committed various types of crime.

than is indicated in the UCR. The NCVS provides detailed information about the circumstances of crimes, the characteristics of the victims, any previous relationship between the offender and the victim, and why the victim may have chosen not to report the crime to the police. The validity of the information produced by the NCVS depends in part on the honesty of those surveyed and their ability to accurately remember what happened. The NCVS, like the UCR, does indicate that crime declined after 1991. While the 2015 NCVS showed a decrease in property crime from the 2014 NCVS, unlike the UCR it did not show a significant change in violent crime between 2014 and 2015 (Bureau of Justice Statistics 2016).

Self-Report Studies

Another significant approach to measuring and studying criminal behavior is self-report surveys (Thornberry and Krohn 2000). These are anonymous surveys in which people are asked to respond to a series of questions concerning whether they have committed various types of crime. The results of **self-report crime studies** typically show that a lot more criminal behavior takes place than is indicated either by official statistics or victimization surveys. However, this approach to gathering data on crime also has significant limitations. One is that respondents may not be truthful by either concealing serious criminal behavior or exaggerating what they have done. Another issue is that self-report studies often have asked questions mainly about relatively minor forms of criminal behavior like drug use or underage use of alcohol.

Electronic Surveillance An emerging new type of data on criminal behavior comes from various forms of video, audio, and cyber surveillance (UNODC 2009). These applications of electronic observation technology continue to spread, providing a new set of data for assessing and dealing with crime.

Police officers

STREET CRIME

Street crime includes crimes of violence like homicide, forcible rape, robbery, and aggravated assault and relatively direct forms of property crime like burglary, larceny theft, and motor vehicle theft. Street crimes are the major focus of the U.S. criminal justice system. Some argue that this is because these crimes are disproportionately committed by low-income people with little power to influence the political system and the making and enforcement of laws. However, another reason is that crimes of violence are widely considered to be the most serious types of crime (Forensic Psychology 2017).

Violent Street Crime

Homicide Homicide, the unlawful taking of a human life, has three forms. First-degree murder is generally a homicide that is planned ahead of time. It is sometimes referred to as cold-blooded murder. An example might be a businessman who hires someone to kill a competitor. Some states also label homicide committed in the course of another serious crime, such as sexual assault, first-degree murder. Second-degree murder is a crime of passion. There is intent to kill, but the decision to kill is made on the spot in an emotionally charged situation, not ahead of time. The other type of homicide is nonnegligent manslaughter, where one person assaults and kills another, but without the intent to kill. For example, if an unarmed person punches someone and that person dies as a result, the charge would likely be nonnegligent manslaughter because, in most cases, this kind of assault would not be expected to result in death.

In 2016 there were 17,250 homicides known to police, resulting in a rate of 5.3 homicide victims per 100,000 U.S. residents, about a 12 percent increase from the 2014 homicide rate, when the rate began to climb. This means that in 2016, a person was murdered in the United States about once every 30.6 minutes (FBI 2017b). Regionally, the homicide rate has historically been low in the Northeast and the upper Midwest and high in the South. In 2016, for example, a person living in Louisiana, the state with the highest homicide rate (11.8), was about nine times more likely to be murdered than a person living in New Hampshire, the state with the lowest homicide rate (1.3).

While the U.S homicide rate is three to four times higher than in most other technologically advanced societies such as Canada, Italy, Britain, and Japan, dozens of lesser-developed countries have higher homicide rates (UNODC 2016). For example, Brazil, Colombia, El Salvador, Guatemala, Mexico, South Africa, and Venezuela have homicide rates in recent years ranging from four to ten times that of the United States (in the case of Honduras, around fifteen times higher). Quimet (2012), analyzing data for 165 nations, found that countries with higher levels of economic inequality and poverty tend to have higher homicide rates.

The U.S. homicide rate began climbing around 1960 and reached its highest level in the twentieth century in 1980, when there were about 10.2 homicide victims per 100,000 U.S. residents. Then in the early 1990s it began a steep decline and was actually slightly below the

street crime Crimes of violence like homicide, forcible rape, robbery, and aggravated assault and relatively direct forms of property crime like burglary, larceny theft, and motor vehicle theft.

1960 rate in 2014. In 1961 a killer was identified (that is, the homicide was "cleared by arrest or exceptional means") in about 94 percent of all U.S. homicides. But by 2016, this had dropped to only 59.4 percent. This meant that in 2016 the perpetrator was not identified for around 7,000 murders. Between 1980 and 2016, more than 200,000 murders were not solved (FBI 2017a; Hargrove 2010). One reason for the drop in the percentage of homicides solved appears to be that the proportion of homicides occurring during the commission of other crimes where the offender and the victim are often strangers may have increased. It is much easier for the police to solve a homicide when the killer and the victim had a previously existing relationship. Also, many drug- and gang-related homicides may not result in an arrest due to lack of witness cooperation in areas where the killings occur (Hargrove 2010). In many American cities, the majority of homicide victims have criminal records. For example, during 2003–2011 about 77 percent of homicide victims in Chicago had a prior arrest record and in 2012 almost 70 percent in New York City did (Thompson 2013). The figure for Indianapolis in 2013 was 79 percent (Shabazz 2014).

Males were 78.4 percent of all homicide victims in 2016. Like the other three UCR violent crimes, persons arrested for homicide are disproportionately young and male. While the median age in the United States in 2016 was 37.9 (U.S. Census 2017f), 73.5 percent of those arrested for homicide were under 35 years of age. In 2016, 88.8 percent of persons arrested for committing homicide in which the sex of the offender was known were male (FBI 2017g). Analyses of data where the sex of both the victim and offender were known and there was one offender killing one victim indicates that in 2016 men killed men in 64.1 percent of homicides, men killed women in 26.1 percent, women killed men in 7.1 percent and women killed women in 2.7 percent. Although the 2016 UCR homicide section did not provide a victim/offender relationship table, the 2015 UCR showed that when women were killed and the relationship to the offender was known, about 36 percent were murdered by husbands or boyfriends. When men were killed, about 2.5 percent were killed by wives or girlfriends. It has been estimated that most homicides involve victims and offenders who had a previously existing relationship of some type. But in 2015 the relationship, if any, in a huge percentage (47.8%) of homicides was unknown. And in another 10.2 percent of homicides it was determined that the victim and offender were strangers (FBI 2017h). Of the remaining homicides, 12.8 percent were family homicides and another 29.2 percent involved other known relationships such a friend or acquaintance. In 2016, about 73 percent of homicides were committed with a firearm (usually a handgun) and 10.6 percent with a knife or other cutting instrument (FBI 2017i).

African Americans are at greater risk of being homicide victims than whites. Although the former are about 14 percent of the U.S. population (U.S. Census 2015a), they were 52.3 percent of all homicide victims in 2016 and 52.6 percent of persons arrested for committing homicide (FBI 2017a). Whites were 43.6 percent of homicide victims and 44.7 percent of those arrested for homicide. In comparison, among persons arrested for all crimes reported in the 2016 UCR, the large majority, 69.6 percent, were white and 26.9 percent were black. In homicides with a single offender and a single victim and the race of both was known, whites killed whites in about 43 percent of homicides, blacks killed blacks in 40 percent, blacks killed whites in 8 percent, and whites killed blacks in 4 percent (other races accounted for the remaining 5 percent). Research in urban areas indicates that killings of whites are more likely to be solved than the killings of African Americans (Flatow 2014). This could be due to several factors. One is that witnesses in the locations where blacks were killed might have been less willing to cooperate with police. It is also possible that less police time and fewer resources are used to solve a homicide when the victim is black compared to when the victim is white. The risk of being murdered in many cities is higher for an African American than a non-Hispanic white. For example, in 2011 African American Milwaukee residents had a homicide rate of 27.9, whereas for Hispanics the rate was 9.7 and for non-Hispanic whites 1.7 (Milwaukee Homicide Review Commission 2012).

Why is the African American homicide rate so much higher than the non-Hispanic white homicide rate? Some argue that there is a significant subculture of violence among many lower-income African Americans that promotes homicide. But many sociologists (DeFronzo 1997; Sampson 1987; Sampson and Wilson 1995) believe that economic factors like high unemployment and concentrated poverty undermine family relations, causing high homicide levels. Parker (2008) shows that the drastic reduction of manufacturing in urban areas had a much greater impact on eliminating industrial jobs for African American men compared to white men. This appeared be a major reason why white homicide rates in the United States began falling after 1980, but black homicide rates did not start to fall until after 1990.

Two especially terrifying forms of homicide are mass murder and serial murder. The FBI defines mass murder as the killing of four or more people, not counting the offender (FBI 2005; Hoyer and Heath 2013), in one basically continuous event. Among the worst are the June 2016 Orlando Pulse nightclub shooting by Omar Mateen, who murdered forty-nine people before being killed by police and the October 2017 Las Vegas massacre by Stephen Paddock, who killed fifty-eight people attending the outdoor Route 91 Harvest music festival. Mass murderers usually kill themselves or are killed by the police.

Serial murderers, in contrast, seldom take their own lives. Criminologists have developed several definitions of serial killers based on factors such as number of victims and motivations. While a number of experts on serial murder define it as the killing of three or more people in separate murders with periods of inactivity in between (Flowers 2013; Holmes and Holmes 1998;), in 2005 the FBI adopted a simplified definition to assist law enforcement: "The unlawful killing of two or more victims by the same offender(s), in separate events" (Morton and Hilts 2005; Ramsland 2013). The United States has been plagued by male and female serial killers of all major racial and ethnic groups (often leading outwardly normal lives while committing their crimes). Notorious examples include truck painter Gary Ridgeway ("The Green River

Killer"), who killed at least forty-nine women; psychology grad and law student Theodore Bundy, thought to have murdered at least thirty women; and construction company owner John Wayne Gacy, who killed at least thirty-three boys and young men. Table 10.1 presents numbers, rates, time frequencies, and clearance rates for four violent and three property crimes of the UCR for 2016.

Rape The FBI reported that in 2016, using the new definition, 130,603 rapes became known to police. The victim knew the offender in most rapes. Sometimes a rape victim may feel too shamed, fearful, or traumatized to report the rape to the police. The police identified the offender in 36.5 percent of the rapes. But since, according to the National Institute of Justice, (2010b) only about 36 percent of rapes are reported, the percentage of all rapes that actually result in identification of an offender may be only around 13 percent. In 2016, of those arrested for rape, 67.6 percent were white, 29.1 percent were black, and 64.3 percent were under the age of thirty-five (FBI 2017a).

The Centers for Disease Control and Prevention's (CDC) *National Intimate Partner and Sexual Violence Survey* (*NISVS*) of 41,174 adults (22,590 women and 18,584 men) selected to be representative of the entire United States was conducted during 2010–2012 (CDC 2017g; Smith et al. 2017). The survey defined rape similarly to the new UCR definition, which includes male victims. The survey asked respondents whether they had experienced completed forced penetration, other nonconsensual penetration due to the influence of drugs or alcohol or being passed out, or attempted forced penetration. The results indicated that

TABLE 10.1	UCR Violent and Property Crimes in the United States, 2016			
	Number	**Rate**	**Time Frequency (One Every)**	**% Cleared by Arrest or Exceptional Means**
Homicide	17,250	5.3	30.6 min.	59.4%
Rape	130,603	40.4	4.0 min.	36.5 %
Robbery	332,198	102.8	1.6 min.	29.6 %
Motor Vehicle Theft	765,484	236.9	41.3 sec.	13.3 %
Aggravated Assault	803,007	248.5	39.4 sec.	53.3 %
Burglary	1,515,096	468.9	20.9 sec.	13.1 %
Larceny Theft	5,638,455	1,745.0	5.6 sec.	20.4 %

Source: FBI Uniform Crime Reports.

almost 23 million American women (19.1 percent of adult women) and 1.7 million men (1.5 percent of adult men) had been the victims of at least one of these types of sexual assaults during their lifetimes. The perpetrators were usually persons the victims knew, such as current or former intimate partners or acquaintances. Only 13 percent of female victims and 20 percent of male victims said the rapists were strangers. The *NISVS* estimated that, on average, about 1,473,000 women and 219,000 men were rape victims at some time in the 12 months before respondents took the survey. Since the UCR listed only 130,603 rapes known to police in 2016, this suggests that law enforcement officials may in reality become aware of less than 10 percent of rapes.

Persons in authority sometimes use their power to commit sexual assault. One of the most disturbing contexts for such rapes is the armed forces. Research indicates that about seventy military persons, women and men, experience forced sexual contact, sexual assault or rape, every day, with most perpetrators escaping punishment (Chemaly 2013). These findings led enraged members of Congress, led by New York senator Kirsten Killibrand, to propose the Military Justice Improvement Act (MJIA) to better protect vulnerable soldiers.

Robbery In 2016 police recorded 332,198 robberies and identified a perpetrator in 29.6 percent of cases(FBI 2017a). Perpetrators used a firearm in about 41.1 percent of robberies. Of those arrested for this offense, 54.5 percent were black, 43.4 percent were white, and 81.3 percent were younger than thirty-five years of age. About 38.9 percent of robberies took place on streets, and 16.6 percent in homes. Banks (4,982 robberies) were targeted in 1.8 percent of robberies, gas/service stations 2.9 percent, convenience stores 6.2 percent, other businesses 15.3 percent, and other locations 18.4 percent.

Aggravated Assault In aggravated assault the victim and the offender tend to be disproportionately men. However, women and children are also often victims. In 2016, the offender was identified by the police in about 53.3 percent of the cases. Of those arrested for aggravated assault, 61.3 percent were under thirty-five years of age. Whites comprised 62.8 percent of those arrested for committing aggravated assault and blacks constituted 33.3 percent (FBI 2017a). In 2016, approximately 25.8 percent of aggravated assaults were committed using firearms.

Street Property Crime

Street property crime includes burglary, larceny theft, and motor vehicle theft, all disproportionately committed by low-income persons. One of the reasons for the decline in these crimes since the early 1990s has been the widespread application of security technologies. Motor vehicles now have various forms of anti-theft devices. Many homeowners pay private security companies to electronically monitor their houses and businesses and/or have installed outdoor lighting systems with motion detectors to illuminate windows and back doors. Tens of thousands of security cameras are positioned in stores, banks, ATM machines, and on homes, streets, and highways. Table 10.2 shows UCR violent and property crime rates from 1960 to 2016.

TABLE 10.2 | UCR Violent and Property Crime Rates from 1960 to 2016

Year	1960	1975	1980	1985	1990	1991	1995	2000	2005	2010	2014	2015	2016
Homicide	5.1	9.6	10.2	8	9.4	9.8	8.2	5.5	5.6	4.8	4.5	4.9	5.3
Rape	9.6	26.3	36.8	37.1	41.2	42.3	37.1	32	31.7	27.5	26.4 (36.6)	28.1 (38.6)	29.6 (40.4)
Robbery	60.1	220.8	251.1	208.5	257	272.7	220.9	144.9	140.7	119.1	102.2	101.9	102.8
Aggravated Assault	86.1	231.1	298.5	302.9	424.1	433.3	418.3	323.6	291.1	252.3	232.5	237.8	248.5
Burglary	508.6	1,532.1	1,684.1	1,287.3	1,235.9	1,252	987.6	728.4	726.7	699.6	542.5	491.4	468.9
Larceny Theft	1,034.7	2,804.8	3,167	2,901.2	3,194.8	3,228.8	3,044.9	2,475.3	2,286.3	2,003.5	1,837.3	1,775.4	1,745
Motor Vehicle Theft	183	473.7	502.2	462	657.8	658.9	560.5	414.2	416.8	238.8	216.2	220.2	236.9

Sources: FBI Uniform Crime Reports (rate for new definition of rape, 2014–2016, in parentheses; 2017a); Disaster Center 2018.

VICTIMLESS CRIME

Victimless crimes are crimes where there is supposedly no victim. The basis for victimless crime law is primarily to maintain what most people consider moral behavior. Moral-order crimes include banned forms of recreational drug use, gambling, and prostitution. However, viewing prostitution as a victimless crime assumes that people willingly engage in prostitution. If people are forced into prostitution, it is not a victimless crime. It is forcible rape. Another issue is whether the effects of some drugs lead to other crimes or impaired capability to perform potentially dangerous tasks, like driving a car or truck.

Outlawing behavior for which there is no real victim can have serious consequences. People who are stigmatized or put in prison for relatively harmless behavior may suffer from the effects for a long time by being denied educational or job opportunities. They may be forced to engage in other crimes to make a living. Society may waste valuable resources in attempts to suppress relatively harmless moral-order crime. The United States has the highest imprisonment rate (number of prisoners per 100,000 residents) of the world's nations per the 2016 *World Prison Brief* (Walmsley 2016) with the exception of Seychelles, a country of around 94,000 people. This is viewed as in part due to U.S. drug laws. Table 10.3 shows imprisonment rates for the United States and a number of other large nations (populations over fifty million) around the world.

victimless crime Crimes where there is supposedly no victim, such as illegal drug use, illegal gambling, and prostitution.

TABLE 10.3	Imprisonment Rates and Rankings for the United States and Other Selected Nations	
Nation	**Rate**	**Rank**
United States	666	2
Russian Federation	424	15
Brazil	318	29
South Africa	291	36
Iran	287	37
Turkey	280	39
Mexico	169	85
Ethiopia	127	124
China	118	134
Egypt	116	136
Italy	95	152
Germany	77	165
Japan	45	203
Nigeria	36	211
India	33	213

Source: Walmsley 2016.

Social Movements: The Movement to Legalize Marijuana

Marijuana was legal in many states until the passage of the federal Marijuana Tax Act of 1937. This law taxed marijuana for medical or industrial uses but made possession or sale of marijuana for any other purpose illegal. There were several reasons why marijuana was declared illegal. One was because it was often used by low-income persons. When some of these persons committed crimes, officials, not wanting to blame poverty and the U.S. economic system, blamed marijuana instead. Also, because African Americans and Mexican immigrant workers disproportionately smoked marijuana, white officials associated marijuana use with what they considered "inferior" racial groups. In addition, economic interests appear to have used the news media and movies, like the 1936 film *Reefer Madness*, to exaggerate and misrepresent the effects of marijuana. The paper industry was threatened by applications of fibers from certain types of cannabis plants (the plant family including marijuana), as was the emerging nylon industry. Also, the alcohol and tobacco industries did not want competition from legal marijuana. In addition, many politicians viewed marijuana as a "gateway" drug that would lead people to use other, "harder" drugs like cocaine and heroin.

Leaders of the movement to legalize marijuana claim that, as a recreational drug, it is less harmful than alcohol and much less harmful than tobacco. Furthermore, research and numerous personal testimonies indicate that marijuana has beneficial medical uses, including helping cancer patients better tolerate treatment. In addition, society has been wasting billions of dollars enforcing anti-marijuana laws, losing out on revenue that could be obtained by taxing a legal marijuana industry, and ruining lives by arresting and imprisoning people for producing, using, or selling marijuana. Activist groups campaigning for the legalization or decriminalization of marijuana include Law Enforcement against Prohibition (www.leap.cc), Students for Sensible Drug Policy (ssdp.org), the Drug Policy Alliance (www.drugpolicy.org), the Marijuana Policy Project (www.mpp.org), the National Organization for the Reform of Marijuana Laws (NORML; norml.org), and Americans for Safe Access (www.safeaccessnow.org).

Surveys indicate that there has been a tremendous change in public opinion toward legalizing marijuana. In the fall of 2013, a national Gallup poll found 58 percent of Americans in favor of legalizing marijuana for adult use (compared to 31 percent in 2001). Sixty-seven percent of those aged 18–29 supported legalization. Only among those over 65 was there a majority against. Over 60 percent of Democrats and independents supported legalization, as did 35 percent of Republicans. A national Pew poll in 2014 found that three-quarters of Americans believe that the legal sale and use of marijuana for recreational use was inevitable. In October 2016, a Gallup national survey found support for legalizing marijuana had climbed to 60 percent of U.S. adults (Ingraham 2016a).

Public support led eight states (Alaska, California, Colorado, Maine, Massachusetts, Nevada, Oregon, and Washington) and the District of Colombia to legalize marijuana for recreational use by 2017. Many other states have legalized it for medical use.

ORGANIZED CRIME

Organized crime refers to people working together to supply an illegal product or service – for example, illicit drugs or illegal gambling opportunities. It also refers to a group using violence to gain an unfair advantage in an otherwise legitimate business, such as killing competitors or damaging their equipment or merchandise. The existence of successful organized crime groups is based on several factors. First, there must be a significant public demand for illegal goods or services. Second, mutual trust must exist among organized crime members, because they are linked together by a bond that transcends the desire to make money, such as extended family ties. Another possible bond is membership in the same ethnic group, especially if that ethnic group has been oppressed. Third, the group must be able to corrupt law enforcement. Fourth is the capacity to use violence to protect business interests, which, because of their illegal nature, cannot be protected by going to the police or courts. A historic opportunity for organized crime to greatly expand was the period between 1920 and 1933 when the federal government prohibited the manufacture and sale of alcoholic beverages. It was during this time that Italian American organized crime groups became much more powerful than ever before. People of many ethnic groups are active in modern U.S. organized crime, with engagement in drug trafficking, international human smuggling, illegal gambling, making high-interest loans (loan sharking), pirating of copyrighted products, financial fraud, money laundering, and other illegal activities. For example, on February 11, 2014, U.S. and Italian criminal justice authorities announced the arrest of twenty-four persons, including alleged members of New York City's Gambino and Bonanno organized crime families, suspected of organizing a plan to ship cocaine and heroin from South America to the Calabria region of Italy and then to North America (Smith-Spark and Messia 2014).

WHITE-COLLAR CRIME

White-collar crime is criminal behavior conducted within otherwise legal businesses or professions (FBI 2017j). These crimes are often not visible to or easily understood by the public or law enforcement. White-collar criminals are often well-educated persons who take advantage of changes in technology – for example, the creation of personal computers and the internet – and inadequate laws or law enforcement to create profitable crimes.

Occupational Crime

Occupational crime is lawbreaking behavior within the context of a legitimate profession. There are many forms of occupational white-collar crime. Embezzlement refers to an employee stealing money from his or her company. Another form is bribery of officials to obtain contracts. Professionals like lawyers and doctors can commit frauds against clients, the government, or insurance companies. For example, some doctors have been accused of engaging in fraud by billing Medicaid or Medicare for services they did not perform or for requiring unnecessary medical tests in return for kickbacks or a share in the profits from the medical labs doing the tests. Insider trading involves a person gaining an illegal advantage over other investors in buying or selling stock by obtaining new information affecting stock value before it is made available to the public. The Ponzi scheme (named after its creator Charles

organized crime People working together to supply an illegal product or service, for example, illicit drugs or illegal gambling opportunities, to the public and/or using violence to gain an unfair advantage in an otherwise legitimate business, such as killing competitors or damaging their equipment or merchandise.

white-collar crime Criminal behavior conducted within otherwise legal businesses or professions.

occupational crime Lawbreaking behavior within the context of a legitimate profession.

Ponzi) involves luring investors with the promise of high rates of return on investments. Investors are then paid their periodic dividends from the funds deposited by new investors rather than nonexistent investment earnings. Continued payments to early investors depend on constantly convincing more people to invest. Eventually the scheme loses the capacity to deliver payments and investors discover that much or all of their original investments are gone. Of the many Ponzi schemes in recent U.S. history, Bernie Madoff's seems the largest, bringing in approximately $65 billion from investors (Yang 2014). Although U.S. white-collar criminals have often received mild punishments, the scale of Madoff's crimes resulted in a prison sentence of 150 years.

Corporate Crime

Corporate crime is any lawbreaking act or omission by a corporation. Corporations that are supposed to compete with each other can break the law by agreeing to fix prices to ensure themselves high profits. The corporate crime of securities fraud involves misrepresenting a corporation's assets to make the company look much stronger and profitable than it actually is. Investors then buy company stock at a highly inflated price. As the value of the stock goes up, corporate executives may receive enormous salaries and bonuses. Just before the truth comes out and stock prices fall, executives may sell off their company stock. One of the biggest examples of this was the Enron energy corporation case that first came to light in 2001. The price of Enron's stock fell from a high of $90 per share on August 23, 2000, to 60 cents on December 31, 2001 (Gilardi 2014). Investors sued to recover an estimated $40 billion in losses, including billions lost from retirement funds (*New York Times* 2007). This crime caused so many people such great hardship that several Enron executives were sent to prison. Another corporate crime is toxic pollution of the environment. Companies have concealed the danger of certain chemicals in products, the workplace, or dumped into the environment. Tobacco companies attempted to deny the health hazards of smoking. Some companies have been accused of knowing harmful materials were injuring workers (asbestos in the case of the Johns-Manville Corporation) or unsafe products harming customers (the Pinto's fuel tank problem in the case of the Ford company) (Hagan 2002; Stout, Ivory, and Wald 2014).

Punishment for White-Collar Crime

Although white-collar criminals steal much more annually than street criminals like robbers, burglars, shoplifters, and car thieves, punishments in the past were often light. Criminologist Frank Hagan (2002) offered several reasons why there has been a low risk of apprehension of white-collar criminals and why, for those charged, punishment has historically been lenient in the United States. Many white-collar crimes tend to be complex, and investigating and successfully prosecuting them often requires specialized training and skills that criminal justice officials may not have. The components of the criminal justice system devoted to white-collar crime are limited. This situation became even more difficult after the 2001 terrorist 9/11 attacks, when many FBI

corporate crime Any lawbreaking act or omission by a corporation.

agents were redirected toward counter-terrorism operations. Gathering sufficient information for prosecution sometimes requires investigators to ask the accused perpetrators for cooperation to make the case. In return, special deals may be offered involving greatly reduced charges and little or no prison time.

Another reason for law enforcement's inability to deal more effectively with white-collar crime is the power of big business. The same corporations committing serious offenses often own or influence news media outlets. News personnel may be fearful of reporting on crimes committed by their corporate owners. Politicians who rely on contributions from white-collar lawbreakers may weaken or eliminate laws and regulations intended to control harmful behavior by corporations. Public opinion surveys indicate, however, that many people believe that certain white-collar crimes, such as fraud, destroying workers' pensions or investors' life savings, polluting the workplace or the environment with poisonous materials, or knowingly selling dangerously unsafe products should be punished harshly (Holtfreter et al. 2008; Rebovich and Kane 2002). In some countries, punishments for white-collar criminals can be severe. In China at least twenty-two men and women were given death sentences in recent years for white-collar crimes such as selling or approving for sale unsafe products that resulted in multiple deaths, stealing huge sums from investors through Ponzi type schemes, embezzling millions of dollars of state funds, and repetitive bribery (Badkar 2013).

cybercrime Any crime committed through use of a computer or the Internet.

CYBERCRIME

Cybercrime is any crime committed through use of a computer or the Internet. It is one of the fastest growing forms of crime worldwide and has become perceived as a serious threat by the American public (Riffkin 2014). Computers have been used to obtain people's personal information, steal millions of dollars from individuals and financial institutions, obtain technological, economic, military, and political secrets, and sabotage laboratory, industrial, business, and military operations and organizations (FBI 2017k).

The FBI refers to one major form of cybercrime as "computer intrusions": gaining partial or total control over someone else's computer. This includes infecting computer systems with viruses to prevent them from operating properly. Many institutions have been targeted, including banks, government departments, 911 operations, and even hospitals, by "ransomware," a malware that enters the organization's computer system and "encrypts, or locks, valuable digital files and demands a ransom to release them" (FBI 2017j). This can seriously disrupt the functioning of the organization, interfere with its ability to fulfill its obligations and harm its reputation. Such attacks can also be launched against individuals' personal computers. In a ransomware

The weapon of cyber criminals

attack an email is sent to the target, who is instructed to click on an element in the email, such as a legitimate-looking attachment or URL, that allows the ransomware to infect the victim's computer system. The ransomware can then potentially spread through an entire network and infect attached computers or backup drives. As access is lost to important files and capabilities, the victim begins to see messages about the attack and a demand for a ransom fee and how to pay it in return for a decryption key.

Many millions of dollars have been stolen from banks by thieves hundreds or thousands of miles away hacking into bank computers, accessing accounts, and then withdrawing and transferring money electronically. Some victimized institutions prefer not to report the thefts to law enforcement agencies to avoid negative publicity, which might discourage future investors or depositors. Spyware may be installed in victims' computers to transmit private information to the perpetrator that can be used to create false identities or fraudulent credit cards or for other illegal purposes. One of the FBI's previous most wanted cybercriminals created spyware in the form of electronic greeting cards. His customers could email the cards to intimate friends or spouses, and when the recipient opened the card she or he unwittingly installed the spyware. The spyware would then provide copies of the victim's future emails to the sender of the electronic greeting card. This was marketed as a way to find out if your partner or spouse was having an affair.

In 2014, Target reported that computer intruders had been able to obtain personal information on at least seventy million of its customers (David and Best 2014). Other corporations and organizations reported similar thefts of confidential customer information. Such information can possibly be used to withdraw money from customers' accounts or take out credit cards or loans in their names. It might also be used to create false identities for criminals. Whereas the average bank robbery in the United States netted the perpetrator $3,531 in 2016, those on the FBI's most wanted cybercriminals list stole as much as $50 million or more without ever using a gun or even physically entering the institutions they victimized (FBI 2017j). Computers can also be used to steal sensitive information. Edward Snowden, a U.S. computer expert, CIA employee, and National Security Agency (NSA) contactor, revealed classified information to media outlets in 2013 describing operational details of global surveillance operations by U.S. intelligence agencies (Spiegel 2013).

Computers are also used to commit sex crimes like transmitting child pornography or advertising sex-tourism trips to countries where adults pay to have sex with young children. Pedophiles use the Internet to approach children to establish online relationships with the intent of later meeting for sex (FBI 2014). Surveys indicate that as many as one in five internet users aged ten to seventeen receive unwanted sexually oriented messages online (Amos 2013). Pedophiles search the Internet for vulnerable kids, often children with family problems, low self-esteem, or money problems. If a child has a Facebook profile or similar site, the pedophile can learn about her or his favorite music and TV shows and pretend to have the same preferences in order to build a friendly relationship (what law enforcement refers to as "grooming"). After days or weeks of this process, the pedophile brings up sexual topics and may ask for revealing pictures and/or getting together for a face-to face-meeting. The FBI and other law enforcement agencies are continually faced with new challenges in their efforts to combat this and other forms of computer crime.

POLITICAL CRIME

Political crime is any crime committed with the intention of influencing politics or government. Street crimes, victimless crimes, organized crimes, white-collar crimes, and computer crimes can also be political crimes if they are intended to accomplish a political goal.

Assassinations

The murder of a major political figure, such as Julius Caesar in 44 BC or Abraham Lincoln in 1865, can change the course of history. It's possible that the Vietnam War would not have taken place if President John F. Kennedy had not been assassinated in 1963. And the war could have ended sooner if his brother Senator Robert Kennedy had not been murdered while running for president in June of 1968. The civil rights movement, the anti-poverty movement and the anti–Vietnam War Movement were all impacted by the loss of Marin Luther King Jr., who was assassinated in April of 1968. Assassinations may be carried out by individuals acting alone, by conspiratorial groups, or by government agents attempting to influence political developments domestically or in other countries. While assassins typically have some type of a political goal, they may also be motivated by other things, like financial gain, a sense of duty, a desire to feel important by killing an important person, or even a psychotic delusion.

Burglaries

Burglaries (and robberies) have also been committed for political reasons. These may be carried out to fund political movements. But in some cases they have obtained politically important information. One of the most significant political burglaries was carried out by eight female and male anti–Vietnam War activists who broke into an FBI office in Media, Pennsylvania, on March 8, 1971 (Pilkington 2014). They stole key documents and then mailed copies to several members of Congress and to major newspapers. Despite pressure from the FBI and the Nixon administration, the *Washington Post* published some of the most important information. The documents revealed that the FBI, then led by J. Edgar Hoover, was operating a nationwide program, called COINTELPRO (counterintelligence). This was a massive effort to gather information on antiwar and African American leaders. But it also involved infiltrating and, through disinformation and other tactics, attempting to disrupt the democratic rights of peace and civil rights activists to organize and express their points of view. One reported action was sending Martin Luther King Jr. a package containing evidence of his alleged extramarital sexual activity. This appeared intended to pressure him into committing suicide (Pilkington 2014). The publicized stolen documents shocked and outraged much of the American public by exposing how the FBI

political crime Any crime committed with the intention of influencing politics or government.

under Hoover was systematically undermining the right of Americans to dissent against their government's policies. Five of those involved in the burglary, knowing that they no longer faced criminal prosecution due to the relevant statute of limitations, decided to come forward 43 years after their break-in. Bonnie Raines indicated she and her fellow burglars decided to reveal their identities partly in support of what they viewed as Edward Snowden's leaking of documents about the massive surveillance activities of the NSA. The 1971 Media, Pennsylvania, burglary has been described as the perfect political crime, as the burglars' goal of exposing the antidemocratic activities of Hoover's COINTEL-PRO succeeded beyond their expectations and they were never caught. But in a sense COINTELPRO itself was also a successful political crime; for years it achieved its goals of disrupting protest groups. And apparently no one involved in the program was ever prosecuted for these antidemocratic activities. Another famous political burglary was the 1972 break-in at the Democratic Party headquarters in the Washington, D.C., Watergate Hotel by Republican Party operatives to gather useful information about the Democratic Party. This led to the forced resignation of President Richard Nixon in 1974 due to charges that he was engaging in obstruction of justice in the criminal investigations of the Watergate affair. Nixon was pardoned by the new president, Gerald Ford, whom Nixon had appointed as his vice president after Nixon's previous vice president, Spiro Agnew, was forced to resign after being charged with accepting bribes while governor of Maryland.

Hacking Political Campaigns and Elections

There have been many instances of groups, organizations, or even governments attempting to influence political developments in other nations openly or covertly. For example, leaders in one nation have sometimes attempted to foster conflict, or assist or defeat a political movement or revolution in another country. When the target nation is a democracy, external groups may channel money or other assistance to political parties or candidates whose goals they favor. U.S. intelligence agencies concluded that modern technology provided a capability for computer hackers to attempt to intervene in the 2016 U.S. presidential election and influence its outcome. According to their investigations, evidence indicated that Russian leaders opposed the Democratic candidate Hillary Clinton because of her strong and repeated criticisms of Russian president Vladimir Putin and his policies (Nance 2016; Scott 2017; Shane 2017). Russian hackers broke into the computer files of the Democratic National Committee, its personnel, and Democratic candidates to steal records, emails, and other communications and information, such as the identities of supporters or donors, credit card numbers, telephone numbers, and media contacts. Many state-level Democratic Party headquarters were also targeted. What all the stolen data was used for is not completely clear. But some material viewed as damaging to Hillary Clinton was steadily released through sources like Wikileaks leading up to the election. The intent appeared to be to increase the likelihood that the Republican candidate, Donald Trump, perceived as expressing more favorable views toward Russia's leader Putin, would be elected.

CHARACTERISTICS OF CRIMINALS

Age

While in the United States people aged fifteen to twenty-four were just slightly over 14 percent of the population, they were 32.3 percent of those arrested for violent crimes and 34.8 percent of those arrested for property crime in 2016. There may be a weaker relationship between age and at least some forms of white-collar crime. For example, the percentage of those in the same age range arrested for fraud was only about 24.3 percent. As noted earlier, white-collar crime is less of a focus of law enforcement than street crime. So the true relationship, if any, between age and major forms of white-collar crime remains unclear.

There are several reasons why people become less likely to commit street crime as they age. One is that getting married and having children may reduce the motivation and opportunity to commit crime. At the same time, these events tend to separate people from crime-promoting learning environments like gangs.

Gender

As noted earlier, males are much more often arrested for violent crime than females. Males are also a majority of those arrested for street property crime. The percentage of persons arrested who are women has been increasing for decades for a number of major crimes, and the trend continued in the twenty-first century (Snyder 2011). For example, between 2006 and 2015 the percentage of persons arrested for violent crimes who were women increased from about 17.8 percent to 20.2 percent and for street property crimes from 32 percent to 38.9 percent (FBI 2016b). Why do men commit more crime than women? One explanation is differences in the way boys and girls are socialized, with boys taught be more competitive and aggressive. Girls, in comparison, are prepared for caretaking roles and are likely to have their behavior much more tightly controlled. Men have more opportunities for crime because of their greater freedom of movement. But social movements for gender equality have brought about more similar patterns of socialization for boys and girls and also, coupled with economic necessity, a huge expansion of female participation in the labor force (allowing women many more opportunities to commit crimes like fraud and embezzlement). Women may also be more motivated to commit crime because they have steadily become a greater percentage of those living in poverty.

Social Class

The UCR does not provide data about the social class of arrested persons. However, research indicates that people arrested for crimes like homicide, aggravated assault, robbery, and burglary generally have low educational attainment (Petit and Western 2004) and tend to be unemployed or employed at very low-income jobs. U.S. prisons are filled mainly with people from low-income backgrounds. And the highest imprisonment rates tend to be in the poorest states like Louisiana (Chang 2012; Prison Policy Initiative 2016). Research shows that as the size of the U.S. prison population grew enormously after 1960, the people being disproportionately imprisoned were individuals lacking a high school diploma (Gao 2014).

But it is important to keep in mind that most people living in low-income neighborhoods are not involved in crime. Studies in the United States and other countries repeatedly show that a relatively small percentage of the general population is responsible for committing the majority of street crimes (Hegarty 2010). The link between social class and street crime, however, does not mean that there is a similar relationship to all forms of criminal behavior. The big white-collar crimes are committed by those with the opportunity to do so. And these are typically well-educated middle- or upper-class persons.

Race and Ethnicity

Race and ethnicity are factors in who commits and who gets arrested for street crime. About 37.5 percent of those arrested for violent crime in 2016 were black, as were 28.1 percent of those arrested street property crime (FBI 2017a). This means that blacks are arrested for these crimes more than twice as often as would be expected on the basis of their percentage of the population. Nationally, blacks are about six times more likely to be in prison than whites (Sentencing Project 2015). Hispanics are also overrepresented among those arrested for street crimes, while non-Hispanic whites are underrepresented and Asian Americans far underrepresented. Three factors appear to play a role in low Asian street crime arrest rates: a cultural emphasis on education, high family income levels, and a much higher percentage of children raised in two-parent households than is the case for non-Hispanic whites, Hispanics, or blacks (Vespa, Lewis, and Kreider 2013).

Why are African-Americans and Hispanics overrepresented among those arrested for street crimes? Major factors likely include poverty, a large percentage of children raised in one-parent households, and the development of distinct cultural traits. About one-third of all black and Hispanic children in the United States grow up in poverty. That's about twice the percentage of white and two-and a-half times the percent of Asian children (Macartney 2011). As noted in Chapter 4, when well-paying manufacturing jobs were removed from many U.S. cities, the proportion of men with incomes that could support families decreased and the percentage of children born outside marriage and then raised in single-parent households rose dramatically (Wilson 1996). Many children grew up with little direct contact with successful male role models, often insufficient supervision, as the parent had to work multiple low-paying jobs to support the family, and severely limited economic opportunities. Anderson (1999), in *The Code of the Street*, and Venkatesh (2006), in *The Underground Economy of the Urban Poor*, also argue that the circumstances of poor inner-city people gave rise to an adaptive culture that fostered deviant norms and patterns of behavior. Goals are to obtain respect from other people and protect oneself from perceived threats. Obtaining respect, according to the "code of street," can include violent and predatory behavior toward others.

Research also indicates that the criminal justice system discriminates against African Americans in multiple ways, from racial profiling to the level of charges filed to the harshness of punishment administered (Alexander 2012). Alexander believes that the justice system, particularly through the so-called war on drugs, has caused the mass incarceration of black males. This functions the way the old Jim Crow system did to deny African Americans access to jobs, social equality, and the right to vote, because people with a criminal record can be legally discriminated against. Thus many African Americans have lifelong difficulty getting a job and improving their education, and, depending on the state, can even be banned from voting. America's criminal justice system functions to economically and politically disadvantage many African Americans, erodes belief in the legitimacy of the system, and pushes some into committing more crime.

Table 10.4 (Prison Policy Initiative 2016) suggests that local economic and environmental factors and geographic segregation may play prominent roles in influencing African American street crime and imprisonment. The excess of black imprisonment over whites is not generally highest in southern states where racial prejudice has historically been most intense but rather in northern states where the African American population tends to be more geographically concentrated in low-income urban areas. The table shows, for example, that a black person is about ten times more likely to be in prison than a white person in Minnesota, Iowa, Vermont, and Wisconsin (states where many African Americans live in central city areas), but only about three times more likely in Mississippi, Georgia, and Alabama (where higher percentages of African Americans live outside central city areas).

TABLE 10.4	State Black-to-White 2010 Imprisonment Ratios
Five Highest States	
West Virginia	11.8
Minnesota	10.8
Iowa	10.7
Vermont	10.1
Wisconsin	9.7
U.S. Average Ratio 5.6	
Five Lowest States	
Hawaii	2.5
Mississippi	3.0
Georgia	3.2
Alabama	3.3
Alaska	3.5

Social Movements: Black Lives Matter Movement

Black Lives Matter demonstration

The Black Lives Matter (BLM) movement was founded by Patrisse Cullors, Opal Tometi, and Alicia Garza shortly after the 2013 acquittal of George Zimmerman, who had shot and killed an unarmed seventeen-year-old African American high school student, Trayvon Martin, walking back from a store. The movement grew in response to further killings of black persons by law enforcement personnel, viewed by many as unjustified. Another factor enraging sectors of the public was the readiness of many police officers to lie to prevent the criminal or incompetent behavior of other police officers from being detected and punished. BLM activists claim the movement seeks not only to end unjustified police shootings but also more generally to end all police brutality, mass incarceration of African Americans, and all forms of racial discrimination in the criminal justice system, as well as other forms of injustice, including mistreatment based on sexual orientation. Some of the notable cases of black persons being killed by police or dying in criminal justice custody include the deaths of Michael Brown in Ferguson, Missouri, Eric Garner in New York City, Tamir Rice in Cleveland, Freddie Grey in Baltimore, Sandra Bland in Waller County, Texas, and Alton Sterling in Baton Rouge.

While BLM can be seen as a re-emergence of the 1960s civil rights movement, it differs in a number of ways. BLM activists have tended to avoid the hierarchical, male-dominated, charismatic leadership model that characterized most previous black activist movements and organizations. Harris (2015:4) notes that BLM participants believe "Charismatic leaders can be co-opted by powerful interests, place their own self-interest above that of the collective, be targeted by government repression, or even be assassinated, as were Martin Luther King and Malcolm X. The dependence of movements on charismatic leaders can therefore weaken them, even lead to their collapse." Instead, BLM activists have tried to use a more group-centered participatory-democracy style of decision making with no single individual in a position of dominance. BLM movement organizations are described as loosely connected independent chapters functioning to rapidly mobilize supporters after questionable police shootings and to influence government officials and politicians running for office. In 2016 the BLM had chapters in 37 U.S. cities plus Toronto (Black Lives Matter 2016).

Like other twenty-first-century movements around the world, the BLM uses social media such as Twitter and Facebook to communicate its ideas and plans, organize, and mobilize people for protests. It also benefits from citizens who use their cell phones to record and post videos of police–civilian interactions.

For example, on July 6, 2016, Philando Castile, an African American school nutrition services supervisor, was shot and killed by a policeman in Falcon Heights, a suburb of St. Paul, Minnesota, while driving with his girlfriend, Diamond Reynolds, and her four-year-old daughter. Apparently acting on the suspicion that Castile fit the description of a robbery suspect, two policemen stopped the car he was driving. According to Reynolds, a police officer then asked Castile for his license and registration. Reynolds said that Castile told the officer that he had a license to carry a weapon and that there was one in the car. Reportedly, as Castile was reaching for his license and registration

Social Movements (*continued*)

the officer told Castile not to move. Although there is apparently no video of what happened at that moment, it is clear that the officer shot Castile, fatally wounding him. Reynolds streamed video and audio of approximately ten minutes of the aftermath of the shooting on Facebook. This instantly publicized the event to millions and showed the behavior of the police following the shooting. The governor of Minnesota, Mark Dayton, expressed shock and stated that he doubted this would have happened if the driver and passengers of the vehicle had been white. He was also dismayed by the reports that the police seemed to be slow in providing medical assistance to Castile and that they handcuffed Reynolds and placed her and her daughter in the back of a police car (Furber and Pérez-Peña 2016). Demonstrations protesting the killing of Castile took place almost immediately in St. Paul and other locations around the country.

In the fall of 2017 dozens of professional football players, following the lead of San Francisco 49ers quarterback and BLM supporter Colin Kaepernick, refused to stand for the national anthem before the start of games (Democracy in America 2017). Many of them decided to kneel instead in support of the goals of the BLM movement.

EXPLAINING CRIME: BIOLOGICAL, PSYCHIATRIC, AND SOCIOLOGICAL THEORIES OF CRIMINAL BEHAVIOR

Biological Factors

In the nineteenth-century Italian physician and criminologist Cesare Lombroso claimed that criminals had unique physical and personality characteristics that were hereditary and "atavistic" (that is, savage, because they were throwbacks to an earlier form of humanity). He believed that criminals were abnormally aggressive and could not abide by the rules of civilized society. Later criminological research showed there was no relation between Lombroso's physical signs of criminality, like having unusually large ears or long arms, and committing crime. However, it's interesting that contemporary research suggests that a tendency to crime may be genetically inherited for some people and that certain personality traits Lombroso said he found in criminals, such as lack of remorse and being less sensitive to pain, appear characteristic of many repeat criminals. Modern research on biological factors and crime includes topics such as genetics, brain abnormalities and injuries, chemical poisoning, unique nervous system characteristics, and chromosomal makeup.

Psychiatric Factors

Psychiatric theories hold that some people commit crimes because of deep-rooted personality characteristics. Many psychiatrists believe that genetic makeup influences personality, causing some people to be relatively insensitive to pain, fearless, and prone to sensation seeking. Most also believe that emotional and physical abuse during childhood can lead to crime-prone personalities. A contemporary psychiatric view is that genetically linked tendencies to fearlessness and sensation seeking can be channeled by loving and supportive parents and other beneficial environmental experiences into positive social activities like piloting jet planes, exploring space, or joining law enforcement to fight crime. But an abusive environment can turn children with the same genetic characteristics into dangerous criminals according to forensic experts like Park Dietz (2012). Psychologists and criminologists refer to the main criminal personality type as the *psychopath* (Babiak and Hare 2007; Dutton 2012; Hare 1999). They estimate that up to 3 percent of males and one percent of females are psychopaths. Psychopathic criminals are a minority of lawbreakers but tend to commit an enormous amount of crime. The most central trait of psychopaths is the absence of feelings of remorse for anything they do. In other words, they lack a conscience. They also appear to experience less fear than other people and to be very convincing and even charismatic liars with a great capacity to deceive others. Certain types of criminals are especially likely to be psychopaths, including serial killers and professional hit men. But many white-collar criminals and some corporate executives also appear to be psychopaths (Babiak and Hare 2007; Dutton 2012). While psychopaths are sane, a much smaller percentage of criminals are psychotic and delusional and do not understand that what they are doing is wrong.

Mass Murderers and Serial Killers When people commit mass murder (the killing of four or more people, not counting the offender, in one continuous event in the same or nearby locations) or serial murder (the killing of two or more people one after another over time with "cooling off" intervals between the killings), we often think that the perpetrator(s) must be mentally ill. Certain circumstances are frequently associated with mass murder (Fox and Levin 2011). The perpetrator has typically experienced a long period of frustration and is or has become relatively socially isolated, with limited emotional support from others. Eventually a "triggering event" occurs, such as the loss of a job, a school problem, a broken relationship, or some other traumatic new frustration. When the perpetrator seeks to strike out at others, he has access to firearms and/or explosives that allow him to kill multiple victims rapidly. There is evidence that in certain situations, such as when a person kills a large group of total strangers, the perpetrator was suffering from schizophrenia, a type of psychosis in which the killer experiences a delusion that motivates the killings. Evidence suggests that two of the most notorious school mass murderers, Seung-Hui Cho at Virginia Tech and Adam Lanza at Sandy Hook Elementary, had serious mental disorders. Mass murderers, however, generally do not appear to be psychopaths.

A large majority of serial killers, however, are psychopaths, while a small minority are psychotic (Douglas and Olshaker 1996, 1997; Ressler and Shachtman 1992). Psychotic serial murderers, probably less than 10 percent of all serial killers, typically suffer from severe paranoid schizophrenia and often believe they have to kill to fulfill some type of a delusionary mission, such as Herbert Mullin, who

Social Movements: Parkland Students Never Again Movement

Student activists March for Our Lives, March 24, 2018

After a gunman used an assault rifle to murder fourteen students, a teacher, a coach, and the athletic director on February 14, 2018, at Marjory Stoneman Douglas High School in Parkland, Florida, the surviving students quickly launched one the most effective social movements of the twenty-first century against gun violence. Several factors help explain the movement's rapid spread and stunning impacts. First, the educational program at the high school uniquely prepared its students to be confident, articulate, and effective speakers, highly informed on gun violence and the gun control controversy, and knowledgeable about politics and legislative process at both the state and federal levels. In fact, every public high school and middle school in the Broward county school system, as well as more than two dozen elementary schools, has a debate program (Gurney 2018). Students at Marjory Stoneman Douglas High had conducted in-depth research on gun laws, the tactics and actions of advocates and opponents of stricter gun control regulations, including the National Rifle Association, and arguments for and against universal background checks in getting ready to participate in debates on gun control in November 2017. As fate would have it, this also prepared them to respond with great speed to the lethal tragedy at their school.

There are other elements that played important roles in the rise and effectiveness of the Parkland students' movement. One was that Parkland followed other large-casualty mass shooting atrocities such as those at Sandy Hook Elementary School, the Pulse nightclub in Orlando, and the Route 91 Harvest country music festival in Las Vegas. These massacres of innocents led to a high level of public frustration with the lack of meaningful action by government officials to stop them from occurring again and again. Another was the relationship among Parkland victims and survivors. They were classmates, study partners, friends, and teammates. The grief of personal loss motivated a communal response of outrage and determination from the survivors (Gomez 2018). Communication technology was also important. Parkland students used the national media and tools like Twitter and Facebook to reach out to the nation and the world.

The Parkland activists also benefited from the fact that the much of the U.S. public had become more supportive of protest and activism than in the past. The massive Women's March on January 21, 2017, showed that millions were outraged with political leaders and ready to act. The emergence and effectiveness of the Me Too movement also served as a model for the high school students. Within days of the shooting, many Parkland students travelled to the Florida state capital, Tallahassee, to demand a ban on the sale of assault rifles like the one used to murder their classmates and friends, the raising of the legal age to buy a firearm from eighteen to twenty-one, and measures to prevent seriously mentally ill persons from obtaining guns.

Dozens of Parkland students appeared on national news programs and on local broadcasts around the country. An international seventeen-minute (one minute for each victim) student walkout was held on March 14, one month after the tragedy. And the Parkland students organized the March 24 anti-gun violence March for Our Lives held

(continued)

Social Movements (*continued*)

in Washington, D.C., and many other cities. Apparently shocked by the Parkland massacre and the student survivors' movement, several businesses raised their age limit for buying guns to twenty-one, and others stopped selling assault rifles. Some companies ended special benefits they had provided to members of the National Rifle Association (NRA) because they perceived the NRA as blocking gun reforms through its influence on and financial backing of pro-NRA government officials. The Florida state legislature enacted some reforms, including raising the age for purchasing guns to twenty-one and providing more money for student mental health services and school safety measures. Students vowed to work to remove from office any government official who did not support common-sense gun control measures. They began developing and circulating lists of office holders who, in their view, refused to accept reasonable gun law reform to be targeted in coming elections for removal from office. As one Parkland student activist put it to such lawmakers, "We are coming after you" (Tarr 2018) at the ballot box.

Victoria Leigh "Vicki" Soto (November 4, 1985–December 14, 2012), first-grade teacher at Sandy Hook Elementary School, shot and killed after throwing herself in front of her students trying to protect them from a mass murderer. Posthumous recipient of the Presidential Citizens Medal

believed he had to kill (he murdered thirteen people) to prevent earthquakes from devastating California. But most male serial killers appear to be sexually motivated psychopaths. Psychopathic sexual sadist serial killers, such as Theodore (Ted) Bundy (at least thirty women killed), experience sexual gratification from torturing and killing another person and crave this experience of power and domination. They have typically had traumatic and often violent childhoods and been the victims of emotional and/or physical abuse. While mass murderers usually kill with firearms, male sexual serial killers typically kill by strangling, stabbing, or bludgeoning their victims to death. Some serial killers, such as the California Zodiac killer and the Honolulu strangler, were never captured. Others were arrested many years after they began killing. The Green River Killer, Gary Ridgeway, admitted to killing the first of his forty-nine victims in 1982 but was not captured until 2001. And the person accused of being the Golden State Killer, Joseph James DeAngelo, believed to have murdered twelve and raped more than forty-five persons between 1974 and 1986, was not apprehended until 2018 (Brueck 2018).

Sociological Factors

Sociological approaches locate the causes of crime in people's social environment. These perspectives hold that environmental factors are responsible for why people who are physiologically and psychiatrically normal commit crime.

Structural-Functional Perspective The French sociologist Emile Durkheim believed that crime could in some ways have positive functions for society. He argued that crime clarifies and reinforces a society's laws because criminal behavior can be pointed out as the opposite of what's lawful and "right." Also, certain crimes can strengthen social bonds and increase social solidarity when people join together for protection and to express mutual outrage at criminal acts. And finally, some crimes can actually help bring about social change. Those engaging in the deviant behavior may provide an attractive example to others discontented with existing laws. This can lead to a movement to change or eliminate a law. For example, the prominent physician and medical spokesperson for CNN, Dr. Sanjay Gupta (2013a, 2013b, 2014), became intrigued by arguments that marijuana had medical benefits. His investigation led him to change his mind about the drug, to support its medical uses, and to widely circulate his findings through documentaries.

Durkheim's analysis, however, is not really an explanation of what causes crime. Later sociologists provided four major structural-functional theories of crime: one attempts to explain motivation for crime, another tries to explain what type of crime a person motivated to commit crime actually engages in, a third attempts to identify what aspects of social structure might prevent people motivated to commit crime from actually doing it, and a fourth offers an explanation for how structural factors can lead to the creation of a new cultural environment that serves as an additional cause of crime. American sociologist Robert Merton's theory holds that when a society's culture defines success in terms of great material wealth but at the same time its social structure denies large numbers of people access to legal means to attain that goal, a condition of structural "strain" exists (Merton 1968). People adapt to their situation in society in one of five ways. Those fortunate enough to have access to legitimate means to achieve material goals become "conformists." Conformists abide by the rules of society and maintain the material goals they were taught to aspire to because they can actually be successful in achieving those goals by using the legitimate means they have access to (like a good education). But people without access to legitimate means to achieve materialistic goals must adapt in some way to alleviate their frustration. One adaptation is "ritualism." Ritualists lack access to legitimate means to achieve high material goals but reduce their frustration by lowering their goals while continuing to obey society's laws. One of the deviant patterns of adaptation to frustration is "retreatism." Retreatists reduce frustration by abandoning both the rules of society and the material goals to which their culture taught them to aspire. They might choose to live in remote rural areas, or they may become heavily involved in drug or alcohol use as part of their pattern of "dropping out" of society. Another pattern of adaptation is "rebellion." Rebels reject both the highly materialistic cultural goals of their society and the unequal structure of opportunities. They seek to replace these with a culture that is less materialistic and more concerned with social justice and a social structure with much more equality of opportunity. The final way of coping with materialistic goals being beyond people's legitimate opportunities is "innovation." This is Merton's major crime-producing adaptation. "Innovators" maintain the high materialistic goals but invent illegal ways to make money to obtain those goals. This includes, for example, forms of organized crime like drug smuggling or selling.

Another structural-functional theory argues that people not only have unequal access to legitimate opportunities but also unequal access to illegal *criminal opportunities* (Cloward and Ohlin 2011). Therefore, the type of crime people actually engage in is determined by what illegal opportunities to which they have access. For example, people with frustrated aspirations living where there is an opportunity to acquire and sell drugs may enter the illegal drug trade. Others may live in an area where the best illegal opportunity is stealing cars. But when there is a lack of both legal and illegal opportunities, people may adapt by becoming "retreatists."

A third structural-functional theory is *"control" theory* (Gottfredson and Hirschi 1990; Hirschi 1969). This theory assumes people regularly experience motivations to commit crime. The key to explaining criminal behavior is learning why some people are inhibited from breaking the law while others aren't. Control theory identifies personal, interpersonal, and institutional control factors. The key control structure is the family environment of the child. Parents must be concerned about the welfare and behavior of the child. They must instruct the child concerning what behavior is permitted or not permitted and consistently supervise and punish the child's bad behavior and reward good behavior. This develops strong self-control in the child and strong *attachments* between parent and child. Attachments control children since they don't want to disappoint parents by engaging in disapproved behavior. As children grow into adults, they gather benefits and establish new social relationships from their rule-abiding behavior like good academic records, jobs, friendships, and their own families that could be damaged by breaking the law. They also develop a positive outlook on society, laws, and government. An additional control factor is a high probability that the government will punish crime rapidly and severely.

Albert Cohen's theory of juvenile delinquency (1955) is a fourth structural-functional approach. Cohen argues that lower-income children tend to fail in the public school system, which is in reality designed for middle-class children. The traumatic frustration of this failure causes them to turn against the dominant culture and create a "**delinquent subculture**" with different norms and values stressing toughness, manliness, and readiness to use violence to gain and keep respect. This subculture helps lower-class kids feel good about themselves. Cohen's theory implies that the frustration of aspirations described in Merton's theory likely results not only in deviant adaptive behaviors but also in criminal subcultures that support and become a separate cause of law-breaking behavior, as described in the next section.

Symbolic-Interactionist Perspective The symbolic-interactionist perspective focuses on learning experiences and also on assignment of and reaction to the label of deviant. Edwin Sutherland (1937) argued in his differential association theory that criminal behavior is simply the result of learning from those with whom we associate and interact. So once criminal subcultures have been created, people introduced into those subcultures are taught both how to commit crimes and rationales for engaging in criminal behavior. Sutherland developed this theory after studying professional burglars and

delinquent subculture A deviant youth subculture with norms and values stressing toughness, manliness, and readiness to use violence to gain and keep respect, which promotes delinquency.

white-collar criminals. The other major interactionist explanation for crime is labeling theory (Goffman 1963; Lemert 1951). Labeling theory holds that once a person is publicly labeled (stigmatized) as a criminal other people will react to the label by discriminating against him or her, for example, by denying employment or friendship. This pushes the stigmatized person into committing more crime. In labeling theory, the crime a person commits due to being stigmatized is called secondary deviance (crime committed before being labeled is called primary deviance).

Conflict Perspective Conflict explanations for crime hold that high levels of power and economic inequality cause crime in multiple ways. Some people engage in crimes like burglary, larceny theft, auto theft, and forms of organized crime like drug dealing to survive economically. Other persons take out their frustrations at being poor and powerless by being violent toward others. This perspective also predicts that powerful people break the law to further enrich themselves because they have little fear of being punished.

The most comprehensive conflict explanation of crime was developed by the Dutch criminologist William Adrian Bonger (Bonger 1905; Antonaccio and Tittle 2007). Bonger argued that capitalism shaped society not only by bringing about structural changes, like industrialization, but also by bringing about cultural changes, like a greater emphasis on materialism and self-centeredness. Capitalist culture fostered what Bonger called an egoistic personality type that pursues personal gain with little concern for the welfare of others. Capitalist structural conditions like inequality and poverty cause crime among the desperately poor. But cultural materialism and egoism cause crime among people of all social classes. In capitalist society, crimes committed by poor people will be punished more harshly than crimes by the wealthy and powerful. This unfairness generates disrespect for the law and police, which becomes an additional cause of crime. Economic insecurity and hardship foster prejudice against competing racial and ethnic groups, sexist discrimination against women, and violent subcultures of distorted masculinity that many men cling to so that they can feel superior to others. According to Bonger's Marxist conflict theory of crime, transforming from a capitalistic society to a relatively equalitarian socialist society would over time solve the crime problem.

The racial/ethnic-conflict view of crime holds that racial and ethnic groups subject to prejudice and discrimination suffer from economic and social disadvantages, which motivate criminal behavior. Members of these groups are treated more harshly by the criminal justice system, stigmatized as criminals, and pushed into more crime by society's reaction to the criminal label.

Feminist-conflict theorists believe that stereotypes of women as inferior to men and as sex objects are responsible for much of the physical and sexual violence against women. Many also argue that gender discrimination limits women's economic opportunities, causing some to engage in criminal activities such as larceny theft, fraud, drug dealing, and prostitution.

CHAPTER REVIEW

What Is Crime?

Crime is any voluntary and intentional behavior or omission that federal, state, or local government designates as a violation of criminal law and for which there is no legally accepted excuse, such as self-defense or insanity.

Measuring the Extent and Forms of Crime

Crime is measured in the United States mainly through official statistics, victimization surveys, and self-report surveys. Official crime statistics come from government sources, primarily the police and courts. The FBI Uniform Crime Reports gathers data from thousands of police departments around the country and focuses mainly on eight crimes: homicide, rape, robbery, aggravated assault, burglary, larceny theft, motor vehicle theft, and arson. Official statistics do not cover all the crime that occurs because often people choose not to report crimes to police. The Justice Department's National Crime Victimization Survey interviews tens of thousands of persons asking if they, their household members, or their businesses were criminally victimized regardless of whether they reported it to police or not. Self-report surveys are anonymous surveys in which people report which and how many crimes they have committed.

Street Crime

The major forms of crime are street crime, victimless moral-order crime, organized crime, white-collar crime, cybercrime and political crime. Street crime includes homicide, rape, robbery, aggravated assault, burglary, larceny theft, and motor vehicle theft. Street crime rates rose from 1960 to 1980 and fluctuated somewhat until 1991. Then crime rates fell to early-1960s levels around 2005 and stayed at those levels or went even lower in much of the country through 2014. Between 2014 and 2016 the property crime rate fell further, while the violent crime rate rose.

Victimless Crime

Victimless moral-order crime includes law-breaking behavior such as recreational drug use, gambling, and prostitution. Critics argue that in the United States drug laws are too harsh, contributing to why the country has the highest rate of imprisonment (number of prisoners per 100,000 residents) of the world's large nations.

Organized Crime

Organized crime involves people working together to make profits by supplying the public with illegal but desired goods and services. The existence of successful organized crime groups is based on several factors: a significant public demand for illegal goods or services; mutual trust among organized crime members, because they are linked together by a bond that transcends the desire to make money, such as extended family ties; the ability to corrupt law enforcement; and the capacity to use violence to protect business interests, which, because of their illegal nature, cannot be protected by going to the police or courts.

White-Collar Crime

White-collar crime is law breaking activity within otherwise legal occupations and businesses such as doctors defrauding Medicare or corporate executives exaggerating their company's assets as part of a securities fraud scheme. White-collar criminals are often well-educated persons who take advantage of changes in technology – for example, the creation of personal computers and the internet – and inadequate laws or law enforcement to create profitable crimes.

Cybercrime

Cybercrime is any crime involving use of a computer or the internet. Many millions of dollars have been stolen from banks by thieves hundreds or thousands of miles away hacking into bank computers, accessing accounts, and then withdrawing and transferring money electronically. Some victimized institutions prefer not to report the thefts to law enforcement agencies to avoid negative publicity, which might discourage future investors or depositors.

Political Crime

Political crime is any crime committed with the intention of influencing politics or government. Street crimes, victimless crimes, organized crimes, white-collar crimes, and computer crimes can also be political crimes if they are intended to accomplish a political goal.

Characteristics of Criminals

The characteristics of most arrested criminals reflect the criminal justice system's focus on street crime. They are disproportionately young, poor, and African American or Hispanic. However, many well-educated and middle- or high-income people commit white-collar, cyber- or political crimes.

Explaining Crime: Biological, Psychiatric, and Sociological Theories of Criminal Behavior

Criminologists have developed biological, psychiatric, and sociological explanations for crime. Biological theories hold that people's biological characteristics cause them to commit crime. Modern biological research on crime focuses on topics such as genetics, brain abnormalities and injuries, unique nervous system characteristics, and chromosomal makeup.

Psychiatric theories hold that some people commit crime because of deep-rooted aspects of their personalities. The psychopathic personality type, characterized by a lack of a conscience and a lack of feelings of remorse, appears especially prone to criminal behavior.

Sociological approaches focus on people's social environment as the cause of crime. Structural-functional theories argue that aspects of social structure and culture can cause or prevent crime. Merton's theory states that people lacking access to legitimate means to achieve materialistic cultural goals become frustrated and turn to crime. Cloward and Ohlin believe that the type of crime people engage in is influenced by their unequal access to illegal criminal opportunities. Control theory states that people motivated to commit crime can be inhibited from doing so by aspects of social structure like attachments to parents and effective law enforcement. Cohen argues that structurally induced frustration can lead to the creation of deviant subcultures.

The symbolic-interactionist perspective emphasizes that people learn either to abide by laws or break laws based on the subcultures they grow up in, who they interact with, and the role models to which they are exposed. Labeling theory argues that once a person is stigmatized by a criminal identity, he or she is pushed into more criminal behavior.

The conflict approach holds that power and economic inequality cause crime in multiple ways. Some low-income people engage in crime to survive. Others take out their frustrations through violence or by numbing their feelings through drug use. Some powerful people are prone to committing profitable white-collar crime because they have no fear of being punished. The Marxist-conflict perspective suggests crime can be reduced through social change that results in greater economic and political equality. Racial/ethnic- and feminist-conflict perspectives of crime argue that criminal behavior can be reduced by eliminating racial/ethnic and sexist discrimination.

KEY TERMS

DISCUSSION QUESTIONS

1. Do you think that having separate criminal justice systems in each state and the District of Columbia is effective, or should there be just one set of laws and criminal justice system for the entire United States? Justify your point of view.

2. What do you think is the most valid source of data on crime: official statistics, victimization surveys, or self-reports? Explain your answer.

3. Which of the major forms of crime is the most serious threat to the United States? How about to you personally? Explain your answer.

4. What do you think would be the most effective way to reduce gun violence in the United States? Justify your point of view.

5. What do you think best accounts for the age, class, and race/ethnic characteristics of most people arrested for crime in the United States? Explain your answer.

6. Do you think that the fight against crime in the United States requires the level of people in prison currently? Should some crimes be punished more harshly than they are now or some crimes less harshly? Justify your views.

7. Which sociological perspective on crime is the best explanation for most crime in U.S. society? Explain your answer.

CHAPTER 11

Globalization, Technology, and Global Inequalities

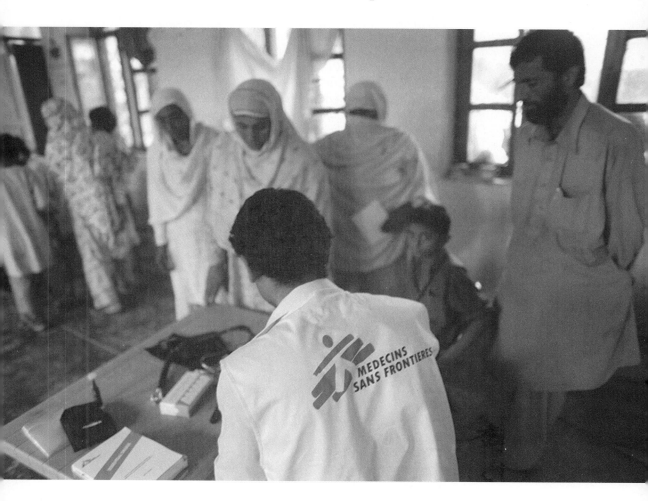

CHAPTER OBJECTIVES

- Explain globalization.
- Explain the role of technology in globalization.
- Describe the positive and negative aspects of globalization.
- Describe the effects of globalization on poverty and inequality.
- Explain how the major sociological perspectives analyze globalization.
- Describe approaches for reducing harmful consequences of globalization.

DOCTORS WITHOUT BORDERS *(Médecins Sans Frontières (MSF)) is a global social movement to bring emergency medical care to people in greatest need because they are the victims of conflict, epidemics, disasters, or exclusion from health care (Doctors without Borders 2017a). MSF was founded in 1971 by a group of French doctors and journalists in the context of civil war and famine in Nigeria and floods in what is now Bangladesh. MSF's first director, Dr. Bernard Kouchner (who later become France's foreign minister), described the group's mission as "It's simple. Go where the patients are," anywhere in the world (Fink, Nossiter, and Kanter 2014). MSF teams of doctors, nurses, and support personnel go to suffering people wherever they are, regardless of political or military boundaries, with or without governmental permission, and provide help, as well as public witness accounts of what they see. Funded by $357 million in contributions from 6.1 million private donors, Doctors without Borders sent 3,202 health workers to 71 countries and hired 32,046 local assistants in 2016 (Doctors without Borders 2017b). Its volunteers have worked in some of the most dangerous places, including Syria, South Sudan, Yemen, the Republic of the Congo, and the Democratic Republic of the Congo, and served in the front lines against the Ebola outbreak in West Africa. Politically neutral, it is the largest of the few groups dedicated to providing urgently needed help to people caught up in medical crises resulting from natural disasters or from armed conflict. MSF-USA accepts qualified applicants without regard to age, race, color, religion, sex, national origin, sexual orientation, disability, or veteran status. Doctors without Borders received the 1999 Noble Peace Prize for its life-saving efforts around the world.*

GLOBALIZATION

Doctors without Borders is one of many examples of globalization. **Globalization** refers to the dramatic increase in the movement of information, people, culture, technologies, goods, services, and money around the world and the increased connectedness and interdependence of peoples and nations (Guillen 2001; World Health Organization 2017c). It is generally viewed as based on two broad and interrelated factors: (1) the increased opening of international borders and (2) modifications in institutions and policies to encourage or ease movement of all of the above things across borders.

The hundreds of sociologists, economists, political scientists, historians, anthropologists, politicians, journalists, and others who have written about globalization have emphasized various dimensions: economic (international trade and finance), political (the creation of international governing or coordinating structures such as the United Nations, European Union, and African Union, and the worldwide growth of democratic political systems), and cultural (the spread of a common world cultural system and developments such as the 2008 adoption of English as the required language for use by flight crews and air traffic controllers working international flights).

globalization The dramatic increase in the movement of information, people, culture, technologies, goods, services, and money around the world and the increased connectedness and interdependence of peoples and nations.

The potential for the development of world culture is enhanced by the fact that by 2010 79 percent of the world's households owned a television set (Oberst 2010) and by 2017 51.7 percent of the world's population (3.89 billion) had access to the internet (Internet World Stats 2017b). However, it's important to note that the poorest people and nations have the least access. In 2017 88.1 percent of the people in North America used the internet, compared to 80.2 percent in Europe, 69.6 percent in Australia/Oceania, 62.4 percent in Latin America and the Caribbean, 58.7 percent in the Middle East, 46.7 percent in Asia, and 31.2 percent in Africa. Another imbalance has to do with sources of information and entertainment available through electronic media. The most dominant internationally tend to be based in Britain and the United States, including the British Broadcasting Company (BBC), Cable Network News (CNN), Music Television (MTV), and Home Box Office (HBO). Television shows originating in the U.S., such as *NCIS* (*Naval Criminal Investigative Services*), *CSI* (*Crime Scene Investigation*), *Criminal Minds*, *Homeland*, and *The Blacklist* have tended to be among the most watched around the world (Adalian 2015). More recently, *The Walking Dead* and *Game of Thrones* have emerged as among the most popular shows worldwide (Lubin 2016; Sarner 2017). This trend has led some social scientists to become concerned that a type of cultural imperialism is taking place in which the values and way of life of Western societies gradually replace those in other parts of the world.

Modern technology provides a means to instantly share events worldwide, from shocking acts of violence like September 11, 2001, or more recent terrorist attacks and mass murders to the sensational openings of Olympic Games in China, the United Kingdom, Brazil, and South Korea. The daily availability of information about people in far-off locations and their problems and achievements provides an opportunity for mutual identification and compassion; perspectives can then transcend national borders and become more global in scope. This can lead to a greater readiness to cooperate internationally, including aiding victims of natural disasters and supporting struggles to alleviate oppression and enhance human rights everywhere.

The globalization process has had profound impacts, such as heightening individuals' sense of economic and political interdependency, and the mutual awareness and knowledge of other cultures among the peoples of the world. Although some have argued that globalization began with European exploration and colonization of the Americas, Africa, and much of Asia, and others with the creation of the United Nations near the end of World War II, Guillen (2001) points out that significant literature on globalization first appeared in the 1960s, increased in the 1970s, and skyrocketed after that.

TECHNOLOGY AND GLOBALIZATION

Expansion of capabilities for transporting people, goods, and resources has been essential to the growth of globalization. Electronic technological advances permit rapid worldwide communication, financial transactions, and cultural sharing.

Transporting People

Larger and more fuel-efficient passenger airliners have made rapid international air travel affordable for an increasing number of persons. In 2016 about 213 million passengers boarded planes in the United States for destinations abroad, an increase of about 11 million (5.5 percent) from 2015 (Bureau of Transportation Statistics 2017). The same trend is happening internationally as more and more people in other countries come to see themselves as cosmopolitan citizens of the world sharing a universal morality and often participating in transnational organizations (Scholz 2015).

Transporting Goods and Resources

Improvements in technology have significantly reduced the costs of transporting manufactured goods, machinery, vehicles, parts, and resources across international borders, helping to propel the globalization process. One of the most crucial innovations was the invention of container shipping (Postrel 2006). Instead of hoisting and lowering individual products or crates to and from the holds of cargo ships, it is much more cost effective to fill long rectangular steel shipping containers with goods. The containers can be placed on truck beds or on train car platforms and brought to ports where they are lifted onto container ships. After reaching destination ports, cranes unload the containers, which can then be placed on trucks or trains for transport to final destinations. By sharply reducing transportation costs, container shipping has vastly increased the amount of international trade and given consumers a wider variety of choices.

Modern container shipping had its beginnings in 1955 when a North Carolinian in the trucking business, Malcolm McLean, purchased a steamship company to implement his idea of transporting truck trailers with their cargos still inside on ships rather than having to unload and reload their contents (World Shipping Council 2017). Implementation of this concept required a number of related technological innovations, including building the 35-foot-long steel containers, new truck trailer platforms onto which the containers could be loaded and unloaded, modifying ships to hold the containers below and above deck, and cranes powerful enough to hoist the containers. But once put into practice, shipping containers reduced the time to load and unload ships to only one-sixth of non-container shipping with only one-third the workers per ship (Ebling 2009). This vastly reduced shipping costs and time, providing a huge boost for global trade.

Communication, Finance, News, Entertainment

Dramatic improvements in communication systems have also played a huge role in globalization. A network of satellites and fiber optic cables under the seas provide the basis for the internet and near instantaneous communication around the world. This allows billions

Special Topics: The Trucker Who Revolutionized Global Trade

Container ship

Malcolm McLean, born in 1914, was the son of a North Carolina farmer, one of seven children. As a teenager he sold the farm's eggs for a small commission. But in the 1930s, when the Great Depression hit, he gave up any plans for college and instead got a job at a gas station. Eventually he saved enough to buy a used truck and began transporting farmer's produce and farm supplies. Calling his thriving business the Mclean Trucking Company, he soon purchased five more trucks and hired drivers while continuing to drive himself (*Economist* 2001). He claimed that the idea for a container that could be detached from a truck, loaded on a ship without unpacking the contents, and then reattached to another truck at the ship's destination came to him in 1937 at the port in Hoboken (Ebling 2009). While waiting most

of the day for his load of cotton bales to be slung from his truck into the hold of a ship, it struck him that it would be much faster if his truck's trailer could simply be lifted onto the ship without being unloaded.

By the mid-1950s, McLean owned one of America's biggest trucking companies and was in a financial position to fulfill his dream of containerized shipping. In 1955 he hired an engineer, Keith Tantlinger, to design 35-foot-long trailer containers that could be detached from a trailer chassis, attached to one another, and stacked on a ship's deck. He also began buying and refitting ships to transport the containers and called his steamship company Sea-Land Industries. McLean's first loaded container ship, the Ideal X, left Port Newark, New Jersey, on April 26, 1956, and arrived at Houston four days later, signaling the beginning of modern container shipping, which would revolutionize and dramatically increase global commerce. Seaports all around the world were fitted with the giant cranes needed to move and stack the large heavy containers. Railroads also got into the container shipping process. New railroad flatcars were designed for 20-foot and 40-foot containers, which could also be moved by cranes between trains and ships. By 2009 more than 90 percent of the world's commercial goods were being shipped by containers, and the carrying capacity and number of container ships continued to grow.

of dollars to be transferred across international borders every day to pay for the purchase of goods and services, build new factories, ports, or apartment buildings, and invest in foreign enterprises. It also facilitates international travel by making it easier to quickly book travel plans and electronically access personal funds in foreign lands. Personal computers and cell phones allow individuals not only to email, phone, text, or video call others almost anywhere on the planet but also to place pictures and videos of their experiences, witnessed events, messages, or ideas on social media or YouTube. Modern news and entertainment networks also contribute to globalization by allowing people in many countries to access foreign news reports, shows, performances, movies, documentaries, and sporting events on their TVs, computers, or mobile devices. Another technological aid to globalization is computer translators that ease communication between peoples speaking different languages.

GLOBALIZATION: POSITIVE AND NEGATIVE VIEWS

Globalization can be viewed as having both positive and negative consequences. Particular nations and social groups enjoy benefits, whereas others may be harmed.

Positive Views of Globalization

Supporters of globalization argue that as national barriers to freedom of movement and trade have been reduced, the more efficient the global division of labor, manufacturing, and optimal use of resources has become (Wolf 2014). Costs of manufactured goods have been lowered and global living standards have risen. The overall world economy has become increasingly productive because investment funding can be directed to whichever country and location has the lowest processing costs and the greatest potential for profit. Advocates of globalization also assert that it has led to the reduction of war among nations and the spread of international cultural understanding. In addition, international organizations have focused attention on important problems like the level of corruption in individual countries and in transnational business operations, transnational organized crimes such as illegal trade in drugs, people, and weapons, and even how aspects of globalization might be harmful. Globalization has also seen the rise of international human rights and service organizations such as Doctors without Borders and Amnesty International.

Negative Views of Globalization

Globalization also has disadvantages (Collins 2010, 2015; Tverberg 2013). Critics argue that globalization based on a **neoliberal free market** (open trade among nations unrestricted by any barriers or regulations) tends to disproportionately benefit the already-rich countries and the wealthier classes within all nations more than the poor, thus increasing economic inequality. Opponents of total free market globalization hold that it allows corporations to move high-wage economic activities to low-wage, less-developed countries, thus shrinking the middle class in advanced countries. In fact, in order to maintain or attract industries and investment from private corporations many countries are forced to continuously limit wages, reduce business taxes, cut welfare assistance, and reduce environmental safeguards, sacrificing the well-being of large sectors of their populations. This global pressure to compete undermines governments' ability to protect their people from the greed and harmful actions of large corporations and wealthy individuals. From this point of view, globalization acts as a form of imperialism, exploiting the poor and increasing inequality between and within nations.

neoliberal free market
Open trade among nations unrestricted by any barriers or regulations.

GLOBALIZATION, ECONOMIC DEVELOPMENT, AND GLOBAL INEQUALITIES

Globalization has likely played a role in reducing extreme poverty. But it concurrently appears to have increased inequality within and between some nations.

Poverty

The percent of people living in poverty around the world has declined significantly (Chandy and Gertz 2011; *Economist* 2013a). Since 1980, international data indicate that extreme poverty has been cut at least in half and median personal income has been rising. This is reflected in the decline in the percentage of the world's population that is undernourished. Data indicate that in the early 1990s a little over one billion people (about 19 percent of the world's population) were undernourished. But by 2016 this had fallen to about 795 million persons (about 11 percent) (World Hunger Education Service 2016). During this period the regions of eastern Asia, southeastern Asia, Latin America, and the Caribbean made the greatest progress in reducing the proportions of their populations undernourished. South Asia, which includes India, Pakistan, and Bangladesh, and Sub-Saharan Africa also improved to a lesser extent. Much of the continuing problem of undernourishment is not due to a lack of food worldwide, but to an inefficient food distribution system that is constrained by the fact that private food suppliers need to make a profit. The number of countries classified as "low income" has also decreased.

The World Bank (2017d) classifies the world's countries into four income categories. In *low-income countries*, the average *gross national income (GNI)* per person is $1,025 or less. In *lower-middle-income countries*, the GNI per person is between $1,026 and $4,035. *upper-middle-income countries* have per person GNI between $4,036 and $12,475. And *high-income-countries* have average GNI of $12,476 or more per person. Indicative of the global decline in poverty, the number of low-income countries shrank between 2000 and 2017 from 66 to 31. In comparison, 52 nations are lower-middle income, 56 upper- middle income, and 79 high income.

The range of average gross domestic product (GDP) per person worldwide ranges from a high of $124,900 in Qatar (an oil-rich monarchy) to a low of $700 in the Central African Republic (CIA 2018c). Many of the countries that continue to have high levels of poverty are *"fragile" states* with characteristics such as weak governments unable to provide basic essential services, development, or law and order to many of their people, very high levels of corruption, and even civil war. Such conditions contribute to the persistence of poverty directly and also by discouraging technical aid, financial assistance, and investment from other countries or international aid organizations. Figure 11.1 shows GDP per person for seventeen selected countries for which 2017 estimates were available and their rank among other nations.

Women Women are 70 percent of the world's poor. In less-developed countries with traditional cultures and intense gender bias, they experience systematic discrimination in employment, control of property and

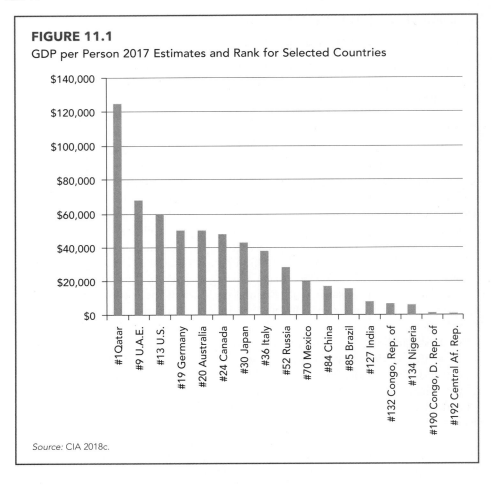

FIGURE 11.1

GDP per Person 2017 Estimates and Rank for Selected Countries

Source: CIA 2018c.

other assets, education, health care, and political participation (Caritas 2017). Women, more often than men, are denied an education or pulled out of school and forced into marriage. Of persons unable to read or write, two-thirds are women.

Children Millions of children live in poverty, and it is estimated that over 7 million children die each year before they reach the age of five (Care 2016). Many of these deaths result from lack of proper nutrition, clean water, sanitation, or needed immunizations. Children who survive these threats but continue to live in areas characterized by extreme poverty are often at grave risk of exploitation and abuse through forced early marriage, child labor, sex trafficking, or being forced into being child soldiers or even slaves.

Child Soldiers The United Nations Children Fund (UNICEF) defines a child soldier as any person younger than eighteen who participates in an armed force or armed group (Becker and Stohl 2015; Kaplan 2005; UNICEF 2017a; United Nations 2015b). Hundreds of thousands of child soldiers, many under age fifteen, have participated in violent conflicts. Armed groups using child soldiers usually operate in countries characterized by high levels of poverty, including Afghanistan, the Central African Republic, the Democratic Republic of the Congo, India, Iraq, Liberia, Mali, Myanmar, Nigeria, South Sudan, Sudan, Somalia, Syria, Uganda, and Yemen. In some countries children serve in only nonstate armed groups; in others they are recruited into government forces as well. In South Sudan alone an estimated 12,000 children in 2015 were active in both nonstate and government armed forces. And in Yemen about one in three fighters in all conflicting forces was under eighteen. But the United States provided military aid to the governments in both countries despite the 2008 Child Soldiers Prevention Act that was intended to limit U.S. military assistance to governments with children in their armies. Cuts in U.S. aid, however, did convince the Democratic Republic of the Congo and Chad to drastically reduce the number of child soldiers operating in their countries (Becker 2015).

Slavery Slavery, unfortunately, continues to exist in many places around the world. The Global Slavery Index (2017) estimated that 45.8 million people were enslaved in 2016. The institution of slavery is often linked to dire poverty. The motivation for modern slavery is typically that slaves constitute a labor force cheaper and more easily controlled than the labor of free persons. The type of slavery that existed in the United States before the Civil War was *chattel slavery*. Chattel slaves are persons who are permanently owned and whose children are automatically born into slavery (this is also called descent slavery). They are treated completely as property to be bought and sold (Abolition Project 2009).

Today almost all slavery is some form of forced labor, which includes any services or work that people are forced to do under threat of some type of punishment (Anti-Slavery International 2017a). Forced labor includes *sex slavery, human trafficking slavery*, and *bonded labor slavery*.

Bonded labor is the most widespread form of forced labor. A bonded labor slave is a person enslaved as a way to pay off a debt. In theory, if the debt is paid off, the person will be free. But in reality the bonded slave's pay is often so low that the debt can never be paid off. In some cases, the debt is passed on to the slave's child or children. Often the person owed the debt determines whom the bonded slave works for, and slavery is enforced by the threat and/or use of violence, or by being kept under surveillance or lock and key. Anti-Slavery.org (2017b) estimates that there are millions of debt bondage slaves, many of them working in agriculture, factories, mills, quarries, or brick kilns in South Asia. Bonded labor exists, despite being illegal, because of persistent poverty and discrimination against certain groups such as the *Dalits* (lowest caste – untouchables) in India and unscrupulous business persons willing to exploit desperate people.

Human trafficking slaves often work as forced laborers or forced sex slaves in developed countries where they live illegally. The traffickers can use violence and threat of disclosure to immigration authorities to control the victims, who typically are inhibited from going to the police out of fear of arrest and deportation. Slavery can also serve the interests of U.S. corporations and consumers, even if unknowingly.

outsourcing The removal of jobs from one country to another, typically to increase profits by taking advantage of lower labor costs.

An Associated Press investigation published in 2015 found evidence that forced laborers (poor migrant workers and children) were sold to factories in Thailand where they processed shrimp that ended up in global supply chains (Mason et al. 2015) servicing Walmart, the world's biggest retailer, and Red Lobster, the world's biggest seafood restaurant.

Income and Wealth Inequality

While it is clear that poverty has declined, economists have debated whether globalization increases or decreases economic inequality between countries and within countries. The evidence seems mixed regarding intercountry inequality and appears to depend in part on which dimension of economic inequality is being examined. Some developing countries(China in particular), have experienced spectacular growth through globalization and have reduced the productivity gap between them and more-advanced nations. Technical advances have also made the residents of many countries more equal in terms of access to the internet, television, and phone and video services. However, as Piketty (2014) has shown, countries with a large surplus of capital often see their wealth grow more rapidly than other nations, increasing internation inequality.

Data show, however, that globalization is one of several factors (including government policies, technological change, and the high growth of capital investments owned by affluent individuals) that can increase inequality within nations. **Outsourcing** jobs to developing nations increases economic inequality in advanced nations by sending well-paying working-class and middle-class type-jobs abroad where labor costs are lower. This has the effect of forcing middle-class people to find new jobs with much lower pay. At the same time, the corporate executives who arranged to outsource middle-class jobs (increasing the profits of their companies by lowering labor costs) were rewarded with higher salaries and large bonuses. Globalization increases inequality in developing nations because foreign investment often recruits skilled workers who are paid relatively high salaries (by the developing country's standards) while the wage level of low skilled workers usually does not increase (Berger 2014; *Economist* 2014). Morcroft (2013) displays data showing that for the period 1988–2008 the income of most citizens in rich countries and the poor in many sub-Saharan African countries remained almost unchanged. But the top 12 percent in the United States, the top 3–6 percent in the United Kingdom, Japan, France, and Germany, and the top 1 percent in Brazil, Russia, and South Africa, as well as the middle classes in emerging economies like China and India, all experienced income increases.

The special feature describes three types of global revolutionary movements, each of whose leaders claimed their movements could solve many of the world's problems, such as exploitation and wealth and income inequalities.

Global wealth inequality

The 85 richest people in the world have more wealth than

the poorest 3.5 billion people **combined.**

GLOBAL CITIZEN

Mobilization for global justice demonstration

Social Movements: Global Revolutionary Movements

A global revolutionary movement has the goal of succeeding in all nations. Be they Marxist, Islamic fundamentalist, or democratic, such movements develop because people experience intense dissatisfaction with situations such as lack of access to education, job and income opportunities, corrupt or repressive regimes, moral/religious issues, foreign exploitation, or some combination of these. Leaders of global revolutionary movements persuade people that the real cause of problems is something that cannot be effectively dealt with by a movement limited to a single nation. The only permanent solution is worldwide revolution (DeFronzo and Gill 2014).

An essential step in a global revolutionary movement is achieving an initial spectacular victory in at least one nation. This draws attention to the movement, increases faith in the revolutionary leadership, expands participation, and raises the probability of future successes (Katz 1997). The crucial initial victories for the global democracy movement were the American Revolution and the French Revolution. The Russian Bolshevik revolution inspired a wave of Marxist revolutionary efforts around the world. And the Islamist

victories in the 1978–1979 Iranian Revolution and the Afghan war against Soviet forces in the late 1980s propelled the Islamic fundamentalist global revolutionary movement.

The Marxist global revolutionary movement asserts that placing control of major economic resources and production in the hands of the people (typically in the form of the people's representatives in government) will lead to true equality of opportunity and the end of class, race, sex, and other types of prejudice and discrimination. Marxist revolutionary ideas were developed by Karl Marx, Frederick Engels, Vladimir Lenin, Leon Trotsky, Mao Zedong, and others. Trotsky especially emphasized the necessity for total world revolution from private to collective control of major economic resources and production.

The central idea of Islamic fundamentalist revolutionary ideology is that Islam must be purified by returning to its original religious principles. This would strengthen Islamic societies so they could compete successfully with non-Islamic societies. Islamic fundamentalism grew in influence because it offered oppressed people a sense of high self-worth and pride. It told them they were adopting a

(continued)

Social Movements (*continued*)

set of beliefs and way of life ordained by God that are inherently superior to the cultures of the more technologically advanced societies. The movement targeted perceived imperialist powers and governments in Islamic nations viewed as collaborating with imperialists.

The two major violent Islamic fundamentalist revolutionary movements were Al Qaeda and ISIS (Islamic State or Islamic State in Iraq and Syria). While both are Sunni Islam in outlook, their means differed significantly. Al Qaeda, Osama bin Laden's organization, focused on striking the "far enemies" like the United States in the 9/11 attacks and Great Britain; ISIS, the group that evolved from Al Qaeda in Iraq, attacked "near enemies," including adherents of Shia Islam, with the aim of establishing a Sunni Islamic state as a base for further operations.

Democracy became the most powerful revolutionary ideal since the end of the eighteenth century (Goldstone 1998a). Thomas Jefferson asserted in the Declaration of Independence (1776) that "all men are created equal, that they are endowed by their creator with certain unalienable Rights, that among these are Life, Liberty and the pursuit of Happiness . . . . That whenever any Form of Government becomes destructive of these ends, it is the Right of the People to alter or to abolish it, and to institute new Government" to ensure "their Safety and Happiness." The message is that democracy is essential to the achievement of global human rights.

During the eighteenth, nineteenth, and early twentieth centuries, most democratic revolutionary movements failed. The post–World War II Cold War between the United States and the Soviet Union became a barrier to democracy. Both states intervened in other nations to keep in place authoritarian regimes that repressed the democratic aspirations of their citizens. The Soviet Union crushed movements for change in Hungary in 1956 and Czechoslovakia in 1968. The United States supported anti-communist right-wing dictatorships in Latin America and elsewhere, even when they had repressed democratic movements or had overthrown elected governments, as in Chile in 1973. Even after the Cold War the United States provided weapons and training to pro-U.S. dictatorships in Saudi Arabia and other oil-rich monarchies. Nevertheless, much of the world has embraced democracy as the best political system.

Global revolutionary movements are not mutually exclusive. For example, the creation of democratic political systems can lead to the elections of leaders favoring socialist economic systems or Islamic fundamentalist systems. Since the most technologically advanced and best-armed nations are democracies, it might be expected that they would be extremely supportive of the global democratic revolutionary movement. However, this is not always the case. Many advanced nations rely on access to energy, mineral, or labor resources of authoritarian regimes and have been willing to supply them with weapons then used to preserve their dictatorships. The success of the global democratic revolutionary movement requires that the most powerful democratic countries support democracy universally rather than only when it favors their interests.

SOCIOLOGICAL PERSPECTIVES ON GLOBALIZATION AND GLOBAL INEQUALITIES

Sociological perspectives emphasize different aspects and consequences of globalization. The structural-functional approach tends to highlight benefits, while the conflict approach focuses attention on unfairness and inequalities. The symbolic-interactionist perspective describes how globalization can affect culture but can also lead to social movements protesting inequalities or other harmful effects of globalization.

Structural-Functional Perspective

According to the structural-functional approach, economic inequalities between nations are linked to technological improvements that increase differentiation of labor, productivity, and wealth. Global inequalities are largely the result of the fact that some nations began modernization and industrializing much earlier than others. Massive rapid gains in technology and productivity soon transformed European nations, the United States, and several other modernizing societies into countries where the majority were middle class and accustomed to experiencing ever-improving lifestyles. In contrast, the majority of residents in countries that lagged behind in industrializing remained poor. As modernizing countries became more and more affluent, economic inequality between nations grew dramatically.

Why did European countries begin modernizing and industrializing first when so many important scientific breakthroughs had previously occurred in other parts of the world (such as the modern number system invented in India and perfected in Arab nations before reaching Europe, and gunpowder invented in China)? The key appears to be that Europe experienced a disruption of its traditional culture and shifted to a culture that was more accepting of social change.

Societies whose members are tightly bound into a traditional culture that inhibits change often fail to effectively exploit the potential of new discoveries or inventions. In comparison, societies with cultures that value science and innovation and expect and accept change have dramatically improved their technologies, the productivity of their economic systems, and the lifestyles and welfare of their people. Arguments have been put forward about what broke the hold of traditional culture in Europe and opened the way for new ideas, greater individualism, science, and progress. One view is that the bubonic plague (the Black Death), which killed an estimated twenty-five million people in Europe between 1347 and 1352 (about one-third of the continent's population at the time; Middleages.net 2011), altered society, setting the stage for the Renaissance and the Protestant Reformation. One impact of the plague was that the conservative hold of religion over people's lives significantly decreased because the church and prayer were unable to prevent the death of loved ones (Decameron 2010). People began to question tradition and look more to reason and science to understand and control the world. This constituted fertile circumstances for the Protestant Reformation. According to Max Weber, one of the theoretical giants of sociology, it was Protestantism, in particular the Calvinist form, that led people to believe that getting rich through hard work, investment, and innovation demonstrated that you were a person destined for salvation. This cultural change encouraged people to support progress and industrialization, which ultimately made European societies wealthy and raised most of their citizens out of poverty.

From the functionalist point of view the way to reduce global inequality is to have the less-developed countries follow the example of the more advanced countries and modernize and industrialize. Rostow (1991) provided a description of this economic growth process, referred to as **modernization theory**.

modernization theory
The theory that states that less-developed countries should go through a multistage modernization process to become technologically advanced, wealthy, and democratic.

Functionalist-Modernization Theory Modernization theory assumes that before modernization begins a traditional society is a social system in which all components interact smoothly. Modernization starts when new technology and information are introduced and begin to change the economy. When this happens other components of the society must also change to ensure the proper functioning of the social system. As more advanced technology is introduced, the formerly traditional society gradually comes to increasingly resemble a modern capitalist nation. This includes adopting the values, legal characteristics, and form of government of advanced capitalist societies. Modernization theory views traditional societies as characterized by emotionally saturated extended family relations that interfere with rational decision making. As societies modernize, their social relations become more impersonal to facilitate the functioning of a capitalist market economy (which the theory views as the type of economy most capable of adapting to new technologies, opportunities, and challenges). Culture changes to put more emphasis on individuality, rational thinking, enterprise, and personal achievement. Stages of development include (Peet and Hartwick 2009):

1. *Traditional Stage.* Society has a low productivity (typically agricultural) economy with a very low percentage of GDP invested in technological and economic growth. The culture has a fatalistic spiritual orientation toward the physical environment rather than a belief in achieving a better life through science and innovation.

2. *Development of Preconditions for Economic "Takeoff".* Traditional societies develop modernization preconditions, including cultural change from values and norms that interfere with progress to valuing progressive change as possible, desirable, and necessary. This could occur through contacts with modern or modernizing countries as well as the creation of an educational system teaching science and new technologies.

3. *Takeoff Period.* After the factors preventing growth have been overcome the society enters the takeoff stage of modernization. The percentage of national income invested in technological and economic growth increases to about 10 percent or more. Over the next decade or two, social and governmental systems change to foster economic growth.

4. *Drive toward Maturity.* During this stage of development, typically lasting about two generations, the society adopts advanced technology throughout its economy, and investment of national income in technological and economic growth reaches up to twenty percent. Annual increase in productivity comes to exceed annual increase in population. Modernization maturity is reached when the country's technical and business knowledge and infrastructure becomes capable of making whatever its citizens need, from medicines to computers and smart phones to advanced military weapons.

5. *Stage of High Mass Consumption.* The production of consumer goods and services comes to dominate the economy, and personal income is high enough for individuals to consume far beyond what is necessary to satisfy essential needs. Funds for providing welfare assistance and retirement benefits often increase.

Modernization theory implies that the way to reduce global inequalities is for poor countries to modernize through adopting neoliberal economic policies in which government regulation of industry, commerce, and business activity is minimized. The resulting free market economy would increase productivity, the country's wealth, and its citizens' incomes.

Criticisms of Modernization Theory One criticism is that parts of modernization theory conflict with reality. Many industrializing societies retained rather than abandoned much of their traditional culture. In fact, pride in traditional cultural heritage appears in some cases to have motivated the drive for industrialization so as to be better able to compete with advanced nations. In addition, some countries have industrialized without adopting governmental systems like those in the United States, Western Europe, or Japan. China, for example, experienced spectacular economic development from 1979 onward under a one-party political system. And much of the economic development in South Korea and Chile took place while military dictatorships held power. Further, a number of developing oil-rich nations in the Middle East are governed by monarchies. Another criticism is that, in reality, advanced nations, beginning during the period of European colonial expansion, have often prevented development in poor nations or steered development to benefit the needs of the advanced nations while leaving most of the local people in poverty. For example, foreign interests exploited Bolivia's mineral wealth for decades. But Bolivia, one of the most resource-endowed nations in the world, remained one of South America's poorest countries.

Conflict Perspective

The conflict approach to globalization and global inequalities focuses on how the actions and policies of powerful nations contribute to maintaining or even increasing inequality between nations. This point of view is expressed in **world systems theory** (Wallerstein 1974, 1979, 1980, 1988) and **dependency theory** (Baran and Sweezy 1966; Dos Santos 1970; Frank 1966, 1969a, 1969b, 1979; Furtado 1963; Sunkel 1972).

World Systems Theory World systems theory claims that global inequality is in great part the result of wealthy nations' domination over and economic exploitation of poor nations. From this point of view, globalization began around 1500 within the framework of an expanding world capitalist system in which European nations grew wealthy and more powerful by feeding on the resources and cheap labor of the Americas, Africa, and large parts of Asia. Once under European control, poor regions were developed to the extent and in the ways that

world systems theory The idea that advanced "core" nations exploit the resources of less developed poor "periphery" nations with the assistance of developing "semi-periphery" nations.

dependency theory The idea that poor nations were purposely made dependent on rich nations so that they can be exploited indefinitely.

core nations The most technologically advanced nations that are economically and militarily powerful and dominate the world system directly or through their multinational corporations.

periphery nations Weak poor nations that provide the world system with minerals, agricultural products, or cheap labor.

semi-periphery nations Partially industrialized nations that extract benefits from periphery societies but pass much of these on to the core nations.

most benefitted the colonial powers. This meant keeping poor countries relatively weak and forcing them to provide their resources and labor at cheap prices, which ensured high profits for the controlling European power.

World systems theory classifies nations into three groups: the **core nations** (the most technologically advanced nations that are economically and militarily powerful and dominate the world system directly or through their multinational corporations), **periphery nations** (weak poor nations that produce little or no modern technology and typically provide the world system with minerals, agricultural products, or cheap labor for manufacturing enterprises moved from high-wage societies), and **semi-periphery nations** (partially industrialized nations that extract benefits from periphery societies but pass much of these on to the core nations). Following World War I the United States was the most powerful of the core nations, a group which also included Britain, France, Germany, several other Western European nations, and Japan. Periphery countries included most nations in Africa and some in Latin America and Asia. Examples of semi-peripheral countries are Brazil, Mexico, South Africa, and Turkey. Over time some countries shifted position in the world system. For example, South Korea advanced from a semi-peripheral country to a technologically advanced core nation. According to world systems theory the wealth derived from the periphery has functioned to decrease class conflict in core nations by improving the lifestyles of workers and has also reduced conflict between core nations.

Dependency Theory Dependency theory compliments world systems theory by arguing that poor nations were purposely made dependent on rich nations so that they can be exploited indefinitely. Dependency theorists believe that the advanced societies used the resources of poor nations to increase their own wealth while restraining the development or even destroying the previous achievements of peoples they had conquered. Elites within poor societies who collaborated with the rich nations enjoyed increasingly affluent lifestyles while most people in their countries remained poor. After colonies became independent nations, they continued to be locked into dependent and exploitive relationships with the former colonizing powers through unfair trade relationships in which the poor (periphery) societies were forced to sell their resources to the rich (core) nations below their true value and

U.S. products on sale in a developing country

purchase products from the rich nations at high prices. Advanced nations structured economic relationships so that they consistently extracted such an excessive flow of wealth from lesser developed countries that no capital accumulation was possible for the former colonies to invest in industrializing or otherwise building their societies' economies in ways that would truly benefit the majority of their peoples. When dependent countries were allowed some industrial development, it was only in ways that served the needs of the advanced nations. Poor countries also became locked into dependency through the mounting debts they owed rich nations.

Criticisms of World Systems and Dependency Theories World systems and dependency theories have been criticized for several reasons. One is that they seem to neglect the power of advances in technology to improve people's lives without necessarily exploiting poor nations. For example, cell phones have allowed many people in poor countries to communicate verbally and visually over long distances without having to spend billions of dollars putting in expensive landline infrastructure. Critics also point out that a number of former colonies, such as South Korea and Hong Kong, became industrial and financial successes. But defenders of world systems and dependency theories argue that South Korea and Hong Kong received immense assistance during the Cold War as part of the advanced capitalist nations' efforts to undermine the Communist Party-led governments of North Korea and China. They also note that technology sold by advanced nations' corporations in poor countries can provide benefits for the seller. For example, residents of poor countries who acquire cell phones must continuously pay for service contracts to use their phones.

Beyond World Systems and Dependency Theories Thomas Piketty (2014), a professor at the Paris School of Economics, has provided new insights into the causes of economic inequality among individuals and nations. Piketty's research indicates that over the last two hundred years the worth of gains from capital (including money generated by invested savings, profits, interest, dividends, and rents) has generally exceeded economic growth. This means that the people and nations with the most accumulated wealth have continuously gotten richer faster than other people and countries. It also indicates that, without any reforms, wealth will become more and more concentrated in the hands of a small percentage of the world's population. Piketty suggests that probably the only way to stop the trend toward an ever-increasing concentration of wealth would be worldwide progressive taxation of capital. He suggests an annual tax of 0.1 to 0.5 percent for fortunes around $1 million, one percent for fortunes between about $1 to 5 million, 2 percent between $6 and 10 million, and so on, with a maximum as high as 5 to 10 percent for fortunes of several hundred million dollars or more.

The special feature describes how globalization has provided new opportunities for persons to conceal wealth from the public and governments.

Racial/Ethnic-Conflict Approach to Global Inequalities The racial/ethnic-conflict perspective points out that the regions of the world European nations set out to explore, conquer, and colonize were inhabited by persons of color many Europeans viewed as racially inferior. While locked in poverty, the resources and labor power of nonwhite peoples made white nations wealthy. The trade and financial systems dominated by rich white nations keeps many nonwhite countries mired in debt. If the residents of poor nations were white, it's doubtful that the technologically advanced societies would have exploited them so unfairly.

Special Topics: The Panama Papers

In April of 2016 world news media broke the story of the so-called Panama Papers, which were believed to shed light on the secretive financial dealings of the superrich, politicians, tyrants, international criminals, and even terrorists. Dozens of investigative journalists around the world read through 11.5 million electronic files from the Panamanian law firm Mossack Fonseca (Peralta 2016). These had been leaked by an unknown person or persons to a German newspaper, *Süddeutsche Zeitung*, which then shared them with the International Consortium of Investigative Journalists. Mossack Fonseca, founded by a German immigrant to Panama, Jürgen Mossack, whose father was a member of the Nazi Waffen-SS, and Ramón Fonseca, a Panamanian who has powerful political ties (Semple, Ahmed, and Lipton 2016), was one of many enterprises in Panama, Barbados, Belize, the British Virgin Islands, the Cayman Islands, Singapore, and other countries accused of assisting clients in concealing wealth through means such as shell corporations (Pellegrini 2016). A shell corporation is a corporation that generally has no significant productive assets, such as manufacturing plants, but instead functions primarily to carry out financial transactions. For example, a person might set up a shell corporation for the purpose of buying real estate, an airplane, or a yacht in the corporation's name, rather than his or her own name. If someone goes to public records to check who owns the property he or she finds the shell corporation's name, not the person behind the shell corporation who is the real owner. Shell corporations are therefore useful for hiding wealth. This is not necessarily illegal. For example, a person might not want the public to know his or her true wealth for privacy reasons.

Shell corporations, however, may be used for illegal purposes. For example, a husband might use a shell corporation to conceal assets from his wife in anticipation of divorce proceedings. Government officials or dictators can use them to hide money they have stolen from their nations, bribes they have received, or shares of stock they own in companies they are supposed to regulate. Criminals can use them to secretly store money gained from illegal activities such as drug dealing, people smuggling, or sex trafficking. Another use of shell corporations is money laundering. For example, someone involved in making money from illegal weapons sales might set up a shell corporation supposedly conducting legitimate business, such as clothing manufacturing. Then the profits from illegal weapons sales are deposited in the shell company and "laundered" by being reported as earnings from the nonexistent legal business of clothing manufacturing.

Sometimes money is shifted among several shell corporations to make discovery of the true sources of income impossible for investigators to uncover. And many people use shell corporations to conceal legal and illegal income and wealth from governments to avoid paying taxes. It is estimated that about 8 percent of the world's total wealth (some $7.6 trillion) is hidden away from governments in secretive financial accounts and instruments like shell corporations, causing a loss of $200 billion a year in tax revenues (Semple et al. 2016), including $37 billion annually in tax losses to the U.S. government (Harding 2016). The disclosure of the Panama Papers has been referred to as the so-called tip of the iceberg of a huge worldwide financial industry that functions to hide the money, property, and business dealings of wealthy people, corrupt business persons and politicians, dictators, and organized criminals.

Feminist-Conflict Approach to Global Inequalities Feminist social scientists believe that global inequality has a significant gender dimension, in that within poor countries women suffer the worst consequences of poverty. Traditional cultures are typically highly male dominated. This often leads to poor men taking out their frustrations in the form of psychological or physical abuse against women. Such men cling to their male privileges as a way of psychologically coping with their otherwise downtrodden status. According to feminist theorists, neoliberal global free market policies involving privatizing public services and water supplies worsened conditions for women in a number of developing areas (Peet and Hartwick 2009). Feminists argue that reducing global inequality can be facilitated by providing women with educational, job, and political opportunities so that they are personally empowered and free of being dependent on men.

Symbolic-Interactionist Perspective

The symbolic-interactionist approach analyzes how increasing interaction among the peoples in societies around the world affects local cultures and the nature of a developing world culture. This includes the question of whether and to what extent a shared world culture is dominated by the values and norms of the most advanced societies. In addition, the symbolic-interactionist approach to global inequalities helps explain why capitalist globalization and inequality have been linked to popular discontent, crime, terrorism, and even revolution. In pre-modernization agricultural societies where poverty is widespread and social mobility is limited, many people are conditioned by a traditional culture to accept their lot in life. But the spread of capitalist modernization has often had a disruptive influence undermining people's feelings of belonging and community. For example, in pre-modernization rural China and Vietnam Confucian norms of communal responsibility and extended family relations put some informal limits on what landlords would charge poor peasants for renting land and interest on loans. But as capitalist business relations began to saturate the countryside in the early twentieth century, landlords, less concerned with the welfare of the poor, increased rents and interest rates on loans. This trend toward coldly maximizing profits heightened economic insecurity and drove many peasants toward socialist movements, leading up to the success of China's Communist Revolution in 1949. More recently, Piketty has made a similar argument for the rise of the terrorist Islamic movement ISIS. Piketty claims that the Middle East's social systems have been undermined by the huge concentration of wealth in a few oil-rich monarchies that have relatively small populations. These dictatorships play key resource, financial, and political roles in the capitalist global economy. Saudi Arabia, Kuwait, the United Arab Emirates, Qatar, Oman, and Bahrain, with about 16 percent of the Middle East's approximately 300 million people, generated almost 60 percent of the region's GDP (Tankersley 2015). Because of the tremendous unequal distribution of oil wealth, tens of millions of Sunni Arabs live impoverished in resource-limited countries while knowing of the typically luxuriant lifestyles of the monarchies' royal families. Piketty believes this situation has generated many recruits for ISIS.

DEALING WITH THE PROBLEMS OF GLOBAL INEQUALITY

Many conservative politicians support the idea that free-market capitalism worldwide can raise productivity to the point where virtually every able-bodied person willing to work can raise her- or himself out of poverty. They point to China, for example, where a rapidly growing economy during the 1990s and the early twenty-first century did reduce dire poverty. Liberal politicians, however, generally believe that unregulated free-market capitalism cannot reduce inequality. Also referring the China case, they note that although extreme poverty was reduced significantly, economic inequality simultaneously rose dramatically, as has been the case in many advanced capitalist societies. One problem, according to left-leaning politicians, is that growing concentration of wealth in a small percentage of the population gives superrich individuals increasing influence over government. They continue to structure laws and policies to protect their wealth and power. In the United States this is reflected in presidential candidates' increasing requirement to attract billionaires to back their campaigns.

Concerned politicians believe that some type of government action is necessary to reduce economic inequality. One proposal focuses on reducing the role of big money in politics through universal public financing of major political campaigns and banning huge financial contributions by individuals or organizations. This would require reversing the 2010 U.S. Supreme Court decision in *Citizens United v. the Federal Election Commission*, in which the five conservative justices ruled to strike down limits and allow enormous private contributions to candidates (Levy 2015).

Another idea is to reduce the outsourcing of manufacturing or other jobs from the United States to other nations and provide incentives for corporations to develop such jobs at home. This proposal could lead to a regrowth of the middle-income sector of the U.S. population. As noted earlier, Piketty's (2014) research indicates that the path toward greater equality must include a global progressive tax on wealth.

Noble Prize Laureate economist Eric Maskin (Berger 2014) suggests that another possible approach to increasing global equality would be for government, nongovernmental organizations, and private foundations to offer job training to workers to acquire skills suitable for well-paying jobs domestically and internationally.

Another approach for reducing economic inequality developed by some Latin American governments is to structure trade and aid relations among rich and poor nations based more on people's welfare than on profit. In 2004 Venezuela and Cuba created the *Bolivarian Alternative for the Americas* (changed to the *Bolivarian Alliance for the Americas, ALBA*, in 2009) to provide an alternative to international neoliberal policies (DeFronzo 2015). Following the election of its first indigenous president, Evo Morales, Bolivia joined ALBA in 2006. Ecuador, led by Rafael Correa, became a member of ALBA in 2009. By 2017 ALBA also included Antigua and Barbuda, Dominica, Grenada, Nicaragua, Saint Kitts and Nevis, Saint Lucia, and Saint Vincent and the Grenadines.

ALBA supports trade relations that prevent poor countries from falling further into debt. It opposes the privatization of essential public services that make these difficult or costly for poor people to obtain. ALBA holds that government provision of services such as water, health care, education, libraries, public transportation, and fire and police services is indispensable for overcoming social inequality. Goals include eliminating poverty, illiteracy, and discrimination against indigenous people, and making health care available free to all unable to pay for it. ALBA proposed that poor countries be assisted in becoming more self-sufficient in food production and economic infrastructure. This would make them less dependent on investment from profit-motivated foreign corporations that tended to continually move production to whereever wages appeared lowest, leaving economic devastation in their wake.

In all likelihood, reducing global inequality will require multiple approaches.

CHAPTER REVIEW

Globalization

Globalization refers to the dramatic increase in the movement of information, people, culture, technologies, goods, services, and money around the world and the increased connectedness and interdependence of peoples and nations.

Technology and Globalization

Advances in technology permit many millions of people to travel internationally. The invention of container shipping helped vastly increase global trade. Satellites, fiber optics, personal computers, and cell phones provide internet communication, facilitating international relationships, financial deals, exchanges of knowledge, and sharing of cultures.

Globalization: Positive and Negative Views

Supporters of globalization believe that the more barriers to freedom of movement and trade are eliminated, the more global living standards will rise. Critics of globalization argue that when it is based on neoliberal free market policies globalization benefits the already-rich countries more than less developed nations and the wealthier classes within all nations.

Globalization, Economic Development, and Global Inequalities

The growth of globalization has been accompanied by a significant decline in extreme poverty. But it has proven difficult to reduce poverty in fragile states. Women and children suffer most from poverty. Many countries with high levels of poverty also suffer from forms of slavery and children serving in armed forces. At the same time that extreme poverty rates have dropped, income and wealth inequality have risen in many countries, concentrating power in a small percentage of the world's population.

Sociological Perspectives on Globalization and Global Inequalities

According to the structural-functional approach, global inequalities largely result from the fact that some nations began modernizing and industrializing much earlier than others. Modernization is seen as proceeding through five stages: traditional stage; development of preconditions for economic take-off; takeoff period; drive toward maturity; and stage of mass consumption.

The conflict approach to globalization and global inequalities focuses on how the actions and policies of powerful nations contribute to maintaining or even increasing inequality between nations. This point of view is expressed in world systems theory and dependency theory. World systems theory classifies nations into three groups: the core (the most technologically advanced nations that are economically and militarily powerful and dominate the world system directly or through their multinational corporations), periphery (weak, poor nations that typically provide the world system with minerals, agricultural products, or cheap labor), and semi-periphery (partially industrialized nations that extract benefits from periphery societies but pass much of these on to the core nations). Dependency theory complements world systems theory by arguing that poor nations were purposely made dependent on rich nations so that they can be exploited indefinitely.

The racial/ethnic-conflict perspective points out that while locked in poverty, the resources and labor power of nonwhite peoples made white nations wealthy. Feminist social scientists believe that global inequality has a significant gender dimension, in that within countries women suffer the worst consequences of poverty.

The symbolic-interactionist approach analyzes cultural change worldwide and also helps explain why capitalist globalization and inequality have often been linked to popular discontent, crime, terrorism, and revolution.

Dealing with the Problems of Global Inequality

Conservative politicians support the idea that free-market capitalism worldwide can raise productivity to the point where virtually every able-bodied person willing to work can raise her- or himself out of poverty. Liberal politicians, however, generally believe that unregulated free-market capitalism disproportionately benefits the already wealthy and increases inequality. One idea to reduce inequality in the United States is to reduce the outsourcing of jobs to other nations and provide incentives for corporations to develop new jobs at home. Another approach is to offer free high-tech training for people to acquire skills suitable for well-paying jobs. Piketty proposes that the path toward greater equality must include a global progressive tax on wealth. Another possible approach is for nations to organize trading networks based more on mutual cooperation rather than on maximizing profit.

KEY TERMS

core nations, p. 308
dependency theory, p. 307
globalization, p. 294
modernization theory, p. 305
neoliberal free market, p. 298

outsourcing, p. 302
periphery nations, p. 308
semi-periphery nations, p. 308
world systems theory, p. 307

DISCUSSION QUESTIONS

1. Do you think that globalization is essentially a beneficial or a harmful process? Justify your point of view.

2. Which technological creation do you think has played the biggest role in bringing about modern globalization? Explain your answer.

3. How could the benefits of globalization be maximized while minimizing its negative effects?

4. Do you think that advanced countries' trade and political relations with lesser-developed countries have been mostly beneficial or mostly harmful to those societies? Why?

5. Which sociological perspective contributes most to our understanding of the key aspects of globalization? Explain your answer.

6. Do you think there should be an effort to try to reduce economic inequality between countries? Justify your point of view.

CHAPTER 12

Population, Urbanization, and Aging

CHAPTER OBJECTIVES

- Describe the major population problems confronting nations around the world and attempts to solve these problems.
- Explain the effects on population of immigration to the United States.
- Identify social problems related to urbanization.
- Explain the effects of aging on the populations of technologically advanced countries.

- Describe responses to population, urbanization, and aging problems.
- Describe sociological perspectives on population, urbanization, and aging.

IMAGINE HOW YOU WOULD FEEL *if your government told you how many children you could have. During much of the nineteenth and twentieth centuries, many of China's people struggled to survive. When droughts, floods, or warfare disrupted agriculture, tens of millions faced famine and starvation. In 1979, one year after launching major market-oriented economic reforms, China's leaders enacted a family-planning policy to significantly reduce* **population growth**. *It became known as the "one-child policy." China's leader at the time, Deng Xiaoping, stated that the policy was needed to make sure "the fruits of economic growth are not devoured by population growth" (Buckley 2015b). This law applied to China's majority ethnic group, the Han Chinese, approximately 92 percent of the population. Minority ethnic groups were still allowed to have two or more children (Rosenberg 2015; Xiaofeng 2007). There were some other exceptions as well. People in rural areas were allowed to have a second child if their first child was a daughter. Also, if both husband and wife were the only child of their parents or if their first child had a birth defect or major health problem, they were allowed to have two children. In the end, about 36 percent of China's people, all living in urban areas, were held to a strict one-child limit. After the implementation of the one-child policy, China's* **fertility rate** *fell from an average of 2.91 children per woman aged fifteen to forty-four in 1978 to 1.55 children in 2012. This much lower rate contributed to slowing China's population growth. In fact, the 2015 fertility rate was below the 2.1 children per woman rate required to maintain the current population level. The government estimated that the one-child policy decreased the number of births in China by about 400 million (Xinhuanet 2014). However, China's success in this area created new problems. The proportion of the population made up of older and retired residents grew while the percentage of young workers shrank. China's leaders eventually realized that the country's economy, which was now vastly larger than when the one-child policy was instated, needed far more productive workers than its meager fertility rate could produce. In addition, the policy resulted in about 40 million more Chinese men than women in 2012 (due to factors such as selective abortion of female fetuses and the abandonment of female infants given up for international adoption), and the government expected that most would be unable to find wives (Levin 2014). How could these new population problems be solved? Increase the number of births. In 2013 government leaders modified the family-planning regulations to allow couples to have two children if either the husband or wife was an only child. In October 2015, China's leaders backed off even further, finally deciding to allow all couples to have two children (Buckley 2015b). Because of the high cost of raising children in China's cities, many couples may not elect to increase the size of their families. And remember, most Chinese couples will still be limited to only two children.*

population growth
Increase in the population of a location, such as a nation, territory, or city, equal to births plus people moving in minus deaths and people moving out.

fertility rate (also called the total fertility rate or TFR) Average number of children per woman aged fifteen to forty-four.

A nation should be able to provide opportunities for all of its people to obtain employment and make a decent living, and its population should be capable of meeting the country's requirements for sustainability and growth. If any one of these conditions is not met, there is need for some type of adjustment. For example, if the number of births in a nation increases greatly within a short time, there may be a lack of resources to provide for the well-being and education of children. On the other hand, a drastic decline in the number of births could lead to a shortage in the coming years of enough people to carry out essential roles in the economy and other major institutions, and pay the taxes necessary to support government and provide for the needs of the society's older citizens no longer in the work force.

This chapter covers topics related to population, **urbanization**, and **aging**, including population change, urban problems, and the aging of populations in technologically advanced nations. It also describes responses to population, urbanization, and aging problems, and sociological approaches to these topics.

POPULATION

The total number of people within a society may increase or decrease. It may also remain the same if the children born and the people moving in equal those who die and the number of people who leave. One of the world's major problems is overpopulation. But while this burdens many nations, others are troubled because their populations are dwindling.

Population Growth Worldwide: Past, Present, and Future

The human race is thought to have originated about 200,000 years ago (Biello 2014). The number of humans on earth in 3000 BC is estimated to have been only around 14 million (U.S. Census 2017a). By 1 AD the population had grown to somewhere between 170 and 400 million. World population increased unevenly in subsequent years to between 600 and 679 million by 1700. The rate of population growth increased with the advent of the scientific, technological, and industrial revolutions, which improved living conditions, increased food production, and cured or prevented previously deadly diseases. It took only 123 years for global population to grow from 1 billion in 1804 to 2 billion in 1927. Less than 50 years later, in 1974, the population had doubled again (United Nations Population Division 2017). Because of factors such as modern birth control methods and increased education and employment of women, the rate of population increase finally has begun to slow. It took just 12 years for the world's population to increase from 6 billion (in 1999) to 7 billion (in 2011), but according to UN estimates it will take 13 years to reach 8 billion, 14 more years

urbanization The movement of people from rural areas into urban areas.

aging Growth in the percentage of older people in a nation's population coupled with the economic, job, health, and psychological issues experienced by many people as they get older.

TABLE 12.1	United Nations Estimates of the Years the World Reached or Will Reach Each One-Billion-Person Population Increase

Year	Population
1804	1 billion
1927	2 billion
1960	3 billion
1974	4 billion
1987	5 billion
1999	6 billion
2011	7 billion
2024	8 billion
2038	9 billion
2058	10 billion
2093	11 billion

Source: U.S. Census 2017a; United Nations Population Division 2017.

to climb to 9 billion, 20 more years to go from 9 to 10 billion, and then 35 more years to reach 11 billion (see table 12.1).

In 2017, the world's population was estimated to be 7.4 billion. There is some disagreement about the maximum number of people the earth can support at current standards of resource consumption using existing technology. Biologist Edward O. Wilson (Cramer 2013) estimates about 10 billion. However, if all people on earth had a European level of resource consumption, some estimate that the earth could sustain only about two billion persons (World Population Balance 2017). Optimists counter by arguing that scientific progress will improve living conditions and allow the planet to support more people in the future (Kucharski 2015).

Regional Differences in Population Growth

Population growth differs significantly among the different regions of the world. African nations tend to have the highest **birth rates** and population growth (World Bank 2017a). Of the top forty highest birth

birth rate Number of live births per 1,000 persons in a population per year.

rate nations in 2016, thirty-six were located in Africa (CIA 2017e). Between 2017 and 2050, Africa is expected to contribute more than half of the world's population growth (United Nations Population Division 2017). All other regions are estimated to have much lower population growth rates, and Europe is actually expected to lose population. If future birth rates correspond to current estimates, the percentage of the world's population residing in Africa will climb from 16.6 percent in 2017 to 40 percent in 2100. The percentages in all other regions except Oceana will decline, as indicated in figure 12.1.

Population Growth in the United States

Since the American Revolution, the population of the United States has grown steadily from high birth rates, lowered death (mortality) rate, immigration, and major acquisitions of new territories such as through the Louisiana Purchase in 1803 and the U.S. victory in the Mexican–American War of 1846–1848, which gained territory that would eventually become the states of California, Utah, and Nevada, as well as parts of the future states of Arizona, Colorado, Kansas, New Mexico, Oklahoma, and Wyoming. When the first U.S. census was conducted in 1790, the total population was estimated at 3,929,214. About 95 percent of Americans lived in rural areas (U-s-history.com 2015).The 1860 census, on the eve of the Civil War, revealed a population of 31,183,582, about 80 percent of whom resided

Resources strained by high population growth

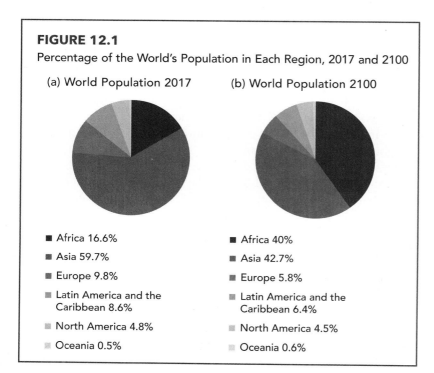

FIGURE 12.1

Percentage of the World's Population in Each Region, 2017 and 2100

(a) World Population 2017

(b) World Population 2100

- Africa 16.6%
- Asia 59.7%
- Europe 9.8%
- Latin America and the Caribbean 8.6%
- North America 4.8%
- Oceania 0.5%

- Africa 40%
- Asia 42.7%
- Europe 5.8%
- Latin America and the Caribbean 6.4%
- North America 4.5%
- Oceania 0.6%

in rural areas (Civil-war.net. 2009). About 13 percent (3,950,528 persons) of the total 1860 U.S. population were slaves, and 1.5 percent (476,748) were free persons of color. By 1900 the country's population had climbed to 76,212,168. The proportion residing in rural areas had fallen to approximately 60 percent. During the twentieth century the U.S. population increased around 1 to 2 percent annually due to birth rates and immigration. Exceptions included the year 1918 (when several hundred thousand U.S. residents died from an influenza epidemic, causing the death rate to temporarily surge by about 27 percent) and the decade of the Great Depression, when growth was notably lower (Celebrezze 1964; Rogers 1920; U.S. Census 2000). In 2016 the U.S. population reached 323,995,528 (CIA 2017f), with nearly 82 percent living in urban areas. The rate of increase in the U.S. population was about 0.78 percent in 2016, with about half of that due to immigration.

The Effect on Population of Immigration to the United States

The United States and the colonies from which it developed were built by immigrants from all over the world, as noted in Chapter 5. Most of the immigrants to the British colonial settlements came from northwestern European countries such as England and Germany. In 1790 the United States enacted the Naturalization Act, which stated that "free white persons" with "good moral character" qualified for U.S. citizenship after residing in the country for two years (Ewing 2012). In the 1840s agricultural disasters in Ireland (the Great Potato Famine) and Germany motivated more European immigration to the United States. It wasn't until after the American Civil War, in 1870, that African immigrants could become U.S. citizens. Many of the early white immigrants were poor people seeking new economic opportunities and political and religious freedom, but a large number became owners of African slaves, who had been brutally stolen from their homelands to work the land, particularly in the South after the expansion of cotton farming in the first half of the nineteenth century. The 1860 census indicated that there were no slaves in 17 states, but almost one-third of all Southern free families owned slaves (civilwarcauses.org 2015; Civil-war.net. 2009) (see table 12.2).

As industrialization accelerated following the Civil War, a new wave brought millions of immigrants from southern and eastern Europe (including Italy, Greece, Poland, Russia, Austria, Hungary, and the Balkan countries) to the United States. The number of people becoming permanent legal residents of the United States per year exceeded one million in 1905, 1906, 1907, 1910, 1913, and 1914. Immigration laws implemented in the 1920s tended to favor people from northwestern Europe and countries in the Western Hemisphere. In the period 1931–1945, during the Great Depression and World War II, there were less than 100,000 new permanent U.S. legal residents each year (Migration Policy Institute 2017). The Immigration Act of 1965 (following close on the heels of the Civil Rights Act of 1964) finally ended the consideration of race, ancestry, or national origin in immigration to the United States. However, the act did limit total immigration from the Eastern Hemisphere to 170,000 per year, with a maximum of 20,000 per country, and 120,000 from the Western Hemisphere with no separate country limit.

TABLE 12.2	Percentage of Free Families Owning Slaves and Percentage of Slaves in the Population	
State	**Percentage of Free Families Owning Slaves in 1860**	**Percentage of Slaves in the Population in 1860**
Mississippi	49%	55%
South Carolina	46%	57%
Georgia	37%	44%
Alabama	35%	45%
Florida	34%	44%
Louisiana	29%	47%
Texas	28%	30%
North Carolina	28%	33%
Virginia	26%	31%
Tennessee	25%	25%
Kentucky	23%	20%
Arkansas	20%	26%
Missouri	13%	10%
Maryland	12%	13%
Delaware	3%	2%

In response to perceptions of increases in illegal immigration, overall annual limits on legal immigrants were raised significantly after 1985. The federal government instituted special screening measures for foreign-born Muslims, Arabs, or South Asians attempting to immigrate to the United States following the 9/11 terrorist attacks in 2001. Figure 12.2 displays the annual average number of new U.S. legal permanent residents from 1960 to 2015.

In 2015 the largest proportion of new legal permanent residents in the United States came from Asia (39.9%), and the next largest (34.8%) came from North America (including Mexico, Central America,

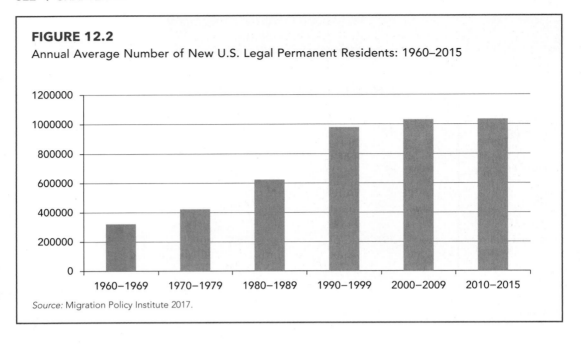

FIGURE 12.2

Annual Average Number of New U.S. Legal Permanent Residents: 1960–2015

Source: Migration Policy Institute 2017.

Canada, and the Caribbean) (Baugh and Witsman 2017). Others included Africans (9.6%), Europeans (8.2%), South Americans (6.9%), Oceanians (0.5%), and those of unknown geographic origin (0.1%). Table 12.3 shows the top twenty countries of origin for new legal permanent residents of the United States in 2015.

TABLE 12.3	Top Twenty Countries of Origin for New Legal Permanent Residents of the United States in 2015

Country of Birth	Number of Persons	Percent of Total
All Countries	1,051, 031	99.9%
Mexico	158,619	15.1%
China, People's Republic of	74,558	7.1%
India	64,116	6.1%
Philippines	56,478	5.4%
Cuba	54,396	5.2%
Dominican Republic	50,610	4.8%

(continued)

TABLE 12.3	Top Twenty Countries of Origin for New Legal Permanent Residents of the United States in 2015 (*continued*)

Country of Birth	Number of Persons	Percent of Total
Vietnam	30,832	2.9%
Iraq	21,107	2.0%
El Salvador	19,487	1.9%
Pakistan	18,057	1.7%
Jamaica	17,642	1.7%
Colombia	17,316	1.6%
Korea, South	17,138	1.6%
Haiti	16,967	1.6%
Bangladesh	13,570	1.3%
Iran	13,114	1.2%
Nepal	12,926	1.2%
Burma	12,808	1.2%
Canada	12,673	1.2%
United Kingdom	12,592	1.2%
All Other Countries	356,025	33.9%

Source: Baugh and Witsman 2017.

Why does the United States grant people born in other countries legal permanent residency? The reason most often cited for seeking legal permanent residency in the United States (by 64.6% of new legal permanent residents in 2015) is a familial relationship with a U.S. citizen or a legal permanent resident of the United States (Baugh and Witsman 2017). Others (13.7%) were accepted because of their occupations or valuable skills. Refugees and political asylum seekers accounted for 14.5 percent and persons winning the US immigration diversity lottery made up about 4.6 percent. (Various other reasons accounted for the remaining approximately 2.7% in 2015.) The annual immigration diversity lottery (also known as the green card lottery) permits interested people from countries around the world that have fewer than 50,000 residents immigrating to the United States over the previous five years to apply for permanent residency. A maximum of 50,000 persons per year from the eligible nations are randomly selected from all those who successfully complete the online application process (Baugh and Witsman 2017; U.S. Citizenship and Immigration Services 2017).

There were an estimated 11.3 million illegal (also referred to as unauthorized or undocumented) immigrants in the United States in 2016 (Krogstad, Passel and Cohn 2017). About 50 percent came from Mexico. Since 2009 the number of illegal immigrants from Mexico has declined, but the numbers from Asia and Central America have increased. Illegal immigrants make up about 5 percent of the overall U.S. labor force, but they comprise about 26 percent of agricultural workers and about 15 percent of construction workers. Just six states – California, Texas, Florida, New York, New Jersey, and Illinois – account for 59 percent of undocumented immigrants.

Social Problems Related to Excessive Population Growth Worldwide

Excessive population has been associated with a wide range of social problems. It may lead to widespread unemployment and poverty and may outstrip the capacity of a country to produce or acquire the food it needs to feed its people. As scarcity causes prices to rise dramatically, large groups of people may not be able to purchase the food necessary for survival, so they may turn to crime or political rebellion. Rapid population growth has preceded a number of revolutions. It contributed to the rebellion of tens of millions of poor peasants against China's Manchu dynasty in the nineteenth and twentieth centuries, paving the way for the successful communist revolution (DeFronzo 2015; Goldstone 1998b). More recently, it has contributed to the high youth unemployment and discontent that drove millions to take to the streets in the Arab uprisings of 2010 and 2011. Excessive population growth has also played a role in motivating thousands to join terrorist groups like ISIS.

Rapid population growth has also been associated with the depletion of natural resources, such as fresh water and fossil fuels. Deforestation may occur as people cut down trees for fuel and to provide more land to grow food. Increases in air and land pollution as fossil fuels are burned and waste is disposed of are also problematic (see Chapter 13).

URBANIZATION

Urbanization is the movement of people from rural areas into urban areas. There is, however, no uniform international definition of urban areas (United Nations 2016). Every country provides its own national census definition of urban, most often based on population size, such as places of 2,000 or more for some countries or 5,000 or more for other countries (Deuskar 2015). But some nations base their definition of urban on population density, the dominant type of economic activity in an area, other factors, or a combination of factors. What this means is that estimates of the percentage of the world's urban population are based on the diverse definitions used by all the world's countries rather than on a common shared definition.

Urbanization Worldwide

The movement of people from rural areas where people are engaged mainly in agricultural production to urban areas where economies are based largely on nonagricultural activities is caused by "pull" and "push" forces. People in the countryside are attracted to cities by factors such as the prospect of higher-paying jobs and business opportunities; educational resources (such as schools and libraries); utilities (including electricity); services (health care, transportation, and police); and forms of entertainment that are less available in rural settings. People are pushed out of rural areas by situations such as a lack of access to land to farm as rural populations grow in size and by limited availability of rural jobs as farming becomes more mechanized and the need for farm labor is reduced. Technological advances and industrialization caused an increase in urbanization in Europe, the United States, and several other countries, such as Australia, Japan, and South Africa, during the eighteenth and nineteenth centuries. In the following centuries, when much of the world's industrial development occurred outside of Europe and the United States, urbanization surged in Asia, Africa, and Latin America. The United Nations estimates that the world's population became slightly more urban than rural in 2007 (World Bank 2017b) and that by 2017 the proportion living in urban areas had climbed to 54.8 percent. In 2016 the United Nations Population Division (2016) identified thirty-one urban areas around the world as "megacities," meaning each had at least 10 million residents. Together they were home to 6.8 percent of the world's population. The megacities and their populations are listed in table 12.4.

TABLE 12.4 | The World's Megacities in 2016

Rank	City, Country	Population
1	Tokyo, Japan	38,140,000
2	Delhi, India	26,454,000
3	Shanghai, China	24,484,000
4	Mumbai (Bombay), India	21,357,000
5	São Paulo, Brazil	21,297,000
6	Beijing, China	21,240,000

(continued)

TABLE 12.4 | The World's Megacities in 2016 (*continued*)

Rank	City, Country	Population
7	Ciudad de México (Mexico City), Mexico	21,157,000
8	Kinki M. M. A. (Osaka), Japan	20,337,000
9	Al-Qahirah (Cairo), Egypt	19,128,000
10	New York-Newark, USA	18,604,000
11	Dhaka, Bangladesh	18,237,000
12	Karachi, Pakistan	17,121,000
13	Buenos Aires, Argentina	15,334,000
14	Kolkata (Calcutta), India	14,980,000
15	Istanbul, Turkey	14,365,000
16	Chongqing, China	13,744,000
17	Lagos, Nigeria	13,661,000
18	Manila, Philippines	13,131,000
19	Guangzhou, Guangdong, China	13,070,000
20	Rio de Janeiro, Brazil	12,981,000
21	Los Angeles-Long Beach-Santa Ana, USA	12,317,000
22	Moskva (Moscow), Russian Federation	12,260,000
23	Kinshasa, Democratic Republic of Congo	12,071,000
24	Tianjin, China	11,558,000
25	Paris, France	10,925,000
26	Shenzhen, China	10,828,000
27	Jakarta, Indonesia	10,483,000
28	Bangalore, India	10,456,000
29	London, United Kingdom	10,434,000
30	Chennai (Madras), India	10,163,000
31	Lima, Peru	10,072,000

Source: United Nations Population Division 2016.

Urbanization in the United States

In 1790, just after ratification of the U.S. Constitution, about 95 percent of U.S. residents lived in rural areas (U.S. Census 2017e). Urbanization was increasing as industry grew in northern cities such as Philadelphia, New York, and Boston. As in other industrializing nations around the world, many rural people were drawn to cities by the promise of manufacturing jobs, better housing and sanitation, greater educational opportunities for their children, better access to medical care, and greater safety because of protection afforded by urban police forces. In addition, improvements in farming technology reduced the need for farm labor, pushing many rural people to look for nonagricultural employment in cities. Since many low-income residents of the Eastern United States had the option of moving to the Western frontiers to establish farms and ranches in territories which would in the future become states, the need for laborers for the booming industrial cities was satisfied in part by new poor immigrants seeking a better life in the United States. Another source of labor for growing industry in the Northern states was the African American population of the South. Once white supremacist rule was re-established in many states of the former Confederacy following the Civil War, economic opportunities for African Americans in the region were extremely limited. Williams (2018) noted that the typical factory worker wage in the North in 1916 was three times what a black rural laborer could make in the South. The demand for industrial workers drew more than six million blacks to northern and western states in what has been called the "Great Migration" from 1916 to 1970 (Williams 2018). Between the 1910 and 1930 censuses, after which the effects of the Great Depression temporarily slowed migration to industrializing cities, the percentages of New York's and Pittsburgh's populations that were African American approximately doubled and for Chicago, Cleveland, and Detroit more than tripled (Gibson and Jung 2005). During this twenty-year period the white populations of these cities also grew, but at a slower pace than the increase of their black populations.

By 2017, 82 percent of Americans lived in urban areas (CIA 2017b). The U.S. Census (2016c) defines two types of urban areas: "urbanized areas" of 50,000 or more people and "urban clusters" of at least 2,500 but less than 50,000 people. Throughout the country there are 486 urbanized areas and 3,087 urban clusters. All those living outside urbanized areas or urban clusters are designated as rural residents. The level of urbanization varies significantly by state (Cox 2016b). The most urbanized states, California and New Jersey, both had about 95 percent of their populations living in urban areas. Four states had less than 50 percent of their populations urbanized: Maine, Mississippi, Vermont, and West Virginia.

Shortly after the end of World War II in 1945, many people started to move out of central cities to the urban areas bordering them, the suburbs. This process of **suburbanization** began for several reasons. As the nation's economy prospered and the postwar baby boom began, many people wanted to own their own homes with spacious yards and lawns for their children. The Federal Housing Administration assisted

suburbanization The settlement of people in suburbs, the urban areas beyond the borders of a neighboring city.

many thousands of returning war veterans in buying homes. Expansion of roads and the highway system, including through the Federal Aid Highway Act of 1956, and the affordability of cars in the postwar years made it easier to live in the suburbs. It is also likely that some whites moved to the suburbs to distance themselves from the growing African American populations of the cities.

Urban Problems Worldwide

Migration to cities can result in temporary (or even permanent) housing shortages, overcrowding, growth of *slums* (substandard housing) and *squatter settlements* (housing on land not owned by the occupants), strain on transportation systems, and sanitation problems that increase the risk of disease, which can spread easily in densely populated neighborhoods.

Another health hazard is that expanding urban industrial centers tend to generate high levels of concentrated pollution. Urbanization can also have less measurable effects, including a breakdown of the sense of community and cooperativeness that are typically part of life in rural villages. The urban environment is characterized by anonymity and heightened materialism, which may lead low-income residents to commit street crimes such as robberies and burglaries, and young people from better off households to engage in theft or fraud motivated by the desire to obtain more and more luxury goods (Chand 2016). Urban areas often provide contexts and customers that facilitate the development and profitability of organized crime. For example, cities such as Rio de Janeiro include mass markets for illicit drugs and prostitution (Glüsing 2013; Grant 2016). In some developing countries, certain urban areas, such as Bangkok, Thailand have become international centers of sex tourism for travelers from other nations (FBI 2016c; Grant 2016). Figure 12.3 shows the percentages of the world's population living in urban areas in 1960 and 2016.

A strained transportation system

FIGURE 12.3

Percentages of World Population Living in Urban or Rural Areas, 1960 and 2016

(a) World Population Urban or Rural, 1960   (b) World Population Urban or Rural, 2016

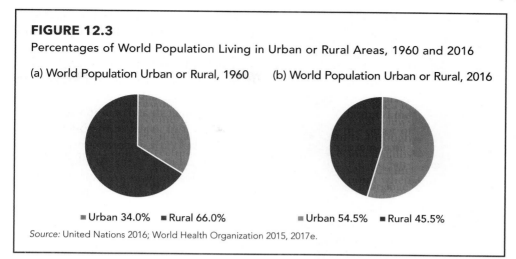

■ Urban 34.0%   ■ Rural 66.0%   ■ Urban 54.5%   ■ Rural 45.5%

Source: United Nations 2016; World Health Organization 2015, 2017e.

Urban Problems in the United States

The United States has a number of urban-related social problems. Beginning in the 1960s, manufacturing plants began moving out of American central cities. Technological advances eliminated some industrial processes and jobs. The advent of the interstate highway system, accelerated by the Federal Aid Highway Act of 1956, helped in allowing industry to locate away from railroad lines because large trucks could transport materials and products to and from certain types of factories. This provided more flexibility to build manufacturing plants in suburban areas. Much industry was also moved from northern cities to southern states, where there were fewer unionized workers and labor costs were lower. Improvements in international transportation shipment, such as container shipping (discussed in Chapter 11), allowed U.S. corporations to shift much of their manufacturing to low-income developing countries where labor costs were a small fraction of what they were in United States, and environmental regulations were often lacking or not enforced. University of Chicago sociologist William Julius Wilson (1997) describes how this process resulted in massive levels of unemployment and poverty, lack of residents' ability to financially support families, and a surge in one-parent households in many American cities. These consequences were in turn linked to increased crime rates and the rise of criminal youth gangs. Another problem for many cities is that departing industries often left behind chemically polluted, environmentally dangerous former factory sites called "brownfields" (described further in Chapter 13).

The loss of tax-paying industries and businesses and the cost of increased social and police services depleted city budgets, limiting funds that could have been used to improve local schools and flawed infrastructure like aging water and sewage systems. High crime rates, poor schools, and, in some cases, racism, motivated many white residents to leave cities for the suburbs. This "white flight" contributed to

Suburban sprawl

hypersegregation of certain urban neighborhoods where residents were overwhelmingly nonwhite and many were poor (Massey and Denton 1988, 1989, 1998).

Suburbanization is also linked to other problems. Many people drive long distances from their homes in the suburbs to their jobs in the cities, leading to traffic jams and increased air pollution from car exhaust. It also increases the likelihood of injury or death from highway accidents. In addition, spending so many hours behind the wheel can be stressful and also leaves much less time for exercise, heightening the risk of obesity (Hoehner et al. 2012).

Another problem associated with suburbanization is what has been termed **suburban (urban) sprawl**. Suburban sprawl is poorly planned suburban development characterized by elements such as the use of large quantities of land to house relatively small numbers of people, destruction of farmland or open green areas, displacement of wildlife, and lack of sidewalks, bike lanes, or proper design to facilitate pedestrian or bicycle travel for work, school, shopping, or other activities. Sprawl promotes heavy reliance on cars, with all the associated problems.

AGING

Aging in the demographic sense refers to the growth of the percentage of older people in a nation's population. In a broader sense, aging also encompasses the economic, job, health, and psychological issues experienced by persons as they grow older. The sections below describe aging and problems related to aging worldwide and in the United States.

Aging Worldwide

The proportion of people age sixty-five or older is growing dramatically in most countries around the world due to lower birth rates and longer life spans, especially in many of the advanced industrial nations. The World Bank (2017c) reported that whereas in 1960 5 percent of world's population was sixty-five or older the percentage grew to 8.5 percent in 2016. But the increase varies significantly by a country's income level. High-income countries went from 9 percent in 1960 to 17 percent in 2016, upper-middle-income countries from 4 to 9 percent, and lower-middle-income countries 4 to 5 percent. But for low-income countries the percent was 3 percent in 1960 and 3 percent in 2016. The reasons for low birth rates and population aging also vary

hypersegregation The very high concentration of people with particular characteristics, typically similar race or ethnicity identities and income levels, in geographical areas.

suburban (urban) sprawl Poorly planned suburban development characterized by elements such as the use of large quantities of land to house relatively small numbers of people, destruction of farmland or open green areas, displacement of wildlife, and lack of sidewalks, bike lanes, or proper design to facilitate pedestrian or bicycle travel.

among countries. They can include the high expense of raising a child and the commitment of many women to full-time careers, leaving less opportunity to raise a child (Kassam et al. 2015; Reville 2016). Another factor in some nations is a poor economy, which means many people lack the incomes necessary to support a family. In particular, the trend toward aging populations affects Japan, the United States, China, the Republic of Korea (South Korea), and virtually all of Europe (CIA 2018b; Goldstone 2010).

Aging in the United States

The World Bank (2017c) data showed that the percentage of the U.S. population sixty-five or older in 1960 was 9 percent but grew to 15 percent in 2016. A decline in birthrates through much of this period, as well as an increase in life span, contributed to the aging of the U.S. population. By 2017 the birth rate in the United States, which had generally been below the level needed to replace the number of people dying since 1971, fell to a thirty-year low (Chappell 2018; Rugaber 2018). The reason the United States has not experienced a loss in population is because of the millions of people immigrating into the country in recent decades. Immigrants are now 17.1 percent of the U.S. labor force.

Aging Problems Worldwide

While Europeans sixty years of age or older are expected to increase 47 percent by 2050, working-age Europeans are projected to decrease by 24 percent, a loss of some 120 million workers. At the same time, as the percentage of active workers needed to grow the economy is shrinking, pension payments to retirees will climb. A similar trend has begun to take place in many developing countries as they increasingly urbanize, technologically improve, and experience declining birth rates and increasing life spans. Some nations with decreasing working-age populations due to lower birth rates have allowed large numbers of young people seeking economic opportunities to enter from poorer nations. In Europe, immigrants have often come from Islamic nations of the Middle East or Africa, leading in some cases to internal tensions between newcomers and prior residents fearing loss of national identity or Christian traditions. In elections, the share of the vote going to anti-immigrant political parties has tended to increase. Another problem generated by aging populations is increased expenditures on health care. Since people sixty and older tend to have increasing needs for health services, medical expenditures are growing significantly (see Chapter 9 on increased life span). Some nations, including Germany, Japan, and Russia, and almost all Eastern European countries, have actually been experiencing population loss. In Japan, more adult diapers are sold than children's diapers (Rugaber 2018). The lack of young adults to join an aging population's workforce also means that fewer individuals are available to serve in the armed forces, which can potentially threaten military security. A nation that continues to lose population year after year may experience economic and military decline.

Table 12.5 shows the thirty-six nations or territories estimated in 2017 to be losing population, as well as the rates of population decline. For most of these, a birth rate below what is necessary to maintain population stability was the primary reason for population loss. For several others, particularly island nations or territories, emigration (people leaving) was an important contributing factor.

TABLE 12.5	Countries or Territories Losing Population: Estimated Annual Percent Loss in 2017
Country or Territory	**Percent Annual Population Loss**
Cook Islands	−2.80%
Puerto Rico	−1.70%
American Samoa	−1.30%
Saint Pierre and Miquelon	−1.10%
Lebanon	−1.10%
Lithuania	−1.10%
Moldova	−1.10%
Latvia	−1.10%
Bulgaria	−.60%
Estonia	−.60%
Serbia	−.50%
Croatia	−.50%
Northern Mariana Islands	−.50%
Micronesia, Federated States of	−.50%
Ukraine	−.40%
Romania	−.30%

(continued)

TABLE 12.5	Countries or Territories Losing Population: Estimated Annual Percent Loss in 2017 (*continued*)
Country or Territory	**Percent Annual Population Loss**
Slovenia	−.30%
Saint Vincent and the Grenadines	−.30%
Montenegro	−.30%
Cuba	−.30%
Hungary	−.30%
Virgin Islands	−.30%
Trinidad and Tobago	−.20%
Armenia	−.20%
Belarus	−.20%
Germany	−.20%
Bosnia and Herzegovina	−.20%
Japan	−.20%
Poland	−.10%
Maldives	−.10%
Greece	−.10%
Russia	−.10%
Tonga	−.10%
Niue (2014 est.)	−.03%
Svalbard (2014 est.)	−.03%
Tokelau (2014 est.)	−.01%

Source: CIA 2017g.

Aging Problems in the United States

The decline in the U.S. birth rate and the growth in the percentage of the aged population pose problems for the economy, government finances, and national security. As in other technologically advanced societies, the percentage of working people in the United States has been shrinking relative to the percentage of retired persons. Since people nearing retirement tend to increase savings rather than spending, the aging population results in a slowdown in the number of people purchasing homes, cars, and other costly items. This tends to limit economic growth (Rugaber 2018). Companies that sell products for children or young adults can also be damaged by an aging population. Toys R Us, for example, which announced in March of 2018 that it would close or sell all of its 735 stores, had in 2017 blamed the dropping birth rate as one possible reason for its financial problems (Garfield 2018). Another issue of the aging U.S. population is the declining number of active workers whose social security taxes go to support those currently receiving social security benefits. About 9 percent of U.S. residents aged sixty-five or over are below the poverty line, but without Social Security it would be 39.2 percent, an additional 15,333,000 in poverty (22 million more in poverty if children and other adults dependent on Social Security or Social Security recipients are included) (Romig 2018). The ratio of workers paying Social Security taxes (which fund benefits) to each person being paid Social Security benefits was 16.5 in 1950, 3.2 in 1980, 2.8 in 2013, and estimated to be about 2.7 in 2018 and only 2.3 in 2030 (Peterson Foundation 2018; Social Security 2018). This means that without some significant changes to the program, Social Security will cease to be able to fulfill its obligations by 2034. In addition, Medicare, the federal health care coverage system for those sixty-five or older, is becoming more and more costly as the percentage of this segment of the population grows. The declining percentage of young adults may also lead to a shortage of people willing to join the U.S. all-volunteer armed forces. Finally, it should be noted that the living conditions of persons sixty-five and older in the United States vary greatly in part as a result of inequalities of opportunity and economic inequalities people have experienced earlier in life. This is reflected in the fact that more than twice the percent of Hispanics and blacks sixty-five and older lived below the poverty line in 2016 compared to non-Hispanic whites and 10.6 percent of women sixty-five and older lived in poverty compared to only 7.6 percent of men (Cubanski et al. 2018).

RESPONSES TO SOCIAL PROBLEMS RELATED TO POPULATION, URBANIZATION, AND AGING

Reduce Population Growth in High-Birth-Rate Countries by Improving Women's Education and Employment Levels

Providing knowledge of and access to effective contraceptive methods for both women and men can help lower a society's fertility rate. Improvement in women's educational levels that allow them to participate in

TABLE 12.6	Total Fertility Rates (TFR), by Level of Women's Education for Specified Less-Developed Regions of the World			
	Level of Education			
	None	Primary	Secondary or Higher	TFR Difference = None − secondary or higher
Sub-Saharan Africa	6.4	5.5	3.7	−2.7
Northern Africa	4.7	3.6	2.8	−1.9
Western Asia	6.4	4.6	3.5	−2.9
Rest of Asia	4.1	3.5	2.7	−1.4
Latin America and the Caribbean	5.8	4.5	2.6	−3.2

Source: United Nations Department of Economic and Social Affairs Population Division 2003.

occupations outside of the home tends to lower fertility rates by providing women with the means to support themselves and by allowing them sources of fulfillment beyond those of the traditional female stereotype of motherhood and housekeeper. Table 12.6 presents total fertility rates for each of the specified less developed regions of the world. The table shows, for example, that in Sub-Saharan Africa the average was 6.4 children per woman with no education compared to an average of 3.7 children per woman with secondary or higher education. Women with secondary or higher education had an average of 2.7 fewer children than women with no education.

Social Movements: Malala's Global Girls' Right to Education Movement

Malala Yousafzai

Malala Yousafzai was born in 1997 in Mingora, a town in the Swat District of northwest Pakistan. Her father, Ziauddin, ran a school near the family's home and worked to increase educational opportunities in Pakistan, which has one of the world's highest rates of children not attending school (UNICEF 2018). He and his daughter Malala became public opponents of the Islamic fundamentalist Taliban's actions to limit education and prevent girls from attending school.

(continued)

Social Movements (*continued*)

As the Taliban tightened its military grip on the Swat District, it banned television, music, and women's shopping. Using an alias, Malala began a BBC Urdu language blog in early 2009 describing what the Taliban was doing in Swat and her fear that her school would be shut down. Later that year, twelve-year-old Malala, her father, and the Taliban repression of female education were the subjects of a documentary entitled *Class Dismissed: The Death of Female Education*, for the *New York Times* (Elleck and Ashraf 2009; Malala Fund 2014). Around the same time, it was revealed that Malala was the writer of the BBC blog. Despite repeated intimidation and death threats, she continued to call for girls' right to education. On October 9, 2012, a gunman boarded her school bus and shot Malala in the head as she and her friends were returning home from school. Malala was rushed to a medical facility in critical condition and soon flown to a hospital in Birmingham, England. She was joined by her family and treated until her release in January 2013. The assassination attempt against Malala was condemned around the world. In November 2012, a little more than one month after the attack on Malala, the Pakistan National Assembly passed a Right To Free and Compulsory Education Bill intended to guarantee free education to Pakistani children aged five to sixteen years of age (*Express Tribune* 2012). Because of Malala's courageous and persistent efforts on behalf of all girls' right to education, in 2014 she became the youngest person ever awarded the Nobel Peace Prize, at age seventeen.

The attempted murder of Malala caused an explosion of support for the global movement to ensure girls and women the right to education. Malala has become a global social activist fighting for the estimated 59 million children (mostly girls) who are denied even a primary formal education because of economic, social, legal, or political factors (UNICEF 2018). One aspect of this international movement is the Malala Fund, which raises money to increase awareness of the beneficial social and economic impacts of girls' education (including greater control over contraception) and to help empower girls to understand their capabilities and demand change.

What are your thoughts?
(1) What do you think should be done about the Taliban or other groups or governments that try to restrict girls' or women's education? (2) Do you think empowering women is important for population control? Why? Why not?

Reduce Problems Related to Urbanization Worldwide

There are several major approaches to reducing social problems related to urbanization. Local government efforts may be directed toward raising funds and enforcing laws. For example, companies that plan to build manufacturing plants in an urban area may be required to minimize the release of harmful substances into the air and dispose of waste without polluting either water or land. Local authorities can also strive to ensure that city budgets fund needed services, such as education and health care, as well as expansions and repairs of crucial infrastructure needed to provide clean water, sewage and trash disposal, energy, and transportation.

Other strategies try to prevent major urban problems by reducing the motivation to move to cities or slowing migration to urban centers. One approach is for government and/or privately owned business interests to undertake large-scale rural development programs that improve the economies, job and income opportunities, and educational and health care services in the countryside. Another option is to couple effective urban planning and development with government-enforced quotas for migration to those cities most vulnerable to deteriorating conditions. This involves matching the construction of urban infrastructure and the availability of crucial services to the flow of urban immigrants. In other words, the government would ensure that the number of people moving to a city each year would roughly correspond to the city's capacity to provide them all with sufficient job opportunities, infrastructure, and services.

Reduce Problems Related to Urbanization in the United States

Several of the most serious urban problems in the United States could be drastically reduced by development programs that expand the number of successful businesses to the point where city economies are capable of providing full employment at wages high enough to lift workers out of poverty and allow them to raise children if they so desire. This would require subsidized free or very low-cost training to give prospective employees necessary high-tech job skills. Achievement of this goal would be expected to reduce poverty and crime and raise municipal revenues, which could then be used to improve schools, rebuild deteriorating infrastructure, and clean up and redevelop former industrial sites for new businesses or residential buildings. Some of the old industrial sites could be turned into parks or other green areas within city boundaries (a process referred to as "de-urbanization").

Other more limited measures have been proposed or attempted to cope with urban problems. One has been referred to as *gentrification*. This involves clearing old buildings of any remaining residents and transforming them into high-priced apartments or condominiums. These are then marketed to professional or business people interested in living close to their place of work rather than having a long commute and also being able to enjoy the entertainments, restaurants, and cultural attractions a city may have to offer. Recruiting such well-paid new residents improves the local economy and increases the flow of tax revenue for the city's budget. While beneficial for city finances, gentrification can also have negative consequences. Removing low-income persons from buildings to be demolished or refurbished without providing suitable alternative residences can force them to live in overcrowded and substandard housing or even become homeless.

The federal government agency established in 1965 to deal with urban issues is the United States Department of Housing and Urban Development (HUD) (Kleniewski and Thomas 2011). Its creation was preceded by the Housing Act of 1949, which expanded the role of the federal government in urban development by providing increased support for mortgage insurance, slum clearance, construction projects, and the building of public housing for low-income persons. HUD's aim is to contribute to the development of inclusive, financially sustainable, and environmentally friendly communities and the availability of affordable housing. One HUD program especially important for cities is the Community Development Block Grants (CDBG). CDBG provides grants to hundreds of city and state governments for projects such as slum removal, construction of new housing for low- or middle-income people, rehabilitation of old residential, commercial, or school buildings, and improvement of infrastructure such as streets, sidewalks, and water and sewer lines (U.S. Department of Housing and Urban Development 2017a).

Other efforts to solve urban problems include Empowerment Zones (EZs) and Community Development Corporations (CDCs). EZs are government-designated areas of high poverty and unemployment where new businesses and job opportunities are badly needed. Within EZs businesses are given special tax incentives (U.S. Department of Housing and Urban Development 2017b). These include tax credits for each of their employees who reside in the EZ and a sizeable tax deduction for certain business equipment. CDCs are nonprofit, community-based organizations that receive funding from the federal Community Economic Development program (Community-wealth. org 2017; Office of Community Services 2017). They are intended to revitalize the areas where they are located, usually low-income neighborhoods. While major aims are developing affordable housing, sustainable businesses, and job opportunities, they are often also involved in projects to improve sanitation, streets, education, and social services. The Obama administration initiated another program for preserving, rehabilitating, building, and operating affordable rental housing for very low-income people, the national Housing Trust Fund (HTF). The HTF gave $174 million to the states in 2016 and scheduled $219 million for 2017 (National Low Income Housing Coalition 2017).

A number of ideas have been suggested to slow the growth of suburban sprawl or reduce some of the problems associated with it. Increasing the attractions of cities and the availability of low-cost urban housing could persuade many people to live in cities rather than suburbs. One way this could be facilitated is through the accelerated conversion of old urban factory sites for new apartments and condominiums. This approach, plus expanded and improved mass transit between a city and its suburbs could significantly limit the number of cars on the road, traffic jams, and air pollution.

New suburban development should be designed to allow and encourage walking or bicycling to parks and stores. Older suburbs could be modified to add features like sidewalks and, where possible, bicycle lanes or separate bicycle trails.

Worldwide Responses to Aging Problems

replacement-level fertility The average number of children born to each woman aged fifteen to forty-four necessary to maintain a stable population size in a country, generally about 2.1 for technologically advanced societies.

European nations typically require a fertility rate of about 2.1 (called **replacement-level fertility**) to maintain a stable population level (BBC 2006). However, factors such as the desire to achieve a good professional standing, make a high income, and have the freedom and leisure time to enjoy it, and the high cost of raising and educating children have led to much lower fertility rates in many European countries and other technologically advanced societies. The World Bank (2017a) reported that in 2015 fertility rates were only 1.5 in Germany, Japan, Serbia, Switzerland, and Ukraine; 1.4 in Italy and Hungary, 1.3 in Greece,

Poland, and Spain; and 1.2 in Portugal, Singapore, and South Korea. In response to such rates, a number of low-fertility-rate nations are providing economic incentives to women and families to have more children (*Direct News* 2014; Kassam et al. 2015; Reville 2016). These include tax breaks, low-cost child care centers, long paid parental leaves, and as much as a year of maternity leave with pay . As noted in the Special Topics feature, Russia provides a large cash bonus payment for a biological or adopted second child.

Technologically advanced societies may consider several possible policies to deal with problems related to their aging populations. You have already learned about one approach: encouraging more people to have children. Governments can give substantial tax breaks or even cash payments to couples to have at least one or two children. Raising children can be made easier if the government and/or private employers provide free child care services and job leave for new parents. Another approach is to permit or even promote the government-managed immigration of young people from developing countries. Goldstone (2010) suggests that this could reduce overpopulation and the threat of social instability in developing states. The immigrants would likely send some of their earnings to their families back home, helping the economy of the developing countries as well. Some would later return to their home countries with new useful skills, knowledge, and work experience, and the immigrants would increase the active workforce and provide a substantial

Special Topics: Russia's Demographic Disaster and Partial Recovery

Following the end of the Cold War and the disintegration of the Soviet Union in 1991, Russia's economy deteriorated rapidly. The Russian gross domestic product (GDP) plummeted by as much as 45 percent (Millar 2000:330). In comparison, between 1929 and 1933, during the Great Depression, the drop in U.S. per capita GDP was "a little less than 25 percent" (Millar 1999:323).

The cost of living rose significantly, and by 1999 40 percent of Russians were living in poverty (World Bank 2004). Many Russians believed that they could no longer afford to raise a child, causing the birth rate to fall so dramatically that by 2002 the death rate (which had risen rapidly due to increases in alcohol- and drug-related deaths, and homicides) exceeded the birth rate by 70 percent (Powell 2002, 344). By 2006 Russia's population of about 142 million was declining by 700,000 each year. Especially given its vast territory (close to twice the size of the United States), a relatively small and shrinking population threatened Russia's ability to maintain a sufficiently large labor force and effective military. In response to the desperate situation, the government called upon its people to have more babies and offered financial incentives, including a $9,200 bonus (in U.S. dollars) to women who would have a second child (Gross 2006). This was later increased to $12,500 for a second child by birth or adoption (*Direct News* 2014). These measures, along with an improved economy that lowered the proportion in poverty to about 15 percent, contributed to a rise in the birth rate. By 2017, Russia's population was still declining but losses had dropped to about 114,000 per year (CIA 2017h).

What are your thoughts?
(1) Do you think that offering couples a payment of $12,500 to have a child would succeed in increasing the number of births?
(2) What other incentives might be effective?

flow of taxes to support the services and pensions of retired workers in the developed countries. However, many of those seeking to immigrate come from African and Islamic nations with significant cultural differences from the populations of technologically advanced nations, which can create other social problems, including religious-ethnic conflicts and the rise of anti-immigrant political movements and parties. Still another approach is that aging population countries that once gave thousands of their children up for adoption by people in other nations, including Russia and South Korea, are prioritizing domestic adoptions.

Responses to Aging Problems in the United States

The United States, along with many other nations, is faced with multiple issues related to aging. One approach is to try to increase the proportion of the population who are active in the labor force paying the taxes necessary to support programs upon which the aged heavily rely, such as Social Security and Medicare. This goal might be achieved if the birth rate were to significantly increase. In the past, a strongly growing economy has led to an increase in births. But improving the economy may not be sufficient if workers cannot afford child care or the costs of educating children. Creating a significant paid maternal and paternal leave system and low-cost or free child care for working parents would likely increase births. Another possible measure for maintaining or increasing the percentage of active workers, one the United States has relied on in the face of declining birth rates for decades to ensure a growing population, is immigration.

For the millions who are sixty-five or over, sufficient funding for growing Medicare expenditures, estimated at $625 billion in 2019 (Amadeo 2018), must be provided. Social Security in 2019 is estimated to cost $1,046 billion ($1.046 trillion). Proposals for protecting Social Security include raising the age at which people can start receiving benefits, reducing benefits to all recipients or to financially affluent persons, and/or funding the program in new ways.

SOCIOLOGICAL APPROACHES TO POPULATION, URBANIZATION, AND AGING

Sociological perspectives provide insights into how social and cultural factors have affected population growth and loss, population aging, and how aspects of population change have influenced society. They also provide varying analyses of the impact of social forces on urbanization, how urbanization has influenced population change, and how urban social problems develop and might be solved.

Structural-Functional Perspective

The structural-functional perspective views population, urbanization, and aging as elements of a coordinated and productive socioeconomic system. Population change (growth or decline) should be in the direction and degree that meets the needs of the social system. For example, if an economy is expanding and requires more participants, the population should be growing at a rate that will provide the required number. As individuals age, they may lose the capacity to perform some of their social roles adequately and may disengage from them. For example, U.S. passenger airline pilots are not allowed to continue flying commercially once they reach the age of sixty-five. After disengagement from one role, another may be entered. Retired airline pilots may become flight simulator instructors.

Two major trends have played roles in altering society and influencing population growth to adapt to the needs of the changing social system: technological progress and urbanization. These processes have contributed to accomplishing the demographic transition, the downward shift in birth and death rates. In western Europe this occurred from the late eighteenth century through to the mid-twentieth century. Death rates were high before the demographic transition because sources of water were often unsafe and medical technology was relatively crude and ineffective. Cultures typically supported high birth rates because many births were needed to ensure that the population grew or at least was maintained in the face of so many deaths. In addition, a high birth rate played a useful role in agricultural societies because children could be used to work the land and tend farm animals. As technology advanced and large-scale industrialization and urbanization got underway, health conditions improved and the death rate dropped for a number of reasons. One is that modern sewage systems protect water sources, which provides greater access to clean, safe drinking water. Another is that new vaccines and better medical treatment more effectively combat disease and prevent people from dying from injuries.

Although death rates fall quickly since people universally want to prolong life, birth rates stay high for an extended period because they are usually rooted in widely shared traditional cultural concepts of gender roles that take a long time to change. Between the beginning and end of the demographic transition in Europe there was a decades-long population explosion just at the time that a massive new labor force was needed to rapidly expand urban industry. Over time, the changed living conditions in urban industrial areas, including longer life spans and the need to provide extensive and expensive educations to give children the capability to be successful at the new jobs in the advancing economic system, cause birth rates to drop, completing the demographic transition. According to the structural-functional perspective, low fertility rates and slow population growth, along with extensive education for children, generally fit the needs of technologically advanced societies. However, if birth rates fall below the level needed to replace those who leave the population through death or emigration, and there is a lack of sufficient immigration of young people from other societies, the proportion of older people in the population will begin to increase (the population will age).

Conflict Perspective

The conflict perspective focuses on the relationships among population, urbanization, and aging and inequalities in education, wealth, and power. As material conditions change in the early stage of the demographic transition, it is generally the wealthiest and most highly educated who break first with outdated fertility traditions and lower their birth rates. Less-educated people remain tied to the old cultural traditions and continue to have high birth rates. This contributes to poverty and crowded conditions in cities that leaves many people without the resources to provide adequately for their children. So the hardships of the demographic transition are borne primarily by those with the least education.

Links between population factors and forms of social conflict are also highlighted by the conflict perspective. For example, periods of increased birth rates cause population explosions and temporary **youth bulges** (increases in the proportion of the population composed of children, teenagers, and young adults.) Youth bulges have often preceded popular uprisings and revolutions throughout history (Goldstone 1998b). If food output does not keep up with population increase, or if an event such as drought, flooding, or war disrupts agricultural production, food shortages can lead to mass distress and insurrections against rulers. A youth bulge also increases the likelihood of rebellion in times of social discontent because unmarried young people are typically less restrained by responsibilities and more likely to engage in potentially risky behavior such as protesting government leaders and their policies. For example, a large U.S. youth bulge coincided with the massive civil rights and anti–Vietnam War protests of the 1960s.

The conflict approach suggests that high levels of economic inequality, poverty, and unemployment motivate lower-income people to oppose immigration for fear of excessive competition for jobs and resources. The conflict perspective also draws attention to the risk of social victimization of elderly persons. In contrast to the structural-functionalist approach, which describes the disengagement of older people from previous economic roles and a shift to new roles or to total retirement and leisure activities, the conflict perspective emphasizes that the weakened economic, physical, or mental states of many elderly people make them vulnerable to abuse by caretakers, neglect by government officials and insurance companies, and exploitation by criminals.

Racial/Ethnic-Conflict Perspective The racial/ethnic-conflict perspective focuses on how racial/ethnic prejudice and discrimination contributes to population, urban, and aging problems. Members of one racial/ethnic group may commit genocide. For example, DNA research indicates that the Native American population of the Americas declined rapidly after the arrival of Europeans (Than 2011) due to factors such as war and enslavement. A relatively recent example of intentional genocide was Hutu extremists' killings of 800,000 men, women and children in Rwanda in 1994. The victims included as much as three-quarters of the Tutsi population, as well as thousands of Hutus who opposed the massacre (United Human Rights Council 2015). In the United States, economic policies coupled with racial and ethnic discrimination contributed to the geographic urban hypersegregation of poor minority areas from affluent white areas, a situation referred to as "American

youth bulge An increase in the proportion of the population composed of children, teenagers, and young adults

apartheid" (Massey and Denton 1998). The racial/ethnic-conflict perspective also emphasizes how the advantages and disadvantages of different racial and ethnic groups add up during the life course, so that among those sixty-five and older the percentage living in poverty is much higher for blacks and Hispanics than for non-Hispanic whites.

Feminist-Conflict Perspective The feminist-conflict perspective focuses on how patriarchal social and cultural systems influence population dynamics through male domination of women. As you have already learned, birth rates tend to be high in countries where most women have been denied educational and workplace opportunities, and knowledge of and access to contraceptive methods. Completion of the demographic transition by achieving a low birth rate is accomplished in part through abandoning the idea that women can only be fulfilled by having many children. Women should be allowed to achieve high levels of education, which can reduce birth rates and limit population growth in developing countries. The feminist perspective also emphasizes how men's advantages help explain why poverty is more common among women, including in urban areas and among people sixty-five and older.

Symbolic-Interactionist Perspective

As you have already learned, the symbolic interactionist perspective emphasizes that what people learn from their culture, and interacting with others influences their attitudes. This includes attitudes toward factors related to population growth, such as family size. Some religions strongly value high fertility rates and discourage or even forbid birth control, emphasizing that having children is the purpose of sexual relations and marriage. People brought up in such cultures tended to believe it is both natural and God's will to have large families. The symbolic-interactionist perspective suggests that interaction with persons who value small families (or exposure to cultures that do) should have the effect of reducing birth rates. Urbanization, living in crowded cities, and the high cost of raising children in urban areas contributed to changing attitudes toward how many children to have. This process helps countries complete the demographic transition and slow population growth, but also leads in many societies to the aging of populations.

CHAPTER REVIEW

Population

Population problems differ among nations. Some of the poorest and least developed are burdened by rapid population growth. Many of the technologically advanced countries are experiencing aging and even population loss. Rapid population growth in less-developed countries has been associated with widespread unemployment, poverty, and malnutrition, and has contributed to loss of natural resources and increased air and land pollution. Africa as a region has the highest birth rates and is expected to contribute about half of the world's population growth between 2015 and 2050.

The U.S. population is still growing, but much of this increase is due to immigration. Since the 1990s, about a million people each year legally immigrate to the United States. In 2015, more legal permanent residents came from Asia than any other region. There are around eleven million illegal immigrants in the United States, the majority from Latin American countries.

Urbanization

More than half the world's population and more than four out of five Americans now live in urban areas. Rapid migration to cities results in housing shortages, overcrowding, growth of slums, strain on transportation systems, and sanitation problems. Expanding urban industrial centers generate high levels of pollution.

In the past the industrialization process drew millions of foreign immigrants and African Americans from southern states to northern American cities in search of new opportunities. Beginning in the 1960s manufacturing plants began moving out of American central cities, causing unemployment to rise dramatically, an increase in one-parent households, and growth of crime and criminal youth gangs. Many middle-class whites had begun moving out of American cities to suburbs after World War II, leading to urban racial and economic hypersegregation. Loss of tax revenue depleted city budgets, limiting funds that could have been used to improve schools and infrastructure like aging water and sewage systems.

Aging

In many advanced industrial nations, the proportion of people age sixty or older is growing dramatically due to lower birth rates and longer life spans. Many technologically advanced countries are actually losing population. The United States also has an aging population, but a relatively high level of immigration has allowed the country to continue growing its population and workforce.

Responses to Social Problems Related to Population, Urbanization, and Aging

One way to reduce birth rates in high birth rates countries is to provide more education and job opportunities for women. Another is providing more knowledge of and better access to contraceptive methods.

An approach to dealing with urbanization problems in developing countries is to reduce the number of people moving to cities by increasing economic opportunities and improving needed services in rural areas. Government quotas offer another option. This approach allows people to move to an urban area only in proportion to the city's capacity to provide job opportunities and necessary services.

U.S. urban problems could be reduced by the expansion of successful urban-based businesses to the point where city economies are capable of providing full employment at wages high enough to lift workers out of poverty and allow them to raise children. Free or very low-cost training could give prospective urban employees necessary high-tech job skills. These measures would reduce poverty and crime and raise municipal revenues, which could then be used to improve schools, rebuild deteriorating infrastructure, and clean up and redevelop former industrial sites for new businesses or residential buildings.

A number of low-birth-rate nations with aging populations are providing incentives to women and families to have more children. Another approach to reversing population loss in low-birth-rate countries is immigration.

In the United States the Social Security and Medicare programs are in danger of being overwhelmed by the growing proportion of the country's aged population. Paid parental leave and free child care have been proposed as ways to increase the birth rate. Social Security and Medicare may be modified by increasing the age at which persons are eligible for these programs, or by reducing benefits to all or possibly just relatively affluent persons.

Sociological Approaches to Population, Urbanization, and Aging

The structural-functional perspective views population, urbanization, and aging as elements of a coordinated and productive socioeconomic system. Population change (growth or decline) should be in the direction and degree that fits with the needs of the social system. The demographic transition, the shift from relatively high birth and death rates to relatively low birth and death rates, brought about in part by urbanization, is a process that helps the population characteristics of societies adapt to the change from low-technology, agricultural-based economies to high-technology, industrial-based economies. One result over the long term can be aging populations, a shrinking labor force, and even population loss.

The conflict perspective focuses on how population problems are related to inequalities in education, wealth and power, and to social conflict. For example, during the demographic transition less-educated people remain tied to the old cultural traditions and continue to have high birth rates for much longer than highly educated people. This contributes to the poorly educated living in poverty and crowded cities without the resources to provide adequately for their children. Thus the hardships of the demographic transition are borne primarily by those with the least education.

The racial/ethnic-conflict perspective focuses on how racial/ethnic prejudice and discrimination contributes to population problems including hypersegregation in U.S. urban areas. The feminist-conflict perspective emphasizes that patriarchal social systems influence population. In countries where most women have been denied educational and workplace opportunities and access to contraceptive methods, birth rates tend to be high. The conflict approach also emphasizes that inequality of opportunities early in life and economic inequalities throughout the life course lead to inequalities among the aged, including much higher levels of poverty among aged black and Hispanic U.S. residents, as well as women compared to non-Hispanic whites and men.

The symbolic-interactionist perspective emphasizes that what we learn from our culture and from interacting with others influences our attitudes toward population growth, population decline, immigration, and aged persons, and whether to have many children, only a few, or none. Urbanization over time affects attitudes toward all of these elements of society.

KEY TERMS

aging, p. 317
birth rate, p. 318
fertility rate, p. 316
hypersegregation, p. 330
population growth, p. 316

replacement-level fertility, p. 338
suburban (urban) sprawl, p. 330
suburbanization, p. 327
urbanization, p. 317
youth bulge, p. 342

DISCUSSION QUESTIONS

1. What measures, if any, should be taken to slow down or stop world population growth?

2. What are the main barriers to women's educational and economic opportunities around the world that influence birth rates and population growth? How can these barriers be overcome?

3. Should countries that are experiencing labor shortages because of their aging populations try to solve this problem by encouraging immigration of young people from other nations or by using another approach? Explain your answer.

4. Do you think that measures should be taken in technologically advanced nations to limit suburbanization? What would such measures be and could they succeed?

5. Should governments in developing countries try to limit migration from rural areas to cities? Explain your position. Can you think of an approach that would be effective in accomplishing this?

6. What measures could be taken to reduce the U.S. urban problem hypersegregation?

7. From your point of view, which sociological perspective is most important in providing insights into the development of population problems and what to do about them? What about urban problems and problems associated with aging populations? Explain your answers.

CHAPTER 13

The Environment

CHAPTER OBJECTIVES

- Describe the major environmental problems facing the United States and the world.
- Describe the concepts of environmental injustice and environmental racism.
- Explain the major sociological perspectives on the environment.
- Explain the causes of environmental problems.
- Describe responses to environmental problems.

THE U.S. NATIONAL OCEANIC *and Atmospheric Administration (NOAA) reported that 2017 was the third-warmest year ever recorded following the record-breaking years of 2016, 2015, and 2014 (Miller 2017; Stapp 2015; U.S. National Oceanic and Atmospheric Administration 2018). In fact, since record keeping started in the 1880s, seventeen of the eighteen hottest years have occurred since 2000. Ocean surface temperatures have increased. High temperatures melted ice in the Arctic and Antarctic regions and raised ocean levels. Long-term temperature increase and lack of sufficient rain and snowfall have caused lakes and reservoirs in a number of states to shrink, reducing the availability of fresh water. At least thirty-nine states are expected to experience water shortages during the next ten years (Kincaid 2015; Megerian, Stevens, and Boxall 2015). Arizona and Nevada, for example, which are both expected to double their 2000 populations by 2030, will be hard pressed to meet increased water needs. And worldwide, the United Nations estimates that within fifteen years almost half the world's population will be living in countries unable to sufficiently satisfy water needs.*

The challenge of providing access to clean water is just one of the world's great environmental problems.

ENVIRONMENTAL PROBLEMS

Global Warming

Global warming refers to the slow but steady warming of the Earth's land, oceans, and atmosphere. Research indicates that the planet's temperature rose by between about 0.7 to 1.4 degrees Fahrenheit over the last 100 years (about 0.4 to 0.8 degrees Celsius) (Live Science 2017). Intergovernmental Panel on Climate scientists have predicted that by the year 2100 average global temperatures could increase by between approximately 2.5 and 10.4 degrees Fahrenheit (about 1.4 and 5.8 degrees Celsius).

What Causes Global Warming? Scientific research indicates that natural factors cannot sufficiently account for global warming (*National Geographic* 2017a). The current pattern and amount of warming can only be explained by including the effects of *greenhouse gases* released into the environment by human activity. Greenhouse gases trap the sun's energy within the Earth's atmosphere. The more there are, the more solar radiation heats the planet rather than being reflected into space. This is the **greenhouse effect**. Most greenhouse gases generated by human activity come from the burning of fossil fuels like gasoline, diesel fuel, home heating oil, natural gas and coal used in vehicles, furnaces, factories, and electricity generation facilities. One gas responsible for global warming is carbon dioxide (CO_2), a product of both animal respiration and fossil fuel combustion. Since plants absorb CO_2, deforestation, like the destruction of rain forests, makes it harder to remove this gas from the atmosphere. Methane from the digestive systems of animals, gases used for refrigeration, and nitrous oxide released from

global warming The slow but steady warming of the Earth's land, oceans, and atmosphere.

greenhouse effect Warming of the Earth caused by solar radiation being trapped by greenhouse gases rather than being reflected into space.

fossil fuel combustion and in the making of fertilizers also contribute to global warming (EPA 2017a).

Consequences of Global Warming The Union of Concerned Scientists (2017) states that global warming leads to some regions suffering long periods of drought, making them vulnerable to severe wildfires and decreasing the availability of fresh groundwater. At the same time, other areas experience increased rainfall and powerful storms. As global heat rises, polar and glacial ice melts, raising ocean levels and threatening coastal areas. The shift in climate toward more frequent extreme weather events is called **climate change**.

Impacts of Increasing Global Energy Use

In 2015 petroleum provided 31.7 percent of the world's energy supply, coal 28.1 percent, and natural gas 21.6 percent. Thus, a total of 81.4 percent came from burning fossil fuels that release greenhouse gases (GHG) and other harmful chemicals and particles into the atmosphere (International Energy Agency 2017). About 4.9 percent was provided by nuclear power plants. Only 13.7 percent of the world's energy came from other sources, such as renewable, including biofuel, hydroelectric, solar, wind, and geothermal. Energy consumed in the United States in January of 2018, as shown in figure 13.1, included 35.5 percent from natural gas, 32.5 percent from petroleum, and 13.9 percent from coal, for a total of about 81.9 percent from burning fossil fuels (U.S. Energy Information Administration 2018b). Nuclear power plants provided 8.1 percent and renewable sources 10 percent.

The U.S. Energy Information Administration (2016) predicted world energy consumption in 2040 will be 48 percent higher than in 2012. Although consumption of renewable energy will increase faster, fossil fuels will still supply about 78 percent of demand. This means that without an acceleration in the availability of renewable energy (or nuclear energy), the amount of CO_2 in the atmosphere will increase by 34 percent.

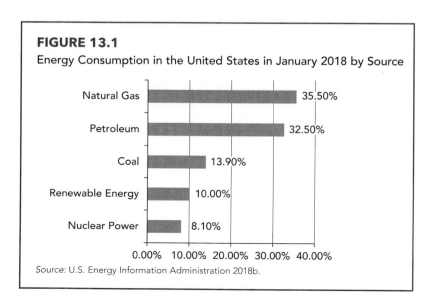

FIGURE 13.1

Energy Consumption in the United States in January 2018 by Source

Natural Gas — 35.50%
Petroleum — 32.50%
Coal — 13.90%
Renewable Energy — 10.00%
Nuclear Power — 8.10%

0.00% 10.00% 20.00% 30.00% 40.00%

Source: U.S. Energy Information Administration 2018b.

climate change The shift in climate toward more frequent extreme weather events such as intense heat waves and powerful storms.

Air Pollution

Air pollution refers to contamination of air by any gases, particles, biological organisms, or other substances that are harmful to people or the environment. The Environmental Protection Agency (EPA) (2017b) identifies six major types of pollutants that damage air quality: ground-level ozone, particles (particulate matter), carbon monoxide, nitrogen oxides, sulfur dioxide, and lead. Ozone is a colorless form of oxygen with three atoms in its molecule, O_3, compared to normal oxygen with two atoms, O_2. In the upper atmosphere ozone acts as a giant sunscreen to protect life on earth from ultraviolet radiation from the sun. But ozone at ground level makes it difficult for people, especially children and people with lung diseases or asthma, to breathe. Ground-level ozone is generated from the interaction of nitrogen oxide and other chemicals produced by industrial facilities, vehicle exhaust, and other sources in the presence of sunlight. Particle pollution refers to the release of very small solid particles or liquid droplets into the atmosphere. These particles are made up of metals, acids or other chemicals, soil, or dust. The smaller the particles the greater the chance that they will pass through the nose and throat and enter the lungs, causing serious damage there or to other parts of the body. Carbon monoxide (CO) is a transparent, odorless gas released into the air during combustion. It harms the body by reducing the delivery of oxygen to the heart and other organs, and at high levels can be lethal. Nitrogen dioxide (NO_2) is one of a number of nitrogen oxides formed from the emissions of vehicles, factories, power plants, and fossil fuel-burning equipment. NO_2 contributes to the formation of ground-level ozone and particle pollution and harms the respiratory system. Sulfur dioxide (SO_2) is a highly reactive gas that also damages the respiratory system. Most SO_2 enters the air from the burning of fossil fuel at power plants and other industrial facilities. Some is generated during the process of separating metals from ore and by locomotives and large ships that burn high-sulfur-content fuel. Lead is a metal that is introduced into the atmosphere through some manufacturing and metal processing operations and from the combustion of aviation gasoline in piston aircraft engines. As noted in Chapter 9, lead poisoning can cause nerve disorders, muscle or joint pain, and infertility, and can interfere with memory and the ability to concentrate.

According to the American Lung Association (ALA 2017), about 39 percent of Americans lived in counties where air pollution was often at dangerous levels during 2013–2015. This represents a significant decline in air pollution since the passage of the Clean Air Act of 1970, which was amended and strengthened in 1990 (EPA 2017c). The level of lead pollution declined because, beginning in the 1970s, the amount of lead permitted in gasoline for cars and trucks was steadily reduced and after 1995 banned completely. Antipollution measures at some industrial facilities and the relocation of many factories to developing countries also contributed to reducing air pollution in the United States. According to the ALA, the most polluted urban areas include Los Angeles, Bakersfield, and Visalia-Porterville-Hanford, California (ALA 2017). Urban areas with the cleanest air include Burlington-South Burlington,

air pollution
Contamination of air by any gases, particles, biological organisms, or other substances that are harmful to people or the environment.

*Fossil fuel combustion
generating air pollution*

Vermont, Cape Coral-Fort Myers-Naples, Florida, Elmira-Corning, New York, and Honolulu, Hawaii.

Global Air Pollution The International Energy Agency (2017) estimates that growth in the world's consumption of energy will occur mainly in developing countries in Asia and Africa as industry and the number of cars, trucks, and other vehicles continues to increase. This means that air pollution is also expected to rise. According to Shirley (2016), the 20 cities with the worst particulate air pollution include 4 in Nigeria, 3 in India, 3 in Pakistan, 3 in Saudi Arabia, 2 in Iran, 2 in Bahrain, 2 in Afghanistan, and 1 in China.

Indoor Air Quality Materials or processes inside or under a residence or workplace building that release harmful gases or particles cause indoor pollution (EPA 2017d). The many potential sources of indoor pollution include: combustion of kerosene, gas, oil, coal, wood, or tobacco; deteriorating asbestos in insulation or roofing shingles; cabinets or furniture made of particular pressed wood materials; certain chemicals used for repainting or remodeling, cleaning, personal care, hobbies, or air freshening; pesticides; and outdoor air pollution that enters buildings. In addition, radon, considered the second leading cause of lung cancer, is the odorless, colorless radioactive gas emitted from the decay of small amounts of uranium found in rock and soil that enters buildings all around the United States (EPA 2017e). Ventilation of buildings that removes indoor pollutants and brings in clean air is one way to improve indoor air quality.

Land Pollution

Land pollution refers to the placement on or into land of any material or substances that are harmful to people or the environment, or render the land difficult or impossible to use. One major cause of land

land pollution The placement on or into land of any material or substances that are harmful to people or the environment, or render the land difficult or impossible to use.

pollution is the disposal of solid waste. This includes garbage, vehicles, appliances, and other equipment, demolition and construction debris, furniture, toys, oil, antifreeze, aerosol cans, paint cans, compressed gas cylinders, metals, tires, and other solid or liquid materials (New York State Department of Environmental Conservation 2017a). Garbage (trash) refers to items we use every day and then throw away, such as food remnants, newspapers and magazines, bottles, product packaging, furniture, clothing, appliances, paint, batteries, and yard trimmings. Each American generated about 4.4 pounds of garbage per day (EPA 2015a). This amounted to 254 million tons of garbage annually for the whole United States, about 34 percent of which was recycled or composted (EPA 2015b). The rest was either incinerated for energy production (about 13 percent) or deposited in landfills (about 53 percent). Landfills are engineered land areas where waste material is buried. They usually have safeguards, such a liner system, to prevent contamination of groundwater. The good news is that the percent of garbage recycled or composted has steadily increased. The percent of garbage recycled or composted in 2013 was more than five times the 6.4 percent in 1960.

Hazardous Waste

Garbage is often nonhazardous waste like food scraps, paper, or cardboard. But much waste material is **hazardous waste**, meaning that it poses a threat to people or the environment (EPA 2017f). Waste material may be hazardous if it is easy to ignite (burns easily), explosive, corrosive, or if it is or contains or can generate a poisonous chemical.

Love Canal The Love Canal neighborhood in Niagara Falls, New York, was one of the most disastrous U.S. hazardous waste sites. The area is named for William T. Love, who in the 1890s attempted to dig a canal to link the upper and lower Niagara River to generate hydroelectric power (De Angelo 2008; Gibbs 2008; Mother Nature Network 2015; New York State Department of Environmental Conservation 2017b). But Nicola Tesla's introduction of alternating current, which allowed electricity to be transmitted over long distances, reduced the need for a local source of power. Only about one mile of the 50-foot-wide canal was dug before the project was abandoned. Between 1942 and 1952 the Hooker Electrochemical Company deposited many barrels of chemical wastes into the canal (an estimated 21,000 tons) and then put a layer of clay on top and sold the land to the local school board for $1. Despite the Hooker Company's warning about buried chemicals, a school and about 800 single-family working-class homes and 240 low-income apartments were constructed over or near the chemical dump. Residents, generally unaware they lived close to thousands of tons of buried chemicals, were mostly blue-collar workers who in 1978 had average annual incomes in the $10,000 to $25,000 range. Beginning in the 1960s, residents started complaining about minor explosions and strange chemical odors. Local news reporters began drawing wider attention to the situation through a series of articles. In 1977, melting snow and heavy rain pushed leaking chemicals into yards and basements. Tests revealed more than eighty chemicals, of which as many as eleven were suspected cancer-causing

hazardous waste Waste that poses a threat to people or the environment.

substances. Evidence also emerged of abnormally high numbers of miscarriages and birth defects among families in the area. In August 1978 about 500 families living in the Love Canal area, led by local housewife Lois Gibbs, formed the Love Canal Home Owners Association (LCHA) to influence government responses to the situation. During the same month, the New York State Department of Health declared that the Love Canal area was a threat to health. This led to a series of federal government actions to remove residents from Love Canal and provide compensation so they could purchase new homes elsewhere.

The federal Comprehensive Environmental Response, Compensation, and Liability Act (CERCLA), enacted on December 11, 1980, was the main legislative reaction to the Love Canal disaster and the concurrent realization that there were hundreds of similar abandoned hazardous waste dumps. CERCLA, also known as Superfund, taxes chemical and petroleum companies in order to fund the cleanup of abandoned or uncontrolled hazardous waste sites (EPA 2016). Since its creation, the Superfund program has located tens of thousands of hazardous waste sites and worked with state and local governments in carrying out cleanups.

Brownfields In 1995 the EPA began a program for dealing with so-called **brownfields** (EPA 2017g) Brownfields are real property (buildings, land, or anything affixed to land), the reuse, redevelopment, or expansion of

brownfields Buildings, land, or anything affixed to land, the reuse, redevelopment, or expansion of which may be affected by the presence or potential presence of a hazardous substance.

Social Movements: Lois Gibbs, Environmental Activist

Lois Gibbs

Lois Marie Gibbs (born 1951) is one of America's foremost environmental activists. In the spring of 1978, she was a twenty-seven-year-old housewife with a high school education in the working-class neighborhood of Love Canal, Niagara, New York. After reading newspaper articles revealing that the 99th Street elementary school, which her sickly child attended, was built next to a huge chemical dump containing toxic and carcinogenic substances, Lois suspected it had something to do with her son's poor health. Angered after she was unable to get the school board to allow her son to attend another school, Lois began speaking to hundreds of other people about their children's health. Convinced that the chemical dump was harming the entire community, in June 1978 she organized the Love Canal Parents Movement, which in August led to the creation of the Love Canal Homeowners Association (Center for Health, Environment

(continued)

Social Movements (*continued*)

and Justice 2015; Gibbs 2008). Lois led her neighbors in the struggle to obtain justice from the city of Niagara, New York State, and the federal government. Their demands to be compensated and relocated were supported by research that indicated high levels of miscarriages, birth defects, and other health problems, particularly among those living closest to flows of liquid outward from the dump, and by news coverage and articles by reporters who kept the story in the public spotlight. Finally, in October 1980 President Jimmy Carter authorized the evacuation of families from the Love Canal area. This was widely viewed as a victory for the grassroots community movement and for the larger environmental movement. The Love Canal Homeowners Association's actions and Lois Gibbs' leadership led to the December 11, 1980, enactment of the Comprehensive Environmental Response, Compensation, and Liability Act, or Superfund Act, which enables the EPA to locate and clean up hazardous waste sites throughout the United States. During the Love Canal community struggle, Lois was contacted by many people around the country in similar situations. In 1981 she formed the Center for Health, Environment and Justice, an environmental crisis center that assists community groups throughout the country with organizing and technical information. CBS aired a two-hour prime time movie called Lois Gibbs: The Love Canal Story, and Lois received honorary degrees from the State University of New York and other colleges and was nominated for a Noble Peace Prize. She continues to speak to audiences nationally and internationally about the danger of toxic chemicals and, in particular, the danger exposure poses to children.

What are your thoughts?

Why is it so difficult for victims to obtain relief from and justice for environmental problems? Who do you think could be the most powerful actor in making corporations worldwide more responsible for environmental protection: governments, the United Nations, international environmental movements, or grassroots organizations? Explain your choice.

---

which may be affected by the presence or potential presence of a hazardous substance. Cleaning up these properties protects the environment, rehabilitates otherwise abandoned or underused facilities, and reduces pressure to build on agricultural land or undeveloped green spaces. By January 2017, the EPA had made 63,900 acres available for reuse.

E-Waste

e-waste Discarded electronic equipment or devices.

E-waste refers to discarded electronic equipment like computers, televisions, DVD players, printers, cell phones, and other mobile devices (EPA 2015c, 2017h). It makes up about 2 percent of municipal waste. Reasons for the increase in e-waste include the popularity of electronic devices like smartphones and the fact that rapid advances in technology continuously generate new models with greater capabilities, resulting in the discarding of old models. Most e-waste has been disposed of in landfills, where they pose a threat to ground water because they contain toxic materials such as barium, beryllium, cadmium, lead, mercury, and various chemical fire retardants (Watson 2013). Greater understanding of the environmental threats posed by e-waste and of the valuable materials that can be recovered from electronic devices such as gold, silver, palladium, and platinum has led to a significant increase in the percentage that are recycled in whole or in part. Much of the recycling occurs in China, where many electronic devices are manufactured. But crude methods and lack of sufficient safeguards has led to significant e-waste contamination at certain recycling locations. Chinese environmental activism, United Nations criticism, and Chinese government action contributed to improved recycling procedures.

Radioactive Material

Radioactive material generates harmful radiation that can cause cancer, genetic defects, or death. Although radioactive material is used in nuclear power plants, certain industries, the construction of nuclear weapons, medical applications, and research, a major problem is the disposal and long-term storage of nuclear waste. Spent nuclear fuel rods from reactors are highly radioactive. Used nuclear fuel includes a significant amount of Plutonium 239, which has a half-life of about 24,100 years, meaning this is how long it takes for its radiation to be reduced by 50 percent (United States Nuclear Regulatory Commission (U.S. NRC) 2017a). There is a plan to transport highly radioactive nuclear waste from around the United States to an underground storage facility at Yucca Mountain in a desert area of Nevada about 90 miles northwest of Las Vegas. But concerns about the safety of the facility, potential contamination of water supplies for Nevada, southern California, and Arizona, and the danger of transporting the waste to Yucca Mountain resulted in an at least temporary suspension of the plan by the Obama administration in 2012. In 2014, however, the NRC determined that the Yucca Mountain site met its requirements (Elias 2017; Worby 2017).

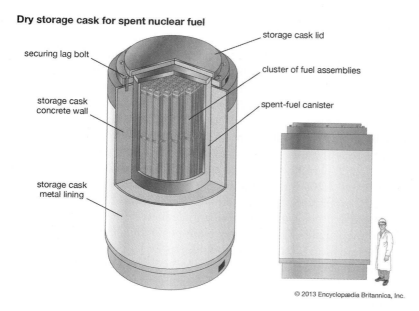

Dry storage cask for spent nuclear fuel

securing lag bolt

storage cask lid

cluster of fuel assemblies

storage cask concrete wall

spent-fuel canister

storage cask metal lining

© 2013 Encyclopædia Britannica, Inc.

Dry cask storage for spent radioactive nuclear fuel rods

U.S. nuclear power plants generate a combined 2,000 to 2,300 metric tons of high-level nuclear fuel waste each year. Because of the lack of a permanent storage facility, more than 76,430 metric tons (84,249 tons) of lethally radioactive nuclear fuel waste are being stored at over one hundred locations in thirty-five states (Nuclear Energy Institute 2014, 2018; United States Nuclear Regulatory Commission 2015, 2016). These supposedly temporary storage sites include operating nuclear power plants and shut-down reactors. U.S. nuclear power plants store used-up nuclear fuel rods in pools of water lined with steel and covered by several feet of concrete for an average of about 10 years. The water cools the fuel rods and helps contain the radiation. Later the spent fuel can be placed in dry cask storage.

The casks are stainless steel cylindrical containers encased in concrete and placed vertically or horizontally on reinforced concrete slabs. The casks are supposed to be able to withstand the impact a jet aircraft crashing into them. In 2017 the Trump administration included a request for $120 million dollars for the process of relicensing the Yucca Mountain project in its national budget proposal so that the spent nuclear power plant fuel could eventually be permanently stored there. Completion of the entire project, including moving the nuclear waste to Yucca Mountain, could cost close to $100 billion.

In addition to extremely radioactive materials, thousands of tons of lower-level, though still dangerous, radioactive materials are stored at various sites. These include mine tailings (the fragments of uranium ore left over after the valuable parts are removed) and equipment, clothing, or other things that have become radioactive through contact with highly radioactive material.

Accidents, terrorism, and traumatic natural events, such as earthquakes, endanger nuclear power plants and stored radioactive material and pose the threat of long-term contamination of the environment. Due to equipment failure and design and instrument problems, the Three Mile Island Unit 2 reactor near Middletown, Pennsylvania, overheated and experienced a partial meltdown of nuclear fuel on March 28, 1979 (U.S. NRC 2014a; EPA 2015d). Some radioactive gas vented into the atmosphere but the containment building remained intact, preventing a more serious release.

The Chernobyl accident of April 26, 1986, in the town of Pripyat, Ukraine, about 65 miles north of Kiev was far more serious and lethal (History.com 2015; U.S. NRC 2014b; World Nuclear Association 2016a). Engineers at Chernobyl Reactor Four disconnected crucial equipment to test a backup water-cooling procedure. But they quickly lost control and made a series of tragic mistakes. As a result, there was a meltdown of the reactor's fuel, partially blowing off the top of the reactor and releasing an estimated 1,200 tons of radioactive particles into the air, endangering parts of Ukraine, Belarus, and Russia. Unlike Three Mile Island, the Chernobyl plant did not have an adequate containment structure around the reactor. At least thirty plant personnel and firemen died in a short time from blast or radiation injuries and, despite the evacuation of approximately 335,000 people from nearby areas, an estimated 5,000 persons died from radiation-related diseases like cancer.

Because the design of the Chernobyl reactors was unique to the Soviet Union, some believed that another nuclear plant accident was unlikely. But on March 11, 2011, a huge magnitude 9.0 earthquake struck off the coast of Honshu Island, Japan, generating an approximately 49-foot tsunami wave that washed over the sea wall that was supposed to protect the Fukushima reactors on shore (Hamada and Tsukimori 2015; World Nuclear Association 2017). The flooding seawater shut down the cooling pumps, causing the three operating reactors to overheat and experience at least partial meltdowns within a few days. Chemical explosions damaged reactor buildings. Radioactive material vented into the air, and huge quantities of radioactive water flowed onto the land and into the sea. More than 160,000 people fled the surrounding areas. The Fukushima disaster demonstrated the vulnerability of nuclear plants to natural events.

Wars and the Environment

Wars and preparation for war can cause significant damage to the environment. Nations that feel threatened by powerful foes have often cared little about protecting the environment in desperate attempts to develop industry and weapons in pursuit of national security. For example, nuclear testing by the United States, the Soviet Union, and other nations during the 1950s and 1960s spewed enormous amounts of radiation into the atmosphere. Military training and exercises using vehicles, ships, and planes contributes to pollution and global warming. Certain tactics used during wars, like burning crops or poisoning water wells to deny an enemy from using them, can have lethal consequences.

Britain sprayed Malayan forests in the 1950s with chemicals to defoliate trees as a means of depriving communist guerrillas of cover (Haberman 2014). The U.S. military used a similar approach from 1962 to 1971 against Viet Cong and North Vietnamese soldiers. American aircraft sprayed about 20 million gallons of defoliants on various parts of South Vietnam, totaling an area the size of Massachusetts. One of the herbicides used, Agent Orange, included a form of toxic dioxin. Although chemical company executives and U.S. officials claimed Agent Orange was not harmful to humans, research showed it was associated with birth defects in lab animals. Scientists began to protest against its use, helping to bring an end to the defoliant program. But there is widespread concern that Agent Orange contamination is responsible for the birth defects of thousands of Vietnamese children as well as birth defects among the children of some of the 2.8 million U.S. military personnel who served in Vietnam. The U.S. government has now accepted responsibility for helping to clean up some locations in Vietnam with high levels of dioxin, like former American military bases where herbicides were stored.

The use of depleted uranium shells in the wars against Iraq appears to have caused another type of environmental damage. When natural uranium is processed to create enriched uranium, with a high content of U-235 for use in nuclear power plants and in making nuclear weapons, what remains is depleted uranium (DU). DU is very low in the U-235 isotope, higher in U-238 than natural uranium, and extremely dense. Its radiation level is about 60 percent that of natural uranium (United Nations Joint Medical Staff 2001). It is also about as chemically toxic as lead if inhaled or ingested into the body (World Nuclear Association 2016b). The arms industries in a number of countries, including the United States and the Russian Federation, have used depleted uranium to make armor for tanks and to make armor-piercing shells. Combined with a little titanium, these shells penetrate armor and then burn, killing vehicle occupants and exploding stored ammunition. In the process, radioactive shell fragments and particles are dispersed into the environment. During the 1990–1991 Gulf War against Iraq and the 2003 U.S.-led invasion of Iraq, U.S. and British forces reportedly fired thousands of DU shells against various targets (Edwards 2013, 2014). Research indicates that there are more than 300 DU-contaminated locations in Iraq and that scrap metal dealers may have inadvertently spread DU to other areas. Iraqi physicians have reported increases in cancer and birth defects.

Water Availability and Quality

Of the Earth's water, the planet's over seven billion people rely on the less than one percent that is liquid fresh water (U.S. Geological Survey 2016). Another two percent of water is frozen in polar caps, permanent snow, ice sheets, and glaciers. About 97 percent is ocean and sea salt water. Fresh water is generated by the hydrologic cycle, which involves water evaporating into the atmosphere and forming clouds that then precipitate water back to earth. This process cleans the water since most pollutants are left behind when water evaporates. Thus, the rain and snow that falls on land to fill lakes, reservoirs, and rivers is relatively pure. Since a sizeable part of the water that evaporates from the oceans precipitates over land, there is a continuous flow of water from land into the oceans (Hubbart 2011).

Much fresh water, however, becomes contaminated by industrial and mine waste, oil and chemical spills, nitrate-based fertilizer and pesticide runoff, untreated sewage, and other sources constituting a health hazard. For example, the United Nations (2013a, 2015a) estimates that 80 percent to 90 percent of the sewage and other wastewater in developing countries is discharged untreated directly into bodies of water. About 800 million people worldwide lack access to freshwater sources that have been "improved" (engineered in some way, for example, transported by pipes, to prevent contamination). According to the United Nations, water use over the last century has been growing at more than twice the rate of population increase; by 2025 up to two-thirds of the worlds' people could be living in areas where it will be difficult to meet water needs. Currently, access to clean water varies significantly among nations. Ninety-eight to 100 percent of people in European nations have access to improved water sources, but in some nations, such as Angola, Chad, the Democratic Republic of the Congo, Ethiopia, Papua New Guinea, and South Sudan, less than 60 percent do (World Bank 2015).

In the United States, local government attempts to cope with water shortages with measures such as limiting the watering of lawns. The EPA (2017i) suggests that Americans can reduce their use of water by washing clothes on the short cycle when possible, taking shorter showers, not

Social Movements: Global Water Justice Movement

Clean water demonstration

The Global Water Justice Movement supports access to clean water and adequate sanitation as basic human rights. It calls on governments around the world to maintain and, where needed, expand public availability of water and sanitation rather than turning these crucial functions over to for-profit private companies (Blue Planet 2015; Global Water Justice Movement 2012). The movement includes social justice and human rights groups, trade unions, environmental organizations, indigenous peoples associations, farmers, community activists and networks, and others sharing the belief that water is a collective resource and that access to it is a basic human right. One of the first major mobilizations to resist water privatization occurred in 2000 in Cochabamba, Bolivia (DeFronzo 2014). The government in 1999 had decided to privatize the water system in Cochabamba (population then about 600,000), Bolivia's third-largest city. Aguas del Tunari, an enterprise owned in great part by Spanish, Italian, and U.S. corporations, took over the city's water service. Water use rates increased by up to 200 percent, forcing poor families to devote as much as 20 to 30 percent of their income just to paying for water (Chávez 2006). Citizens formed the Coalition for the Defense of Water and Life. Major protests against privatization beginning in April 2000 involved work strikes and roadblocks that basically shut the city down. These popular actions forced the government to reverse privatization and bring water service in Cochabamba back under public control. This victorious mass uprising against water privatization in Bolivia helped inspire other protests against water-privatization around the world. The Cochabamba uprising and the Global Water Justice Movement helped draw international attention to water and sanitation issues. The UN estimates that 800 million people lack access to safe water. In 2010, the United Nations General Assembly voted that access to clean water and sanitation is a basic human right fundamental to life (BBC 2010; United Nations 2010). One hundred and twenty-two nations, among them Bolivia, Brazil, China, France, Germany, Russia, and Spain, voted in favor, while none voted against and forty-one abstained, including Australia, the United Kingdom, and the United States. The resolution also called on countries and organizations to provide financial and technological assistance to developing countries so that clean water and effective sanitation can be available to all.

Activist organizations within the Water Justice Movement have fought vigorously against water privatization. The Transnational Institute stated that in the last 15 years 237 cities and towns in thirty-seven countries, including fifty-eight in the United States, have reversed privatization and brought water access services back under public control (Barlow 2015).

Despite the 2010 UN water resolution and the Water Justice Movement, privatization of water services continued to occur. And in some locations, such as Detroit, municipal water access was cut off to many residents because of unpaid water bills (Blue Planet 2015; Gottesdiener 2015). The goal of guaranteeing universal access to safe water and adequate sanitation is still far from being achieved.

What are your thoughts?
Should government or private for-profit companies supply water to the public?

running the water while brushing teeth, and other measures. The box feature describes the global movement to ensure access to clean water.

Acid Rain Acid rain refers to the precipitation of nitric and sulfuric acids from the atmosphere onto land and bodies of water (EPA 2017j). Some of this acid enters the atmosphere from natural sources, such as volcanoes. But much of it comes from the burning of fossil fuels. In the United States, for example, about two-thirds of sulfur dioxide and one-quarter of nitric oxides in the atmosphere come from electric power plants burning coal or other fossil fuels.

Acid rain can damage plants and poison fish in bodies of water. In 1984, researchers found that acid rain from far-away urban areas had killed off the fish in hundreds of lakes in the six-million-acre New York Adirondack Park. But after passage of the 1990 Clean Air Act amendments forced a reduction of pollution from coal power electric plants, acid rain and the acid levels of Adirondack lakes decreased. In the fall of 2005, one of the dead Adirondack lakes, Brooktrout Lake, was successfully restocked with trout, showing that government action to reduce acid rain could be effective (Esch 2006).

Dangers to Biodiversity

Biodiversity refers to the different forms of life. One major study concluded that there are about 8.74 million species of life on earth, about 1.23 million of which have been described and catalogued (Mora et al. 2011). Harmful pollution and clearing land and rain forests for cities, industry, and agriculture, as well as overhunting and overfishing, have eliminated or threaten to eliminate many species. The United Nations (2013b) estimates that between 1970 and 2000, the planet lost 32 percent of its land and marine species. And freshwater ecology suffered the worst damage to biodiversity. Maintaining a high level of biodiversity is important for several reasons. First, biodiversity helps purify water and provide nutrients for fertilizing soil. Second, taking advantage of a wide variety of species, biologists can modify food crops with genes from other plants to make them more productive or more resistant to disease and insects. Third, scientists exploring the wide range of life forms have and continue to find substances that can cure or more effectively treat diseases. For example, aspirin is derived from the White Willow tree native to Europe and western and central Asia (Veeresham 2012). Paclitaxel, derived from the Pacific Yew tree, is used to treat lung, ovarian, and breast cancer. And artemisinin from the Chinese sweet wormwood tree is used to fight drug-resistant malaria.

environmental justice The condition in which all people have the same level of protection from environmental hazards and have equal access to decision making on healthy living, learning, and work environments.

environmental injustice The condition in which lower-income persons and other groups are relatively powerless to ensure themselves a healthy environment and are more likely to be exposed to environmental hazards.

ENVIRONMENTAL INJUSTICE

The EPA (2017k) describes **environmental justice** as all people having the same level of protection from environmental hazards and having equal access to decision making on healthy living, learning, and work environments. **Environmental injustice** is the condition in which lower-income persons and other groups are relatively powerless to ensure themselves a healthy environment and are more likely to be exposed to environmental hazards. **Environmental racism** is the condition in which racial or ethnic minorities are relatively powerless to ensure themselves a healthy environment and are more likely to be exposed to environmental hazards. Due to limited financial resources or outright discrimination, these groups have often been forced to reside in areas close to sources of pollution or to contaminated industrial sites and waste dumps.

Research in the United States (Katz and *Environmental Health News* 2012; Lees 2014) indicates that the greater the percentage of poor people, Hispanics, African Americans, or Asians in an area, the higher the probability that harmful chemicals like nitrates are in the air. Furthermore, the disadvantage for poor minority communities varies geographically, tending to be highest in states or parts of states with a lot of industry (Badger 2014). For example, the area called "cancer alley" in Louisiana, where some 150 petrochemical companies and seventeen refineries are located has a disproportionately African American population (Hayoun 2015).

In most countries around the world, lower-income persons are at greater risk from environmental hazards such as impure or chemically polluted drinking water. Sometimes the jobs available to them, like taking apart discarded electronic items shipped to their countries from

environmental racism The condition in which racial or ethnic minorities are relatively powerless to ensure themselves a healthy environment and are more likely to be exposed to environmental hazards.

Special Topics: The British Petroleum *Deepwater Horizon* Oil Spill

Burning Deepwater Horizon oil rig

In the spring of 2010 the Deepwater Horizon oil rig off the coast of Louisiana in the Gulf of Mexico, leased by British Petroleum (BP) but owned and operated by the Transocean drilling company, was floating 4,993 feet above an oil well that penetrated 18,000 feet beneath the sea floor (Pallardy 2015). On April 20, natural gas broke through a concrete barrier installed by the Halliburton Corporation. The natural gas travelled up the rig's conduit pipe to the rig and exploded, killing eleven workers and injuring seventeen. The rig sank on April 22, and oil poured from the well into the gulf at a rate of as much as 60,000 barrels per day, according to U.S. government officials. A series of repair measures carried out over several months succeeded in slowing the flow by mid-July. Scientists estimated that by that point over 4 million barrels of oil had already leaked into the gulf. Through a method involving drilling a new shaft to intersect with the leaking oil well and then pumping in cement, the leak was declared totally sealed on September 19.

By then an oil slick covered thousands of square miles of the Gulf of Mexico, and oil and tar balls polluted as much as 1,100 miles

(continued)

Special Topics (*continued*)

of shoreline in Louisiana, Alabama, Mississippi, and Florida. Some of the floating oil was burned or siphoned off the sea surface by skimmer ships, and 1.8 million gallons of chemical emulsifier was poured on unrecovered oil to make it easier for bacteria to consume. Manual efforts were employed to remove the oil that reached land. Beyond being an enormous environmental catastrophe, the oil spill caused immense economic damage. Much of the gulf fishing industry was shut down for months. And polluted beaches caused shoreline tourism to suffer devastating loses.

BP, which lost billions of dollars of its stock value and also spent $40 billion in repair, clean-up, and related costs, set up a $20 billion fund to compensate those affected by the spill. Most of this money was dispersed by 2013. The total number of animals harmed by the oil spill has not been fully determined, but it is clear that tens of thousands, including turtles, dolphins, whales, and aquatic birds, were killed.

The Deepwater Horizon spill resulted in criminal charges and civil law suits. A BP engineer charged with deleting hundreds of text messages believed relevant to the disaster was convicted of obstruction of justice in 2013. The Department of Justice (DOJ) reached an agreement with BP in 2012 on fourteen criminal charges, including eleven counts of felony manslaughter for the workers killed and violations of environmental laws, requiring the company to pay $4.5 billion in penalties and fines. A little more than half of this was to go to the National Fish and Wildlife Foundation. BP also consented to paying the Securities Exchange Commission more than half a billion dollars for misleading stockholders about the size of the oil spill. Transocean agreed to pay a one-billion-dollar civil penalty and $400 million in criminal penalties. In 2014 a civil court ruled that BP was 67 percent responsible for the spill, Transocean 30 percent, and Halliburton 3 percent.

Then, in July of 2015, a court settlement was reached between BP and the federal government, the states of Alabama, Florida, Louisiana, Mississippi, and Texas, and more than 400 local governments in coastal areas where the oil spill damaged tourism, devastated fishing, and greatly reduced government revenue from taxes (Robertson, Schwartz, and Pérez-Peña 2015). BP agreed to pay $18.7 billion, including $12.6 billion for environmental violations and damage.

But some political leaders, including Florida Senator Bill Nelson, and environmental activists and groups question whether BP should be required to pay a lot more, especially since the company was found to have been grossly negligent and since it is possible that serious health or environmental damage from the spill may be discovered in the future (St. Myer 2015; Sheppard 2015).

What are your thoughts?
Do you think that offshore oil drilling is worth the risk of environmental accidents?

more-affluent nations, expose them to toxic chemicals. Their homes are often close to smoke-belching factories, with industrial waste dumped into nearby rivers. Their welfare may be sacrificed as local governments seek rapid economic development or business managers bribe officials not to enforce regulations. Foreign corporations can often damage the environment with little fear of punishment, or if ordered to pay damages or penalties, use high-priced law firms to get them reduced or to delay paying. For example, in 2013 an Ecuadorian court stated that the Chevron oil corporation should pay Ecuadorian farmers $9.5 billion for polluting the Ecuadorian rain forest and the Amazon, damaging their livelihood.

But in 2014 the company won an appeal in a Manhattan federal court, potentially reducing or totally eliminating any payments on the grounds that lawyers for the farmers had submitted false evidence and engaged in other irregularities, although a lawyer for the farmers denied committing fraud (Krauss 2014). The box feature describes one of the most damaging environmental disasters.

Environmental movement demonstrator

SOCIOLOGICAL PERSPECTIVES ON THE ENVIRONMENT

The structural-functional perspective sees environmental problems as stemming from human progress and looks to new technologies and behavioral and cultural changes to solve them. The conflict approach views the capitalist economic system as creating many of the world's environmental problems and that, worldwide, people with the least power are most exposed to environmental hazards. Symbolic interactionists see people's conceptions of environmental problems as linked to their values and communication with others.

Structural-Functional Perspective

The structural-functional perspective views exploitation of the environment as a natural component of economic progress. Humanity's ingenuity and technological innovations succeed through drawing on and transforming environmental resources. Extracting resources and discharging waste into the environment become seen as problems when people view resources as finite and fear the effects of a damaged environment. The structural-functional approach sees environmental problems as latent dysfunctions resulting from efforts to improve human welfare and living standards. The solution is to create better technology that will produce energy from new or renewable resources and generate far less pollution. Some functionalists also believe that cultural values and norms must change to effectively reduce environmental problems. Unbridled materialism, which supports the continuous acquisition of possessions and unnecessarily wastes resources and generates heavy pollution, should be replaced by a concern for **sustainable development**. Sustainable development refers to using resources to promote human welfare in ways that protect the environment and allow it to support human development indefinitely.

Conflict Perspective

The economic-conflict perspective argues that the capitalist economic system has created, directly and indirectly, many of the world's environmental problems and that people with the least power and wealth are most vulnerable to being exposed to environmental hazards. Businesses try to maximize profits and also compete successfully with rival compa-

sustainable development Using resources to promote human welfare in ways that protect the environment and allow it to support human development indefinitely.

nies; in their efforts to cut costs they attempt to obtain resources from the environment and dispose of waste in the cheapest possible ways. The most environmentally reckless companies are likely to drive others out of business. Government regulation is one possible way to prevent capitalists from destroying the environment. But in capitalist societies, wealthy business interests can shape laws to protect polluters, prevent effective enforcement of what laws there are, and hire lawyers to minimize punishment. Regardless of the environmental harm they do, business leaders are virtually never criminally prosecuted. If penalized at all, it's likely to be some type of fine. The conflict view notes that capitalist nations took control of vast areas of the world and exploited their resources with little concern for the environment. The conflict approach also states that some lesser-developed nations, including a number with more socialist economic systems, also damaged their environments in crash efforts to quickly catch up with the advanced capitalist nations. An implication of the conflict approach is that less emphasis on maximizing profits and less international conflict would reduce environmental problems.

The racial/ethnic-conflict perspective points out that within the United States low-income minority persons are more likely to suffer from health problems caused by hazardous waste. The exploitation of resources with little regard for the environment in countries with non-white populations also suggests racism on the part of those responsible.

The feminist-conflict perspective holds that male-dominated patriarchal society plays a major role in creating environmental problems. According to this view, the traditional masculine orientation is to aggressively dominate and exploit both women and nature (Miles 2013; Tong 2013). Women, in contrast, tend to be more cooperative with and supportive of others. This general caring orientation extends to the environment. The feminist environmental movement, ecofeminism, focuses on major environmental problems, such as water shortages and poor water quality and how living near hazardous waste dumps and sources of pollution affect women and children. They also note that women, including Rachel Carson, author of the environmental classic *Silent Spring* (2002), and Lois Gibbs and her associates in the Love Canal protest movement, have played leading roles in building the environmental movement. Ecofeminists believe that having more women in positions of power in government and the economy will contribute greatly to solving environmental problems.

Symbolic-Interactionist Perspective

Symbolic interactionists emphasize that environmental problems and potential solutions are linked to people's knowledge, values, and attitudes shaped through interaction with others and messages conveyed through the media. One concern is that U.S. culture puts too great an emphasis on individualism and materialism while the environment is a collective resource. A greater cultural focus on community could foster more recycling, preference for fuel-efficient or electric cars, and other environment friendly behavior.

The symbolic-interactionist perspective also examines how people define and explain environmental problems, try to bring attention to them, and how they propose to solve them. In the process of making the public aware of an issue, environmental activists try to gain media coverage, present convincing evidence, and get assistance from authoritative sources like biologists and other scientists to support their claims. But when powerful interests feel threatened by an emerging environmental movement, they typically respond with a countermessage. For example, when environmentalists called for reducing the use of coal as an energy source, coal supporters came up with the expression "clean coal" to suggest that there were new ways to burn coal that would release much less pollution into the atmosphere. They also pointed out that the United States needs coal as a relatively cheap way to produce much of its electricity and that thousands of Americans are employed in the coal industry. Critics argue that current technology for cleaner coal burning is not effective enough, too expensive, and presents the problem of how to dispose of the CO_2 and toxic chemicals removed from coal. In 2014, for example, the founder of an energy company claiming to have developed clean-coal technology was convicted of defrauding investors of $57 million (Welbes 2014).

In efforts to improve their image regarding the environment, some companies engage in "greenwashing." Greenwashing is when a company that is actually damaging the environment or including potentially harmful substances in its products uses advertising, public relations, or other means to portray itself as protecting the environment. Some environmentalists view the clean-coal campaign as greenwashing. Other examples include claims of biodegradability of bottles or plastic bags that are exaggerated or unsubstantiated or cases in which a company highlights a positive action it has taken, while in reality this it outweighed by the overall damage its practices do to the environment (Kewalramani and Sobelsohn 2012). The box feature describes how neglected infrastructure and flawed government contributed to an environmental disaster.

Special Topics: Flint, Michigan, Environmental Disaster

Protesting the Flint environmental disaster

The Flint, Michigan, water crisis is one of the greatest environmental catastrophes in U.S. history. Many have citied it as a prime example of environmental class prejudice and racism. Flint in 1908 was the birthplace of General Motors (GM). For decades the city flourished as a major producer of automobiles. Its population grew to 200,000 and in 1978 GM's Flint facilities employed 80,000 workers (Sterbenz and Fuchs 2013). However, in the 1980s GM began moving factories to Mexico, where wages were much lower. It drastically decreased operations in Flint, reducing its work force there to 8,000

(continued)

Special Topics (*continued*)

by 2006. The city fell deeply into debt, the unemployment rate surged, and the population declined to about 99,000 (57 percent black and 42 percent below the poverty line). Much property was abandoned, and the city's violent crime rate became more than four times the national average (FBI 2017m; Schneider and Householder 2016).

In response to Flint's economic crisis, the conservative Republican state government took over the city's finances in 2011 and tried to cut its budget and expenditures. One way was to switch the city's drinking water from Lake Huron water, which Flint paid around a million dollars per month to obtain from Detroit's water system, to water from the Flint River. The highly acidic Flint River water, estimated by Virginia Tech researchers to be about nineteen times more corrosive than Lake Huron water, was supposed to be treated with anticorrosive chemicals so that it would not leach poisonous lead from the old pipes servicing thousands of homes (Yan 2016). A federal lawsuit on behalf of Flint's residents would later charge that the Michigan Department of Environmental Quality (DEQ) did not carry out effective anticorrosion treatment of the river water. In April 2014 the state switched Flint's water supply to the Flint River. By May many city residents complained about the water coming out of their faucets, saying it was often brown or yellow and smelled and tasted bad. But officials told the people the water was okay. Despite continuing reports of illnesses and complaints about the water, the federal regional EPA official, as late as July 2015, reportedly still was not certain if there was a serious problem with the water. In August 2015 a group of researchers from Virginia Tech conducted their own tests and released their findings to the public. They found high levels of lead in the water and concluded this was because the pipes were corroding and leaching lead into the water supply. But the Michigan DEQ refused to accept the researchers' conclusions that the high lead content was due to corrosion and leaching (Yan 2016). In September 2015 pediatrician

Dr. Mona Hanna-Attisha and her research team found that the levels of lead in children living in certain parts of Flint had doubled and in some cases tripled. While the legal maximum lead allowed in water was 15 parts per billion, a test indicated that water coming into one Flint home had almost 400 parts per billion (Keating 2016). Effects of lead poisoning can include memory loss, muddled thinking, and fatigue. What is especially terrifying is that as many as 9,000 Flint children are likely to suffer long-term developmental effects from lead poisoning. These can include lower IQ scores and behavioral problems such as attention deficit hyperactivity disorder (LaPook 2016). Even after exposure to lead ends, the harmful effects can last for years or be permanent, and there appear to be no drugs to cure the developmental harm caused by lead. The expectation is that many of the children have been harmed for life, will need remedial education, and may never reach what would have been their full potentials if they had not been poisoned by Flint River water.

Finally in October 2015, after the horrible damage done to Flint's children, the governor announced that the state would switch the city from the contaminated river water back to Lake Huron water. The following month a federal lawsuit was filed against the state of Michigan, the governor, and various other state officials on behalf of the people of Flint. In 2016 it was estimated that it will cost $55 million to replace the lead pipes in Flint. But the human cost is much greater. On April 20, 2016, the first criminal charges were filed in the case when three people, two Michigan DEQ officials and one Flint water official, were accused of tampering with evidence and other offenses (Davey and Pérez-Peña 2016; Domonoske and McCallister 2016).

What are your thoughts?

Why do you think government officials failed to protect the people of Flint from contaminated water?

CAUSES OF ENVIRONMENTAL PROBLEMS

Population Growth

Population growth increases both the consumption of resources and environmental pollution. During 2015 the world's population increased by approximately 78 million people, or a rate of about 1.1 percent in a year. The good news is that this is half the 2.2 percent rate of population increase in 1962 (U.S. Census 2015b). The population growth rate declined due to both wider and more effective use of contraceptive methods and rising marriage age. The rate is projected to fall below 1 percent in 2020 and under 0.5 percent in 2050. But even with the declining rate of increase, the world's population will climb from 7.4 billion in 2017 to 8 billion in 2024. Population, however, is only one key factor. Also important are what resources people use and how they are consumed.

Technological Progress, Urbanization, and Economic Development

The consumption of natural resources by ancient humans, first through hunting and gathering and then rudimentary farming, had little impact on the environment. But technological progress leading to urbanization and industrialization gave rise to serious environmental problems. There is some evidence, however, that the relationship between economic development and pollution is curvilinear (Acar and Tekee 2014; Skaza and Blais 2013). That is, as technology advances from simple tools, pollution increases and tends to reach its worst levels as a nation comes to rely on heavy industries powered by burning wood, coal, and oil, belching enormous quantities of toxic gasses and particulate matter into the environment and generating harmful solid waste. But as technology and the economy continue to develop, the amount of pollution generated in the most advanced nations begins to decline for several reasons. One is that as people in democratic countries begin to demand that the environment be protected their governments tend to impose regulations that reduce pollution like requiring more energy-efficient, higher-mileage cars and trucks. Another factor is that science can be used to tap renewable energy resources and create technologies like hydrogen-burning motors that produce little or no pollution. Still another element is that corporations often relocate high-pollution heavy industry to developing nations where labor costs are low and environmental regulations weak or unenforced.

Militarism and International Competition

All around the world the threat of military confrontation and fear of foreign economic competition or exploitation has motivated arms races, including atmospheric nuclear weapons tests, and rapid industrialization drives with little regard for negative environmental consequences. The groundwater and land in and around military bases and support facilities have often become polluted with toxic substances such as gasoline from leaking tanks, carcinogenic degreasing chemicals, cleaning fluids, and stored or discarded weapons materials. In the United States about 141 of the EPA's approximately 1,200 Superfund sites were associated with the Department of Defense (Nazaryan 2014). International rivals of the United States like Russia and China also experienced extensive environmental pollution resulting from crash military and economic development efforts. A study released in 2015 by Berkeley Earth, a research organization, found that outdoor air pollution contributed to the deaths of 1.6 million people in China annually, or about 4,400 each day (Levin 2015).

Materialist Consumerism

Materialist consumerism is the cultural belief that obtaining prized material possessions is essential to high self-esteem and a happy life. In societies with highly materialistic cultures, advertising media promote the idea that happiness depends on purchasing the latest products with the newest features. Much of the economic activity in such societies results in unnecessarily rapid depletion of resources and the generation of a high level of waste as "obsolete" items are continuously discarded in favor of the latest trends. But by its nature, the materialistic quest for happiness can never fully succeed because people are always presented with some new "must-have" product (Goldberg 2006).

Excessive Individualism

Excessive individualism means continuously putting selfish personal desires and interests above community welfare, including nature's collective resources and the environment. This includes careless disposal of waste, driving a vehicle when mass transportation is available, buying unnecessary products just to keep up with changing fashions, or neglecting to recycle. Cultures with excessive individualism result in selfish individual behaviors harmful to the environment and in powerful wealthy nations exploiting the resources and poisoning the environment of weaker developing countries. In 2015, Pope Francis expressed such ideas in his encyclical letter *On Care of Our Common Home* (Pope Francis 2015), in which he calls on people and wealthy nations to turn away from excessive individualism and toward a more caring orientation regarding others around the world and humanity's common resources, the environment and climate.

materialist consumerism The cultural belief that obtaining prized material possessions is essential to high self-esteem and a happy life.

excessive individualism Continuously putting selfish personal desires and interests above community welfare, including nature's collective resources and the environment.

RESPONDING TO ENVIRONMENTAL PROBLEMS

Our review of causes of environmental problems suggests some obvious ways to protect the environment. These include slowing population growth and cultural changes to reduce materialist consumerism and excessive individualism. Other important responses to environmental problems are described below.

Environmental Education

Environmental education programs teach about the importance of the environment and the ways in which ecological systems work and are impacted by human activity. Environmental education plays a central role in protecting the environment by allowing students and the general public to become more aware of the nature and causes of environmental problems and how changes in individual behavior, government policies, and corporate practices can have major benefits. By promoting greater appreciation for the value of the natural environment, educational efforts foster environmentally friendly behavior such as recycling, lower use of resources and production of waste and pollution, and more environmental activism and efforts at repairing or preventing damage to the environment.

Environmental Activism

According to a Gallup poll (2018) conducted in March 2017, about 17 percent of respondents (which translates to about 41 million U.S. adults) described themselves as "active participants" in the environmental movement. Another 45 percent described themselves as "sympathetic, but not active" (approximately another 110 million adults). Major environmental movement organizations include the Sierra Club, founded in 1892, the Audubon Society (1905), the National Parks Conservation Association (1919), the National Wildlife Federation (1936), the Nature Conservancy (1951), the World Wide Fund for Nature (1961), the National Resources Defense Council, (1970) and Greenpeace (1972). These and many similar organizations attempt to lobby and put pressure on local, state, and federal governments to pursue environment-friendly policies.

Environmental activists span a wide range of ideologies, from religious to anarchist beliefs, motivating adherents to protect nature. Activist organizations engage in actions such as demonstrations, petition drives, and mobilizing supporters to vote for environmentally friendly candidates. The FBI (2008) described two radical environmental organizations as domestic terrorist groups (meaning engagement in unlawful use or threatened use of violence to achieve political goals), the Earth Liberation Front (ELF) and the Animal Liberation Front (ALF). The ELF supported "monkeywrenching," a term referring to sabotage and or destruction of activities or property viewed as harmful. Monkeywrenching has included tree spiking (placing metal or ceramic spikes in trees to damage saws), sabotage of logging or construction equipment, arson, or other types of damage to property. ALF opposes harming any animals, human or nonhuman. Its members acted against entities that exploited animals for research or profit, including animal research laboratories, the fur business, and mink farms. The FBI reports that ALF and ELF, sometimes apparently working together, committed hundreds of crimes, resulting in tens of millions of dollars in damage.

The funding of environmental organizations is a popular form of philanthropy. But critics claim that the at least $10 billion in contributions since 2000 accomplished little because the money went largely to old movement organizations rather than grassroots groups in communities suffering from serious environmental damage (Montague 2012).

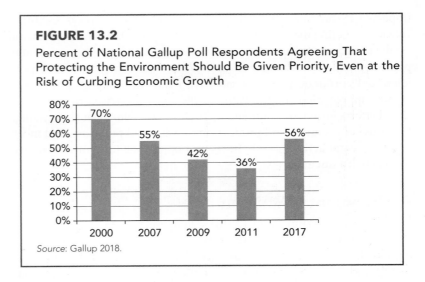

FIGURE 13.2

Percent of National Gallup Poll Respondents Agreeing That Protecting the Environment Should Be Given Priority, Even at the Risk of Curbing Economic Growth

Source: Gallup 2018.

The results of public opinion surveys suggest that by 2017 the environmental movement had lost some of its past support. For example, according to national Gallup polls (2018), while 82 percent of Americans supported stronger enforcement of federal environmental regulations in 2007, only 69 percent did in 2017. Similarly, while 81 percent favored setting tighter emission and pollution standards for businesses and industry in 2001, only 67 percent did in 2017. Seventy-nine percent favored the government spending more money for developing solar and wind power in 2001; 72 percent did in 2017. In addition, while 78 percent of respondents considered themselves "an environmentalist" in 1991, only 42 percent did in 2016. Survey results indicate that attitudes toward protecting the environment are affected by economic conditions. In 2000, 70 percent of national Gallup poll respondents agreed that protecting the environment should be given priority, even at the risk of curbing economic growth. This fell to 55 percent in 2007, and then after the economic recession that began in 2008 the percent favoring prioritizing the environment fell to 42 percent in 2009 and to only 36 percent in 2011, rising to 56 percent in 2016 and 2017 as the economy improved.

Green Energy and Technology

Green technology allows us to access green energy, energy that is renewable and does not cause pollution. Green technology also attempts to eliminate pollution from the use of fossil nonrenewable energy sources.

Solar Power Solar power refers to using the sun's energy for power production and/or use. The simplest method is where the sun heats material that then distributes the heat where needed. For example, black painted metal plates can be placed on a roof to absorb the sun's heat. Circulating water through tubes in the heated plates then provides hot water for the home. Some substances, such as silicon, can convert a

green technology
Technology that allows us to access green energy, energy that is renewable and does not cause pollution.

fraction of the sun's energy that strikes them into electricity. Silicon semiconductors are used to make photovoltaic cells that generate electricity from sunlight. A third way is to use mirrors to focus sunlight into superhot light beams that boil water to propel steam turbine electric generators.

Geothermal Power Geothermal power is energy derived by tapping the Earth's internal heat from molten rock known as magma. The first geothermal production of electricity occurred in Larderello, Italy, in 1904 (*National Geographic* 2017b). In some places, such as near active volcanoes or hot springs, this energy can be exploited near the Earth's surface, but elsewhere special wells must be drilled a mile or more deep to reach the heat that can drive steam-powered electricity-generating turbines.

Wind Power Wind power uses wind to turn electric generators, typically through tall windmills, that produce no pollution at all. Electricity-generating windmills have been installed all around the world, often in flat windswept areas or on bodies of water. Energy kites are an alternate system designed to provide wind produced electricity at a lower cost than windmills. The kites, made of lightweight materials and electronics, fly about 800 feet up, where the winds are stronger and steadier, and send electricity by a tether line to a ground station (Alternative Energy 2017). Small windmills are also used in some locations to reduce household or farm electricity bills.

Biofuel Biofuel is fuel made from living organisms, typically plants. One major example is ethanol, a type of alcohol that can be blended with gasoline for use in cars and trucks. But vehicles with specialized engines, common in the nation of Brazil, can operate solely on ethanol. In the United States ethanol is typically made from corn; in Brazil it is made from sugarcane. Biodiesel is another biofuel that can be made from plant oils, such as palm oil or soybean oil, or from animal fat, to power diesel engines. Ethanol and biodiesel fuel emit fewer particulates into the atmosphere than petroleum-based fuels, contributing less pollution to urban areas (Earth Talk 2015). Also, plant-generated biofuels do not directly add to global warming because the CO_2 released when they burn is the CO_2 absorbed from the air by biofuel plants.

However, there are significant limitations to the use of biofuels. First, research indicates that it actually takes more energy to grow certain biofuel crops, like corn, than the biofuel yields when used. Another problem is that to play a major role in providing energy, huge amounts of agricultural land would have to be diverted from food to fuel production (Conca 2014), thus raising the cost of remaining food crops and/or causing food shortages. One possible better source for biofuel is algae oil produced in salt water.

Nuclear Fusion Nuclear fusion, the sun's process of energy generation and the principle behind the hydrogen bomb, holds the promise of unlimited energy with virtually no pollution (Cleary 2015). Nuclear fusion power plants, unlike current nuclear fission reactors, would not leave radioactive waste behind. The problem is that controlled nuclear fusion, in which atoms of light elements like hydrogen are smashed together at very high speeds to form other elements and in the process release enormous energy, has proved to be a very difficult and expensive technological task. Yet many nations and private companies are hard at work trying to achieve this revolutionary technological breakthrough.

Electric and Hydrogen-Powered Vehicles Electric and hydrogen-powered vehicles do not pollute the areas where they operate. They therefore have significant potential to reduce urban pollution. For electric vehicles like the Tesla to become more widely used, battery technology must be improved to provide faster charging and more mileage per charge. Hydrogen fuel-cell vehicles are powered by motors that use electricity generated by cells in the vehicle that combine hydrogen gas with oxygen. The only emission from this process is water. The fuel tanks of hydrogen vehicles can be filled in only a few minutes, and they can run longer than other electric vehicles (Reuters 2014). But hydrogen fuel cells are relatively expensive.

Carbon Capture and Storage

CO_2 capture and storage (sequestration, CCS) refers to removing CO_2 from power plants or industrial facilities using fossil fuels like coal, oil, or natural gas, compressing and transporting the CO_2 to a suitable location, and then sending it down well shafts as much as a mile or more beneath impenetrable rock into porous areas where it can be permanently stored (EPA 2017l). CCS is being done in some locations and could have a significant impact in reducing CO_2 emissions if carried out on a large scale. But critics fear that some of the buried CO_2 could escape into the atmosphere. Furthermore, if a destructive event like an earthquake suddenly caused the rapid release of huge amounts of stored

CO_2 the results could be catastrophic. Rather than spend hundreds of millions of dollars on CCS, which might unnecessarily prolong the use of fossil fuels, many scientists suggest increasing funding for expanding nonpolluting renewable energy sources.

International Government Policies

Many developing nations view rapid industrialization as the only way to improve standards of living and raise large percentages of poor residents out of poverty. Leaders of these countries often feel that it is unfair that their efforts be impeded by environmental regulations that did not exist when the most advanced societies industrialized. A number of scientists believe that the advanced industrial nations should provide technology and economic assistance to low-income countries to help them industrialize without severely damaging the environment.

There have been numerous international agreements aimed at protecting the environment. The most important include the 1985 Vienna Convention for the Protection of the Ozone and the 1987 Montreal Protocol on Substances that Deplete the Ozone Layer, ratified by all UN recognized nations (EPA 2012). Together these agreements were aimed at significantly reducing the use of ozone-damaging chlorofluorocarbons (CFCs) around the world.

The Kyoto Protocol, adopted in Kyoto, Japan, in 1997, is a major international agreement within the United Nations Framework Convention on Climate Change that commits ratifying parties to the reduction of greenhouse gas (GHG) emissions (United Nations 2014). Viewing the most advanced nations' industries as primarily responsible for high levels of GHG in the atmosphere, the Kyoto Protocol places greater responsibility for GHG emissions reductions on the highly developed countries. By 2014, 191 nations had ratified the Kyoto Protocol, but the United States was not one of them.

In December 2015, the United States and 194 other countries took a major step toward slowing the emission of GHG and the warming of the earth by adopting the Paris Climate Agreement (Cañete 2015; Davenport 2015). The participants committed themselves to taking measures such as reducing the use of fossil fuel and developing and increasing the use of nonpolluting energy sources. The goal is to limit global heat increase to less than 2 degrees Celsius (less than 3.8 degrees Fahrenheit) above Earth's pre-industrial level and ideally below 1.5 Celsius (2.7 degrees Fahrenheit). The United States pledged to reduce its GHG emissions at least 26 percent below 2005 levels by 2025 (Shear 2017). But on June 1, 2017, President Trump announced that the United States would withdraw from the Paris Climate Agreement because abiding by it would damage the U.S. economy and undermine the country's sovereignty.

U.S. Government Policies

The federal government has taken several major actions to protect the environment. The Wilderness Act of 1964 provided for the evaluation and designation of millions of acres of American land as protected wilderness areas (Digest of Federal Resource Laws 2017). The same year, Congress passed the Land and Water Conservation Fund Act, which provides funds to federal, state, and local government to purchase land, water, and wetlands to protect the environment and for public recreational use (U.S. Forest Service 2017). Then the Nixon administration took a major step toward greater protection of the environment with the creation of the Environmental Protection Agency (EPA) in 1970. The EPA was to establish and enforce standards suitable for fulfilling national environmental goals, gather data on the harmful effects of various forms of pollution and on ways to reduce or eliminate them, and provide guidance for the development or modification of environmental policies (EPA 1992). The EPA was also to assist other organizations with preventing environmental pollution through funding, technology, or other means.

Congress also passed the important Clean Air Act in 1970 and proceeded to amend it in 1977 and 1990 to expand its scope (EPA 2017c). This act was intended to reduce the emission of pollutants into the air from various sources. The EPA notes that although after the act's passage U.S. energy consumption increased by 47 percent and population by 53 percent, emissions of six common pollutants decreased by 72 percent. In 1972 Congress amended the 1948 Federal Water Pollution Control Act into the Clean Water Act (CWA). The CWA regulates the quality standards for surface waters such as rivers, streams, lakes, and wetlands, and also controls discharges of pollutants into U.S. waters (EPA 2017m).

In 1973 Congress passed the Endangered Species Act (ESA; National Wildlife Federation 2015). The ESA gives the federal government responsibility to protect "endangered species" (species that are likely to become totally extinct or extinct within a large portion of species' geographical territory), "threatened species" (species that will probably be endangered in the near future), and "critical habitat" (environments crucial to the existence of an endangered or threatened species). Over 1,360 plants and animals came to be listed as endangered or threatened in the United States. Another significant environmental law is the Food Quality Protection Act of 1996. This legislation amended earlier pesticide laws to create more consistent, scientifically based regulations (Cornell University 2017). It requires a single health test standard for all pesticides and for repeated re-evaluation of pesticides.

One important federal measure for protecting the environment is the setting of required fuel-efficiency standards for vehicles. The Corporate Average Fuel Economy (CAFE) program, first enacted by Congress in 1975 and amended by later legislation, set a target of an average of 35.5 miles per gallon by 2016. But in 2012 the Obama administration set a new requirement of 54.5 miles per gallon for the 2025 model year (Vlasic 2012).

The federal government has also provided financial aid for increasing energy efficiency and use of renewable energy. Congress, as part of the 2009 American Recovery and Reinvestment Act, included the Energy Efficiency and Conservation Block Grant Program (EECBG) to assist city, county, and state governments in implementing energy efficiency and conservation efforts to reduce fossil-fuel emissions and overall energy use (Energy.gov 2017; Catalog of Federal Domestic Assistance 2015).

A widely used but controversial antipollution program is cap-and-trade. The government sets a pollution "cap" (limit) for how much of various air pollutants a company can release into the atmosphere. A company that lowers its emissions of pollutants below its cap can then "trade" (sell its unused pollution capacity) to another company for cash. Thus, there is a financial incentive for businesses to try decrease their own emissions in order to make profits by selling their unused level of pollution. The buyers can then increase their emission of pollutants beyond the caps that were set for them. The expectation is that the drive for profits from selling unused pollution capacity will have the effect of reducing overall air pollution in the long run and immediately in areas where the companies emitting below their caps are located. One controversial aspect of the program, however, is that people living near companies that purchase pollution capacity are likely to be exposed to increased levels of pollution (Walker 2012).

U.S. environmental policies and the EPA were affected by the election of Republican Donald Trump as president in 2017. Trump stated that he would expand coal production and the extraction of other fossil fuels to improve the economy and make the United States more energy independent. He and other Republican leaders raised doubts about the validity of climate change. Trump met with U.S. auto corporation executives, raising expectations that the Obama administration's motor vehicle mileage efficiency goals would be reduced or scrapped. And the Trump administration's Secretary of the EPA, Scott Pruitt, had opposed a number of EPA policies and had sued the EPA repeatedly in his former position as attorney general of Oklahoma (*New York Times* 2017). A national Gallup survey conducted during March 1–5, 2017, found that only 36 percent thought that Trump was doing a good job protecting the nation's environment; 57 percent responded that he was doing a poor job. In comparison, a national Gallup survey conducted during March 2–6, 2016 had found that 54 percent thought that Obama was doing a good job protecting the nation's environment, while 39 percent responded that he was doing a poor job (Gallup 2018). In June 2017, after Trump announced that he would withdraw the United States from the Paris Climate Agreement, a *Washington Post*-ABC News poll found that only 28 percent of respondents supported withdrawing while 59 percent opposed (*Washington Post* 2017).

CHAPTER REVIEW

Environmental Problems

Global warming, the ongoing warming of the Earth's land, oceans, and atmosphere, is caused in part by human activity releasing greenhouse gases such as CO_2 into the air. Global warming is linked to climate change, including the extreme weather events of intense heat waves and powerful storms.

Global heating melts polar and glacial ice, raising ocean levels and flooding coastal regions, while drying interior areas and increasing the likelihood of severe wildfires. About 81.4 percent of the world's energy and 81.9 percent of U.S. energy comes from burning fossil fuels that release greenhouse gases and other harmful chemicals and particles into the atmosphere. Many Americans live in areas where air pollution is often at dangerous levels. Globally, air pollution is rising most rapidly in developing countries where industries and the numbers of cars and trucks are increasing. Land pollution includes solid waste, hazardous waste, and e-waste. Radioactive material constitutes another major environmental threat. Wars and preparation for war have caused major environmental damage. Nations have often neglected the environment in developing weapons and waging war. Two of the modern examples were the use of Agent Orange in the Vietnam War and depleted uranium shells in the 1991 Gulf War and the 2003 Iraq War.

The availability and quality of fresh water is insufficient in many countries and is increasingly threatened in others. Globally, much water is contaminated by industrial wastes, pesticide runoff, untreated sewage, and other harmful materials. The burning of fossil fuels contributes to the production of acid rain that poisons lakes and other bodies of water. Certain human activities threaten biodiversity. A high level of biodiversity contributes to a healthy environment and provides resources for the protection and improvement of food crops and the development of medicines.

Environmental Injustice

Environmental injustice and environmental racism refer to relatively powerless groups being more exposed to environmental hazards and having little ability to do anything about it. This is a worldwide problem and includes situations in which advanced nations' economic activities exploit the resources and harm the environment of lesser developed countries.

Sociological Perspectives on the Environment

The structural-functional perspective views human exploitation of the environment as necessary for economic progress. Extracting resources and discharging waste become viewed as problems when resources are seen as finite and escaping the effects of the damaged environment is believed to be impossible. Some functionalists believe that society will develop new technologies to eliminate environmental problems. Others think that cultural change, in particular shifting from self-centered individualism to a more community-oriented concern for achieving sustainable development, will also have to be part of the solution.

The economic-conflict perspective holds that to maximize profits by cutting costs, capitalist businesses attempt to obtain resources from the environment and dispose of waste in the cheapest ways possible. This view implies that less emphasis on maximizing profits would reduce environmental problems. The racial/ethnic-conflict perspective emphasizes that relatively powerless African American and Hispanic minorities are more likely to suffer from health problems caused by hazardous waste. Internationally, corporations from the United States and European countries exploit the resources of nonwhite peoples with little regard for the environmental damage they cause. The feminist-conflict perspective holds that the traditional masculine orientation is to dominate and exploit both women and nature. In contrast, women tend to be more supportive of others and the environment. Having more women in positions of power in government and the economy will contribute significantly to solving environmental problems.

The symbolic-interactionist approach emphasizes that environmental problems and potential solutions are linked to people's knowledge, values, and attitudes shaped through interaction with others and the media. This perspective also focuses on how people bring attention to environmental issues, how competing groups try to define and explain them, and how they propose to solve them.

Causes of Environmental Problems

There are multiple causes of environmental problems. Population growth increases the consumption of resources and environmental pollution. Economic development has also increased resource use and pollution. Fear of being militarily or economically overwhelmed by foreign enemies has motivated nations to engage in crash militarization and industrialization programs with little concern for environmental consequences. Materialist culture promotes unnecessarily rapid depletion of resources and a high level of waste, as "obsolete" items are continuously discarded in favor of the latest trends. Excessive individualism damages the environment by placing selfish personal interests above community welfare, including nature's collective resources, the environment, and climate.

Responding to Environmental Problems

Social responses to environmental problems include slowing population growth, cultural changes to reduce materialism and excessive individualism, environmental education, environmental activism, and scientific innovations. Green technology includes solar power, geothermal power, wind power, biofuel, nuclear fusion, and electric- and hydrogen-powered vehicles.

Major international agreements, such as the 1985 Vienna Convention, the 1987 Montreal Protocol, the 1997 Kyoto Protocol, and the 2015 Paris Climate Agreement are aimed at getting nations to cooperate in protecting the environment.

The U.S. government has taken several major actions to safeguard the environment. This includes passing laws to protect wilderness areas and legislation to create the EPA, decrease air and water pollution, and protect biodiversity. But after the 2016 presidential election, federal government assessment of environmental issues appeared to change.

KEY TERMS

air pollution, p. 350
brownfields, p. 353
climate change, p. 349
environmental injustice, p. 360
environmental justice, p. 360
environmental racism, p. 361
e-waste, p. 354
excessive individualism, p. 368

global warming, p. 348
greenhouse effect, p. 348
green technology, p. 370
hazardous waste, p. 352
land pollution, p. 351
materialist consumerism, p. 368
sustainable development, p. 363

DISCUSSION QUESTIONS

1. Do you think global warming is actually taking place? Why or why not? Why do you think this has become a political issue?

2. What do you consider the greatest threats to the global environment? Justify your choices.

3. What are the greatest threats to the environment in your state or community?

4. How can we end environmental injustice and environmental racism?

5. Overall, which sociological perspective is most helpful for identifying the solutions to environmental problems? Justify your answer.

6. What actions or policies do you favor to provide greater protection for the environment? Explain your choices.

CHAPTER 14

Drug Abuse and Human Trafficking

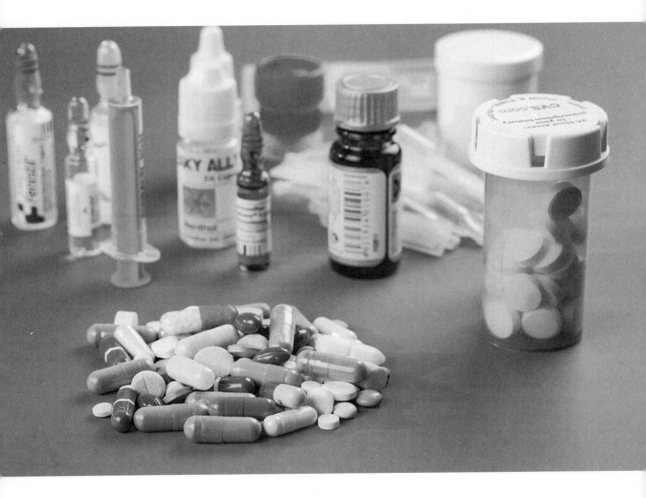

CHAPTER OBJECTIVES

- Explain what drugs and drug abuse are.
- Describe the levels and effects of drug abuse.
- Explain why people use drugs.
- Describe efforts to reduce drug abuse.
- Describe forms and characteristics of human trafficking.
- Describe efforts to combat human trafficking.

PEOPLE ARE CONTINUOUSLY BOMBARDED *with messages telling them that they need to use drugs for a variety of reasons: treating ailments, preventing aging, stopping hair loss, losing weight, building muscles, enhancing mood, and improving performance. But drugs are often misused. One of the biggest drug scandals involves major league baseball players using drugs to improve performance. Investigations indicate the many players used performance-enhancing drugs (PEDs) from the late 1980s through the early 2000s. During this period the number of home runs hit per game reached a high point. Although no player had hit more than 60 home runs in a single season since 1961 (when Roger Maris hit 61), three players later accused of using PEDs exceeded this number. Sammy Sosa hit 66 home runs in 1998, 63 in 1999, and 64 in 2001; Mark McGwire hit 70 in 1998 and 65 in 1999; and Barry Bonds hit 73 in 2001! None of these players will likely ever be admitted to the Baseball Hall of Fame because of widespread belief that their achievements were due to the unfair advantage of PEDs. The introduction of harsh penalties for PED use was followed by a drastic decline in both home runs and runs per game (Branch 2014). In the 2014 baseball season, the average runs scored per game was about 21 percent lower than in 2000 and home runs 25 percent lower.*

WHAT IS A DRUG?

A **drug** is any substance, other than food or water, that affects the functioning, development, or condition of the body. They can affect thought processes, awareness, sensations, emotions, performance, and health. For thousands of years, millions of people have used naturally occurring substances as cures for illnesses, to alter perception or feelings, or to otherwise affect the body. Eventually, many synthetic chemicals were created. Commonly used legal drugs include alcohol, aspirin, and caffeine. Tens of millions of people drink coffee in the morning to help get ready for the day or to stay up late studying for exams. And millions take aspirin to relieve headaches or low-dose aspirin daily to help prevent heart disease and cancer.

Many people distinguish between "good" drugs, which are legal and assumed to be beneficial or at least harmless if not used to excess, and "bad" drugs which are illegal, like cocaine and heroin, and viewed as causing harm and addiction. But there are wide variations in the perception of how harmful drugs are and what government drug policy should be. And as noted in Chapter 10, public opinion on drugs can change significantly. The sale of alcohol was criminalized from 1920 to 1933 but then re-legalized. Similarly, marijuana went from being legal to illegal and appears to be undergoing a widespread process of becoming legal again.

Further, drugs that are seen as dangerous in one culture may be viewed as beneficial in another. In Bolivia, for example, the coca plant (from which cocaine is made) is used by the country's indigenous majority. The leaves are chewed or boiled in water to make tea to prevent altitude sickness, alleviate the sensation of hunger, or act as a stimulant.

drug Any substance, other than food or water, that affects the functioning, development, or condition of the body.

Drug abuse (also known as substance abuse) is the use of a drug that is illegal or use of a legal drug in amounts or in ways harmful to the user or others. For example, using a drug in a way that results in inability to fulfill occupational obligations would typically be viewed as abuse. Another variety of drug abuse is using a mood- or behavior-altering drug that impairs ability to drive a car or pilot an airplane. Drug abuse can also include taking a substance to boost performance illegally or in violation of rules by which the person is bound, such as use by professional athletes in certain sports.

Extent of Drug Use Internationally

International surveys in 2008 by the World Health Organization (WHO) (CBS News 2008) and in 2013 by the Global Drug Survey (Winstock 2014) together interviewed almost 133,000 people in twenty-six countries. The findings reveal that alcohol, tobacco, and caffeine are the most widely used legal drugs. Marijuana is by far the most widely used illegal drug, with cocaine a distant second. The results indicate that alcohol consumption is much greater in Europe, Japan, and the Americas than in the Middle East, Africa, or China. Tobacco use is very high in Middle Eastern countries like Egypt, Lebanon, and Jordan, where as many as 40 to 50 percent (or more) of men smoke (Malik 2009). In China an estimated 28.1 percent of population (more than 300 million people) smokes (World Health Organization 2017d). This includes about 52.9 percent of Chinese men and 2.4 percent of Chinese women. And in the United States about 16.7 percent of adult (eighteen or over) men and 13.6 percent of adult women are "current smokers" who smoke cigarettes "every day or some days" (Centers for Disease Control 2017a).

The international WHO drug survey (Degenhardt et al. 2008) of 54,000 adults in Belgium, China, Colombia, France, Germany, Israel, Italy, Japan, Lebanon, Mexico, Netherlands, New Zealand, Nigeria, South Africa, Spain, Ukraine, and the United States revealed that the United States and New Zealand had the "highest" percentages of respondents reporting ever using marijuana during their lifetime (about 42 percent). The United States also had the highest percentage reporting using cocaine at least once during their lifetime (16 percent), four times the percentage of the next highest country, New Zealand. Interestingly, in the Netherlands, a country with significantly more liberal drug laws than the United States and New Zealand, only about 20 percent reported having used marijuana and only 2 percent cocaine.

Drug Use in the United States

According to the National Institute on Drug Abuse (2017a), 10.6 percent of U.S. residents age twelve or over reported using an illicit drug at least once during the month in 2016 preceding their interview. A similar national survey in 2012 (National Center for Health Statistics 2014) found that males and females in the twelve to seventeen age category used illicit drugs about equally. But for all age groups combined, men

drug abuse The use of a drug that is illegal or a legal drug in amounts or in ways harmful to the user or others.

TABLE 14.1	Percentages of Persons in the United States Age 12 or over Reporting Lifetime, Past Year, and Past Month Use of Illegal and Legal Drugs in 2016		
Drug	**Lifetime**	**Past Year**	**Past Month**
Alcohol	80.2	64.8	50.7
Cigarettes	57.4	22.7	19.1
Smokeless Tobacco	16.1	4.4	3.3
Any Illegal Drug	48.5	18.0	10.6
Marijuana/Hashish	44.0	13.9	8.9
Cocaine	14.4	1.9	0.7
Crack Cocaine	3.3	0.3	0.2
Heroin	1.8	0.4	0.2
Hallucinogens	15.4	1.8	0.5
LSD	9.6	0.7	0.1
MDMA-Ecstasy	6.9	0.9	0.2
Inhalants	9.1	0.6	0.2
Methamphetamine	5.4	0.5	0.2

Source: National Institute on Drug Abuse 2017a.

were almost 70 percent more likely to use illicit drugs than women. In the eighteen to twenty-five age category, slightly over 21 percent reported illicit drug use, a higher percentage than any other age group. White Americans were slightly less likely to report using illicit drugs than African Americans or Hispanic Americans. But Asian Americans were far less likely to use illicit drugs than any other ethnic or racial group.

Alcohol

Alcohol is the most widely used recreational drug in the United States. About 80 percent of Americans age twelve or older reported at least some alcohol use in 2016 and nearly 51 percent at least monthly (National Institute on Drug Abuse 2017a). Although the legal age for purchasing drinking alcohol in the United States is twenty-one, about 27 percent of young people aged twelve to seventeen claim to have used alcohol, and 9.2 percent reported monthly use. Alcohol, a depressant that affects the central nervous system and slows brain activity, is generally safe unless consumed excessively or in inherently dangerous situations such as operating a car, boat, or plane. The Centers for Disease Control (CDC 2017i) refers to "excessive drinking" as including "**binge drinking**" and "heavy drinking," defined in terms of the number of drinks consumed in a given time period. In addition, the CDC refers to drinking alcohol while pregnant or underage as excessive drinking.

A "drink" (CDC 2017i) is any one of the following: 12 ounces of beer (5 percent alcohol content); 8 ounces of malt liquor (7 percent alcohol content); 5 ounces of wine (12 percent alcohol content); or 1.5 ounces of 80 proof (40 percent alcohol content) distilled spirits or liquor (e.g., gin, rum, vodka, or whiskey). The CDC defines "binge drinking" as drinking that brings the blood alcohol concentration level to 0.08 percent or more. For women this would typically involve consuming four or more drinks during a single occasion (generally during a period of two hours or less) and for men five or more drinks during a single occasion. Heavy drinking is defined for women as eight or more drinks per week and for men as fifteen or more drinks per week. Research indicates that one in six adult Americans binge drinks around four times a month, consuming an average of eight drinks on each occasion (CDC 2017j). Not surprisingly, binge drinking is associated with higher risks of car crashes, falls, burns and drowning, firearm injuries, sexual assault, unintended pregnancy, domestic violence, and alcohol poisoning. In the long term, it's linked to birth defects, liver disease, and cardiovascular disease.

One significant concern is drinking among young people. Each year an estimated 599,000 students between the ages of eighteen and twenty-four experience unintended injuries related to alcohol, and 1,825 of them die (National Institute on Alcohol Abuse and Alcoholism 2015). A further 690,000 are assaulted by other students who have been drinking. And around 97,000 college students are victimized by alcohol-related sexual assault or date rape.

The American College Health Association (2017a, 2017b) asked questions about alcohol use in its spring 2017 survey of 63,497 students at 92 colleges and universities in all 50 states and the District of Columbia. The results indicated that about 66.7 percent of students used alcohol within the 30 days preceding their taking of the survey. And 31.5 percent of all students surveyed reported that they had consumed five or more drinks in a single sitting at least once in the two weeks before taking the survey. Although the percent of college women who drink alcohol is virtually the same as for men, men increasingly exceed women as the level of drinking increases from light to moderate to heavy drinking. The survey also found that among students who reported drinking alcohol within the 12 months preceding the survey, 35.2 percent reported doing something while drinking that they later regretted,

binge drinking Drinking that brings the blood alcohol concentration level to 0.08 percent or more. For women this would typically involve consuming four or more drinks and for men five or more drinks during a period of two hours or less.

21.5 percent had unprotected sex, 12.3 percent physically injured themselves, 2 percent got into trouble with the police, 1.2 percent physically injured another person, 0.3 percent reported they had sex with someone without that person's consent, and 2.4 percent said that someone had sex with them without their consent. In addition, 3.4 percent seriously considered suicide.

Tobacco and Nicotine

Unlike alcohol, there seems to be no safe way to use tobacco. The active drug in tobacco, nicotine, is highly addictive, and many of the chemicals present in tobacco or produced when tobacco burns are toxic and carcinogenic. The risk for developing lung cancer is about twenty-five times greater for men who smoke cigarettes and twenty-six times higher for women compared to men and women who have never smoked, respectively (CDC 2017k). Smoking cigarettes also increases the risk of developing many other types of cancer, including of the mouth, esophagus, larynx, pancreas, cervix, urinary bladder, and kidney. Smoking also increases by two to four times the risk of coronary heart disease, the leading cause of death in the United States, and the risk of stroke. Nonsmokers who are exposed to secondhand smoke also have an increased risk of coronary heart disease and cancer. Smoking also increases the likelihood of pregnancy complications, premature birth, low-birth-weight infants, stillbirth, and sudden infant death syndrome. In total, about 480,000 people die from smoking each year in the United States, more than the combined deaths from illegal drugs, alcohol use, motor vehicle injuries, firearms, and HIV/AIDS. Despite all the health damage and premature deaths due to tobacco use, millions of adult Americans continue to smoke. And there has been a persisting trend for many teenagers and young adults to begin smoking (National Institute on Drug Abuse 2017a).

Cannabis: Marijuana, Hashish

Cannabis-derived substances, marijuana and hashish, are the most widely used illegal drugs in the United States About 44 percent of the U.S. population age twelve or over have tried marijuana, hashish, or both, according to the National Institute on Drug Abuse (2017a). And an estimated 8.9 percent use marijuana or hashish at least once a month. The psychoactive component in marijuana and hashish is THC (tetrahydrocannabinol). While marijuana is made from the flowers and certain leaves of the female marijuana plant, hashish is made from the resin-producing parts of the plant and has a significantly higher concentration of THC.

People use these drugs by smoking them or eating them as ingredients in foods like brownies or cookies. Most users of marijuana or hashish believe the drugs help them relax and experience a sense of euphoria, and can often stimulate appetite. But there is some evidence that heavy use is associated with sluggishness, disorientation, or even paranoia. Another concern is that marijuana and hashish can be

Poster supporting legalization of marijuana

gateway drugs leading to the use of other illegal drugs. Critics argue that most users of these drugs do not go on to be regular users of heroin or cocaine and that heavy use of legal drugs like alcohol and tobacco can also precede cocaine or heroin use.

As noted in Chapter 10, marijuana was made illegal by the federal Marijuana Tax Act of 1937. But in 2013 and 2014, national opinion surveys showed that a clear majority of Americans eighteen and over supported the legalization of marijuana (CNN 2014). Support for legalization had been 43 percent in 2012, 34 percent in 2002, 26 percent in 1996, and just 16 percent in 1987. In 2014 the only major demographic groups with majorities still opposed to legalization were Republicans, southerners, and people over sixty-five. Men were somewhat more in favor than women, and about two-thirds of those eighteen to forty-nine supported legalization. Public support resulted in eight states (Alaska, California, Colorado, Maine, Massachusetts, Nevada, Oregon, and Washington), and the District of Colombia legalizing marijuana for recreational use by 2017.

Cocaine

Cocaine is a powerful stimulant (National Institute on Drug Abuse 2017b) that heightens alertness, induces feelings of excitement and euphoria, and can reduce appetite. It also has a strong potential for addiction. It is present, along with other chemicals, in the leaves of the coca plant. Indigenous people in Bolivia and Peru chew coca leaves and drink tea made from coca leaves, as they have done for hundreds of years, to increase alertness and energy, experience euphoric feelings, and suppress hunger pangs during food shortages.

A German scientist successfully isolated cocaine from coca leaves for the first time in 1855. Many Europeans and Americans initially believed that cocaine was a beneficial drug, and it was for a time included in some medicines and drinks, including Mariani Wine and, between 1886 to 1906, Coca-Cola.

Cocaine was promoted by some employers who believed it helped their workers work longer and more productively and over time cocaine use became more prevalent among blue-collar workers and lower income-persons. Upper- and middle-class bias against the lower classes may have played a role in a wave of local, state, and federal laws that effectively banned cocaine in the early twentieth century. Most important was the Harrison Narcotics Act of 1914. Another factor was that much of the public came to believe that cocaine was a major cause of violent crime and other crimes like prostitution.

In the 1980s the amount of cocaine coming into the United States increased dramatically, and prices fell. Crack cocaine use surged, particularly among African Americans. Crack is a crystallized material made by mixing powder cocaine with another substance, usually baking soda, and heating the mixture until it forms small "rocks." This hard or

gateway drug A drug whose use is thought to lead to the use of one or more other illegal drugs.

solid form of cocaine, also known as "base," "rock," and "gravel," can be smoked. This introduces the cocaine into the blood stream more rapidly, producing a quick, intense high. Crack is believed to be more addictive than powdered cocaine. Some law enforcement authorities also believe that use of crack cocaine is associated with violent crime. However, the violence linked to crack cocaine may also be due to conflict between gangs involved in the drug trade.

Methamphetamine

Methamphetamine, like cocaine, is a stimulant. Taken in low does, it increases alertness, energy and the ability to concentrate in fatigued persons, and can elevate mood and induce a feeling of euphoria. High doses or long-term use can lead to psychosis and other problems like addiction or even cerebral hemorrhage. When methamphetamine was first sold by a Berlin drug company in 1938, a high-ranking German general saw it as a miracle drug that could both help exhausted pilots and soldiers stay awake and boost their morale (Hurst 2013). The German military command provided millions of methamphetamine tablets (called *Panzerschokolade*, "tank chocolate") to the armed forces. The German users of the drug were the first to become aware of its long-term, often devastating effects. Many soldiers became addicted and experienced bouts of dizziness, sweating, depression, and hallucinations. Some even died of heart failure or shot themselves during psychotic episodes. Even though government health officials wanted to limit methamphetamines, the Nazi regime continued providing the drug to try to get the most out of their pilots and troops.

Today methamphetamine is a relatively easy and inexpensive drug to produce and is sold under names like "meth," "speed," "crank," "crystal," or "ice." Many people worldwide became aware of methamphetamine through watching the hugely popular American TV series Brea*king Bad*, in which a terminally ill high school chemistry teacher with money problems and a former student team up to make and sell the drug with ultimately brutal and tragic consequences.

Heroin and Other Opioids

Opioids are "natural or synthetic chemicals that interact with opioid receptors on nerve cells in the body and brain, and reduce the intensity of pain signals and feelings of pain" (CDC 2017l). They include the illegal drug heroin and legally available pain medications such as oxycodone, hydrocodone, morphine, and codeine. Heroin is a compound that releases morphine into the body. Morphine is derived from the opium produced by poppy plants. Heroin users report that the drug boosts their self-esteem and creates feelings of warmth, contentment, and even euphoria. Despite the fact that by the fall of 2014 the United States had spent $7.6 billion on poppy plant eradication and incentives for new crops in Afghanistan as part of its then-thirteen-year war effort, that country supplied at least 80 percent of the world market for opium (Bienaimé 2014; Martinez and Siegel 2014). Although almost all nations

opioid epidemic The dramatic growth in opioid drug use and deaths since 1999.

now severely regulate or ban the sale of opium, morphine, and heroin, in the nineteenth century there was an enormous international opium trade in which businessmen from Great Britain were major players. When the Chinese government banned opium being brought to China from Britain's India and Burma colonies and burned a shipment of British opium, Britain launched a series of successful opium wars against China between 1839 and 1860. The victorious British forced China to allow the opium trade, which Chinese leaders claim led to tens of millions more opium addicts. And the British punished China by requiring it to give up Hong Kong Island, provide Chinese territory for British personnel who would be subject to British rather than Chinese law, and pay millions of dollars in reparations.

While the use of some illegal drugs in the United States has fallen, heroin use has been on the rise. According to the U.S. Substance Abuse and Mental Health Services Administration (SAMHSA), while there were 90,000 first-time heroin users in 2002, there were 156,000 first-time users in 2012 (about a 73 percent increase) (DiSalvo 2014). For the nation as a whole, the CDC reported that in 2015 heroin-related deaths surpassed gun homicide deaths for the first time (Ingraham 2016b).The growth in heroin use may be due in part to heroin being substituted for prescription painkillers because the price of painkillers rose while the price of heroin fell. Deaths from prescription opioid drugs like oxycodone, hydrocodone, and methadone also rose, more than quadrupling between 1999 and 2015. The CDC (2017m) has labeled the dramatic growth in opioid drug use and deaths the **opioid epidemic**. Ninety-one Americans die from opioid overdose everyday (including heroin and prescribed opioids). Total drug overdose deaths in 2015, about 47,000 (approximately six in ten from opioids), exceeded the number of people killed in car accidents, 38,000 (Smialek 2017).

Noting the growth in heroin use in western Massachusetts at the conclusion of his CNN program *Parts Unknown Massachusetts*, Anthony Bourdain (2014) commented that many Americans were relatively unconcerned with the imprisonment on drug charges of large masses of minority young men and women and what this has done to their lives. But the increase in heroin use by whites has shocked many into viewing heroin as a more universal issue requiring a better approach than the heavily punitive strategy of the past.

Opioid saturation of the United States

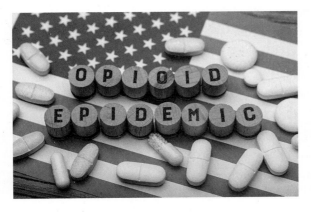

Prescription Drugs

Some medications that physicians prescribe to treat illnesses or other medical conditions have mind-altering properties. Because of this, many people abuse these drugs by taking them in amounts or for purposes not intended by a physician (National Institute on Drug Abuse 2017d). Another form of prescription drug abuse occurs when a person other than the person for whom the medicine was prescribed uses it for a nonmedical purpose. Commonly abused medicines include painkillers such as oxycodone (Oxycontin) and hydrocodone (Vicodin) and depressants for treating anxiety and sleep disorders such as diazepam (Valium).

Hallucinogens: LSD, Peyote, and MDMA

Hallucinogens are drugs that cause significant distortions in people's perceptions of reality (hallucinations). Under the influence of hallucinogens, people may feel sensations, hear sounds, or see things that are not real. LSD (d-lysergic acid diethylamide) is one of the most powerful hallucinogens (National Institute on Drug Abuse 2016a). Discovered in 1938, it is made from lysergic acid found in ergot, a fungus that grows on grains, particularly on rye. Hallucinations and bizarre behavior caused by eating rye bread with ergot very possibly played a major role in the mass executions of thousands of alleged "witches" in Europe during the Middle Ages. LSD is usually sold as a tablet, and sometimes in liquid form. It was most popular in the 1960s and early 1970s, when many young people were alienated from adult society. LSD psychedelic "trips" could last for as long as 12 hours. Users of LSD may experience several emotions simultaneously or swing quickly from one emotion to another. Large doses can produce visual hallucinations or delusions or the feeling of seeing sounds or hearing colors. Some users feel a sense of despair, have terrifying thoughts, or have "flashbacks," which are repetitions of part of a previous drug experience, sometimes as long as a year or more later. LSD was used in secret government experiments and research, sometimes on unknowing subjects, in efforts to develop better interrogation techniques or even recruit enemy agents or soldiers.

Peyote cactus contains the chemical mescaline. The hallucinogenic effects of a dose, which can also be produced synthetically, can last 12 hours. Some mushrooms that grow in tropical areas contain the hallucinogen psilocybin. After eating these mushrooms, hallucinogenic effects can last 6 hours. MDMA (3, 4-methylenedioxy-methamphetamine) (Ecstasy or Molly) is also often classified as a hallucinogen. It is a psychoactive synthetic drug that produces effects similar to both the stimulant methamphetamine and the hallucinogen mescaline, such as feelings of increased energy, emotional empathy toward others, euphoria, and sensory and time perception distortions (National Institute on Drug Abuse 2016b).

Steroids

Anabolic steroids, or, more precisely, anabolic (constructive) androgenic (masculinizing) steroids, are synthetic derivatives of the male hormone testosterone (ESPN 2014). This steroid helps the body retain ingested protein, aiding in the building of muscles. Despite the fact that taking nonmedically prescribed steroids is illegal, many athletes have taken anabolic steroids to increase muscles and strength. Anabolic steroids are designed to accomplish the bodybuilding functions of testosterone. While healthy males typically produce under 10 milligrams of testosterone per day (and females very small amounts), some athletes may use hundreds of milligrams of steroids per day.

Possible bad effects from anabolic steroids in men include pain in urinating, and, ironically, reduced sperm count and impotence; for women undesirable effects can include voice deepening and facial hair. Both men and women may experience rapid weight gain, bloated appearance, acne, liver damage, heightened cholesterol levels, and premature heart attacks and strokes. But unlike most other drugs, the negative side effects of anabolic steroids may not become apparent for months or even many years.

Inhalants

The National Institute on Drug Abuse (2012, 2017c) notes that although parents are concerned about discouraging their children from using drugs like cocaine and heroin, they sometimes pay little attention to the dangers from common household products with solvents or aerosols like glues, deodorant sprays, hair sprays, cleaning fluids, lighter fluid, and nail polish remover. Many children try to become intoxicated by inhaling the vapors from these chemical sources. Research shows that almost 22 million Americans aged twelve or older have tried inhalants at least once in their lives. One NIDA survey indicates that about 13 percent of 8th graders have tried inhalants. Use of inhalants can damage the brain, heart, liver, and kidneys, and can even cause death.

PROBLEMS RELATED TO DRUG ABUSE

Drug abuse is linked to a number of problems. These include making people more likely to commit crime, including child neglect and abuse. The demand for illegal drugs also fosters the development of organized crime to supply them.

Crime

Heavy alcohol use appears to obstruct rational thinking and remove inhibitions to engaging in violence, as well as other dangerous or risky behaviors. Research shows that alcohol was a factor in the homicides committed by 40 percent of those imprisoned for the crime of murder (National Council on Alcoholism and Drug Dependence 2017). Alcohol is more likely to be involved in homicide, aggravated assault, and rape than any other drug. Two-thirds of violence victims who were assaulted by an intimate (such as a current or former spouse, boyfriend or girlfriend) reported that alcohol was involved.

Other forms of criminal behavior associated with drugs are robbery and burglary (engaged in by persons trying to obtain the money to buy drugs), the illegal business of supplying drugs, and crimes resulting from competition among suppliers. Because millions of U.S. residents want to buy illegal drugs, many people engage in the organized crime business of importing, growing, manufacturing, or distributing drugs. Groups competing to supply illegal drugs may engage in violent competition with one another. During the rise of crack cocaine use in the United States during the 1980s there was a dramatic increase in the number of young people in youth gangs selling the drug. While the number of all homicide victims in the United States grew by 25 percent during the

Special Topics: Mexican Organized Crime, Corruption, and the Massacre of Forty-Three College Students

Demonstrators protesting the disappearance of 43 Mexican students

Extreme economic inequality, poverty, and lack of legitimate opportunities have provided a fertile environment for the growth of Mexican drug cartels. As in many societies, police typically do not interfere with important businesses and may even assist them. In the poorest parts of Mexico, this is the often the illegal business of providing drugs for the huge U.S. market.

Approximately 100,000 people are known to have died since 2007 due to organized crime violence, and thousands more simply disappeared (*New York Times* 2014). A Human Rights Watch investigation in 2013 found strong evidence that in 149 of 250 examined disappearance cases, government personnel appear to have played a role.

One of the most barbaric mass murders carried out by organized crime with apparent police assistance occurred on September 26, 2014, in the city of Iguala, State of Guerrero, 120 miles south of Mexico City. Forty-three college students were murdered. Authorities say that Iguala is dominated by a criminal gang called the Guerreros Unidos (United Warriors), which controls many of the local police (Krauze 2014). Dozens of students from the left-wing Ayotzinapa teachers college, the Escuela Normal Rural Raúl Isidro

Burgos, arrived in Iguala on the 26th to solicit for donations and to commandeer buses in order to travel. Students had done this before and returned the buses on their way home. The college, founded in 1926, has a leftist orientation and culture that views Marx, Lenin, and Che Guevara as heroes (Krauze 2014). The students are mostly the idealistic sons of poor farmers (Grillooct 2014) committed to a socioeconomic transformation of Mexico to benefit lower-income groups. Drug dealers and corrupt officials oppose the students largely because political protests and revolutionary activism are considered bad for the drug business. Investigating officials have concluded that Iguala's mayor thought the students would disrupt a speech to be given by his wife and ordered the police to stop them (*New York Times* 2014). Police then attacked the students in a shootout that left six people dead, and turned the surviving students over to drug gang members, who murdered them and disposed of the bodies. The mass slaughter of the students enraged millions and led to huge demonstrations against what protestors viewed as ineffective and corrupt government officials, political parties, and police. The mayor of Iguala, his wife, and a number of police officers and gang members were arrested. Many people demanded a new Mexican revolution to destroy what they called the narco-state (a country dominated by drug cartels and corrupt politicians and officials) and to provide more equality of opportunity.

What are your thoughts?

What is more to blame for Mexican groups that supply illegal drugs to the United States, the millions of Americans who buy illegal drugs or U.S. drug laws that make supplying drugs illegal? Explain your answer.

crack epidemic between 1985 and 1992, there was a 71 percent increase in the number of white homicide victims aged fifteen to nineteen and a 156 percent increase in the number of African American homicide victims in this age category (FBI 1986, 1993)!

The cost of drugs also motivates many low-income drug users to engage in various forms of theft and in prostitution to purchase drugs. According the National Council on Alcoholism and Drug Dependence (2017), nearly 50 percent of all the persons locked up in jails or prisons are clinically addicted. The feature describes how the illegal drug business has affected Mexico.

Drugs and the Family

Parental substance abuse can lead to an unstable, chaotic, and unpredictable home environment, resulting in child abuse (Child Welfare Information Gateway 2016, 2017). Millions of children live with at least one parent who is dependent on alcohol or illegal drugs. These children are at greater risk of maltreatment, physical, emotional, and social problems, and engaging in substance abuse themselves. Drug-abusing parents who neglect or otherwise mistreat their children can interfere with their ability to form secure bonds or attachments, leading to mistrust of others and unwillingness to learn from adults and to an abnormally limited ability to feel remorse for harming others. Recognition of the links between parental substance abuse and child maltreatment led many states to enact laws focusing on the exposure of children to parental involvement with drugs. In twenty states, for example, the production or possession of methamphetamine in the presence of a child is a felony. The same is true in ten states for the production or possession of any controlled substance in the presence of a child.

WHY DO PEOPLE USE DRUGS?

People who use drugs do so for a variety of biological, psychological, economic, and sociological reasons (National Institute on Drug Abuse 2014).

Physical or Psychological Problems Many substances are used to deal with illnesses, injuries, and disabilities. Therapeutic functions of drugs include relieving pain, preventing seizures, and reducing the effects of mental disorders such as schizophrenia.

Performance Enhancement Some drugs are taken in the belief that they enhance physical or mental performance or provide energy, alertness, and the ability to fight fatigue. Some persons who have set records or won championships in sports have later been accused of taking PEDs, including winners of the Tour de France and Olympic gold medals (CNN 2017b).

Escaping Stress or the Effects of Trauma Many people suffer from the long-term effects of traumatic events such as child physical or sexual abuse or wartime experiences. Some take drugs to relieve post-traumatic stress. People may also take drugs to reduce anxiety during or in anticipation of stressful situations. For example, a politician might have a drink before giving a speech, a surgeon before performing an operation, or a policeman before working undercover.

Recreation Often drugs are taken for recreational purposes. For example, people may consume wine or beer or smoke marijuana at a party to feel more relaxed and sociable.

Controversial Psychological Aims Since certain drugs can affect thought processes, some people take drugs with the goal of altering their consciousness and/or perception or to achieve what they believe will be a unique experience.

Pressure to Socially Conform Many people use to drugs primarily to conform to the perceived expectations of others. For example, freshmen going to their first college parties may feel pressured to fit in by taking a toke on a marijuana joint being passed around or to take a bite out of a "magic" marijuana brownie to please a new roommate or boyfriend or girlfriend.

Cultural Tradition Some drug use is part of people's ethnic cultures or religions. As noted earlier, some indigenous people in Bolivia chew coca leaves and drink coca tea as traditional ways to relieve altitude sickness and hunger.

SOCIOLOGICAL PERSPECTIVES ON DRUG ABUSE

The structural-functional perspective attempts to identify any positive functions drug use has for society, while the conflict approach focuses on the role inequality plays in causing drug use and in affecting which drugs are illegal and how drug laws are enforced. The symbolic- interactionist perceptive emphasizes how interaction and learning affect what people think and do about drugs.

Structural-Functional Perspective

While many drugs are intended to treat illness and disease, some other drugs also appear to have positive functions for society. For example, ingesting caffeine in coffee, soda pop, or chocolate can make people wake up faster and overcome fatigue, helping them to drive vehicles more safely, get to work on time, and be more productive. Occasional moderate use of alcohol may help increase social solidarity by helping people socialize and get to know each other better. And some drugs also help people under stress or suffering from the effects of trauma survive and contribute to society. It is also clear that the sale and production of both legal and illegal drugs provides jobs and income for tens of thousands of people. On the other hand, drug abuse can result in major dysfunctions for society, such as those described in the earlier section, "Problems Related to Drugs."

Conflict Perspective

The conflict approach holds that economic, political, and social inequalities influence both drug use and the regulation of drugs. This perspective argues that economic insecurity and stress, coupled with feelings of frustration, hopelessness, and powerlessness, motivate disadvantaged people to engage in drug abuse as a means of escape. Thus, the level of drug abuse could be reduced by reducing structural inequalities. The legality of a drug and the severity of drug law enforcement have historically been greatly affected by the political power and social status of those who most use that particular drug, and by whether powerful interest groups benefit from a drug being legal or illegal. For example, the producers of tobacco products have used their power to downplay the enormous damage done by this extremely harmful drug, and to keep it legal. Making certain drugs illegal benefitted the owners of the legal alcohol and tobacco industries by helping them monopolize the legal recreational drug market.

The racial/ethnic-conflict perspective notes that some drugs that became illegal in the United States were used disproportionately by lower-income persons and minorities. For example, racial/ethnic-conflict theorists point out that opium smoking, engaged in by Chinese immigrant workers in the western United States, was declared illegal through a succession of government actions beginning with a San Francisco law passed in 1874 (PBS 1998). Marijuana, used disproportionately by Hispanic and African Americans, was made illegal through the federal Marijuana Tax Act of 1937. This benefitted white men in competition for jobs with other groups because minorities could be stigmatized as users of illicit harmful drugs.

Symbolic-Interactionist Perspective

Symbolic interactionists note that drugs viewed as beneficial and a normal part of life or even religious practice in one culture can be defined as harmful and destructive in another. People learn about drugs and whether and how to use them from communicating with others. This observation suggests that shared views about a drug may not be entirely due to the properties of the drug but are in part be due to learning experiences.

SOCIAL RESPONSES TO THE DRUG PROBLEM

A wide range of responses have been implemented or proposed for dealing with drug abuse. These include attempts to eliminate the production of illegal drugs, cut off drug supply lines, and prosecute and imprison drug suppliers and users. Other efforts include educating people to the dangers of drug abuse, providing treatment for drug abusers, attacking the root causes of drug abuse, or even legalizing and regulating the use of currently illegal drugs.

The War on Drugs

war on drugs U.S. efforts to reduce illegal drug use by educating people about drugs, stopping the manufacture of illicit drugs, preventing the flow of foreign drugs into the United States, prosecuting and punishing those who sell or use illegal drugs, and providing treatment for persons addicted to drugs.

The United States for decades has publicly committed itself to reducing illegal drug use by stopping the manufacture of illicit drugs, preventing the flow of foreign drugs into the United States, and prosecuting and punishing those who sell or use illegal drugs. This so-called **war on drugs** has cost the United States at least one trillion dollars since it was launched by President Richard Nixon in 1971 (Branson 2012). But the war on drugs confronts tremendous obstacles. Most important is the significant demand for drugs in the United States. This is the underlying cause of the profitability of the drug trade. Another is the limitations on police, which inhibit their power to conduct searches. This is especially true when drug consumers are white and middle or upper class.

Destroying Foreign Production

U.S. efforts to significantly reduce the cultivation of poppies, coca, and marijuana appear to have had only limited success. The supply of illegal drugs for the U.S. market remains high. Although the U.S. militarily occupied Afghanistan for more than 16 years, and, as noted earlier, spent billions of dollars on poppy eradication programs, that country continued to supply most of the world's opium. Bolivia rejected U.S. efforts to drastically reduce its coca crop.

Interdiction

U.S. efforts to stop the flow of drugs across its borders have been only partially successful since there appears to be a continuing large supply for American buyers. Resources and procedures are too limited for agencies like the Coast Guard, the DEA, and the Customs Department to adequately inspect the tens of millions of vehicles and boats entering the United States each year along the country's 7,478 miles of borders with Mexico and Canada and 12,387 miles of coastline. During the 1980s surge of cocaine into the United States, some evidence suggests that drug interdiction efforts were undermined by the Reagan administration's efforts to supply counterrevolutionaries trying to overthrow the Sandinista revolutionary government in Nicaragua. Critics claimed that people flying weapons to the Honduran-based contras would fly back with illegal drugs for the U.S. market (Grim 2011; PBS 1988). The feature provides an example of global links between drugs and politics.

Prosecution and Punishment

Many Americans advocate severe punishment for drug dealers. Enforcement of tough drug laws has contributed to dramatically increasing the U.S. prison population. As indicated in Chapter 10, the United States had the highest imprisonment rate (number of inmates per 100,000 population) of any nation except for tiny Seychelles. The loss of industrial jobs in major U.S. urban centers motivated tens of thousands to enter the drug trade, helping to explain why the prison system is disproportionately populated by the poor and minorities.

Education

Antidrug education programs are intended to provide accurate information about drugs and their effects so that young people can make informed decisions about whether to use them or not. The Foundation

Special Topics: Drugs, Monarchs, and the Contra War

Big money influences politics and government. And large-scale drug distribution networks can, like legal corporations, generate a lot of money that finds its way into the pockets of politicians, government officials, and even some whose job it is to enforce laws and protect the public. There is strong evidence that in the 1980s, drug money, along with millions from oil-rich monarchies, helped finance a war that the American people and Congress opposed but that then-President Reagan supported. In 1979 the leftist Sandinista revolutionaries overthrew the Somoza regime in Nicaragua. After Ronald Reagan became president in 1981, his administration, through the CIA, began funding and arming conservative Nicaraguan counterrevolutionaries (contras) who sought to overthrow the new revolutionary government. But contra atrocities and the CIA–contra mining of Nicaragua's harbors infuriated many in Congress. A member of the House of Representatives, Berkley Bedell of Iowa, stated, "If the American people could have talked with the common people of Nicaragua whose women and children are being indiscriminately tortured and killed by terrorists (contras) financed by the American taxpayer, they would rise up in legitimate anger and demand that support for this criminal activity be ended at once" (*New York Times* 1983:1). In response to such reports the House of Representatives banned further military assistance to the contras (DeFronzo 2015). But operatives for the Reagan administration sought other ways to continue providing support. One was to approach oil-rich monarchal dictatorships for money for the contras. The Saudi regime reportedly provided significant assistance. Another method was to secretly sell weapons to Iran in violation of the United States's own ban on weapons sales to that country in what became known as the Iran–contra affair. The price was highly inflated and some of the profits were diverted to the contras. Six employees of the Reagan administration accused of involvement in aspects of the weapons sales to Iran were convicted of crimes, pled guilty, or had charges pending. They were all granted pardons by President George H. W. Bush (Johnston 1992). Another who had been convicted had the conviction overturned on appeal "because he had been granted limited immunity for his Congressional testimony, and that testimony was deemed to have influenced witnesses at his trial" (U-S-History.com 2017). A third source of funds appears to have come from bringing cocaine into the United States. Investigations indicated that some contras who transported weapons for contra units brought cocaine to the United States, with little inference from law enforcement (Ruiz-Marrero 2014; PBS 1988). Further, a PBS documentary (1988) also indicated that a drug cartel contributed millions of dollars to the contras. The huge flow of cocaine into the United States in the 1980s fueled the crack-cocaine epidemic that severely damaged people in low-income, predominately minority urban communities.

What are your thoughts?

Should money from the sale of illegal drugs or from oil monarchies be used to support a U.S. president's goals when other funds are not available? Explain your point of view.

for a Drug-Free World (2017) provides teaching resources worldwide to educators to counter the prodrug pitches and lures of drug dealers. The Drug Abuse Resistance Education program (DARE) involves police officers giving talks on the dangers of drugs to students in schools. However, a number of studies indicate that the DARE program has not been as effective as hoped (PBS 2014c).

Treatment

A number of approaches have been developed to help people overcome drug addiction. Methadone (a synthetic opioid) is a chemical treatment for heroin addiction (National Institute on Drug Abuse 2016c). Advocates of methadone treatment say it prevents the distressing withdrawal symptoms that otherwise follow ceasing to use heroin and that it provides less of a high than heroin. Counseling is oriented toward helping people deal with individual problems that might otherwise cause them to use drugs. Group programs like Narcotics Anonymous, inspired by Alcoholics Anonymous, involve people supporting one another's efforts to give up drugs. Workplace and campus programs utilize multiple methods coupled with regular drug testing as a further deterrent to drug use.

Attacking Root Causes of Drug Abuse

While educational programs can help people resist peer pressure to use drugs, they may be of limited effectiveness when traumatic stress is the root cause of drug use. Research indicates, for example, that perceived deteriorating economic conditions are linked to a surge in drug overdose deaths among white working-class people in the United States (Smialek 2017). Thus, efforts to reduce or eliminate child abuse, war, and poverty, all sources of traumatic stress that can increase the likelihood of drug use, are crucial elements in creating a world free of drug abuse.

An Alternative to the War on Drugs

Rather than waging the costly punitive war on drugs that has led to other enormous problems, such as mass incarceration of poor and minority people and expanded organized crime domestically and internationally, a sweeping alternative policy might be to legalize some or all drugs and regulate them, as is the case for alcohol, tobacco, and prescription drugs. Proponents of this approach claim it would eliminate the organized crime networks that currently supply the markets for drugs like marijuana, cocaine, methamphetamine, and heroin, along with violence associated with their illegal business activity. In addition, legalization would provide governments with large new revenues through taxation and licensing fees while simultaneously saving society the vast sums that are currently spent on fighting a futile war on drugs and on incarcerating, feeding, and providing services for the hundreds of thousands imprisoned for drug offences. Legalization would also allow government agencies to test drugs to make sure they do not contain toxic contaminants.

Opponents of legalization argue that public opinion does not support the legalization of currently illicit drugs other than marijuana. Further, they fear that legalization would lower the price of drugs, encourage businesses selling drugs to advertise for new customers, and ultimately increase the number of drug users. The question of what to do about drugs remains one of the most difficult and divisive issues facing society.

WHAT IS HUMAN TRAFFICKING?

Drugs are among a number of things trafficked illegally within nations and across international borders. A more tragic commerce is the trade in human beings.

The United Nations Office on Drugs and Crime (UNODC 2017b) defines "Trafficking in Persons as the recruitment, transportation, transfer, harboring or receipt of persons, by means of the threat or use of force or other forms of coercion, of abduction, of fraud, of deception, of the abuse of power … for the purpose of exploitation."

In response to **human trafficking**, the U.S. government enacted the Trafficking Victims Protection Act (TVPA) in 2000, which attempts to combat both international and domestic trafficking, expand protection of victims, and increase prosecution of traffickers. It also attempts to increase awareness of the problem (Dess 2013). The TVPA (U.S. State Department 2017:3) defines "severe forms of trafficking in persons" as

1. "sex trafficking in which a commercial sex act is induced by force, fraud, or coercion, or in which the person induced to perform such an act has not attained 18 years of age, or;

2. the recruitment, harboring, transportation, provision or obtaining of a person for labor or services, through the use of force, fraud, or coercion for the purpose of subjection to involuntary servitude, peonage, debt bondage, or slavery."

The TVPA also states that "[a] victim need not be physically transported from one location to another for the crime to fall within this definition."

A number of countries include the illegal sale of human organs as a form of human trafficking (U.S. State Department 2017). UNODC (2017b) also states that all nations should in addition include the following as criminal human trafficking: attempts to commit one or more of the trafficking offences, participating as an accomplice to a trafficking offence, and ordering or organizing others to commit a trafficking offence. UNODC (2017c) also reports that about 71 percent of human trafficking victims are female and about 28 percent are children.

It's important to understand that human trafficking occurs within nations as well as across international borders. In the U.S, for example, a pimp who has acquired a young woman in one city may sell her to a pimp in another city or state. Human trafficking and human smuggling are related, but not the same thing. First, human smuggling refers to people moved illegally across national borders, but as noted above much trafficking in persons occurs within a country. Second, people who are smuggled across borders often are not forced or coerced, but willingly desire to enter another nation illegally.

Dimensions of Human Trafficking

Estimates of the number of trafficked persons vary widely. This is partly because the activity is secretive, law enforcement personnel often have not been adequately trained to recognize trafficked individuals, and also because trafficking victims may be unable, unwilling, or too afraid to report their situation to the police or may believe the police will do

human trafficking The use of force, fraud, or coercion to make a person commit a commercial sex act and/or the recruitment, harboring, transportation, provision, or obtaining of a person for labor or services through the use of force, fraud, or coercion for the purpose of subjection to involuntary servitude.

nothing to help them. The U.S. Department of Health and Human Services (2017) cites estimates of the number of persons trafficked annually worldwide as high as 27 million persons. Former Secretary of State John Kerry stated in the 2014 State Department Trafficking in Persons Report that there were more that 20 million victims of human trafficking globally (U.S. State Department 2014). The inadequacy of law enforcement is reflected in the fact that authorities were able to identify only about 66,520 trafficking victims worldwide in 2016 and only 14,897 prosecutions were reported, with 9,071 convictions (U.S. State Department 2017). Estimates of the number of persons trafficked in the United States annually range up to 45,000 (McCabe 2013:145). The U.S. State Department (2017:420) states that "the United States is a source, transit and destination country for men, women, transgender individuals, and children – both U.S. citizens and foreign nationals – subjected to sex trafficking and forced labor. Trafficking occurs in both legal and illegal industries, including in commercial sex, hospitality services, traveling sales crews, agriculture, seafood, manufacturing, janitorial services, construction, restaurants, health care,

Anti-human-trafficking poster

care for persons with disabilities, salon services, fairs and carnivals, peddling and begging, drug smuggling and distribution, and child care and domestic work."

In 2016 the U.S. Department of Justice (DOJ) initiated 241 human trafficking prosecutions against 531 defendants (U.S. State Department 2017). The DOJ got convictions against 439 traffickers, 425 predominantly involved in sex trafficking and 14 predominantly in labor trafficking. Sentences were from 12 months to life in prison. The William Wilberforce Trafficking Victims Protection Reauthorization Act of 2008 required the FBI to begin collecting human trafficking offense data (FBI 2017n). Although not all police departments around the United States are participating in reporting this type of crime to the FBI, results show that in addition to DOJ trafficking investigations (and those by other federal agencies such as the Department of Defense) many local law enforcement agencies are also involved in combating human trafficking. In 2016 law enforcement agencies in thirty-four states reported becoming aware of 1,196 cases of human trafficking, of which suspected perpetrators were identified in 654.

CAUSES OF HUMAN TRAFFICKING

Several factors contribute to human trafficking. Tremendous economic inequality within nations means that there are millions of desperately poor people seeking a way to survive, many of whom are victims of abuse within their own households. Wars also force many to leave their homes, land, and jobs to escape the violence. These people are often susceptible to traffickers' false lures of legitimate jobs. Lack of rights and education for women in certain nations makes them especially vulnerable.

Special Topics: Sex Trafficking and Sex Slavery

Sex trafficking takes place throughout the United States and worldwide. Traffickers often use debt bondage, lies, violence, threats, and other methods to force children, women, and men into prostitution (Polaris 2014). Sex traffickers sometimes establish a romantic relationship with a runaway, who is often the victim of prior emotional, physical, or sexual abuse, or extreme poverty, promising a better life. In reality the trafficker employs several tactics, such as economic leverage, threats, and force, to coerce the victim into prostitution. International sex traffickers often promise the victim a good-paying job or refuge from war or political persecution. But after being smuggled into another country, the vulnerable undocumented immigrant is told to engage in prostitution to pay back the trafficker. The trafficked victims work in escort services, massage parlours, strip clubs, brothels, hotels and motels, on the street, and at truck stops. Women working in brothels and fake massage businesses may have paid sex with six to ten men per day.

Another venue for sex trafficking is bars and brothels near military bases. The South Korean government is accused by former prostitutes of promoting prostitution around U.S. military bases. The reported reasons were to encourage continued U.S. military presence and to obtain income from the commercial sex business while South Korea was in the process of becoming a developed nation (Rowland and Chang 2014). Even in 2014, despite prostitution being illegal in South Korea, enforcement appeared weak (Kim 2014).

Conquering armies have sexually exploited people in the places they occupied. In 2014 and 2015, the Islamic State of Iraq and Syria (ISIS, also called the Islamic State of Iraq and the Levant, ISIL) captured large swaths of territory including numerous towns and cities in Syria and Iraq. In areas ISIS controlled, many non-Islamic women were forced into "marriages" with ISIS fighters. In particular, women of the Yizidi religious minority were raped and treated as sexual slaves (Balkiz and Dewan 2017; Watson 2014). In October 2017, a Kurdish women's military unit participated in the successful effort to liberate Raqqa, the ISIS capital in Syria. Fighting to free women and fellow Kurds from ISIS oppression, they lost thirty of their comrades in the battle.

Unscrupulous persons in positions of power often sexually exploit vulnerable people. One notorious case involved the three-term Republican mayor Phillip Giordano of Waterbury, Connecticut. Giordano, a former Marine, lawyer, and state representative, was also the Republican Party's candidate for the U.S. Senate in 2000, losing to Democratic senator Joe Lieberman (Leukhardt and Mahony 2001). In 2001, during a municipal corruption investigation, FBI surveillance discovered that Giordano was seeking sex with young girls using an interstate communication device, his cell phone. In 2003 he was convicted in federal court of using the power of his governmental office to engage in oral sex with two girls aged eight and ten years old and sentenced to thirty-seven years in federal prison (Cowan 2003).

What are your thoughts?

What do you think should be done to fight sex trafficking and sex slavery?

Very poor families may sell children to traffickers. The tremendous inequality between nations also plays a role. Prostitution is generally frequent in areas near foreign military bases, as was the case for the U.S. military in the Philippines (Cottingham et al. 2013; McCabe 2013). Traffickers also profit by providing women as sex slaves to brothels and "massage" businesses in wealthy countries. Others make money through international sex tourism in countries with high levels of poverty, such as Thailand, the Philippines, and Cambodia. Cottingham et al. (2013)

cite an estimate that prostitution and sex trafficking constitute about 14 percent of Thailand's gross domestic product. Traffickers use the internet to advertise sex with their victims. In many cases, corruption and lack of effective law enforcement means traffickers have little fear of being punished (U.S. State Department 2017). The same is true for sex tourists. Increased ease of international travel facilitates trafficking and sex tourism. In sum, poverty, economic and gender inequality, lack of deterrence, and elements of globalization and modern technology all contribute to human trafficking. The feature describes aspects and examples of sex trafficking and sex slavery.

SOCIOLOGICAL PERSPECTIVES ON HUMAN TRAFFICKING

The structural-functional perspective attempts to identify any positive functions human trafficking has for society. The conflict approach focuses on the roles poverty and inequality play in causing human trafficking and making particular people or groups especially vulnerable to becoming victims. The symbolic-interactionist perceptive emphasizes how traffickers lure and manipulate victims and what has to be done to help victims survive trafficking.

Structural-Functional Perspective

The structural-functional approach tends to view business activity, including human trafficking, as developing to meet some market demand or other economic interests. It implies that trafficking can provide income for the economies of poor nations and that forced labor trafficking may also relieve labor shortages in some industries or keep them profitable and operating by supplying cheap labor.

Conflict Perspective

The conflict perspective focuses on the how economic, political, and gender inequalities promote human trafficking and interfere with attempts to address the issue. Extreme poverty motivates some families to sell a child to traffickers so that other family members have a chance to survive. It also makes desperate people vulnerable to traffickers' false promises of legitimate job opportunities far from home. The income trafficking and prostitution brings to poor nations, as well as corruption and bribery, influences the politically powerful to ignore or even support trafficking. The racial/ethnic-conflict perspective notes that the higher level of poverty among people of color, coupled with racial or ethnic discrimination, contributes to minority youth being especially vulnerable to becoming trafficking victims. Furthermore, this perspective argues that law enforcement historically tended to neglect trafficking victims of color. The feminist-conflict perspective emphasizes that lack of education and job opportunities for women outside the home in strongly patriarchal societies makes many women relatively easy targets for traffickers. The sexual objectification of women's bodies in many cultures also contributes to their becoming the victims of trafficking.

Symbolic-Interactionist Perspective

The symbolic-interactionist perspective focuses on the role person-to-person interaction and learning experiences play in human trafficking. Women who are lured into prostitution by traffickers find themselves dependent on the trafficker in their new environment. They are often isolated from family and friends and lack income because the trafficker or pimp takes the money from acts of prostitution. The trafficker may induce the victim to take drugs to control him or her and intensify dependency. In such circumstances the victim often becomes emotionally tied to the trafficker and susceptible to adopting the identity and attitudes the trafficker desires, like believing there is no way out of the situation. A trafficked person may be told that she or he will receive better treatment if she or he assists the trafficker in controlling other victims. Cottingham et al. (2013) note that successfully liberating sexually trafficked persons often requires convincing them that economic opportunities and psychological benefits are sufficient outside of the situation of bondage and prostitution for them to survive escaping the traffickers.

SOCIAL RESPONSES TO HUMAN TRAFFICKING

The United Nations has called on member states to fight human trafficking. Individual countries, including the United States, have developed policies to combat trafficking and rescue victims.

International

The United Nations Trafficking in Persons Protocol (UNTIP) or the Protocol to Prevent, Suppress and Punish Trafficking in Persons, Especially Women and Children is a major attempt to combat human trafficking. It is a protocol or supplement to the United Nations (Palermo) Convention against Organized Crime (UNODC 2017a). The UNTIP protocol entered into force on December 25, 2003. As of December 4, 2017, it had been ratified by 172 UN members (United Nations 2017b). The protocol is intended to assist countries in creating anti-trafficking strategies and laws and through UNODC aid in their implementation.

United States: Federal and States

The TVPA states that sexually exploited persons under the age of eighteen should be recognized and treated as victims by authorities. The act, however, was criticized as inadequate because in the years following its passage the number of traffickers prosecuted was low and assistance and protection for victims were viewed as insufficient. Partly in response to the limitations of the TVPA, the DOJ published the Model State Anti-Trafficking Criminal Statute in 2004, intended as a guide for state legislators to create state laws to deal with human trafficking. In 2015 Congress passed a new anti-trafficking law with bipartisan support, The Justice for Victims of Trafficking Act of 2015, which President Obama signed into law (Byrnes 2015; U.S. Superintendent of Documents 2015). This act is intended to help victims of trafficking serve as witnesses and recover from trauma and build new lives by providing them with financial assistance.

By December 5, 2016, all fifty states had enacted anti-trafficking criminal laws (National Conference of State Legislatures 2017b). The state laws are important because more resources are needed to address trafficking than the federal government has available and because local and state police are more likely to encounter and detect trafficking in their daily work and be able to apprehend traffickers and free victims (Dess 2013). States can provide additional funding for the needed special training of law enforcement personnel, for investigations, and for helping victims. While the federal government often focuses on large-scale trafficking operations, the additional enforcement by states can expand anti-trafficking efforts to address small-scale trafficking.

An example of a state anti-trafficking law is the Massachusetts Trafficking Law of 2011. It criminalizes three forms of trafficking: sex trafficking, forced labor trafficking, and trafficking in human organs (Dess 2013). While a step forward in fighting trafficking, critics point to limitations. For example, according to Dess (2013) the law does not require that police be given training on child sex trafficking, and it permits, under certain conditions, that minors engaged in prostitution be charged with a criminal or delinquent act. But the prosecution will in effect be stopped as long as the child complies with receiving court-required services. Otherwise the court has the discretion to proceed with the prosecution of the child. Many concerned about trafficking argue that it is wrong to further victimize a trafficking victim by charging her or him with a crime because her or his behavior is the result of coercion. But others contend that the criminal justice system needs the threat of criminal conviction to convince trafficking victims to cooperate in prosecutions of traffickers and to participate in rehabilitation programs.

Cross (2013) argues that anti-trafficking laws should include at least three elements to make them more effective and avoid dual victimization of trafficking victims. First, laws must require mandatory human trafficking training for law enforcement officers so that they can more effectively detect and investigate trafficking and treat trafficked persons as victims, not criminals. Second, laws should provide that if a trafficked person is forced into engaging in a criminal activity such as prostitution, she or he should not be criminally charged. Third, if a person has been convicted of a crime such as prostitution in the past but it can be shown that this was because the person was the victim of human trafficking, that conviction should be vacated (that is, erased from the person's records).

Another innovation is that several states, including Arkansas, Kansas, Ohio, and Washington, have enacted laws requiring truck drivers be trained in how to recognize signs of human trafficking, such as a group of women in an SUV clearly being dominated or controlled by a male traveling companion, so that they can quickly notify authorities to investigate (King 2017; Sweeney 2017). Suggestions have also been made that similar training be required for motel and hotel workers.

THE MOVEMENT AGAINST HUMAN TRAFFICKING

Internationally and in the United States there are dozens of groups and organizations, both secular and religious, involved in the movement to end human trafficking. They engage in efforts to make the public aware and outraged over sexual and labor exploitation. They also push governments to enact and enforce laws against trafficking and support United Nations efforts to combat it. One organization that has taken even more direct action against human traffickers is Operation Underground Railroad (OUR). Founded in 2013, OUR includes former U.S. CIA personnel, Navy Seals, Green Berets, and Special Ops operatives that, in coordination with local law enforcement, lead or assist efforts to identify and rescue victims (OUR 2017a, 2017b, 2017c). The organization reported rescuing more than 500 children from sex traffickers by early May 2016 and many more since then. Successful OUR operations have been conducted in Asia, Latin America, and Africa, as well as in the United States, with dozens of accused traffickers arrested. OUR also produced a 2016 documentary movie, *The Abolitionists*, that describes dimensions of sex trafficking worldwide and efforts to combat it and rescue victims.

Slavery and human trafficking existed in the United States from its inception. The nineteenth-century abolitionist movement that sought to rescue blacks from chattel slavery was the anti-human-trafficking movement of that era. But in the early twentieth century a new anti-trafficking movement emerged that focused on combating "white slavery" (Butler 2015). Racism and sexism limiting economic opportunity had led to a disproportionate number of women of color being involved in prostitution. But it was the perceived increasing number of white prostitutes that alarmed the white majority of the population and sparked the anti-white-slavery movement. According to Butler (2015) the United States anti-trafficking movement continued to focus more on white victims of sex trafficking into the twenty-first century. She notes, however, that when Obama became president there was a greater recognition of the role of racial disadvantage in making minority youth especially vulnerable to sex trafficking. Federal policy also shifted toward viewing those forced into prostitution as victims requiring assistance rather than as persons who should simply be punished as lawbreakers.

The modern U.S. anti-trafficking movement has led to laws in several states requiring police officers and trucker drivers to be trained to recognize signs of human trafficking, as described elsewhere in this chapter. In fact, a branch of the anti-human-trafficking movement, Truckers against

Trafficking (TAT) – The Freedom Drivers Project, developed among the nation's three million truck drivers. Created in 2009, TAT encourages truck drivers to be aware of the signs of human trafficking and to immediately report possible trafficking to authorities (Truckers against Trafficking 2017). Since TAT began, thousands of truckers have contacted police about suspected human trafficking situations.

CHAPTER REVIEW

What Is a Drug?
A drug is any substance, other than food or water, that affects the functioning, development, or condition of the body. Drug abuse is the use of a drug that is illegal or the use of a legal drug in amounts or in ways harmful to the user or others. Excessive alcohol consumption is strongly linked to violent crime, vehicle and other accidents, and liver and other diseases. However, any level of tobacco smoking is harmful, and even just breathing smoke produced by other persons increases the risk of diseases such as cancer.

Problems Related to Drug Abuse
The cost of buying illegal drugs motivates people to commit crimes like robbery, burglary, and prostitution. Groups involved in manufacturing, importing, or selling illegal drugs have often engaged in acts of violence and in the corruption of politicians and law enforcement.

Why Do People Use Drugs?
People use drugs for relief from pain, physical or psychological therapy, performance enhancement, escaping from the effects of trauma, and recreation. Many people also use drugs as part of their cultural traditions or in order to conform to peer expectations.

Sociological Perspectives on Drug Abuse
The structural-functional approach emphasizes potential benefits of drug use, such as how caffeine can increase alertness and how other drugs may have physical or psychological benefits. The conflict approach focuses on how economic, political, and social inequalities generate frustration leading to

drug use as a way of coping with stress and hopelessness. This perspective also highlights how powerful interests play a role in determining which drugs are legal and how drug laws are enforced. The symbolic-interactionist perspective considers how factors such as culture, communication, and learning experiences influence the perception, use, and legal status of drugs.

Social Responses to Drug Abuse
The "war on drugs" has emphasized destroying foreign production, interdiction of drug shipments, prosecution and punishment of sellers and users, education, and treatment. Reducing inequality and extreme poverty have typically not been major components of the war on drugs.

What Is Human Trafficking?
Human trafficking includes forced prostitution and other forms of sexual exploitation, as well as slavery, forced labor or services, and the forced or coerced removal of human organs. Estimates of the number of people trafficked globally are in the tens of millions and in the United States in the tens of thousands.

Causes of Human Trafficking
Extreme poverty, economic and gender inequality, lack of deterrence, and aspects of globalization and modern technology all appear to contribute to human trafficking.

Sociological Perspectives on Human Trafficking
The structural-functional perspective on human trafficking implies that trafficking can provide income for the economies of poor nations and can relieve labor shortages. The

conflict perspective focuses on how economic, political, and gender inequalities promote human trafficking as desperately poor people fall victim to traffickers' false promises of legitimate job opportunities. The racial/ethnic-conflict perspective notes that minority youth are especially vulnerable to becoming trafficking victims. The feminist-conflict perspective emphasizes that lack of education and legitimate job opportunities for women often makes them easy targets for traffickers. The symbolic-interactionist perspective focuses on the roles person-to-person interaction and learning experiences play in human trafficking and in the rehabilitation of victims.

Social Responses to Human Trafficking

The United Nations Trafficking in Persons Protocol is a major international measure to combat human trafficking by assisting countries in creating and implementing anti-trafficking strategies and laws. The 2000 U.S. federal Trafficking Victims Protection Act attempts to combat both international and domestic trafficking by mandating punishment for traffickers, providing assistance to trafficking victims, and increasing awareness of trafficking. By the end of 2016, all fifty states had enacted anti-trafficking laws and some required human trafficking training for law enforcement officers and truck drivers.

KEY TERMS

binge drinking, p. 382
drug, p. 379
drug abuse, p. 380
gateway drugs, p. 384

human trafficking, p. 396
opioid epidemic, p. 386
war on drugs, p. 392

DISCUSSION QUESTIONS

1. What do you think would be the best approach for reducing problems caused by drug abuse? Why?

2. Which sociological perspective do you think is most helpful for explaining drug abuse? In what ways?

3. Which social response to drug abuse do you think is most effective? Explain your position.

4. Which sociological perspective do you think is most helpful for explaining human trafficking? Why?

5. Which social response to human trafficking do you think is most effective? Explain your answer.

CHAPTER 15

War, Rebellion and Terrorism

CHAPTER OBJECTIVES

- Explain the concepts of war, rebellion, and terrorism.
- Explain sociological perspectives on war and rebellion.
- Explain the causes of war and rebellion.
- Describe the consequences of war and rebellion.
- Describe strategies to establish and maintain peace.
- Describe major forms of terrorism, the causes of terrorism, and different approaches to combating terrorism.

AL QAEDA PLANNED THE SEPTEMBER 11, 2001, attacks on New York City and Washington, D.C. at bases in Afghanistan. Less than two months later, U.S. forces invaded Afghanistan to oust the Al Qaeda-allied Taliban regime and capture or kill Osama bin Laden and his associates. This began the longest war in U.S. history, a conflict fought with high-tech weapons on one side and suicide bombers on the other. Few incidents illustrate the nature of the war more than the December 30, 2009, terrorist attack at Forward Operating Base Chapman in Khost, Afghanistan, that took the lives of five CIA personnel, two American contractors, and two others. They were killed by a suicide bomber, Humam Khalil Abu Mulal al Balawi, a Jordanian doctor. In 2009, Balawi convinced the Jordanian General Intelligence Department and American intelligence agents that he had information about the location of one of Al Qaeda's top leaders (Riedel 2010). In reality, Balawi was working for Al Qaeda. On December 30, he was allowed to enter the CIA's base at Khost without being searched. As he approached CIA agents, he detonated explosives hidden on his body, killing them and his Jordanian case officer and wounding many others. It was the second-most lethal attack ever on the CIA, exceeded only by the 1983 bombing of the U.S. embassy in Beirut that took the lives of eight CIA officers. Balawi believed that the U.S. and Jordanian governments were helping Israel oppress the Palestinians and that attacking the CIA would make him a holy martyr.

A video the suicide bomber left behind revealed his motivations, his strategy of deception, and his farewell to his family. The Khost attack exemplifies the lethal threat that Americans and anti–Al Qaeda Afghans face. Suicide bombers are among the few threats that can occasionally defeat U.S. high-tech weapons. This tactic has also been repeatedly used by ISIS, which developed from Al Qaeda in Iraq, in its operations in the Middle East and other regions (Al Arabiya 2017). But the intelligence provided by genuine undercover agents that penetrate Al Qaeda networks is central to identifying targets for drone attacks in the U.S. war on terrorism (Riedel 2010).

War is one of history's oldest social problems. Pinker (2011), in his extensive review of research on human conflict, showed that in the distant past warfare often resulted in the deaths of large percentages of the warring groups' populations. He argues that as strong modern states developed, the percentage of populations killed in war tended to decrease. World War II, with its mass bombings of cities and "racial" persecutions of certain civilian groups like Jews, temporarily reversed this long-term trend. In modern times, even though nuclear weapons have given governments the means to destroy many millions of people, or even wipe out most of the world's population, the frequency of wars has decreased, especially among states with strong governments. Wars in the twenty-first century, when they do occur, tend to be civil wars (like the Nepalese civil war that ended in 2006, the Syrian civil war that began in 2011, or the Ukrainian civil war that started in 2014) or invasions of militarily inferior states by stronger powers (such as the U.S.-led invasion of Iraq in 2003, and the Israeli incursions into Lebanon in 2006 and Gaza in 2014).

BASIC CONCEPTS: WAR, REBELLION, AND TERRORISM

War is violent conflict between nations, between different groups, or between nations and groups. World War II was primarily a war between nations, such as when Nazi Germany invaded the Soviet Union on June 22, 1941, and when Japan attacked the United States at Pearl Harbor on December 7, 1941. In comparison, after Portugal ended its colonial rule of Angola in 1975, opposing Angolan groups fought each other in a civil war until a peace agreement in 2002. In the modern war on terror, nations like the United States are in conflict with violent groups like Al Qaeda.

Rebellion is a violent or nonviolent effort on the part of a large number of people to resist the policies of or totally overthrow their country's government or ruler. When Americans fired on British troops seeking to confiscate their weapons at Lexington and Concord, Massachusetts, on April 19, 1775, they launched a rebellion against the British monarchy that became the American Revolution. A **revolution** is a rebellion that results in the change of one or more basic institutions. The American Revolution changed the whole system of government in the thirteen colonies from monarchy to democratic republic.

Terrorism is the use of violence or the threat of violence to achieve a political goal. It can be used by individuals, groups, or governments. The Nazi German and Stalinist Soviet regimes exemplified government terrorism by using violence to eliminate political opponents. The post–Civil War Ku Klux Klan was a group that used terrorist violence to restore white political and social dominance over much of the American South after the Civil War. An example of an individual terrorist was Harvard University graduate and former mathematics professor at the University of California at Berkeley Theodore "Ted" Kaczynski, the "Unabomber" (the name given to an originally unknown bomb maker who attacked people at universities and airlines). From 1978 to 1995 he killed three persons and wounded twenty-three by sending homemade package bombs to professors and various individuals associated with advanced technology.

America's Wars

The United States has been involved in more than forty wars and foreign interventions. Table 15.1 shows the twelve deadliest wars in U.S. history. The number of deaths listed includes both those that occurred in combat and from related causes like disease in the war zones or mistreatment while a prisoner of war. Almost one percent of the population of the thirteen colonies died in the American Revolution. The Civil War, America's deadliest conflict, took over 600,000 lives, about 2 percent the country's population at the time.

SOCIOLOGICAL PERSPECTIVES ON WAR AND REBELLION

Structural-Functional Perspective

The structural-functional perspective holds that wars or rebellions occur when people believe they will result in greater benefits than con-

war Violent conflict between nations, between different groups, or between nations and groups.

rebellion A violent or nonviolent effort on the part of a large number of people to resist the policies of or totally overthrow their country's government or ruler.

revolution A rebellion that results in the change of one or more basic institutions.

terrorism The use of violence or the threat of violence to achieve a political goal.

TABLE 15.1	Total American Deaths in Selected Major U.S. Wars

Rank	War	Years	Deaths	Deaths per Population
1	American Civil War	1861–1865	625,000	1.988% (1860)
2	World War II	1941–1945	405,399	0.307% (1940)
3	World War I	1917–1918	116,516	0.110% (1920)
4	Vietnam War	1964–1973	58,151	0.03% (1970)
5	Korean War	1950–1953	36,516	0.02% (1950)
6	American Revolutionary War	1775–1783	25,000	0.899% (1780)
7	War of 1812	1812–1815	20,000	0.345% (1810)
8	Mexican–American War	1846–1848	13,283	0.057% (1850)
9	Iraq War	2003–2017	4,528	0.001% (2016)
10	Philippine–American War	1899–1913	4,196	0.006% (1900)
11	Spanish–American War	1898	2,446	0.004% (1898)
12	Afghan War	2001–2017	2,407	0.001% (2016)

Source: The Military Order of the Purple Heart 2009; Icasualties.org 2017.

tinued peace. Wars have been launched to acquire resources and expand territory. A successful war can generate wealth for the victorious society and provide more soldiers for its army and workers for its industries and farms. Many social scientists believe that warfare played the key role in forcing small political entities, like ancient city-states, to combine into modern nations and that large states were absolutely essential for industrialization and the creation of advanced technology. Successful rebellions can have the positive functions of removing incompetent, ineffective, or corrupt leaders or, in some cases, providing large numbers of people with greater benefits, like educational and economic opportunities, than they had before.

Structural functionalism also states that war can have unintended functions. Inventions developed to fight an enemy can impact society. For example, during World War II, Germany, England, Italy, and the United States all developed jet technology. After the war, jet engines enabled the commercial airline industry to greatly expand and provide cheaper airfares, dramatically increasing the ability of hundreds of millions of people to travel domestically and internationally. Nuclear reactors, employed in the U.S. Manhattan Project to develop the atomic bomb, became the basis for nuclear power plants. And radar technology unexpectedly provided the basis for the invention of the microwave oven.

War can provide opportunities for previously disadvantaged groups. The shortage of workers caused by millions of men serving in the armed forces brought millions of women into the industrial labor force during World War II, where they helped produce weapons, vehicles, and aircraft, and proved they were just as intelligent and capable as men. Also, large numbers of African Americans participated in the armed forces and received training and new opportunities. Groups like the Tuskegee Airmen, African American pilots who flew Red Tail P-51 fighters against the Nazi German air force, shattered stereotypes of racial inferiority. While bringing women into the labor force and racial minorities into the armed forces were intended to help win the war, unintended consequences included contributing to the development of the postwar civil rights and women's movements.

Conflict Perspective

The conflict perspective views inequalities between nations and between people within nations as causes of wars and rebellions. The leaders of powerful nations are freer to resort to war when they think their targets are much weaker and unable to effectively strike back or defend themselves. Russia, China, the United States, and Great Britain have all had major disagreements but have not gone to war with one another since the Korean War, when China entered on North Korea's side. Each has a powerful, nuclear-armed military that could inflict enormous damage on an opponent. Thus, mutually assured destruction (MAD) has prevented war among the military giants. But these countries have engaged in military conflict against much weaker nations. Russia invaded Hungary in 1956, Czechoslovakia in 1968, Afghanistan in 1979, Georgia in 2008, and annexed Crimea from the Ukraine in 2014. Great Britain attacked Egypt in 1956, fought Argentina over the Falkland Islands in 1982, invaded Iraq in 2003, and attacked Libya in 2011. China fought Vietnam in 1979. And the United States has had a long record of conflict in much smaller countries since the end of World War II, including Vietnam during 1963–1973, the Dominican Republic in 1965, Cambodia in 1970, Grenada in 1983, Panama in 1989, Iraq in 1991, Serbia in 1999, Afghanistan during 2001–2017, and Iraq during 2003–2017.

Inequalities within societies can also facilitate war making. If the governing figures and their families are insulated from the risk of war, they may be more prone to launch them. In addition, limited opportunity for large numbers of people in a society with high inequality motivates the disadvantaged to seek military service. In the United States, where service in the military became voluntary after the draft was ended in 1973, military enlistees come disproportionately from the lower-middle class and working class and from among the children of military veterans. The vast majority of government leaders, including members of Congress, have no military experience. Those most in favor of war or military intervention are often nonveterans. Matthew Farwell, an Afghan war veteran who writes for *Rolling Stone*, used the term "chicken hawks" to refer to such people in a June 5, 2014, CNN interview ("hawkish" – in favor of war, but too "chicken" to participate themselves).

Conflict theorists point to the Iraq War to illustrate their point of view. The Bush administration took advantage of anger over Al Qaeda's 9/11 attacks to launch an invasion of oil-rich Iraq, which had nothing to do with Al Qaeda. The main reason given for the invasion was that Iraq had weapons of mass destruction (WMDs). This was false. In reality, the Iraqi armed forces were so weakened by years of international sanctions that they were a virtual pushover for U.S., British, and allied forces. In other words, conflict theorists argue that Iraq was invaded not because it was militarily strong and a danger to the United States but because it was weak and had a tremendous amount of valuable energy resources. Conflict theorists also argue that the costs of the war, the way the war was waged, and its outcome also verify their point of view. The Iraq War cost the American taxpayers as much as two trillion dollars, over 4,500 Americans killed, and many thousands wounded. The big beneficiaries of the taxpayer-financed war were United States and other foreign corporations that came to Iraq to provision occupation forces, rebuild facilities, and extract oil.

The conflict perspective also views a high level of economic inequality as a factor that can lead to rebellion. This can occur if people decide that the existing level of inequality is unjust and can be reduced through a successful rebellion.

Symbolic-Interactionist Perspective

The symbolic-interactionist approach is concerned with the meanings people develop for war and rebellion and how these promote or inhibit conflict. Many societies tell their citizens that wars and rebellions are sometimes inevitable. In the United States children are taught that the American Revolution was necessary to win independence and democracy, that the Civil War was necessary to abolish slavery, and that the United States and its allies' victory in World War II saved the world from fascist and racist domination. Children also learn about war through playing at war with toy weapons, watching war movies, and playing electronic games where the player tries to annihilate countless enemies. Government leaders provide reasons for going to war, and vilify the other side. For example, when the George W. Bush administration invaded Afghanistan in October 2001, the justification was that Al Qaeda had launched the 9/11 attacks from there, that ousting the Taliban regime and occupying the country was necessary to prevent terrorists from using Afghan territory, and that the Taliban was both an Al Qaeda ally and a repressive extremist religious movement that imposed a terrorist regime on the Afghan people, especially women. Few Americans would argue with that assessment. But the story is much different for the 2003 invasion of Iraq.

Baghdad under attack

The Bush administration claimed Iraq had WMDs that threatened the United States and its allies, and administration supporters argued Iraq was behind 9/11. Despite evidence before the invasion that both of these claims were incorrect, most news media uncritically accepted and broadcast these false assertions. However, some news sources were better at accurately informing their viewers or listeners than others. Worldpublicopinion.org (2003) reported on polls conducted from June through September 2003 by the Program on International Policy at the University of Maryland and Knowledge Networks. This research showed that about 48 percent of Americans wrongly believed that Saddam Hussein's regime had been connected to Al Qaeda, 25 percent mistakenly thought that world public opinion backed the U.S. invasion, and 22 percent believed that WMDs had been found in Iraq. Only 23 percent of those with none of the misperceptions supported the Iraq war, while 86 percent who had all three misperceptions did. Furthermore, the research showed that accuracy of information about Iraq was related to the news source from whence it came. Among those people whose primary news source was National Public Radio or the Public Broadcasting Service, about 77 percent had none of the three misperceptions, while the proportion of viewers with no misperceptions whose primary news source was CNN or NBC was 45 percent, and Fox 20 percent.

CAUSES OF WAR AND REBELLION

Wars and rebellions have occurred for a number of reasons. Perceived threats have motivated wars. In 1967 Israel anticipated attacks from Egypt, Syria, and Jordan. It launched a preemptive war, devastating its opponents' air forces on the ground. Israel won the war in six days. A nation's leaders have started wars to gain territory, resources, and economic advantages. European countries fought wars that had them take control of much of Asia and Africa. The most successful, Great Britain, boasted that "the sun never sets on the British empire" because it spanned the entire globe. Britain structured the economies of countries it dominated. When the Chinese destroyed a shipment of opium brought to China by British businessmen, Britain attacked China, won the 1839–1842 Opium War, and forced China to accept the opium trade. British businessmen who shipped the drug to China profited. Armament inequalities among nations encouraged leaders of the more powerful to attack militarily inferior societies for gain with little fear of effective retaliation or resistance. The German Nazis, who believed that British subjugation of so much of the world proved Aryan racial superiority, invaded the Soviet Union in the summer of 1941 to obtain what Hitler called "*lebensraum*" (living room) for the German people, along with vast stretches of fertile land and energy resources. Another motivation for war is to overthrow an enemy government. Iraq invaded Iran in 1980 with the goal of bringing down Iran's religious fundamentalist government, which was encouraging Shia Iraqis to rebel against Saddam Hussein's Iraqi regime.

Wars have also occurred for religious reasons. Islamic armies conquered vast territories following the death of the Prophet Mohammad. In the Middle Ages, Christian countries launched the Crusades to recover the Holy Lands. Later, Catholics and Protestants slaughtered one another in European religious wars, and in the twenty-first century Christians and Muslims have fought in Africa, and Shia and Sunni Muslims have attacked each other in the Middle East.

Terrorist acts have led to major wars. The most famous was the assassination of the heir to the Austro-Hungarian throne, Archduke Franz Ferdinand in 1914, by a Serbian assassin. This prompted Austria-Hungary to attack Serbia, and then other major nations to declare war on one another, launching World War I. A more recent example was the U.S. invasion of Afghanistan after Al Qaeda terrorists based there carried out the 9/11 terrorist attacks.

Extreme nationalism and racial and ethnic conflicts have also led to war. Nazi Germany invaded Poland in 1939 supposedly to rescue the German-speaking minority there from Polish persecution, precipitating World War II in Europe. Later, the Nazis invaded the Soviet Union to obtain land and resources for the self-proclaimed racially superior Germans. Ethnic rivalry has prompted numerous violent conflicts in Africa, including Hutu extremists' slaughter of at least 500,00 Tutsi and moderate Hutus in Rwanda in 1994.

Leaders can also start wars in an attempt to divert attention from domestic problems. The Russian czar launched a war against Japan in 1904 hoping to unite quarreling Russians against a common enemy in a victorious war. Instead, Japan won and internal conflict in Russia increased.

Finally, some wars occur because of the apparent lack of an alternative course of action, such as when one nation is attacked by another. When the Japanese bombed Pearl Harbor on December 7, 1941, the United States had no alternative but to declare war on Japan.

Wars can play a role in starting rebellions and vice versa. The repeated defeats of Russian armies by Germany during World War I weakened the authority of the czar's government, helping to bring about the Russian Revolution. The Japanese invasion of China in the 1930s unintentionally helped the Chinese Communist Revolution succeed. Some revolutions have been followed by wars. For example, after the French Revolution, other European countries attacked France in a counterrevolutionary effort trying to reinstate the French monarchy.

Rebellions are motivated by intense discontent with government policies and leaders. Rebellions that become revolutions aiming for sweeping institutional change like the total replacement of a society's political system or economic system are likely to succeed when five factors exist at the same time (DeFronzo 2015). The first is that a large part of the population becomes very dissatisfied with existing conditions and believes that the problems can be solved if the political and/or economic arrangements in the society are changed. The second factor is that a division opens up among people with leadership characteristics (elites) in the society so that they no longer unanimously support the existing system. Some elites instead come to support revolution and provide the discontented mass of the population with leadership, organization, a clear conception of what's wrong with society and what needs to be changed (an ideology), and a plan for how to do it. The third necessary element is that a shared motivation for revolution develops that unites different groups and classes in favor of the revolution. The fourth factor is that the existing government becomes weakened and unable to carry out important functions or cope with the rebellion. And the fifth element is that other countries are unwilling or unable to intervene to prevent the success of the revolution.

For example, in the late 1970s many people in Iran were frustrated over increasing inequality and a repressive monarchy that seemed to serve foreign interests. Many of the country's prominent academic, labor union, and religious leaders turned against the Iranian shah's regime and provided leadership for the emerging revolution. Most Iranians, despite their differing views about what a future Iran should look like, were united by their intense opposition to what they viewed as a brutal and corrupt monarchy. The regime's power deteriorated rapidly because many soldiers refused orders to attack anti-government protestors. And no nations intervened to help the monarchy crush the revolution and stay in power. The regime collapsed, and the shah fled the country. The new government was hostile toward the United States for supporting the shah's dictatorship for many years.

WAR, REBELLION, REVOLUTION, AND SOCIAL CHANGE

Wars, rebellions, and revolutions brought about dramatic social change, shaping many aspects of the modern world. Alexander the Great's conquests spread Greek culture to many lands, and later the victories of Julius Caesar and his successors did the same for Roman culture and technology. This provided a foundation for tribal peoples in places like Britain and Germania to eventually rise into powerful nations. On the other hand, conquests by the Mongols arguably crippled the development of Islamic Arab civilization with the destruction of Baghdad in 1258.

European colonial conquests changed the culture, political systems, and economies of South and Central America, Africa, and huge sections of Asia, and promoted a form of globalization dominated by the most technologically advanced nations. World War I resulted in the destruction of the Austro-Hungarian and Ottoman Empires and the expansion of the territory held by the British and the French.

The enormous financial penalties imposed on Germany by the victorious nations drove many Germans to support Adolf Hitler and the Nazis, who promised to save the nation, rescue the economy, and restore German honor. The Nazis' aggression cost the lives of tens of millions of people during World War II. Following the war, revolutions against colonial rule broke out in lands controlled by the weakened British and French Empires, setting in motion another tsunami of social change.

The U.S. Volunteer Armed Forces

Modern weapons allow armed forces in technologically advanced societies to be simultaneously smaller, more destructive, and better protected. This allows the United States and other nations to maintain a totally volunteer military. Young people with no inclination to serve in the armed forces are free not to because there is no draft. This results in the armed forces being relatively unrepresentative of the entire population. Those who enlist are more likely to come from rural areas and from southern or western states (with the major exception of California) (DeFronzo 2010). And children of military veterans are much more likely to enlist than other young people. Eikenberry and Kennedy (2013) argue that there is a danger that the United States is developing "a self-perpetuating military caste, sharply segregated from the larger society and with its enlisted ranks disproportionately recruited from the disadvantaged." Advanced technology also contributes to the civilian–military divide by making the individual soldier more lethal and efficient, allowing for war making to be less costly in terms of lives. Technology such as remotely piloted drone aircraft economizes both personnel and expense and can lead to lack of public comprehension and concern about the use of force. The volunteer armed force, its advanced weapons, and fewer personal consequences of war for the vast majority of Americans give the president greater freedom to resort to military force. Eikenberry and Kennedy (2013) note the while there were nineteen U.S. military deployments during the twenty-seven years after World War II while the United States still had the draft, there were 144 military deployments between 1973 and 2013 in the era of the volunteer armed forces.

Private Military Companies (PMCs)

Employing mercenary soldiers began thousands of years ago (Singer 2008:20). But governments' hiring of private soldiers declined significantly by the twentieth century. There was one civilian employee for every six

U.S. soldiers in the Vietnam conflict (Miller 2006: 75). But as the U.S. armed forces shrank after the Cold War, reliance on private personnel increased. The number of private contractors supporting U.S. troops in Iraq in 2006 was estimated at about 1 per 2.6 American soldiers (Miller 2006:76). Singer (2008:8–18) notes that private military companies (PMCs) are active in virtually every part of the world.

Blackwater

The Blackwater PMC (which changed its name to Xe in 2009 and then became known as Academi in 2011) was founded by Eric Prince, a former Navy Seal, in 1997 (Scahill 2007). The name comes from the black water at its training site on thousands of acres of the North Carolina Great Dismal Swamp. Several events spurred its growth. First was the April 20, 1999, Columbine High School mass murders. After Columbine, Blackwater used a mock school building, R U Ready High School, complete with the sound of screaming students, to train hundreds of SWAT police officers (Scahill 2007:36–37). The next was the October 12, 2000, suicide attack on the USS *Cole*, a guided-missile destroyer, at Aden, Yemen. Blackwater received a contract worth about $35.7 million to train Navy personnel to protect ships and naval facilities. And the 9/11 attacks resulted in a greater surge of Blackwater contracts. Blackwater and similar companies supplement the government's military but also give it a relatively covert capability to intervene in other countries through hiring private soldiers rather than openly using U.S. forces.

Deaths and Injuries of War

Wars have killed and injured tens of millions. During World War II, at least 50 million were killed (White 2011). For the Soviet Union alone the number was over 20 million, about half of whom were civilians. Wars also inflict psychological injuries that can include nightmares, depression, and behavioral problems. In 2014, investigations revealed that the U.S. Veteran's Administration was failing to provide adequate health care services to U.S. veterans to the extent that dozens died while waiting to receive medical treatment (Bronstein, Griffin, and Black 2014). The feature describes sexual violence in war and within armed forces.

Economic Devastation and Political Impacts

Wars also cause enormous destruction and economic devastation. The First World War so devastated Russia that many of its people supported the revolution that overthrew the country's monarchy and brought the Communists to power. The victory of revolutionaries in Russia inspired revolutionary movements in other countries, such as China.

Mao Zedong, leader of the Chinese revolution

Social Movements: War, Sexual Violence, and the Movement to End Sexual Assault in the Military

There have been an untold number of war-related rapes. Some rapes are the acts of criminal psychopaths who take advantage of wartime chaos to commit rapes. But sometimes rape is more widespread. Soldiers may commit rape to terrorize an enemy or kidnap women to serve as sex slaves.

Rape has been used a weapon of war in many countries, including Bangladesh, Bosnia and Herzegovina, Cambodia, Cyprus, the Democratic Republic of the Congo, Liberia, Rwanda, Somalia, and Uganda. The United Nations (1996) points out that the harm inflicted on women by rapists is also an attack on families, communities, and cultures. The military rapists' intent is to demoralize their opponents by assaulting mothers, sisters, and daughters, attempting to shame both the victims and other family members who were unable to protect them. In some wars, thousands of girls and women were forced into prostitution. During World War II, the Japanese were accused of forcing thousands of non-Japanese women into sex slavery.

Sexual violence also takes place within armies, as some men attempt to assert physical domination over women soldiers and even other male soldiers. The U.S. armed forces (Steinhauer 2013) released the results of a survey of active-duty military personnel, which indicated that in fiscal year 2012, 6.1 percent of the 203,000 active-duty women in the U.S. armed forces (12,100 women) experienced "unwanted sexual contact," as did 1.2 percent of the 1.2 million active-duty men (13,900 men) (U.S. Department of Defense 2013:11). Only about 13 percent of these incidents were reported to authorities. Military women were significantly more likely to be the victims of sexual assault than women in the general population (Steinhauer 2013). In its 2014 and 2016 surveys of military personnel, the Defense Department (2018) switched from measuring "unwanted sexual contact" to measuring "sexual assault." The Defense Department

reports there has been progress in reducing sexual assault in the armed forces. The surveys, which are conducted once every two years, indicated that in 2014, 4.9 percent of military servicewomen and 0.9 percent of men had been the victims of sexual assault (Defense Department 2018). For 2016 the survey results were 4.3 percent for women and 0.6 percent for men. The Defense Department concludes that between 2012 and 2016 the prevalence of sexual assault against women declined by 30 percent and against men by 50 percent. During the same period, the Defense Department states that the reporting of sexual assault increased by 88 percent, suggesting that service members had gained more confidence in the Defense Department's sexual assault response system. However, the number of reported cases of sexual assault in the military grew from 4,794 in 2016 to 5,277 in 2017, a ten-percent increase (U.S. Department of Defense 2018). The movement to end sexual assault of American soldiers by American soldiers was spurred by the 2013 Academy Award nominated documentary The Invisible War, which dealt with rape within the U.S. military. The film notes that a female soldier in combat zones "is more likely to be raped by a fellow soldier than killed by enemy fire," that "among all active-duty female soldiers, 20 percent are sexually assaulted" during their military service, and that there was a "systemic cover-up of military sex crimes" (PBS 2012b). After watching The Invisible War, Secretary of Defense Leon Panetta and members of Congress moved to improve sexual assault investigations in the armed forces. A number of U.S. women senators, led by Senator Kirsten Gillibrand, Democrat of New York, called for having all sex offenders in the military discharged from service and taking adjudication of sexual assault cases outside the military chain of command. The 2015 National Defense Authorization Act contained provisions intended to improve

Social Movements (*continued*)

the ability of victims of sexual assault in the armed forces to obtain justice. These included efforts to ensure improved legal representation rights for alleged victims and greater protection from retaliation for bringing a charge of sexual assault (Vergun 2015).

What are your thoughts?

How should sexual assault by soldiers be dealt with around the world? How should sexual assault by military personnel against military personnel within the U.S. armed forces be dealt with?

World War I and the financial punishments imposed on defeated Germany bankrupted the country. Economic hardship and desire for revenge motivated millions of Germans to vote the Nazi Party and Hitler into power in the 1930s, setting the stage for World War II. During the 1980s, Iraq fell 80 billion dollars into debt during its war against Iran, a country with three times Iraq's population. In 1990, Iraq, under Saddam Hussein, invaded oil-rich Kuwait in an unsuccessful attempt to eliminate the debt it owed Kuwait, gain more oil revenue, and save its deteriorating economy. This action led to wars with the United States in 1991 and 2003, and the overthrow of Saddam Hussein's regime and his execution. Resistance to the American occupation included an Al Qaeda-affiliated group that evolved into ISIS. In the United States, public dissatisfaction over the Iraq War and its enormous financial and human costs contributed to the election of a war opponent, Barack Obama, as president in 2008.

War Crimes

War crimes are human rights abuses that violate widely shared international standards of conduct concerning war, such as launching a war of aggression, harming civilians, executing prisoners, removing whole racial or ethnic categories from specified areas ("ethnic cleansing"), sexual abuse, torture, and the use of banned weapons like poison gas. International law recognizes three major types of war crimes: crimes against peace, "traditional" war crimes, and crimes against humanity (*Legal Dictionary* 2018). Crimes against peace include the planning and waging of a war of aggression against another nation. Traditional war crimes are acts that violate widely accepted rules of warfare covering the rights and responsibilities of conflicting states, prisoners of war, occupying powers, combatants, and civilians. Traditional war crimes also include using internationally banned weapons. War crimes against humanity include the persecution, forcible removal, enslavement, and/or extermination of people based on their race, ethnicity, religion, sexual preference, or some other identifiable characteristic.

Before and during World War II, the German Nazis imprisoned, worked to death, or executed millions in Germany and the countries German armies occupied for racial or political reasons. The victims included Jews, Romanis, communists (such as captured political officers in the Soviet military), and many other prisoners of war. In some countries occupied by German forces, thousands of local racists and fascists

war crimes Human rights abuses that violate widely shared international standards of conduct concerning war and include crimes against peace, "traditional" war crimes, and crimes against humanity.

assisted the Nazis or actually carried out the murders themselves. The Nazis were notorious for collective punishment, executing groups of civilians for acts of resistance by others against Nazi occupation.

The Japanese military was also accused of committing horrible war crimes during World War II. These included the mass murder of captured soldiers and civilians, mistreatment of prisoners of war, and rape in occupied areas on an enormous scale, including the forced sexual slavery of tens of thousands of Korean, Chinese, and Philippine "comfort women."

Nazi and Japanese wartime leaders were tried after the allied victory at Nuremberg, Tokyo, and other locations. These trials helped expand the concept of war crimes to include crimes against peace and against humanity (History.com 2018; PBS 2014a).

During the Vietnam War, hundreds of thousands of civilians were killed by opposing combatants. The worst known mass killing of civilians by U.S. forces, the My Lai Massacre (Allison 2012; PBS 2010; Peers et al. 1976) carried out on March 16, 1968, resulted in the deaths of between 347 and 504 persons, mainly children and women aged one to over eighty. The massacre was reported to senior military commanders by American helicopter pilot Hugh Thompson. He and his crew members Glenn Andreotta and Lawrence Colburn observed U.S. soldiers shooting unarmed civilians and landed, trying to convince an army officer, Lieutenant William Calley, to halt the slaughter. Later when they observed more killings, the helicopter crew landed between a group of civilians and U.S. soldiers advancing toward them. Thompson left the helicopter and ordered his crew to open fire on the American soldiers if they shot at either the civilians or him. He and his crew, with the help of other helicopter pilots, were able to save about a dozen women and children. Some military authorities tried to cover up My Lai and the only person convicted in the atrocity was Lieutenant Calley. He served only about three-and-a-half years of what was originally a life sentence and was pardoned by President Richard Nixon in 1974. American war crimes in Vietnam seemed to be mainly the responsibility of individuals or groups of soldiers; the cover-ups of these crimes appeared more institutional and systematic.

According to standards established by the post–World War II trials of German and Japanese fascist leaders, many Americans believe that former president George W. Bush, former vice president Dick Cheney, and other members of their administration should have been charged with a crime against peace for invading Iraq in 2003 on false accusations that it possessed WMDs. A notorious traditional war crime occurred at Abu Ghraib prison. This came to light when photographs showed male and female U.S. military personnel abusing captured prisoners (Leung 2004).

The United Nations International Criminal Court (ICC) has the power to deal with war crimes, crimes against humanity, and genocide (International Criminal Court 2014, 2017). But the ICC's jurisdiction is limited to events occurring after July 1, 2002, when it officially became active. In

Anti-Iraq war demonstration in Hollywood

addition, at least one of three other conditions must be met: the accused person is a national of a country accepting the authority of the ICC; the crime took place on the territory of a country accepting of the authority of the ICC; or the United Nations Security Council refers the situation to the ICC, regardless of the location where the crime took place or the nationality of the accused person. Over 120 countries have accepted the jurisdiction of the ICC. But many nations have not, including the United States, the Russian Federation, the People's Republic of China, and India. While President Bill Clinton favored the United States accepting ICC jurisdiction, President George W. Bush instructed the State Department to inform the United Nations' secretary general that the United States would not approve the ICC treaty (*Legal Dictionary* 2018). The feature describes issues concerning the ICC.

Special Topics: Should the United States Participate in the International Criminal Court?

International Court of Justice in the Hague, Holland

After the Second World War, leaders of Nazi Germany and imperial Japan were tried for crimes including launching wars of aggression and committing mass murder. This inspired the idea that war and human rights abuses could be prevented if there was a standing international court with the authority to punish those who committed such crimes. In 1998 the Rome Treaty created the International Criminal Court (ICC). But the court can only operate in countries that have ratified the treaty or in instances when it is directed to act by the United Nations. Although more than 120 nations have ratified the ICC, many countries, including the United States, have not (Onishi 2017).

While supportive of the ideals of the ICC, U.S. administrations from Bill Clinton on have expressed concerns with how it might operate in practice. One issue is the possibility that the ICC, for political reasons, could prosecute U.S. officials, soldiers, or other American nationals located abroad. In 2016, 193,442 U.S. active-duty military personnel were stationed outside the United States (Bialik 2017). There may be more operating secretly. Another concern emphasized by the George W. Bush administration is that the ICC could violate U.S. national sovereignty over criminal justice for American citizens (BBC 2015; Schaefer and Groves 2009). However, there are at least two other reasons why the U.S. government is reluctant to ratify the ICC. One is that the United States invaded Iraq in 2003 without UN permission, in opposition to overwhelming world public opinion, and on false accusations that Iraq possessed weapons of mass destruction. The ICC could conceivably prosecute American leaders for launching an aggressive war that resulted in tens of thousands of deaths if the United States were to ratify the ICC. Another likely concern is maintaining sufficient enlistment levels for America's volunteer armed forces. The possibility of prosecution by the ICC for misconduct in other countries could significantly impede recruitment and threaten the viability of the volunteer military.

The United States has also taken a series of actions to prevent the ICC from prosecuting American citizens. One was the passage of

(continued)

Special Topics (*continued*)

the American Servicemembers' Protection Act (ASPA). This authorized the use of U.S. military force to free any Americans or citizens of U.S.-allied countries being held by the ICC (Human Rights Watch 2002). The law also provides for withdrawing U.S. military assistance from countries that ratify the ICC treaty and restricting American participation in the United Nations' peacekeeping operations unless the U. S. obtains immunity from ICC prosecution. Another major strategy used to protect U.S. citizens from the ICC is to take advantage of the ICC treaty's Article 98, which states that the ICC may not request a country to turn over a person if that action would be inconsistent with the nation's obligations under an agreement with another nation (Georgetown Law Library 2014). Thus the United States has established bilateral immunity agreements with more than 100 countries to ensure that those states will not turn over American citizens to the ICC for prosecution. Despite U.S. government opposition to the ICC, public opinion polls repeatedly indicated that a majority of Americans favor U.S. participation in the court (Columbia University Institute for Study of Human Rights 2017). Without American support the ICC has been largely limited to trying persons the United States consents to have prosecuted, such as a number of individuals accused of human rights abuses in the former Yugoslavia and in several African countries. The perceived unfairness in the operation of the ICC has led several African countries to consider withdrawing from the ICC (Onishi 2017).

What are your thoughts?
Should the United States participate in the International Criminal Court? Why or why not?

STRATEGIES TO ESTABLISH AND MAINTAIN PEACE

Efforts to promote and maintain peace include ensuring punishment for those starting a war and improved defensive capabilities to discourage attacks. In addition, pro-peace strategies encompass disarmament and nuclear nonproliferation agreements, mediation to resolve serious disagreements among nations, and fairer distribution of resources and opportunities.

Deterrence

One argument for preventing war and war crimes is deterrence. This is the belief that individuals or nations will not start wars if they are convinced that they will be severely punished for doing so. This is the logic behind the ICC and sanctions imposed by the United Nations against a perpetrator. But anyone of the five permanent members of the United Nations Security Council (China, Great Britain, France, the Russian Federation, and the United States) can veto any proposed action of the United Nations. This of course means that the United Nations cannot realistically deter military action by any of these powerful nations. Historically, individual nations have tried to deter other nations from attacking them by building up strong military forces and by forming defensive alliances with other countries. With the advent of atomic weapons, the use of which could kill hundreds of millions, devastate the warring nations, and poison the environment, peace between major nuclear powers was said to have been maintained because of the fear of mutually assured destruction.

Improved Defensive Capabilities

Another approach to preventing war is to stop attacking weapons from being able to reach their targets through high-tech antimissile and anti-aircraft systems. Interceptor missiles are designed to destroy incoming missiles or aircraft. Other proposed defenses include satellite-based laser beams, microwave-emitting missiles that destroy enemy electronics and guidance systems, and satellite interceptors.

Disarmament and Nuclear Nonproliferation

Many argue that mutually agreed disarmament and preventing the spread of nuclear weapons can prevent war. This approach can conceivably reduce the destructiveness of war, if not stop wars from occurring. On the other hand, the leaders of some nations may believe that possessing nuclear weapons can actually protect their nations from attack. North Korean leaders concluded that if Iraq had nuclear weapons in 2003, the United States probably would not have invaded. In response, they rapidly pushed to develop and publicly test a nuclear weapon in 2006, assuming this would make an invasion of North Korea less likely. North Korea continued its nuclear weapons program and claimed to have developed and successfully tested hydrogen (fusion) bombs in 2016 and 2017, which are far more powerful the atomic (fission) bombs, and intercontinental ballistic missiles for delivering nuclear weapons (Griffiths and Dewan 2017). The Trump administration threatened possible military action against North Korea and, along with assistance from South Korea, announced that it intended to negotiate a denuclearization of the Korean peninsula with North Korea (Associated Press 2018).

Resolving Underlying Conflicts through Mediation and Oversight by the United Nations or other Unbiased Parties

Some wars have been prevented or ended with the help of a third party perceived to be unbiased by the opposing sides. For example, the 1946–1954 French–Indochina War was settled by an international commission in Geneva in 1954. In the late 1980s, the United Nations and the Organization of American States worked out a settlement of the civil war in Nicaragua (DeFronzo 2015). UN troops then helped maintain the peace until new elections were held in 1990. In 1998, U.S. Senator George Mitchell successfully mediated a peace settlement of the civil war in Northern Ireland (Mitchell 2001). And in 2016, after four years of negotiations in Havana, Cuba, assisted by Chile, Cuba, Norway, and Venezuela, the Marxist Revolutionary Armed Forces of Colombia and the Colombian government signed a peace agreement ending a 52-year-long civil war that had cost the lives of more than 220,000 (Colombia Reports 2016; Reuters 2016).

Fairer Distribution of Resources

A high level of inequality within nations has been linked to the outbreak of revolutions when a large mass of people becomes outraged at what they perceive as an unfair system. Improving the living conditions and opportunities of disadvantaged persons can reduce the motivation for rebellion, especially when there is a shared acceptance of the political system as legitimate.

Internationally, since wealthy nations are typically heavily armed, there is little possibility that the leaders of a poor nation would dare attack a wealthy one. More probable is that individuals within a poor nation might form militant groups to carry out violent terrorist attacks against rich countries. Thus, a more equitable distribution of resources between societies may be one way to combat terrorism.

TERRORISM

Terrorism, as noted, earlier, is the use of violence or the threat of violence to achieve a political goal. Whereas combatants in war are supposed to act according to international law and norms of warfare, terrorists engage in acts that violate such rules. Their actions can include hijackings, kidnappings, assassinations, mass murder, car and truck bombings, and suicide bombings. The targets for terrorist acts may be members of some specific group like government or military officials, or much larger categories like all members of a particular political party, religion, or ethnic group. The terrorists' goals might be to remove one or a few persons from power in the hope that this will bring about changes they favor. Or it might be to draw attention to a particular cause or encourage popular opposition to a ruling group and set the stage for a mass-participation revolution. It is often said that whether acts of violence are terrorism depends in part on your political viewpoint. People who engage in politically motivated violence may be viewed as terrorists if you oppose their goals but "freedom fighters" if you support their goals. But the type of violence used has separate significance. The label terrorist is most likely to be applied when the attacks are on members of broad population groups viewed as innocent civilians.

The issue of who is a terrorist has sometimes been widely contested, even within the United States. During the 1980s for example, President Reagan provided support and weapons for counterrevolutionary Nicaraguans, or "contras," trying to overthrow the revolutionary Sandinista government in Nicaragua. The contras were accused of executing captured Nicaraguan soldiers and some civilians. Many Democrats in Congress called the contras terrorists. At the same time, President Reagan called the contras freedom fighters.

How Many Terrorists Are There?

The U.S. National Counterterrorism Center (NCTC) database of known or suspected terrorists, the Terrorist Identities Datamart Environment (TIDE), included 1.1 million names (NCTC 2017; Sullivan 2014). Among them were 25,000 people who are U.S. citizens or legal permanent residents.

Types of Terrorism

Transnational terrorism refers to a terrorist or a terrorist organization operating in more than one country. For example, while Al Qaeda originated in Afghanistan and Pakistan, it spread to and carried out attacks in other nations, such as the 1998 bombing of U.S. embassies in Kenya and Tanzania, the bombing of the U.S. guided-missile destroyer *USS Cole* in a Yemeni port in 2000, the 9/11 attacks in New York and Washington, D.C. in 2001, and numerous acts of violence in Europe, Africa, and the Middle East. *State-sponsored terrorism* is a form of transnational terrorism in which a government in one nation provides support for people who commit terrorist acts in another nation. The United States accused Iran of supporting groups it considers terrorist, such as the Shia Lebanese organization Hezbollah (U.S. State Department 2016). On the other hand, Iran accused Israel and the United States of supporting a series of assassinations of its nuclear scientists between 2010 and 2012 (Cowell and Gladstone 2012). Sometimes state support for a violent group can backfire if that group later turns around and uses violence against its former benefactor. For example, during the 1980s the United States provided crucial support, including antiaircraft missiles, for Islamic militants fighting against a leftist government in Afghanistan and its allied Soviet military forces. This operation was a huge strategic success for the United States in the Cold War because the U.S. aid ensured that the Soviets would be unable to win the war. This defeat further discredited the communist government, contributing to its fall from power and the dissolution of the Soviet Union in 1991. But Osama bin Laden and other Islamic volunteers who had been on the winning side in Afghanistan formed themselves into Al Qaeda and, aided by the Islamic extremist Taliban government that came to power in Afghanistan, soon began terrorist attacks against the United States, whom it wanted to drive from the Middle East and punish for supporting Israel.

Domestic terrorism refers to a terrorist or terrorist organization that originated and operates in one country. The most lethal act of domestic terrorism in U.S. history occurred on April 19, 1995, when a truck bomb destroyed the Alfred P. Murrah Federal Building in Oklahoma City. The bombing killed 168 people, including 19 children, and injured hundreds (Federal Bureau of Investigation 2017). This bombing was carried out by Timothy McVeigh. McVeigh was a decorated army veteran who had fought in the 1991 Gulf War against Iraq. He became angry at U.S. government actions that he considered dictatorial and brutal, in particular the federal government's 1993 siege of the Branch Davidian sect in Waco, Texas, which resulted in the deaths of five federal agents and eighty-one sect members, including eighteen children. McVeigh appeared to have been inspired in part by a novel, *The Turner Diaries*, about white-supremacist revolutionaries who destroyed the FBI's Washington, D.C. national headquarters with a truck bomb (Thomas 2001). This book was and is widely read by extremist anti-government conservatives and white supremacists. While left-wing terrorists, such as the Weather Underground, the Symbionese Liberation Army, and the Black Liberation Army, carried out acts of violence, right-wing terrorists like McVeigh and members of white nationalist groups like the Ku Klux Klan

Bombed Oklahoma City federal building

and the Order (Silent Brotherhood) caused far more deaths. White supremacist Wade Michael Page shot and killed six members of the Sikh faith at a Sikh temple in Oak Creek, Wisconsin, on August 5, 2012, and wounded four others, including a police lieutenant, before being killed by another police officer (CBS/AP 2012). On June 17, 2015, Dylann Roof, a young man accused of being a white supremacist, shot and killed nine people at the Emanuel African Methodist Episcopal Church in Charleston, South Carolina (Sanchez and O'Shea 2016). He was captured and later sentenced to death. An apparently politically motivated shooting took place on June 14, 2017, when a former supporter of Democratic presidential candidate Bernie Sanders, James T. Hodgkinson, shot and wounded four persons, including Republican House Majority Whip Steve Scalise of Louisiana, at a morning baseball practice session for Republican members of Congress in Alexandria, Virginia (Hermann 2017). Hodgkinson was shot and killed by police.

State repressive terrorism is a type of domestic terrorism in which a government uses violence within its borders to crush political opposition or other social groups. Methods have included mass arrests, torture, and murder. The Italian dictator Benito Mussolini, the founder of fascism, and his fellow fascists used such terror to maintain control of Italy beginning in 1922. The Communist leader Joseph Stalin engaged in state terror on a much larger scale in the Soviet Union. Adolf Hitler and his Nazis used state terror to dominate Germany and eliminate what they considered inferior racial groups. It's important to note that all three of these regimes enjoyed significant popular support during much of their existence because they seemed to achieve some important goals many people supported: many Italians praised Mussolini for bringing social stability and efficiency to Italy and for suppressing both the communists and the mafia; millions of Russians credited Stalin with rapidly industrializing the USSR; and millions of Germans adored Hitler for restoring German honor after the defeat of World War I and reviving the economy before the outbreak of World War II. State terrorism is never the work of only one person. Enormous numbers of Italians, Soviets, and Germans carried out acts of state terror on behalf of their dictatorial governments. The same was true for the brutal regime of Pol Pot in Cambodia, certain right-wing military officials and associates in Chile, Argentina, El Salvador, and Guatemala, the apartheid-era government in South Africa, and various authoritarian leaders in the Middle East.

THE ROOT CAUSES OF TERRORISM

There are multiple causes of terrorist violence. Psychopathic personality types among government and military leaders and among individual political activists may engage in terrorism. But much terrorist violence is linked to sociological and historical factors.

Inequality, Poverty, and Perception of Unfair Treatment

Discrimination, extreme inequality, and poverty can contribute to the development of terrorist groups. People with little hope of a better future can sometimes be persuaded to strike out at those they perceive deserve blame. The decades-long hardships of Arab Palestinians in the Gaza Strip and the West Bank, who suffered from high poverty and unemployment rates (CIA 2016a; 2016b), played a role in why many Palestinians carried out acts of terrorism against Israelis. Nationalist revolutionaries like the Palestinians struggling to establish their own independent state have frequently engaged in acts of terrorism against occupying forces which, in turn, have often carried out violent reprisals against the revolutionaries and those who support them.

Extremist Ideologies

Ideologies make assertions about the causes of hardships, such as discrimination and poverty, and also often prescribe actions to address these problems. Racism, ethnocentric extremism, and religious extremism are among the types of ideologies that attempt to justify acts of terrorism. Racist concepts define the members of certain groups as biologically inferior and as threats to the "purity" of the supposedly "superior" race. This idea motivated much of the Nazis' terrorism. Ethnocentric extremism asserts that ethnic groups are superior or inferior in terms of their cultures and also encompasses vengeance for historic crimes that members of one ethnic group are accused of having committed against members of another. This type of extremism played a role in the Hutu massacre of Tutsis and moderate Hutus in Rwanda in 1994. Religious extremism has also motivated and justified acts of terrorism (Combs 2012). Christians tortured and killed many Muslims and Jews during the Crusades and the Inquisition, and Catholics and Protestants did the same to each other for decades after the Protestant Reformation. In the twenty-first century hundreds of Muslims participated in terrorist attacks against Christians and Jews as well as other Muslims. Religion-motivated terrorism is facilitated by several factors, such as the belief that God is on your side, that the violence is God's will, that the targets are "enemies of God," and that any innocent victims are part God's plan, who will be made happy in the afterlife. A belief that God will reward "martyrs," those who give their lives in the struggle, also motivates many who carry out acts of violence, such as suicide bombers.

Asymmetry of Power

Another element that can promote terrorism is an asymmetry of power: that is, opponents differ greatly in their ability to inflict damage, at least in the initial period of the conflict. Typically, an existing government has far more power and capability for violence than its adversaries and can be tempted to use repressive state terrorism to crush opposition because its leaders have little or no fear of retribution. The weak party in the conflict may employ terrorism because it lacks other means to attack a powerful foe. The contrasting perspectives of state terrorism and insurgent (rebel) terrorism are reflected in the classic film *The Battle of Algiers*, which covers the French conflict with Algerian revolutionaries fighting for their country's independence. Revolutionaries exploded bombs in French civilian areas in Algeria. When asked by a reporter whether it was cowardly to have women use their baskets and handbags to plant bombs to kill French civilians, a captured Algerian revolutionary leader, Larbi Ben M'hidi, replied:

"Doesn't it seem to you even more cowardly (for the French) to drop napalm bombs on unarmed villages, so that there are a thousand times more innocent victims... . Give us your bombers (your airplanes), and you can have our baskets" (Internet Movie Database 2014). The feature describes two religious extremist movements whose members engaged in terrorist violence.

Social Movements: Islamic Fundamentalist Terrorist Movements: Al Qaeda and ISIS

World Trade Center South Tower exploding after being struck by a hijacked airliner on 9/11, 2001

Al Qaeda, the Sunni Islamic extremist movement that carried out the 9/11 terrorist attacks against the United States, was born in the struggle against Soviet occupation of Afghanistan in the 1980s. Osama bin Laden, a Saudi citizen, and tens of thousands of other Arabs volunteered to go to Afghanistan to drive the Russians out. With help from the United States, Pakistan, and Saudi Arabia, Islamists forced the Soviets to withdraw in 1989. Around that time, Bin Laden created Al Qaeda, "the base," a database and communication network of Islamic volunteers who had fought in Afghanistan that could be mobilized

for future conflicts. Believing the Americans intended to permanently occupy the Middle East, Bin Laden turned Al Qaeda against the United States in the 1990s. In retaliation for 9/11, the United States invaded Afghanistan in October 2001 and ousted the repressive Taliban regime, which had provided training sites for bin Laden and Al Qaeda. Relying heavily on Special Forces operations and drone aircraft missiles, the United States decimated Al Qaeda's leadership. But individuals trained or inspired by Al Qaeda repeatedly tried to attack the United States, including an Afghan immigrant's attempt to bomb the New York City subway system in September 2009; the November 5, 2009, killings of thirteen soldiers at Fort Hood, Texas, by a U.S. Army major; the December 25, 2009, attempted bombing of an airliner arriving in Detroit by a Nigerian man; and the attempt of a Connecticut Pakistani American man to bomb Times Square on May 1, 2010 (Mazzetti, Tavernise, and Healy 2010).

Although on May 1, 2011, U.S. Navy Seals found and killed Osama bin Laden at his walled compound in Abbottabad, Pakistan, Al Qaeda-type armed groups remained active in Iraq, Libya, Mali, Somalia, Syria, Yemen, and other countries. One of the most serious new terrorist threats came to

Social Movements (*continued*)

world attention in 2014 when a successor to Al Qaeda in Iraq, the Islamic State in Iraq and Syria (ISIS) established control over much of Iraq and Syria. ISIS, also known as the Islamic State (IS), and the Islamic State in Iraq and the Levant (ISIL), received support from tens of thousands of Iraqi Sunni Arabs who believed they were being persecuted by Iraq's Shia-dominated, U.S- supported regime, barred from meaningful participation in government, and denied resources (Lister 2014; Nance 2016; Weiss and Hassan 2015). The ISIS leader, Abu Bakr al Baghdadi, said to have a Ph. D. in Islamic Studies from an Iraqi university, was held in prison by U.S. forces for four years until his release in 2009. He is believed to have successfully reorganized Al Qaeda in Iraq into ISIS after it had been devastated during the American occupation.

ISIS wants to create an Islamic caliphate, initially covering Iraq and Syria, but then expanding to other Islamic countries and beyond. A caliphate is the concept of a sovereign state of all Muslims governed by a caliph under Islamic law (sharia). Viewed as the successor to the Prophet Mohammad, the caliph is seen as the supreme religious and political leader. ISIS imposes its version of Sharia law in areas it controls. This includes separating girls from boys in schools, making women wear the veil in public, and having Sharia courts mete out often brutal "justice." ISIS is accused of carrying out mass executions of Iraqi and Syrian soldiers and forcing non-Muslims to convert to Islam, pay special taxes, flee their homes, or face severe punishment, including execution. ISIS executed American journalist James Foley in August of 2014 after a demanded ransom was not paid and the United States began air strikes against ISIS forces in Iraq (Chandler 2014).

ISIS declared that Abu Bakr al-Baghdadi is the caliph and true leader of all Muslims everywhere (Al Jazeera 2014). Much more than was the case for Al Qaeda under Osama bin Laden, ISIS organized large-scale military formations with the aim of conquering territory and forcibly establishing a Sunni Muslim caliphate. Although the armed forces of several nations, including the United States, Russia, Iran, Iraq, and Syria, recovered significant territory from ISIS and battled to destroy the organization, ISIS supporters carried out brutal and devastating terrorist attacks in multiple countries including in Paris on January 7, 2015 (Charlie Hebdo), and November 13, 2015 (Bataclan night club), in San Bernardino, California, on December 2, 2015 (Inland Regional Center), in Belgium on March 22, 2016 (Brussels Airport and Maalbeek Metro Station), and in Orlando, Florida on June 12, 2016 (Pulse nightclub).

What are your thoughts?
What do you think would be the most effective ways to deal with Al Qaeda and ISIS?

COMBATING TERRORISM

Multiple strategies have been developed to combat terrorism. These include defensive measures, denying terrorists' sanctuaries, refusing to make deals with terrorists, killing or capturing terrorists, and addressing the underlying causes of terrorism.

Defend against Terrorism

Defending against terrorism means employing various security measures to prevent terrorist attacks (Combs 2012; Pillar 2002). These include security screening at airports and other transportation facilities, nuclear power plants, water supplies, and other potential targets. Electronic surveillance and penetration of communication systems worldwide is another significant, though sometimes controversial, approach, to detecting and stopping terrorist attacks. The Patriot Act, passed by the U.S. Congress shortly after the September 11, 2001, attacks, permitted more extensive surveillance. While supporters believe this helped prevent terrorist attacks, critics claimed that the act gave the government too much power to violate people's personal privacy and that government personnel often exceeded, without fear of punishment, what they were legally permitted to do.

Deny Terrorists Sanctuary

The United States has imposed economic penalties on nations suspected of aiding or harboring terrorists and invaded Afghanistan in October 2001 to destroy Al Qaeda bases. But the U.S.-led invasion of Iraq in March 2003 created conditions that resulted in the emergence of new terrorist groups. In addition, the civil wars which began in 2011 in Syria and Libya appear to have spawned additional terrorist organizations. The United States aided in ousting ISIS from Iraqi and Syrian cities and towns in 2016 and 2017. Intelligence gathering, drone warfare, and special forces actions are major means for attempting to disrupt terrorist operations.

Make No Deals with Terrorists

A stated U.S. policy is to refuse to give in to the demands of terrorists. The fear is that to give in would reward terrorists for actions such as kidnapping and holding hostages and encourage more such behavior in the future. In reality, however, this policy has not always been followed. For example, while condemning Iran for supporting terrorism and convincing other nations to stop selling Iran weapons during the Iran–Iraq War, the Reagan administration secretly sold missiles to Iran, apparently as part of an agreement to win the release of Americans being held prisoner by Iran-allied groups in Lebanon (PBS 2014).

Kill or Capture Terrorists

Another approach to fighting terrorism is to kill or apprehend persons who have carried out acts of terrorism or are planning to do so. On May 1, 2011, members of U.S. Navy Seal Team Six killed Al Qaeda leader Osama bin Laden in Abbottabad, Pakistan (CNN 2013b). And on June 17, 2014, Ahmed Abu Khattala, accused of playing a major role in the September 11, 2012, attack in Benghazi that killed U.S. Ambassador to Libya Chris Stevens and three other Americans, was captured by U.S. forces (Associated Press 2014b). The United States and some other nations have used armed drone aircraft to kill dozens of suspected terrorists in countries such as Pakistan and Yemen (Dilanian 2016; Sledge 2014). However, it seems clear that many innocent people have also died in such attacks.

The treatment of captured alleged terrorists by U.S. personnel has been a subject of controversy. A 2009 national Pew Forum survey found that about 49 percent of American adults said that the use of torture on "suspected terrorists is 'often' or 'sometimes' justified" (CNN 2009). In 2014, the U.S. Senate issued a report accusing the CIA of engaging in brutal treatment of terror suspects after the September 11, 2001, attacks.

Methods used included "slapping, humiliation, exposure to cold, sleep deprivation and the near-drowning technique known as waterboarding" (Dilanian 2014). The report also concluded that "the harm caused by the use of these techniques outweighed any potential benefit." In reference to the report, President Obama said that "we did some things that were contrary to our values.... We tortured some folks" (Bruce 2014).

Address the Causes of Terrorism

Another approach to preventing terrorism is to attempt to eliminate the social conditions and cultural factors that give rise to terrorism in the first place, the so-called root-causes of terrorism. This means providing all peoples with democracy, secure human rights, and the right of self-determination of their political futures, "alleviating political repression, bringing relief from depraved rulers, and economically supplying the means to escape from poverty and improve living standards" (Cohen 2006:867). People who suffer from horrible conditions and are desperate for relief are vulnerable to the appeal of religious or secular ideologies that justify terrorist violence by dehumanizing those perceived to oppress them.

CHAPTER REVIEW

Basic Concepts: War, Rebellion, and Terrorism

War is armed conflict between nations, between different groups, or between nations and groups. Rebellion is a violent or nonviolent effort on the part of a large number of people to resist or totally overthrow their country's government. Terrorism is the use of violence or the threat of violence to achieve a political goal. It can be used against or by individuals, groups, or governments.

Sociological Perspectives on War and Rebellion

The structural-functional perspective holds that war or rebellion occur when people believe war or rebellion will result in greater benefits than continuing peace. The conflict perspective views inequalities as major causes of war and rebellion. The symbolic-interactionist approach is concerned with the meanings people develop for war or rebellion and how these promote or inhibit conflict.

Causes of War and Rebellion

Wars and rebellions have occurred for a number of reasons. Perceived threats have motivated nations to launch preemptive attacks on other countries. A nation's leaders have started wars to gain territory, resources, and economic advantages, especially when the targeted societies were militarily incapable of effectively defending themselves. Another motivation for war is to overthrow a hostile government. Wars have also been launched for religious reasons or because of ethnic rivalries. Terrorist acts, such as the assassination of the heir to the Austro-Hungarian throne, Archduke Franz Ferdinand, in 1914 by a Serbian, have also led to wars. And wars have occurred because there appeared to be no alternative course of action.

Rebellions occur when large numbers of people want to resist the policies of or totally overthrow their country's government or ruler. A revolution, a rebellion that results in the replacement of one or more basic institutions, is likely to succeed when a large part of the population becomes very dissatisfied with existing conditions, a division opens up among elites so that some support revolution, a shared motivation for revolution develops that unites different groups, the existing government becomes unable to carry out basic functions, and other countries are unwilling or unable to intervene to prevent the success of the revolution.

War, Rebellion, Revolution, and Social Change

Wars, rebellions, and revolutions have caused great social change. For example, European colonial conquests changed the culture, political systems, and economies of South and Central America, Africa, and huge sections of Asia. War-related technologies like radar and jet engines have also changed society. The ideologies of successful revolutions often spread internationally. For example, the democratic ideas of the American and French Revolutions circulated around the world.

Strategies to Establish and Maintain Peace

Strategies to establish and maintain peace include ensuring punishment for those who resort to war and improved defensive capabilities to prevent attacks. Pro-peace strategies also encompass disarmament and nuclear nonproliferation agreements, third-party mediation to peacefully resolve serious disagreements among nations, and fairer distribution of resources and opportunities.

Terrorism

Major forms of terrorism include transnational, state-sponsored, domestic, and state repressive terrorism.

The Root Causes of Terrorism

Some terrorists may have serious personality disorders. But terrorism also stems from sociological and historical factors such as a category of people suffering from inequality, poverty, and discrimination. Asymmetry of power and the spread of dehumanizing extremist ideologies can also promote terrorism.

Combating Terrorism

Defending against terrorism involves security measures, denying terrorists secure territories in which to organize and operate, refusing to make deals with terrorists, and apprehending or killing terrorists. A further approach to combating terrorism is to attempt to eliminate the social and cultural conditions that give rise to terrorism in the first place. This means providing all peoples with democracy, secure human rights, the right of self-determination of their political future, and ending political and economic oppression.

KEY TERMS

rebellion, p. 407
revolution, p. 407
terrorism, p. 407

war, p. 407
war crimes, p. 417

DISCUSSION QUESTIONS

1. Should war and rebellion be avoided at all cost, or are they sometimes necessary or justified? Explain your answer.

2. Which sociological perspective is most useful for explaining wars and rebellions? Why?

3. What do you think are the main contemporary causes of war?

4. Which wars and revolutions do you think have brought about the most social change? Explain your answer.

5. What do you think is the best way to maintain peace around the world? Explain your answer.

6. What do you think is the major cause of terrorism worldwide? What about in the United States? Explain your answers.

GLOSSARY

A

absolute deprivation theory The idea that social movements develop when people are unable to obtain adequate food, shelter, or other basic needs.

absolute poverty Not having access to basic things, including food, clean water, clothing, housing, sanitation, health care, and education, needed to survive and maintain health and well-being.

affirmative action programs Policies aimed at recruiting minority persons to make up for past discrimination and create a workforce or student body more representative of the entire population.

African American freedom movement The struggle for equal rights for African Americans throughout American history.

aging Growth in the percentage of older people in a nation's population coupled with the economic, job, health, and psychological issues experienced by many people as they get older.

AIDS Acquired immunodeficiency syndrome.

air pollution Contamination of air by any gases, particles, biological organisms, or other substances that are harmful to people or the environment.

alternative movements Social movements that aim to change a single type of behavior.

anomie State of lacking meaningful or useful norms (also referred to as normlessness).

apartheid A system of segregation in South Africa.

applied research (also called evaluation research) Testing the effectiveness of any program, strategy, or policy intended to affect society.

arranged marriage Marriages where a third party, typically the families of the persons to be married, take the leading role in selecting a marriage partner but in which the proposed parties to the marriage are free to decide whether to go through with it.

assimilation The process through which a culturally distinct group gradually adopts the dominant culture in a society.

autonomous marriage A marriage in which persons freely chose who to marry.

B

binge drinking Drinking that brings the blood alcohol concentration level to 0.08 percent or more. For women this would typically involve consuming four or more drinks and for men five or more drinks during a period of two hours or less.

birth rate Number of live births per 1,000 persons in a population per year.

birth rate The number of live births per 1,000 members of a population per year.

blended family A family with a stepparent, stepsibling, or half-sibling.

bourgeoisie In Marx's theory, the wealthy business owners.

brownfields Buildings, land, or anything affixed to land, the reuse, redevelopment, or expansion of which may be affected by the presence or potential presence of a hazardous substance.

C

capitalism The economic system in which resources, industry and businesses, and other means of producing goods or services are privately owned, the primary motive for economic activity is profit, and most goods and services are sold and bought in competitive markets.

capitalist-socialist societies Nations with predominantly capitalist economies where resources, businesses, and industries are mainly privately owned but which adopted measures advocated by socialist movements such as universal public education for children, publicly funded health care systems, and social security retirement systems.

charismatic leader A type of leader who emotionally inspires others through words and actions by presenting the movement as an essential moral struggle.

charter school A publicly funded school, often managed by a private company contracted by government, that is able to operate more independently of the school system in order to try new educational methods.

child abuse Physical, sexual, psychological, or emotional maltreatment or neglect of a child (a person under age eighteen), especially by a person or persons responsible for the child's well-being.

cisgender identity Having a gender identity that is the same as the person's sex identity assigned at birth (the same as her or his physical sex characteristics).

cisnormativity The individual or institutional assumption that everyone is cisgender and cisgender identities are superior to transgender identities.

claim An argument that a condition or behavior is harmful.

claims maker An expert in a related field, someone with personal experience, or a social activist who tries to assemble evidence supporting a claim that a condition or behavior is a social problem.

climate change The shift in climate toward more frequent extreme weather events such as intense heat waves and powerful storms.

coalescence The second stage of a social movement, in which it becomes more organized and develops resource-gathering capabilities.

Colonialism A process in which a typically more technologically advanced nation subdues and dominates the people of a lesser-developed area in order to benefit from their resources.

color-blind racial discrimination (also referred to as color-blind racism) Behavior or institutional practices that have the effect of discriminating against people of a certain race even though the publicly stated basis for differential treatment is not race.

coming out The process of identifying and accepting one's own sexual orientation or gender identity (coming out to oneself) and of publicly acknowledging it to others (coming out to others).

conflict perspective A conceptual approach that views society as characterized by inequalities that advantage some groups and disadvantage others, leading to conflict and the potential for social change.

conglomerate A corporation that operates in multiple economic sectors.

conservative movement A social movement with the goal of maintaining things the way they are.

core nations The most technologically advanced nations that are economically and militarily powerful and dominate the world system directly or through their multinational corporations.

corporate crime Any lawbreaking act or omission by a corporation.

corporation A business organization that is given a charter by a government recognizing it as a separate legal entity having rights, assets, responsibilities, and liabilities separate from those of its owners or employees.

crime Any voluntary and intentional behavior or omission that federal, state, or local government designates as a violation of criminal law and for which there is no legally accepted excuse, such as self-defense or insanity.

critical race theory A conflict approach stating that because racism is profoundly integrated into American institutions, culture, and everyday social life and activities, the only way to spread awareness of and remove it is through the insights and narratives of people of color.

culture of poverty The concept that in response to long-term structural conditions like unemployment, minimum wage jobs, and poor-quality schools, poor people develop a subculture of values, norms, beliefs, attitudes, and behaviors that help them adapt to their situation.

culture The knowledge, ways of thinking, shared understandings of behavior, and physical objects that characterize a people's way of life.

cybercrime Any crime committed through use of a computer or the internet.

D

death (mortality) rate Number of deaths per 1,000 persons in a population per year.

deinstitutionalization The shift to treating persons designated as mentally ill in settings other than as residents in mental hospitals.

delinquent subculture A deviant youth subculture with norms and values stressing toughness, manliness, and readiness to use violence to gain and keep respect, which promotes delinquency.

demise The fifth stage of a social movement, in which it comes to an end because it has achieved its goal, lost popular support, or been repressed.

demographic transition The shift from high birth and death rates to low birth and death rates in a society.

demographic transition The shift from high birth rates and high death rates to low birth rates and low death rates.

dependency theory The idea that poor nations were purposely made dependent on rich nations so that they can be exploited indefinitely.

dependent variable The variable whose value is determined by the independent variable.

deviant behavior Behavior that is inconsistent with deeply and widely held norms, expectations, or standards but is not necessarily unlawful.

digital divide The division between those having or not having technologically advanced devices such as personal computers and smartphones that provide access to information and the ability to communicate with people almost anywhere in the world.

discrimination Treating people a certain way because they are members of a particular social category.

doing gender How people try to display masculinity or femininity through attitudes, traits, clothing, symbols, and behaviors that represent the gender they want to present to others.

drug abuse The use of a drug that is illegal or a legal drug in amounts or in ways harmful to the user or others.

drug Any substance, other than food or water, that affects the functioning, development, or condition of the body.

E

economic-conflict perspective A conflict perspective that focuses on factors such as poverty, the concentration of power in the hands of the wealthy, and the profit motive of capitalist culture as major causes of social problems.

egalitarian family Families in which the partners have equal influence in decision making and share equally in family-centered activity such as child-rearing and housework.

elder abuse Any behavior that harms or causes serious risk of harm to a vulnerable "senior" adult.

environmental injustice The condition in which lower-income persons and other groups are relatively powerless to ensure themselves a healthy environment and are more likely to be exposed to environmental hazards.

environmental justice The condition in which all people have the same level of protection from environmental hazards and have equal access to decision making on healthy living, learning, and work environments.

environmental racism The condition in which racial or ethnic minorities are relatively powerless to ensure themselves a healthy environment and are more likely to be exposed to environmental hazards.

epidemiological transition The shift in the cause of death in a society from being predominantly infectious disease to chronic disease.

ethnicity A social category of people who share the same cultural heritage, often involving a common language and a common religion.

e-waste Discarded electronic equipment or devices.

excessive individualism Continuously putting selfish personal desires and interests above community welfare, including nature's collective resources and the environment.

experiment The type of research in which the independent variable is manipulated to see if this is followed by the predicted change in the dependent variable while controlling for other factors thought to affect the dependent variable.

F

false consciousness A lack of understanding about the existence or cause of a harmful condition or behavior.

family A group of two or more people who are recognized by others as a family and identify themselves as a family.

feminist-conflict perspective A conflict perspective that focuses on gender inequality as the cause of social problems.

fertility rate (also called the total fertility rate or TFR) Average number of children per woman aged fifteen to forty-four.

field research A type of research that involves gathering data on what is assumed to be natural behavior in a real-world setting.

focus group A group discussion, usually one to two hours in length, in which group members are asked to focus on a selected topic under the guidance of a researcher who acts as a moderator and facilitator.

forced marriage Marriages in which one or both persons do not giving free consent to marry but are instead forced into the marriage by third parties, such as parents or religious leaders.

fragmentation The fourth stage of a social movement, in which it breaks apart, typically after a period of some success, because movement participants disagree about whether essential goals have really been achieved.

framing theory The idea that a social movement emerges because of framing: the process of describing a social movement in such a way that it makes sense, appeals to as many people as possible, and fulfills one or more deeply held values.

functional illiteracy The lack of the level of reading or writing skills necessary to carry out everyday tasks.

G

gateway drug A drug whose use is thought to lead to the use of one or more other illegal drugs.

gender A social construct that it is the product of people learning from their culture and interactions with others what behaviors and psychological traits are expected of men or women.

gender binary The cultural belief that men and women have distinct personality traits, capabilities, and strengths and weaknesses.

gender identity How one's sense of gender corresponds to biological sex characteristics.

genocide The deliberate attempt to annihilate, in whole or in part, a racial, ethnic, national, or religious group.

Gini coefficient A measure of income inequality that ranges from zero (meaning everyone has the same income) to one (meaning a single person has all the income).

glass ceiling An invisible and often subtle yet powerful barrier of male prejudice and "old boy" networks that prevent female promotion beyond a certain level.

global warming The slow but steady warming of the Earth's land, oceans, and atmosphere.

globalization The dramatic increase in the movement of information, people, culture, technologies, goods, services, and money around the world and the increased connectedness and interdependence of peoples and nations.

green technology Technology that allows us to access green energy, energy that is renewable and does not cause pollution.

greenhouse effect Warming of the Earth caused by solar radiation being trapped by greenhouse gases rather than being reflected into space.

H

hate crime A criminal offense against a person or property motivated in whole or in part by an offender's bias against a race, religion, disability, sexual orientation, ethnicity, gender, or gender identity.

hazardous waste Waste that poses a threat to people or the environment.

heteronormativity The individual or institutional assumption that everyone is heterosexual and heterosexual orientation is superior to other sexual orientations.

historical and comparative research Sociological analyses and comparisons of societies.

HIV Human immunodeficiency virus.

homelessness Not having a home to call your own and instead having to spend nights in homeless shelters, on the streets, or in makeshift shelters made of various discarded materials.

household All people who occupy a housing unit together regardless of relationship.

human trafficking The use of force, fraud, or coercion to make a person commit a commercial sex act and/or the recruitment, harboring, transportation, provision, or obtaining of a person for labor or services through the use of force, fraud, or coercion for the purpose of subjection to involuntary servitude.

hypersegregation The very high concentration of people with particular characteristics, typically similar race or ethnicity identities and/or wealth levels, in geographical areas.

hypothesis A prediction derived from a theory about how one variable is related to another variable.

I

identity movement A social movement aimed at creating a new identity for an oppressed group that provides a sense of empowerment, pride, self-confidence, and equality.

immigration The movement of people into a country from another to take up residence.

incipiency The first stage of a social movement, which begins when a large number of people become distressed by a particular situation.

income The money a person receives from working, investments, or other sources.

independent variable The variable that a theory says determines the value of another variable.

infant mortality rates The number of deaths during the first year of life per 1,000 live births per year.

innovative (liberal) movement A social movement that intends to introduce something new with regard to culture, patterns of interaction, policies, or institutions.

institutional discrimination The operation of institutions in a way that discriminates against a category of people.

institutional racism The operation of institutions in a way that discriminates against people on the basis of race.

institutionalization The third stage of a social movement, in which the government takes official notice of the movement and tries to cope with it and the movement establishes one or more geographically extensive or even national social movement organizations.

intellectual leader A type of leader who provides a social movement with ideology explaining the problem, its cause, and the need for action.

intimate partner abuse Psychological abuse, economic abuse, physical violence, and sexual abuse occurring between spouses or former spouses, cohabiting couples, or boyfriends and girlfriends.

K

kinship Being related to another person through common ancestry (sharing common DNA) or marriage or adoption.

L

land pollution The placement on or into land of any material or substances that are harmful to people or the environment, or render the land difficult or impossible to use.

latent functions Unintended and often hidden or not well-understood functions.

leadership theory The idea that the emergence and success of social movements requires exceptional leaders.

literature review A researcher's review of previous research on her or his topic of interest.

M

magnet school A free public elementary, middle, or high school run by school districts or groups of school districts that has an attractive central educational focus such as science, technology, engineering, mathematics, or fine and performing arts.

managerial leader A type of leader who transforms the ideals and goals of the movement into organization and coordinated action.

manifest functions Intended and publicly recognized functions.

materialist consumerism The cultural belief that obtaining prized material possessions is essential to high self-esteem and a happy life.

matriarchal family Families that are mother centered and in which the mother has the greatest influence.

mental illness Any one of a number of thinking or mood disorders resulting in impaired functioning and/or debilitating feelings of distress.

minorities Categories of people who are subjected to disadvantages such as barriers to educational, employment, or political opportunities because of their physical or cultural characteristics, or other reasons such as sexual orientation.

modernization theory The theory that states that less-developed countries should go through a multistage modernization process to become technologically advanced, wealthy, and democratic.

monogamous marriage Marriage between only two persons.

multicultural pluralism A social environment in which no group is socially disadvantaged and racial and ethnic groups maintain a high level of cultural distinctiveness.

multifactor theory The idea that a social movement emerges and is shaped by multiple factors including communication, discontent, shared beliefs, dramatic events, movement leadership's ability to mobilize people, and the response of those in power.

N

National Crime Victimization Survey (NCVS) A national survey of tens of thousands of Americans asking them if they, their household members, or their businesses had been criminally victimized, regardless of whether they reported it to police.

National Incident-Based Reporting System (NIBRS) A more comprehensive and detailed crime data system intended to replace the UCR.

nativist movement A movement that aims to prevent people viewed as racially, culturally, or morally different, or otherwise threatening to the interests of residents, from entering a country.

neoliberal free market Open trade among nations unrestricted by any barriers or regulations.

new social movements Social movements that arose during the second half of the twentieth century and are concerned with moral and quality-of-life issues and the establishment of new collective identities.

news objectivity The extent to which news personnel and institutions present stories truthfully and without bias to the public.

newsworthiness The extent to which a story has the qualities, such as significance, proximity, prominence, human interest, and timing, to merit being presented to the public through news media.

O

objective element Reality of the existence of a condition or behavior recognized as a social problem.

occupational crime Lawbreaking behavior within the context of a legitimate profession.

official crime statistics Crime statistics that come from government sources, primarily the police and the courts.

opioid epidemic The dramatic growth in opioid drug use and deaths since 1999.

organized crime People working together to supply an illegal product or service, for example, illicit drugs or illegal gambling opportunities, to the public and/or using violence to gain an unfair advantage in an otherwise legitimate business, such as killing competitors or damaging their equipment or merchandise.

outsourcing The removal of jobs from one country to another, typically to increase profits by taking advantage of lower labor costs.

P

participant observation A type of research that involves the researcher actually participating in the activities of the people she or he is observing.

patriarchal family Families in which the father has the greatest influence in making decisions for the family and its members.

periphery nations Weak poor nations that provide the world system with minerals, agricultural products, or cheap labor.

pluralism The view that political power is exercised by ordinary Americans through elections and through the organizations they support.

political crime Any crime committed with the intention of influencing politics or government.

political opportunities theory The idea that political context is key in explaining social movements and their effects on society.

polygamous marriage Marriage to two or more spouses.

population growth Increase in the population of a location, such as a nation, territory, or city, equal to births plus people moving in minus deaths and people moving out.

power elite According to Mills, the power elite are people occupying the top positions in major business corporations, the federal government, and the armed forces who made the most important decisions. According to Domhoff, the dominant power elite are the economic elite.

prejudice Prejudgment of people before getting to know them personally, often involving negative feelings, attitudes, and stereotypes directed toward every individual in an entire race, ethnic group, religion, social class, or other social group.

proletariat In Marx's theory, the working class, composed of all workers from unskilled to highly trained who sell their labor for a wage.

R

race A socially constructed category of persons who share one or more physical traits such as skin color that affect access to political rights, economic opportunities, and other forms of resources and power.

racial and ethnic pluralism A social environment in which all racial and ethnic categories have the same level of civil rights, economic opportunity, and respect, regardless of their level of assimilation to the dominant culture.

racial profiling The practice of targeting people for suspicion of crime based on their race, ethnicity, religion, or national origin rather than on observing or detecting them engaged in a specific behavior.

racial/ethnic-conflict perspective A conflict perspective that focuses on discrimination based on skin color or ethnic heritage as the cause of social problems.

racism The belief that people of one race are superior to people of another race or of all other races.

reactionary movement A social movement that seeks to resurrect cultural elements, patterns of behavior, or institutions of the past.

rebellion A violent or nonviolent effort on the part of a large number of people to resist the policies of or totally overthrow their country's government or ruler.

redemptive movements Social movements that encourage people to adopt a new moral-religious outlook that will affect a wide range of personal behaviors.

reform movement A social movement that calls for changes in patterns of behavior, culture, and/or policy, but does not try to replace entire social institutions.

relative deprivation theory The idea that living conditions or political limitations only become intolerable when people come to view them as unacceptable relative to their conception of the way they think things should be.

relative poverty Having so much less in material goods and style of life than others that people are seen as "poor" in terms of social standards even if they do not suffer absolute poverty.

replacement-level fertility The average number of children born to each woman aged fifteen to forty-four necessary to maintain a stable population size in a country, generally about 2.1 for technologically advanced societies.

research question The topic that the researcher wants to investigate.

resource mobilization theory The idea that people motivated to create a social movement must have access to necessary resources to succeed.

revival An additional stage of some social movements that occurs if they re-emerge in the same or a modified form.

revolution A rebellion that results in the change of one or more basic institutions.

revolutionary movement A social movement that aims to bring about great structural change by replacing one or more major social institutions.

ruling class According to Domhoff, the economic power elite.

S

sample the persons chosen for a study to represent a larger population you want to learn about.

school segregation The division of students by race, ethnicity, and/or class into different schools.

school voucher programs Programs that provide taxpayer funds to the parents of school children to use in paying all or partial tuition at private (or in some cases public) schools of their choice.

secondary data analysis A type of research that involves analyzing data that have been collected by others.

segregation The separation of a race, ethnic group, class, religious group, or other group from the rest of society

self-report crime studies Anonymous surveys in which people are asked whether they have committed various types of crime.

semi-periphery nations Partially industrialized nations that extract benefits from periphery societies but pass much of these on to the core nations.

sex Being biologically (physically) male or female in terms of a person's chromosomal, chemical, reproductive, and anatomical characteristics such as external genitalia.

sexism Prejudice or discrimination against a person on the basis of sex or gender identity.

sexual orientation A person's sexual attraction and/or emotional-romantic attraction to persons of the opposite sex, same sex, or both sexes.

slavery A situation in which one person is owned by another and must do whatever the latter demands.

social class system A social and economic stratification system typically based on both birth and achievement within which it is possible to move either up or down.

social disorganization A structural-functional perspective that sees problems being caused by social change that occurs too quickly, or anything else that disrupts the functioning of social institutions.

social dysfunction A structural-functional perspective asserting that harmful conditions may be created by the positive functions of social institutions.

social institution A continuing pattern of social relationships intended to fulfill people's basic needs and aspirations and carry out functions essential to the operation of society.

social mobility The upward or downward movement on the economic ladder within a lifetime or between generations.

social movement A persistent and organized effort involving the mobilization of large numbers of people to work together to either bring about what they believe to be beneficial social change or resist or reverse what they believe to be harmful social change.

social pathology A structural-functional perspective that likens society to a living organism that can be healthy, evolve to a higher state, or become ill.

social problem A condition or a type of behavior that many people believe is harmful.

social stratification Inequality among people with regard to important social factors including access to education, income, property, power, and prestige.

social structure Relatively stable patterns of social behavior and relationships among people.

socialism Ideally, an economic and social system characterized by equality of opportunity and social justice in which major resources and industries are socially (collectively) owned and health care, education, and basic nutrition are provided to all either freely or at low cost.

socialist-capitalist societies Nations where resources and major industries are owned primarily by the state but where a significant expansion of capitalist business activity from selling crops in open markets to owning industries and businesses for profit has taken place.

sociological imagination The ability to relate the most personal elements and problems of an individual's life to social forces and the flow of history.

stereotype A set of expectations for the behavior, moral character, capabilities, or limitations of a person based on their membership in a social category.

strategy A general approach for achieving movement goals.

street crime Crimes of violence like homicide, forcible rape, robbery, and aggravated assault and relatively direct forms of property crime like burglary, larceny theft, and motor vehicle theft.

structural-functional perspective A conceptual framework that views society as a system of interdependent parts carrying out functions crucial to the well-being of the other parts and the system as a whole.

student movement A social movement in which students are the main or leading participants.

subculture A specific set of values, norms, beliefs, symbols, and behaviors shared by a group of people unique enough to significantly distinguish them from the other members of a culture.

subjective element Level of public concern about a condition or behavior recognized as a social problem.

suburban (urban) sprawl Poorly planned suburban development characterized by elements such as the use of large quantities of land to house relatively small numbers of people, destruction of farmland or open green areas, displacement of wildlife, and lack of sidewalks, bike lanes, or proper design to facilitate pedestrian or bicycle travel.

suburbanization The settlement of people in suburbs, the urban areas beyond the borders of a neighboring city.

survey research A type of research that involves asking people questions about a topic.

sustainable development Using resources to promote human welfare in ways that protect the environment and allow it to support human development indefinitely.

symbolic-interactionist perspective A sociological perspective that focuses on the analysis of person-to-person interaction and the actual meanings people give to their experiences and environments.

T

tactics The immediate actions used to implement a strategy.

terrorism The use of violence or the threat of violence to achieve a political goal.

theory An explanation for the existence of particular social conditions or patterns of behavior.

transgender identity Having a gender identity that is the opposite of the person's physical sex characteristics.

transnational movements Social movements active in more than one country.

true consciousness Awareness of the existence and real cause of a harmful condition or behavior and that this harmful condition or behavior can be eliminated if people work together.

U

Uniform Crime Reports (UCR) FBI-compiled crime statistics based on crime data supplied by thousands of law enforcement agencies around the United States.

under-five-child-mortality rate The number of children dying under five years old per 1,000 live births.

urbanization The movement of people from rural areas into urban areas.

V

variable Anything that can have two or more values and can be measured in some way.

victimless crime Crimes where there is supposedly no victim, such as illegal drug use, illegal gambling, and prostitution.

W

war crimes Human rights abuses that violate widely shared international standards of conduct concerning during war and include crimes against peace, "traditional" war crimes, and crimes against humanity.

war on drugs U.S. efforts to reduce illegal drug use by educating people about drugs, stopping the manufacture of illicit drugs, preventing the flow of foreign drugs into the United States, prosecuting and punishing those who sell or use illegal drugs, and providing treatment for persons addicted to drugs.

war Violent conflict between nations, between different groups, or between nations and groups.

wealth The total worth of all assets a person owns minus any debts he or she has.

white privilege Advantages that white persons enjoy, often without awareness, over nonwhite persons.

white-collar crime Criminal behavior conducted within otherwise legal businesses or professions.

working poor People who work and earn a wage, but whose earnings are near or below the poverty level.

world systems theory The idea that advanced "core" nations exploit the resources of less developed poor "periphery" nations with the assistance of developing "semi-periphery" nations.

Y

youth bulge An increase in the proportion of the population composed of children, teenagers, and young adults.

REFERENCES

Abbott, Karen. 2014. *Liar, Temptress, Soldier, Spy: Four Women Undercover in the Civil War*. New York: Harper Collins.

Abolition Project. 2009. "What Is Slavery?" (http://abolition.e2bn.org/slavery_40.html).

Acar, Sevil and Mahmut Tekee. 2014. "Economic Development and Industrial Pollution in the Mediterranean Region: A Panel Data Analysis." Topics in Middle Eastern and African Economies 16 (1):65–95 (www.luc.edu/orgs/meea/volume16/pdfs/Acar-Tekce.pdf).

Acuna, Kristen. 2012. "AGE DISCRIMINATION ON TV: 10 Anchors Who Were Replaced by Younger Women." Business Insider, August 8 (www.businessinsider.com/age-discrimination-on-tv-10-anchors-who-were-replaced-by-younger-women-2012-8).

Adalian, Josef. 2015. "The Most Popular U.S. TV Shows in 18 Countries around the World." *Vulture*, December 2 (www.vulture.com/2015/12/most-popular-us-tv-shows-around-the-world.html).

Adams, Chris. 2015. "Cuba First among Nations to End Mother-to-Child HIV, Syphilis" Idaho Statesman, June 30 (http://www.idahostatesman.com/2015/06/30/3876083/cuba-first-among-nations-to-end.html).

Addati, Laura, Naomi Cassirer, and Katherine Gilchrist. 2014. Maternity and Paternity at Work Law and Practice across the World. Geneva: International Labor Office (www.ilo.org/wcmsp5/groups/public/–dgreports/–dcomm/–publ/documents/publication/wcms_242615.pdf).

Addati, Laura, Naomi Cassirer, and Katherine Gilchrist. 2014. *Maternity and Paternity at Work: Law and Practice across the World.*, Geneva Switzerland: International Labour Organization (http://www.ilo.org/global/publications/ilo-bookstore/order-online/books/WCMS_242615/lang–en/index.htm).

Administration on Aging. 2015. "What is Elder Abuse?" (www.aoa.gov/AoA_programs/Elder_Rights/EA_Prevention/whatIsEA.aspx).

Adorno, Theodor W., Else Frenkel-Brunswik, Daniel J. Levinson, and R. Nevitt Sanford. 1993. *The Authoritarian Personality*. New York: Norton.

AFL-CIO. 2017. "Labor History Timeline" (https://aflcio.org/about/history).

———. 2018. "Highest-Paid CEOs" (https://aflcio.org/paywatch/highest-paid-ceos).

Al Arabiya. 2017. "ISIS Militants Launched an Attack on Iraqi Forces in the al-Rafei Neighborhood in Mosul on Wednesday Morning Using Five Suicide Care Bombs" (http://english.alarabiya.net/en/News/middle-east/2017/05/17/ISIS-attacks-Iraqi-forces-in-Mosul-with-five-suicide-car-bombs.html).

Al Jazeera. 2014. "Sunni rebels declare new 'Islamic caliphate." June 30 (www.aljazeera.com/news/middleeast/2014/06/isil-declares-new-islamic-caliphate-201462917326669749.html).

Al Mukhtar, Sarah, Michael Gold and Larry Buchanan. 2018. "After Weinstein: 71 Men Accused of Sexual Misconduct and their Fall from Power." New York Times, February 8 (https://www.nytimes.com/interactive/2017/11/10/us/men-accused-sexual-misconduct-weinstein.html).

Alexander, Michelle. 2012. *The New Jim Crow: Mass Incarceration in the Age of Colorblindness*. New York: New Press.

Allison, William Thomas. 2012. My Lai: An American Atrocity in the Vietnam War. Baltimore, MD: Johns Hopkins University Press.

Alterman, Eric. 2012. "Springsteen's Political Voice." *Nation*, April 30, 294:11–12, 14–15.

Alternative Energy. 2017. "Wind Power" (http://www.alternative-energy-news.info/technology/wind-power/).

Amadeo, Kimberly. 2018. "Current U.S. Federal Government Spending." *Balance*, March 23 (https://www.thebalance.com/current-u-s-federal-government-spending-3305763).

Amato, Paul. R. 1993. "Children's Adjustment to Divorce: Theories, Hypotheses, and Empirical Support." *Journal of Marriage and the Family* 55(1):23–38.

———. 2000. "The Consequences of Divorce for Adults and Children." *Journal of Marriage and the Family* 62(4):1269–1287.

Amato, Paul R. and Jacob Cheadle. 2005. "The Long Reach of Divorce: Divorce and Child Well-Being across Three Generations." *Journal of Marriage and the Family* 67(1):191–206.

American Association of University Women. 2016. "The Simple Truth about the Gender Pay Gap." Spring (www.aauw.org/research/the-simple-truth-about-the-gender-pay-gap/).

American Bar Association Commission on Domestic Violence. 2007. "Domestic Violence Arrest Policies by State" (www.americanbar.org/content/dam/aba/migrated/domviol/docs/Domestic_Violence_Arrest_Policies_by_State_11_07.authcheckdam.pdf).

American College Health Association. 2017a. "American College Health Association National College Health Assessment: Spring 2017 Reference Group Data Report" (http://www.acha-ncha.org/docs/NCHA-II_SPRING_2017_REFERENCE_GROUP_DATA_REPORT.pdf).

———. 2017b. "American College Health Association National College Health Assessment: Spring 2017 Reference Group Executive Summary" (http://www.acha-ncha.org/docs/NCHAII_SPRING_2017_REFERENCE_GROUP_EXECUTIVE_SUMMARY.pdf).

American Humane Association. 2013. "Mary Ellen Wilson" (www.americanhumane.org/about-us/who-we-are/history/mary-ellen-wilson.html).

American Lung Association (ALA). 2017. "Key Findings: State of the Air 2017" (http://www.lung.org/our-initiatives/healthy-air/sota/key-findings/).

American Psychiatric Institute. 2013. *The Diagnostic and Statistical Manual of Mental Disorders, 5th Edition: DSM-5.* Arlington, VA: American Psychiatric Publishing.

American Psychological Association Zero Tolerance Task Force. 2008. "Are Zero Tolerance Policies Effective in the Schools?" *American Psychologist*, December 2008 (www.apa.org/pubs/info/reports/zero-tolerance.pdf).

American Psychological Association. 2008. "For a Better Understanding of Sexual Orientation and Homosexuality" (www.apa.org/topics/lgbt/orientation.pdf).

———. 2011. "Sex, Gender, Gender Identity, Sexual Orientation" (www.apa.org/pi/lgbt/resources/sexuality-definitions.pdf).

———. 2018. "Education and Socioeconomic Status" (http://www.apa.org/pi/ses/resources/publications/education.aspx).

American Sociological Association. 2013. "ASA Files Amicus Brief with U.S. Supreme Court in Same-Sex Marriage Cases." www.asanet.org/press/asa_files_amicus_brief_in_same-sex_marriage_cases.cfm.

Amos, Deborah. 2013. "Online with a Sexual Predator." ABC News, August 14 (http://abcnews.go.com/WNT/story?id=130735).

Anderson, Elijah. 1999. *Code of the Street: Decency, Violence, and the Moral Life of the Inner City.* New York: W. W. Norton.

Anderson, L. R. 2016. "Divorce Rate in the U.S.: Geographic Variation, 2015." National Center for Family and Marriage Research. (https://www.bgsu.edu/ncfmr/resources/data/family-profiles/anderson-divorce-rate-us-geo-2015-fp-16-21.html).

Andrews, Evan. 2015. "9 Things You May Not Know about Elizabeth Cady Stanton." *History*, November 12 (http://www.history.com/news/9-things-you-may-not-know-about-elizabeth-cady-stanton).

Anti-Defamation League. 2016. "State Hate Crime Statutory Provisions" (http://archive.adl.org/learn/hate_crimes_laws/map_frameset.html).

Anti-Slavery.org. 2017a. "What Is Modern Slavery?" (https://www.antislavery.org/slavery-today/).

———. 2017b. "What Is Bonded Labour?" (https://www.antislavery.org/slavery-today/bonded-labour/).

Antonaccio, Olena and Charles R. Tittle. 2007. "A Cross-National Test of Bonger's Theory of Criminality and Economic Conditions." *Criminology* 45(4): 925–958.

Archibold, Randal C. 2010. "Arizona Enacts Stringent Law on Immigration." *New York Times*, April 23 (www.nytimes.com/2010/04/24/us/politics/24immig.html).

Associated Press. 2010. "Obama Signs Repeal of 'Don't Ask, Don't Tell.'" NBCNEWS.com, December 22 (www.nbcnews.com/id/40777922/ns/politics-white_house/t/obama-signs-repeal-dont-ask-dont-tell/#.Vv6S7npFfIU).

———. 2012. "Report: Minority Students Face Harsher Punishments." Fox News (www.foxnews.com/us/2012/03/06/report-minority-students-face-harsher-punishments/).

———. 2014a. "Coming Soon to a Menu Near You: Calories Counts." Crain's Chicago Business, November 25 (www.chicagobusiness.com/article/20141125/NEWS07/141129875/coming-soon-to-a-menu-near-you-calorie-counts).

———. 2014b. "Libyan Militant Accused in Benghazi Attack in US Custody." Telegram.com. June 17 (www.telegram.com/article/20140617/NEWS/306179759/1116).

———. 2016. "Companies Thinking Twice About North Carolina over LGBT rights." ABC15, April 1 (www.abc15.com/news/national/companies-thinking-twice-about-north-carolina-over-lgbt-rights).

———. 2018. "The Latest: Trump Doesn't Like Kim Jung Un's Attitude Change." May 22 (https://wtop.com/asia/2018/05/the-latest-commemorative-coin-issued-of-kim-trump-meeting/).

Axios. 2017. "Gerrymandering Gives GOP Huge Structural Advantage." June 2015. (https://www.axios.com/gerrymandering-gives-gop-huge-structural-advantage-2447889907.html).

Babbie, Earl. 2016. *The Basics of Social Research.* Boston, MA: Cengage Learning.

Babiak, Paul and Robert D. Hare. 2007. *Snakes in Suits: When Psychopaths Go to Work.* New York: Harper Business.

Badger, Emily. 2014. "Pollution Is Segregated, Too." Washington Post, April 15 (www.washingtonpost.com/news/wonkblog/wp/2014/04/15/pollution-is-substantially-worse-in-minority-neighborhoods-across-the-u-s/).

Badkar, Mamta. 2013. "22 Chinese People Who Were Handed the Death Sentence for White Collar Crime." Businessinsider.com, July 15 (www.businessinsider.com/chinese-white-collar-criminals-death-sentence-2013–7?op=1).

Balkiz, Ghazi and Angela Dewan. 2017. "The Women Fighters Who Helped Defeat ISIS in Raqqa." CNN, October 22 (http://www.cnn.com/2017/10/20/middleeast/raqqa-kurdish-female-fighters/index.html).

Baltzell, E. Digby. 1987. *The Protestant Establishment: Aristocracy and Caste in America.* New Haven, CT: Yale University Press.

Baran, Paul and Paul Sweezy. 1966. *Monopoly Capitalism.* New York: Monthly Review Press.

Barlow, Maude. 2015. "The Water Crisis Comes Home." *Nation*, August 3–10:12–14.

Barner, Mark R. 1999. "Sex-Role Stereotyping in FCC-Mandated Children's Educational Television." *Journal of Broadcasting & Electronic Media* 43(4):551–564.

Barnett, Cynthia. 2013. "The Measurement of White Collar Crime Using Uniform Crime Reporting (UCR) Data. Washington, DC: Federal Bureau of Investigation (http://www.fbi.gov/stats-services/about-us/cjis/ucr/nibrs/nibrs_wcc.pdf).

Batley, Melanie. 2014. "FBI Investigating High-Speed Trading for Insider Information." Newsmax, April 1 (www.newsmax.com/Newsfront/FBI-WallStreet-insidertrading-highspeed/2014/04/01/id/563028/).

Baugh, Ryan and Katherine Witsman. 2017. U.S. Lawful Permanent Residents: 2015 (https://www.dhs.gov/sites/default/files/publications/Lawful_Permanent_Residents_2015.pdf).

BBC. 2006. "The EU's Baby Blues." March 27 (http://news.bbc.co.uk/2/hi/europe/4768644.stm).

———. 2010. "UN Declares Clean Water a 'Fundamental Human Right.'" July 29 (www.bbc.com/news/world-us-canada-10797988).

———. 2011. "Egypt Internet Activist Wael Ghonim: 'I am Not a Hero.'" February 8 (www.bbc.co.uk/news/world-middle-east-12396147).

———. 2014. "Egypt Police Jailed Over 2010 Death of Khaled Siad." March 3 (http://www.bbc.com/news/world-middle-east-26416964).

———. 2015. "What Does the International Criminal Court Do?" June 25 (www.bbc.com/news/world-11809908).

BBC World Service. 2010. "Poverty Most Serious World Problem, Says Global Poll" (http://www.globescan.com/news_archives/bbcWorldSpeaks-2010/).

———. 2011. "Unemployment Is the World's Fastest Rising Fear – Survey" (http://www.bbc.co.uk/news/business-16108437).

Becker, Jo and Rachel Stohl. 2015. "U.S. Must Get Tough over Child Soldiers." *Human Rights Watch*, September 28 (www.hrw.org/news/2015/09/28/us-must-get-tough-over-child-soldiers).

Beeman, Angie. 2006. "Women's Movement of the United States." Pp. 940–954 in *Revolutionary Movements in World History*, edited by James DeFronzo. Santa Barbara, CA: ABC-CLIO.

Bendery, Jennifer. 2014. "Obama Signs Executive Order on LGBT Job Discrimination." *Huffington Post*, July 21 (www.huffingtonpost.com/2014/07/21/obama-gay-rights_n_5605482.html).

Berger, Nahuel. 2014. "Theorist Eric Maskin: Globalization Is Increasing Inequality." World Bank, June 23 (www.worldbank.org/en/news/feature/2014/06/23/theorist-eric-maskin-globalization-is-increasing-inequality).

Berman, John and Enjoli Francis. 2010. "What Makes a Family? Children, Say Many Americans." ABC News, September 15. http://abcnews.go.com/WN/defines-family-children-americans-survey/story?id=11644693.

Bernard, Tara Siegel. 2013. "In Paid Family Leave, U.S. Trails Most of the Globe." New York Times, February 22 (www.huffingtonpost.com/2013/02/04/maternity-leave-paid-parental-leave-_n_2617284.html).

Bernstein, Mary. 2002. "Identities and Politics: Towards a Historical Understanding of the Lesbian Gay Movement." *Social Science History* 26(3):531–581.

Berryman, Phillip. 1987. *Liberation Theology: Essential Facts about the Revolutionary Movement in Latin America—and Beyond*. Philadelphia, PA: Temple University Press.

Best, Joel. 2013. *Social Problems*. New York: W. W. Norton.

Bialik, Kristen. 2017. "U.S. Active-Duty Military Presence Overseas Is at Its Smallest in Decades." Pew Research Center, December 13 (http://www.pewresearch.org/fact-tank/2017/08/22/u-s-active-duty-military-presence-overseas-is-at-its-smallest-in-decades/).

Biello, Shannon. 2014. "The X and Y of Human Origins: Using Y Chromosome Sequencing Data to Explore Human Evolution." National Human Genome Research Institute, July 3 (www.genome.gov/27555170).

Bienaimé, Pierre. 2014. "The Failure of a Major Mission in Afghanistan in Two Charts." *Business Insider*, October 24 (www.businessinsider.com/the-uss-failure-to-end-afghanistans-opium-trade-2014–10).

Biography. 2014. "Linda Brown" (www.biography.com/people/linda-brown-21134187).

———. 2016. "Tammy Baldwin" (www.biography.com/people/tammy-baldwin-21027897).

Black Lives Matter. 2016. (http://blacklivesmatter.com/).

Black, Debra. 2013. "Forced Marriages: A Hidden Problem in Canada." Star, September 20. (www.thestar.com/news/investigations/2013/09/20/forced_marriages_a_hidden_problem_in_canada.html).

Bleakley, Amy, Michael Hennessey, and Martin Fishbein. 2006. "Public Opinion on Sex Education in Schools." *Archives of Pediatrics and Adolescent Medicine* 160 (11):1151–1156.

Blow, Charles M. 2012. "The Curious Case of Trayvon Martin." *New York Times*, March 16. (http://www.nytimes.com/2012/03/17/opinion/blow-the-curious-case-of-trayvon-martin.html).

Blue Planet. 2015. "Water Shutoffs in Detroit" (www.blue-planetproject.net/index.php/home/local-campaigns/detroit/).

Bobo, Lawrence D., Camille Z. Charles, Maria Krysan, and Alicia D. Simmons. 2012. "The Real Record on Racial Attitudes." Pp. 38–83 in *Social Trends in American Life*, edited by Peter V. Marsden. Princeton, NJ: Princeton University Press.

Bonger, William Adrian. 1905. [1916]]. *Criminality and Economic Conditions*. Translated by Henry P. Horton. Boston, MA: Little, Brown.

Bonilla-Silva, Eduardo. 2018. *Racism without Racists*. Lanham, MD: Rowman & Littlefield.

Boonstra, Heather. 2002. "Teen Pregnancy: Trends and Lessons Learned." *Guttmacher Report on Public Policy* 5(1):1–4.

Booth, Barbara. 2015. "One of the Most Dangerous Places for Women in America." CNBC, September 22 (www.cnbc.com/2015/09/22/college-rape-crisis-in-america-under-fire.html).

Borzelleca, Daniel. 2012. "The Male-Female Ratio in College." Forbes, February 16 (www.forbes.com/sites/ccap/2012/02/16/the-male-female-ratio-in-college).

Bourdain, Anthony. 2014. "Anthony Bourdain Parts Unknown: Massachusetts." November 9 (http://transcripts.cnn.com/TRANSCRIPTS/1411/09/abpu.02.html).

Bramlett, Matthew D. and Stephen J. Blumberg. 2007. "Family Structure and Children's Physical and Mental Health." *Health Affairs* 26(2):549–558 (http://content.healthaffairs.org/content/26/2/549.full).

Branch, John. 2014. "Many Strikeouts, Fewer Runs as Pitchers Take Control." New York Times, September 30 (www.nytimes.com/2014/10/01/sports/baseball/as-batting-numbers-shrivel-eyes-turn-to-the-mound.html?_r=0).

Branson, Richard. 2012. "War on Drugs a Trillion Dollar Failure." CNN, December 7 (www.cnn.com/2012/12/06/opinion/branson-end-war-on-drugs/index.html).

Breiding, Matthew J., Sharon G. Smith, Kathleen C. Basile, Mikel L. Walters, Jieru Chen, and Melissa T. Merrick. 2014. "Prevalence and Characteristics of Sexual Violence, Stalking, and Intimate Partner Violence Victimization – National Intimate Partner and Sexual Violence Survey, United States, 2011." Centers for Disease Control and Prevention. (www.cdc.gov/mmwr/preview/mmwrhtml/ss6308a1.htm?s_cid=s-s6308a1_e).

Breslow, Jason M. 2012. "By the Numbers: Dropping Out of High School." PBS, September 21. www.pbs.org/wgbh/pages/frontline/education/dropout-nation/by-the-numbers-dropping-out-of-high-school/.

Briggs, Helen. 2013. "Biological Clue to Why Women Live Longer than Men." British Broadcasting Company (BBC), May 15 (www.bbc.com/news/health-22528388).

Britt, Robert Roy. 2009. "14 Percent of U.S. Adults Can't Read." Live Science, January 10. http://www.livescience.com/3211-14-percent-adults-read.html

Broich, John. 2017. "How the Nazis Destroyed the First Gay Rights Movement." Conversation, July 4 (http://theconversation.com/how-the-nazis-destroyed-the-first-gay-rights-movement-80354).

Bronstein, Scott, Drew Griffin, and Nelli Black. 2014. "VA Deaths Covered Up to Make Statistics Look Better, Whistle-Blower Says." CNN, June 24 (www.cnn.com/2014/06/23/us/phoenix-va-deaths-new-allegations/index.html).

Broussard, Meredith. 2015. "When Cops Check Facebook." *Atlantic*, April 19. https://www.theatlantic.com/politics/archive/2015/04/when-cops-check-facebook/390882/

Brownmiller, Susan. 1975. *Against Our Will: Men, Women and Rape*. New York: Bantam Books.

Bruce, Mary. 2014. "Obama Says 'We Tortured Some Folks.'" ABC News, August 1 (http://abcnews.go.com/blogs/politics/2014/08/obama-says-we-tortured-some-folks/).

Brueck, Hilary. 2018. "The Suspected Golden State Killer Was Finally Caught Because His Relative's DNA Was Available on a Genealogy Website." Business Insider, April 27. (http://www.businessinsider.com/golden-state-killer-caught-because-relatives-dna-online-2018-4).

Bryant, John Hope. 2015. "Obama's Proposal for Free Community College: Reconnecting Education with Aspiration." *Huffington Post*, January 25 (http://www.huffingtonpost.com/john-hope-bryant/obamas-proposal-for-free-_b_6533436.html).

Buchheit, Paul. 2014. "4 Ways Privatization Is Running Our Education System." Salon, February 19. www.salon.com/2014/02/19/4_ways_privatization_is_ruining_our_education_system_partner/

Buckley, Cara. 2015a. "'American Sniper' Fuels a War on the Home Front." New York Times, January 28. www.nytimes.com/2015/01/29/movies/awardsseason/american-sniper-fuels-a-war-on-the-home-front.html?_r=0

Buckley, Chris. 2015b. "China Ends One-Child Policy, Allowing Families Two Children." New York Times, October 29 (http://www.nytimes.com/2015/10/30/world/asia/china-end-one-child-policy.html?emc=edit_th_20151030&nl=todaysheadlines&nlid=38763373&_r=0).

Bump, Philip. 2015. "When Did Black Americans Start Voting So Heavily Democratic?" *Washington Post*, July 7 (https://www.washingtonpost.com/news/the-fix/wp/2015/07/07/when-did-black-americans-start-voting-so-heavily-democratic/?utm_term=.12175aed3593).

Bureau of Justice Assistance. 2011. "Plea and Charge Bargaining: Research Summary." U.S. Department of Justice, January 24 (https://www.bja.gov/Publications/PleaBargainingResearchSummary.pdf).

Bureau of Justice Statistics. 2013. "Serious Intimate Partner Violence against Females Declined 72 Percent from 1994 to 2011." (www.bjs.gov/content/pub/press/ipvav9311pr.cfm).

———. 2016. "Data Collection: National Crime Victimization Survey (NCVS)" (https://www.bjs.gov/index.cfm?ty=dcdetail&iid=245).

———. 2017. "How Many Persons in the U.S. Have Ever Been Convicted of a Felony?" (https://www.bjs.gov/index.cfm?ty=qa&iid=404).

Bureau of Labor Statistics. 2013. "International Comparisons of Annual Labor Force Statistics, 1970–2012." June 7. (www.bls.gov/fls/flscomparelf/lfcompendium.pdf).

———. 2017. "Union Members Summary" (https://www.bls.gov/news.release/union2.nr0.htm).

Bureau of Transportation Statistics. 2017. "Corrected BTS Statistics Release: 2016 Traffic Data for U.S. Airlines and Foreign Airlines U.S. Flights" (https://www.bts.gov/newsroom/corrected-bts-statistics-release-2016-traffic-data-us-airlines-and-foreign-airlines-us).

Burton, Neel. 2015. "When Homosexuality Stopped Being a Mental Disorder." *Psychology Today*, September 18 (https://www.psychologytoday.com/us/blog/hide-and-seek/201509/when-homosexuality-stopped-being-mental-disorder).

Butler, Cheryl Nelson. 2015. "The Racial Roots of Human Trafficking." UCLA Law Review 62:1464–1514 (https://www.uclalawreview.org/racial-roots-human-trafficking/).

Byrnes, Jesse, 2015. "Obama Signs Anti-Trafficking Bill into Law." *The Hill*, May 29 (https://thehill.com/blogs/blog-briefing-room/news/243519-obama-signs-anti-trafficking-law).

Caldwell, Alicia. 2017. "A Look at Trump's Executive Order on Refugees, Immigration." Yahoo News, January 27 (https://www.yahoo.com/news/look-trumps-executive-order-refugees-immigration-004600231–politics.html).

Campaign Finance Institute (CFI). 2016. "Table 2: Individual Donors to 2016 Presidential Candidates through January 31, 2016" (www.cfinst.org/pdf/federal/president/2016/M3/Presidential_M3_Table2.pdf).

———. 2018. "The Cost of Winning a House and Senate Seat, 1986–2016"; "House Campaign Expenditures 1974–2016"; "Senate Campaign Expenditures, 1974–2016" (http://cfinst.org/data.aspx).

Cañete, Miguel Arias. 2015. "The Paris Agreement: The World Unites to Fight Climate Change" (https://ec.europa.eu/clima/policies/international/negotiations/paris_en).

Cantor, David, Bonnie Fisher, Susan Chibnall, and Reanne Townsend 2015. *Report on the AAU Campus Climate Survey on Sexual Assault and Sexual Misconduct*. Rockville, MD: Westat (www.aau.edu/uploadedFiles/AAU_Publications/AAU_Reports/Sexual_Assault_Campus_Survey/Report%20on%20the%20AAU%20Campus%20Climate%20Survey%20on%20Sexual%20Assault%20and%20Sexual%20Misconduct.pdf).

Care. 2016. "Child Survival" (http://www.care.org/work/health/children).

Caritas. 2017. "Women and Development" (http://www.caritas.org.au/learn/global-poverty-issues/women-and-development).

Carmichael, Mary. 2006. "How It Began: HIV Before the Age of Aids." *PBS Frontline* (www.pbs.org/wgbh/pages/frontline/aids/virus/origins.html).

Carson, Clayborne, ed. 2001. *The Autobiography of Martin Luther King, Jr.* New York: Warner Books.

———. 2006. "African American Freedom Struggle." Pp. 12–29 in *Revolutionary Movements in World History*, edited by James DeFronzo. Santa Barbara, CA: ABC-CLIO.

Carson, Rachel. 2002. *Silent Spring*. Boston, MA: Houghton Mifflin Company.

Carter, Susan B. 2003. "Labor Force for Historical Statistics of the United States, Millennial Edition." University of California Project on the Historical Statistics of the United States, Center for Social and Economic Policy, September. (http://economics.ucr.edu/papers/papers04/04–03.pdf).

Carty, Victoria. 2015. *Social Movements and New Technology*. Boulder, CO: Westview.

Castillo, Michelle, 2013. "U.S. Has Highest First-Day Infant Mortality out of Industrialized World, Group Reports." CBS News, May 7 (http://www.cbsnews.com/news/us-has-highest-first-day-infant-mortality-out-of-industrialized-world-group-reports/).

Catalano, Shannan. 2013. "Intimate Partner Violence: Attributes of Victimization, 1993–2011." (www.bjs.gov/content/pub/pdf/ipvav9311.pdf).

Catalog of Federal Domestic Assistance. 2015. "Energy Efficiency and Conservation Block Grant Program (EECBG)" (www.cfda.gov/?s=program&mode=form&tab=step1&id=31cd65f48a09072cc06c2a4423f4086b).

Cauchon, Dennis. 2011. "Student Loans Outstanding Will Exceed $1 Trillion This Year." USA Today, October 25 (http://www.usatoday.com/money/perfi/college/story/2011–10-19/student-loan-debt/50818676/1).

Cavanagh, Shannon E. and Aletha C. Huston. 2008. "The Timing of Family Instability and Children's Social Development." *Journal of Marriage and the Family* 70(5):1258–1270.

CBS News. 2006. "Ready for a Woman President?" February 3 (www.cbsnews.com/news/ready-for-a-woman-president/).

———. 2008. "U.S. Leads the World in Illegal Drug Use July 1" (www.cbsnews.com/news/us-leads-the-world-in-illegal-drug-use).

———. 2011. "60 Minutes – Wael Ghonim and Egypt's New Age Revolution." February 13 (https://www.youtube.com/watch?v=LxJK6SxGCAw).

———. 2012. "Supreme Court Doubles Down on "Citizens United." CBSNEWS, June 25 (www.cbsnews.com/8301–503544_162–57459906-503544/supreme-court-doubles-down-on-citizens-united/).

CBS/AP. 2012. "Sikh Temple Shooting Suspect Wade Michael Page Was White Supremacist." CBS News, August 6 (https://www.cbsnews.com/news/sikh-temple-shooting-suspect-wade-michael-page-was-white-supremacist/).

Cecere, David. 2009. "New Study Finds 45,000 Deaths Annually Linked to Lack of Health Coverage." Harvard Gazette, September 17 (http://news.harvard.edu/gazette/story/2009/09/new-study-finds-45000-deaths-annually-linked-to-lack-of-health-coverage/).

Celebrezze, Anthony J. 1964. The Change in Mortality Trend in the United States. National Center for Health Statistics, Series 3, Number 1 (https://www.cdc.gov/nchs/data/series/sr_03/sr03_001acc.pdf).

Center for American Women and Politics – Rutgers Eagleton Institute of Politics. 2018. "Results: Women Candidates in the 2018 Elections." November 14 (http://cawp.rutgers.edu/sites/default/files/resources/results_release_5bletterhead5d_1.pdf).

Centers for Disease Control and Prevention (CDC). 2011. "Obesity" (www.cdc.gov/chronicdisease/resources/publications/AAG/obesity.htm).

———. 2013. *Health, United States, 2012: With Special Feature on Emergency Care*. www.cdc.gov/nchs/data/hus/hus12.pdf.

———. 2015a. "Tobacco-Related Mortality." www.cdc.gov/tobacco/data_statistics/fact_sheets/health_effects/tobacco_related_mortality/.

———. 2015b. "HIV in the United States" (www.cdc.gov/hiv/statistics/overview/ataglance.html).

———. 2015c. "Intimate Partner Violence: Consequences." (www.cdc.gov/ViolencePrevention/intimatepartnerviolence/consequences.html).

———. 2016. *Health, United States, 2015: Black or African American Population*. https://www.cdc.gov/nchs/data/hus/2015/016.pdf.

———. 2017a. "Obesity in Adults." https://www.cdc.gov/vitalsigns/AdultObesity/index.html.

———. 2017b. "About HIV/AIDS." https://www.cdc.gov/hiv/basics/whatishiv.html.

———. 2017c. "HIV in the United States: At a Glance." https://www.cdc.gov/hiv/statistics/overview/ataglance.html.

———. 2017d. "Life Expectancy." https://www.cdc.gov/nchs/fastats/life-expectancy.htm.

———. 2017e. "Mental Health Basics." www.cdc.gov/mentalhealth/basics.htm.

———. 2017f. Unmarried Childbearing" (https://www.cdc.gov/nchs/fastats/unmarried-childbearing.htm).

———. 2017g. "Findings from the National Intimate Partner and Sexual Violence Survey 2010–2012 State Report." https://www.cdc.gov/violenceprevention/pdf/NISVS-StateReportFactsheet.pdf.

———. 2017h. "Current Cigarette Smoking among Adults in 2015" (https://www.cdc.gov/tobacco/data_statistics/fact_sheets/adult_data/cig_smoking/index.htm).

———. 2017i. "Alcohol and Public Health: Frequently Asked Questions." https://www.cdc.gov/alcohol/faqs.htm#bingeDrinking.

———. 2017j. "Fact Sheets – Binge Drinking." www.cdc.gov/alcohol/fact-sheets/binge-drinking.htm.

———. 2017k. "Health Effects of Cigarette Smoking." https://www.cdc.gov/tobacco/data_statistics/fact_sheets/health_effects/effects_cig_smoking/index.htm.

———. 2017l. "Opioids." https://www.cdc.gov/drugoverdose/opioids/terms.html.

———. 2017m. "Understanding the Epidemic: Drug Overdose Deaths in the United States Continue to Increase in 2015." https://www.cdc.gov/drugoverdose/epidemic/index.html.

———. 2018. "Poverty and Infant Mortality – United States 1988". (https://www.cdc.gov/mmwr/preview/mmwrhtml/00039818.htm).

Center for Divorce Education. 2017. "Divorce Education." (https://www.divorce-education.com/).

Center for Health, Environment and Justice. 2015. "About Lois" (http://chej.org/about/our-story/about-lois/).

Center for Healthcare Finance Information. 2015. "Administrative Costs." http://health-financing.com/administrative%20costs.htm.

Centers for Medicare and Medicaid Services (CMS). 2018. "National Health Expenditures 2016 Highlights" (https://www.cms.gov/Research-Statistics-Data-and-Systems/Statistics-Trends-and-Reports/NationalHealthExpendData/NationalHealthAccountsHistorical.html).

Center for Women and Politics. 2017. "Gender Differences in Voter Turnout" (http://www.cawp.rutgers.edu/facts/voters/turnout).

Central Intelligence Agency (CIA). 2016a. "Gaza Strip" (https://www.cia.gov/library/publications/the-world-factbook/geos/gz.html).

———. 2016b. "West Bank" (https://www.cia.gov/library/publications/the-world-factbook/geos/we.html).

———. 2017a. "Life Expectancy at Birth." *World Factbook*. https://www.cia.gov/library/publications/the-world-factbook/rankorder/2102rank.html.

———. 2017b. "HIV/AIDS – Adult Prevalence Rate." World Factbook. www.cia.gov/library/publications/the-world-factbook/rankorder/2155rank.html.

———. 2017c. "Bolivia." CIA World Factbook (https://www.cia.gov/library/publications/the-world-factbook/geos/bl.html).

———. 2017d. "Literacy." *CIA World Fact Book.* https://www.cia.gov/library/publications/the-world-factbook/fields/2103.html.

———. 2017e. "Birth Rate." World Factbook (https://www.cia.gov/library/publications/the-world-factbook/rankorder/2054rank.html).

———. 2017f. "United States." *World Factbook* https://www.cia.gov/library/publications/the-world-factbook/geos/us.html.

———. 2017g. "Country Comparison: Population Growth Rate." World Factbook https://www.cia.gov/library/publications/the-world-factbook/rankorder/2002rank.html#cw.

———. 2017h. "Russia." World Factbook. https://www.cia.gov./library/publications/the-world-factbook/geos/rs.html.

———. 2018a. "Country Comparison: Infant Mortality Rate." World Factbook (https://www.cia.gov/library/publications/the-world-factbook/rankorder/2091rank.html).

———. 2018b. *World Factbook*. https://www.cia.gov/library/publications/the-world-factbook/fields/2018.html.

———. 2018c. "Country Comparison: GDP – Per Capita (PPP)." *World Factbook* (https://www.cia.gov/library/publications/the-world-factbook/rankorder/2004rank.html).

Chadbourn, Margaret. 2016. "ACLU Sues Over Controversial North Carolina Transgender Bathroom Law." ABC News, March 28 (http://abcnews.go.com/US/aclu-sues-controversial-north-carolina-transgender-bathroom-law/story?id=37976188).

Chalabi, Mona. 2017. "Who Are the Three-Quarters of Adult Americans Who Didn't Vote for Trump?" *Guardian*, January 18 (https://www.theguardian.com/us-news/2017/jan/18/american-non-voters-election-donald-trump).

Chand, Smriti. 2016. "11 Major Problems of Urbanization in India" (http://www.yourarticlelibrary.com/urbanisation/11-major-problems-of-urbanisation-in-india/19880/).

Chandler, Adam. 2014. "The U.S. Refused to Pay ISIL's Ransom Demands for James Foley." *MSN News*, August 21 (http://news.msn.com/world/the-us-refused-to-pay-isils-ransom-demands-for-james-foley-1?ocid=ansnews11).

Chandy, Laurence and Geoffrey Gertz. 2011. "Two Trends in Global Poverty." Brookings Institute (www.brookings.edu/research/opinions/2011/05/17-global-poverty-trends-chandy).

Chang, Cindy. 2012. "Louisiana Is the World's Prison Capital." Times-Picayune, May 29. www.nola.com/crime/index.ssf/2012/05/louisiana_is_the_worlds_prison.html.

Chapman, Chris, Jennifer Laird, Nicole Ifill, and Angelina Kewal Ramani. 2011. *Trends in High School Dropout and Completion Rates in the United States: 1972–2009 (NCES 2012–006).* U.S. Department of Education. Washington, DC: National Center for Education Statistics. nces.ed.gov/pubs2012/2012006.pdf.

Chappell, Bill. 2018. "U.S. Births Dip To 30-Year Low; Fertility Rate Sinks Further Below Replacement Level." NPR, May 17 (https://www.npr.org/sections/thetwo-way/2018/05/17/611898421/u-s-births-falls-to-30-year-low-sending-fertility-rate-to-a-record-low).

Chávez, Franz. 2006. "Cochabamba's 'Water War,' Six Years On." Inter Press Service, November 8 (ipsnews.net/print.asp?idnews=35418).

Chemaly, Soraya. 2013. "Why Pass MJIA? 50 Facts about Sexual Assault in the U.S. Military." Huff Post Politics, November 15. www.huffingtonpost.com/soraya-chemaly/military-sexual-assault-facts_b_4281704.html.

Chen, Grace. 2014. "What is a Magnet School?" *Public School Review*, December 23. www.publicschoolreview.com/blog/what-is-a-magnet-school.

Children's Defense Fund. 2016. "Child Defense Fund." (www.childrensdefense.org/about/).

Child Labor Public Education Project. 2016. "Child Labor in U.S. History." (www.continuetolearn.uiowa.edu/laborctr/child_labor/about/us_history.html).

Child Trends. 2017. "High School Dropout Rates" (https://www.childtrends.org/indicators/high-school-dropout-rates/).

Child Trends Data Bank. 2015a. "Births to Unmarried Women." (www.childtrends.org/?indicators=births-to-unmarried-women).

———. 2015b. "Family Structure." www.childtrends.org/?indicators=family-structure.

———. 2015c. "Child Maltreatment." (www.childtrends.org/?indicators=child-maltreatment).

———. 2018. "Births to Unmarried Women" (https://www.childtrends.org/indicators/births-to-unmarried-women/).

Child Welfare Information Gateway. 2016. *Parental Drug Use as Child Abuse*. Washington, DC: U.S. Department of Health and Human Services, Children's Bureau. https://www.childwelfare.gov/pubPDFs/drugexposed.pdf.

———. 2017. "Substance Use by Parents and Caregivers." https://www.childwelfare.gov/topics/can/factors/contribute/parentcaregiver/substance/.

Chishti, Muzaffar and Michelle Mittelstadt. 2016. "Unauthorized Immigrants with Criminal Convictions: Who Might Be a Priority for Conviction?" Migration Policy

Institute, November (http://www.migrationpolicy.org/news/unauthorized-immigrants-criminal-convictions-who-might-be-priority-removal).

Chuck, Elizabeth. 2017. "#Me Too: Hashtag Becomes Anti-Sexual Harassment and Assault Rallying Cry." NBC News, October 16 (https://www.nbcnews.com/storyline/sexual-misconduct/metoo-hashtag-becomes-anti-sexual-harassment-assault-rallying-cry-n810986).

Civil-War.net. 2009. "The Civil War Home Page" (www.civil-war.net/pages/1860_census.html).

Civilwarcauses.org. 2015. "Selected Statistics on Slavery in the United States" (http://civilwarcauses.org/stat.htm).

Clawson, Heather J., Nicole Dutch, Amy Solomon, and Lisa Goldblatt Grace. 2017. "Human Trafficking into and within the United States: A Review of Literature" U.S. Department of Health and Human Services (https://aspe.hhs.gov/report/human-trafficking-and-within-united-states-review-literature).

Clear Bankruptcy. 2017. "10 Leading Causes of Bankruptcy." http://www.clearbankruptcy.com/financial-literacy/10-leading-causes-of-bankruptcy.aspx#

Cleary, Daniel. 2015. "Exclusive: Secretive Fusion Company Claims Reactor Breakthrough." *Science Magazine*, August 24 (http://news.sciencemag.org/physics/2015/08/secretive-fusion-company-makes-reactor-breakthrough).

Clement, Scott and Robert Barnes. 2015. "Poll: Gay-Marriage Support at Record High." Washington Post, April 23. (www.washingtonpost.com/politics/courts_law/poll-gay-marriage-support-at-record-high/2015/04/22/f6548332-e92a-11e4-aae1-d642717d8afa_story.html?postshare=1281429790315216).

Cloward, Richard A. and L. E. Ohlin. 2011. *Delinquency and Opportunity: A Study of Delinquent Gangs*. New York: Routledge.

CNN. 2009. "Survey: Support for Terror Suspect Torture Differs among the Faithful." April 30 (www.cnn.com/2009/US/04/30/religion.torture/).

———. 2011. "California Governor Signs Bill Requiring Schools to Teach Gay History." July 15 (www.cnn.com/2011/US/07/14/california.lgbt.education/index.html).

———. 2012. "President: Exit Polls." December 10 (http://www.cnn.com/election/2012/results/race/president/).

———. 2013a. "By the Numbers: Women in the U.S. Military." January 24 (www.cnn.com/2013/01/24/us/military-women-glance/index.html).

———. 2013b. "Bin Laden's Death: How the Story Unfolded." May 1 (www.cnn.com/2013/05/01/world/bin-laden-recap/index.html).

———. 2014. "CNN Poll: Support for Legal Marijuana Soaring." January 6. http://politicalticker.blogs.cnn.com/2014/01/06/cnn-poll-support-for-legal-marijuana-soaring/.

———. 2015a. "Nearly 90 Percent of Americans Have Health Coverage." April 13. http://money.cnn.com/2015/04/13/news/economy/obamacare-uninsured-gallup/index.html.

———. 2015b. "Read the Opinion: Supreme Court Upholds Obamacare Subsidies." June 25. www.cnn.com/2015/06/25/politics/scotus-opinion-document-aca-subsidies/index.html.

———. 2016. "Election 2016: Exit Polls." November 23.

———. 2017a. "Trump Condemns 'Hatred, Bigotry and Violence on Many Sides' in Charlottesville." August 13 (http://www.cnn.com/2017/08/12/politics/trump-statement-alt-right-protests/index.html).

———. 2017b. "Performance Enhancing Drugs in Sports Fast Facts." May 28. http://www.cnn.com/2013/06/06/us/performance-enhancing-drugs-in-sports-fast-facts/index.html.

Coffman, Katherine B., Lucas C. Coffman, and Keith M. Marzilli Ericson. 2013. "The Size of the LGBT Population and the Magnitude of Anti-Gay Sentiment are Substantially Underestimated." National Bureau of Economic Research. NBER Working Paper no. 19508, October (www.nber.org/papers/w19508).

Cohen, Albert. 1955. *Delinquent Boys*. New York: Free Press.

Cohen, Albert K. 2006. "Terrorism." Pp. 862–868 in *Revolutionary Movements in World History*, edited by James DeFronzo. Santa Barbara, CA: ABC-CLIO.

Cohen, Lon S. 2010. "6 Ways Law Enforcement Uses Social Media to Fight Crime." Mashable.com, March 17. http://mashable.com/2010/03/17/law-enforcement-social-media/.

College Board. 2017. "Table 2: Average Tuition and Fees and Room and Board (Enrollment-Weighted) in Current Dollars and in 2016 Dollars, 1971–72 to 2016–17." Trends in Higher Education: Tuition and Fees and Room and Board over Time (https://trends.collegeboard.org/college-pricing/figures-tables/tuition-fees-room-and-board-over-time).

Collins, Mike. 2010. "The Pros and Cons of Globalization." Manufacturing.net, June 28 (https://www.manufacturing.net/article/2010/06/pros-and-cons-globalization).

———. 2015. "The Pros and Cons of Globalization." Forbes, May 6 (https://www.forbes.com/sites/mikecollins/2015/05/06/the-pros-and-cons-of-globalization/#5e486131ccce).

Collins, Patricia Hill. 2008. *Black Feminist Thought*. New York: Routledge.

Collins, Randal. 1998. "Capitalism." Pp. 72–73 in *The Encyclopedia of Political Revolutions*, edited by Jack Goldstone. Washington, DC: Congressional Quarterly.

Colombia Reports. 2016. "Colombia's 2012–2016 Peace Talks: Fact Sheet." September 25. https://colombiareports.com/colombia-peace-talks-fact-sheet/.

Columbia University Institute for Study of Human Rights. 2017. "American Public Support for the ICC." https://www.amicc.org/public-opinions-and-polls.

Combahee River Collective. 1978. "Combahee River Collective Statement" (http://circuitous.org/scraps/combahee.html).

Combs, Cindy C. 2012. *Terrorism in the Twenty-First Century*. Upper Saddle River, NJ: Pearson Education.

Community-Wealth.org. 2017. "Community Development Corporations (CDCs)." http://community-wealth.org/strategies/panel/cdcs/index.html.

Conca, James. 2014. "It's Final – Corn Ethanol Is of No Use." *Forbes*, April 20 (www.forbes.com/sites/jamesconca/2014/04/20/its-final-corn-ethanol-is-of-no-use/).

Congressional Budget Office. 2018. "The Distribution of Household Income, 2014" (https://www.cbo.gov/publication/53597).

Congressional Record. 2009. Children's Health Insurance Program Reauthorization Act of 2009. www.cms.gov/Regulations-and-Guidance/Health-Insurance-Reform/HealthInsReformforConsume/downloads/CHIPRA.pdf.

Constitution of the Plurinational State of Bolivia. 2009. pdba.georgetown.edu/Constitutions/Bolivia/bolivia09.html.

Consumerism Commentary. 2013. "2011 Federal Income Tax Brackets and Marginal Rates" (http://www.consumerismcommentary.com/federal-income-tax-brackets-and-marginal-rates/).

Convissor, Kate. 2014. "Why Kids Drop Out of School." EduGuide. http://www.eduguide.org/article/why-kids-drop-out-of-school.

Cook, Charlie. 2016. "Democrats Need to Reach Out to the Heartland." Cook Political Report. December 23 (https://cookpolitical.com/story.pdf/10203).

Corak, Miles. 2016. "Economic Mobility." The Stanford Center on Poverty and Inequality. Pathways, the Poverty and Inequality Report 2016: 51–57 (https://inequality.stanford.edu/sites/default/files/Pathways-SOTU-2016-Economic-Mobility-3.pdf).

Cornell University. 2017. "Food Quality Protection Act" (http://pmep.cce.cornell.edu/fqpa/).

Cornell University Law School. 2016. "Prince v. Massachusetts." (www.law.cornell.edu/supremecourt/text/321/158).

Cornuelle, Kimberly and Richard Pillard. 2010. "Nature versus Nurture: The Biology of Sexuality." *BU Today*, November 16 (www.bu.edu/today/2010/nature-vs-nurture-the-biology-of-sexuality/).

Coser, Lewis A. 1977. *Masters of Sociological Thought.* Long Grove, Il: Waveland Press.

Cossman, Jeralyn Sittig. 2004. "Parents' Heterosexism and Children's Attitudes toward People with AIDS." *Sociological Spectrum* 24(3):319–339.

Cottingham, Marci, Thomas Nowak, Kay Snyder, and Melissa Swauger. 2013. "Sociological Perspective: Underlying Causes." Pp. 51–72 in *Human Trafficking*, edited by Mary C. Burke. New York: Routledge.

Cowan, Alison Leigh. 2003. "Ex-Mayor Gets 37 Years in Prison for Abusing 2 Girls." New York Times, June 14. www.nytimes.com/2003/06/14/nyregion/ex-mayor-gets-37-years-in-prison-for-abusing-2-girls.html?ref=philip_a_giordano.

Cowell, Alan and Rick, Gladstone. 2012. "Iran Reports Killing of Nuclear Scientist in "Terrorist" Blast." New York Times, January 11. www.nytimes.com/2012/01/12/world/middleeast/iran-reports-killing-of-nuclear-scientist.html?pagewanted=all&_r=0.

Coy, Maddy. 2014. "Pornographic Performances: A Review of Research on Sexualisation and Racism in Music Videos." *Imkann*, July (https://dl.dropboxusercontent.com/u/85173313/Pornographic%20Performances%20FINAL%20Aug%202014.pdf).

Cox, John Woodrow. 2016a. "Why Sex Assault Reports Have Spiked at the Naval Academy, West Point and the Air Force Academy." *Washington Post*, March 11 (www.washingtonpost.com/news/checkpoint/wp/2016/03/11/why-sex-assault-reports-have-spiked-at-the-naval-academy-west-point-and-the-air-force-academy/).

Cox, Wendell. 2016b. "America's Most Urban States." *New Geography*. March 8 (http://www.newgeography.com/content/005187-america-s-most-urban-state).

Cramer, Menno. 2013. "How to Save the World According to Edward O. Wilson." International Society of Biourbanism. http://www.biourbanism.org/save-world-according-edward-o-wilson/.

Craven, James. 2009. "DeFronzo Defends Constitutionality of Campaign Finance Reform Law." New Britain Herald, August 31 (www.centralctcommunications.com/newbritainherald/news/article_c25790fe-d994-5001-885f-9c3cdd71ea42.html).

Crenshaw, Kimberlé. 2016. *On Intersectionality: Essential Writings*. New York: New Press.

Crenshaw, Kimberlé and Bim Adewunmi. 2014. "Kimberlé Crenshaw on Intersectionality: 'I Wanted to Come up with an Everyday Metaphor That Anyone Could Use.'" New Statesman. April 2 (www.newstatesman.com/lifestyle/2014/04/kimberl-crenshaw-intersectionality-i-wanted-come-everyday-metaphor-anyone-could).

Crompton, Louis. 1976. "Homosexuals and the Death Penalty in Colonial America." *Journal of Homosexuality* 1(3):277–293.

Cross, Allison L. 2013. "Slipping through the Cracks: The Dual Victimization of Human-Trafficking Survivors." *McGeorge Law Review* 44(2):395–422.

Crossman, Ashley. 2017. "Understanding the Meaning of the 'American Melting Pot.'" Thought Co. (https://www.thoughtco.com/melting-pot-definition-3026408).

Cubanski, Juliette, Kendall Orgera, Anthony Damico, and Tricia Neuman. 2018. "How Many Seniors Are Living in Poverty? National and State Estimates under the Official and Supplemental Poverty Measures in 2016." Henry J. Kaiser Family Foundation, March 2. https://www.kff.org/report-section/how-many-seniors-are-living-in-poverty-national-and-state-estimates-under-the-official-and-supplemental-poverty-measures-in-2016-data-note/.

Cunningham, Nicole. 2013. "Lori Haas, Mother of Virginia Tech Shooting Victim: "We Hold the Moral Authority and Our Elected Leaders Need to Listen to Us." Moms Demand Action for Gun Sense in America, April 16. http://momsdemandaction.org/faces-of-courage/lori-haas-mother-of-virginia-tech-shooting-victim-we-hold-the-moral-authority-and-our-elected-leaders-need-to-listen-to-us/.

Curwen, Thomas, Jason Song, and Larry Gordon. 2015. "What's Different about the Latest Wave of College Activism." Los Angeles Times. November 18 (http://www.latimes.com/local/education/la-me-campus-unrest-20151118-story.html).

Cutler, David, Elizabeth Wikler, and Peter Basch. 2012. "Reducing Administrative Costs and Improving the Health Care System." *New England Journal of Medicine* 367(November):1875–1878. www.nejm.org/doi/full/10.1056/NEJMp1209711.

Dahl, Robert and Douglas E. Rae. 2005. *Who Governs?* New Haven, CT: Yale University Press.

Dalen, James. E. 2009. "Only in America: Bankruptcy due to Health Care Costs." *American Journal of Medicine* 122(8):699.

Daley, David. 2016. *Rat F**ked: The True Story behind the Secret Plan to Steal America's Democracy*. New York: Liveright Publishing.

———. 2017. *Rat F**ked: Why Your Vote Doesn't Count*. New York: Liveright.

Darling-Hammond, Linda. 2018. "What Teacher Strikes Are Really About." CNN, April 27, 2018. https://www.cnn.com/2018/04/27/opinions/teacher-strikes-more-than-pay-darling-hammond-opinion/index.html.

Davenport, Coral. 2015. "Nations Approve Landmark Climate Accord in Paris." *New York Times*, December 12 (https://www.nytimes.com/2015/12/13/world/europe/climate-change-accord-paris.html).

Davey, Monica and Richard Pérez-Peña. 2016. "Flint Water Crisis Yields First Criminal Charges." *New York Times*, April 20. http://www.nytimes.com/2016/04/21/us/first-criminal-charges-are-filed-in-flint-water-crisis.html?_r=0

David, Javier E. and Izzy Best. 2014. "Target: Stolen information Involved at Least 70 Million People." CNBC.com www.cnbc.com/id/101323479.

Davies, James C. 1962. "Toward A Theory of Revolution." *American Sociological Review* 27(February):5–19.

Davis, Kingsley and Wilbert E. Moore. 1945. "Some Principles of Stratification." *American Sociological Review* 10(2):242–249.

Davis, Susan. 2017. "'Me Too' Legislation Aims to Combat Sexual Harassment in Congress." *NPR*, November 15 (https://www.npr.org/2017/11/15/564405871/me-too-legislation-aims-to-combat-sexual-harassment-in-congress).

de Anda, Diane. 2006. "Baby Think It Over: Evaluation of an Infant Simulation Intervention for Adolescent Pregnancy Prevention." *Health and Social Work* 31(1):26–35.

De Angelo, Laura. 2008. "Love Canal, New York." Encyclopedia of Earth. www.eoearth.org/view/article/154300/

Decameron Web. 2010. "Social and Economic Effects of the Plague" (www.brown.edu/Departments/Italian_Studies/dweb/plague/effects/social.php).

DeFronzo, James and Jungyun Gill. 2014. "Revolution without Borders: Global Revolutionaries, Their Messages and Means." Pp. 739–758 in *Sage Handbook of Globalization*, edited by Manfred B. Steger, Paul Battersby, and Joseph M. Siracusa. Thousand Oaks, CA: Sage.

DeFronzo, James. 1997. "Welfare and Homicide." *Journal of Research in Crime and Delinquency* 34(3):395–406.

———. 2008. *"Revolutionaries." Oxford Encyclopedia of the Modern World*. Oxford, UK: Oxford University Press. http://www.mywire.com/a/Oxford-Enc-Modern-World/Revolutionaries/9500098/.

———. 2010. *The Iraq War: Origins and Consequences.* New York: Routledge.

———. 2015. *Revolutions and Revolutionary Movements.* New York: Routledge.

Degenhardt, Louisa, Wai-Tat Chiu, Nancy Sampson, Ronald C. Kessler, James C. Anthony, Matthias Angermeyer, Ronny Bruffaerts, Giovanni de Girolamo, Oye Gureje, Yueqin Huang, Aimee Karam, Stanislav Kostyuchenko, Jean Pierre Lepine, Maria Elena Medina Mora, Yehuda Neumark, J. Hans Ormel, Alejandra Pinto-Meza, Jose Posada-Villa, Dan J. Stein, Tadashi Takeshima, and J. Elisabeth Wells. 2008. "Toward a Global View of Alcohol, Tobacco, Cannabis, and Cocaine Use: Findings from the WHO World Mental Health Surveys." *PLoS Medicine* 5(7):1053–1067.

Deming, David. 2009. "Early Childhood Intervention and Life-Cycle Skill Development: Evidence from Head Start." *American Economic Journal: Applied Economics* 1(3):111–134.

Democracy in America Blog. 2017. "Taking a Knee: Donald Trump Sparks Protests on Football Fields across America." *Economist*, September 25. https://www.economist.com/blogs/democracyinamerica/2017/09/taking-knee.

DeNavas-Walt, Carmen, Bernadette D. Proctor, and Jessica C. Smith. 2011. "Income, Poverty and Health Insurance Coverage in the United States: 2010." Current Population Reports, September (www.census.gov/prod/2011pubs/p60-239.pdf).

Dess, Melissa. 2013. "Walking the Freedom Trail: An Analysis of the Massachusetts Human Trafficking Statute and Its Potential to Combat Child Sex Trafficking." *Boston College Journal of Law & Social Justice* 33(1):147–182 (lawdigitalcommons.bc.edu/cgi/viewcontent.cgi?article=1030&context=jlsj).

Deuskar, Chandan. 2015. "What does 'Urban' Mean?" World Bank. June 2 (http://blogs.worldbank.org/sustainablecities/what-does-urban-mean).

Dick, Kirby and Amy Ziering. 2012. The Invisible War (www.invisiblewarmovie.com/).

Dietz, Park. 2012. *The Iceman Interviews*. New York: HBO.

Digest of Federal Resource Laws of Interest to the U.S. Fish and Wildlife Service. 2017. "Wilderness Act." www.fws.gov/laws/lawsdigest/wildrns.html.

Dilanian, Ken. 2014. "State Dept.: 'No American Is Proud' of CIA Tactics." Associated Press, July 31. http://news.msn.com/us/state-dept-no-american-is-proud-of-cia-tactics.

———. 2016. "Should the CIA Use Drones to Kill ISIS Targets?" NBC News, March 24. http://www.nbcnews.com/storyline/isis-uncovered/should-cia-use-drones-kill-isis-targets-n543666.

Direct News. 2014. "Can Government Incentives Reverse Falling Birth Rates?" June 27. http://national.deseretnews.com/article/1769/can-government-incentives-reverse-falling-birth-rates.html.

DiSalvo, David. 2014. "Why Is Heroin Abuse Rising while Other Drug Abuse Is Falling?" Forbes, January 14 http://www.forbes.com/sites/daviddisalvo/2014/01/14/why-is-heroin-abuse-rising-while-other-drug-abuse-is-falling/

Disaster Center. 2018. "United States Crime Rates" http://www.disastercenter.com/crime/uscrime.htm).

Divorcepapers.com. 2015. "Divorces per 1,000 Married Women, 1940–2012." (http://divorcepapers.com/wp-content/uploads/2015/04/divorce-rate-women.jpg).

Doctors without Borders. 2017a. "Doctors without Borders." http://www.doctorswithoutborders.org/about-us/?ref=nav-footer.

———. 2017b. *International Activity Report 2016. www.msf.ca/en/article/*international-activity-report-2016

Dollard, John. 1980. *Frustration and Aggression*. Westport, CT: Praeger.

Domhoff, G. William. 2012. "The Class-Domination Theory of Power" (http://www2.ucsc.edu/whorulesamerica/power/class_domination.html).

———. 2013. *Who Rules America*. New York: McGraw-Hill.

Domonoske, Camila and Doreen McCallister. 2016. "3 Face Criminal Charges over Flint Water Crisis." NPR, April 20. http://www.npr.org/sections/thetwo-way/2016/04/20/474931189/criminal-charges-to-be-filed-in-flint-water-crisis-reports-say.

Donohue, John J., Abhay Aneja, and Kyle D. Weber. 2017. "Right to Carry Laws and Violent Crime: A Comprehensive Assessment Using Panel Data and a State-

Level Synthetic Controls Anaysis." National Bureau of Economic Research (June): NBER Working Paper No. 23510 (http://www.nber.org/papers/w23510).

Dos Santos, Theontonio. 1970. "The Structure of Dependence." *American Economic Review* 60(May):231–236.

Dougherty, Jill. 2016. "The Reality Behind Russia's Fake News." CNN, December 2. http://edition.cnn.com/2016/12/02/politics/russia-fake-news-reality/.

Douglas, John and Mark Olshaker. 1996. *Mind Hunter.* New York: Pocket Star Books.

———. 1997. *Journey into Darkness.* New York: Pocket Star Books.

Dovidio, John F. and Gaertner, Samuel L. 1999. "Reducing Prejudice: Combating Intergroup Biases." *Current Directions in Psychological Science* 8(4):101–105.

Dream Act Portal. 2017. "The Dream Act" (https://dreamact.info/).

Dreier, Peter. 2001. "The Campus Anti-Sweat Shop Movement." American Prospect, December 19. http://prospect.org/article/campus-anti-sweatshop-movement.

Drum, Kevin. 2017. "The Real Story behind All Those Confederate Statues." Mother Jones, August 15 (http://www.motherjones.com/kevin-drum/2017/08/the-real-story-of-all-those-confederate-statues/).

Dubois, W. E. B. 1935. *Black Reconstruction in America: 1860–1880.* New York: Harcourt, Brace.

Duneier, Mitchell. 2000. *Sidewalk.* New York: Farrar, Straus and Giroux.

Durkheim, Emile. 1892. *The Division of Labor in Society.* New York: The Free Press, 1997.

———. 1893 (1997). *The Division of Labor in Society.* New York: Free Press.

Dutton, Kevin. 2012. *The Wisdom of Psychopaths.* New York: Scientific American.

Dye, Jessica, Joseph Ax, and Jim Finkle. 2013. "Huge Cyber Bank Theft Spans 27 Countries." Reuters, May 9. www.reuters.com/article/2013/05/09/net-us-usa-crime-cybercrime-idUSBRE9480PZ20130509.

Earth Talk. 2015. "The Pros and Cons of Biofuels." *Environmental Magazine.* http://environment.about.com/od/fossilfuels/a/biofuels.htm.

Ebling, Charles W. 2009. "Evolution of a Box." *Invention and Technology* 23(4):8–9.

Economist. 2001. "Malcolm Purcell McLean, Pioneer of Container Ships." May 31. www.economist.com/node/638561.

———. 2013a. "How Did the Global Poverty Rate Halve in 20 Years?" June 2. www.economist.com/blogs/economist-explains/2013/06/economist-explains-0.

———. 2013b. "The Fraying Knot." January 12. (www.economist.com/news/united-states/21569433-americas-marriage-rate-falling-and-its-out-wedlock-birth-rate-soaring-fraying).

———. 2014. "Why Globalisation May Not Reduce Inequality in Poor Countries." September 2. www.economist.com/blogs/economist-explains/2014/09/economist-explains-0.

Educator Resources. 2013. "Martin Luther King, Jr., and Memphis Sanitation Workers" (www.archives.gov/education/lessons/memphis-v-mlk/).

Edwards, Rob. 2013. "Iraq's Depleted Uranium Clean-Up to Cost $30m as Contamination Spreads." *Guardian*, March 6. www.theguardian.com/environment/2013/mar/06/iraq-depleted-uranium-clean-up-contamination-spreads.

———. 2014. "US Fired Depleted Uranium at Civilian Areas in 2003 Iraq War, Report Finds." *Guardian*, June 19 (www.theguardian.com/world/2014/jun/19/us-depleted-uranium-weapons-civilian-areas-iraq)n.

Eikenberry, Karl W. and David M. Kennedy. 2013. "Americans and Their Military, Drifting Apart." New York Times, May 26. www.nytimes.com/2013/05/27/opinion/americans-and-their-military-drifting-apart.html?pagewanted=all&_r=1&pagewanted=print&.

Elias, Thomas D. 2017. "Will Yucca Mountain Be the Answer to Nuclear Waste?" Orange County Register, May 2. http://www.ocregister.com/2017/05/02/will-yucca-mountain-be-the-answer-to-nuclear-waste/.

Elleck, Adam B. and Irfan Ashraf. 2009. "Class Dismissed: The Death of Female Education." *New York Times* (https://www.nytimes.com/video/world/asia/100000001835296/class-dismissed-malala-yousafzais-story.html).

Elsevier Health Sciences. 2009. "Over 60% of US Bankruptcies Attributable to Medical Problems." Disabled World, June 7. http://www.disabled-world.com/disability/statistics/medical-expenses-bankruptcy.php.

Encyclopedia Britannica. 2017. "Susan B. Anthony: American Suffragist." https://www.britannica.com/biography/Susan-B-Anthony.

Energy.gov. 2017. "Energy Efficiency and Conservation Block Grant Program." https://www.energy.gov/eere/wipo/energy-efficiency-and-conservation-block-grant-program.

Engels, Friederich. 1884 . *The Origin of the Family, Private Property and the State.* New York: Random House, 2010.

Environmental Protection Agency (EPA). 1992. "*The Guardian*: Origins of the EPA." www2.epa.gov/aboutepa/guardian-origins-epa.

———. 2012. "The Montreal Protocol on Substances that Deplete the Ozone Layer." www.epa.gov/ozone/intpol/

———. 2015a. "Municipal Solid Waste." www.epa.gov/waste/nonhaz/municipal/.

———. 2015b. "Recycling Basics." www2.epa.gov/recycle/recycling-basics.

———. 2015c. "Statistics on the Management of Used and End-of-Life Electronics." www.epa.gov/osw/conserve/materials/ecycling/manage.htm.

———. 2015d. "Nuclear Incidents: Three Mile Island Nuclear Plant." www.epa.gov/radiation/rert/tmi.html.

———. 2016. "Superfund: CERCLA Overview." https://www.epa.gov/superfund/superfund-cercla-overview.

———. 2017a. "Greenhouse Gas Emissions." https://www.epa.gov/ghgemissions/overview-greenhouse-gases.

———. 2017b. "Criteria Air Pollutants" https://www.epa.gov/criteria-air-pollutants.

———. 2017c. "Overview of the Clean Air Act and Air Pollution." https://www.epa.gov/clean-air-act-overview.

———. 2017d. "The Inside Story: A Guide to Indoor Air Quality." https://www.cpsc.gov/Safety-Education/Safety-Guides/Home/The-Inside-Story-A-Guide-to-Indoor-Air-Quality/.

———. 2017e. "Radon." https://www.epa.gov/radon.

———. 2017f. "Resource Conservation and Recovery Act (RCRA) Laws and Regulations." https://www.epa.gov/rcra.

————. 2017g. "Brownfields." https://www.epa.gov/brownfields.

————. 2017h. "Cleaning Up Electronic Waste (E-Waste)." https://www.epa.gov/international-cooperation/cleaning-electronic-waste-e-waste.

————. 2017i. "Water Sense." https://www.epa.gov/watersense.

————. 2017j. "Acid Rain." https://www.epa.gov/acidrain.

————. 2017k. "Environmental Justice." https://www.epa.gov/environmentaljustice.

————. 2017l. "Carbon Dioxide Capture and Sequestration: Overview." https://19january2017snapshot.epa.gov/climatechange/carbon-dioxide-capture-and-sequestration-overview_.html.

————. 2017m. "Summary of the Clean Water Act." https://www.epa.gov/laws-regulations/summary-clean-water-act

Epatko, Larisa and Nora Daly. 2014. "Demonstrators Coordinate Using Social Media as Hong Kong Pretests Swell." PBS Newshour, September 29. http://www.pbs.org/newshour/rundown/protests-swell-in-hong-kong/.

Equalrightsamendment.org. 2016. "The Equal Rights Amendment" (http://equalrightsamendment.org/).

Erasing76crimes.com. 2015. "79 Countries Where Homosexuality Is Illegal" (http://76crimes.com/76-countries-where-homosexuality-is-illegal/).

Ertelt, Steven. 2016. "States Pass More Pro-Life Laws Saving Babies from Abortion in Last 5 Years Than the Previous 15." LifeNews.com, January 4. www.lifenews.com/2016/01/04/states-pass-more-pro-life-laws-saving-babies-from-abortions-in-last-5-fives-than-the-previous-15/.

Esch, Mary. 2006. "Dead Lake Comes Back to Life, at Least for Now." NBC News, June 8. www.nbcnews.com/id/13049814/ns/world_news-world_environment/t/dead-lake-comes-back-life-least-now/#.Vcdf3-9RHIU

ESPN. 2014. "Anabolic Steroids." September 6. http://espn.go.com/special/s/drugsandsports/steroids.html

European Commission. 2010. *Poverty and Social Exclusion Report. Brussels*, Belgium: European Commission (ec.europa.eu/*commfrontoffice/publicopinion/archives/ebs/ebs_355_en.pdf*).

Ewing, Walter A. 2012. "Opportunity and Exclusion: A Brief History of U.S. Immigration Policy." Immigration Policy Center. January (www.immigrationpolicy.org/sites/default/files/docs/opportunity_exclusion_011312.pdf).

Ewing, Maura. 2017. "Do Right-to-Carry Gun Laws Make States Safer?" *Atlantic*, June 24 (https://www.theatlantic.com/politics/archive/2017/06/right-to-carry-gun-violence/531297/).

Express Tribune. 2012. "NA Passes Right to Free and Compulsory Education Bill." November 13 (http://tribune.com.pk/story/464989/na-passes-right-to-free-and-compulsory-education-bil)

Eyerman, Ron and Andrew Jamison. 1998. *Music and Social Movements: Mobilizing Traditions in the Twentieth Century*. Cambridge, UK: Cambridge University Press.

Falini, Lauren. 2013. "5 Ways Families Can Fight Obesity." Philly.com, September 25. www.philly.com/philly/blogs/healthy_kids/5-ways-families-can-fight-obesity-.html.

Familyfacts.org. 2016. "Unwed Childbearing Has Increased Dramatically, Regardless of Mother's Age." (http://familyfacts.org/charts/207/unwed-childbearing-has-increased-dramatically-regardless-of-mothers-age).

Farley, Robert. 2017. "Fact Check: Trump Claims Massive Voter Fraud; Here's the Truth." *USA Today*. January 26 (https://www.usatoday.com/story/news/politics/2017/01/26/fact-check-trumps-bogus-voter-fraud-claims-revisited/97080242/).

Featherstone, Liza. 2002. *Students gainst Sweatshops*. London: Verso.

Fedders, Barbara. 2010. "Mandatory Arrest for Domestic Violence: A Universal Solution?" (http://academic.udayton.edu/health/01status/violence02.htm).

Federal Bureau of Investigation (FBI). 1986. *Crime in the United States 1985*. Washington, DC: U.S. Department of Justice.

————. 1993. *Crime in the United States 1992*. Washington, DC: U.S. Department of Justice.

————. 2005. "Serial Murder: Multi-Disciplinary Perspectives for Investigators" (https://www.fbi.gov/stats-services/publications/serial-murder).

————. 2008. "Putting Intel to Work against ELF and ALF Terrorists." www.fbi.gov/news/stories/2008/june/ecoterror_063008.

————. 2014. "Child Predators." www.fbi.gov/news/stories/2011/may/predators_051711.

————. 2016a. "Hate Crimes – Overview" (https://www.fbi.gov/about-us/investigate/civilrights/hate_crimes/overview).

————. 2016b. "Table 33: Ten-Year Arrest Trends by Sex, 2006–2015." *Crime in the United States 2015*, https://ucr.fbi.gov/crime-in-the-u.s/2015/crime-in-the-u.s.-2015/tables/table-33.

————. 2016c. "Confronting the Child Sex Trade in Southeast Asia." September 16 (https://www.fbi.gov/news/stories/report-from-thailand-part-1).

————. 2017a. Crime in the United States 2016. https://ucr.fbi.gov/crime-in-the-u.s/2016/crime-in-the-u.s.-2016/resource-pages/about-ucr.

————. 2017b. *Crime in the United States 2016:Tables by Title*. https://ucr.fbi.gov/crime-in-the-u.s/2016/crime-in-the-u.s.-2016/topic-pages/tables/table-1.

————. 2017c. "Law Enforcement Officers Killed and Assaulted" https://www.fbi.gov/news/stories/2016-leoka-report-released.

————. 2017d. "Uniform Crime Reporting Statistics: About the Uniform Crime Reporting Program" https://www.ucrdatatool.gov/abouttheucr.cfm.

————. 2017e. "Offenses Known to Law Enforcement by State by City, 2016." https://ucr.fbi.gov/crime-in-the-u.s/2016/crime-in-the-u.s.-2016/tables/table-6/table-6.xls/view.

————. 2017f. Uniform Crime Reporting Program: National Incident-Based Reporting System. "FBI Releases 2015 Crime Statistics from the National Incident-Based Reporting System, Encourages Transition." https://ucr.fbi.gov/nibrs/2015/resource-pages/nibrs-2015_summary_final-1.pdf.

————. 2017g. "Expanded Homicide." https://ucr.fbi.gov/crime-in-the-u.s/2016/crime-in-the-u.s.-2016/topic-pages/expanded-homicide.

————. 2017h. "Expanded Homicide: Murder by Relationship, Percent Distribution, Volume by Relationship, 2015." https://ucr.fbi.gov/crime-in-the-u.s/2015/crime-in-the-u.s.-2015/offenses-known-to-law-enforcement/expanded-homicide.

———. 2017i "Murder Victims by Weapon, 2012–2016." https://ucr.fbi.gov/crime-in-the-u.s/2016/crime-in-the-u.s.-2016/tables/expanded-homicide-data-table-4.xls

———. 2017j. "White Collar Crime" https://www.fbi.gov/about-us/investigate/white_collar.

———. 2017k. "Cyber Crime." https://www.fbi.gov/about-us/investigate/cyber.

———. 2017l. "Oklahoma City Bombing." https://www.fbi.gov/history/famous-cases/oklahoma-city-bombing.

———. 2017m. *2016 Crime in the United States.* https://ucr.fbi.gov/crime-in-the-u.s/2016/crime-in-the-u.s.-2016/tables/table-6/table-6-state-cuts/michigan.xls.

———. 2017n. "Human Trafficking." *Uniform Crime Reports 2016.* https://ucr.fbi.gov/crime-in-the-u.s/2016/crime-in-the-u.s.-2016/additional-publications/human-trafficking.

———. 2017o. "Expanded Homicide." (https://ucr.fbi.gov/crime-in-the-u.s/2015/crime-in-the-u.s.-2015/offenses-known-to-law-enforcement/expanded-homicide).

———. 2017p. "Crime in the United States im/ucr.fbi.gov/crime-in-the-u.s/2015/crime-in-the-u.s.-2015/tables/table-4).

Federal Student Aid. 2017. "Types of Aid." U.S. Department of Education (https://studentaid.ed.gov/sa/types).

Feldman, Carol and Emily Swanson. 2018. "Poll: Amid Strikes across the U.S., Americans Back Teacher Raises." AZ Central, April 23. https://www.azcentral.com/story/news/local/arizona-education/2018/04/23/amid-strikes-americans-back-teacher-raises/542334002/.

Finchelstein, Federico. 2014. *The Ideological Origins of the Dirty War.* New York: Oxford University Press.

FindLaw. 2016. "United States Supreme Court: *In Re Winship,* (1970)." (http://caselaw.findlaw.com/us-supreme-court/397/358.html).

Fink, Sheri, Adam Nossiter, and James Kanter. 2014. "Doctors without Borders Evolves as It Forms the Vanguard in Ebola Fight." *New York Times,* October 10. www.nytimes.com/2014/10/11/world/africa/doctors-without-borders-evolves-as-it-forms-the-vanguard-in-ebola-fight-.html.

Finkelhor, David, Lisa Jones, Anne Shattuck, and Kei Seito. 2013. "Updated Trends in Child Maltreatment, 2012." (www.unh.edu/ccrc/pdf/CV203_Updated%20trends%202012_2_12_31.pdf).

Fishel, Justin. 2017. "US Intelligence Agency Leaders Squarely Blame Election Hacking on Russia." ABC News, January 10. http://abcnews.go.com/Politics/fbi-director-testify-russia-hacking-opens-door-grilling/story?id=44674836.

Fisher, Gordon M. 1997. "Development and History of the U.S. Poverty Thresholds – A Brief Overview." Newsletter of the Government Statistics Section and the Social Statistics Section of the American Statistical Association, Winter:6–7. (http://aspe.hhs.gov/poverty/papers/hptgssiv.htm).

Flatow, Nicole. 2014. "City Murders Are Twice as Likely to Be Solved When the Victim Is White Instead of Black." Think Progress, January 7. http://thinkprogress.org/justice/2014/01/07/3125001/york-city-police-solved-murders-white-victim/.

Flowers, R. Barri. 2013. *The Dynamics of Murder.* Boca Raton, FL: CRC Press.

Foley, Ellse. 2015. "Why Some Cities Don't Rush to Turn Over Undocumented Immigrants to the Feds." HuffPost, July 9 (https://www.huffingtonpost.com/2015/07/09/sanctuary-cities-law-enforcement_n_7765058.html).

Food Research and Action Center. 2011. "Food Insecurity and Obesity: Understanding the Connection." Spring (http://frac.org/pdf/frac_brief_understanding_the_connections.pdf).

Foran, John. 2005. *Taking Power: On the Origins of Third World Revolutions.* Cambridge: Cambridge University Press.

Forced Marriage Unit. 2015. "What Is Forced Marriage?" Foreign and Commonwealth Office, United Kingdom. (www.gov.uk/government/uploads/system/uploads/attachment_data/file/325920/FCO_FM2014_A6_web.pdf).

Forensic Psychology. 2017. "Public Opinion about Crime." http://criminal-justice.iresearchnet.com/forensic-psychology/public-opinion-about-crime/.

Foundation for a Drug Free World. 2017. "Who We Are." www.drugfreeworld.org/about-us/about-the-foundation.html.

Fox, James Alan and Jack Levin. 2011. *Extreme Killing: Understanding Serial and Mass Murder.* Thousand Oaks, CA: Sage.

Fraley, R. Chris and Marie E. Heffernan. 2013. "Attachment and Parental Divorce: A Test of the Diffusion and Sensitive Period Hypotheses." *Personality and Social Psychology Bulletin* 39(9):1199–1213.

Frank, Andre Gunder. 1966. "The Development of Underdevelopment." *Monthly Review* 18(September): 17–31.

———. 1969a. *Latin America: Underdevelopment or Revolution?* New York: Monthly Review Press.

———. 1969b. *Capitalism and Underdevelopment in Latin America.* New York: Monthly Review Press.

———. 1979. *Dependent Accumulation and Underdevelopment.* New York: Monthly Review Press.

Frey, William H. 2018. "The U.S. Will Become "Minority White" in 2045, Census Projects." *Brookings,* March 14 (https://www.brookings.edu/blog/the-avenue/2018/03/14/the-us-will-become-minority-white-in-2045-census-projects/).

Friedman, Zack. 2018. "Student Loan Debt Statistics in 2018: A $1.5 Trillion Crisis." *Forbes,* June 13. https://www.forbes.com/sites/zackfriedman/2018/06/13/student-loan-debt-statistics-2018/#721e90e57310.

Fullerton, Andrew. 2006. "Inequality, Class and Revolution." Pp. 408–412 in *Revolutionary Movements in World History, Vol.2,* edited by James DeFronzo. Santa Barbara, CA: ABC-CLIO.

Furber, Matt and Richard Pérez-Peña. 2016. "After Philando Castile's Killing, Obama Calls Police Shootings 'an American Issue.'" *New York Times,* July 7. http://www.nytimes.com/2016/07/08/us/philando-castile-falcon-heights-shooting.html?_r=0.

Furtado, Celso. 1963. *The Economic Growth of Brazil.* Berkeley, CA: University of California Press.

Gadalla, Tahany M. 2009. "Impact of Marital Dissolution on Men's and Women's Income: A Longitudinal Study." Journal of Divorce and Remarriage 50(1):55–65. (www.rdc-cdr.ca/sites/default/files/income_paper.pdf).

Gallup. 2014. "Arkansas, Kentucky Report Sharpest Drops in Uninsured Rate." August 5. www.gallup.com/poll/174290/arkansas-kentucky-report-sharpest-drops-uninsured-rate.aspx#1.

———. 2016. "Gay and Lesbian Rights" (www.gallup.com/poll/1651/Gay-Lesbian-Rights.aspx).

———. 2017. "Most Important Problem." Gallup, March 30 (http://www.gallup.com/poll/1675/Most-Important-Problem.aspx).

———. 2018. "Environment" (https://news.gallup.com/poll/1615/environment.aspx).

Gamboa, Suzanne. 2013. "Housing Discrimination Persists Subtly for Minorities, HUD Study Finds." *Huffington Post*, July 13 (www.huffingtonpost.com/2013/06/11/housing-discrimination-persists-subtly-hud-study-finds_n_3423747.html).

Gao, George. 2014. "Chart of the Week: The Black-White Gap in Incarceration Rates." Pew Research Center, July 18. http://www.pewresearch.org/fact-tank/2014/07/18/chart-of-the-week-the-black-white-gap-in-incarceration-rates/.

Garces, Eliana, Thomas Duncan, and Janet Currie. 2002. "Long-Term Effects of Head Start." *American Economic Review* 92(4):999–1012.

Garfield, Leanna. 2018. "Toys R Us Says Millennials Not Having Kids Hurt the Company – and It Could Be Because Of A Looming 'Demographic Time Bomb.'" Business Insider, March 21. http://www.businessinsider.com/toys-r-us-closes-millennials-babies-birth-rate-2018–3.

Gates, Gary J. and Frank Newport. 2013a. "Special Report: 3.4% of U.S. Adults Identify as LGBT." Gallup, February 15 (www.gallup.com/poll/158066/special-report-adults-identify-lgbt.aspx).

———. 2013b. "LGBT Percentage Highest in D.C., Lowest in North Dakota." *Gallup*, February 15 (www.gallup.com/poll/160517/lgbt-percentage-highest-lowest-north-dakota.aspx).

Gautney, Heather and Adolph Reed, Jr. 2015. "Bernie Sanders's 'College for All' Plan Is Fair, Smart and Achievable." *Nation*, December 2 https://www.thenation.com/article/bernie-sanderss-college-for-all-plan-is-fair-smart-and-achievable/).

Georgetown Law Library. 2014. "International Criminal Court – Article 98 Agreements Research Guide." www.law.georgetown.edu/library/research/guides/article_98.cfm.

Gibbs, Lois Marie. 2008. "History: Love Canal: The Start of a Movement." Boston University School of Public Health. www.bu.edu/lovecanal/canal/.

Gibson, Campbell and Kay Jung. 2005. "Historical Census Statistics on Population Totals by Race, 1790 to 1990, and by Hispanic Origin, 1970 to 1990, for Large Cities and Other Urban Places in the United States." United States Census, Population Division Working Paper No. 76 February. https://www.census.gov/population/www/documentation/twps0076/twps0076.html.

Gibson, Kate. 2016. "Paid Parental Leave: Finally Coming to America?" *CBS Money Watch*, April 7 (http://www.cbsnews.com/news/paid-parental-leave-finally-coming-to-america/).

Gilardi. 2014. "Enron Corporation (ENRN Q) Common Stock Historical Price Table: Daily prices from 01/ 01/1997 to 12/ 31/2002." www.gilardi.com/pdf/enro13ptable.pdf.

Gilbert, Dennis L. 2018. *The American Social Class Structure in an Age of Growing Inequality*, 10th ed. Thousand Oaks, CA: Sage.

Gill, Jungyun and James DeFronzo. 2009. "A Comparative Framework for the Analysis of International Student Movements." *Social Movement Studies* 8(3):203–224.

Ginley, Caitlin. 2012. "Grading the Nation: How Accountable in Your State?" iWatch News by The Center for Public Integrity, March 19. (http://www.iwatchnews.org/2012/03/19/8423/grading-nation-how-accountable-your-state).

Gladstone, Rick. 2014. "W.H.O. Assails Delay in Ebola Vaccine." New York Times, November 3. www.nytimes.com/2014/11/04/world/africa/ebola-cure-delayed-by-drug-industrys-drive-for-profit-who-leader-says.html?_r=0.

Global Center for Pluralism. 2016 (http://pluralism.ca/en/programs/experiences/canada.html).

Global Freedom Struggle. 2013. "Memphis Sanitation Workers Strike." (http://mlk-kpp01.stanford.edu/index.php/encyclopedia/encyclopedia/enc_meredith_james_howard_1933).

Global Slavery Index. 2017. https://www.globalslaveryindex.org/findings/.

Global Water Justice Movement. 2012. "Global Water Justice Movement Call to Action for Governments on the Implementation of the Human Right to Water." http://focusweb.org/content/global-water-justice-movement-call-action-governments-implementation-human-right-water.

GLSEN (The Gay, Lesbian, and Straight Education Network). 2012. *Playgrounds and Prejudice: Elementary School Climate in the United States*. New York: GLSEN and Harris Interactive.

Glüsing, Jens. 2013. "Ex Rio Drug Queen Recalls Life of Crime." *Der Spiegel*, March 27. http://www.spiegel.de/international/world/former-brazilian-favela-queen-recalls-life-in-rio-drug-trade-a-891072.html.

Goffman, Irving. 1963. *Stigma*. Englewood Cliffs, NJ: Prentice Hall.

Goldberg, Robert A. 1991. *Grassroots Resistance: Social Movements in Twentieth Century America*. Belmont, CA: Wadsworth Publishing Company.

Goldberg, Carey. 2006. "Materialism is Bad for You, Studies Say." New York Times, February 8. www.nytimes.com/2006/02/08/health/08iht-snmat.html.

Goldfarb, Kara. 2018. "The Lavender Scare: The U.S. Government's Anti-Gay Purge." *All That's Interesting*, June 13 (https://allthatsinteresting.com/lavender-scare).

Goldfrank, Walter L. 1979. "Theories of Revolution and Revolution without Theory: The Case of Mexico." *Theory and Society* 7(January–March):135–165.

Goldstone, Jack. 1980. "Theories of Revolution: The Third Generation." *World Politics* 32(3):425–453.

———. 1982. "The Comparative and Historical Study of Revolutions." *Annual Review of Sociology* 8:187–207.

———. 1998a. "Democracy." Pp. 131–132 in *The Encyclopedia of Political Revolutions*, edited by Jack Goldstone . Washington, DC: Congressional Quarterly.

———. 1998b. "Population." Pp. 403–405 in *The Encyclopedia of Political Revolutions*, edited by Jack A. Goldstone. Washington, DC: Congressional Quarterly.

————. 2010. "The New Population Bomb: Four Mega-trends That Will Change the World." *Foreign Affairs* 89(January/February):31–43.

Gomez, Alan. 2018. "The Parkland Survivors Started a Movement When They Took on Gun Violence. Here's how it happened." USA Today, February 22. https://www.usatoday.com/story/news/nation/2018/02/22/parkland-survivors-started-movement-when-they-took-gun-violence-heres-how-happened/361297002/.

Goodwin, Jeff. 2001. *No Other Way Out: States and Revolutionary Movements, 1945–1991.* Cambridge: Cambridge University Press.

Gornick, Janet C. 2007. "Atlantic Passages: How Europe Supports Working Parents and Their Children." *American Prospect* 18(3):A19–A20. (http://prospect.org/article/atlantic-passages).

Gottesdiener, Laura. 2015. "The Water Belongs to the People." *Nation,* 3–10:20–24.

Gottfredson, Michael and Travis Hirschi. 1990. *A General Theory of Crime.* Redwood City, CA: Stanford University Press.

Goyette, Braden. 2012. "Cheat Sheet: How Super PACs Work, and Why They're So Controversial." *New York Daily News,* January 13 (www.nydailynews.com/news/politics/cheat-sheet-super-pacs-work-controversial-article-1.1005804).

Grant, Jaime M, Lisa A. Mottet, and Justine Tanis. 2011. *Injustice at Every Turn: A Report of the National Transgender Discrimination Survey.* Washington, DC: National Center for Transgender Equality and National Gay and Lesbian Task Force.

Grant, Lara. 2016. " The Most Popular Countries for Sex Tourism." Oyster.com, *Huffington Post,* October 1. http://www.huffingtonpost.com/oyster/the-most-popular-countrie_b_8067520.html.

Gravé-Lazi, Lidar. 2014. " 2012 PISA Test: Israeli Students Receive Low Scores in Problem Solving Skills." Jerusalem Post, April 1. http://www.jpost.com/National-News/2012-PISA-test-Israeli-students-receive-low-scores-in-problem-solving-skills-347195.

Gray, Lucinda and Laurie Lewis 2015 "Public School Safety and Discipline: 2013–14." National Center for Education Statistics. https://nces.ed.gov/pubs2015/2015051.pdf.

Greif, Jim. 2010. "Weisburd Wins Criminology's Top Prize for His Policing Research" (http://news.gmu.edu/articles/470).

Griffiths, James and Angela Dewan. 2017. "What Is a Hydrogen Bomb and Can North Korea Deliver One?" CNN, September 22. https://www.cnn.com/2017/09/03/asia/hydrogen-bomb-north-korea-explainer/index.html

Grillooct, Joan. 2014. "Mexico's Deadly Narco-Politics." New York Times, October 9. www.nytimes.com/2014/10/10/opinion/mexicos-deadly-narco-politics.html.

Grim, Ryan. 2011. "Kerry: CIA Lied About Contra-Cocaine Connections." *Huffington Post,* May 25 www.huffingtonpost.com/2009/05/21/kerry-cia-lied-about-cont_n_206423.html.

Gross, Daniel. 2006. "Children for Sale." Slate, May 24. www.slate.com/articles/business/moneybox/2006/05/children_for_sale.html.

Grych, John H. 2005. "Interparental Conflict as a Risk Factor for Child Maladjustment: Implications for the Development of Prevention Programs." *Family Court Review* 43(1):97–108.

Grynbaum, Michael M. and John Koblin. 2016. "Gretchen Carlson of Fox News Files Harassment Suit Against Roger Ailes." New York Times, July 6 (https://www.nytimes.com/2016/07/07/business/media/gretchen-carlson-fox-news-roger-ailes-sexual-harassment-lawsuit.html).

Guardian. 2016. "Gay Rights in the U.S., State by State" (www.theguardian.com/world/interactive/2012/may/08/gay-rights-united-states).

Guerin, Bill. 2006. "Labor Pains in Indonesia." *Asia Times,* April 25. http://www.atimes.com/atimes/Southeast_Asia/HD25Ae02.html.

Guillen, Mauro F. 2001. "Is Globalization Civilizing, Destructive or Feeble? A Critique of Five Key Debates in the Social Science Literature." *Annual Review of Sociology* 27:235–260.

Gunier, Lani, Richard Hasen, David Savage, and Ilya Shapiro. 2013. "What Changes After Supreme Court Ruling on Voting Rights Act." National Public Radio (www.npr.org/2013/06/25/195557564/what-changes-after-supreme-court-ruling-on-voting-rights-act).

Gupta, Sanjay. 2013a. "Why I Changed My Mind on Weed." CNN, August 8. www.cnn.com/2013/08/08/health/gupta-changed-mind-marijuana/index.html.

————. 2013b. "Weed." CNN, August 24. www.youtube.com/watch?v=B4GUkzTnFG0.

————. 2014. "Weed 2." CNN, March 11. www.youtube.com/watch?v=tAFu-Ihwyzg.

Gurney, Kyra. 2018. "Last Fall, They Debated Gun Control in Class. Now, They Debate Lawmakers on TV." Miami Herald, February 25. http://www.miamiherald.com/news/local/education/article201678544.html

Gurr, Ted Robert. 1970. *Why Men Rebel.* Princeton, NJ: Princeton University Press.

Gutgold, Nichola A. 2010. "Women in Television News Still Face Ageism in the United States." Roman and Littlefield, January 5 (http://rowmanblog.typepad.com/rowman/2010/01/women-in-television-news-still-face-ageism-in-the-united-states.html).

Guttmacher Institute. 2007. "Abstinence-Only Programs Don't Work, New Study Shows." (www.guttmacher.org/media/inthenews/2007/04/18/).

————. 2011. "States Enact Record Number of Abortion Restrictions in First Half of 2011." July 13. http://www.guttmacher.org/media/inthenews/2011/07/13/index.html.

————. 2012. "Facts on American Teens' Sources of Information about Sex." (www.guttmacher.org/pubs/FB-Teen-Sex-Ed.html).

Haberman, Clyde. 2014. "Agent Orange's Long Legacy, for Vietnam and Veterans." New York Times, May 11. www.nytimes.com/2014/05/12/us/agent-oranges-long-legacy-for-vietnam-and-veterans.html?_r=0.

Hagan, Frank. 2002. *Introduction to Criminology.* Belmont, CA: Wadsworth.

Haider-Markel, Donald P. and Joslyn R. Mark. 2008. "Beliefs about the Origins of Homosexuality and Support for Gay Rights: An Empirical Test of Attribution Theory." *Public Opinion Quarterly* 72(2):291–310.

Hall, Amber. 2015. "Gun Owners Face Much Higher Murder Risks, Researchers Said. Then the NRA Silenced

Them." MSN News, April 13. http://www.msn.com/en-us/news/us/gun-owners-face-much-higher-murder-risks-researchers-said-then-the-nra-silenced-them/ar-AAaUFQx?ocid=mailsignout.

Hamada, Kentaro and Tsukimori Osamu. 2015. "Tokyo Electric Executives to Be Charged over Fukushima Nuclear Disaster." Reuters, July 31. www.reuters.com/article/2015/07/31/us-japan-nuclear-prosecution-idUSKCN0Q50FJ20150731?feedType=RSS&feedName=topNews&utm_source=twitter.

Hamilton, Mykol C., David Anderson, Michelle Broaddus, and Kate Young. 2006. "Gender Stereotyping and Under-Representation of Female Characters in 200 Popular Children's Picture Books: A Twenty-first Century Update." *Sex Roles* 55(December):757–765.

Hammond, Betsy. 2013. "Lesbian and Gay Students Subjected to Slurs, Shoves in Oregon Schools, Survey Says." *Oregonian*, June 13 (www.oregonlive.com/education/index.ssf/2013/03/lesbian_and_gay_students_subje.html).

Han, Chong-Suk. 2008. "No Fats, Femmes, or Asians: The Utility of Critical Race Theory in Examining the Role of Gay Stock Stories in the Marginalization of Gay Asian Men." *Contemporary Justice Review* 11(1):11–22.

Handley, Antoinette. 2004. "The New South Africa, a Decade Later." *Current History* 103(May):195–201.

Harding, David J. 2003. "Counterfactual Models of Neighborhood Effects: The Effect of Neighborhood Poverty on Dropping Out and Teenage Poverty." *American Journal of Sociology* 109(3):676–719.

Harding, Luke. 2016. "Mossack Fonseca: Inside the Firm that Helps the Super-Rich Hide Their Money." *Guardian*, April 8. www.theguardian.com/news/2016/apr/08/mossack-fonseca-law-firm-hide-money-panama-papers.

Hare, Robert. 1999. *Without Conscience*. New York: Guilford Press.

Hargrove, Thomas. 2010. "Murder Mysteries: Percentage of Killings That Go Unsolved Has Risen Alarmingly across the United States." *TCPALM*, May 21.

Harris, Fredrick C. 2015. "The Next Civil Rights Movement?" Dissent, Summer 2015. https://www.dissentmagazine.org/article/black-lives-matter-new-civil-rights-movement-fredrick-harris.

Hastings, Deborah. 2015. "2 Former Vanderbilt Football Players Found Guilty on All Counts in Brutal Rape Case." *New York Daily News*, January 28, www.nydailynews.com/news/national/vanderbilt-athletes-found-guilty-rape-article-1.2094226.

Hayoun, Massoud. 2015. "China's Louisiana Purchase: Environmental Concerns in 'Cancer Alley.'" Al Jazeera, January 28. http://america.aljazeera.com/articles/2015/1/28/chinese-methanol-plant-in-louisiana-cancer-alley.html.

Healthcare.gov. 2016. "*Medicaid*." (https://www.healthcare.gov/).

Healthinsurancecompanies.org. 2015. "Health Insurance Costs." www.healthinsurancecompanies.org/costs.

Hedgpeth, Dana. 2017. "Charlottesville City Council Votes Unanimously to Remove Another Confederate Statue." Chicago Tribune, September 6 (http://www.chicagotribune.com/news/nationworld/ct-charlottesville-confederate-statue-20170906-story.html).

Hegarty, Tim. 2010. "Power Law Distribution and Solving the Crime Problem." *Police Chief* 77(December):28–36.

Hegewisch, Ariane and Maxwell Matite. 2013. "The Gender Wage Gap by Occupation." Institute for Women's Policy Research (IWPR), April (www.iwpr.org/publications/pubs/the-gender-wage-gap-by-occupation-and-by-race-and-ethnicity-2013?searchterm=occupations).

Hegewisch, Ariane and Asha DuMonthier. 2016. "The Gender Wage Gap: 2015." Institute for Women's Policy Research (IWPR), March (www.iwpr.org/publications/pubs/the-gender-wage-gap-2015-earnings-differences-by-race-and-ethnicity/).

Heinrich, Katie and Daniel Arkin. 2017. "What Is DACA? Here's What You Need to Know About the Program Trump Is Ending." NBC News, September 5 (https://www.nbcnews.com/storyline/immigration-reform/what-daca-here-s-what-you-need-know-about-program-n798761).

Helpguide.org. 2016. "Step-Parenting and Blended Families." (www.helpguide.org/articles/family-divorce/step-parenting-blended-families.htm).

Hendrick, Bill. 2008. "Smoking Rate Is Declining in the U.S." WebMD. www.webmd.com/smoking-cessation/news/20081113/smoking-rate-is-declining-in-us.

Herek, Gregory M. 2012. "Facts about Homosexuality and Mental Health." http://psychology.ucdavis.edu/faculty_sites/rainbow/html/facts_mental_health.html.

Herman, Judith W., Julie K. Waterhouse, and Julie Chiquoine. 2011. "Evaluation of an Infant Simulator Intervention for Teen Pregnancy Prevention." *Journal of Obstetrics, Gynecologic, and Neonatal Nursing* 40(3):322–328.

Hermann, Peter. 2017. "Gunman Who Shot Steve Scalise Cased Baseball Field for Weeks before Rampage." *Chicago Tribune*, October 6. http://www.chicagotribune.com/news/nationworld/ct-steve-scalise-shooting-20171006-story.html.

Hermanns, Deborah. 2014. "Germany Is Scrapping Tuition Fees – Why Can't England?" *Guardian*, October 7. (http://www.theguardian.com/commentisfree/2014/oct/07/germany-scrapping-tuition-fees-england).

Hernandez, Daphne C., Emily Pressler, Cassandra Dorius, and Katherine Stamps Mitchell. 2014. "Does Family Instability Make Girls Fat? Gender Differences between Instability and Weight." *Journal of Marriage and Family* 76(1):175–190.

Herron, Arika. 2018. "Teachers are striking across the country, but not in Indiana. Why not?" *IndyStar*, April 10. https://www.indystar.com/story/news/education/2018/04/10/teacher-strikes-2018-across-country-but-not-indiana-why-not/491170002/.

Himmelstein, David. U., Deborah Thorne, Elizabeth Warren, and Steffie Wollhandler. 2009. "Medical Bankruptcy in the United States, 2007: Results of a National Study." *American Journal of Medicine* 122(8):741–746.

Hirschi, Travis. 1969. *Causes of Delinquency*. Oakland, CA: University of California Press.

History.com. 2015. "Nuclear Disaster at Chernobyl." www.history.com/this-day-in-history/nuclear-disaster-at-chernobyl.

———. 2018. "Nuremberg Trials." www.history.com/topics/world-war-ii/nuremberg-trials.

History.org. 2016. "Timeline: Women in the U.S. Military" (www.history.org/History/teaching/enewsletter/volume7/images/nov/womenmilitary_timeline.pdf).

Hobbes, Michael. 2014. "Why Did AIDS Ravage the U.S. More than Any Other Developed Country?" New Republic, May 12. www.newrepublic.com/article/117691/aids-hit-united-states-harder-other-developed-countries-why.

Hoehner, Christine M., Carolyn E. Barlow, Peg Allen, and Mario Schootman. 2012. "Commuting Distance, Cardiorespiratory Fitness, and Metabolic Risk." *American Journal of Preventive Medicine* 42(6):571–578. https://www.ncbi.nlm.nih.gov/pmc/articles/PMC3360418/.

Hoffman, Beatrix. 2003. "Health Care Reform and Social Movements in the United States." *American Journal of Public Health* 93(1):75–85.

Holmes, Ronald M. and Stephen T. Holmes. 1998. *Contemporary Perspectives on Serial Murder*. Thousand Oaks, CA: Sage.

Holsti, Ole. R. 1999. "A Widening Gap between the U.S. Military and Society? Some Evidence, 1976–1996." *International Security* 23(3):5–42.

———. 2001. "Of Chasms and Convergences: Attitudes and Beliefs of Civilians and Military Elites at the Start of the New Millennium." Pp. 15–99 in *Soldiers and Civilians: The Civil-Military Gap and American National Security*, edited by Peter D. Feaver and Richard H. Kohn. Cambridge, MA: MIT Press.

Holtfreter, Kristy, Shanna Van Slyke, Jason Bratton, and Marc Gertz. 2008. "Public Perceptions of White-Collar Crime and Punishment." *Journal of Criminal Justice* 36(1):50–60.

Honey, Michael K. 2007. *Going Down Jericho Road*. New York: Norton.

Hook, Janet. 2015. "Support for Gay Marriage Hits All-Time High – WSJ/NBC News Poll." *Wall Street Journal*, May 9. (http://blogs.wsj.com/washwire/2015/03/09/support-for-gay-marriage-hits-all-time-high-wsjnbc-news-poll/).

Horwitz, Sari. 2007. "8 Minutes after 911 Call, A Rescue from Madness." Washington Post, June 22. www.washingtonpost.com/wp-dyn/content/article/2007/06/21/AR2007062102497_2.html.

House of Representatives. 2017. "Party Breakdown" (https://pressgallery.house.gov/member-data/party-breakdown).

Hoyer, Meghan and Brad Heath. 2013. "Mass Killings Occur in USA Once Every Two Weeks." USA Today, December 2. www.usatoday.com/story/news/nation/2012/12/18/mass-killings-common/1778303/.

Hubbart, Jason A. 2011. "Hydrologic Cycle." Encyclopedia of Earth. www.eoearth.org/view/article/153627/.

Huffington Post Education. 2012. "Mississippi Sex Education: Majority of School Districts Choose Abstinence-Only Curriculum." July 30. (www.huffingtonpost.com/2012/07/30/mississippi-sex-education_n_1719882.html).

Huffington Post. 2013. "Marriage Rate Declines to Historic Low, Study Finds." July 22. (www.huffingtonpost.com/2013/07/22/marriage-rate_n_3625222.html).

Human Rights Campaign. 2016a. "Statewide Non-Discrimination in Adoption Laws" (www.hrc.org/state_maps).

———. 2016b. "Statewide Employment Laws and Policies" (www.hrc.org/state_maps).

Human Rights Watch. 2002. "U.S.: 'Hague Invasion Act' Becomes Law." August 4. www.hrw.org/news/2002/08/03/us-hague-invasion-act-becomes-law.

Hundley, Kris, Susan Taylor Martin, and Connie Humburg. 2012. "Florida 'Stand Your Ground' Law Yields Some Shocking Outcomes Depending on How Law Is Applied." *Tampa Bay Times*, June 1 (https://www.journalnow.com/news/local/florida-stand-your-ground-law-yields-some-shocking-outcomes-depending/article_36990777–2363-59e2-af13-ef1a0158b192.html).

Hunter, Margaret. 2011. "Shake It, Baby, Shake It: Consumption and the New Gender Relation in Hip-Hop." *Sociological Perspectives* 54(1):15–36.

Hurst, Fabienne. 2013. "WWII Drug: The German Granddaddy of Crystal Meth." Spiegel Online International. May 30. http://www.spiegel.de/international/germany/crystal-meth-origins-link-back-to-nazi-germany-and-world-war-ii-a-901755.html.

Icasualties.org. 2017. "'Operation Iraqi Freedom' and 'Operation Enduring Freedom/Afghanistan.'" http://www.icasualties.org/.

Immigration and Customs Enforcement (ICE). 2017. "Criminal Alien Program" (https://www.ice.gov/criminal-alien-program).

Infoproc. 2015. "Life Expectancies." http://www.bing.com/images/search?q=native+american+women+life+-expectancy&id=C1882581910144D7EB8361CEF-FB5A9917D8CA153&FORM=IQFRBA#view=-detail&id=981CCD3A9A050516DE0EF22A33E-CF14EF43572ED&selectedIndex=15.

Ingraham, Christopher. 2016a. "Gallup: Support for Marijuana Legalization Surges to New Highs." *Washington Post*, October 19. https://www.washingtonpost.com/news/wonk/wp/2016/10/19/gallup-support-for-marijuana-legalization-surges-to-new-highs/?utm_term=.2df8b90be6cf.

———. 2016b. "Heroin Deaths Surpass Gun Homicides for the First Time, CDC Data Shows." Washington Post, December 8. https://www.washingtonpost.com/news/wonk/wp/2016/12/08/heroin-deaths-surpass-gun-homicides-for-the-first-time-cdc-data-show/?utm_term=.04271c3a1dd6.

Institute for Women's Policy Research. 2016. "The Gender Wage Gap by Occupation and by Race and Ethnicity 2015" (https://iwpr.org/wp-content/uploads/wpallimport/files/iwpr-export/publications/C440.pdf).

Internal Revenue Service (IRS) 2016a. *2012 Statistics of Income – Corporation Income Tax Returns*. Washington, DC: IRS (https://www.irs.gov/pub/irs-soi/12coccr.pdf).

———. 2016b. "State and Local Governments with Earned Income Tax Credit (https://www.irs.gov/credits-deductions/individuals/earned-income-tax-credit/states-and-local-governments-with-earned-income-tax-credit).

———. 2017. "Earned Income Tax Credit" (https://www.irs.gov/credits deductions/individuals/earned-income-tax-credit).

International Criminal Court (ICC). 2014. "Jurisdiction and Admissibility." http://www.icc-cpi.int/en_menus/icc/about%20the%20court/icc%20at%20a%20glance/Pages/jurisdiction%20and%20admissibility.aspx.

———. 2017. "International World Court." https://www.icc-cpi.int/about?ln=en.

International Energy Agency. 2017. Key World Energy Statistics. https://www.iea.org/publications/freepublications/publication/KeyWorld2017.pdf.

Internet Movie Database. 2014. *The Battle of Algiers* www.imdb.com/title/tt0058946/quotes.

Internet World Stats. 2017a. "Internet Usage Statistics." March 25. http://www.internetworldstats.com/stats.htm

———. 2017b. "Internet Users in the World by Regions – June 30, 2017." http://www.internetworldstats.com/stats.htm.

Inter-Parliamentary Union. 2017. "Women in National Parliaments" (www.ipu.org/wmn-e/classif.htm).

Isaacs, Julia B., Isabel V. Sawhill, and Ron Haskins, 2008. Getting Ahead or Losing Ground: Economic Mobility in America. Washington, DC: The Bookings Institution (http://www.brookings.edu/research/getting-ahead-or-losing-ground-economic-mobility-in-america).

Jackson, D. Amari. 2017. "Can Anyone Hear My Plea? Race, Criminal Justice and the 97 Percent Who Never Got Their Day in Court." *Atlanta Black Star*, February 18 (http://atlantablackstar.com/2017/02/18/can-anyone-hear-plea-race-criminal-justice-97-never-got-day-court/).

Jacobs, David, Zhenchao Qian, Jason T. Carmichael, and Stephanie L. Kent. 2007. "Who Survives on Death Row: An Individual and Contextual Analysis." *American Sociological Review* 72(4):610–632.

James, Brian. 2016. "What Is Divorce Mediation?" *Mediate.* (www.mediate.com/articles/jamesB1.cfm).

Jefferson, Thomas. 1776[2007]. *Declaration of Independence.* London: Verso.

Jenkins, J. Craig. 1983. "Resource Mobilization Theory and the Study of Social Movements." *Annual Review of Sociology* 9(August):527–553.

Jewkes, Rachel. 2002. "Intimate Partner Violence: Causes and Prevention." *Lancet* 359(9315):1423–1429. (www.sciencedirect.com/science/article/pii/S0140673602083575).

Johnston, Angus. 2014. "American Student Protest Timeline 2014–2015." https://studentactivism.net/2014/12/04/american-student-protest-timeline-2014–15/.

Johnston, David. 1992. "Bush Pardons 6 in Iran Affair, Aborting a Weinberger Trial; Prosecutor Assails 'Cover Up.'" *New York Times*, December 25. http://www.nytimes.com/books/97/06/29/reviews/iran-pardon.html

Jones, Jeffrey M. 2013. "Same-Sex Marriage Support Solidifies Above 50% in U.S." *Gallup*, May 13. (www.gallup.com/poll/162398/sex-marriage-support-solidifies-above.aspx).

Kaiser Family Foundation. 2012. Massachusetts Health Care Reform: Six Years Later. https://kaiserfamilyfoundation.files.wordpress.com/2013/01/8311.pdf.

———. 2017. "Distribution of Physicians by Gender." http://kff.org/other/state-indicator/physicians-by-gender/?currentTimeframe=0&sortModel=%7B%22colId%22:%22Location%22,%22sort%22:%22asc%22%7D.

Kalmijn, Matthijs. 2015. "How Childhood Circumstances Moderate the Long-Term Impact of Divorce on Father-Child Relationships." *Journal of Marriage and the Family* 77(4):921–938.

Kaplan, Eben. 2005. Child Soldiers around the World." *Council on Foreign Relations*, December 2. www.cfr.org/human-rights/child-soldiers-around-world/p9331#p7.

Kaplan, George A., Elsie R. Pamuk, John W. Lynch, Richard D. Cohen, and Jennifer L. Balfour. 1996. "Income in Inequality and Mortality in the United States: Analysis of Mortality and Potential Pathways." *British Medical Journal* 312(April):999–1003.

Kaplan, Larry. 2017. "States' Approach to Sanctuary Cities Hits Nonprofits Serving Undocumented Populations." Nonprofit Quarterly, May 15 (https://nonprofitquarterly.org/2017/05/15/states-approach-sanctuary-cities-hits-nonprofits-serving-undocumented-populations/).

Kassam, Ashifa, Rosie Scammell, Kate Connolly, Richard Orange, Kim Willsher, and Rebecca Ratcliffe. 2015. "Europe Needs Many More Babies to Avert a Population Disaster." *Guardian* August 22 https://www.theguardian.com/world/2015/aug/23/baby-crisis-europe-brink-depopulation-disaster.

Katz, Cheryl and Environmental Health News. 2012. "People in Poor Neighborhoods Breathe More Hazardous Particles." Scientific American, November 1. www.scientificamerican.com/article/people-poor-neighborhoods-breate-more-hazardous-particles/.

Katz, Mark N. 1997. *Revolutions and Revolutionary Waves.* New York: St. Martin's Press.

Kaup, Brent Z. 2010. "A Neoliberal Nationalization? The Constraints on Natural-Gas-Led Development in Bolivia." *Latin American Perspectives* 37(3):123–138.

Kearney, Melissa S. and Phillip B. Levine. 2014. " Teen Births Are Falling: What's Going On?" Brookings Institute Policy Brief (March) (www.brookings.edu/~/media/research/files/reports/2014/03/teen%20births%20falling%20whats%20going%20on%20kearney%20levine/teen_births_falling_whats_going_on_kearney_levine.pdf).

Keating, 2016. "How Sick Are the Kids in Flint? Inside the Shocking Health Effects of the Devastating Water Crisis." People, January 28. www.people.com/article/outcome-lead-poisoning-flint-michigan-water-crisis.

Keaton, Susan. 2013. "Women Now 1 of 4 UMC clergy in U.S." UMC Connections, December 4 (http://umcconnections.org/2013/12/04/women-now-1-4-umc-clergy-u-s/).

Kellermann, Arthur L. and Frederick P. Rivara. 2013. "Silencing the Science on Gun Research." *Journal of the American Medical Association* 309(6):549–550. http://jama.jamanetwork.com/article.aspx?articleid=1487470.

Kelly, Heather. 2012. "Police Embrace Social Media as Crime-Fighting Tool." CNN, August 30. www.cnn.com/2012/08/30/tech/social-media/fighting-crime-social-media/index.html.

Kennedy, Sheela and Steven Ruggles. 2014. "Breaking Up Is Hard to Count: The Rise of Divorce in the United States, 1980–2010." *Demography* 51(2):587–598.

Kewalramani, Devika and Richard J. Sobelsohn. 2012. "'Greenwashing': Deceptive Business Claims of 'Eco-Friendliness.'" *Forbes*, March 20. www.forbes.com/sites/realspin/2012/03/20/greenwashing-deceptive-business-claims-of-eco-friendliness/.

Kidder, Jeffrey L. 2005. "Style and Action: A Decoding of Bike Messenger Symbols." *Journal of Contemporary Ethnography* 34(2):344–367.

Kids Count Data Center. 2014. "Children in Single-Parent Families by Race." http://datacenter.kidscount.org/data/tables/107-children-in-single-parent-families-by-race?loc=1#detailed/1/any/false/868,867,133,38,35/10,168,9,12,1,13,185/432,431

Kim, Daniel. 2014. "Prostitution/Sex Industry in South Korea." Daily Opinion International, January 31. www.dailyopinioninternational.com/2014/01/prostitutionsex-industry-in-south-korea.html.

Kimmel, Michael S. 2008. *Guyland*. New York: Harper Collins.

Kincaid, Ellie. 2015. "California Isn't the Only State with Water Problems." Business Insider, April 21. www.businessinsider.com/americas-about-to-hit-a-water-crisis-2015–4.

King, Donna. 2017 "How Truckers, Hotel Workers Can Fight Human Trafficking." North State Journal, April 17. http://nsjonline.com/article/2017/04/how-truckers-hotel-workers-can-fight-sex-trafficking/.

Kipling, Rudyard. 1899. "The White Man's Burden" (http://historymatters.gmu.edu/d/5478/).

Kirkwood, Thomas. 2010. "Why Women Live Longer." Scientific American, October 1. www.scientificamerican.com/article/why-women-live-longer/.

Kite, M. E. and Whitley, Jr., B. E. 1996. "Sex Differences in Attitudes toward Homosexual Persons, Behaviors and Civil Rights: A Meta-Analysis." *Personality and Social Psychology Bulletin* 22(4):336–352.

Klein, Joel. 2014a. *Lessons of Hope*. New York: Harper Collins.

Klein, Rebecca. 2014b. "New York Students Inch Upward on Common Core Tests, but Most Are Still Failing." *Huffington Post*, August 14. www.huffingtonpost.com/2014/08/14/new-york-common-core-scores-2014_n_5679545.html.

Kleniewski, Nancy and Alexander R. Thomas. 2011. *Cities, Change & Conflict*. Belmont, CA: Wadsworth.

Kopczuk, Wojciech, Emmanuel Saez and Jae Song. 2010. "Earnings Inequality and Mobility in the United States: Evidence from Social Security Data since 1937." *Quarterly Journal of Economics* 125(1):91–128.

Koppan, Tal. 2017. "Trump Ends DACA but Gives Congress Window to Save It." CNN, September 5 (http://www.cnn.com/2017/09/05/politics/daca-trump-congress/index.html).

Kost, Kathryn and Stanley Henshaw. 2014. "U.S. Teenage Pregnancies, Births and Abortions, 2010: National and State Trends by Age, Race and Ethnicity." Guttmacher Institute (May) (www.guttmacher.org/pubs/USTPtrens10.pdf).

Kozol, Jonathan. 1991. *Savage Inequalities: Children in America's Schools*. New York: Crown Publishers.

———. 2005. *The Shame of the Nation: The Restoration of Apartheid Schooling in America*. New York: Three Rivers Press.

———. 2012. *Savage Inequalities*. New York: Broadway Books.

———. 2013. *Fire in the Ashes: Twenty-Five Years among the Poorest Children in America*. New York: Broadway Books.

Krauss, Clifford. 2014. "Big Victory for Chevron Over Claims in Ecuador." New York Times, March 4. www.nytimes.com/2014/03/05/business/federal-judge-rules-for-chevron-in-ecuadorean-pollution-case.html?_r=0.

Krauze, Enrique. 2014. "Mexico's Barbarous Tragedy." New York Times, November 10 www.nytimes.com/2014/11/10/opinion/enrique-krauze-mexicos-barbarous-tragedy.html?_r=0.

Krehely, Jeff. 2011. "Polls Show Huge Public Support for Gay and Transgender Workplace Protections." *Center for American Progress*, June 2 (www.americanprogress.org/issues/lgbt/news/2011/06/02/9716/polls-show-huge-public-support-for-gay-and-transgender-work-place-protections/).

Krogstad, Jens Manuel, Jeffrey S. Passel, and D'Vera Cohn. 2017. "5 Facts about Illegal Immigration in the U.S." Pew Research Center, April 27 (http://www.pewresearch.org/fact-tank/2017/04/27/5-facts-about-illegal-immigration-in-the-u-s/).

Krueger, Alan B. 2012. "The Rise and Consequences of Inequality in the United States." Chairman, Council of Economic Advisors. White House, January 12 (http://www.whitehouse.gov/sites/default/files/krueger_cap_speech_final_remarks.pdf).

Krugman, Paul. 2012. "The Great Gatsby's Curve." New York Times, January 15 (http://krugman.blogs.nytimes.com/2012/01/15/the-great-gatsby-curve/).

Kucharski, Adam. 2015. "Will the Earth Ever Fill Up? We've Predicted and Broken Population Limits for Centuries." *Nautilus*, October 1. http://nautil.us/issue/29/scaling/will-the-earth-ever-fill-up.

Kusnetz, Nicholas. 2015. "State Integrity 2015: Only Three States Score Higher than D+ in State Integrity Investigation; 11 Flunk." Center for Public Integrity (https://www.publicintegrity.org/2015/11/09/18693/only-three-states-score-higher-d-state-integrity-investigation-11-flunk).

Lahrichi, Kamilia. 2015. "How Tobacco Companies Are Aggressively Pushing into the Middle East." Your Middle East, April 15 www.yourmiddleeast.com/culture/how-tobacco-companies-are-aggressively-pushing-into-the-middle-east_31454.

LaMar L. and Kite, M. 1998. "Sex Differences in Attitudes toward Gay Men and Lesbians: A Multidimensional Perspective. *Journal of Sex Research* 35(2):189–196.

Lamothe, Dan. 2015. "In Historic Decision, Pentagon Chief Opens All Jobs in Combat Units to Women." Washington Post, December 3 (www.washingtonpost.com/news/checkpoint/wp/2015/12/03/pentagon-chief-to-announce-how-womens-roles-in-the-military-will-expand/).

Landau, Elizabeth. 2009. "Study: Average Preemie Cost $49,000 in First Year." CNN, March 17. www.cnn.com/2009/HEALTH/03/17/premature.babies/index.html

Långström, Niklas., Qazi Rahman, Eva Carlström, and Paul Lichtenstein. 2010. "Genetic and Environmental Effects on Same-Sex Sexual Behavior: A Population Study of Twins in Sweden." *Archives of Sexual Behavior* 39(1):75–80.

Langton, Lynn, Marcus Berzofsky, Christopher Krebs, and Hope Smiley-McDonald. 2012. "Victimizations Not Reported to the Police, 2006–2010." U.S. Department of Justice. National Crime Victimization Survey, Special

Report (August). http://www.bjs.gov/content/pub/pdf/vnrp0610.pdf.

LaPook, Jonathan, 2016. "Doctors Explain the Long-Term Health Effects of Flint Water Crisis." CBS News, January 19. www.cbsnews.com/news/doctors-explain-the-long-term-health-effects-of-flint-water-crisis/.

———. 2017. "March for Science Global Rally Takes Aim at Trump, Environmental Cuts." CBS News, April 22 (http://www.cbsnews.com/news/march-for-science-earth-day-2017-rallies-protesters-environment/).

Lavy, Victor and Edith Sand. 2015. "On the Origins of Gender Human Capital Gaps: Short and Long Term Consequences of Teachers' Stereotypical Biases." National Bureau of Economic Research, Working Paper Number 20909 (January) (www.nber.org/papers/w20909).

Lee, Valerie E. and Susanna Loeb. 1995. "Where Do Head Start Attendees End Up? One Reason Why Preschool Effects Fade Out." *Educational Evaluation and Policy Analysis* 17(1):62–82.

Lees, Kathleen. 2014. "Environmental Injustice: Pollution Higher in Poor, Minority Communities." Science World Report, April 17. www.scienceworldreport.com/articles/14064/20140417/environmental-injustice-pollution-often-segregated-to-poor-minority-communities.htm.

Legal Dictionary. 2018. "War Crimes." https://legal-dictionary.thefreedictionary.com/War+Crimes.

Legal Information Institute. 2010. "Citizens United v. the Federal Election Commission (No. 08 – 205)" (www.law.cornell.edu/supct/html/08–205.ZS.html).

Leighley, Jan E. and Jonathan Nagler. 2006. "Unions, Voter Turnout, and Class Bias in the U. S. Electorate, 1964–2004" (www.nyu.edu/gsas/dept/politics/faculty/nagler/leighley_nagler_unions06.pdf).

Lemert, Edwin M. 1951. *Social Pathology.* New York: McGraw-Hill.

Lengermann, Patricia Madoo and Gillian Niebrugge. 2007. *The Women Founders: Sociology and Social Theory, 1830–1930.* Long Grove, IL: Waveland Press.

Leukhardt, Bill and Edmund Mahony. 2001. "Unmasked: The Depravity Within." *Hartford Courant, December* 16, p. A1, pp. A18–A24.

Leung, Rebecca. 2004. "Abuse of Iraqi POWs by GIs Probed." CBS 60 Minutes. www.cbsnews.com/news/abuse-of-iraqi-pows-by-gis-probed/.

Levin, Dan. 2014. "Many in China Can Now Have a Second Child, but Say No." New York Times, February 25. www.nytimes.com/2014/02/26/world/asia/many-couples-in-china-will-pass-on-a-new-chance-for-a-second-child.html.

———. 2015. "Study Links Polluted Air in China to 1.6 Million Deaths a Year." *New York Times,* August 13. www.nytimes.com/2015/08/14/world/asia/study-links-polluted-air-in-china-to-1–6-million-deaths-a-year.html?_r=0.

Levitt, Steven D. 2004. "Understanding Why Crime Fell in the 1990s: Four Factors that Explain the Decline and Six that Do Not." *Journal of Economic Perspectives* 18(1):163–190.

Levy, Gabrielle. 2015. "How Citizens United Has Changed Politics in 5 Years." U.S. News, January 21. www.usnews.com/news/articles/2015/01/21/5-years-later-citizens-united-has-remade-us-politics?page=2.

Lewis, Jamie M. and Rose M. Kreider. 2015. "Remarriage in the United States." (www.census.gov/content/dam/Census/library/publications/2015/acs/acs-30.pdf).

Lewis, Kristen and Sarah Burd-Sharps. 2013–2014. Measure of America of the Social Science Research Council. www.measureofamerica.org/wp-content/uploads/2013/06/MOA-III.pdf.

Lewis, Oscar. 1966. "The Culture of Poverty." *Scientific American* 215(4):19–25.

Library of Congress. 2017. "The Indian Removal Act" (https://www.loc.gov/rr/program/bib/ourdocs/Indian.html).

Lindenmeyer, Kristie. 2008. "Teen Pregnancy." *Encyclopedia of Children and Childhood in History and Society.* (www.faqs.org/childhood/So-Th/Teen-Pregnancy.html).

Lipset, Seymour Martin. 1981. *Political Man.* Baltimore, MD: John Hopkins University Press.

Lister, Tim. 2014. "ISIS: The First Terror Group to Build an Islamic State?" June 12. www.cnn.com/2014/06/12/world/meast/who-is-the-isis/index.html.

Live Science. 2017. "Global Warming: News, Facts, Causes & Effects." http://www.livescience.com/topics/global-warming.

Living Wage Calculator. 2016. Massachusetts Institute of Technology (http://livingwage.mit.edu/).

Llobrera, Joseph and Bob Zahradnik. 2004. "A Hand Up." Center on Budget and Policy Priorities (www.cbpp.org/cms/?fa=view&id=277).

LoBianco, Tom. 2015. "Obama to Tout Community College Plan in Indiana." *Indianapolis Star,* February 5 (www.usatoday.com/story/news/politics/2015/02/05/obama-to-tout-community-college-plan-in-indiana/22945231/).

Lohr, Kathy. 2008. "Poor People's Campaign: A Dream Unfulfilled." NPR, June 19. http://www.npr.org/templates/story/story.php?storyId=91626373.

Lorenz, Frederick O., K. A. S. Wickrama, Rand D. Conger, and Glen H. Elder. 2006. "The Short-Term and Decade-Long Effects of Divorce on Women's Midlife Health." *Journal of Health and Social Behavior* 47(2):111–125.

Los Angeles Times. 2017. "Annotated Transcript: President Trump's Address to a Joint Session of Congress." March 2.

Lubin, Gus. 2016. "The 25 Hottest TV Shows in the World Right Now." *Business Insider,* December 2. http://www.businessinsider.com/hottest-tv-shows-around-the-world-right-now-2016–12.

Lynskey, Dorian. 2011. *33 Revolutions per Minute: A History of Protest Songs, from Billie Holiday to Green Day.* New York: Ecco.

Macartney, Suzanne. 2011. "Child Poverty in the United States 2009 and 2010: Selected Race Groups and Hispanic Origin." American Community Survey Briefs, November. www.census.gov/prod/2011pubs/acsbr10-05.pdf.

MacDorman, Marian F. and T. J. Mathews. 2011. "Understanding Racial and Ethnic Disparities in U.S. Infant Mortality Rates." *NCHS Data Brief,* No. 74, September 2011. CDC. www.cdc.gov/nchs/data/databriefs/db74.pdf.

Madland, David and Nick Bunker. 2012. "Unions Boost Economic Mobility in U.S. Sates." Center for American Progress Action Fund, September 20 (http://www.americanprogressaction.org/wp-content/uploads/2012/09/MadlandBunkerUnions-2.pdf).

Magnet Schools. 2014. "What are Magnet Schools?" www.magnet.edu/about/what-are-magnet-schools.

Malala Fund. 2014. "Malala Yousafzai." www.malala.org/malalas-story/.

Malik, Sana. 2009. "Through the Smoke: Tobacco Use in the Middle East" Institute for Social Policy and Understanding, April 1. cehs.unl.edu/edpsych/npcada/tobacco-use-middle-east.

Mangahas, Mahar. 2013. "Stubborn Poverty in the U.S., Too." Philippine Daily Inquirer, September 20 (http://opinion.inquirer.net/61555/stubborn-poverty-in-the-us-too).

Mangino, Matthew T. 2014. "How Plea Bargains Are Making Jury Trials Obsolete." *Crime Report*, January 4 (https://thecrimereport.org/2014/01/07/2014-01-how-plea-bargains-are-making-jury-trials-obsolete/).

Maps of the World. 2015. "Matriarchies around the World." (www.mapsofworld.com/around-the-world/matriarchy.html).

Martin, Claire, 2014. "Out of Tragedy, a Protective Glass for Schools." New York Times, December 27. www.nytimes.com/ … /out-of-tragedy-a-protective-glass-for-schools.html.

Martin, Joyce A., Brady E. Hamilton, Stephanie J. Ventura, Michelle J. K. Osterman, and T. J. Mathews. 2013. "Births: Final Data for 2011."National Vital Statistics Reports 62(1):1–70. (www.cdc.gov/nchs/data/nvsr/nvsr62/nvsr62_01.pdf).

Martinez, Luis and Benjamin Siegel. 2014. "Afghan Opium Trade Thriving despite – or with Help of – US $7 Billion Effort." ABC News, October 21. http://abcnews.go.com/Politics/afghan-opium-trade-thriving-us-billion-effort/story?id=26351064.

Martinez, Michael and Alexandra Meeks. 2015. "Feds Fight 'Maternity Tourism' with Raids on California 'Maternity Hotels'" CNN, March 4 (http://www.cnn.com/2015/03/03/us/maternity-tourism-raids-california/index.html).

Marx, Karl. 1867. *Das Kapital*. Miami, FL: Synergy International of the Americas, 2007.

———. 1875 (1994). "Critique of the Gotha Program." Pp. 315–332 in *Karl Marx: Selected Writings*, edited by Lawrence H. Simon. Indianapolis, IN: Hackett Publishing.

Marx, Karl and Frederick Engels. 1848. The Communist Manifesto, 1888 English ed. (http://www.gutenberg.org/files/61/61.txt).

Marx, Karl and Friedrich Engels. 1848 (1998). *The Communist Manifesto*. New York: Signet Classics.

Mason, Margie, Robin McDowell, Martha Mendoza, and Esther Htusan. 2015. "Global Supermarkets Selling Shrimp Peeled by Slaves." Associated Press, December 14 (https://www.ap.org/explore/seafood-from-slaves/global-supermarkets-selling-shrimp-peeled-by-slaves.html).

Massey, Douglas S. and Nancy A. Denton. 1988. "Suburbanization and Segregation in U.S. Metropolitan Areas." *American Journal of Sociology* 94(3):592–626.

———. 1989. "Hypersegregation in U.S. Metropolitan Areas: Black and Hispanic Segregation along Five Dimensions." *Demography* 26(3):373–391.

———. 1998. *American Apartheid: Segregation and the Making of the Underclass*. Cambridge, MA: Harvard University Press.

Matza, Michael. 2017. "Your Immigrant Ancestors Came Here Legally? Are You Sure?" Philadelphia Inquirer, June 25 (http://www.philly.com/philly/news/breaking/your-immigrant-ancestors-came-here-legally-are-you-sure-20170625.html).

Mauss, Armand L. 1975. *Social Problems as Social Movements*. Philadelphia, PA: J. B. Lippincott.

Mayor, Adrienne. 2014. *Amazons: Lives and Legends of Warrior Women across the Ancient World*. Princeton, NJ: Princeton University Press.

Mazzetti, Mark, Sabrina Tavernise, and Jack Healy. 2010. "Suspect, Charged, Said to Admit to Role in Plot." New York Times, May 4. www.nytimes.com/2010/05/05/nyregion/05bomb.html.

McAdam, Doug, John D. McCarthy and Mayer N. Zald, eds. 1996. *Comparative Perspectives on Social Movements: Political Opportunities, Mobilizing Structures, and Cultural Framings*. Cambridge: Cambridge University Press.

McAdam, Doug. 1982. *Political Process and the Development of Black Insurgency, 1930–1970*. Chicago: The University of Chicago Press.

———. 1986. Recruitment to High Risk Activism: The Case of Freedom Summer. *American Journal of Sociology* 92(1):64–90.

———. 1997. "Tactical Innovation and the Pace of Insurgency." Pp. 340–356 in *Social Movements: Readings on Their Emergence, Mobilization, and Dynamics*, edited by Doug McAdam and David A. Snow. Los Angeles, CA: Roxbury Publishing.

McCabe, Kimberly A. 2013. "Common Forms: Sex Trafficking." Pp. 133–148 in *Human Trafficking*, edited by Mary C. Burke. New York: Routledge.

McCarthy, Justin. 2014a. "Americans' Views on Origins of Homosexuality Remain Split." Gallup, May 28 (www.gallup.com/poll/170753/americans-views-origins-homosexuality-remain-split.aspx).

———. 2014b. "In U.S., Adult Obesity Rate Now at 27.7%." Gallup, May 22. http://www.gallup.com/poll/170264/adult-obesity-rate.aspx.

McDonald, Michael. 2018. "Voter Turnout Demographics." United States Election Project, University of Florida. (http://www.electproject.org/home/voter-turnout/demographics).

McKirdy, Euan. 2017. "Tens of Thousands Protest Jailing of Hong Kong Pro-Democracy Leaders." CNN. August 21. http://www.cnn.com/2017/08/20/asia/hong-kong-protests-joshua-wong/index.html.

McShane, Larry. 2016. "Roger Ailes Resigns as Fox News Chairman amid Sexual Harassment Allegations, Rupert Murdoch to Take the Reins." New York Daily News, July 21 (http://www.nydailynews.com/new-york/roger-ailes-kicked-fox-news-headquarters-office-article-1.2720469).

Mediacollege.com. 2015. "What Makes a Story Newsworthy?" www.mediacollege.com/journalism/news/newsworthy.html.

Medicare.gov. 2017. "What Is Medicare?" https://www.medicare.gov/sign-up-change-plans/decide-how-to-get-medicare/whats-medicare/what-is-medicare.html.

Medina, Jennifer. 2010. "Standards Raised, More Students Fail Tests." New York Times, July 28. www.nytimes.com/2010/07/29/education/29scores.html?pagewanted=all&_r=0.

Medline Plus. 2015. "Poisoning. Toxicology, Environmental Health." www.nlm.nih.gov/medlineplus/poisoningtoxicologyenvironmentalhealth.html.

MEDTV. 2015. "Obesity and Heart Disease." http://heart-disease.emedtv.com/heart-disease/obesity-and-heart-disease.html.

Megerian, Chris, Matt Stevens, and Bettina Boxall. 2015. "Brown Orders California's First Mandatory Water Restrictions: 'It's a Different World.'" Los Angeles Times, April 1. www.latimes.com/local/lanow/la-me-ln-snowpack-20150331-story.html#page=1.

Melber, Ari. 2013. "Why Is There No Punishment for Racial Profiling?" MSNBC, July 30 (http://www.msnbc.com/msnbc/presumed-guilty-why-there-no-punishment).

Mendes, Elizabeth. 2011. "Smoking Rates Remain Highest in Kentucky, Lowest In Utah." Gallup, November 17. www.gallup.com/poll/150779/Smoking-Rates-Remain-Highest-Kentucky-Lowest-Utah.aspx#1.

Merton, Robert K. 1957. *Social Theory and Social Structure*. New York: The Free Press.

———. 1968. *Social Theory and Social Structure*. New York: Free Press.

Meyer, David S. 2004. "Protest and Political Opportunities." *Annual Review of Sociology* 30:125–145.

Middleages.net. 2011. "*The Black Death: Bubonic Plague*." www.themiddleages.net/plague.html.

Migration Policy Institute. 2017. "Legal Immigration to the United States, 1820–Present." www.migrationpolicy.org/programs/data-hub/charts/Annual-Number-of-US-Legal-Permanent-Residents.

Miles, Kathryn. 2013. "Eco-Feminism." Encyclopaedia Brtainnica. www.britannica.com/topic/ecofeminism.

Military Order of the Purple Heart, Department of Pennsylvania. 2009. "United States Casualties of War." www.mophdepartmentpa.org/United%20States%20Casualties%20of%20War.pdf.

Millar, James R. 1999. "The De-development of Russia." *Current History* 98(October):322–327.

———. 2000. "Can Putin Jump-Start Russia's Stalled Economy?" *Current History* 99(October):329–333.

Miller, T. Christian. 2006. *Blood Money*. New York: Little, Brown, and Company.

Miller, Brandon. 2017. "2016 Was the Hottest Year on Record – Again." CNN, January 18. http://www.cnn.com/2017/01/18/world/2016-hottest-year/index.html.

Mills, C. Wright. 1959. *The Sociological Imagination*. New York: Oxford University Press.

———. 1967. *The Power Elite*. New York: Oxford University Press.

Milwaukee Homicide Review Commission. 2012. "2011 Homicides and Nonfatal Shootings Data Report for Milwaukee, WI." http://city.milwaukee.gov/ImageLibrary/Groups/cityHRC/reports/2011Reportv6.pdf.

Minimum-wage.org. 2018. "Federal Minimum Wage for 2017, 2018" (https://www.minimum-wage.org/federal).

Mishel, Lawrence and Jessica Schieder. 2017. "CEO Pay Remains High Relative to the Pay of Typical Workers and High-Wage Earners." Economic Policy Institute, July 20 (https://www.epi.org/publication/ceo-pay-remains-high-relative-to-the-pay-of-typical-workers-and-high-wage-earners/).

Mississippi Legislature. 2011. "House Bill No. 999." (http://billstatus.ls.state.ms.us/documents/2011/pdf/HB/0900-0999/HB0999SG.pdf).

Mitchell, George. 2001. *Making Peace*. Berkeley, CA: University of California Press.

Moller, Stephanie, David Bradley, Evelune Huber, Francois Nielson, and John D. Stephens. 2003. "Determinants of Relative Poverty in Advanced Capitalist Democracies." *American Sociological Review* 68(1):22–25.

Montague, Peter. 2012. "Why the Environmental Movement Is Not Winning." *Alternet*, February 24. www.alternet.org/story/154290/why_the_environmental_movement_is_not_winning.

Mora, Camilo, Derek P. Tettensor, Sina Adl, Alastair G. B. Simpson, and Boris Worm. 2011. "How Many Species Are There on the Earth and in the Ocean?" *PLoS Biology* 9(8):1–8 (https://journals.plos.org/plosbiology/article?id=10.1371/journal.pbio.1001127).

Morcroft, Greg. 2013. "Global Income Inequality: The Story in Charts." International Business Times, December 24. www.ibtimes.com/global-income-inequality-story-charts-1519376.

Morgan, David L. 1996. *Focus Groups as Qualitative Research*. Thousand Oaks, CA: Sage Publications.

Morris, Aldon. 1986. *Origins of the Civil Rights Movement: Black Communities Organizing for Change*. New York: Free Press.

Morton, Robert J. and Mark A. Hilts. 2005. "Serial Murder." Federal Bureau of Investigation (https://www.fbi.gov/stats-services/publications/serial-murder/serial-murder-1).

Moss-Racusin, Corinne A., John F. Dovidio, Victoria L. Brescoll, Mark J. Graham, and Jo Handelsman. 2012. "Science Faculty's Subtle Gender Biases Favor Male Students." *Proceedings of the National Academy of Science* 109(41):16,474–16,479.

Mother Nature Network. 2015. "America's 10 Worst Man-Made Environmental Disasters: Love Canal." www.mnn.com/earth-matters/wilderness-resources/photos/americas-10-worst-man-made-environmental-disasters/love.

Moveon.org. 2017. "*Abolish the Electoral College*." (http://petitions.moveon.org/sign/abolish-the-electoral-6).

Nadeau, Carey and Amy K. Glasmeier. 2016. "Minimum Wage: Can an Individual or Family Survive on It?" *Living Wage Calculator*, January 16 (http://livingwage.mit.edu/articles/15-minimum-wage-can-an-individual-or-a-family-live-on-it).

Nader, Ralph. 2013. "21 Ways the Canadian Health Care System Is Better than Obamacare." *Counterpunch*, November 22 (https://www.counterpunch.org/2013/11/22/21-ways-the-canadian-health-care-system-is-better-than-obamacare/).

Names Project Foundation. 2016. "The AIDS Memorial Quilt: History of the Quilt" (http://www.aidsquilt.org/about/the-aids-memorial-quilt).

Nance, Malcolm. 2016. *Defeating ISIS: Who They Are, How They Fight, What They Believe*. New York: Skyhorse Publishing.

Nance, Malcolm. 2016. *The Plot to Hack America*. New York: Skyhorse Publishing.

National Alliance to End Homelessness. 2016. "State of Homelessness in America 2016" (http://www.endhomelessness.org/library/entry/SOH2016).

National Archives. 2016. "Teaching with Documents – Photographs of Lewis Hine: Documentation of Child Labor." (https://www.archives.gov/education/lessons/hine-photos).

National Cancer Institute. 2012. "Obesity and Cancer Risk." www.cancer.gov/about-cancer/causes-prevention/risk/obesity/obesity-fact-sheet.

National Center for Education Statistics (NCES). 2015a. "Bachelor's, Master's, and Student and Discipline Division: 2012–13" (http://nces.ed.gov/programs/digest/d14/tables/dt14_318.30.asp).

———. 2015b. *Indicators of School Crime and Safety: 2014.* http://nces.ed.gov/pubs2015/2015072.pdf.

———. 2016a. "Educational Institutions." https://nces.ed.gov/fastfacts/display.asp?id=84.

———. 2016b. "The School Drop Out Rate." http://nces.ed.gov/programs/coe/indicator_coj.asp.

———. 2016c. "Incidence of Victimization at School and Away from School." https://nces.ed.gov/programs/crimeindicators/ind_02.asp.

———. 2016d. "Violent Deaths at School and Away from School." https://nces.ed.gov/programs/crimeindicators/ind_01.asp.

———. 2016e. "Percentage of High School Dropouts among Persons 16 to 24 Years Old (Status Dropout Rate), by Income Level, and Percentage Distribution of Status Dropouts, by Labor Force Status and Years of School Completed: 1970 through 2015" (https://nces.ed.gov/programs/digest/d16/tables/dt16_219.75.asp).

———. 2017a. "Number and Enrollment of Public Elementary and Secondary Schools, by School Level, Type and Charter and Magnet Status: Selected Years, 1990–91 through 2015–16 (https://nces.ed.gov/programs/digest/d17/tables/dt17_216.20.asp).

———. 2017b. "The Condition of Education: Public High School Graduation Rates" (https://nces.ed.gov/programs/coe/indicator_coi.asp).

National Center for Health Statistics. 2014. *Health, United States, 2013: With Special Feature on Prescription Drugs.* Hyattsville, MD: National Center for Health Statistics (https://www.ncbi.nlm.nih.gov/pubmed/24967476).

National Conference of State Legislatures (NCSL). 2015a. "Obesity Statistics in the United States." www.ncsl.org/research/health/obesity-statistics-in-the-united-states.aspx

———. 2015b. "Health Insurance: Premiums and Increases." www.ncsl.org/research/health/health-insurance-premiums.aspx#Exchange_premiums.

———. 2017a. "Health Insurance: Premiums and Increases." http://www.ncsl.org/research/health/health-insurance-premiums.aspx.

———. 2017b. "Human Trafficking State Laws." http://www.ncsl.org/research/civil-and-criminal-justice/human-trafficking-laws.aspx.

———. 2017c. "School Vouchers." www.ncsl.org/research/education/school-choice-vouchers.aspx.

———. 2018. "State Minimum Wage Legislation" April 14 (http://www.ncsl.org/research/labor-and-employment/state-minimum-wage-chart.aspx).

National Council on Alcoholism and Drug Dependence. 2017. "Alcohol, Drugs and Crime." http://ncadd.org/index.php/for-youth/drugs-and-crime/230-alcohol-drugs-and-crime.

National Counterterrorism Center (NCTC). 2017. "NCTC: Who We Are." https://www.dni.gov/index.php/nctc-who-we-are.

National Education Administration. 2015. "Safe Schools for Everyone: Gay, Lesbian, Bisexual, and Transgender Students" (www.nea.org/tools/30420.htm).

National Geographic. 2017a. "Causes of Global Warming?" http://www.nationalgeographic.com/environment/global-warming/global-warming-causes/.

———. 2017b. "Geothermal Energy." http://www.nationalgeographic.com/environment/global-warming/geothermal-energy/.

National Heart, Lung, and Blood Institute. 2017. "Body Mass Index Table 1." https://www.nhlbi.nih.gov/health/educational/lose_wt/BMI/bmi_tbl.htm.

National Institute of Justice. 2009. "The National Elder Mistreatment Study." (www.ncjrs.gov/pdffiles1/nij/grants/226456.pdf).

———. 2010a. "The Prevalence of Elder Abuse." (www.nij.gov/journals/265/Pages/elder-abuse-prevalence.aspx).

———. 2010b. "Reporting of Sexual Violence Incidents." https://www.nij.gov/topics/crime/rape-sexual-violence/Pages/rape-notification.aspx.

———. 2018. "Racial Profiling" (https://nij.gov/topics/law-enforcement/legitimacy/pages/racial-profiling.aspx).

National Institute on Alcohol Abuse and Alcoholism. 2015. "College Drinking." http://niaaa.nih.gov/alcohol-health/special-populations-co-occurring-disorders/college-drinking.

National Institute on Drug Abuse. 2012. "Inhalants: Letter from the Director." https://www.drugabuse.gov/publications/research-reports/inhalants/letter-director.

———. 2014. "Drugs, Brains, and Behavior: The Science of Addiction." https://www.drugabuse.gov/publications/drugs-brains-behavior-science-addiction/drug-abuse-addiction.

———. 2016a. "Hallucinogens." https://www.drugabuse.gov/publications/drugfacts/hallucinogens.

———. 2016b. "MDMA (Ecstasy/Molly)." https://www.drugabuse.gov/publications/drugfacts/mdma-ecstasy-molly.

———. 2016c. "Treatment Approaches for Drug Addiction." https://www.drugabuse.gov/publications/drugfacts/treatment-approaches-drug-addiction.

———. 2017a. "National Survey on Drug Use and Health." https://www.drugabuse.gov/national-survey-drug-use-health.

———. 2017b. "Cocaine." https://www.drugabuse.gov/drugs-abuse/cocaine.

———. 2017c. "Inhalants." https://www.drugabuse.gov/publications/drugfacts/inhalants.

———. 2017d. "Prescription Drugs and Cold Medicines." https://www.drugabuse.gov/drugs-abuse/prescription-drugs-cold-medicines.

———. 2017e. "National Survey of Drug Use and Health." https://www.drugabuse.gov/national-survey-drug-use-health.

National Low Income Housing Coalition. 2017. "National Housing Trust Fund." http://nlihc.org/issues/nhtf.

National Student Campaign against Hunger and Homelessness. 2016. "Homelessness in the U.S" (http://studentsagainsthunger.org/homelessness-in-the-u-s/).

National Wildlife Federation. 2015. "Endangered Species Act." www.nwf.org/Wildlife/Wildlife-Conservation/Endangered-Species-Act.aspx.

Nazaryan, Alexander. 2014. "The US Department of Defense Is One of the World's Biggest Polluters." Newsweek, July 17. www.newsweek.com/2014/07/25/us-department-defence-one-worlds-biggest-polluters-259456.html.

NBC News. 2015. "Doctors Hope Thawing Relations Bring Cuban Diabetes Drug 'Herberprot' to U.S." July 21. http://www.nbcnews.com/nightly-news/video/doctors-hope-thawing-relations-bring-cuban-diabetes-drug–herberprot–to-u.s.-483127363926.

Nepstad, Sharon Erikson. 1997. "The Process of Cognitive Liberation: Cultural Synapses, Links, And Frame Contradictions in the U.S.-Central America Peace Movement." *Sociological Inquiry* 67(4):470–487.

Neuman, W. Lawrence. 2011. *Social Research Methods: Qualitative and Quantitative Approaches*. Saddle River, NJ: Pearson Education.

New York State Department of Environmental Conservation. 2017a. "What Is Solid Waste?" http://www.dec.ny.gov/chemical/8732.html.

———. 2017b. "Love Canal." http://www.dec.ny.gov/chemical/72562.html.

New York Times. 1983. "Key House Member Fears U.S. Breaks Law in Nicaragua," April 14:1.

———. 2007. "Enron Shareholders Look to SEC for Support in Court." www.nytimes.com/2007/05/10/business/worldbusiness/10iht-enron.1.5648578.html?_r=0.

———. 2009. "A Loss for Voting Rights." August 4 (www.nytimes.com/2009/08/05/opinion/05wed3.html?_r=0).

———. 2012. "Wrongly Turning Away Ex-Offenders." November 3 (www.nytimes.com/2012/11/04/opinion/sunday/voting-rights-former-felons.html?ref=felony-disenfranchisement).

———. 2014. "Law and Order in Mexico." November 11. www.nytimes.com/2014/11/12/opinion/murder-in-mexico.html?_r=0.

———. 2016. "Million-Dollar Donors in the 2016 Presidential Race." February 9 (www.nytimes.com/interactive/2016/us/elections/top-presidential-donors-campaign-money.html?_r=0).

———. 2017. "Pruitt v. EPA: 14 Challenges of EPA Rules by the Oklahoma Attorney General." https://www.nytimes.com/interactive/2017/01/14/us/politics/document-Pruitt-v-EPA-a-Compilation-of-Oklahoma-14.html?_r=0.

Newport, Frank and Gary J. Gates. 2015. "San Francisco Metro Area Ranks Highest in LGBT Percentage." Gallup, March 20 (www.gallup.com/poll/182051/san-francisco-metro-area-ranks-highest-lgbt-percentage.aspx).

Newton, Huey P. 1971. "The Black Panther Party." Pp. 200–204 in *Racial* Conflict, edited by Gary T. Marx. Boston, MA: Little, Brown and Company.

Ngai, Mae M. 2004. *Impossible Subjects: Illegal Aliens and the Making of Modern America*. Princeton, NJ: Princeton University Press.

Norton, Michael I. and Dan Ariely. 2011. "Building a Better America – One Wealth Quintile at a Time." *Perspectives on Psychological Science* 6(1):9–12.

Novacic, Ines. 2015. "Despite Opposition, Syrian Refugee Families Strive for Better Lives in the U.S." CBS News, November 16. (www.cbsnews.com/news/syrian-refugees-resettle-in-america/).

NPR Online. 2001. "Poverty in America." NPR/Kaiser/Kennedy School Poll (www.npr.org/programs/specials/poll/poverty/staticresults1.html).

NPR. 2016. "What You Need to Know About the Alt-Right Movement." August 16 (http://www.npr.org/2016/08/26/491452721/the-history-of-the-alt-right).

Nuclear Energy Institute. 2014. "Used Nuclear Fuel in Storage." www.nei.org/CorporateSite/media/Images/Infographics/Used-Fuel-Storage.png?width=9482&height=7327&ext=.png.

———. 2018. "Used Fuel Storage and Nuclear Waste Fund Payments by State" (https://www.nei.org/resources/statistics/used-fuel-storage-and-nuclear-waste-fund-payments).

O'Brien, John. 2018. "State AGs Unite For #MeToo Movement, but Changing Federal Law Could Be Slippery Slope." *Forbes*, February 23 (https://www.forbes.com/sites/legalnewsline/2018/02/23/state-ags-unite-for-metoo-movement-but-changing-federal-law-could-be-slippery-slope/#296ed1e665b7).

Oberst, Gerry. 2010. "ITU Satellite Goals." *Broadcasting via Satellite*, September 1.

OECD. 2016. "OECD Income Distribution Database (IDD): Gini, Poverty, Income, Methods and Concepts" (www.oecd.org/els/soc/income-distribution-database.htm).

OECD Key Indicators. 2016. "OECD Heath Statistics, Current Expenditure on Health, Per Capita." http://www.oecd.org/els/health-systems/health-data.htm.

Office of Community Services. 2017. "Community Economic Development (CED)." https://www.acf.hhs.gov/ocs/programs/ced.

Office of the Clerk, House of Representatives. 2013, http://clerk.house.gov/.

Olick, Diana. 2014. "Where to Put Your Cash? A House or a Stock?" CNBC, December 8 (https://www.cnbc.com/2014/12/08/where-to-put-your-cash-a-house-or-a-stock.html).

Oliver, Pamela. 2008. "Repression and Crime Control: Why Social Movement Scholars Should Pay Attention to Mass Incarceration as a Form of Repression." *Mobilization* 13(1):1–24.

Omnibus Consolidated Appropriations Bill. HR 3610, Pub L No. 104–208. 1996. http://www.gpo.gov/fdsys/pkg/PLAW-104publ208/pdf/PLAW-104publ208.pdf.

Onishi, Norimitsu. 2017. "South Africa Reverses Withdrawal from International Criminal Court." *New York Times*, https://www.nytimes.com/2017/03/08/world/africa/south-africa-icc-withdrawal.html.

Operation Underground Railroad (OUR). 2017a. "Operation Underground Railroad." http://ourrescue.org/.

———. 2017b. "Operation Underground Railroad: OUR Stories." http://ourrescue.org/blog/category/operations/.

———. 2017c. *The Abolitionists*. http://theabolitionists-movie.com/.

Orfield, Gary, John Kucsera, and Genevieve Siegel-Hawley. 2012. "E Pluribus… Separation: Deeping Double Segregation for More Students." Civil Rights Project (September) https://civilrightsproject.ucla.edu/research/k-12-education/integration-and-diversity/

mlk-national/e-pluribus ... separation-deepening-double-segregation-for-more-students.

Ourdocuments.gov. 2013. "Transcript of Voting Rights Act (1965) (http://www.ourdocuments.gov/doc.php?-flash=true&doc=100&page=transcript).

Pallardy, Richard. 2015. "Deep Water Horizon Oil Spill of 2010." *Encyclopedia Britannica* (https://www.britannica.com/event/Deepwater-Horizon-oil-spill-of-2010).

Palm Center. 2009. "Nations Allowing Gays to Serve Openly in Military (www.palmcenter.org/research/nations%20allowing%20service%20by%20openly%20gay%20people).

Palmer, Griff and Michael Cooper. 2012. "How Maps Helped Republicans Keep an Edge in the House." *New York Times*, December 14 (https://www.nytimes.com/2012/12/15/us/politics/redistricting-helped-republicans-hold-onto-congress.html).

Parker, Karen F. 2008. *Unequal Crime Decline*. New York: New York University Press.

Parsons, Talcott and Robert Bales. 1956. *Family Socialization and Interaction Process*. New York: Routledge.

Payson-Denney, Wade. 2015. "Secretary Duncan Unveils Plan to Revamp No Child Left Behind." CNN, January 13. http://www.cnn.com/2015/01/12/politics/duncan-no-child-left-behind-revamp/index.html.

Pearson, Catherine. 2013. "7 Surprising Health Conditions That Affect Women More than Men." *Huffington Post*, August 5. www.huffingtonpost.com/2013/08/05/health-conditions-women_n_3695162.html.

Peers, William R., Joseph Goldstein, Burke Marshall, and Jack Schwartz. 1976. *The My Lai Massacre and Its Cover-Up: Beyond the Reach of Law? The Peers Commission Report*. New York: Free Press.

Peet, Richard and Elaine Hartwick. 2009. *Theories of Development*. New York: Guilford Press.

Pellegrini, Christina. 2016. "Panama Papers: A Game of Hide and Seek Using Shell Companies." Globe and Mail, April 5. www.theglobeandmail.com/report-on-business/panama-papers-a-game-of-hide-and-seek-using-shell-companies/article29522301/.

Peralta, Eyder. 2016. "Panama Papers: Here's What You Need to Know (So Far)" NPR, April 4. www.npr.org/sections/thetwo-way/2016/04/04/472985787/heres-what-you-need-to-know-so-far-about-panama-papers.

Peralta, Stacy. 2009. *Crips and Bloods: Made in America*. New York: Docurama Films.

Perez, Chris. 2017. "Federal Contractor Busted for Leaking Top Secret NSA Docs Russian Hacking." *New York Post*, June 5. http://nypost.com/2017/06/05/top-secret-nsa-doc-details-russian-election-hacking-effort-report/.

Perrin, Andrew and Maeve Duggin. 2015. "Americans' Internet Access: 2000–2015." Pew Research Center, June 26. http://www.pewinternet.org/2015/06/26/americans-internet-access-2000–2015/.

Peter G Peterson Foundation. 2018. "Selected Charts on the Long-Term Fiscal Challenges of the United States." *https://www.pgpf.org/sites/default/files/PGPF-Chart-Pack.pdf*.

Petit, Becky and Bruce Western. 2004. "Mass Imprisonment and the Life Course: Race and Class Inequality in U.S. Incarceration." *American Sociological Review* 69(April):151–169.

Pew Research Center. 2010. "The Decline of Marriage and the Rise of New Families." November 18. (www.pewsocialtrends.org/2010/11/18/the-decline-of-marriage-and-rise-of-new-families/).

———. 2011. "A Portrait of Stepfamilies." (www.pewsocialtrends.org/2011/01/13/a-portrait-of-stepfamilies/).

———. 2012a. "Economic Mobility of the States." Pew Research Center, May 10 (http://www.pewstates.org/research/data-visualizations/economic-mobility-of-the-states-85899381539).

———. 2012b. "Religion and Attitudes toward Same-Sex Marriage." February 7 (www.pewforum.org/2012/02/07/religion-and-attitudes-toward-same-sex-marriage/).

———. 2013. "A Survey of LGBT Americans." June 13 (www.pewsocialtrends.org/2013/06/13/a-survey-of-lgbt-americans/).

———. 2014a. "Gender" Religious Landscape Study. (www.pewforum.org/religious-landscape-study/gender-composition/).

———. 2014b. "Record Share of Americans Have Never Married." September 24. (www.pewsocialtrends.org/2014/09/24/record-share-of-americans-have-never-married/).

———. 2015a. "U.S. Catholics Open to Non-Traditional Families." (http://www.pewforum.org/2015/09/02/u-s-catholics-open-to-non-traditional-families/).

———. 2015b. "The American Family Today." (http://www.pewsocialtrends.org/2015/12/17/1-the-american-family-today/).

———. 2017. "Changing Attitudes on Gay Marriage." *Public Opinion on Same Sex Marriage* (http://www.pewforum.org/fact-sheet/changing-attitudes-on-gay-marriage/).

Philipps, Dave. 2014. "Inquiry Urged on Air Force Academy's Handling of Sexual Assault Cases." *New York Times*, August 20 www.nytimes.com/2014/08/21/us/senators-urge-review-in-handling-of-air-force-academy-sex-assault-cases.html).

Philly.com. 2013. "Mother Jones' 'Children's Crusade' Returns to Philadelphia." August 17. (www.philly.com/philly/blogs/TODAY-IN-PHILADELPHIA-HISTORY/Mother-Jones-.html#fP1eI9s3H8vLu8t8.99).

Picchi, Aimee. 2016. "Congrats, Class of 2016: You're the Most Indebted Yet." CBS News. http://www.cbsnews.com/news/congrats-class-of-2016-youre-the-most-indebted-yet/.

Pichardo, Nelson A. 1997. "New Social Movements: A Critical Review." *Annual Review of Sociology* 23:411–430.

Piketty, Thomas. 2014. *Capital in the Twenty-First Century*. Cambridge, MA: Harvard University Press.

Pilkington, Ed. 2014. "Burglars in 1971 FBI Office Break-In Come Forward after 43 Years." *Guardian*, January 7. www.theguardian.com/world/2014/jan/07/fbi-office-break-in-1971-come-forward-documents

Pillar, Paul R. 2002. "Fighting International Terrorism: Beyond September 11th." *Defense Intelligence Journal* 11(1):17–26.

Pinker, Steven. 2011. *The Better Angels of Our Nature: Why Violence Declined*. New York: Penguin Group.

PISA. 2017. Program for International Student Assessment. (https://nces.ed.gov/surveys/pisa/pisa2015/index.asp).

Planas, Roque. 2012. "Why Voter Turnout in U.S. Lags behind Latin America." *Huffington Post*, November 8 (www.huffingtonpost.com/2012/11/08/voter-turn-out-latin-america_n_2093819.html).

Polaris. 2014. "Human Trafficking." www.polarisproject.org/human-trafficking/overview.

Pollack, Eileen. 2013. "Why Are There Still So Few Women in Science?" New York Times, October 3 (www.nytimes.com/2013/10/06/magazine/why-are-there-still-so-few-women-in-science.html?pagewanted=all&_r=2&).

Pope Francis. 2015. On Care of Our Common Home. www.hillheat.com/articles/2015/06/18/full-english-translation-of-pope-francis-climate-and-environmental-encyclical-laudato-si-chapter-six#6.

Postero, Nancy. 2010. "Morales's MAS Government: Building Indigenous Popular Hegemony in Bolivia." *Latin American Perspectives* 37(3):18–34.

Postrel, Virginia. 2006. "The Container That Changed the World." New York Times, March 23. www.nytimes.com/2006/03/23/business/23scene.html?pagewanted=print&_r=0.

Powell, David. 2002. "Death as a Way of Life: Russia's Demographic Decline." *Current History* 101(October):344–348.

Prison Policy Initiative. 2016. "Breaking Down Mass Incarceration in the 2010 Census: State-By-State Incarceration Rates by Race/Ethnicity." http://www.prisonpolicy.org/reports/rates.html

Prothero, Arianna. 2017. "What Are School Vouchers and How Do They Work?" Education Week, January 26 http://www.edweek.org/ew/issues/vouchers/index.html.

Prudence Crandall Center. 2016. "Services." (http://prudencecrandall.org/services/).

Public Broadcasting Service (PBS). 1988. "Guns, Drugs and the CIA." www.pbs.org/wgbh/pages/frontline/shows/drugs/archive/gunsdrugscia.html.

———. 1998. "Opium throughout History". https://www.pbs.org/wgbh/pages/frontline/shows/heroin/etc/history.html

———. 2010. "My Lai". *American Experience*. WGBH. https://www.pbs.org/wgbh/americanexperience/films/mylai/.

———. 2011. "Stonewall Uprising." *American Experience*. https://www.pbs.org/video/american-experience-stonewall-uprising/.

———. 2012a. "The Mormons: Polygamy and the Church." www.pbs.org/mormons/peopleevents/e_polygamy.html.

———. 2012b. *The Invisible War*. www.pbs.org/independentlens/invisible-war/film.html.

———. 2013a. " 'The Untouchables,' Why Major Wall Street Players Haven't Been Criminally Prosecuted for Wrong Doing Related to the 2008 Financial Meltdown." PBS Frontline, January 22 (www.pbs.org/wgbh/pages/frontline/untouchables).

———. 2013b. "Milestones in the Gay Rights Movement." www.pbs.org/wgbh/americanexperience/features/timeline/stonewall/.

———. 2014a. "The Tokyo War Crimes Trials (1946–1948)." //www.pbs.org/wgbh/amex/macarthur/peopleevents/pandeAMEX101.html.

———. 2014b. "The Iran-Contra Affair." www.pbs.org/wgbh/americanexperience/features/general-article/reagan-iran/.

———. 2014c. "How Effective Is DARE?" www.pbs.org/wgbh/pages/frontline/shows/dope/dare/.

Quimet, Marc. 2012. "A World of Homicides: The Effect of Economic Development, Income Inequality, and Excess Infant Mortality on the Homicide Rate for 165 Countries in 2010." *Homicide Studies* 16(3):238–258.

Quota Project. 2017. "Gender Quotas around the World" (http://www.quotaproject.org/).

Radu, Sintia. 2017. "How #Me Too Has Awoken Women around the World." *U.S. News and World Report*, October 25 (https://www.usnews.com/news/best-countries/articles/2017–10-25/how-metoo-has-awoken-women-around-the-world).

Raiz, Lisa. 2006. "College Students' Support of Rights for Members of the Gay Community." *Journal of Poverty* 10 (2): 53–75.

Ramsland, Katherine. 2013. "Defining 'Serial Killer': So Much Confusion." Psychology Today, April 15. http://www.psychologytoday.com/blog/shadow-boxing/201304/defining-serial-killer-so-much-confusion.

Ravitch, Diane. 2013. *Reign of Error: The Hoax of the Privatization Movement and the Danger to America's Public Schools*. New York: Alfred A. Knopf.

———. 2014. "New York Schools: The Roar of the Charters." New York Review of Books, March 27. www.nybooks.com/blogs/nyrblog/2014/mar/27/new-york-charters-against-deblasio/.

Raymond, Alan G. 2007. The 2006 Massachusetts Health Care Reform Law: Progress and Challenges after One Year of Implementation. Massachusetts Health Policy Forum, Brandeis University http://masshealthpolicyforum.brandeis.edu/publications/pdfs/31-May07/MassHealthCareReformProgess%20Report.pdf.

Reality Works Experiential Learning Technology. 2016. "Real Care Baby." (www.realityworks.com/products/realcare-baby).

Rebovich, D. J. and J. L. Kane 2002. "An Eye for an Eye in the Electronic Age: Gauging Public Attitudes toward White-Collar Crime and Punishment." *Journal of Economic Crime Management* 1:1–19.

Rector, Robert. 2012. "Marriage: America's Greatest Weapon against Child Poverty." *Heritage Foundation*, September 5. (www.heritage.org/research/reports/2012/09/marriage-americas-greatest-weapon-against-child-poverty).

Reed, Adolph Jr. 2005. "Free Higher Education: Interview with Adolph Reed, Jr." Solidarity, March–April (http://www.solidarity-us.org/node/289).

Reed, Adolph Jr. and Heather Gautney. 2015. "Higher Ed for Bernie." Common Dreams, October 22 (https://www.commondreams.org/views/2015/10/22/higher-ed-bernie).

Regalsky, Pablo. 2010. "Political Processes and the Reconfiguration of the State in Bolivia." *Latin American Perspectives* 37(3): 35–50.

Reiss, Ira L. 2016. "Commentary on van Anders (2015): A Sociological Perspective." *Archives of Sexual Behavior* 45(3):509–511.

Religioustolerance.org. 2015. "Women as Clergy" (www.religioustolerance.org/femclrg13.htm).

———. 2016. "Policies of 47 Christian Faith Groups towards Homosexuality" (www.religioustolerance.org/hom_chur2.htm).

Republican Governors Association. 2013. http://www.rga.org/homepage/governors/.

Resmovits, Joy. 2015. "No Child Left Behind Rewrite Should Limit Standardized Testing, Duncan Says." Huffpost Politics, January 12. http://www.huffingtonpost.com/2015/01/12/no-child-left-behind-2015_n_6453092.html.

Ressler, Robert K. and Tom Shachtman. 1992. *Whoever Fights Monsters*. New York: St. Martin's Press.

Reuters. 2014. "Japan Moves to Fast-Track Cars Powered by Hydrogen Fuel Cells." New York Times, June 25. www.nytimes.com/2014/06/26/business/international/japan-bets-big-on-cars-powered-by-hydrogen-fuel-cells.html?_r=0.

———. 2016. "Colombia's Government and FARC Rebels Agree to New Peace Deal." *Guardian*, November 12. https://www.theguardian.com/world/2016/nov/13/colombias-government-and-rebel-movement-agree-new-peace-terms.

Reville, William. 2016. "Why Is Europe Losing the Will to Breed?" *Irish Times*, May 19. https://www.irishtimes.com/news/science/why-is-europe-losing-the-will-to-breed-1.2644169.

Rich, Motoko. 2014a. "Administration Urges Restraint in Using Arrest or Expulsion to Discipline Students." New York Times, January 8. www.nytimes.com/2014/01/09/us/us-criticizes-zero-tolerance-policies-in-schools.html.

———. 2014b. "School Data Finds Pattern of Inequality Along Racial Lines." New York Times, March 21. www.nytimes.com/2014/03/21/us/school-data-finds-pattern-of-inequality-along-racial-lines.html?_r=0.

Riedel, Bruce. 2010. "Khost CIA Attack: Lessons One Year Later." Daily Beast, December 29. www.thedailybeast.com/articles/2010/12/29/khost-cia-attack-lessons-one-year-later.html.

Riffkin, Rebecca. 2014. "Hacking Tops List of Crimes Americans Worry about Most." *Gallup News*, October 27. http://news.gallup.com/poll/178856/hacking-tops-list-crimes-americans-worry.aspx.

Rios, Edwin. 2017. "The Battle over School Choice Is Happening in State Houses across America." *Mother Jones*, March 8. http://www.motherjones.com/politics/2017/03/school-voucher-bills-across-country.

Ripley, Amanda. 2013. *The Smartest Kids in the World*. New York: Simon and Schuster.

Robers, Simone, Jana Kemp, Amy Rathbun, Rachel E. Morgan, and Thomas D. Snyder. 2014. *Indicators of School Crime and Safety: 2013*. National Center for Education Statistics, Bureau of Justice Statistics. (June) nces.ed.gov/pubs2014/2014042.pdf.

Robert Wood Johnson Foundation. 2008. "Gaps in Infant Mortality Rates by Mother's Education: How Do States Compare?" www.commissiononhealth.org/PDF/tab6_78.pdf.

Robertson, Campbell, John Schwartz, and Richard Pérez-Peña. 2015. "BP to Pay $18.7 Billion for Deepwater Horizon Oil Spill." *New York Times*, July 2. www.nytimes.com/2015/07/03/us/bp-to-pay-gulf-coast-states-18-7-billion-for-deepwater-horizon-oil-spill.html.

Rogers, Sam. L. 1920. Mortality Statistics 1918. Department of Commerce, Bureau of Census. https://www.cdc.gov/nchs/data/vsushistorical/mortstatsh_1918.pdf.

Romig Kathleen . 2018. "Social Security Lifts More Americans above Poverty Than Any Other Program." Center on Budget and Policy Priorities, November 5 (https://www.cbpp.org/research/social-security/social-security-keeps-22-million-americans-out-of-poverty-a-state-by-state).

Rosenberg, Matt. 2015. "China One Child Policy Facts." Geography. http://geography.about.com/od/china-maps/a/China-One-Child-Policy-Facts.htm.

Rosenberg, Robin. 2013. "Abnormal Is the New Normal." *Slate Medical Examiner*, April 12. www.slate.com/articles/health_and_science/medical_examiner/2013/04/diagnostic_and_statistical_manual_fifth_edition_why_will_half_the_u_s_population.html.

Rosenthal, Ron and Richard Flacks. 2012. *Playing for Change: Music and Musicians in the Service of Social Movements*. Boulder, CO: Paradigm Publishers.

Rostow, Walt Whitman. 1991. *The Stages of Economic Growth: A Non-Communist Manifesto*. Cambridge, UK: Cambridge University Press.

Rothenberg, Paula S. 2015. *White Privilege*. New York: Worth Publishers.

Rothwell, Jonathan T., and Pablo Diego-Rosell. 2016. "Explaining Nationalist Political Views: The Case of Donald Trump." *Social Science Research Network*, November 6 (https://papers.ssrn.com/sol3/papers.cfm?abstract_id=2822059).

Rowe, Nelson. 2016. "NY Governor Bans Non-Essential Travel to North Carolina." Tri-County Sun Times, April 1 (http://thevillagessuntimes.com/2016/04/01/ny-governor-bans-non-essential-travel-to-north-carolina/).

Rowland, Ashley and Yoo Kyong Chang. 2014. "Former Prostitutes Who Served US Troops Sue South Korea." Stars and Stripes, July 18. www.stripes.com/news/former-prostitutes-who-served-us-troops-sue-south-korea-1.294069.

Rugaber, Christopher. 2018. "U.S. Birth Rate Drops to Lowest Point in 30 Years." Chicago Sun-Times, May 17. https://chicago.suntimes.com/health/u-s-birth-rate-drops-to-lowest-point-in-30-years/.

Ruiz-Marrero, Carmelo. 2014. "Three. Decades Later: The CIA, the Contras and Drugs." Counterpunch, October 29. www.counterpunch.org/2014/10/29/the-cia-the-contras-and-drugs/.

Rupar, Terri. 2014. "Here Are the 10 Countries Where Homosexuality May Be Punished by Death." Washington Post, February 24 (www.washingtonpost.com/blogs/worldviews/wp/2014/02/24/here-are-the-10-countries-where-homosexuality-may-be-punished-by-death).

Russell Sage Foundation. 2013. "The Rise of Women: Seven Charts Showing Women's Rapid Gains in Educational Achievement" (www.russellsage.org/blog/rise-women-seven-charts-showing-womens-rapid-gains-educational-achievement).

Sampson, Robert J. 1987. "Urban Black Violence: The Effect of Male Joblessness and Family Disruption." *American Journal of Sociology* 93(2):348–382.

Sampson, Robert J. and William Julius Wilson. 1995. "Toward a Theory of Race, Crime and Urban Inequality." Pp. 37–56 in *Crime and Inequality*, edited by John

Hagan and Ruth Peterson. Stanford, CA: Stanford University Press.

Sanchez, Ray and Keith O'Shea. 2016. "Mass Shooter Dylann Roof, with a Laugh, Confesses, 'I Did It.'" CNN, December 10. https://www.cnn.com/2016/12/09/us/dylann-roof-trial-charleston-video/index.html.

Sanger-Katz, Margot. 2015. "Income Inequality: It's Also Bad for Your Hralth." Onhealthylife.com.www.onhealthylife.com/income-inequality-its-also-bad-for-your-health-new-york-times/.

Sarner, Lauren. 2017. "The 20 Most Popular TV Shows in the World Right Now." *Inverse Entertainment*, May 19. https://www.inverse.com/article/31808-walking-dead-game-of-thrones-thirteen-reasons-why-arrow-top-20-shows-world.

SAT. 2008. SAT 2008 College – Bound Seniors – Total Group Profile Report. http://media.collegeboard.com/digitalServices/pdf/research/Total_Group_Report_CBS_08.pdf.

——. 2016. SAT 2016 College – Bound Seniors – Total Group Profile Report. https://secure-media.collegeboard.org/digitalServices/pdf/sat/total-group-2016.pdf.

Sawhill, Isabel and Joanna Venator. 2015. "Is There a Shortage of Marriageable Men?" Brookings Institute, Center on Children and Families at Brookings, September. (www.brookings.edu/~/media/research/files/papers/2015/09/ccf-policy-breif/56-shortage-of-marriageable-men.pdf).

Scahill, Jeremy. 2007. *Blackwater: The Rise of the World's Most Powerful Mercenary Army*. New York: Nation Books.

Schaefer, Brett D. and Steven Groves. 2009. "The U.S. Should Not Join the International Criminal Court." Heritage Foundation, August 17. www.heritage.org/research/reports/2009/08/the-us-should-not-join-the-international-criminal-court.

Schemo, Diana Jean. 2003. "Rate of Rape at Academy Is Put at 12% in Survey." New York Times, August 29 (www.nytimes.com/2003/08/29/national/29ACAD.html?th).

Schmidt, Peter. 2009. "Growth in International Enrollments Slows at U.S. Graduate Schools." Chronicle of Higher Education, September 16. http://chronicle.com/article/Growth-in-International/48421/.

Schneider, Roger and Mike Householder. 2016. "Would Flint's Water Crisis Happen in a Wealthier City?" Associated Press, January 22. www.freep.com/story/news/local/michigan/flint-water-crisis/2016/01/22/would-flints-water-crisis-happen-wealthier-city/79157868/.

Schoenborn, Charlotte. 2004. "Marital Status and Health: United States, 1999–2002." Advance Data from Vital and Health Statistics, Number 351, CDC. December 15 (www.cdc.gov/nchs/data/ad/ad351.pdf).

Scholz, Bettina R. 2015. *The Cosmopolitan Potential of Exclusive Associations*. Lexington, MA: Lexington Books.

Schulte, Brigid. 2014. "The U.S. Ranks Last in Every Measure When It Comes to Family Policy, in 10 Charts." *Washington Post*, June 23. (www.washingtonpost.com/blogs/she-the-people/wp/2014/06/23/global-view-how-u-s-policies-to-help-working-families-rank-in-the-world/).

Schumaker, Erin. 2015. "Cuba's Had a Lung Cancer Vaccine for Years, and Now It's Coming to the U.S." *Huffington Post*, May 14. www.huffingtonpost.com/2015/05/14/cuba-lung-cancer-vaccine_n_7267518.html.

Scommegna, Paola. 2013. "Exploring the Paradox of U.S. Hispanics' Longer Life Expectancy." Population Reference Bureau. www.prb.org/Publications/Articles/2013/us-hispanics-life-expectancy.aspx.

Scott, Eugene. 2017. "10 Most Damning Findings from Report on Russian election Interference." CNN, January 7. http://www.cnn.com/2017/01/07/politics/intelligence-report-russian-interference/index.html.

Seccombe, Karen T. 2007. *Families in Poverty*. New York: Pearson.

——. 2012. *Exploring Marriage and the Family*. New York: Pearson.

Semple, Kirk, Azam Ahmed, and Eric Lipton. 2016. "Panama Papers Leak Casts Light on a Law Firm Founded on Secrecy." New York Times, April 6 (www.nytimes.com/2016/04/07/world/americas/panama-papers-leak-casts-light-on-a-law-firm-founded-on-secrecy.html?nlid=64748605&_r=0).

Seniors Health Insurance. 2015. "Prescription Drug Costs in the U.S. vs Canada." www.seniors-health-insurance.com/drug-costs-compared-us-canada.php.

Sentencing Project. 2015. "Trends in U.S. Corrections." http://sentencingproject.org/doc/publications/inc_Trends_in_Corrections_Fact_sheet.pdf.

——. 2017. "Trends in U.S. Corrections" (http://www.sentencingproject.org/publications/trends-in-u-s-corrections/).

Shabazz, Abdul-Hakim. 2014. "Killers, Victims Often Have Something in Common – Crime Record." Indianapolis Star, January 3. www.indystar.com/article/20140102/OPINION/301020020/Killers-victims-often-something-common-crime-record.

Shalby, Colleen. 2017. "Trump Called 'Fake News' Media an Enemy of the American People. Here's What Else Has Made the Public Enemies List." *Los Angeles Times*, February 17. http://www.latimes.com/politics/washington/la-na-essential-washington-updates-donald-trump-called-fake-news-media-1487377442-htmlstory.html.

Shane, Scott. 2017. "Russian Intervention in American Election Was No One-Off." New York Times, January 6. https://www.nytimes.com/2017/01/06/us/politics/russian-hacking-election-intelligence.html.

Shannon, Sarah, Christopher Uggen, Melissa Thompson, Jason Schnittker, and Michael Massoglia. 2011. "Growth in the Ex-Felon and Ex-Prisoner Population, 1948–2010." Paper presented at the Annual Meeting of the Population Association of America, Washington, DC (http://paa2011.princeton.edu/papers/111687).

Shapiro, Ari. 2010. "Bill Eases Penalty for Crack Cocaine Possession." NPR, March 18 (www.npr.org/templates/story/story.php?storyId=124795401).

Shear, Michael D. 2017 "Trump Will Withdraw U.S. from Paris Climate Agreement." New York Times, June 1. https://www.nytimes.com/2017/06/01/climate/trump-paris-climate-agreement.html.

Sheppard, Kate. 2015. "DOJ Announces $18.7 Billion Settlement with BP Over Gulf Spill." *Huffington Post*, July 2. www.huffingtonpost.com/2015/07/02/bp-settlement-civil-gulf_n_7713832.html?utm_hp_ref=bp-oil-spill.

Sherman, Lawrence W. and Richard A. Berk. 1984. "The Specific Deterrent Effects of Arrest for Domestic Assault." *American Sociological Review* 49(2):261–272.

Sheth, Sonam. 2017. "More than 3 Million People Believed to Have Protested on the Day after Trump's Inauguration." *Business Insider*, January 25 (http://www.businessinsider.com/more-than-3-million-people-marched-on-saturday-for-the-womens-march-2017–1).

Shipler, David K. 2005. *The Working Poor*. New York: Vintage Books.

Shirley, Adam. 2016. "Which Are the World's Most Polluted Cities?" *World Economic Forum*, May 12. https://www.weforum.org/agenda/2016/05/which-are-the-world-s-most-polluted-cities/

Shupak, Amanda. 2015. "50 Years of Research on TV Violence and Little Progress." CBS News, January 6. www.cbsnews.com/news/50-years-of-research-on-tv-violence-and-little-progress/.

Sigle-Rushton, Wendy, Torkild Hovde Lyngstad, Patrick Lie Andersen, and Øystein Kravdal. 2014. "Proceed with Caution? Parents' Union Dissolution and Children's Educational Achievement." *Journal of Marriage and the Family* 76(1):161–174.

Silver, Nate. 2012. *The Signal and the Noise*. New York: Penguin Press.

Singer, P. W. 2008. *Corporate Warriors: The Rise of the Privatized Military Industry*. Updated ed. Ithaca, NY: Cornell University Press.

Skaza, Jonathan and Brian Blais. 2013. "The Relationship between Economic Growth and Environmental Degradation: Exploring Models and Questioning the Existence of an Environmental Kuznets Curve." Working Paper Series, The Center for Global and Regional Economic Studies at Bryant University (http://web.bryant.edu/~bblais/pdf/SSRN-id2346173.pdf).

Sledge, Matt. 2014. "One Year After Obama's Big Drone Speech, Many Promises Left Unkept," *Huffington Post*, May 27. www.huffingtonpost.com/2014/05/27/obama-drone-speech_n_5397904.html.

Smelser, Neil J. 1962. *Theory of Collective Behavior*. New York: The Free Press.

Smialek, Jeanna. 2017. "Deaths of Despair" Are Surging Among the White Working Class." *Bloomberg*, March 23. https://www.bloomberg.com/news/articles/2017-03-23/white-working-class-death-rate-to-be-elevated-for-a-generation.

Smith, Adam. 1776 (2012). *The Wealth of Nations*. Hollywood, FL: Simon and Brown.

Smith, Casey. 2017. "Is This the Golden Age of College Student Activism." *USA Today College*, March 22. http://college.usatoday.com/2017/03/22/is-this-the-golden-age-of-college-student-activism/.

Smith, Michelle R. 2013. "50 Years Later, Kennedy's Vision for Mental Health Not Realized." *Seattle Times*, October 21. www.seattletimes.com/nation-world/50-years-later-kennedyrsquos-vision-for-mental-health-not-realized/.

Smith, Sharon G., Jieru Chen, Kathleen C. Basile, Leah K. Gilbert, Melissa T. Merrick, Nimesh Patel, Margie Walling, and Anurag Jain. (2017). *The National Intimate Partner and Sexual Violence Survey (NISVS): 2010–2012 State Report*. Atlanta, GA: National Center for Injury Prevention and Control, Centers for Disease Control and Prevention.

Smith-Spark, Laura and Hada Messia 2014. "Gambino, Bonano Family Members Arrested in Joint U.S.–Italy Anti-Mafia Raid." Fox61, February 11 (https://fox61.com/2014/02/11/gambino-bonanno-family-members-arrested-in-joint-us-italy-anti-mafia-raids/comment-page-1/).

Sneed, Tierney. 2014. "Study: Thank Hollywood for the Drop in Smoking." U.S. News and World Report. April 4. www.usnews.com/news/articles/2014/04/04/study-drop-in-smoking-on-tv-in-line-with-decline-in-us-tobacco-use.

Snow, David A. and Robert D. Benford. 1988. "Ideology, Frame Resonance, and Participant Mobilization." *International Social Movements Research* 1:197–217.

Snow, David A., E. Burke Rochford Jr., Steven K. Worden, and Robert D. Benford. 1986. "Frame Alignment Processes, Micromobilization, and Movement Participation." *American Sociological Review* 51:464–481.

Snyder, Howard N. 2011. *Arrest in the United States, 1980–2009*. Washington, DC: U.S. Department of Justice. www.bjs.gov/content/pub/pdf/aus8009.pdf.

Social Security. 2018. "Social Security History." https://www.ssa.gov/history/ratios.html.

Sokou, Katerina. 2013. "Housing Discrimination Persists in U.S. in More Subtle Ways, HUD Report Says." *Washington Post*, June 11 (http://articles.washingtonpost.com/2013–06-11/business/39892388_1_housing-discrimination-housing-bias-housing-units).

Solijonov, Abdurashid. 2016. "Voter Turnout Trends around the World." International Institute for Democracy and Electoral Assistance(https://www.idea.int/sites/default/files/publications/voter-turnout-trends-around-the-world.pdf).

Somashekhar, Handhya. 2014. "Health Survey Gives Government Its First Large-Scale Data on Gay, Bisexual Population." Washington Post, July 15 (www.washingtonpost.com/national/health-science/health-survey-gives-government-its-first-large-scale-data-on-gay-bisexual-population/2014/07/14/2db9f4b0-092f-11e4-bbf1-cc51275e7f8f_story.html).

Spiegel Online International. 2013. "Edward Snowden Interview: The NSA and Its Willing Helpers." July 8. www.spiegel.de/international/world/interview-with-whistleblower-edward-snowden-on-global-spying-a-910006.html.

St. Myer, Thomas. 2015. "Senator Voices Concerns over BP Oil Spill Settlement." Pensacola News Journal, August 5. www.pnj.com/story/news/local/pensacola/beaches/2015/08/05/senator-voices-concerns-bp-oil-spill-settlement/31181749/

Stanford University News Service. 1995. "Biological Basis of Sexual Orientation." March 10 (www.news.stanford.edu/pr/95/950310Arc5328.html).

Stapp, Kitty. 2015. "2014 Another Record-Shattering Year for Climate." Inter Press Services, July 17, 2015. www.globalissues.org/news/2015/07/17/21266.

Statista. 2018a. "Infant Mortality Rate in the United States in 2013, by Race and Ethnicity of Mother." https://www.statista.com/statistics/260521/infant-mortality-rate-in-the-us-by-race-ethnicity-of-mother/.

———. 2018b. Shares of Household Income Quintiles in the United States from 1970 to 2016" (https://www.statista.com/statistics/203247/shares-of-household-income-of-quintiles-in-the-us/).

Steele, Emily and Michael S. Schmidt. 2017. "Bill O'Reilly Is Forced Out at Fox News." New York Times, April 19 (https://www.nytimes.com/2017/04/19/business/media/bill-oreilly-fox-news-allegations.html).

Steinhauer, Jennifer. 2013. "Sexual Assaults in Military Raise Alarm in Washington." New York Times, May 7. www.nytimes.com/2013/05/08/us/politics/pentagon-study-sees-sharp-rise-in-sexual-assaults.html?page-wanted=all&_r=0.

Sterbenz, Christina and Erin Fuchs. 2013. "How Flint Michigan Became the Most Dangerous City in America." Business Insider, June 16. www.businessinsider.com/why-is-flint-michigan-dangerous-2013-6.

Stohr, Greg. 2015. "Gay Marriage Legalized by Top U.S. Court in Landmark Ruling." Bloomberg Business, June 26. (www.bloomberg.com/news/articles/2015-06-26/gay-marriage-legalized-nationwide-by-u-s-supreme-court-ibdovxv1).

Stopbullying.gov. 2014. "Effects of Bullying." www.stopbullying.gov/at-risk/effects/index.html.

Storey, Tim. 2010. "GOP Makes Historic State Legislative Gains in 2010." Rasmussen Reports, December 10 (http://www.rasmussenreports.com/public_content/political_commentary/commentary_by_tim_storey/gop_makes_historic_state_legislative_gains_in_2010).

Stout, Hilary, Danielle Ivory, and Matthew L. Wald. 2014. "Auto Regulators Dismissed Defect Tied to 13 Deaths." New York Times, March 8. www.nytimes.com/2014/03/09/business/auto-regulators-dismissed-defect-tied-to-13-deaths.html?_r=0.

Student Loan Hero. 2017. "A Look at the Shocking Student Loan Debt Statistics for 2017" (https://studentloanhero.com/student-loan-debt-statistics/).

Sullivan, Eileen. 2014. "U.S. Database of Suspected Terrorists Doubled in Recent Years." Associated Press, August 5. www.pbs.org/newshour/rundown/u-s-database-suspected-terrorists-doubled-recent-years/.

Sun, Yongmin and Yuanzhang Li. 2002. "Child Well-Being during Parents' Marital Disruption Process: A Pooled Time-Series Analysis." Journal of Marriage and the Family 64(2):472–488.

———. 2009. "Postdivorce Family Stability and Changes in Adolescents' Academic Performance: A Growth-Curve Model." Journal of Family Issues 30(11):1527–1555.

Sunkel, Osvaldo. 1972. "Big Business and Dependencia." Foreign Affairs 50(April):517–531.

Sutherland, Edwin. 1937. The Professional Thief. Chicago: University of Chicago Press.

Sweeney, Erica. 2017. "The Truckers Who Are Taking on Human Trafficking." City Lab, November 14. https://www.citylab.com/transportation/2017/11/the-truckers-taking-on-human-trafficking/545927/.

Tan, Avianne. 2015. "Syrian Refugee Family Finds a Home in Connecticut after Being Denied Entry in Indiana." ABC News, November 18. (http://abcnews.go.com/US/syrian-refugee-family-finds-home-connecticut-denied-entry/story?id=35277871).

Tanenhaus, Sam. 2013. "Original Sin: Why the GOP Is and Will Continue to Be the Party of White People." New Republic, February 16, 2013 (http://www.newrepublic.com/article/112365/why-republicans-are-party-white-people).

Tankersley, Jim. 2015. "Thomas Piketty Might Have the Most Controversial Theory for What's Behind the Rise of ISIS." Washington Post, November 30. www.businessinsider.com/thomas-piketty-might-have-the-most-controversial-theory-for-whats-behind-the-rise-of-isis-2015-11.

Tarr, Delaney. 2018. "Survivor to Lawmakers: We Are Coming after You." CNN, February 19. https://www.cnn.com/videos/us/2018/02/21/delaney-tarr-parkland-massacre-survivor-sot.cnn.

Tarrow, Sidney. 1992. "Mentalities, Political Cultures, and Collective Action Frames: Constructing Meanings through Action." Pp. 174–202 in Frontiers of Social Movement Theory, edited by Aldon D. Morris and Carol McClurg Mueller. New Haven, CT: Yale University Press.

Taub, Amanda. 2016. "'White Nationalism', Explained." New York Times, November 21 (https://www.nytimes.com/2016/11/22/world/americas/white-nationalism-explained.html?_r=0).

Than, Ker. 2011. "Massive Population Drop Found for Native Americans, DNA Shows." National Geographic News, December 5. http://news.nationalgeographic.com/news/2011/12/111205-native-americans-europeans-population-dna-genetics-science/.

Thomas, Jo. 2001. "Behind a Book that Inspired McVeigh." New York Times, June 9. www.nytimes.com/2001/06/09/us/behind-a-book-that-inspired-mcveigh.html.

Thomas, Lauren. 2017. "The Number of Americans without Health Insurance Rose in First Quarter 2017." CNBC, April 11. http://www.cnbc.com/2017/04/11/the-number-of-americans-without-health-insurance-rose-in-first-quarter-2017.html.

Thomas, W. I. and Dorothy Swaine Thomas. 1928. The Child in America. New York: Alfred Knopf.

Thompson, Michael. 2013. "Most Murder Victims in Big Cities Have Criminal Record." WND (WorldNetDaily). March 4. http://mobile.wnd.com/2013/03/most-murder-victims-in-big-cities-have-criminal-record/#ARMfesMy7l7qBG8q.99.

Thornberry, Terrence P. and Marvin D. Krohn. 2000. "The Self-Report Method for Measuring Delinquency and Crime." Criminal Justice 2000. https://www.ncjrs.gov/criminal_justice2000/vol_4/04b.pdf.

Thrush, Glenn and Maggie Haberman. 2017. "Trump Gives White Supremacists an Unequivocal Boost." New York Times, August 15 (https://www.nytimes.com/2017/08/15/us/politics/trump-charlottesville-white-nationalists.html).

Thrush, Glenn. 2011, "Ohio Senate Bill 5's Repeal Buoys Dems." Politico, November 8 (http://dyn.politico.com/printstory.cfm?uuid=8B5F60E1-5DCF-4E8B-95A9-65E20F927A9A).

Tilly, Charles. 1978. From Mobilization to Revolution. Reading, MA: Addison-Wesley.

Tilove, Jonathan 2008. "Obama Made Inroads with White Voters except in Deep South: The Role of Race." Times-Picayune, November 8 (www.nola.com/news/index.ssf/2008/11/obama_made_inroads_with_white.html).

Time. 2013. "The 100 Most Influential Persons in the World" (2011). http://time100.time.com/.

Tong, Rosemarie Putnam. 2013. Feminist Thought. Boulder, CO: Westview.

Tough, Paul. 2013. *How Children Succeed*. New York: Mariner Books.

Toumayan, Michael. 2015. "Majority of Americans Oppose LGBT Discrimination." Human Rights Campaign, June 12 (www.hrc.org/blog/majority-of-americans-oppose-lgbt-discrimination).

Tozzi, John. 2013. "Doctors Order More Lab Tests When They Own the Labs." Bloomberg www.bloomberg.com/bw/articles/2013–07-16/doctors-order-more-lab-tests-when-they-own-the-labs.

Tribune News Service. 2016. "U.S. Official: Hackers Targeted Voter Registration Systems of 20 States." *Chicago Tribune*, September 30. http://www.chicagotribune.com/news/nationworld/.

Truckers against Trafficking (TAT). 2017. Truckers against Trafficking – Freedom Drivers Project. http://www.truckersagainsttrafficking.org/freedom-drivers-project-homepage/.

Trueman, C. N. 2011. "The White Rose Movement." *History Learning Site* (http://www.historylearningsite.co.uk/nazi-germany/the-white-rose-movement/).

Trulia. 2017. "Greenwich, CT Real Estate" (trulia.com/ct/greenwich).

Truman, Jennifer L. and Rachel E. Morgan. 2016. "Criminal Victimization, 2015." Bureau of Justice Statistics, October 20. https://www.bjs.gov/index.cfm?ty=pbdetail&iid=5804.

Turner, Jonathan, Leonard Beeghley, and Charles H. Powers. 2006. *The Emergence of Sociological Theory*. Belmont, CA: Wadsworth Publishing.

Tverberg, Gail. 2013. "Twelve Reasons Why Globalization Is a Huge Problem." *Our Finite World*, February 22. https://ourfiniteworld.com/2013/02/22/twelve-reasons-why-globalization-is-a-huge-problem/.

UCLA Higher Education Research Institute. 2016. "The American Freshman: National Norms Fall 2015." https://www.heri.ucla.edu/monographs/TheAmericanFreshman2015.pdf.

Uggen, Christopher, Ryan Larson, and Sarah Shannon. 2016. "6 Million Lost Voters: State-Level Estimates of Felony Disenfranchisement, 2016." *Sentencing Project*, October 6.

UNESCO. 2015. "Adult and Youth Literacy." UNESCO Institute for Statistics. http://www.uis.unesco.org/literacy/Documents/fs32-2015-literacy.pdf.

Union of Concerned Scientists. 2017. "Global Warming Impacts." http://www.ucsusa.org/our-work/global-warming/science-and-impacts/global-warming-impacts#.WRCiwNwpDIU.

United Human Rights Council. 2015. "Genocide in Rwanda." www.unitedhumanrights.org/Genocide/genocide_in_rwanda.htm.

United Nations. 1996. "Sexual Violence as a Weapon of War." www.unicef.org/sowc96pk/sexviol.htm.

———. 2010. "General Assembly Adopts Resolution Recognizing Access to Clean Water, Sanitation as Human Right, by Recorded Vote of 122 in Favour, None against, 41 Abstentions." July 28. www.un.org/press/en/2010/ga10967.doc.htm.

———. 2013a. "The Major Sources of Water Pollution Are from Human Settlements and Industrial and Agricultural Activities." http://www.unwater.org/fileadmin/user_upload/watercooperation2013/doc/Factsheets/water_quality.pdf.

———. 2013b. "Water and Biodiversity." www.unwater.org/fileadmin/user_upload/watercooperation2013/doc/Factsheets/water_and_biodiversity.pdf www.unwater.org/fileadmin/user_upload/watercooperation2013/doc/Factsheets/water_quality.pdf.

———. 2014. "Kyoto Protocol." http://unfccc.int/kyoto_protocol/items/2830.php.

———. 2015a. "The United Nations World Water Development Report 2015: Water for a Sustainable World" http://unesdoc.unesco.org/images/0023/002318/231823E.pdf.

———. 2015b. "Children and Armed Conflict." www.un.org/ga/search/view_doc.asp?symbol=A/69/926&Lang=E&Area=UNDOC.

———. 2016. "United Nations Demographic Yearbook 2015" (https://unstats.un.org/unsd/demographic/products/dyb/dybsets/2015.pdf).

———. 2017a. "Global Issues Overview." (www.un.org/en/sections/issues-depth/global-issues-overview/).

———. 2017b. "Status of a Protocol to Prevent, Suppress and Punish Trafficking in Persons, Especially Women and Children, Supplementing the United Nations Convention against Transnational Organized Crime." https://treaties.un.org/pages/ViewDetails.aspx?src=TREATY&mtdsg_no=XVIII-12-a&chapter=18&clang=_en.

United Nations Children's Fund (UNICEF). 2003. "Declaration of the Rights of the Child." (www.unicef.org/malaysia/1959-Declaration-of-the-Rights-of-the-Child.pdf).

———. 2013. Committing to Child Survival: A Promise Renewed. www.apromiserenewed.org/files/APR_Progress_Report_2013_9_Sept_2013.pdf.

———. 2015. *Committing to Child Survival: A Promise Renewed.* https://www.unicef.org/publications/files/APR_2015_9_Sep_15.pdf.

———. 2016. "Children's Protection and Civil Rights." (www.unicef.org/specialsession/about/sgreport-pdf/sgrep_adapt_part2c_eng.pdf).

———. 2017a. "At Least 65,000 Children Released from Armed Forces and Groups over the Last Ten Years, UNICEF." https://www.unicef.org/media/media_94892.html.

———. 2017b. *UNICEF Innocenti Report Card 14: Children in the Developed World.* (https://www.unicef.org.nz/stories/innocenti-report-card-14).

———. 2018. "Rapid Acceleration of Progress Is Needed to Achieve Universal Primary Education." https://data.unicef.org/topic/education/primary-education/.

United Nations Department of Economic and Social Affairs Population Division. 2003. "Population, Education and Development" (www.un.org/esa/population/publications/concise2003/Concisereport2003.pdf).

United Nations High Commission on Refugees (UNHCR). 2013. "Fractured Families." (http://unhcr.org/FutureOfSyria/fractured-families.html).

United Nations Joint Medical Staff. 2001. "WHO Guidance on Exposure to Depleted Uranium." World Health Organization. www.who.int/ionizing_radiation/en/Recommend_Med_Officers_final.pdf.

United Nations Office on Drugs and Crime (UNODC). 2017a. "United Nations Convention against Transnational Organized Crime and the Protocols Thereto." http://www.unodc.org/unodc/en/organized-crime/intro/UNTOC.html.

———. 2017b. "Human Trafficking." http://www.unodc.org/unodc/en/human-trafficking/what-is-human-trafficking.html.

———. 2017c. "Report: Majority of Trafficking Victims Are Women and Girls; One-Third Children." https://www.un.org/sustainabledevelopment/blog/2016/12/report-majority-of-trafficking-victims-are-women-and-girls-one-third-children/.

United Nations Population Division. 2016. "The World's Cities in 2016" (http://www.un.org/en/development/desa/population/publications/pdf/urbanization/the_worlds_cities_in_2016_data_booklet.pdf).

———. 2017. *World Population Prospects: 2017.* (https://esa.un.org/unpd/wpp/Publications/Files/WPP2017_KeyFindings.pdf).

United Students Against Sweatshops. 2017. http://usas.org/.

United We Dream. 2017. "Dream Act 2017" (https://unitedwedream.org/).

UNODC (United Nations Office for Drugs and Crime). 2009. Current Practices in Electronic Surveillance in the Investigation of Serious and Organized Crime. http://www.unodc.org/documents/organized-crime/Law-Enforcement/Electronic_surveillance.pdf.

———. 2016. "International Homicide, Counts and Rates per 100,000 Population." https://data.unodc.org/#state:1.

UNOS Transplant Living. 2015. "Costs." http://transplantliving.org/before-the-transplant/financing-a-transplant/the-costs/.

USA Today. 2017. "Transcript of President Trump's Inauguration Speech." January 20 (http://www.usatoday.com/story/news/nation/2017/01/20/his-own-words-president-trumps-inaugural-address/96836330/).

U.S. Bureau of Labor Statistics. 2015. "American Time Use Survey Summary." June 24 (www.bls.gov/news.release/atus.nr0.htm).

———. 2016. "Usual Weekly Earnings Summary Economic News Release." USDL-16–0111, Table 9 (www.bls.gov/news.release/pdf/wkyeng.pdf).

U.S. Census. 2000. "Historical National Population Estimates: July 1, 1900 to July 1, 1999." www.census.gov/popest/data/national/totals/pre-1980/tables/popclockest.txt.

———. 2011a. "What Is the Difference between Households and Families?" www.census.gov/hhes/www/income/about/faqs.html.

———. 2011b. "Same-Sex Couple Households." September. (http://www.census.gov/prod/2011pubs/acsbr10-03.pdf).

———. 2011c. Overview of Race and Hispanic Origin: 2010 (2010 Census Briefs) (www.census.gov/prod/cen2010/briefs/c2010br-02.pdf).

———. 2011d. The Hispanic Population: 2010 (2010 Census Briefs) (www.census.gov/prod/cen2010/briefs/c2010br-04.pdf).

———. 2012a. "Table 134. National Health Expenditures – Summary: 1960 to 2009." www.census.gov/compendia/statab/2012/tables/12s0134.pdf.

———. 2012b. "U.S. Census Bureau Projections Show a Slower Growing, Older, More Diverse Nation a Half Century from Now." December 12 (https://www.census.gov/newsroom/releases/archives/population/cb12-243.html).

———. 2013. "Poverty: 2000 to 2012" (https://www.census.gov/prod/2013pubs/acsbr12-01.pdf).

———. 2014. "American Indian and Alaska Native Population: 2000 and 2010" (https://www.census.gov/prod/cen2010/briefs/c2010br-10.pdf).

———. 2015a. "American Community Survey Demographic and Housing Estimates." https://factfinder.census.gov/faces/tableservices/jsf/pages/productview.xhtml?src=bkmk.

———. 2015b. "World Population Growth Rates: 1950–2050" www.census.gov/population/international/data/idb/worldgrgraph.php.

———. 2016a. "Enrollment Status of the Population 3 Years and over, by Sex, Age, Race, Hispanic Origin, Foreign Born, and Foreign-Born Parentage: October 2015." *Current Population Survey 2015* https://census.gov/data/tables/2015/demo/school-enrollment/2015-cps.html.

———. 2016b. American Community Survey, 2014. "Percent of Related Children Under 18 Years below the Poverty Level in the Past 12 Months: States and Puerto Rico" (http://factfinder.census.gov/faces/tableservices/jsf/pages/productview.xhtml?src=bkmk).

———. 2016c. "Growth in Urban Population Outpaces Rest of Nation, Census Bureau Reports." https://www.census.gov/newsroom/releases/archives/2010_census/cb12-50.html

———. 2017a. "Income and Poverty in the United States: 2016" (https://www.census.gov/library/publications/2017/demo/p60-259.html).

———. 2017b. "Voting and Registration in the Election of November 2016." (https://www.census.gov/data/tables/time-series/demo/voting-and-registration/p20-580.html).

———. 2017c. "Poverty Thresholds" (https://www.census.gov/topics/income-poverty/poverty.html).

———. 2017d. "Historical Estimates of World Population." https://www.census.gov/population/international/data/worldpop/table_history.php.

———. 2017e. "Population: 1790 to 1990." https://www.census.gov/population/censusdata/table-4.pdf.

———. 2017f. "The Nation's Older Population Is Still Growing, Census Bureau Reports." https://census.gov/newsroom/press-releases/2017/cb17-100.html.

———. 2017g. "People Reporting Ancestry." 2009–2011 American Community Survey 3-Year Estimates (https://factfinder.census.gov/faces/tableservices/jsf/pages/productview.xhtml?pid=ACS_11_3YR_B04006&prodType=table).

———. 2018a. "Older People Projected to Outnumber Children for First Time in U.S. History" (https://www.census.gov/newsroom/press-releases/2018/cb18-41-population-projections.html).

———. 2018b. "ACS Demographic and Housing Estimates 2012–2016 American Community Survey 5 Year Estimates" (https://factfinder.census.gov/faces/tableservices/jsf/pages/productview.xhtml?src=bkmk).

———. 2018c. "Poverty Thresholds." (https://www.census.gov/data/tables/time-series/demo/income-poverty/historical-poverty-thresholds.html).

U.S. Citizenship and Immigration Services. 2017. "DV Lottery and Different Ways to Apply for a US Green Card." https://www.us-immigration.com/greencard/Green-Card-Lottery.html.

U.S. Department of Agriculture. 2017. "Supplemental Nutritional Assistance Program." (https://www.fns.usda.gov/snap/retailer-apply).

U.S. Department of Defense. 2013. Department of Defense Annual Report on Sexual Assault in the Military: Fiscal Year 2012. May 3. www.sapr.mil/public/docs/reports/FY12_DoD_SAPRO_Annual_Report_on_Sexual_Assault-VOLUME_ONE.pdf.

———. 2014. Military Health System Review. www.health.mil/Military-Health-Topics/Access-Cost-Quality-and-Safety/MHS-Review.

———. 2016. "DoD Military Service Academies: APY 14–15, Sexual Assault Reports" (http://sapr.mil/public/docs/reports/MSA/APY_14–15/SAPRO_MSA_DoD_Infographic.pdf).

———. 2018. *Department of Defense Annual Report on Sexual Assault in the Military: Fiscal Year 2017*. April 27. http://sapr.mil/index.php/reports.

U.S. Department of Education. 2017. "Title IX and Sex Discrimination." http://www2.ed.gov/about/offices/list/ocr/docs/tix_dis.html.

U.S. Department of Energy. 2016. "Bolivia" (http://www.eia.gov/beta/international/country.cfm?iso=BOL).

U.S. Department of Health and Human Services. 2012. TANF, Ninth Report to Congress (www.acf.hhs.gov/sites/default/files/ofa/9th_report_to_congress_3_26_12.pdf).

———. 2015. "Trends in Teen Pregnancy and Child-bearing" (www.hhs.gov/ash/oah/adolescent-health-topics/reproductive-health/teen-pregnancy/trends.html).

———. 2016. "Teen Pregnancy and Childbearing." (www.hhs.gov/ash/oah/adolescent-health-topics/reproductive-health/pregnancy-and-childbearing.html).

———. 2017. "Office of Family Assistance: Work Participation Rates – Fiscal Year 2016".

———. 2018a. "Poverty Guidelines" (https://aspe.hhs.gov/poverty-guidelines).

———. 2018b. "Poverty Guidelines and Determining Eligibility for Participation in Head Start Programs" (https://eclkc.ohs.acf.hhs.gov/eligibility-ersea/article/poverty-guidelines-determining-eligibility-participation-head-start).

———. 2018c. "Office of Head Start: Head Start Programs" (https://www.acf.hhs.gov/ohs/about/head-start).

———. 2018d. Child Maltreatment 2016. (www.acf.hhs.gov/cb/research-data-technology/statistics-research/child-maltreatment).

U.S. Department of Housing and Urban Development. 2013a. "An Overview of Homeless Clients: Income, Employment and Other Income Sources" (www.huduser.org/publications/homeless/homelessness/ch_2e.html).

———. 2013b. "Rental Assistance" (http://portal.hud.gov/hudportal/HUD?src=/topics/rental_assistance).

———. 2014. "HUD Reports Homelessness in U.S. Continues to Decline." October 30 (http://portal.hud.gov/hudportal/HUD?src=/press/press_releases_media_advisories/2014/HUDNo_14–135).

———. 2017a. "Community Development Block Grant Program" https://www.hud.gov/program_offices/comm_planning/communitydevelopment/programs.

———. 2017b. "Empowerment Zones." https://www.hud.gov/hudprograms/empowerment_zones.

U.S. Department of Justice. 2017. "Uniform Crime Reporting Offense Definitions." https://www.ucrdatatool.gov/offenses.cfm.

U.S. Energy Information Administration. 2016. *International Energy Outlook 2016*. https://www.eia.gov/outlooks/ieo/pdf/0484(2016).pdf.

———. 2018a. "Residential Energy Consumption Survey (RECS)" (http://www.eia.gov/consumption/residential/).

———. 2018b. "April 2018 Monthly Energy Review." *https://www.eia.gov/totalenergy/data/monthly*.

U.S. Forest Service. 2017. "The Land and Water Conservation Fund and Your National Forests." www.fs.fed.us/land/staff/LWCF/.

U.S. Geological Survey. 2016. "How Much Water Is on Earth?" https://water.usgs.gov/edu/gallery/global-water-volume.html.

U-S-History.com. 2015. "U.S. Population: 1790–2000: Always Growing." www.u-s-history.com/pages/h980.html.

———. 2017. "Oliver North." http://www.u-s-history.com/pages/h3696.html.

U.S. House of Representatives. 2017a. "Directory of Representatives" (www.house.gov/representatives/).

———. 2017b. "The Women's Rights Movement, 1848–1920." http://history.house.gov/Exhibitions-and-Publications/WIC/Historical-Essays/No-Lady/Womens-Rights/.

U.S. National Oceanic and Atmospheric Administration (NOAA). 2018. "NOAA: 2017 Was 3rd Warmest Year on Record for the Globe: NOAA, NASA Scientists Confirm Earth's Long-Term Warming Trend Continues." January 18 (https://www.noaa.gov/news/noaa-2017-was-3rd-warmest-year-on-record-for-globe).

U.S. Nuclear Regulatory Commission (NRC). 2014a. "Backgrounder on the Three Mile Island Accident." www.nrc.gov/reading-rm/doc-collections/fact-sheets/3mile-isle.html.

———. 2014b. "Backgrounder on Chernobyl Nuclear Power Plant Accident. www.nrc.gov/reading-rm/doc-collections/fact-sheets/chernobyl-bg.html.

———. 2015. "Backgrounder on Radioactive Waste." https://www.nrc.gov/reading-rm/doc-collections/fact-sheets/radwaste.html.

———. 2016. "Storage of Spent Nuclear Fuel." https://www.nrc.gov/waste/spent-fuel-storage.html.

———. 2017a. "Backgrounder on Plutonium." https://www.nrc.gov/reading-rm/doc-collections/fact-sheets/plutonium.html.

U.S. Senate. 2018. www.senate.gov/general/contact_information/senators_cfm.cfm?OrderBy=party&Sort=ASC.

U.S. State Department. 2014. Trafficking in Persons Report: June 2014. www.state.gov/documents/organization/226844.pdf.

———. 2016. "Foreign Terrorist Organizations." Bureau of Counterterrorism. http://www.state.gov/j/ct/rls/other/des/123085.htm.

———. 2017. Trafficking in Persons Report: June 2017. https://www.state.gov/documents/organization/271339.pdf.

U.S. Superintendent of Documents. 2015. "Justice for Victims of Trafficking Act of 2015." https://www.gpo.gov/fdsys/pkg/BILLS-114s178enr/pdf/BILLS-114s178enr.pdf.

U.S. Supreme Court. 2013. Shelby County, Alabama v. Holder, Attorney General, ET AL (www.supremecourt.gov/opinions/12pdf/12–96_6k47.pdf).

van Anders, Sari M. 2015. "Beyond Sexual Orientation: Integrating Gender/Sex and Diverse Sexuality via Sexual Configurations Theory. *Archives of Sexual Behavior* 44(5):1177–1213.

Van Ausdale, Debra and Joe R. Feagin. 2001. *The First R: How Children Learn Race and Racism.* Lanham, MD: Rowman & Littlefield.

Veeresham, Ciddi. 2012. "Natural Products Derived from Plants as a Source of Drugs." Journal of Advanced Pharmaceutical Technology & Research 3(4):200–201. www.ncbi.nlm.nih.gov/pmc/articles/PMC3560124/.

Venkatesh, Sudhir Alladi. 2006. *Off the Books: The Underground Economy of the Urban Poor.* Cambridge. MA: Harvard University Press.

Ventura, Stephanie J., Brady E. Hamilton, and T. J. Mathews. 2014. "National and State Patterns of Teen Births in the United States, 1940–2013." National Vital Statistics Reports 63(4):1–34. (www.cdc.gov/nchs/data/nvsr/nvsr63/nvsr63_04.pdf).

Vergun, David. 2015. "Legislation Changes UCMJ for Victims of Sexual Assault." *Army News Service,* January 7. https://www.army.mil/article/140807/Legislation_changes_UCMJ_for_victims_of_sexual_assault/.

Vespa, Jonathan, Jamie M. Lewis, and Rose M. Kreider. 2013. "America's Families and Living Arrangements: 2012." August www.census.gov/prod/2013pubs/p20-570.pdf.

Vlasic, Bill. 2012. "U.S. Sets Higher Fuel Efficiency Standards." New York Times, August 28. www.nytimes.com/2012/08/29/business/energy-environment/obama-unveils-tighter-fuel-efficiency-standards.html.

Volscho, Thomas W. and Nathan J. Kelly. 2012. "The Rise of the Super-Rich: Power Resources, Taxes, Financial Markets, and the Dynamics of the Top 1 Percent, 1949 to 2008." *American Sociological Review* 77(5):679–699.

Wade, Lisa and Myra Marx Ferree. 2015. *Gender: Ideas, Interactions and Institutions.* New York: Norton.

Wagner, Peter and Wendy Sawyer. 2018. "Mass Incarceration: The Whole Pie 2018" Prison Policy Initiative. (https://www.prisonpolicy.org/reports/pie2018.html).

Waldfogel, Jane. 2001. "Policies toward Parental Leave and Child Care." *Future of Children* 11(1):99–111, tables 1 and 2 (http://futureofchildren.org/futureofchildren/publications/docs/11_01_06.pdf).

Walker, John. 2012. "California Cap and Trade: Conservation, Controversy, and Big Money." U.S. Green Chamber of Commerce. www.usgreenchamber.com/blog/california-cap-and-trade-conservation-controversy-and-big-money/.

Walker, Tim. 2016. "Why Are 19 States Still Allowing Corporal Punishment in Schools?" *NEA Today.* October 17. (http://neatoday.org/2016/10/17/corporal-punishment-in-schools/).

Wallerstein, Immanuel. 1974. *The Modern World System, Vol. 1.* New York: Academic Press.

———. 1979. *The Capitalist World Economy.* New York: Cambridge University Press.

———. 1980. *The Modern World System, Vol. 2.* New York: Academic Press.

———. 1988. *The Modern World System, Vol. 3.* New York: Academic Press.

Walmsley, Roy. 2016. "Highest to Lowest – Prison Population Rate." *World Prison Brief.* Institute for Criminal Policy Research. Birkbeck University of London. http://prisonstudies.org/highest-to-lowest/prison_population_rate?field_region_taxonomy_tid=All&=Apply.

Warren and Kerwin. 2017. "The 2,000 Mile Wall in Search of a Pure: Since 2007 Visa Overstays Have Outnumbered Undocumented Border Crossers by Half a Million." Center for Immigration Studies (http://cmsny.org/publications/jmhs-visa-overstays-border-wall/).

Washington Post. 2010. "The Fair Sentencing Act Corrects a Long-Time Wrong in Cocaine Cases." August 3 (http://www.washingtonpost.com/wpdyn/content/article/2010/08/02/AR2010080204360.htm).

———. 2017. "Most Americans Oppose Trump's Withdrawal from Paris Accord." *Washington Post-ABC News Poll* June 2–4, 2017, June 7. https://www.washingtonpost.com/page/2010–2019/WashingtonPost/2017/06/05/National-Politics/Polling/release_474.xml?tid=a_inl.

Watson, Ivan. 2013. "China: The Electronic Wastebasket of the World." CNN, May 30. www.cnn.com/2013/05/30/world/asia/china-electronic-waste-e-waste/index.html.

———. 2014. "'Treated Like Cattle': Yazidi Women Sold, Raped, Enslaved by ISIS." CNN World. November 7. www.cnn.com/2014/10/30/world/meast/isis-female-slaves/index.html.

Weber, Max. 1904–1905. *The Protestant Ethic and the Spirit of Capitalism.* New York: Routledge Classics, 2001.

———. 1915 (2014). "The Social Psychology of Religions." Pp. 195–204 in, *Sociological Theory in the Classical Era,* edited by Laura Desfor Edles and Scott Appelrouth Thousand Oaks, CA : Sage Publications.

———. 1924 (1964). *The Theory of Social and Economic Organization.* New York: Free Press.

Weiner, Rachel. 2017. "Virginia State Troopers Killed in Charlottesville Helicopter Crash Remembered as Heroes." Boston Globe, August 13 (https://www.msn.com/en-us/news/us/virginia-state-troopers-killed-in-charlottesville-helicopter-crash-remembered-as-heroes/ar-AAq136D).

Weisburd, David. 2005. "Hot Spots Policing Experiments and Criminal Justice Research: Lessons from the Field." *Annals* 599(May):220–245.

Weiss, Michael and Hassan Hassan. 2015. *ISIS: Inside the Army of Terror.* New York: Regan Arts.

Weissman, Dick. 2010. *Talkin' 'Bout a Revolution: Music and Social Change in America.* London, UK: Backbeat Books.

Weitz, Rose. 2013. *The Sociology of Health, Illness, and Health Care: A Critical Approach.* Boston, MA: Wadsworth.

Welbes, John. 2014. "Bixby Energy Founder Walker Convicted on All Counts." Twincities.com Pioneer Press, March 5. www.twincities.com/ci_25281112/verdict-reached-bixby-energy-fraud-trial.

Western, Bruce and Christopher Wildeman. 2009. "The Black Family and Mass Incarceration." Annals of the American Academy of Political and Social Science 261 (January):221–242. (http://prisonstudiesproject.org/wpcontent/uploads/2011/07/west_wild_blackfamincarc20091.pdf).

White House Briefing Room. 2014. "FACT SHEET: U.S. Response to the Ebola Epidemic in West Africa." September 16. www.whitehouse.gov/the-press-office/2014/09/16/fact-sheet-us-response-ebola-epidemic-west-africa.

———. 2015. "After Five Years of the Affordable Health Care Act, More than 16 Million Americans Have Gained Health Coverage." April 29. www.whitehouse.gov/healthreform/relief-for-americans-and-businesses.

White House. 2012. "Remarks by the First Lady and the President at Final Campaign Rally – Des Moines, IA" November 5 (http://www.whitehouse.gov/the-press-office/2012/11/06/remarks-first-lady-and-president-final-campaign-rally-des-moines-ia).

———. 2013. "Inaugural Address by President Barack Obama." January 21. (www.whitehouse.gov/the-press-office/2013/01/21/inaugural-address-president-barack-obama).

———. 2014. Fiscal Year 2014 Budget of the U.S. Government (www.whitehouse.gov/sites/default/files/omb/budget/fy2014/assets/budget.pdf).

White, Matthew. 2011. "Source List and Detailed Death Tolls for the Primary Megadeaths of the Twentieth Century." http://necrometrics.com/20c5m.htm.

Whitley, Bernard E. and Mary E. Kite. 2009. The Psychology of Prejudice and Discrimination. Belmont, CA: Cengage.

Whittington, Leslie and James Alm. 2003. "The Effects of Public Policy on Marital Status in the United States." Pp.75–104 in Marriage and the Economy: Theory and Evidence from Advanced Industrial Societies, edited by Shoshanna A. Grossbard-Schectman. Cambridge, UK: Cambridge University Press.

Will, Michelle. 2018. "See How Your State's Average Teacher Salary Compares." Education Week, April 24. http://blogs.edweek.org/edweek/teacherbeat/2018/04/teacher_pay_2017.html.

Williams, C. P. Sarah and My Health News Daily. 2011. "Why Women Report Being in Worse Health than Men." Scientific American, December 30. www.scientificamerican.com/article/why-women-report-being-in/.

Williams, Christine L. 1992. "The Glass Escalator: Hidden Advantages for Men in the 'Female' Professions." Social Problems 39(3):253–267.

Williams, Yohuru. 2018. "The Great Migration." History.com. September 20 (http://www.history.com/topics/black-history/great-migration).

Wilson, Helen W. and Cathy Spatz Widom. 2010. "Does Physical Abuse, Sexual Abuse, or Neglect in Childhood Increase the Likelihood of Same-Sex Sexual Relationships and Cohabitation? A Prospective 30-year Follow-Up." Archives of Sexual Behavior 39(1):63–74.

Wilson, William J. 1987. The Truly Disadvantaged: The Inner City, the Underclass, and Public Policy. Chicago, IL: University of Chicago Press.

———. 1996. When Work Disappears: The World of the New Urban Poor. New York: Knopf.

———. 1997. When Work Disappears: The World of the New Urban Poor. New York: Vintage Press.

———. 2009. More Than Just Race: Being Black and Poor in the Inner City. New York: W. W. Norton.

———. 2010. More Than Just Race. New York: W. W. Norton.

Wingfield, Adia Harvey. 2009. "Racializing the Glass Escalator: Reconsidering Men's Experiences with Women's Work." Gender and Society 23(1):5–26.

Winstock, Adam. 2014. "The Global Drug Survey 2014 Findings." The Global Drug Survey 2014. www.globaldrugsurvey.com/facts-figures/the-global-drug-survey-2014-findings/.

Wolf, Martin. 2014. "Shaping Globalization." Finance & Development 51(3):22–25. http://www.imf.org/external/pubs/ft/fandd/2014/09/pdf/wolf.pdf.

Wolf, Richard and Kevin McCoy. 2016. "Voters in Key States Face Long Lines, Equipment Failures." USA Today Network, North Jersey (http://archive.northjersey.com/news/voters-in-key-states-face-long-lines-equipment-failures-1.1689331).

Wolfers, Justin, David Leonhardt, and Kevin Quealy. 2015. "1.5 Million Missing Black Men." New York Times, April 20. (www.nytimes.com/interactive/2015/04/20/upshot/missing-black-men.html).

Wolff, Edward N. 2017. "Household Wealth Trends in the United States, 1962 to 2016: Has Middle Class Wealth Recovered?" Working Paper 24085. National Bureau of Economic Research: November (http://www.nber.org/papers/w24085).

Wong, Alia. 2015. "The Renaissance of Student Activism." Atlantic. May 21. https://www.theatlantic.com/education/archive/2015/05/the-renaissance-of-student-activism/393749/.

Wood, Jennie. 2016. "A History of Women in the U.S. Military" (http://www.infoplease.com/us/military/women-history.html).

Woodhandler, Steffie, Terry Campbell, and David U. Himmelstein. 2003. "Costs of Health Care Administration in the United States and Canada." New England Journal of Medicine 349(8):768–775.

Worby, Rebecca. 2017. "Is Yucca Mountain Back from the Dead?" High Country News, May 8. http://www.hcn.org/articles/is-yucca-mountain-back-from-the-dead.

World Bank. 2004. Poverty Assessment Report on Russia. www.worldbank.org.

———. 2015. "Improved Water Source (% of Population with Access)." http://data.worldbank.org/indicator/SH.H2O.SAFE.ZS/countries/1W?display=default.

———. 2017a. "Fertility Rate, Total (Births Per Woman)." http://data.worldbank.org/indicator/SP.DYN.TFRT.IN.

———. 2017b. "Urban Population (% of Total)." United Nations Population Divisions World Urbanization Prospects. https://data.worldbank.org/indicator/SP.URB.TOTL.IN.ZS.

———. 2017c. "Population Ages 65 and Above (% of Total)" https://data.worldbank.org/indicator/SP.POP.65UP.TO.ZS.

———. 2017d. "Country and Lending Groups." https://datahelpdesk.worldbank.org/knowledgebase/articles/906519-world-bank-country-and-lending-groups.

World Economic Forum. 2015. The Global Gender Gap Report 2015. (www.weforum.org/reports/global-gender-gap-report-2015).

World Health Organization (WHO). 2013. Global and Regional Estimates of Violence against Women. Executive Report – (www.who.int/reproductive-health/publications/violence/9789241564625/.en/). Full Report– (http://apps.who.int/iris/bitstream/10665/85239/1/9789241564625_eng.pdf?ua=1).

———. 2015. "Urban Population Growth." http://www.who.int/gho/urban_health/situation_trends/urban_population_growth_text/en/.

———. 2017a. "The Top Ten Causes of Death." http://www.who.int/mediacentre/factsheets/fs310/en/.

———. 2017b. "Number of People (All Ages) Living With HIV." (http://www.who.int/gho/hiv/epidemic_status/cases_all/en/).

———. 2017c. "Globalization." www.who.int/trade/glossary/story043/en/.

———. 2017d. "Tobacco in China." http://www.wpro.who.int/china/mediacentre/factsheets/tobacco/en/.

———. 2017e. "Urban Population Growth." http://www.who.int/gho/urban_health/situation_trends/urban_population_growth/en/.

World Hunger Education Service. 2016. "2016 World Hunger and Poverty Facts and Statistics." http://www.worldhunger.org/2015-world-hunger-and-poverty-facts-and-statistics/#hunger-number.

World Nuclear Association. 2016a. "Chernobyl Accident 1986." http://www.world-nuclear.org/information-library/safety-and-security/safety-of-plants/chernobyl-accident.aspx.

———. 2016b. "Uranium and Depleted Uranium." www.world-nuclear.org/info/Nuclear-Fuel-Cycle/Uranium-Resources/Uranium-and-Depleted-Uranium/.

———. 2017. "Fukushima Accident." http://www.world-nuclear.org/information-library/safety-and-security/safety-of-plants/fukushima-accident.aspx.

World Population Balance. 2017. "Current Population Is Three Times the Sustainable Level." http://www.worldpopulationbalance.org/3_times_sustainable.

World Shipping Council. 2017. "The History of Containerization." www.worldshipping.org/about-the-industry/history-of-containerization.

Worldpublicopinion.org. 2003. "Misperceptions, the Media and the Iraq War: Study Finds Widespread Misperceptions on Iraq Highly Related to Support for War." October 2 (http://worldpublicopinion.net/misperceptions-the-media-and-the-iraq-war/).

———. 2005. "Americans on the Darfur Crisis and ICC." March 1. www.worldpublicopinion.org/pipa/articles/btjusticehuman_rightsra/109.php.

Wright, Amy Nathan. 2007. "Civil Rights "Unfinished Business": Poverty, Race, and the 1968 Poor People's Campaign." PhD dissertation: University of Texas (http://repositories.lib.utexas.edu/bitstream/handle/2152/3230/wrighta71412.pdf?sequence=2).

Xiaofeng, Guan. 2007. "Most People Free to Have More (than One) Child." China Daily, July 11. www.chinadaily.com.cn/china/2007–07/11/content_5432238.htm.

Xinhuanet. 2014. "11 Million Couples Qualify for a Second Child." July 10. http://news.xinhuanet.com/english/video/2014–07/10/c_133475240.htm.

Yan, Holly. 2016. "Timeline of the Flint Water Crisis." CNN, March 3. www.cnn.com/2016/01/20/health/flint-water-crisis-timeline/index.html.

Yang, Stephanie. 2014. "5 Years Ago Bernie Madoff Was Sentenced to 150 Years in Prison – Here's How His Scheme Worked." *Business Insider*, July 1. http://www.businessinsider.com/how-bernie-madoffs-ponzi-scheme-worked-2014–7.

Yavorsky, Jill E., Claire M. Kamp Dush, and Sarah J. Schoppe-Sullivan. 2015. "The Production of Inequality: The Gender Division of Labor across the Transition to Parenthood." *Journal of Marriage and the Family* 77(June):662–679.

Yee, Vivian, Kenan Davis, and Jugal K. Patel. 2017. "Here's the Reality about Illegal Immigrants in the U.S." *New York Times*, March 6 (https://www.nytimes.com/interactive/2017/03/06/us/politics/undocumented-illegal-immigrants.html?smid=fb-shareII).

Young, Saundra. 2014. "Kids Deal with Vomiting, Burning Eyes Working on Tobacco Farms." CNN, May 18. (www.cnn.com/2014/05/17/health/hrw-children-tobacco-workers-report/index.html).

Youth Risk Behavior Survey. 2018. "Trends in the Prevalence of Behaviors that Contribute to Violence on School Property, National YRBS: 1991–2017." https://www.cdc.gov/.../yrbs/pdf/trends/2017_violence_trend_yrbs.pdf.

Zinn, Howard. 2003. *A People's History of the United States.* New York: Harper Perennial Modern Classics.

Zumbrun, Josh. 2014. "SAT Scores and Income Inequality: How Wealthier Kids Rank Higher." Wall Street Journal, October 7. http://blogs.wsj.com/economics/2014/10/07/sat-scores-and-income-inequality-how-wealthier-kids-rank-higher/.

CREDITS

INDEX

Note: Page numbers with *f* indicate figures and those with *t* indicate tables.